KARL MARX
FREDERICK ENGELS

COLLECTED WORKS
VOLUME
7

KARL MARX
FREDERICK ENGELS

COLLECTED
WORKS

LAWRENCE & WISHART

LONDON

KARL MARX
FREDERICK ENGELS

Volume
7

MARX AND ENGELS: 1848

1977

LAWRENCE & WISHART

LONDON

This volume has been prepared jointly by Lawrence & Wishart Ltd., London, International Publishers Co. Inc., New York, and Progress Publishers, Moscow, in collaboration with the Institute of Marxism-Leninism, Moscow.

Editorial commissions:
GREAT BRITAIN: Jack Cohen, Maurice Cornforth, Maurice Dobb, E. J. Hobsbawm, James Klugmann, Margaret Mynatt.
USA: James S. Allen, Philip S. Foner, Dirk. J. Struik, William W. Weinstone.
USSR: for Progress Publishers — N. P. Karmanova, V. N. Sedikh, M. K. Shcheglova, T. Y. Solovyova, Y. V. Yeremin; for the Institute of Marxism-Leninism — P. N. Fedoseyev, L. I. Golman, A. I. Malysh, A. G. Yegorov, V. Y. Zevin.

ISBN 0 85315 352 3

First printing 1977

Printed in the Union of Soviet Socialist Republics in 1976

Contents

KARL MARX AND FREDERICK ENGELS

March-November 1848

KARL MARX AND FREDERICK ENGELS

ARTICLES FROM THE *NEUE RHEINISCHE ZEITUNG*

June 1-November 7, 1848

June

Contents

July

September

Contents

APPENDICES

Contents

XI

NOTES AND INDEXES

ILLUSTRATIONS

TRANSLATORS

GREGOR BENTON: Articles 11, 14, 34, 43, 77, 81, 86, 88, 93, 97, 100-02, 109, 111, 113, 115, 119, 121-24, 128, 143

CLEMENS DUTT: Articles 42, 44; Appendices 2, 6, 8, 9, 11, 12, 14-16, 20-22, 24, 25, 29-32, 34-39

BARBARA RUHEMANN: Article 3; Appendices 1, 5, 7, 10, 13, 17, 18, 23, 26-28, 33

SALO RYAZANSKAYA: Articles 5, 6, 9, 18, 26, 29, 41, 46, 51, 53, 54, 71, 76, 83, 84, 89, 96, 99, 104-06, 112, 114, 116-18, 127, 140, 142, 144, 145; Appendices 3, 4, 19

KAI SCHOENHALS: Articles 7, 8, 10, 12, 13, 15-17, 19-25, 27, 28, 30-33, 35-40, 45, 47-50, 52, 55-70, 72-75, 78-80, 82, 85, 87, 90-92, 94, 95, 98, 103, 107, 108, 110, 120, 125, 126, 129-39, 141

CHRISTOPHER UPWARD: Article 146

Preface

The seventh volume of the *Collected Works* of Karl Marx and Frederick Engels covers the period from March to November 1848. It is the first of three volumes (Vols. 7-9) containing their writings during the revolutionary years 1848 and 1849.

The series of revolutions of this period arose primarily from the crisis of feudalism and absolutism, which still prevailed in a considerable part of Europe. Emerging bourgeois society needed to rid itself of feudal relics and abolish such legacies of the feudal age as the political dismemberment of Germany and Italy and the national oppression of the Poles, Hungarians and other European nations that were striving for independence.

Feudalism had already been swept away in France by the revolution of 1789-94. But another bourgeois revolution became inevitable when the rapacious rule of the financial aristocracy, the top crust of the bourgeoisie, and the political monopoly it enjoyed began to hamper the further development of capitalism.

Unlike previous bourgeois revolutions, those of 1848 and 1849 took place when fundamental social contradictions had already developed within bourgeois society and when the proletariat had already entered the political arena. The deepening conflict between proletariat and bourgeoisie—a conflict which became especially acute in France, and also in England, the most advanced capitalist country at that time—left its imprint on the revolutionary events of that period, influenced their course and determined their specific character.

Marx and Engels in these years made clear the organic unity of their revolutionary theory and practice. They were by no means merely detached observers, but played a very active and practical part in the revolutionary events themselves. They demonstrated their qualities as dedicated revolutionary writers, pamphleteers and true tribunes of the people, who organised and led the democratic and proletarian movements and headed the vanguard of the working class.

The revolutions of 1848-49 were indeed the first crucial practical test for Marxism both as the scientific world outlook of the working class and as a political movement. Revolutionary epochs, with their rapidly and drastically changing situations, the sharp demarcations of class forces and the powerful rise of the revolutionary activities of the masses are always testing times for party doctrines and ideologies. For Marxism this test in 1848-49 demonstrated the solid foundation and viability of its theoretical and tactical principles. Equally it exposed sectarian and dogmatic features of petty-bourgeois utopian socialism and the theoretical and tactical weaknesses of many of the bourgeois and petty-bourgeois democrats.

Before 1848 what had been of paramount importance in Marxism had been the creation of its general theoretical basis — its philosophy, the working out of its dialectical and materialist method to analyse social phenomena. But now immediate problems of political strategy and tactics had urgently to be solved. And Marx and Engels were able accurately to define the intrinsic nature of the tempestuous events of the revolutionary years by clearly revealing the class forces at work, and in many cases to predict the further course and the after-effects of the events. The political programme they put forward at various stages of the revolution expressed the basic requirements of social change. It was a programme to prepare the ground for further social advance by a consistent and complete bourgeois-democratic revolution.

The analysis of current events by Marx and Engels in 1848-49 permanently enriched revolutionary theory with new conclusions and general principles derived from actual experience of the class struggle waged by the masses and, in particular, by the proletariat. Lenin was later to emphasise that "their participation in the mass revolutionary struggle of 1848-49 ... was their point of departure when determining the future pattern of the workers' movement and democracy in different countries. It was to this point that they always returned in order to determine the essential nature of the different classes and their tendencies..." (V. I. Lenin, *Collected Works*, Vol. 13, Moscow, 1962, p. 37).

The volume opens with the "Demands of the Communist Party in Germany" drawn up by Marx and Engels in the name of the Central Authority of the Communist League. This set forth concrete political objectives for the proletariat in the German revolution which began with uprisings in Prussia and other German states in March 1848. And running like a single thread throughout was the sense of the indissoluble connection of the class interest of the proletariat with the national interest. The first demand was for the establishment of a single and indivisible German republic. Marx and Engels saw in the abolition of the economic and political dismemberment of the country, which was divided into some three dozen large and small states, and in the creation of a single democratic German state the necessary precondition for further progress. This demand was then closely linked with another — for the abolition of feudal oppression, the liberation of the peasants from all feudal services and the destruction of the whole economic base of the rule of the nobility. The full programme of the "Demands" provided for the democratisation of the entire economic and political system of the country — the creation of a truly democratic and representative legislative assembly, the introduction of universal suffrage, fundamental legal reforms, universal free education, and universal arming of the people as the sure means to defend their democratic rights.

Marx and Engels looked forward to the heightening and intensification of the revolutionary wave, carried forward by the resolute and rising struggle of the German proletariat, the lower middle class in the towns and the small peasants. These they saw as the social forces which could carry through a successful bourgeois-democratic revolution. And this viewpoint was a very important element of the emerging Marxist doctrine of permanent revolution, for which the starting point was the sweeping away of all survivals of feudalism but for which the goal was the overthrow of the capitalist system effected in the interests of the working class and of all exploited people. They saw in the successful bourgeois-democratic revolution the prologue to a proletarian revolution. And accordingly they outlined in the "Demands" a number of transitional measures, such as the transformation of feudal estates into state property and the organisation of large-scale agriculture on these confiscated lands, the nationalisation of the mines and of all means of transport, provision of work for all workers and state maintenance for those unable to work.

Thus in the "Demands of the Communist Party in Germany" the general propositions just announced in the *Manifesto of the Communist Party* were already expressed in concrete terms adapted to the specific situation in one country and the particular conditions of the German revolution of 1848-49.

The bulk of the volume consists of articles by Marx and Engels written after their return to Germany and published in the *Neue*

Rheinische Zeitung between June 1 and November 7, 1848. These were articles not just to record and interpret but to influence events. They reflect Marx's and Engels' direct participation in the revolutionary struggle and the tactics they used during the German and the European revolution.

The *Neue Rheinische Zeitung* was an organ of democracy—but, as Engels wrote, of "a democracy which everywhere emphasised in every point the specific proletarian character" (see "Marx and the *Neue Rheinische Zeitung*, 1848-1849" written in 1884). This trend of the paper was determined by the specific historical features of the German revolution, the actual alignment of class forces, in which the level of development reached by the German proletariat, its weakness and lack of organisation, made it impracticable to set up immediately a mass proletarian party. Two or three hundred members of the Communist League, scattered throughout the country, could not exert any substantial influence on the broad masses of the people. Marx and Engels, accordingly, decided to take their stand on the extreme Left wing of the democratic movement.

Although the *Neue Rheinische Zeitung* carried the banner of democracy, it was nevertheless the official organ of no particular democratic organisation. From the very first days of the revolution Marx and Engels criticised the weaknesses and errors of the German democrats, their inconsistencies and vacillations, and also their inclination to go to extremes and to engage in "revolutionary adventures". Even before returning from Paris, Marx and Engels strongly opposed a scheme drawn up by Herwegh, Bornstedt and other petty-bourgeois democrats to invade Germany with a volunteer corps in order to start a republican uprising. The documents published in this volume (e.g. "Letter to Étienne Cabet, Editor of the *Populaire*" and "To the Committee of the German Democratic Society in Paris") show up the real nature of this plan. As a matter of principle, Marx and Engels repudiated any such adventurous and conspiratorial schemes to "export the revolution". They consistently upheld the proletarian point of view within the general democratic movement. And so they tried to draw the petty-bourgeois democrats into the genuine revolutionary mass struggle and get them to adopt a firmer and more consistent course. At the same time they drew their followers' attention to the importance of organising workers' associations and the political education of the proletariat, indispensable prerequisites for the creation of a workers' mass party.

Marx and Engels defended their line against, in particular, the sectarian views of Gottschalk and his supporters. These had completely failed to understand the tasks facing the proletariat in the bourgeois-democratic revolution, and had come out against the workers taking any part in the general democratic movement. They were against the struggle for democratic political demands and against joint action with the democrats. The beginning of the conflict between Marx, together with those who shared his convictions, and Gottschalk is reflected in the "Minutes of the Meeting of the Cologne Community of the Communist League" (see this volume, p. 542). Marx and Engels likewise rejected the tactics of Stephan Born, who wanted to circumscribe the fight of the working class by setting it strictly occupational economic goals, which would in fact have diverted the proletariat from the general political tasks that confronted the German people. Though they did not publicly criticise Born's opportunism, since his endeavour to unite the various workers' associations helped to consolidate the forces of the proletariat, they emphatically protested against any attempt to equate Born's programme and tactics with the course pursued by the *Neue Rheinische Zeitung* (see "The *Concordia* of Turin").

The editorial board of the *Neue Rheinische Zeitung*, which was headed by Marx, became the true headquarters of the militant proletariat. It became in effect the leading centre of the Communist League, directing the political activity of its members throughout Germany during the revolutionary period. The paper's revolutionary propaganda, its unmasking of the counter-revolutionary forces and their abettors, and its defence of democratic demands, won the editors immense prestige in democratic circles of Germany and beyond her borders as courageous fighters for the interest of the people. "Outside, throughout the Reich," Engels wrote later, "wonder was expressed that we carried on our activities so unconcernedly within a Prussian fortress of the first rank, in the face of a garrison of 8,000 troops and in the face of the guardhouse" (Marx and Engels, *Selected Works* in three volumes, Vol. 3, Moscow, 1970, p. 171).

The *Neue Rheinische Zeitung*'s stand against the arbitrary behaviour of the courts, the police and the military, against the victimisation of those who took part in the revolutionary movement and against attempts to muzzle the press (see for example the articles "Hüser", "Arrests", "The Attempt to Expel Schapper", "Public Prosecutor 'Hecker' and the *Neue Rheinische Zeitung*", and others) found widespread support. The paper's great popularity was largely due to its brilliant journalism, its militancy, its precise language, the wide use it made of political exposure, and the devastating sarcasm with which it attacked the enemies of the revolution.

Not only did the *Neue Rheinische Zeitung* disseminate revolutionary
ideas, it also promoted the organisation of the masses and helped
them acquire courage, endurance and readiness for resolute action.
The example its editors themselves set by their practical activity in
the workers' and democratic organisations of the Rhineland (such as
the Cologne Workers' Association and the Cologne Democratic
Society), and their constant efforts, by means of the newspaper
and through personal contacts, to exert a revolutionary influence
on the German proletarian and democratic movement also played
a great part in rallying people around the revolutionary standard.

The *Neue Rheinische Zeitung* carried comments not only on vital
questions of the German revolutionary movement but also on those
of the European one. In their articles Marx and Engels sought to
analyse all important aspects of social development during the
revolutionary epoch. They saw the revolution in broad historical
perspective, as a phase of universal history, and so understood the
interconnectedness of widely dispersed events as separate links in a
single chain.

The *Neue Rheinische Zeitung*, supporting as it did the revolutionary
actions in many countries, was rightly regarded as the revolutionary
organ not only of German democracy, but also of European
democracy. It was the first influential popular newspaper to voice
the class interests of the European proletariat and to formulate the
democratic and socialist aims of the international proletarian
struggle for emancipation. No wonder that progressive leaders of
the contemporary European labour movement expressed their
admiration for its consistent revolutionary trend. The Chartist
Northern Star of June 24, 1848, for instance, wrote: "The *Neue
Rheinische Zeitung* ..., which announces itself 'the organ of democracy', is conducted with singular ability and extraordinary boldness;
and we hail it as a worthy, able, and valiant comrade in the
grand crusade against tyranny and injustice in every shape and
form."

The paper's proletarian and internationalist attitude became
especially evident during the uprising of the Paris workers in June
1848. It was the only newspaper in Germany, and practically in the
whole of Europe, that from the very outset firmly sided with the
insurgents, and fearlessly took their part against the slander and
abuse showered on them by the ruling classes and their press.
A series of articles and comments by Engels is devoted to the June
uprising, as is also one of the most powerful of Marx's articles, "The
June Revolution". These articles, which were written while the
events were still in progress or immediately afterwards, are imbued

with fighting spirit and at the same time they contain a profound analysis of the causes of the uprising and of its historical significance.

In his article on "The June Revolution" Marx shows the fundamental difference between this uprising and all previous revolutions. It was aimed at the system of exploitation itself, and was the first major manifestation of the profound class contradictions inherent in bourgeois society, "civil war in its most terrible aspect, the war of labour against capital" (see this volume, p. 147). Marx states that the uprising was the predictable consequence of developments in France after February 22 to 24, when the workers and artisans of Paris toppled the July monarchy and set up a bourgeois republic; it was the proletarian masses' reply to the bourgeois attack on their rights. The June events, as Marx demonstrates, destroyed the illusion that universal brotherhood and harmony prevailed in bourgeois society. They revealed the irreconcilable contradictions between the capitalist class and the proletariat, and proved that the only way to emancipate the workers was by the revolutionary overthrow of capitalism. It was this that constituted the world-historic significance of the June uprising, despite the serious defeat the workers suffered.

The military aspects of the June events were examined in Engels' articles, "Details about the 23rd of June", "The 23rd of June", "The 24th of June", "The 25th of June", "The *Kölnische Zeitung* on the June Revolution" and "The June Revolution (The Course of the Paris Uprising)", which describe the June uprising as "the first decisive battle of the proletariat" (see this volume, p. 143) and which contain a number of important observations about the nature, the significance and the methods of street and barricade fighting under the conditions existing at that time. These articles provided the basis of the Marxist theory of armed insurrection. Engels admired not only the heroism and selflessness of the barricade fighters, but also the ability of the Paris workers to acquire the necessary practical military skill and knowledge. He wrote: "It is quite remarkable how quickly the workers mastered the plan of campaign, how well-concerted their actions were and how skilfully they used the difficult terrain" (see this volume, p. 159).

Marx and Engels realised from the start that the June uprising in Paris was an event of European importance and regarded it as a turning-point in the European revolution. They pointed out that the insurgents' victory would have radically changed the balance of forces to the advantage of the revolution in all countries. Their defeat, on the other hand, encouraged the counter-revolutionaries everywhere. The French bourgeoisie, by crushing the insurrection, fought in fact on the same side as feudal and absolutist reaction in Europe, which was beginning to lift up its head again.

After June 1848 Marx and Engels continued attentively to follow events in France and to discuss them in the pages of the *Neue Rheinische Zeitung* ("Proudhon's Speech against Thiers", "The Paris *Réforme* on the Situation in France", and other articles). Their articles on France show that they still expected a new revolutionary upsurge, in which the French proletariat was to play a leading part. Marx and Engels stressed the connection and interdependence existing between the revolutions in the different European countries. And for this very reason they judged that a victory of the French workers would be of decisive importance, for it would give a new and powerful impetus to the revolutionary struggles of the people in the other European countries. They hoped that this victory would make it easier to carry through to the end the bourgeois-democratic revolution in Germany and would pave the way for a proletarian revolution throughout Europe.

Engels wrote later that their expectations at that time of a proletarian revolution in the near future were due to some extent to their having overestimated the level of economic development in Europe and also the degree of organisation and class consciousness reached by the proletariat at that time. But neither the objective nor the subjective prerequisites of the revolution were then mature enough for the liquidation of the capitalist mode of production.

The attention of the *Neue Rheinische Zeitung* was, however, invariably focussed on Germany, on the course of the revolution in the German states and the driving forces of the German revolutionary movement and its perspectives.

In their analysis of the immediate outcome of the German March revolution of 1848 Marx and Engels emphasised that the revolution had not been carried through to the end (e.g. in the articles on "The Berlin Debate on the Revolution", "The Debate on Jacoby's Motion" and "The Suppression of the Clubs in Stuttgart and Heidelberg"). Although in Vienna on March 13, in Berlin on March 18 and 19, and also in various other German states the people forced the monarchs to make a number of concessions (they promised to adopt constitutions, to convene national assemblies and to form liberal or semi-liberal governments) they failed to achieve a decisive victory over feudalism. The entire political structure and the entire civil service and police apparatus were left intact. "The Bastille ... has not yet been stormed," wrote the *Neue Rheinische Zeitung*, stressing that the decisive battle had not yet been won (see this volume, p. 89).

The reason for this half-heartedness of the German revolution was, according to the founders of Marxism, the policy pursued by the liberal bourgeoisie after it had attained power. The German bourgeoisie, scared by the determination of the masses, and especially by the revolutionary action of the French proletariat, betrayed the interests of the people. "The big bourgeoisie, which was all along anti-revolutionary, concluded a defensive and offensive alliance with the reactionary forces, because it was afraid of the people, i.e. of the workers and the democratic bourgeoisie" (see this volume, p. 74). In the articles which dealt with the debates in the Prussian National Assembly and analysed the policy of the Camphausen-Hansemann Ministry and the Auerswald-Hansemann Ministry, which replaced it in July 1848, Marx and Engels firmly opposed the "agreement theory", which the leaders of the Prussian liberal bourgeoisie advanced to justify their compromises with the feudal and monarchical forces (see, *inter alia*, "The Government of Action", "The Crisis and the Counter-Revolution").

Marx and Engels clearly foresaw that two antithetical courses were possible after the March uprising. One was that designed to carry the revolution further in the interest of the broad masses of the people, by radically abolishing all feudal and monarchical institutions, all vestiges of feudalism, first of all in agriculture, just as they had been abolished by the French revolution between 1789 and 1794. The other, pursued by the German liberals, was designed to curtail the revolutionary movement and to come to an arrangement with the feudal aristocracy. The second course, the *Neue Rheinische Zeitung* warned, would inevitably lead to a monarchical counter-revolution and to the partial or complete restoration of the state of affairs which had existed before the March revolutionary events.

Marx and Engels waged a tireless struggle to solve the principal task facing the German revolution — the national unification of the country. In a number of articles (e.g. "The Programmes of the Radical-Democratic Party and of the Left at Frankfurt", "The *Zeitungs-Halle* on the Rhine Province") they expressed their opposition to plans hatched by the German liberals to unite Germany under the hegemony of Prussia or Austria, and likewise to the setting up of a federal state on Swiss lines, a project that had found wide support in democratic circles. Marx and Engels demonstrated that only the establishment of a truly united and truly democratic state could entirely abolish the economic division and political fragmentation of Germany, together with all survivals of medieval particularism and local isolation. Such centralisation, carried through on a really democratic basis, would, they thought, create favourable conditions for a genuine consolidation of the German proletariat, and of the German revolutionary movement, too, which was greatly hampered by separatist tendencies and by parochial narrow-mindedness. They advocated the unification of Germany "from below". It should be brought about by the revolutionary onslaught of the people on the decaying absolutist system in the states of the German Confederation, and above all in Prussia and Austria. "Germany," Engels wrote, "must become *one* state not only in word but in deed. And to bring this about it is necessary above all that there should be 'neither an Austria nor a Prussia' " (see this volume, p. 400).

Marx and Engels pointed out that Germany's unification was a European problem, and that it could only be achieved in the course of a struggle waged by the revolutionary forces of the European countries against the internal and external forces of reaction, and above all against the counter-revolutionary rulers of Britain and against Russian Tsarism then acting as the principal gendarme of Europe.

It was from this revolutionary point of view that they approached the question of Schleswig-Holstein. According to the *Neue Rheinische Zeitung*, the national liberation movement in the duchies of Schleswig and Holstein, which were ruled by the Danish King and inhabited mainly by Germans, had become part of the struggle for the unification of Germany into a single democratic state. The Prussian Government, which by the logic of events was involved in the Schleswig-Holstein war waged by the German Confederation against Denmark, tried to come to an arrangement with the Danish Government; it was prepared to sacrifice German national interests, not only in response to the pressure exerted by Britain and Russia, who supported the Danish Crown, but also because it wanted to disengage the Prussian troops so as to be able to employ them against the masses of the people in Prussia itself. This treacherous policy of the Prussian Government, carried on with the collusion of the Prussian and German liberal bourgeoisie, was unequivocally exposed by Marx and Engels, who regarded it as a fatal concession to the counter-revolutionary powers and an obstacle to German unity. "Prussia, England and Russia," wrote Engels in the article "The Danish-Prussian Armistice", "are the three powers which have greater reason than anyone else to fear the German revolution and its first result—German unity: Prussia because she would thereby cease to exist, England because it would deprive her of the possibility of exploiting the German market, and Russia because it would spell the advance of democracy not only to the Vistula but even as far as the Dvina and the Dnieper. Prussia, England and Russia have conspired against Schleswig-Holstein, against Germany and against the revolution" (see this volume, pp. 424-25).

A revolutionary war against Tsarism and the other reactionary forces in Europe was regarded by Marx and Engels not only as a means to defend the revolution but as a condition of its further development. They reasoned that in the course of such a war the resistance of the people to the counter-revolutionary forces within the country was also bound to grow and that the preconditions for revolutionary outbursts could come into being even in those countries where popular discontent had not yet led to overt revolutionary action. The news about Russia's unstable internal situation — disturbances taking place in various districts, rising discontent in St. Petersburg etc. — received in Germany and printed in the *Neue Rheinische Zeitung* (see "The Russian Note") justified the hope that, in the event of such a war, a revolutionary outbreak might occur even in the Tsarist Empire.

For Marx and Engels power was the fundamental question in every revolution. And in the *Neue Rheinische Zeitung* they firmly upheld the concept of the sovereignty of the people and the establishment of a people's democratic government as conditions indispensable for the consolidation of the victory of the revolutionary masses and the implementation of the tasks facing the revolutionary movement. These ideas run through "The Assembly at Frankfurt", one of their first articles to appear in the *Neue Rheinische Zeitung*. Subsequently the concept of the people's sovereignty was continually returned to by them and, on the basis of the experience gained in the revolutionary struggle, further developed and made more concrete at every stage in the German revolution — at the time of the political crisis in Prussia caused by the action of the people in Berlin on June 14, during the intensification of the fight between the counter-revolutionary and the democratic forces in September, and during the October uprising in Vienna and the ensuing events.

Already the experience of the first months of the revolution convinced Marx and Engels of the necessity to abolish all the old administrative, military and judicial authorities, thoroughly purge the entire government apparatus, and end the rule of the bureaucracy, which was especially powerful in Prussia (see "The Agreement Session of July 4" and other articles). They saw in the arming of the people, who stood up against the counter-revolutionary soldiery, the principal guarantee of the sovereignty of the people (see "The Agreement Assembly Session of June 17", "The Civic Militia Bill" and other articles).

Marx and Engels, who regarded mass revolutionary struggle as the decisive factor in carrying through the revolution, vigorously supported all who fought in the revolutionary battles, e.g. the Viennese workers who fought again on the barricades in May 1848 to compel the ruling circles to make new concessions; the workers of Berlin who in June 1848 stormed the arsenal to obtain weapons and to repulse the counter-revolutionary conspirators; and the insurgents in Frankfurt am Main who rose in September 1848 in protest against the ratification of the infamous armistice with Denmark by the Frankfurt Assembly.

On the other hand, Marx and Engels emphasised again and again that a premature or badly prepared uprising would only result in defeat and thus strengthen the counter-revolutionary forces. For example, in the articles "Cologne in Danger" and "The 'Revolution of Cologne'" they urged the Cologne workers not to allow the Prussian Government to provoke them to action, but to preserve their forces for the decisive battle. The explanatory campaign conducted by Marx and Engels and their comrades-in-arms in Cologne in fact prevented the destruction of the democratic movement in the Rhine Province during the September crisis.

According to the editors of the *Neue Rheinische Zeitung*, revolutionary action from below must be matched by a vigorous policy in the representative institutions created by the revolution, which should act as constituent assemblies in the name of the people. Marx and Engels fought for the creation of democratic representative bodies, which would reflect the will of the masses, be closely connected with them and rely on their support. By stressing that deputies elected by the people should be accountable to the people and carry out its wishes, they upheld the right of the revolutionary people to exert pressure on elected assemblies and to demand that they adopt effective revolutionary decisions and take steps to implement them ("Freedom of Debate in Berlin" and other articles).

In a number of articles dealing with the German National Assembly and also in a series devoted to the debates in the Prussian National Assembly, Marx and Engels sharply criticised the conduct of the liberal majorities. Because all drastic measures were sabotaged by the liberals, the Frankfurt and Berlin assemblies, which failed to appeal to the masses and never assumed real power, engaged only in futile verbal disputes and became merely pitiable imitations of representative assemblies. The deputies representing the democratic bourgeoisie and petty bourgeoisie, who formed the Left wing in these assemblies, failed to display sufficient energy either. Marx and Engels often rebuked the parliamentary leaders of the "Left" and the leaders of democratic organisations for their indecision and their refusal openly to side with the people. (See, for example, Marx's article "Appeal of the Democratic Congress to the German People".) They stressed the detrimental effect of the constitutional illusions in the grip of which many Left-wing politicians still remained, and their unfounded hope of carrying through radical measures by parliamentary means alone, without the support of the revolutionary masses.

During the September days Marx and Engels, who were convinced that the conciliatory policy of the Berlin and Frankfurt assemblies merely led to ever increasing concessions to the counter-revolution, coined the slogan of the revolutionary dictatorship of the people to express the concept of the people's sovereignty during the revolution. In the article "The Crisis and the Counter-Revolution" Marx wrote: "Every provisional political set-up following a revolution requires a dictatorship, and an energetic dictatorship at that" (see this volume, p. 431). For the editors of the *Neue Rheinische Zeitung* this dictatorship constituted power genuinely wielded by the people: this power is by its very nature democratic and at the same time bold and vigorous, capable of crushing all counter-revolutionary conspiracies, of abolishing the monarchy and feudal landownership, and of ensuring the complete victory of the bourgeois-democratic revolution. That Marx and Engels firmly rejected the sectarian interpretation of revolutionary power as the arbitrary dictatorship of a small group of men is evident from the speech against Weitling which Marx made at the meeting of the Cologne Democratic Society on August 4, 1848 (see this volume, pp. 556-57).

The participation of the masses of the peasantry in the revolutionary struggle was regarded by Marx and Engels as a most important condition for the extension and consolidation of the democratic front. They thought that the spontaneous actions of the peasants which were taking place all over Germany should be rendered organised and purposeful. In such articles as "Patow's Redemption Memorandum", "Debate about the Existing Redemption Legislation" and others Marx and Engels set forth the agrarian programme of the *Neue Rheinische Zeitung*. They called upon the peasants to fight for the immediate and complete abolition without compensation of all feudal services. They vehemently denounced the Prussian liberal bourgeoisie, which was betraying the peasants "who are its *natural allies*,.... without whom it cannot stand up to the aristocracy" (see this volume, p. 295), because it was afraid that to abolish feudal property might lead to attacks on bourgeois property. Marx and Engels, who spoke for the proletariat, the consistently revolutionary class, were convinced champions of the anti-feudal peasant movement, which they regarded as one of the principal motive forces of the bourgeois-democratic revolution.

The struggle for the liberation of the oppressed nations was likewise in the eyes of Marx and Engels integrally connected with this revolution. They welcomed with enthusiasm the upsurge of the national liberation movement among the Poles, Czechs, Hungarians and Italians, and saw in them allies in the fight against feudal and absolutist counter-revolution.

In the articles "Germany's Foreign Policy", "German Foreign Policy and the Latest Events in Prague" and others, Marx and Engels took their stand for the genuine freedom and the brotherhood of all nations and again denounced the German bourgeoisie, which carried on the oppressive national policy of the Hohenzollerns and the Habsburgs. "A revolutionised Germany ought to have renounced her entire past," wrote Engels, "especially as far as the neighbouring nations are concerned. Together with her own freedom, she should have proclaimed the freedom of the nations hitherto suppressed by her" (see this volume, p. 92). According to Marx and Engels the German people could become a free democratic nation only if they supported the liberation movements of the oppressed nations. "Germany will liberate herself to the extent to which she sets free neighbouring nations" (see this volume, p. 166).

The founders of Marxism fought resolutely and consistently for the restoration of an independent Poland and pressed for an alliance of German democrats with the revolutionary wing of the Polish movement, which was fighting not only for national resurrection and liberation but also for the radical democratic reorganisation of Poland. The policy of the Prussian Government, which first provoked a national uprising in Posen and then crushed it, and which under the pretext of "reorganisation" had formally incorporated the greater part of Posen into Germany, was castigated by Engels, in particular in the series of articles entitled "The Frankfurt Assembly Debates the Polish Question". Marx and Engels condemned the attitude of the liberal majority in the Frankfurt National Assembly which sanctioned the new partition of Poland.

In the just-mentioned series of articles on the Polish question, Engels showed that the restoration of the Polish state on a democratic basis would be in the interest of German and international democracy. It would, moreover, strike a heavy blow at the three counter-revolutionary powers — Prussia, Austria, and

Russia—who had shared in the partitioning of Poland. Thus it would help bring about a change in the balance of power in favour of the revolution; and this in turn would make it easier for the Germans "to eradicate patriarchal feudal absolutism in Germany" (see this volume, p. 351).

The national liberation struggle waged by the Czech people in the summer of 1848 was enthusiastically supported by the *Neue Rheinische Zeitung*. The potential revolutionary significance of this uprising against the arbitrary rule of the Austrian Government and the Czech feudal aristocracy was stressed by Engels in "The Prague Uprising" and "The Democratic Character of the Uprising". The *Neue Rheinische Zeitung* bitterly denounced the massacre of the Prague insurgents which the brutal Austrian soldiery carried through with the connivance of the German liberal bourgeoisie, and pointed out that the crushing of the uprising was bound to have serious consequences for the Czech democratic movement and the German revolution. And it is true that after the tragic events in Prague the leadership of the Czech movement passed entirely into the hands of liberal aristocrats and bourgeois, who looked to the Austrian monarchy and the Russian Tsar for assistance.

Warm sympathy for the Italian people, which was fighting for its freedom and independence, was expressed in a letter written by Marx to the editorial board of the Italian democratic newspaper *Alba* and in several articles of the *Neue Rheinische Zeitung* in which the revolutionary events in Italy were analysed. The Italian revolution, which began with the popular uprising in Sicily in January 1848, was confronted with serious problems. The country consisted of a conglomeration of large and small states, a considerable number of which were oppressively ruled by Austria. The progressive development of Italy was only possible if she liberated herself from foreign domination and abolished the feudal and monarchical regimes. But the Italian liberals, who at the time controlled the Italian movement, were trying to unite the country "from above" within the framework of a constitutional monarchy to be headed by Charles Albert, the King of Sardinia. Marx and Engels called upon the Italian people to take the leadership of the national liberation movement into their own hands, to free themselves from the tutelage of the liberals and monarchists and to frustrate all dynastic intrigues. In many of his articles Engels demonstrated that the self-seeking policy of Charles Albert and his supporters, which counteracted the truly popular resistance to the Austrians, was largely responsible for the reverses the Italians suffered during the Austro-Italian war. He observed that only a revolutionary people's war could end Austrian domination over Italy.

The articles on the national question which Marx and Engels wrote in 1848 constitute, in sum, an important set of statements making clear their internationalist attitude towards national liberation movements.

Among the most important events of the German and European revolution was the uprising of the Viennese people in October 1848, when for three weeks the workers, students and democratic intellectuals withstood the onslaught of numerically stronger reactionary forces. Marx and Engels believed that the outcome of this rising was bound to affect substantially the fate of the revolution not only in Germany but also in Europe. Marx called the June uprising in Paris the first act of the revolutionary drama, and the October uprising in Vienna the second act (see this volume, p. 505). He emphasised that the Viennese workers had played an outstanding part in this revolutionary battle (ibid., p. 595).

A number of articles published in this volume ("Revolution in Vienna", "The *Frankfurter Oberpostamts-Zeitung* and the Viennese Revolution", "The Viennese Revolution and the *Kölnische Zeitung*", "The Latest News from Vienna, Berlin and Paris" and "The Victory of the Counter-Revolution in Vienna") and also the speeches delivered by Marx at the committee meetings of the Cologne Workers' Association on October 16 and November 6, 1848, are devoted to the Viennese uprising and analyse the causes which led to its defeat. The principal cause, according to Marx, was the fact that the liberal bourgeoisie in Austria and in Germany deserted the revolution. Vienna was captured "only as a result of the manifold betrayal on the part of the bourgeoisie" (see this volume, p. 598). Marx concluded, moreover, that the failure of the German democrats to organise and lead a popular movement in support of the Viennese insurgents had disastrous consequences. The Viennese events confirmed, indeed, Marx's and Engels' conviction that the treacherous tactics of the bourgeoisie had urgently to be countered by rallying all truly revolutionary forces for the decisive battle against the counter-revolutionary offensive.

Marx and Engels also paid attention to those European countries which, although not directly involved in the revolutionary upheaval, were in one way or another affected by it. In "The *Kölnische Zeitung* on the State of Affairs in England" and other articles about Britain, the *Neue Rheinische Zeitung* exposed the social conflicts which existed in Britain behind the façade of bourgeois and aristocratic security and stability, and the intensification of these conflicts as the result of the revolutionary upsurge in the whole of Europe. It stressed the magnitude of the class movement of the British workers who were fighting under the Chartist banner, and it described this fight against the official British establishment as the war of "the organised party of the proletariat against the organised political power of the bourgeoisie" (see this volume, p. 297). It was in the true spirit of proletarian internationalism that Marx and Engels supported the Chartists, who were persecuted by the authorities in 1848, and defended them against the slanderous accusations made by the bourgeois press. They also backed the fight for an independent Ireland, one of the principal hotbeds of revolutionary discontent in the British Isles (see "Cologne in Danger", "The *Neue Berliner Zeitung* on the Chartists").

The articles "The 'Model State' of Belgium" and "The Antwerp Death Sentences" outline the consequences of capitalist development in Belgium, where it was proceeding in an apparently peaceful and constitutional way. But the rule of the liberal bourgeoisie, which was able to crush the incipient republican movement in 1848, had, as is pointed out in these articles, caused the conditions of the workers to deteriorate substantially, and pauperism and criminality to increase. It also strengthened political reaction in the country, so that brutal repressive measures were taken against democrats and socialists, with arrests and deportations of political emigrants. Marx and Engels adduce the example of this bourgeois "model" state to show that in order to preserve its domination and prevent a revolution the ruling bourgeoisie is prepared to resort to the most arbitrary and subtle police methods, which can compete with any that are practised under feudal and absolutist monarchies.

Engels' unfinished sketch "From Paris to Berne" is published at the end of this volume. After being compelled to leave Germany at the end of September 1848, and after his subsequent deportation from Belgium to France, Engels decided to walk from Paris to Switzerland, where he wrote these travel notes. Considerable space is devoted to a description of the French peasants and their way of life and thinking. Engels notes the antipathy of the French peasants to the revolution of 1848 and to the revolutionary movement in the towns, and especially in Paris, together with their Bonapartist sympathies and illusions. This he attributes to the peasants' parochialism and political backwardness. And he adds that the demagogic exploitation of the peasants' proprietary instincts by the bourgeoisie, and the fiscal policy of the Provisional Government, which went against the interests of the peasants and alienated them from the revolution, were also largely responsible for this antipathy.

The Appendices contain a number of documents which illustrate the many-sided revolutionary activity of Marx and Engels in 1848 and their practical work among the people. They comprise papers relating to the Communist League, the Cologne Democratic Society and the Cologne Workers' Association, among the leaders of which were Marx and Engels and their comrades-in-arms. Reports of speeches delivered by Marx and Engels in these organisations and at public meetings are also included: though brief and incomplete, these give some idea of the content of the speeches. The Appendices comprise also a series of documents showing how the *Neue Rheinische Zeitung* came into being, and throwing light on the police and court proceedings against its editors and the difficult conditions (they were persecuted by the government authorities and slandered by the "loyal" press) in which Marx and Engels published this newspaper of the revolutionary proletariat.

* * *

The collection of articles written by Marx and Engels in 1848 and 1849 which is presented in Volumes 7 to 9 of this edition is more complete than any previously published. Not only the writings of Marx and Engels which appeared in Volumes 5 and 6 of the Russian and German editions of their *Collected Works* are included, but also many articles from the *Neue Rheinische Zeitung* which more recent research carried out in the USSR and the GDR has shown to have been also written by them. Included, too, are a number of documents relating to their activity in workers' and other democratic organisations. This volume contains 16 articles and notes — e.g. "Defeat of the German Troops at Sundewitt", "The Question of Union", "The Downfall of the Camphausen Government", "Reichensperger", "The Milan Bulletin", "Miscellaneous", "The Cologne Committee of Public Safety"—which have never before been published in any edition of the *Collected Works* of Marx and Engels. Of the 146 articles forming the main section of the volume, 103 are published in English for the first time. The Appendices consist entirely of material not previously published in English.

A specific feature of this volume is the fact that in a number of cases it has not been possible to establish whether a given article was written by Marx or by Engels. Since most of the articles published in the *Neue Rheinische Zeitung* are unsigned and none of the manuscripts have been preserved, the question of which of them wrote it is, indeed, generally difficult to answer. And many of the articles seem in any case to be their joint work. In those cases where up to now it has proved impossible to ascertain which one of them wrote a particular item, no name is given at the end of the article.

The titles of the articles from the *Neue Rheinische Zeitung* are printed according to the table of contents given in the paper. Those supplied by the editors are in square brackets. Those works included in this volume which have been previously published in English are given either in new or in carefully revised translations. Peculiarities in the presentation of the text of some articles, in particular the manuscripts, are described in the notes.

All the texts have been translated from the German except where otherwise indicated.

The volume was compiled and the preface, notes and subject index written by Tatyana Vasilyeva and edited by Lev Golman (Institute of Marxism-Leninism of the CC CPSU). The indexes of names and of books and periodicals mentioned or quoted were prepared by Galina Kostryukova (Institute of Marxism-Leninism of the CC CPSU).

The translations were made by Gregor Benton, Clemens Dutt, Barbara Ruhemann, Salo Ryazanskaya, Kai Schoenhals and Christopher Upward, and edited by Margaret Mynatt and Barbara Ruhemann (Lawrence & Wishart), Salo Ryazanskaya, Yelena Chistyakova, Margarita Lopukhina and Maria Shcheglova (Progress Publishers) and Vladimir Mosolov, scientific editor (Institute of Marxism-Leninism of the CC CPSU).

The volume was prepared for the press by Lyudgarda Zubrilova (Progress Publishers).

KARL MARX
and
FREDERICK ENGELS

March-November 1848

Karl Marx and Frederick Engels

DEMANDS OF THE COMMUNIST PARTY
IN GERMANY [1]

"Workers of all countries, unite!"

1. The whole of Germany shall be declared a single and indivisible republic.

2. Every German, having reached the age of 21, shall have the right to vote and to be elected, provided he has not been convicted of a criminal offence.

3. Representatives of the people shall receive payment so that workers, too, shall be able to become members of the German parliament.

4. Universal arming of the people. In future the armies shall be simultaneously labour armies, so that the troops shall not, as formerly, merely consume, but shall produce more than is necessary for their upkeep.

This will moreover be conducive to the organisation of labour.

5. Legal services shall be free of charge.

6. All feudal obligations, dues, corvées, tithes etc., which have hitherto weighed upon the rural population, shall be abolished without compensation.

7. Princely and other feudal estates, together with mines, pits, and so forth, shall become the property of the state. The estates shall be cultivated on a large scale and with the most up-to-date scientific devices in the interests of the whole of society.

8. Mortgages on peasant lands shall be declared the property of the state. Interest on such mortgages shall be paid by the peasants to the state.

9. In localities where the tenant system is developed, the land rent or the quit-rent shall be paid to the state as a tax.

4 Karl Marx and Frederick Engels

The measures specified in Nos. 6, 7, 8 and 9 are to be adopted in order to reduce the communal and other burdens hitherto imposed upon the peasants and small tenant farmers without curtailing the means available for defraying state expenses and without imperilling production.

The landowner in the strict sense, who is neither a peasant nor a tenant farmer, has no share in production. Consumption on his part is, therefore, nothing but abuse.

10. A state bank, whose paper issues are legal tender, shall replace all private banks.

This measure will make it possible to regulate the credit system in the interest of the people *as a whole*, and will thus undermine the dominion of the big financial magnates. Further, by gradually substituting paper money for gold and silver coin, the universal means of exchange (that indispensable prerequisite of bourgeois trade and commerce) will be cheapened, and gold and silver will be set free for use in foreign trade. Finally, this measure is necessary in order to bind the interests of the conservative bourgeoisie to the Government.[a]

11. All the means of transport, railways, canals, steamships, roads, the posts etc. shall be taken over by the state. They shall become the property of the state and shall be placed free at the disposal of the impecunious classes.

12. All civil servants shall receive the same salary, the only exception being that civil servants who have a *family* to support and who therefore have greater requirements, shall receive a higher salary.

13. Complete separation of Church and State. The clergy of every denomination shall be paid only by the voluntary contributions of their congregations.

14. The right of inheritance to be curtailed.

15. The introduction of steeply graduated taxes, and the abolition of taxes on articles of consumption.

16. Inauguration of national workshops. The state guarantees a livelihood to all workers and provides for those who are incapacitated for work.

17. Universal and free education of the people.

It is to the interest of the German proletariat, the petty bourgeoisie and the small peasants to support these demands with all possible energy. Only by the realisation of these demands will the millions in

---

[a] The leaflet published in Cologne has "cause of the revolution" instead of "Government".— *Ed.*

Forderungen

der

Kommunistischen Partei

in

Deutschland.

„Proletarier aller Länder vereinigt Euch!"

1. Ganz Deutschland wird zu einer einigen, untheilbaren Republik erklärt.

2. Jeder Deutsche, der 21 Jahre alt, ist Wähler und wählbar, vorausgesetzt daß er keine Kriminalstrafe erlitten hat.

3. Die Volksvertreter werden besoldet, damit auch der Arbeiter im Parlament des deutschen Volkes sitzen könne.

4. Allgemeine Volksbewaffnung. Die Armeen sind in Zukunft zugleich Arbeiter-Armeen, so daß das Heer nicht blos, wie früher, verzehrt, sondern noch mehr produzirt, als seine Unterhaltungskosten betragen. Dieß ist außerdem ein Mittel zur Organisation der Arbeit.

5. Die Gerechtigkeitspflege ist unentgeltlich.

6. Alle Feudallasten, alle Abgaben, Frohnden, Zehnten, 2c., die bisher auf dem Landvolke lasteten, werden ohne irgend eine Entschädigung abgeschafft.

7. Die fürstlichen und andern feudalen Landgüter, alle Bergwerke, Gruben, u. s. w., werden in Staatseigenthum umgewandelt. Auf diesen Landgütern wird der Ackerbau im Großen und mit den modernsten Hilfsmitteln der Wissenschaft zum Vortheil der Gesammtheit betrieben.

8. Die Hypotheken auf den Bauerngütern werden für Staatseigenthum erklärt. Die Interessen für jene Hypotheken werden von den Bauern an den Staat gezahlt.

9. In den Gegenden, wo das Pachtwesen entwickelt ist, wird die Grundrente oder der Pachtschilling als Steuer an den Staat gezahlt.

Alle diese unter 6, 7, 8 und 9 angegebenen Maaßregeln werden gefaßt, um öffentliche und andere Lasten der Bauern und kleinen Pächter zu vermindern, ohne die zur Bestreitung der Staatskosten nöthigen Mittel zu schmälern und ohne die Produktion selbst zu gefährden.

Der eigentliche Grundeigenthümer, der weder Bauer noch Pächter ist, hat an der Produktion gar keinen Antheil. Seine Konsumtion ist daher ein bloßer Mißbrauch.

10. An die Stelle aller Privatbanken tritt eine Staatsbank, deren Papier gesetzlichen Kurs hat.

Diese Maaßregel macht es möglich, das Kreditwesen im Interesse des ganzen Volkes zu regeln und untergräbt damit die Herrschaft der großen Geldmänner. Indem sie nach und nach Papiergeld an die Stelle von Gold und Silber setzt, verwohlfeilert sie das unentbehrliche Instrument des bürgerlichen Verkehrs, das allgemeine Tauschmittel, und erlaubt, das Gold und Silber nach außen hin wirken zu lassen. Diese Maaßregel ist schließlich nothwendig, um die Interessen der konservativen Bourgeois an die Revolution zu knüpfen.

11. Alle Transportmittel: Eisenbahnen, Kanäle, Dampfschiffe, Wege, Posten, 2c., nimmt der Staat in seine Hand. Sie werden in Staatseigenthum umgewandelt und der unbemittelten Klasse zur unentgeltlichen Verfügung gestellt.

12. In der Besoldung sämmtlicher Staatsbeamten findet kein anderer Unterschied statt, als der, daß diejenigen mit Familie, also mit mehr Bedürfnissen, auch ein höheres Gehalt beziehen als die Uebrigen.

13. Völlige Trennung der Kirche vom Staate. Die Geistlichen aller Konfessionen werden lediglich von ihrer freiwilligen Gemeinde besoldet.

14. Beschränkung des Erbrechts.

15. Einführung von starken Progressivsteuern und Abschaffung der Konsumtionssteuern.

16. Errichtung von Nationalwerkstätten. Der Staat garantirt allen Arbeitern ihre Existenz und versorgt die zur Arbeit Unfähigen.

17. Allgemeine, unentgeltliche Volkserziehung.

Es liegt im Interesse des deutschen Proletariats, des kleinen Bürger- und Bauernstandes, mit aller Energie an der Durchsetzung obiger Maaßregeln zu arbeiten. Denn nur durch Verwirklichung derselben können die Millionen, die bisher in Deutschland von einer kleinen Zahl ausgebeutet wurden und die man weiter in der Unterdrückung zu erhalten suchen wird, zu ihrem Recht und zu derjenigen Macht gelangen, die ihnen, als den Hervorbringern alles Reichthums, gebührt.

Das Comité:

Karl Marx. Karl Schapper. H. Bauer. F. Engels.
J. Moll. M. Wolff.

Demands of the Communist Party in Germany,
leaflet published in Cologne in 1848

Germany, who have hitherto been exploited by a handful of persons and whom the exploiters would like to keep in further subjection, win the rights and attain to that power to which they are entitled as the producers of all wealth.

The Committee:
Karl Marx, Karl Schapper, H. Bauer, F. Engels,
J. Moll, W. Wolff

Written between March 21 and 24, 1848

First published as a leaflet in Paris on March 24 or 25, 1848, in the supplement to the *Berliner Zeitungs-Halle* No. 82, on April 5, 1848, and in a number of other German newspapers; it was repeatedly reprinted during the revolution and after its defeat, in particular as a leaflet in Cologne issued not later than September 10, 1848

Printed according to the text of the *Berliner Zeitungs-Halle* collated with the leaflet issued in Cologne

Karl Marx and Frederick Engels

LETTER TO ÉTIENNE CABET, EDITOR OF THE *POPULAIRE*[2]

Citizen Cabet,

Would you be so kind as to insert the attached Declaration in the next number of the *Populaire*. The point is not to let the Communist Party be made responsible for an enterprise and conduct which have already reawakened in a part of the German nation the old national and reactionary prejudices against the French people. The Alliance of German Workers,[a] an association of various workers' societies in all European countries, which counts among its members Mr. Harney and Mr. Jones, the English Chartist leaders, is composed entirely of communists and openly professes itself communist. The so-called German Democratic Society in Paris[3] is essentially anti-communist insofar as it claims not to recognise the antagonism and struggle between the proletarian and bourgeois classes. It is, therefore, a question of making a protest and a declaration in the interests of the Communist Party. And it is this which makes us anticipate your compliance. (This note is strictly confidential.)

Fraternal greetings,

Frederick Engels
Karl Marx

The undersigned committee considers it its duty to inform the various branches of the *Alliance of German Workers* in the different European countries that it has in no way participated in the proceedings, posters and proclamations to appeal to the French

---

[a] This refers to the Communist League.— *Ed.*

citizens for clothes, arms and money. The *German Workers' Club*[4] is the only one in Paris which maintains relations with the *Alliance*, and it has nothing in common with the society in Paris, called the *Society of German Democrats*, whose leaders are Herr Herwegh and Herr von Bornstedt.

The Central Committee of the Alliance of German Workers

(signed) *K. Marx, K. Schapper, H. Bauer,
F. Engels, J. Moll, W. Wolff*

Written at the end of March 1848

First published in English in the journal *Science and Society*, 1940, Vol. IV, No. 2

Printed according to the manuscript

Translated from the French

10

Karl Marx and Frederick Engels

[TO THE COMMITTEE OF THE GERMAN DEMOCRATIC SOCIETY IN PARIS]

To Herr Bornstedt and Others[5]

Paris, April 1, 1848
22 rue Neuve Saint Augustin

Copy

The following will serve as a reply to the note of Herr Bornstedt and others which was this morning left with Marx:

1. Marx has not the least intention of rendering anybody an account for any German newspaper article.

2. Marx has not the least intention of giving an account to any committee or deputation of the German Democratic Society with which he has nothing to do.

3. If Herr Bornstedt and Herr Herwegh demand explanations in their *personal capacity* and not as members of any committee or society, then Herr Bornstedt has already once before privately and also once publicly been told to whom they should address themselves.

First published in Russian in: Marx and Engels, *Collected Works,* first ed., Vol. XXV, Moscow, 1934

Printed according to a copy in Engels' hand

Published in English for the first time

Karl Marx

TO THE EDITOR OF THE NEWSPAPER *L'ALBA*[6]

Dear Sir,

A new daily newspaper will be published in Cologne from the first of June; it will be called *Neue Rheinische Zeitung* and will be edited by Herr Karl Marx. This paper will advocate in these latitudes the same democratic principles that *L'Alba* represents in Italy. There can therefore be no doubt about the line we shall take on the questions now pending between Italy and Austria. We shall defend the cause of Italian independence, we shall fight to the death Austrian despotism in Italy as in Germany and Poland. We extend a fraternal hand to the Italian people and want to prove to them that the German nation entirely repudiates the policy of oppression which in your country is carried through by the same men who in our country too have always combated freedom. We shall do our utmost to promote the union of, and good understanding between, two great and free nations which have, until now, been led to believe by a nefarious system of government that they were each other's enemy. We shall therefore demand the immediate withdrawal from Italy of the brutal Austrian soldiery, and that the Italian people be placed in a position to express its sovereign will in the question of the form of government which it wants to choose.

In order to enable us to follow Italian affairs, and in order to give you the opportunity of judging the sincerity of our promises, we suggest an exchange of papers. Thus we propose to send you the *Neue Rheinische Zeitung* every day and to receive from you *L'Alba* regularly. We hope that you will accept this proposal and ask you to start sending us *L'Alba* as soon as possible so that already in our first issues we can make use of it.

If you wish to send us other information as well we should be pleased to receive it, and assure you that anything likely to serve the cause of democracy in any country will be given our most careful consideration.

Fraternal greetings.

> For the editorial board of the *Neue Rheinische Zeitung*
>
> Dr. *Karl Marx*, Editor

Written at the end of May 1848

First published in the newspaper
L'Alba No. 258, June 29, 1848

Printed according to the newspaper

Translated from the Italian

KARL MARX
and
FREDERICK ENGELS

ARTICLES
FROM THE *NEUE RHEINISCHE ZEITUNG*

June 1-November 7, 1848

Neue Rheinische Zeitung.
Organ der Demokratie.

| № 1. | Köln, Donnerstag, 1. Juni | 1848. |

[STATEMENT OF THE EDITORIAL BOARD OF THE *NEUE RHEINISCHE ZEITUNG*][7]

Originally the date of publication of the *Neue Rheinische Zeitung* was to be the first of July, and arrangements with correspondents etc. were made with that date in view.

But since the renewed insolence of the reactionaries foreshadows the enactment of German September Laws[8] in the near future, we have decided to make use of every available day and to publish the paper as from June the first. Our readers will therefore have to bear with us if during the first days we cannot offer the abundant variety of news and reports that our widespread connections should enable us to do. In a few days we shall be able to satisfy all requirements in this respect too.

Editorial Board:
Karl Marx, editor-in-chief
Heinrich Bürgers ⎫
Ernst Dronke ⎪
Friedrich Engels ⎬ editors
Georg Weerth ⎪
Ferdinand Wolff ⎪
Wilhelm Wolff ⎭

Written not later than May 31, 1848

First published in the *Neue Rheinische Zeitung* No. 1, June 1, 1848

Printed according to the newspaper

3-3447

THE ASSEMBLY AT FRANKFURT[9]

Cologne, May 31. For a fortnight Germany has had a Constituent National Assembly elected by the German people as a whole.

The German people won its sovereign status by fighting in the streets of almost all cities and towns of the country, and especially on the barricades of Vienna and Berlin. It exercised this sovereignty in the elections to the National Assembly.

The first act of the National Assembly should have been to proclaim loudly and publicly this sovereignty of the German people.

Its second act should have been the drafting of a German Constitution based on the sovereignty of the people and the elimination from the regime actually existing in Germany of everything that contradicted the principle of the sovereignty of the people.

During the whole of its session the Assembly ought to have taken all necessary measures to frustrate any reactionary sallies, to maintain the revolutionary basis on which it depends and to safeguard the sovereignty of the people, won by the revolution, against all attacks.

Though the German National Assembly has met about a dozen times already, it has done none of these things.

But it has ensured the salvation of Germany by the following great deeds.

The National Assembly realised that it must have rules, for it knew that when two or three Germans get together they must have a set of rules, otherwise chair legs will be used to decide matters. And now some schoolmaster had foreseen this contingency and drawn up special standing orders for this High Assembly. A motion was submitted to adopt this scheme provisionally; though most deputies had not read it, the Assembly adopted it without more ado, for what would become of Germany's representatives without regulations? *Fiat reglementum partout et toujours!*[a]

Herr Raveaux of Cologne tabled a quite simple motion dealing with conflicts between the assemblies at Frankfurt and at Berlin.[10] But the Assembly debates the final standing orders, and although Raveaux's motion is urgent, the standing orders are still more urgent. *Pereat mundus, fiat reglementum!*[b] However, the elected philistines in their wisdom cannot refrain from making a few remarks concerning Raveaux's motion, and while they are debating whether the standing orders or the motion should take precedence, they have already produced up to two dozen amendments to this motion. They ventilate the thing, talk, get stuck, raise a din, waste time and postpone voting from the 19th[c] to the 22nd of May. The matter is brought up again on the 22nd, there is a deluge of new amendments and new digressions, and after long-winded speeches and endless confusion they decide that the question, which was already placed on the agenda, is to be referred back to the sections. Thus the time has happily slipped by and the deputies leave to take their meal.

On May 23 they first wrangle about the minutes, then have innumerable motions read out again, and just when they are about to return to the agenda, that is, to the beloved standing orders, Zitz of Mainz calls attention to the brutal acts of the Prussian army and the despotic abuses of the Prussian commandant at Mainz.[d] What had occurred was an indubitable and successful sally on the part of reaction, an event with which the Assembly was especially competent to deal. It ought to have called to account the presumptuous soldier who dared threaten to shell Mainz almost within sight of the National Assembly, it ought to have protected the unarmed citizens of Mainz in their own houses from the atrocities of a soldiery which had been forced upon them and incited against them. But Herr Bassermann, the waterman of Baden,[e] declares that these are trifles. Mainz must be left to its fate, the whole is more important, the Assembly meets here to consider a set of standing orders in the interests of Germany

---

[a] Let there be regulations everywhere and always.— *Ed.*
[b] Engels paraphrases a motto of the German Emperor Ferdinand I: "*Fiat justitia et pereat mundus*" (let justice be done, though the world perish).— *Ed.*
[c] The *Neue Rheinische Zeitung* has "the 18th", evidently a misprint.—*Ed.*
[d] See this volume, pp. 20 and 23.—*Ed.*
[e] A pun on the words *Bassermann* and *Wassermann* (waterman).—*Ed.*

as a whole — indeed, what is the shelling of Mainz compared with this! *Pereat Moguntia, fiat reglementum!*[a] But the Assembly is soft-hearted, it elects a commission that is to go to Mainz to investigate matters and — it is again just the right time to adjourn and dine.

Finally, on May 24, we lose the parliamentary thread altogether. The standing orders would seem to have been completed or to have got lost, at any rate we hear nothing more about them. Instead we are inundated by a veritable flood of well-intentioned motions in which numerous representatives of the sovereign people obstinately demonstrate the limited understanding of a loyal subject.[11] Then follow applications, petitions, protests etc., and in the end the national torrent of hog-wash finds an outlet in innumerable speeches skipping from one subject to another. The fact, however, that four committees have been set up should not be passed over in silence.

Finally Herr Schlöffel asked for the floor. Three German citizens, Esselen, Pelz and Löwenstein, had been ordered to leave Frankfurt that very day, before 4 p.m. The wise and all-knowing police asserted that these gentlemen had incurred the wrath of the townspeople by their speeches in the Workers' Association and must therefore clear out. And the police dare to do this after the German right of citizenship was proclaimed by Preparliament[12] and even after it was endorsed in the draft Constitution[b] of the seventeen "trusted men" (*hommes de confiance de la diète*).[13] The matter is urgent. Herr Schlöffel asks to be allowed to speak on this point. He is refused permission. He asks for the floor to speak on the urgency of the subject, which he is entitled to do according to the standing orders, but on this occasion it was a case of *fiat politia, pereat reglementum!*[c] Naturally, for it was time to go home and eat.

On the 25th, the flood of tabled motions caused the thought-laden heads of the deputies to droop like ripe ears of corn in a downpour. Two deputies then attempted once more to raise the question of the expulsion, but they too were not allowed to speak, even about the urgency of the matter. Some of the documents received, especially one sent by Poles, were much more interesting than all the motions of the deputies. Finally the commission that had been sent to Mainz was given the floor. It announced that it could not report until the following day; moreover it had, of course, arrived too late: 8,000

---

[a] Let there be regulations, though Mainz perish.— *Ed.*
[b] F. Weichsel, *Deutschlands Einheit und der Entwurf des Deutschen Reichsgrundgesetzes.—Ed.*
[c] Let polity prevail, though the regulations perish.— *Ed.*

Prussian bayonets had restored order by disarming 1,200 men of the civic guard. Meantime, there was nothing for it but to pass on to the agenda. This was done promptly, the item on the agenda being Raveaux's motion. Since in Frankfurt this had not yet been settled, whereas in Berlin it had already lost all significance because of Auerswald's decree,[14] the National Assembly decided to defer the question till the next day and to go and dine.

On the 26th innumerable new motions were introduced and after that the Mainz commission delivered its final and very indecisive report. Herr Hergenhahn, ex-people's representative and *pro tempore* Minister, presented the report. He moved an extremely moderate resolution, but after a lengthy debate the Assembly concluded that even this mild proposal was too strong and resolved to leave the citizens of Mainz to the tender mercies of the Prussians commanded by a Hüser, and "in the hope that the Government will do its duty" the Assembly passed on to the agenda, that is the gentlemen left to have a meal.

Finally, on May 27, after lengthy preliminaries over the minutes, Raveaux's motion was discussed. There was some desultory talk until half past two and then the deputies went to dine, but this time they assembled again for an evening session and at last brought the matter to a close. Because of the extreme tardiness of the National Assembly, Herr Auerswald had already disposed of Raveaux's motion, therefore Herr Raveaux decided to support an amendment proposed by Herr Werner, which settled the question of the people's sovereignty neither in the affirmative nor in the negative.

Our information concerning the National Assembly ends here, but there is every reason to assume that after having taken this decision the meeting was adjourned and the deputies went to dine. If they were able to do this so early, they have to thank Robert Blum, who said:

"Gentlemen, if you decide to pass on to the agenda today, then the whole agenda of this Assembly may be cut short in a very curious manner."

Written by Engels on May 31, 1848   Printed according to the newspaper

First published in the *Neue Rheinische Zeitung* No. 1, June 1, 1848

HÜSER[15]

Cologne, May 31. With the aid of old fortress regulations and antiquated confederate laws Herr Hüser in Mainz has invented a new method to turn Prussians and other Germans into still greater slaves than they were before May 22, 1815.[16] We are advising Herr Hüser to take out a patent for his new invention which would undoubtedly be very profitable. For according to this method two or more drunken soldiers are sent out, who of course will, of their own accord, pick a quarrel with citizens. The authorities intervene and arrest the soldiers; this is sufficient to enable the commandants of each fortress to declare a state of siege for their respective towns, to confiscate all weapons and to leave the inhabitants to the mercy of the brutal soldiery. This plan would be particularly lucrative in Germany since there are more fortresses here directed against the internal enemy than against the enemy from abroad. It would be especially lucrative here since any publicly paid fortress commandant, a Hüser, a Roth von Schreckenstein or a similar feudal name, may dare more than even a king or an emperor, since he can curb the freedom of the press, since he can, for example, forbid the citizens of Mainz (who are not Prussians) to express their antipathy against the King of Prussia and the Prussian political system.

Herr Hüser's project is only part of the grand plan of the Berlin reactionaries who seek to disarm as rapidly as possible all civic guards (particularly along the Rhine), thus step by step annihilating the nascent popular armed forces and delivering us defenceless into the hands of an army that consists mostly of soldiers from other

Neue Rheinische Zeitung.
Organ der Demokratie.

№ 1.   Köln, Donnerstag, 1. Juni   1848.

Die "Neue Rheinische Zeitung" erscheint vom 1. Juni an täglich.
Der Abonnementspreis beträgt: Für das Vierteljahr in Köln 1 Thlr. 15 Sgr.; für alle übrigen Orte Preußens 2 Thlr. 3 Sgr. 9 Pf. Außerhalb Preußens mit Zuschlag des fremden Zeitungsporto's.
Das Abonnement für den Monat Juni kann nur unter gleichzeitiger Bestellung des nächsten Quartals (Juli, August, September) geschehen. Der Preis dieses viermonatlichen Abonnements beträgt: Für Köln 2 Thlr.; auswärts 2 Thlr. 25 Sgr.
Man abonnirt bei allen Postanstalter und Buchhandlungen des In- und Auslandes; — für Köln in der Expedition der Zeitung bei Hrn. W. Clouth, St. Agatha 12, Köln.

Fernere Aktienzeichnungen werden entgegen genommen in der Expedition der Zeitung. Auswärtige werden gebeten, sich ebenfalls dorthin franco zu wenden.

Insertionsgebühren.

Für die vierspaltige Petitzeile oder deren Raum . . . . 1 Sgr. 6 Pf.

Die Expedition der "Neuen Rheinischen Zeitung."

Das Erscheinen der Neuen Rheinischen Zeitung war ursprünglich auf den ersten Juli festgesetzt. Die Arrangements mit den Correspondenten ꝛc. waren auf diesen Termin getroffen.

Da jedoch bei dem erneuten frechen Auftreten der Reaktion deutsche September-gesetze in naher Aussicht stehen, so haben wir jeden freien Tag benutzen wollen, und erscheinen schon mit dem ersten Juni. Unsre Leser werden es uns also nachsehen müssen, wenn wir in den ersten Tagen an Nachrichten und mannigfaltigen Correspondenzen noch nicht das reichhaltige Material liefern, wozu unsere ausgedehnten Verbindungen uns befähigen. In wenig Tagen werden wir auch hierin allen Anforderungen genügen können.

Redaktions-Comité.

Karl Marx, Redakteur en Chef.
Heinrich Bürgers,
Ernst Dronke,
Friedrich Engels,   Redakteure.
Georg Weerth,
Ferdinand Wolff,
Wilhelm Wolff,

Uebersicht.

...

Humoristische Skizzen aus dem deutschen Handelsleben.
Von Georg Weerth.
Der Herr Preiß in Röthen.

...

Amtliche Nachrichten.

...

Deutschland.

...

First page of the *Neue Rheinische Zeitung* No. 1

parts who can easily be stirred up, or are already stirred up, against us.

. This has happened in Aachen, Trier, Mannheim and Mainz and can also occur elsewhere.

Written by Engels on May 31, 1848

Printed according to the newspaper

First published in the *Neue Rheinische Zeitung* No. 1, June 1, 1848

[THE LATEST HEROIC DEED OF THE HOUSE OF BOURBON]

The House of Bourbon has not yet reached the end of its glorious career. True, its white flag has recently been rather besmirched and its withering lilies are drooping sadly enough. Charles Louis of Bourbon bartered away one dukedom[a] and had to abandon a second one[b] ignominiously; Ferdinand of Bourbon lost Sicily and in Naples was forced to grant a Constitution to the revolution. Louis Philippe, although only a crypto-Bourbon, nevertheless went the way of all French-Bourbon flesh across the Channel to England. But the Neapolitan Bourbon has avenged the honour of his family brilliantly.

The Chambers are convened at Naples. The opening day is to be used for the decisive battle against the revolution. Campobasso, one of the main police chiefs of the notorious Del Carretto, is surreptitiously recalled from Malta. Large bands of armed *Sbirri*, led by their old ringleaders, again patrol Toledo Street for the first time in a long while. They disarm the citizens, rip off their coats and force them to cut off their moustaches. May 14, the opening day of the Chambers, draws near. The King demands that the Chambers should pledge themselves under oath not to change anything in the Constitution he has granted. They refuse. The national guard declares itself for the deputies. Negotiations take place, the King gives way and the Ministers resign. The deputies demand that the King should publicise his concessions in the form of an ordinance. The King promises such an ordinance for the following day. During

---

[a] Lucca.— *Ed.*
[b] Parma.— *Ed.*

the night, however, all troops stationed in the vicinity of Naples move into the city. The national guard realises that it has been betrayed and throws up barricades which are manned by 5,000 to 6,000 men. But they are opposed by 20,000 soldiers, partially Neapolitans and partially Swiss, equipped with 18 cannon. Between them stand the 20,000 *lazzaroni*[17] of Naples who are not participating for the time being.

On the morning of the 15th, the Swiss are still declaring that they will not attack the people. One of the police agents, however, who has mingled with the people, fires upon the soldiers in the Strada de Toledo. Thereupon fort St. Elmo at once hoists the red flag and on this signal the soldiers rush at the barricades. A horrible massacre begins. The national guards defend themselves heroically against the superior strength of four to one and against the cannon shots of the soldiers. Fighting rages from 10 a.m. until midnight. The people would have won in spite of the numerical superiority of the soldiery had the miserable conduct of the French Admiral Baudin not induced the *lazzaroni* to join the royal side.

Admiral Baudin was lying with a fairly large French fleet before Naples. A simple but timely threat to fire upon the castle and the forts would have forced Ferdinand to yield. But Baudin, one of Louis Philippe's old servants who was used to the earlier period of the *entente cordiale*[18] when the existence of the French fleet was merely tolerated, remained inactive, thereby causing the *lazzaroni*, who were already leaning towards the people, to join the troops.

This action of the Neapolitan lumpenproletariat decided the defeat of the revolution. Swiss guardsmen, Neapolitan soldiers and *lazzaroni* combined pounced upon the defenders of the barricades. The palaces along Toledo Street, which had been swept clean with grape-shot, collapsed under the cannon-balls of the troops. The frantic mob of victors tore into the houses, stabbed the men, speared the children, violated the women only to murder them afterwards, plundered everything in sight and then set fire to the pillaged dwellings. The *lazzaroni* proved to be the greediest and the Swiss the most brutal. The base acts and barbarities accompanying the victory of the well-armed and four times stronger Bourbon mercenaries and the always *sanfedistic*[19] *lazzaroni* over the nearly destroyed national guard of Naples, are indescribable.

Eventually, things went too far even for Admiral Baudin. Droves of refugees arrived on his ships and told of the events in the city. The French blood of his sailors was brought to boiling point. Now at last, when the victory of the King was assured, he contemplated a bombardment. The slaughter gradually came to an end. Once no longer murdered in the streets but limited oneself to pillage and rape. The prisoners, however, were led off to the forts and shot without further ado. It was all over by midnight. Ferdinand's absolute rule was restored in fact and the honour of the House of Bourbon was purified with Italian blood.

That is the latest heroic deed of the House of Bourbon and as always it is the Swiss who are fighting the people on behalf of the Bourbons. On August 10, 1792, on July 29, 1830, and during the Neapolitan battles of 1820,[20] everywhere we find the descendants of Tell and Winkelried serving as mercenaries in the pay of the royal family whose name has for years been synonymous throughout Europe with that of absolute monarchy. Now all this will of course soon come to an end. After long disputes, the more civilised cantons have succeeded in prohibiting the military capitulations.[21] The sturdy sons of the original free Swiss League will have to give up kicking Neapolitan women with their feet, revelling in the pillage of rebellious towns and, in case of defeat, being immortalised by Thorwaldsen's lions like the fallen of August 10.

The House of Bourbon, however, may for the time being breathe a sigh of relief. Nowhere has the reaction which set in again after February 24[a] achieved such a decisive victory as at Naples and this in spite of the fact that the first of this year's revolutions began precisely in Naples and Sicily. The revolutionary tidal wave, however, which has inundated Old Europe, cannot be checked by absolutist conspiracies and coups d'état. By his counter-revolution of May 15, Ferdinand of Bourbon has laid the cornerstone of the Italian republic. Already Calabria is in flames, in Palermo a Provisional Government has been formed and the Abruzzi will also erupt. The inhabitants of all the exploited provinces will move upon Naples and, united with the people of that city, will take revenge on the royal traitor and his brutal mercenaries. And when Ferdinand falls he will at least have had the satisfaction of having lived and died a true Bourbon.

Written by Engels on May 31, 1848   Printed according to the newspaper

First published in the *Neue Rheinische*   Published in English for the first
Zeitung No. 1, June 1, 1848   time

---

[a] On February 24, 1848, Louis Philippe was overthrown.— *Ed.*

THE DEMOCRATIC PARTY[22]

Cologne, June 1. Every new organ of public opinion is generally expected to show enthusiasm for the party whose principles it supports, unqualified confidence in the strength of this party, and constant readiness either to give the principles the cover of real power, or to cover up real weaknesses with the glamour of principles. We shall not live up to these expectations, We shall not seek to gild defeats with deceptive illusions.

The democratic party has suffered defeat; the principles which it proclaimed at the moment of victory are called in question; the ground it has actually won is being contested inch by inch; much has been lost already and soon the question will arise—what is left?

What is important for us is that the democratic party should understand its position. People may ask why we are concerned with a party, why we do not concentrate on the aims of the democratic movement, the welfare of the people, the happiness of all without distinction.

For such is the law and usage of struggle, and only from the *struggle* of parties can the future welfare arise—not from seemingly clever compromises or from a hypocritical alliance brought about despite conflicting views, interests and aims.

We demand of the democratic party that it grasp the significance of its position. This demand springs from the experience of the past months. The democratic party has allowed the elation of its first victory to go to its head. Intoxicated with the joy of being able at last to proclaim its principles openly for all to hear, it imagined that one had merely to proclaim these principles for them to be immediately realised. It did not go beyond this proclamation after its first victory and the concessions which directly followed it. But while the party was lavish with its ideas and treated as a brother everyone who did not immediately dare to challenge them, the others—those who retained or obtained power—were active. And their activity is not to be made light of. Keeping their principles to themselves and divulging only those parts that were directed against old conditions already overthrown by the revolution, they carefully held the movement in check, ostensibly in the interests of the evolving legal system and the establishment of formal order. They made seeming concessions to the advocates of the old order to secure their support for their own plans; then they gradually built up the basic elements of their own political system and thus succeeded in occupying an intermediate position between the democratic party and the defenders of absolutism, on the one hand advancing and on the other retarding the movement, being at once progressive—as regards the absolutists—and reactionary—as regards the democrats.

This is the party of the prudent, moderate bourgeoisie, and by this party the people's party, in its first intoxication, allowed itself to be taken in till finally it began to see things in their true light after having been contemptuously spurned, after all sorts of reprehensible intentions had been imputed to it, and its members denounced as agitators.[23] Then it perceived that it had actually achieved nothing but what the gentlemen of the bourgeoisie regarded as compatible with their own well-understood interests. Set in conflict with itself by an undemocratic electoral law and defeated in the elections, the party now has against it two elected bodies; the only doubtful thing about them is, which of them will more strongly oppose its demands. Consequently, the enthusiasm of the party has of course melted away and has been replaced by the sober recognition of the fact that a powerful reaction has gained control, and this, strangely enough, happened before any revolutionary action took place.

Although all this is undoubtedly true, it would be dangerous if the bitter feeling engendered by the first and partly self-induced defeat were to impel the democratic party now to revert to that wretched idealism, which is unfortunately characteristic of the German temperament, and according to which a principle that cannot be put into practice immediately is relegated to the distant future while for the present its innocuous elaboration is left to the "thinkers".

We must clearly warn against those hypocritical friends who, while declaring that they agree with the principles, doubt whether they are practicable, because, they allege, the world is not yet ready for them, and who have no intention of making it ready, but on the contrary prefer to share the common lot of the wicked in this wicked earthly life. If these are the crypto-republicans whom the *Hofrat* Gervinus fears so much, then we whole-heartedly agree with him: "Such men are dangerous."[a]

Written by Marx on June 1, 1848

First published in the *Neue Rheinische Zeitung* No. 2, June 2, 1848

Printed according to the newspaper

---

[a] Shakespeare, *Julius Caesar*, Act I, Scene 2.—*Ed.*

CAMPHAUSEN'S STATEMENT
AT THE SESSION OF MAY 30 [24]

Cologne, June 2. *Post et non propter,*[a] in other words Herr *Camphausen* did not become Prime Minister *because of* the March revolution but *after* that revolution. On May 30, 1848, in a most solemn manner and with many protestations, displaying as it were a mysterious carriage of the body to cover the defects of the spirit,[b] Herr Camphausen has revealed this subsequent significance of his Ministry to the Berlin Assembly which sprang from an agreement between him and the indirect electors.

The *thinking friend of history*[c] states that "the Government which was formed on March 29 met soon *after* an occurrence whose significance has not been and will not be misjudged by it".

Herr Camphausen's assertion that he *did not* form a Government *before* March 29 finds confirmation in the issues of the *Preussische Staats-Zeitung* published during the last few months. It may be assumed with confidence that a date, which indicates at least the chronological point of departure of Herr Camphausen's ascension into heaven, possesses great "significance", particularly for Herr Camphausen. What comfort it must be for the fallen barricade fighters to know that their cold corpses serve as visible sign and index finger pointing to the Government of March 29! *Quelle gloire!*[d]

---

[a] After and not because of.— *Ed.*

[b] Laurence Sterne, *The Life and Opinions of Tristram Shandy, Gentleman,* Vol. I, ch. XI.— *Ed.*

[c] An ironical allusion to the subtitle of Karl von Rotteck's *Allgemeine Geschichte vom Anfang der historischen Kenntniss bis auf unsere Zeiten. Für denkende Geschichtsfreunde* (General History from the Beginning of Historical Knowledge Until Our Time. For Thinking Friends of History).— *Ed.*

[d] What honour!— *Ed.*

In one word: after the March revolution, a Camphausen Ministry was formed. This same Camphausen Ministry recognises the "*great significance*" of the March revolution, at least it does not *misjudge* it. The revolution itself is a trifle — its *significance* is what matters! It *signifies* precisely the Camphausen Ministry, at least *post festum*.[a]

"This occurrence" — the formation of the Camphausen Ministry or the March revolution? — "belongs to the most essential contributing factors in the transformation of our *internal* political structure."

Is this passage supposed to mean that the March revolution is "an essential contributing factor" to the formation of the Government of March 29, i.e. the Camphausen Government; or is it supposed merely to say: the Prussian March revolution has revolutionised Prussia! Such a solemn tautology may perhaps be expected from a "*thinking friend of history*"!

"The Government recognises that we stand at its beginning" (namely of the transformation of our internal political conditions) "and that we have a long road ahead of us."

In a word, the Camphausen Ministry recognises that it still has a long way *to travel*, i.e. it is looking forward to a *long* life. Brief is art, i.e. the revolution, and long is life,[b] i.e. the Ministry that came after. It gratuitously recognises itself. Or is one to interpret Camphausen's words in some other way? One would certainly not attribute to the *thinking friend of history* the trivial explanation that nations who stand at the beginning of a new historical epoch stand at the beginning and that the road which lies *ahead* of every epoch will be just as long as the *future*.

So much for the *first* part of the laborious, grave, ceremonious, thorough and considered oration of Prime Minister Camphausen. It may be summarised in the following three statements: *After* the March revolution — the Camphausen Ministry. The Camphausen Ministry has great significance. A long road lies *ahead* of the Camphausen Ministry!

Now for the *second* part.

"By no means have we judged the situation to be such," lectures Herr Camphausen, "that a complete upheaval has resulted from this occurrence" (the March revolution), "that the entire structure of our state has been overthrown, that everything that exists has ceased to be legal and that all conditions must be placed on a new legal basis. On the contrary. The Government agreed from the moment of its initial meeting to regard it as essential for its own future that the then convoked

---

[a] After the event. — *Ed.*

[b] Modified quotation from Goethe's *Faust*, Erster Teil, "Nacht". — *Ed.*

United Diet[25] meet in reality, regardless of the petitions received opposing such a course, and that the new constitution evolve from the existing structure with the legal machinery offered by it without the bond which ties the old to the new being severed. This incontestably correct policy has been maintained. The electoral law has been submitted to the United Diet and passed with its advice. Later on, the attempt was made to induce the Government to alter this law on its own authority, in particular to change the indirect electoral system into a direct one. The Government did not yield. The Government did not act in a dictatorial way; it could not and *would* not act in such a way. The electoral law has in fact been implemented strictly according to the letter. It was on the basis of this electoral law that the electors and deputies were chosen. You are here on the basis of this electoral law with the power to agree with the Crown on a Constitution which it is to be hoped will endure in the future."

A kingdom for a doctrine! A *doctrine* for a kingdom![a]

First there is the "occurrence"—a bashful euphemism for *revolution*. Afterwards there comes the doctrine and dupes the "occurrence".

The illegal "occurrence" turned Herr Camphausen into the *responsible* Prime Minister, i.e. into a creature that had no place and no meaning within the old state of affairs, within the existing structure. We override the old by a *salto mortale* and, fortunately, we find a responsible Minister. The responsible Minister however is even more fortunate in discovering a doctrine. With the first breath of life of a *responsible Prime Minister* the absolute monarchy died and rotted. Among the latter's victims was to be found primarily the blessed "*United Diet*", that disgusting mixture of Gothic delusion and modern deception.[b] The "United Diet" was the "dear faithful follower", the "pet" of the absolute monarchy. Just as the German republic can only celebrate its entry over the body of Herr Venedey, so the responsible Ministry can only enter over the body of the "dear faithful follower". The responsible Minister now picks out the lost body or conjures up the *ghost* of the dear faithful "United Diet", the ghost indeed makes an appearance, but unfortunately hovers suspended in the air, going through all sorts of bizarre capers because it can no longer find any *ground* under its feet, since the old *foundation of law and trust* has been swallowed up by the "occurrence" of the earthquake. The master magician reveals to the ghost that he has summoned it so as to settle its estate and to be able to act the loyal heir. The ghost cannot find enough praise for these polite manners because in ordinary life the deceased are not permitted to issue posthumous testaments. The most highly flattered ghost nods like a pagod to all that the master magician orders, takes a bow at the exit

---

[a] Modified quotation from Shakespeare's *King Richard III*, Act V, Scene 4.— *Ed.*
[b] Heinrich Heine, *Deutschland. Ein Wintermärchen*, Caput XVII.— *Ed.*

and disappears. The law on indirect elections[26] is its posthumous testament.

The doctrinal trick by which Herr Camphausen "has evolved the new constitution from the existing structure with the legal machinery offered by it" develops as follows: ·

An illegal occurrence turns Herr Camphausen into an *illegal* person within the meaning of the "existing structure" and of the "old state of affairs": that is into a responsible Prime Minister, a *constitutional Minister.* The constitutional Minister illegally transforms the *anti-constitutional,* dear faithful *"United Diet", based on the estates,* into a *constituent* assembly. The dear faithful "United Diet" creates unlawfully the law of indirect elections. The law of indirect elections creates the Berlin Chamber, the Berlin Chamber draws up the Constitution and the Constitution produces all successive chambers from here to eternity.

Thus, a goose is transformed into an egg and an egg into a goose. Thanks to the Capitol-saving cackling,[27] the nation soon realises, however, that the golden eggs of Leda, which it laid in the revolution, have been stolen. Not even Deputy *Milde* seems to be the bright conspicuous Castor, son of Leda.

Written by Marx on June 2, 1848   Printed according to the newspaper

First published in the *Neue Rheinische Zeitung* No. 3, June 3, 1848

DEFEAT OF THE GERMAN TROOPS AT SUNDEWITT[28]

Schleswig. So the German troops have once again been beaten, once again the German-Prussian policy has suffered a brilliant defeat! This is the outcome of all those solemn promises of a strong, united Germany!—The time that could have been used to press home the initial victory they let slip by in useless negotiations which the enemy only entered into under duress in order to gain time for renewed resistance. And when Russia declared that she would intervene if Jutland were not evacuated, they still failed to recognise what lay behind the offer of an armistice, they lacked the courage to accept the impending conflict, the long-awaited and unavoidable conflict with Russia. Indeed, the proponents of a policy of force were at a loss, they gave in like cowards and during the *retreat* the "brave" guards were defeated by the "little" Danes! If this is not a case of open treason, then it is a manifestation of such immense incompetence that in any case the management of the whole affair must be placed in other hands. Will the National Assembly in Frankfurt at last feel compelled to do what it should have done long since, that is take over foreign policy itself? Or will it here too—"in the trust that governments perform what are the duties of their office"—proceed to the order of the day?

There follows the report of the Danish attack at Sundewitt,[a] taken from the *Schleswig-Holsteiner Zeitung.*

Rendsburg, May 29. Yesterday (Sunday, the 28th) was assigned to the relief of confederate troops on outpost duty outside Alsen.[b] This information must have

---

[a] The Danish name is Sundeved.—*Ed.*
[b] The Danish name is Als.—*Ed.*

reached the Danes, who are generally well served by their spies in that region. Considerably reinforced by troops that in the last few days had once more been brought over from Fünen[a] to Alsen, they carried out a landing on this side of the river the full significance of which the Germans do not seem to have grasped, since their attention was taken up with the coming on and off guard of their own troops. Soon after the stationing of the new pickets the Germans suddenly found themselves under heavy attack beneath the Düppel[b] Heights from a greatly superior force of Danish infantry and artillery, while at the same time the appearance of a number of ships and gunboats west of Erkensund (near Alnver and Treppe) gave the impression that a landing was also to be carried out there. Clearly this was an attempt by the Danes to split the German forces, but they achieved only a slight measure of success. On the Düppel Heights a fierce battle ensued in which both sides suffered heavy casualties, some of them fatal, as a result of cannon-fire (it is not yet possible to give figures). The Danes fought famously. Their numbers are put at 8,000 men, who took up battle-stations under cover of the deck-guns and flanked by cannon on land, while our men can scarcely have numbered 7,000. It was several hours before the battle was decided, when at last, around 7 o'clock in the evening, the German troops were forced to begin the retreat via Gravenstein northwards to Quars, while the Danes got to within an hour's march of Gravenstein, where our rearguard had stopped.

Written by Engels on June 2, 1848

First published in the *Neue Rheinische Zeitung* No. 3, June 3, 1848

Printed according to the newspaper

Published in English for the first time

---

[a] The Danish name is Fyn.—*Ed.*
[b] The Danish name is Dybbøl.—*Ed.*

QUESTIONS OF LIFE AND DEATH

Cologne, June 3. The times are changing and we are changing with them. That is a short saying with which our Ministers *Camphausen* and *Hansemann* are also well acquainted. Oh, what they had to put up with from government officials and marshals[29] when they were still modest deputies sitting on the school bench of a provincial diet! And how they were kept on a leash like fifth formers in the Rhenish Provincial Diet by His Most Serene Highness, form-master Solms-Lich! Although they were permitted to indulge in a few exercises in elocution after they had been promoted to the sixth form, to the United Diet,[30] how they were even then disciplined by their schoolmaster, Herr Adolf von Rochow, with the cane presented to him from on high! How meekly they had to take the impertinences of a Bodelschwingh, how attentively they had to admire the broken German of a Boyen, and how limited an understanding of a loyal subject they were obliged to display in face of the crude ignorance of a Duesberg!

Things have changed now. The 18th of March has put an end to all the pedantic political schooling and the pupils of the Provincial Diet have announced their graduation. Herr Camphausen and Herr Hansemann have become Ministers and are delighted to feel their great importance as "indispensable persons".

Everybody that has come in contact with them has been made to feel just how "indispensable" they consider themselves to be and how audacious they have become since their release from school.

They immediately began to re-establish provisionally their old schoolroom, the United Diet. It was here that the grand act of transition from bureaucratic grammar school to constitutional university was to take place, the solemn presentation, with all due formality, to the Prussian people of their certificate of maturity.

The people declared in numerous memoranda and petitions that they did not want to have anything to do with the United Diet.

Herr Camphausen replied (e.g. during the session of the Constituent Assembly on May 30[a]) that the convocation of the Diet was of *vital importance* to the Ministry and that was that.

The Diet met, a dejected, contrite assembly which despaired of the world, of God and of itself. The Diet had been given to understand that it was merely to adopt the new electoral law; but Herr Camphausen demanded of it not only a paper law and indirect elections, but also twenty-five million in cash. The curiae become confused, they begin to doubt their competence and stammer disjointed objections. There is nothing they can do, however, since after deliberation Herr Camphausen has made up his mind, and if the money is not granted and the "vote of confidence" is withheld Herr Camphausen will depart for Cologne and abandon the Prussian monarchy to its fate. The thought of such a possibility brings cold sweat to the foreheads of the gentlemen of the Diet, all resistance ceases and the vote of confidence is passed with a bitter-sweet smile. These twenty-five million—currency in the airy realm of dreams[b]—clearly show where and how they were enacted.

The indirect elections are proclaimed. A wave of speeches, petitions and deputations rises against them. The ministerial gentlemen reply: the Ministry stands or falls with the indirect elections. After that everything becomes calm once more and both parties can go to sleep.

The Agreement Assembly[c] meets. Herr Camphausen is resolved that an address should be made in reply to his speech from the throne. Deputy Duncker is to make the proposal. A discussion begins during which a pretty lively opposition to the address emerges. Herr Hansemann is bored by the everlasting, confused cross-talk of the clumsy assembly; it becomes unendurable to his sense of parliamentary tact and he declares curtly that they could be spared all this: either an address is forthcoming and in that case all is well, or no address is made and the Ministry resigns. Nevertheless, the debate goes on and finally Herr Camphausen himself steps up to the rostrum to confirm that the question of the address is of vital importance to the Ministry. Finally, when this also has no effect,

---

[a] See this volume, pp. 30-32.—*Ed.*

[b] Heinrich Heine, *Deutschland. Ein Wintermärchen*, Caput VII.—*Ed.*

[c] i.e. the Prussian National Assembly convened on May 22, 1848.—*Ed.*

Herr Auerswald also rises and asserts for the third time that the Ministry stands or falls with the address. The assembly was now sufficiently convinced and, of course, voted for the address.

Thus, our "responsible" Ministers have, within two months, already acquired that experience and self-possession necessary for the conduct of an assembly which M. Duchâtel, who certainly is not to be belittled, gained only after several years of intimate dealing with the last but one French Chamber of Deputies. For some time past M. Duchâtel, too, when the Left bored him with its lengthy tirades, used to declare: the Chamber is free to vote for or against, but we shall resign if it votes against. Thereupon, the timorous majority, for which M. Duchâtel was the "most indispensable" man in the world, flocked around its threatened ringleader like a flock of sheep in a thunderstorm. M. Duchâtel was a frivolous Frenchman and played this game until it became too much for his fellow countrymen. Herr Camphausen is a stalwart and composed German and he will know how far he can go.

Of course, one can save both time and arguments by this method if one is as sure of one's supporters as Herr Camphausen is of the "agreers". The opposition is pretty effectively silenced if every issue is made a question of confidence. That is why this method is most suitable for determined men like Duchâtel and Hansemann who know once and for all what they want and who find all further useless palaver unbearable. This little earthly expedient, however, as our Prime Minister will find out by experience, is not at all suitable for men with debating skills who love "to expound and exchange their views about the past, the present, and the future as well, in great debates" (Camphausen, session of May 31), for men who stand their ground on principles and grasp the meaning of current events with the acumen of philosophers, for elevated minds such as Guizot and Camphausen. He should let his Duchâtel-Hansemann handle such matters and keep to the more elevated sphere where we take such a delight in observing him.

Written on June 3, 1848

First published in the *Neue Rheinische Zeitung* No. 4, June 4, 1848

Printed according to the newspaper

Published in English for the first time

THE CAMPHAUSEN GOVERNMENT[31]

Cologne, June 3. It is well known that the French National Assembly of 1789 was preceded by an assembly of notables which was composed of the *estates* like the Prussian United Diet. In the decree by which he convoked the National Assembly, Minister Necker referred to the expressed desire of the notables to call together the Estates-General. Thus, Minister Necker held a significant advantage over Minister Camphausen. He did not have to wait for the storming of the Bastille or the overthrow of the absolute monarchy in order afterwards to link the old and new in a doctrinaire fashion so that he could laboriously maintain the *illusion* that France had achieved the new Constituent Assembly by the legal machinery of the old constitution. He possessed still other advantages. He was Minister of France and not Minister of Lorraine and Alsace, whereas Herr Camphausen is not Minister of Germany but Minister of Prussia. And in spite of all these advantages Minister Necker did not succeed in transforming a revolutionary movement into a tranquil reform. The serious malady could not be cured by attar of roses.[a] Herr Camphausen will succeed even less in changing the character of the movement by an artificial theory that draws a straight line of succession between his Ministry and the old conditions which prevailed in the Prussian monarchy. No device can transform the March revolution and the German revolutionary movement as a whole into *incidents* of more or less consequence. Was Louis Philippe elected King of the French *because* he was a Bourbon?

---

[a] Heinrich Heine, *Deutschland. Ein Wintermärchen*, Caput XXVI (paraphrased).—*Ed.*

Was he chosen *although* he was a Bourbon? One may remember that this question divided the parties shortly after the July revolution.[32] And what did the question prove? It proved that the revolution itself was called in question and that the interests of the new ruling class and its political representatives were not the interests of the revolution.

The same significance must be ascribed to the statement of Herr Camphausen that his Government had been brought into the world not *by* the March revolution but *after* the March revolution.

Written by Marx on June 3, 1848　　　　　　　Printed according to the newspaper

First published in the *Neue Rheinische Zeitung* No. 4, June 4, 1848

THE QUESTION OF UNION

Throughout the whole of North Italy various plots and schemes are being hatched, on the one hand to unite the smaller states with Sardinia and on the other to prevent that union. These intrigues are very similar to those for hegemony in Germany. Charles Albert is seeking to establish an Italian Prussia "on the broadest possible basis", from Nice to Trieste. The affair is of absolutely no national importance; on both sides it is a question of local interests and the gratification of provincial vanities, such as can only be removed through the creation of a united and indivisible Italy. Until then, the decisive factor will continue to be the needs of the moment, and these are *for* union, since this would bring about, at least in some measure, a certain concentration of forces for the struggle against Austria.

Written by Engels on June 2, 1848

First published in the *Neue Rheinische Zeitung* No. 4, June 4, 1848

Printed according to the newspaper

Published in English for the first time

THE WAR COMEDY

Schleswig-Holstein. Indeed, the annals of all history know of no such campaign, no such striking alternation between the force of arms and diplomacy as our current unitedly-German-national war against little Denmark! All the great deeds of the old imperial army with its six hundred commanders, general staffs and military councils, the mutual chicaneries of the leaders of the 1792 coalition, the orders and counter-orders of the blessed Royal and Imperial War Council, are serious and touchingly tragic events compared to the warlike comedy which the new German federal army[33] is performing in Schleswig-Holstein to the resounding laughter of all Europe.

Let us briefly trace the plot of this comedy.

The Danes advance from Jutland and land troops in North Schleswig. The Prussians and Hanoverians occupy Rendsburg and the Eider line. The Danes, who, in spite of all the German bragging, are an alert and brave people, quickly attack and in a *single* battle drive the army of Schleswig-Holstein back towards the Prussians. The latter calmly look on.

At last, Berlin gives the order to advance. The united German troops attack the Danes and at Schleswig overwhelm them by their numerical superiority. The victory was brought about primarily by the Pomeranian guardsmen who handled their rifle-butts as skilfully as they had done previously at Grossbeeren and Dennewitz.[34] Schleswig is conquered once more and Germany is jubilant at the heroic deed of her army.

In the meantime, the Danish fleet which numbers less than twenty ships of any size, seizes the German merchant vessels, blockades all

German ports, and covers the crossings to the islands to which
the army withdraws. Jutland is abandoned and partially occupied by Prussian troops who demand an indemnity of 2 million
speciestaler.

Before a single taler of the indemnity has been received, however,
England sends proposals for mediation on the basis of a withdrawal
and the neutrality of Schleswig, and Russia sends threatening Notes.
Herr Camphausen falls right into this trap and, on his orders, the
Prussians, drunk with victory, withdraw from Veile to Königsau, to
Hadersleben, Apenrade[a] and Flensburg. The Danes, who till then
had vanished, reappear at once. They pursue the Prussians day and
night, throw their withdrawal into confusion, make landings
everywhere, defeat the troops of the 10th Federal Corps at Sundewitt[b] and retreat only before superior numbers. In the engagement of May 30, rifle-butts, swung this time by the solid arms
of Mecklenburgers, again proved decisive. The German inhabitants flee with the Prussians, all North Schleswig is · abandoned to devastation and plunder, and the *Danebrog*[c] flies once
more over Hadersleben and Apenrade. It is obvious that Prussian
soldiers of all ranks obey orders in Schleswig just as they do in
Berlin.

Suddenly there comes an order from Berlin: the Prussians are to
advance again. Now they merrily advance northward once more, but
the comedy still has long to run. We want to wait and see where the
Prussians will this time receive orders to retreat.

In short, it is a genuine quadrille, a military ballet which the
Camphausen Ministry is having performed for its own amusement
and for the glory of the German nation.

We must not forget, however, that it is the burning villages of
Schleswig which supply the illumination for the stage and that it is
the cries for vengeance from Danish marauders and partisans which
provide the chorus for this performance.

The Camphausen Ministry has on this occasion demonstrated its
high calling to represent Germany abroad. Schleswig, twice abandoned to Danish invasions through the fault of this Ministry, will
gratefully remember the first diplomatic experiment of our "responsible" Ministers.

---

[a] The Danish names are Kongeaa, Haderslev, Aabenraa.—*Ed.*
[b] See this volume, pp. 34-35.—*Ed.*
[c] Danish flag.— *Ed.*

Let us have confidence in the wisdom and energy of the Camphausen Ministry!

Written by Engels on June 4, 1848

First published in the *Neue Rheinische Zeitung* No. 5, June 5, 1848

Printed according to the newspaper

Published in English for the first time

THE REACTION

Cologne, June 5. The dead ride fast.[a] Herr Camphausen disavows the revolution and the reaction dares to suggest to the Agreement Assembly that the revolution should be stigmatised as a riot. On June 3, a deputy[b] moved that a monument be erected for the soldiers who died on March 18.

Written on June 5, 1848

First published in the *Neue Rheinische Zeitung* No. 6, June 6, 1848

Printed according to the newspaper

Published in English for the first time

---

[a] Gottfried Bürger, "Lenore".—*Ed.*
[b] Karl Richter.—*Ed.*

COMITÉ DE SÛRETÉ GÉNÉRALE IN BERLIN[35]

Cologne, June 5. Now Berlin, too, has its *Comité de sûreté générale* just as Paris had in the year 1793. There is, however, one difference: the Paris committee was revolutionary, whereas the one in Berlin is reactionary. For according to an announcement which appeared in Berlin, "the authorities entrusted with the maintenance of order" have found it necessary "to join in a combined effort". They have therefore appointed a Committee of Public Safety which has taken up residence in Oberwallstrasse. This new administrative body is composed as follows: 1. President: Puttkamer, director in the Ministry of the Interior; 2. Commandant Aschoff, the former commander-in-chief of the civic militia; 3. Chief of Police Minutoli; 4. Public Prosecutor Temme; 5. Burgomaster Naunyn and two councillors; 6. The chairman of the City Council and three city councillors; 7. Five officers and two soldiers of the civic militia. The committee will

"take notice of all events which disturb or threaten to disturb public order and it promises to subject the facts to a profound and thorough investigation. While circumventing old and inadequate means and methods, and avoiding unnecessary correspondence, the committee will agree upon suitable steps and initiate the rapid and energetic implementation of the necessary orders by the various organs of the administration. Only such joint co-operation can bring speed and safety, combined with the requisite circumspection, into the conduct of business which is often very difficult in the present circumstances. In particular, however, the civic militia, which has assumed the protection of the city, will be enabled, *when required, to lend appropriate weight to the decisions made with its advice by the authorities.* With full confidence in the participation and collaboration of all inhabitants, particularly the honourable (!) estate of artisans *and* (!) workers, the deputies, *free of all party views and aims,* begin their laborious task and hope that they may be able to fulfil it, preferably by the peaceful method of mediation, so that the well-being of all may be assured".

The very unctuous, ingratiating, humbly pleading language used leads one to suspect that what is being formed here is a centre for reactionary activities against the revolutionary people of Berlin. The composition of this committee changes this suspicion to certainty. There is first of all Herr Puttkamer, who as Chief of Police became well known for his expulsions. As under the bureaucratic monarchy, no high authority without at least *one* Puttkamer. Then there is Herr Aschoff, who, because he is as rude as a drill-sergeant and on account of his reactionary intrigues, came to be so hated by the civic militia that it decided to remove him. He has now indeed resigned. Then we come to Herr Minutoli, who in 1846 saved the fatherland in Posen[a] by discovering the Polish conspiracy[36] and who recently threatened to expel the compositors when they were striking because of wages disagreements.[37] Then there are the representatives of two bodies that have become extremely reactionary: the Municipal Government and the City Council, and, finally, among the civic militia officers the arch-reactionary Major Blesson. We hope that the people of Berlin will by no means let themselves be held in tutelage by this arbitrarily constituted committee of reaction.

The committee, by the way, has already started its reactionary activity by asking that the popular procession, announced for yesterday (Sunday),[b] to the grave of those killed in March should be called off since this would be a demonstration and demonstrations in general are held to be an evil.

Written on June 5, 1848

First published in the *Neue Rheinische Zeitung* No. 6, June 6, 1848

Printed according to the newspaper

Published in English for the first time

---

[a] The Polish name is Poznań.—*Ed.*
[b] June 4, 1848.—*Ed.*

THE PROGRAMMES
OF THE RADICAL-DEMOCRATIC PARTY
AND OF THE LEFT AT FRANKFURT[38]

Cologne, June 6. Yesterday we acquainted our readers with the "reasoned manifesto of the radical-democratic party in the Constituent National Assembly at Frankfurt am Main".[39] Today they will find the manifesto of the Left under the heading Frankfurt. At first sight the two manifestos appear to be almost identical except in form, as the radical-democratic party has a clumsy editor and the Left a skilful one. On closer scrutiny, however, several substantially different points stand out. The manifesto of the radicals demands a National Assembly to be set up "*without any property qualification* and by *direct elections*", that of the Left wants it to be convened by "*free universal elections*". *Free universal elections* exclude *property qualifications*, but by no means exclude the *indirect* method of election. In any case why use this vague and ambiguous term?

We encounter once more this greater latitude and flexibility in the demands of the Left compared with the demands of the radical party. The Left wants

"an executive Central Authority elected *by* the National Assembly for a definite period and responsible to it".

It does not say whether this Central Authority has to be elected *from the ranks of the National Assembly*, as the manifesto of the radicals expressly states.

Finally the manifesto of the Left calls for the immediate definition, proclamation and maintenance of the basic rights of the German people against all possible encroachments by individual governments. The manifesto of the radicals is not content with this. It declares that

"all political power of the federal state is now concentrated in the Assembly which must *immediately* bring into operation the various forces and political institutions falling within its jurisdiction, and direct the home and foreign policies of the federal state".

Both manifestos agree that the "drafting of the German Constitution should be left solely to the National Assembly" and the governments debarred from taking part in it. Both agree that "without prejudice to the people's rights to be proclaimed by the National Assembly" it should be left to the individual states to choose their form of government, whether that of a constitutional monarchy or a republic. Both finally agree that Germany should be transformed into a confederation or a federative state.

The manifesto of the radicals at least expresses the *revolutionary* nature of the National Assembly. It demands appropriate revolutionary action. Does not the mere existence of a *Constituent* National Assembly prove that *there is no longer* any Constitution? But if there is no Constitution, then there is no Government either. And if there is no longer any Government, the National Assembly must govern. Its first move should have been a decree of seven words: " *The Federal Diet*[40] *is dissolved for ever."*

A Constituent National Assembly must above all be an *active*, revolutionarily active assembly. The Assembly at Frankfurt is engaged in parliamentary school exercises and leaves it to the governments to act. Assuming that this learned gathering succeeds, after mature consideration, in framing the best of agendas and the best of constitutions, of what use is the best agenda and the best Constitution if the governments meanwhile have placed bayonets on the agenda?

Apart from the fact that it was the outcome of *indirect* elections, the German National Assembly suffers from a specifically German malady. It sits at Frankfurt am Main, and Frankfurt am Main is merely an ideal centre, which corresponded to the hitherto ideal, that is merely imaginary, German unity. Frankfurt am Main moreover is not a big city with a large revolutionary population backing the National Assembly, partly defending it, partly spurring it on. It is the first time in world history that the Constituent Assembly of a big nation holds its sessions in a small town. This is the result of Germany's previous history. While the French and English national assemblies met on volcanic ground—Paris and London—the German National Assembly considered itself lucky to find *neutral* ground, where in the most comfortable peace of mind it could ponder over the best Constitution and the best agenda. Yet the present state of affairs in Germany offered the Assembly an opportunity to overcome the drawbacks of its unfortunate physical situation. It only needed everywhere to counter dictatorially the reactionary encroachments by obsolete governments in order to win over public opinion, a power against which all bayonets and rifle-butts would be ineffective. Instead Mainz, almost within sight of the Assembly, is abandoned to the arbitrary actions of the army, and German citizens from other parts of the country are exposed to the chicanery of the philistines in Frankfurt.[a] The Assembly bores the German people instead of inspiring it or being inspired by it. Although there is a *public* which for the time being still looks with good-natured humour upon the antics performed by the spectre of the resurrected Diet of the Holy Roman Empire,[41] there is no *people* that can find its own life reflected in the life of the Assembly. Far from being the central organ of the revolutionary movement, the Assembly, up till now, was not even its echo.

If the National Assembly forms a Central Authority from its own midst, little satisfaction can be expected from such a Provisional Government, in view of the Assembly's present composition and the fact that it let the favourable moment slip by. If it forms no Central Authority, it puts its seal to its own abdication and will be scattered to the winds at the first stir of a revolutionary current.

It is to the credit of both the programme of the Left and that of the radical group that they have grasped this necessity. Both exclaim with Heine:

> "For when I consider the matter with care,
> We don't need an Emperor really."[b]

Because it is so difficult to decide *"who* shall be emperor", and because there are as many good reasons for an elected emperor as there are for an hereditary emperor, even the conservative majority of the Assembly will be compelled to cut the Gordian knot by electing *no emperor at all.*

It is incomprehensible how the so-called radical-democratic party can advocate, as the ultimate constitutional structure of Germany, a *federation* of constitutional monarchies, small principalities and tiny republics, i.e. a federal state consisting of such heterogeneous elements, headed by a republican Government—for this is what the central body agreed to by the Left really amounts to.

First of all the German Central Government elected by the National Assembly must undoubtedly be set up *alongside* the governments

---

[a] See this volume, pp. 16-19.—*Ed.*

[b] Heinrich Heine, *Deutschland. Ein Wintermärchen*, Caput XVI.—*Ed.*

which still actually exist. But its struggle against the separate governments begins as soon as it comes into existence, and in the course of this struggle either the Central Government and the unity of Germany are wrecked, or the separate governments with their constitutional princes or petty republics are destroyed.

We do not make the utopian demand that at the outset a *united indivisible German republic* should be proclaimed, but we ask the so-called radical-democratic party not to confuse the starting point of the struggle and of the revolutionary movement with the goal. Both German unity and the German Constitution can result only from a movement in which the internal conflicts and the war with the East will play an equally decisive role. The final act of constitution cannot be *decreed*, it coincides with the movement we have to go through. It is therefore not a question of putting into practice this or that view, this or that political idea, but of understanding the course of development. The National Assembly has to take only such steps as are practicable in the first instance.

Nothing can be more confused than the notion advanced by the editor of the democratic manifesto—for all his assurances that "everybody is glad to get rid of his confusion"—that the *federal state of North America* should serve as a model for the German Constitution.

Leaving alone the fact that all its constituent parts have a similar structure, the United States of America covers an area equal to that of civilised Europe. Only a *European* federation would be analogous to it. But in order to federate with other states Germany must first of all become *one* state. The conflict between centralisation and federalism in Germany is a conflict between modern culture and feudalism. Germany fell into a kind of bourgeoisified feudalism at the very moment the great monarchies arose in the West; she was moreover excluded from the world market just when this market was opened up to the countries of Western Europe. Germany became impoverished while the Western countries grew rich; she became countrified while they became urbanised. Even if Russia did not knock at the gates of Germany, the economic conditions alone would compel the latter to introduce rigorous centralisation. Even from a purely bourgeois point of view, the solid unity of Germany is a primary condition for her deliverance from her present wretchedness and for the building up of her national wealth. And how could modern social problems be solved in a territory that is split into 39 small states?

Incidentally, the editor of the democratic programme does not bother about such a minor question as material economic conditions.

He relies on the concept of federation in his reasoning. *Federation* is an *alliance of free* and *equal partners. Hence* Germany must be a *federal state.* But cannot the Germans unite in *one* great state without offence to the concept of an alliance of free and equal partners?

Written on June 6, 1848   Printed according to the newspaper

First published in the *Neue Rheinische Zeitung* No. 7, June 7, 1848

THE AGREEMENT DEBATES IN BERLIN [42]

Cologne, June 6. The *negotiations for an agreement* etc. are making most satisfactory progress in Berlin. Motions follow motions and most of them are even submitted five or six times to make quite sure that they are not lost on their long way through the sections and committees. At every opportunity the greatest number of preliminary questions, secondary questions, interpolated questions, supplementary questions, and main questions is raised. Whenever one of these great or small questions is taken up, an informal conversation ensues between the delegates "on the floor" and the President, the Ministers etc., thus creating a welcome pause between the demanding "great debates". Especially those anonymous agreers whom the stenographer is in the habit of designating as "votes", love to express their opinions during such genial discussions. These "votes", by the way, are so proud of their right to vote that sometimes *they vote both yes and no* as happened on June 2. Alongside this idyll, however, there arises with all the grandeur of tragedy the battle of the great debate, a battle which is not only conducted verbally from the rostrum but is joined by the chorus of the agreers with drumming, murmuring, and confused shouting. Each time the drama ends, of course, with a victory for the virtuous Right and is almost always decided by the conservative army calling for a vote.

During the session of June 2 Herr *Jung* questioned the Foreign Minister about the extradition treaty with Russia.[43] It is known that already in 1842, public opinion forced the abrogation of the extradition treaty, which was, however, renewed during the reaction of 1844. It is known that the Russian Government orders extradited persons to be knouted to death or to be exiled to Siberia. It is known that the agreed extradition of common criminals and vagabonds offers the desired pretext for the delivery of political refugees into the hands of the Russians.

Foreign Minister *Arnim* replied:

"Surely, no one will object to the extradition of deserters, since it is an accepted practice between friendly states mutually to extradite such people."

We take notice that according to our Minister Russia and Germany are "friendly states". The massive armies which Russia is concentrating along the Bug and Niemen rivers have no other intention, to be sure, than to liberate "friendly" Germany as soon as possible from the terror of the revolution.

"The decision to extradite criminals, by the way, rests in the hands of the courts so that there is every guarantee that the accused will not be extradited before the conclusion of the criminal investigation."

Herr Arnim tries to make the Assembly believe that Prussian courts investigate the evidence which has been gathered against the accused. The opposite is true. Russian or Russian-Polish judicial authorities send a decision to the Prussian judicial authorities, indicting the fugitive. The Prussian court is obliged to check merely the authenticity of this document and if it proves to be genuine, the extradition has to take place. Thus, "there is every guarantee" that the Russian Government has only to beckon to its judges in order to get hold of every fugitive with the aid of Prussian chains as long as the fugitive has not yet been indicted for political offences.

"It goes without saying that *our own subjects* will not be extradited."

"Our own subjects", feudal Baron von Arnim, cannot be extradited under any circumstances because there are no longer "subjects" in Germany since the people took the liberty of emancipating themselves on the barricades.

"Our own subjects"! Are we, who elect assemblies and prescribe sovereign laws to kings and emperors, "subjects" of His Majesty the King of Prussia?

"Our own subjects"! If the Assembly had even a spark of the revolutionary pride to which it owes its existence, it would have drummed the servile Minister off the rostrum and the ministerial bench in a single outburst of indignation. Instead it calmly allowed the stigmatising expression to go unchallenged. Not the slightest protest was heard.

Herr *Rehfeld* questioned Herr Hansemann about the *Seehandlung's*[44] renewed buying up of wool and about the advantages enjoyed by British buyers over German buyers as a result of the discount offered to the British. The wool industry, depressed by the general crisis, expected to gain at least some small benefit by purchasing at this year's very low wool prices. Along comes the *Seehandlung* and drives up the price of wool by its enormous purchases in bulk. At the same time it offers to facilitate considerably the purchases of British buyers by discounting bills of exchange drawn on London—a measure which is also quite apt to raise the price of wool by attracting new buyers and which gives significant advantages to foreign over domestic purchasers.

The *Seehandlung* is a legacy of absolute monarchy which used it for all sorts of purposes. For twenty years it has caused the 1820 Law on Government Debts [45] to remain an illusion and it has meddled in trade and industry in a most disagreeable fashion.

The question asked by Herr *Rehfeld* is basically of little interest to democracy. It concerns a profit of several thousand talers more or less for either wool producers or wool manufacturers.

The wool producers are almost exclusively large landed proprietors, i.e. feudal lords from Brandenburg, Prussia, Silesia and Posen.

The wool manufacturers are for the most part big capitalists, i.e. gentlemen of the big bourgeoisie.

Hence, the price of wool is a matter not of general interest but of class interests. The question is whether the big landed aristocracy will profit to the exclusion of the big bourgeoisie or whether it will be the other way around.

Herr Hansemann who has been sent to Berlin as the representative of the big bourgeoisie, the party now in power, betrays it to the landed aristocracy, the conquered party.

The only interest which this entire matter holds for us democrats lies in the fact that Herr Hansemann has taken up the cause of the conquered party, that he does not support the merely conservative class but the *reactionary* class. We admit that we did not expect such behaviour from the bourgeois Hansemann.

Herr *Hansemann* assures us, to begin with, that he is no friend of the *Seehandlung* and then adds: Neither the purchasing business nor the mills of the *Seehandlung* can be stopped suddenly. Concerning wool purchases, there are treaties by which the *Seehandlung* ... is committed to buy up a certain amount of wool this year. I believe that if during any year such purchases are not harmful to private trade, it is certainly the case this year (?) ... because otherwise the prices would drop too low.

The entire speech shows that Herr Hansemann is not comfortable while delivering it. He had been induced to do a favour to the

Arnims, Schaffgotsches and Itzenplitzes to the detriment of the wool manufacturers, and he must now defend his rash step with the arguments of modern political economy which is so unmerciful to the interests of the aristocracy. He knows better than anyone else that he is making a fool of the Assembly.

"Neither the purchasing business nor the mills of the *Seehandlung* can be stopped suddenly." Thus, the *Seehandlung* buys wool and lets its mills work at full speed. If the mills of the *Seehandlung* "cannot be stopped" suddenly then the sales obviously also cannot be ended. Thus, the *Seehandlung* will put its woollen products on the market, glut the already overstocked market and depress the already sinking prices even more. In a word, it will make the current commercial crisis even worse and take away the last few remaining customers from the wool manufacturers in order to supply the landed gentry of Brandenburg etc. with money for their wool.

Concerning the English bills of exchange, Herr Hansemann delivers a brilliant tirade describing the enormous advantages which will accrue to the entire country when English guineas flow into the pockets of the landed gentry of Brandenburg. We will of course not discuss these remarks seriously. What we cannot understand is that Herr Hansemann was able to maintain a straight face during his speech.

The same session also debated a committee which is to be formed because of Posen. Concerning that, tomorrow.

Written by Engels on June 6, 1848

First published in the *Neue Rheinische Zeitung* No. 7, June 7, 1848

Printed according to the newspaper

Published in English for the first time

THE AGREEMENT DEBATES

Cologne, June 6. At the *Berlin agreement session* of the 2nd, Herr *Reuter* moved the appointment of a committee of inquiry into the causes of the civil war in Posen.[46]

Herr *Parrisius* demands an immediate debate on this motion.

The President[a] gets ready to call for a vote when Herr *Camphausen* recalls that there has as yet been no debate on Herr *Parrisius'* motion:

"May I remind you that the passage of this" (Reuter's) "motion would mean the acceptance of an *important political principle* which is certainly entitled (*sic!*) to a test in the sections."

We are put in suspense about the "important principle" contained in Reuter's motion, a secret which Herr Camphausen is not disclosing for the time being.

While we have to show patience in this respect, a complacent debate develops between the Chairman (Herr *Esser,* Vice-President) and several "votes" as to whether or not a debate is permissible on Parrisius' motion. Herr Esser here debates with arguments which sound strange in the mouth of the President of a *soi-disant* National Assembly: "*I was under the impression* that it is permissible to discuss any matter that the Assembly is called upon to decide."

"I was under the impression"! Man proposes and Herr Camphausen disposes by drafting standing orders that nobody can understand and having them adopted provisionally by his Assembly.

Herr Camphausen was gracious this time. He had to have the debate. Parrisius' and Reuter's motions might have been passed without debate, i.e. an indirect vote of no confidence would have

---

[a] Karl Milde.— *Ed.*

been rendered against him. And, still worse, what would have become of his "important political principle" without a debate?

Hence, a discussion takes place.

Herr *Parrisius* wants an immediate debate on the main motion so that no time is lost and the committee may possibly report before the debate on the address. Otherwise judgment would be made in the address without any factual knowledge about Posen.

Herr *Meusebach* opposes this move although as yet rather mildly.

But now Herr *Ritz* rises impatiently to put an end to Reuter's subversive motion. He is a royal Prussian *Regierungsrat* and will not tolerate that assemblies, even if they are assemblies for the purpose of agreement, meddle in his special field. He knows of but one authority entitled to do so: the *Oberpräsidium*. He prefers the system of successive appeals to everything else.

"What," he exclaims, "do you, gentlemen, intend to send a commission to Posen? Do you intend to *turn* yourselves into *administrative* or *judicial authorities?* Gentlemen, I cannot perceive from this motion what you are trying to accomplish. Are you going to demand an inspection of the files of the commanding general" (what outrage!) "or the judicial authorities" (horrible!) "or perhaps even the administrative authorities?" (In contemplating that possibility, the *Regierungsrat* is at his wits' end.) "Do you want the investigation to be conducted by an improvised committee" (which perhaps has never taken an examination) "dealing with all these matters *which nobody yet clearly understands?*" (Herr Ritz probably only appoints committees to investigate matters which everybody clearly understands.) "This important issue *on which you arrogate to yourselves rights which do not belong to you....*" (Interruption.)

What is one to say to this *Regierungsrat* of sterling worth, to this personification of red tape who has no guile! He is like that provincial character in Cham's little cartoon who, upon arriving in Paris after the February revolution, sees posters with the inscription "*République française*" and runs to the Public Prosecutor-General to denounce these agitators against the royal Government. That man had slept through the entire period.

Herr Ritz, too, has been asleep. The thundering words "committee of inquiry for Posen" roughly shake him awake and, still drowsy with sleep, the astonished man exclaims: "Do you wish to arrogate to yourselves rights which do not belong to you?"

Herr *Duncker* regards a committee of inquiry as superfluous "since the committee on the address must demand the necessary clarifications from the Ministry". As if it were not precisely the job of the committee to compare the "clarifications" of the Ministry with the facts.

Herr *Bloem* spoke of the urgency of the motion. The question ought to be settled before there are deliberations on the address. There had been talk about improvised committees. Herr Hansemann had the previous day similarly improvised a question of confidence and still a vote had been taken.

Herr *Hansemann*, who had probably thought about his new financial plan during the entire unedifying debate, was rudely awakened from his golden dreams by the mention of his name. He evidently had no idea what it was all about but his name had been mentioned and he had to speak. Only two points of contact had remained in his memory: the speeches of his superior, Camphausen, and Herr *Ritz*. After mouthing a few platitudes about the question of the address he composed the following rhetorical masterpiece from these two speeches:

"Precisely because we do not yet know all the tasks which the committee will have to perform, whether it will dispatch some of its own members to the Grand Duchy, whether it will have to take care of this or that matter, *all this proves the great importance of the question that is under discussion* (!). To decide this question here and now right away would mean to *decide one of the most important political questions in an improvised fashion.* I do not believe that the Assembly will want to tread this path and I am confident that it will be careful etc."

What contempt Herr Hansemann must have for the entire Assembly to be able to fling such conclusions at this body! We want to appoint a committee which will perhaps have to go to Posen and maybe not. Just because we do not know whether it must remain in Berlin or go to Posen, the question whether a committee ought to be appointed at all is of *great importance*. And because it is of great importance, it is one of the *most important political* questions!

Which question, however, this most important political question is, Herr Hansemann keeps to himself for the time being, just as Herr Camphausen does not reveal his important political principle. Let us be patient once more!

The effect of Hansemann's logic is so crushing that everybody at once begins clamouring for a termination of the debate. Now the following scene ensues:

Herr *Jung* demands the right to speak against the closing of the debate.

The President: It seems to me inadmissible to permit you to speak on this.

Herr *Jung*: It is customary everywhere to have the right to speak against the closing of a debate.

Herr *Temme* reads out Article 42 of the provisional standing orders according to which Herr Jung is correct and the President incorrect.

Herr *Jung* is allowed to speak: I am against closing the debate because the Minister was the last person to speak. The words of a

Minister are of the greatest importance because they attract a great party to one side, because a great party does not like to disavow a Minister....

A general, long-drawn-out aha! aha! arises. A terrific uproar begins on the Right.

Commissioner of Justice *Moritz* exclaims from the floor: I move that Jung be called to order since he has offended *the entire Assembly by resorting to personalities!*(!)

Another voice from the "Right" shouts: I second the motion and I protest against....

The uproar grows constantly. *Jung* does his best but finds it impossible to make himself heard. He calls upon the President to uphold his right to speak.

President: Since the Assembly has decided, my duties are over.(!!)

Herr *Jung*: The Assembly has not decided. You must first call for a formal vote.

Herr *Jung* is forced to yield. The noise does not abate until he has left the rostrum.

President: The last speaker *seems* (!) to have spoken against the termination of the debate. The question is whether someone else still wants to speak for closure.

Herr *Reuter*: The debate for and against closure has already taken up 15 minutes of our time. Should we not leave it on the table?

Thereupon the speaker again takes up the urgency of setting up a committee which compels Herr Hansemann to rise once more and to explain at last his "most important political question".

Herr *Hansemann*: Gentlemen! We are dealing with one of the *greatest political questions*, i.e. whether the Assembly has the desire to venture upon a path that *may involve it in considerable conflicts!*

At last! Herr Hansemann, as a consistent Duchâtel, promptly declares once again that it is a *question of confidence*. For him all questions have only one significance, namely whether they are questions of confidence, and a question of confidence is for him naturally the "greatest political question".

This time Herr *Camphausen* does not seem to be satisfied with this simple method of curtailment. He takes the floor.

"It should be observed that the Assembly could already be informed" (about Posen) "if the deputy had chosen to ask the *question*" (but the deputies wanted to ascertain the facts for themselves). "That would be the *quickest* method of obtaining clarification" (but of what kind?).... "I close with the explanation that the motion simply means that the Assembly ought to decide *whether we should form committees of inquiry for one or another purpose.* I agree entirely that the question must be *thoroughly considered and examined,* but I do not want it so suddenly here and now to become a topic for debate."

Thus, the "important political principle" turns out to be the question whether the Agreement Assembly has the right to form committees of inquiry or whether it will refuse itself this right!

The French Chambers and English Houses have all along formed such committees (select committees) to conduct an inquiry (*enquête,* parliamentary inquiry)[a] and respectable Ministers have never raised objections to them. Without such committees, ministerial responsibility is an empty phrase. But Herr Camphausen contests this right of the members of the Agreement Assembly!

Enough. Talking is easy but voting is difficult. The debate is closed and a vote is to be held. Numerous difficulties, doubts, sophistries and moral scruples make their appearance. But we shall spare our readers the details. After a great deal of speech-making, Parrisius' motion is rejected and Reuter's is sent to the sections. May its ashes rest in peace.

Written by Engels on June 6, 1848

First published in the *Neue Rheinische Zeitung* No. 8, June 8, 1848

Printed according to the newspaper

Published in English for the first time

---

[a] In the German original the terms "select committees" and "parliamentary inquiry" are given in English in brackets after the German.— *Ed.*

THE QUESTION OF THE ADDRESS

Cologne, June 7. The Berlin Assembly thus has decided to send an address to the King to give the *Government* an opportunity to express its views and to vindicate its administration up to now. It is not to be a vote of thanks along the lines of the old Diet, not even an attestation of respect: His Majesty, according to the admission of His Majesty's "responsible ones", only offers the "most suitable" and "best" *occasion* to bring the principles of the majority "into line" with those of the Government.

If in essence the person of the King represents a mere medium of exchange—we refer once again to the very words of the Prime Minister [a]—a voucher which merely expedites the business in hand, that person is by no means irrelevant to the form of the negotiations. In the first place the representatives of the popular will are thereby put into direct touch with the Crown, a fact from which, as already evident in the debate on the address, it is easy to infer the recognition of the agreement theory, the renunciation of popular sovereignty. In the second place, however, one would hardly address a sovereign to whom one is required to pay one's respect in the same manner as one would address the Ministers. Greater reserve of expression will prevail and hints will take the place of plain words, particularly since it is still up to the Government to decide whether a slight censure is compatible with its continued existence. It may well be, however, that the difficult questions which throw the contradictions into the boldest relief will be touched upon only superficially or not at all. It will be easy to arouse fears of a premature break with the

---

[a] Ludolf Camphausen.— *Ed.*

Crown perhaps accompanied by serious consequences, and this could be covered up by the assertion that it was not desirable to prejudge matters awaiting more thorough discussion at a later date.

Thus, sincere respect either for the person of the monarch or the monarchical principle in general, apprehension about going too far, and fear of anarchical tendencies offer inestimable advantages to the Ministry during the debate on the address and Herr Camphausen had good reason to call the opportunity "most suitable" and "best" for winning a strong majority.

The question is now whether the people's representatives are inclined to enter into this obedient, dependent relationship. The Constituent Assembly has already greatly weakened its position by failing on its own initiative to call the Ministers to account about their provisional government up to now; that should have been its first task, for it was ostensibly convoked at such an early date because the orders of the Government were to be based upon the indirect will of the people. Indeed, it seems now, *after* it has assembled, that it is supposed to be there merely "for the purpose of agreeing with the Crown upon a Constitution which, it is hoped, will endure in the future".

But instead of proclaiming its true mission from the very start, by proceeding in this way, the Assembly has tolerated the humiliation of being compelled by the Ministers to accept a statement of accounts. It is remarkable that not a single one of its members countered the proposal for the formation of an address committee with a demand that the Ministry appear before the Chamber *without* a special "occasion", solely for the purpose of rendering an account of its activities up to now. And yet this was the only compelling argument against an address, since on all other counts the Ministers were completely right to demand one.

Written on June 7, 1848

First published in the *Neue Rheinische Zeitung* No. 8, June 8, 1848

Printed according to the newspaper

Published in English for the first time

A NEW PARTITION OF POLAND[47]

Cologne, June 8. The new demarcation line of Herr von Pfuel in Posen is a new rape of Poland. It limits the part· that is to be "reorganised" to less than a third of the entire Grand Duchy and joins the far larger part of Great Poland to the German Confederation. The Polish language and nationality are to be recognised only in a small strip along the Russian border. This strip consists of the Wreschen and Pleschen[a] districts and parts of the districts of Mogilno, Wongrowiec, Gnesen, Schroda, Schrimm, Kosten, Fraustadt, Kröben, Krotoschin, Adelnau and Schildberg.[b] The other parts of these districts as well as the entire districts of Buk, Posen, Obornik, Samter, Birnbaum, Meseritz, Bomst, Czarnikow, Chodziesen, Wirsitz, Bromberg, Schubin,[c] and Inowroclaw are transformed without more ado into German soil by the decree of Herr von Pfuel. And yet there is no doubt that even within this "territory of the German Confederation", the majority of the inhabitants still speak Polish.

The old demarcation line at least gave the Poles the River Warta as their frontier. The new one restricts that part of Poland which is to be reorganised by another quarter. Both "the *desire*" of the Minister of War[d] to exclude from reorganisation a three to four mile strip of territory around the fortress of Posen and the wish of various

---

[a] The Polish names are Września, Pleszew.— *Ed.*

[b] Wągrowiec, Gniezno, Środa, Śrem, Kościan, Wschowa, Krobia, Krotoszyn, Odolanów, Ostrzeszów.— *Ed.*

[c] Poznań, Oborniki, Szamotuły, Międzychód, Międzyrzecz, Babimost, Czarnków, Chodziez, Wyrzysk, Bydgoszcz, Szubin.— *Ed.*

[d] August Kanitz.— *Ed.*

towns such as Ostrowo[a] etc. to be joined to Germany, serve as convenient pretexts for this measure.

The desire of the Minister of War is perfectly natural. First one steals the city and fortress of Posen which lies ten miles deep inside Polish territory; then one finds the new theft of a three-mile strip desirable so as not to be disturbed in the enjoyment of the previously stolen territory. This further acquisition of land leads again to all sorts of small adjustments, and so one has the best occasion to propel the German frontier further and further towards the Russian-Polish border.

The desire to be incorporated expressed by "German" towns may be explained as follows: all over Poland, Germans and Jews form the main part of the artisans and merchants; they are the descendants of immigrants who fled their homeland for the most part because of religious persecutions. Founding towns in the midst of Polish territory, they have shared for centuries all the vicissitudes of the Polish realm. These Germans and Jews, a very large minority in the country, are trying to make use of the country's present situation to gain mastery. They plead their *German* nature; they are no more German than the German Americans. Annexing them to Germany would entail the suppression of the language and nationality of more than half of Posen's Polish population and especially that part of the province in which the national insurrection raged with the greatest violence and intensity, i.e. the districts of Buk, Samter, Posen and Obornik.

Herr von Pfuel declares that he will regard the new frontier as finally settled as soon as the Ministry ratifies it. He mentions neither the Agreement Assembly nor the German National Assembly who after all have also a word to say when it comes to settling the boundary of Germany. But no matter whether the Ministry, the Agreement Assembly, or the Frankfurt Assembly ratify the decision of Herr von Pfuel, the demarcation line will not be "finally settled" so long as two other powers have not ratified it as well: the German nation and the Polish nation.

Written by Engels on June 8, 1848   Printed according to the newspaper

First published in the *Neue Rheinische*   Published in English for the first
Zeitung No. 9, June 9, 1848   time

---

[a] The Polish name is Ostrów Wielkopolski.—*Ed.*

THE SHIELD OF THE DYNASTY

Cologne, June 9. Herr Camphausen, according to the reports of German newspapers, poured out his overflowing heart to his agreers on the 6th of this month. He gave

> "not so much a brilliant speech as one *that flowed from the innermost recesses of his heart*, a speech which reminds one of the passage in St. Paul which reads: 'Though I speak with the tongues of men and of angels, and have not charity, I am become as sounding brass!'[a] His speech was full of that holy emotion that we call love ... it spoke inspiringly to the inspired ones, the applause did not seem to come to an end ... and a prolonged intermission was necessary to surrender oneself to and absorb its total impact".[b]

And who was the hero of this speech that was full of love and flowed from the innermost recesses of the heart? Who was the subject that inspired Herr Camphausen so much that he spoke inspiringly to the inspired ones? Who was the Aeneas of this Aeneid of June 6?

Who else but the *Prince of Prussia!*

One can read in the stenographic report how the poetic Prime Minister describes the journeys of the modern son of Anchises, how he acted on the day when

> —holy Ilium fell in the fighting,
> Priam too, and the folk of the King, skilled javelin-thrower,[c]

how after the fall of squirearchical Troy, and after a long odyssey on both water and land, he at last arrived at the shores of modern

---

[a] 1 Corinthians 13:1.—*Ed.*
[b] *Kölnische Zeitung* No. 161, June 9, 1848.—*Ed.*
[c] Homer, *Iliad*, IV, 164-65, and VI, 448-49 (paraphrased).—*Ed.*

Carthage where he was received in a most friendly fashion by Queen Dido; how he fared better than Aeneas the First since there was a Camphausen who did his utmost to restore Troy and rediscovered the sacred "legal basis", how Camphausen finally permitted Aeneas to return to his Penates and how joy once more reigns in the halls of Troy.[48] One has to read all this as well as countless poetic embellishments so as to feel what it means when an inspirer speaks to inspired ones.

This entire epic, by the way, only serves Herr Camphausen as a pretext for a dithyramb on himself and his own Ministry.

"Yes," he exclaims, "we believed that we were acting in the spirit of the Constitution when *we* took the place of a high personage, when *we* ourselves posed as the personages against whom all attacks were to be directed.... And so it happened. We placed ourselves as a shield before the dynasty and drew all dangers and attacks upon ourselves."

What a compliment for the "high personage" and what a compliment for the "dynasty"! The dynasty would have been lost without Herr Camphausen and his six paladins. As what a mighty "dynasty deeply rooted in the people" must Herr Camphausen regard the House of Hohenzollern, to speak in such a fashion! Verily, if Herr Camphausen had spoken less "inspiringly to the inspired ones", had he been less "full of that holy emotion that we call love", or had he only let his Hansemann speak who is content with "sounding brass"—it would have been better for the dynasty!

"Gentlemen, I am not saying this, however, with challenging pride but rather with the humility that arises from the conviction that the great task with which you and we are entrusted can only be solved if the spirit of *gentleness* and *conciliation* descends also upon this Assembly, if we can find besides your justice also your forbearance."

Herr Camphausen is correct in pleading for gentleness and forbearance from an Assembly which itself is in such need of gentleness and forbearance from the public!

Written on June 9, 1848   Printed according to the newspaper

First published in the *Neue Rheinische*   Published in English for the first
Zeitung No. 10, June 10, 1848   time

COLOGNE IN DANGER

Cologne, June 10. The lovely holiday of Whitsuntide had arrived, the fields were green, the trees were blossoming [a] and as far as there are people who confuse the dative with the accusative,[b] preparations were made to pour out the holy spirit of reaction over all lands in a *single* day.

The moment is well chosen. In Naples guard lieutenants and Swiss mercenaries have succeeded in drowning the young liberty in the people's blood.[c] In France, an Assembly of capitalists fetters the Republic by means of Draconic laws[49] and appoints General Perrot, who ordered the shooting at the Hôtel Guizot on February 23, commandant of Vincennes. In England and Ireland masses of Chartists and Repealers[50] are thrown into gaol and unarmed meetings are dispersed by dragoons. In Frankfurt the National Assembly itself now appoints the triumvirate which the blessed Federal Diet proposed and the Committee of Fifty rejected.[51] In Berlin the Right is winning blow by blow through numerical superiority and drumming, and the Prince of Prussia declares the revolution null and void by moving back into the "property of the entire nation".[52]

Troops are being concentrated in Rhenish Hesse; the heroes who won their spurs fighting the republican partisans in the Lake district[53] are encamped all around Frankfurt. Berlin is invested, Breslau [d] is

---

[a] The beginning of Goethe's "Reineke Fuchs" (paraphrased).—*Ed.*

[b] An allusion to a grammatical mistake commonly made by people speaking the Berlin dialect.—*Ed.*

[c] See this volume, pp. 24-26.—*Ed.*

[d] The Polish name is Wroclaw.—*Ed.*

besieged and we shall presently discuss how things stand in the Rhine Province.

The reaction is preparing a big coup.

While there is fighting in Schleswig, while Russia sends threatening Notes and gathers 300,000 men at Warsaw, troops are inundating Rhenish Prussia even though the bourgeoisie of the Paris Chamber once again proclaims "peace at any price"!

According to the *Deutsche Zeitung, fourteen entire* infantry regiments (the 13th, the 15th,* the 16th, the 17th, the 25th, the 26th, the 27th, the 28th, the 30th, the 34th, the 35th, the 38th, the 39th, and the 40th), i. e. *a third* of all the Prussian line and guard infantry (45 regiments), are located in Rhenish Prussia, Mainz and Luxembourg. Some of these forces are fully mobilised for war, the rest have been reinforced by calling up a third of the reserves. Besides these there are three uhlan regiments, two hussar regiments and one dragoon regiment as well as a regiment of cuirassiers that is expected to arrive shortly. In addition there is the major part of the 7th and 8th artillery brigades of which at least half are already mobilised (i.e. each battery of foot-artillery has now 121 horses instead of 19, or 8 instead of 2 horse-drawn cannon). In addition a third company has been formed for Luxembourg and Mainz. These troops are drawn up in a wide arc which extends from Cologne and Bonn to Koblenz and Trier and to the French and Luxembourg frontiers. All fortresses are being armed, the moats are stockaded, and the trees of the glacis are razed either completely or in the line of fire.

And what is the situation here in *Cologne?*

The forts of Cologne are fully armed. The artillery platforms are being extended, the embrasures are being cut and the cannon have arrived and are being set up. Work continues on these projects every day from 6 in the morning until 6 in the evening. It is even said that the cannon were driven out of the city during the night *with wheels wrapped in rags* so as to avoid all noise.

The arming of the city wall started at the Bayen Tower and has already advanced to Bastion No. 6, i.e. half the wall has been fortified. On Sector 1, 20 cannon have already been brought up.

Cannon are installed above the gate of Bastion No. 2 (at the Severin gate). They need only to be turned around to bombard the city.

The best proof that these armaments are only ostensibly directed against an external enemy but in reality are aimed *at Cologne itself* lies

---

* This is not quite correct since the 13th remains in part and the 15th entirely in Westphalia but they are able to get here by train within a few hours.— *Note by Engels.*

in the fact that here the trees of the glacis have everywhere been left standing. In the event of the troops having to evacuate the city and retreat into the forts, the cannon of the city wall are thereby rendered useless against the forts, whereas the mortars, howitzers and twenty-four pounders of the forts are in no way hindered from lobbing grenades and shells over the trees and into the city. The distance of the forts from the city wall is only 1,400 paces and enables the forts to pour shells that can travel up to 4,000 paces into any part of the city.

Now as to the measures which are *pointed directly against the city*.

The *arsenal* opposite the government building is being *evacuated*. The rifles are nicely wrapped up in order not to attract attention, and are brought into the forts.

Artillery ammunition is brought into the city in *rifle crates* and deposited in bomb-proof magazines all along the city wall.

While we are writing all this, *rifles with bayonets* are being distributed to *the artillery*, although it is a well-known fact that artillery units in Prussia receive no training with these weapons.

Part of the infantry is already in the forts. All of Cologne knows that each company received 5,000 ball-cartridges the day before yesterday.

The following arrangements have been made in case of a clash with the people:

At the first alarm, the 7th (Fortress) Artillery Company is to move into the forts.

Battery No. 37 will then also move out to face the city. This battery has already been equipped fully "ready for war".

The 5th and 8th artillery companies will remain in town for the time being. These companies have 20 shells in each of their caissons.

The hussars are moving from Deutz to Cologne.

The infantry occupies the Neumarkt, the Hahnen gate and the Ehren gate so as to cover the retreat of all troops from the city, and thereafter is also to withdraw into the forts.

The higher officers are moreover doing everything in their power to inculcate in these troops the traditional Prussian hatred for the new order. Nothing is easier during the present state of mounting reaction than to launch, under the pretext of denouncing agitators[54] and republicans, the most vicious attacks against the revolution and the constitutional monarchy.

Yet Cologne has never been calmer than precisely in recent times. Except for an insignificant gathering in front of the house of the *Regierungspräsident* and a brawl in the Heumarkt, nothing has occurred for the past four weeks that so much as even alarmed the civic militia in any way whatever. Thus all these measures are *completely unprovoked.*

We repeat: after these otherwise totally incomprehensible measures, after the troop concentrations around Berlin and Breslau, which have been confirmed to us by letters, after the inundation with troops of the Rhine Province, which the reactionaries hate with such passion, we cannot doubt that reactionary forces are preparing a big general coup.

The eruption here in Cologne seems to have been fixed for *Whit Monday.* The rumour is being assiduously spread that things will "start moving" on that day. They will try to provoke a small row so as to call the troops out immediately, threaten the city with bombardment, disarm the civic militia, arrest the chief agitators, in short to maltreat us in the fashion of Mainz and Trier.[a]

We warn the workers of Cologne earnestly not to fall into this trap set for them by the reactionaries. We urgently plead with them *not to give* the old-Prussian party *the slightest pretext* for placing Cologne under the despotism of martial law. We beg them *to let Whit Sunday and Whit Monday pass in an especially tranquil atmosphere* and thereby frustrate the entire scheme of the reactionaries.

If we give the reaction a pretext for attacking us we will be lost and our fate will be the same as that of the inhabitants of Mainz. If they should feel compelled to attack us and if they really dare to stage an assault, the inhabitants of Cologne will have plenty of opportunity to prove that they too will not hesitate for one moment to defend the gains of March 18 with their blood and lives.

Postscript. Just now the following orders have been issued:

No watchword will be announced during the two *Whitsuntide holidays* (whereas usually it was issued with special solemnity). The troops will *remain confined to barracks* where the officers will receive the watchword.

As of today, the fortress and auxiliary artillery companies as well as the infantry garrison of the forts will obtain, in addition to their normal rations, daily bread rations for four days in advance *so that they will always have in hand food for eight days.*

The artillery will begin *rifle* practice already at seven o'clock this evening.

Written by Engels on June 10, 1848	Printed according to the newspaper
First published in the *Neue Rheinische Zeitung* No. 11, June 11, 1848	Published in English for the first time

---

[a] See this volume, pp. 20 and 23.—*Ed.*

AN ADMISSION OF INCOMPETENCE
BY THE ASSEMBLIES OF FRANKFURT AND BERLIN

Cologne, June 11. *Both assemblies, the one in Frankfurt and the one in Berlin, have solemnly put on record their admission of incompetence. One assembly, by its vote on the question of Schleswig-Holstein, recognises the Federal Diet as its superior authority.*[55] *The other, by its decision to reject Deputy Berends' motion and by passing to the substantiated order of the day, not only repudiates the revolution,*[a] *but expressly admits that it is solely empowered to agree upon the Constitution* and thereby recognises the basic principle underlying the draft of the Constitution that has been proposed by the Camphausen Government. Both assemblies have given a correct appraisal of their worth. They are both *incompetent.*

Written on June 11, 1848

First published in the *Neue Rheinische Zeitung* No. 12-13, June 13, 1848

Printed according to the newspaper

Published in English for the first time

---

[a] See this volume, pp. 75-86.—*Ed.*

THE BERLIN DEBATE ON THE REVOLUTION[56]

[*Neue Rheinische Zeitung* No. 14, June 14, 1848]

Cologne, June 13. At last the Agreement Assembly has made its position clear. It has rejected the idea of revolution and accepted the theory of agreement.

The matter the Assembly had to decide was this.

On March 18 the King promised a Constitution, introduced freedom of the press together with caution money,[57] and made a series of proposals in which he declared that Germany's unity must be achieved by the merging of Germany in Prussia.

These sum up the real content of the concessions made on March 18. The fact that the people of Berlin were satisfied with this and that they marched to the palace to thank the King is the clearest proof of the necessity of the March 18 revolution. Not only the state, its *citizens* too had to be revolutionised. Their submissiveness could only be shed in a sanguinary liberation struggle.

A well-known "misunderstanding"[58] led to the revolution. There was indeed a misunderstanding. The attack by the soldiers, the fight which continued for 16 hours and the fact that the people had to force the troops to withdraw are sufficient proof that the people completely *misunderstood* the concessions of March 18.

The results of the revolution were, on the one hand, the arming of the people, the right of association and the sovereignty of the people, won *de facto*; on the other hand, the retention of the monarchy and the Camphausen-Hansemann Ministry, that is a Government representing the big bourgeoisie.

Thus the revolution produced two sets of results, which were bound to diverge. The people was victorious; it had won liberties of a pronounced democratic nature, but direct control passed into the hands of the big bourgeoisie and not into those of the people.

In short, the revolution was not carried through to the end. The people let the big bourgeoisie form a Government and the big bourgeoisie promptly revealed its intentions by inviting the old Prussian nobility and the bureaucracy to enter into an alliance with it. Arnim, Kanitz and Schwerin became members of the Government.

The big bourgeoisie, which was all along anti-revolutionary, concluded a defensive and offensive alliance with the reactionary forces, because it was afraid of the people, i.e. of the workers and the democratic bourgeoisie.

The united reactionary parties began their fight against democracy by *calling the revolution in question*. The victory of the people was denied, the famous list of the "seventeen dead soldiers"[59] was fabricated, and those who had fought on the barricades were slandered in every possible way. But this was not all. The United Diet convoked before the revolution was now actually convened by the Government, in order *post festum* to fabricate a legal transition from absolutism to the Constitution. Thus the Government openly repudiated the revolution. It moreover invented the theory of agreement, once more repudiating the revolution and with it the sovereignty of the people.

The revolution was accordingly really called in question, and this could be done because it was only a partial revolution, only the beginning of a long revolutionary movement.

We cannot here go into the question as to why and to what extent the present rule of the big bourgeoisie in Prussia is a necessary transitional stage towards democracy, and why, directly after its ascent to power, the big bourgeoisie joined the reactionary camp. For the present we merely report the fact.

The Agreement Assembly had now to declare whether it recognised the revolution or not.

But to recognise the revolution under these circumstances meant recognising the democratic aspects of the revolution, which the big bourgeoisie wanted to appropriate to itself.

Recognising the revolution at this moment meant recognising the *incompleteness* of the revolution, and consequently recognising the democratic movement, which was directed against some of the results of the revolution. It meant recognising that Germany was in the grip of a revolutionary movement, and that the Camphausen Ministry, the theory of agreement, indirect elections, the rule of the big capitalists and the decisions of the Assembly itself could indeed be regarded as unavoidable transitional steps, but by no means as final results.

The debate on the recognition of the revolution was carried on by both sides with great prolixity and great interest, but with remarkably little intelligence. One seldom reads anything so unedifying as these long-winded deliberations, constantly interrupted by noisy scenes or fine-spun arguments about standing orders. Instead of the great passion of party strife, we have a cool, placid temper which threatens at any moment to sink to the level of amiable colloquy; instead of the biting edge of argument we have interminable and confused talk rambling from one subject to another; instead of trenchant retorts we have tedious sermons on the essence and nature of morality.

Nor has the Left particularly distinguished itself in these debates.[60] Most of its speakers repeat one another; none of them dare tackle the question resolutely and speak their mind in frank revolutionary terms. They are always afraid to give offence, to hurt or to frighten people away. Germany would have been in a sorry plight if the people who fought on March 18 had not shown more energy and passion in battle than the gentlemen of the Left have shown in the debate.

[*Neue Rheinische Zeitung* No. 15, June 15, 1848]

Cologne, June 14. Deputy *Berends* from Berlin opened the debate by moving:

"In recognition of the revolution, the Assembly declares that those who fought on March 18 and 19 have rendered a genuine service to their country."

The form of the motion, the classical-Roman laconic style, which was revived by the great French Revolution, was quite appropriate.

On the other hand, the way in which Herr *Berends* argued in support of his motion was all the more inappropriate. He spoke not in a revolutionary but in a placating manner. He had to vindicate the anger of the insulted barricade fighters in the face of an Assembly of reactionaries and yet he calmly delivered a completely dry lecture as if he still spoke as a teacher to the Berlin Craftsmen's Association. The cause he had to defend was quite simple and quite clear but the arguments he advanced were the most confused imaginable.

Herr *Berends* begins:

"Gentlemen, recognition of the revolution is entirely in the nature of things (!). Our Assembly is itself an eloquent recognition of the great movement which has swept through all the civilised countries of Europe. The Assembly is a product of this revolution, and consequently its existence is the actual recognition of the revolution."

Firstly. It is by no means a question of recognising in general that the "great movement which has swept through all the civilised countries of Europe" is a fact; it would be quite superfluous and meaningless to recognise this. It is rather a question of recognising the Berlin street battle, which is passed off as a revolt, as a genuine, real revolution.

Secondly. The Assembly in Berlin is in one respect indeed a "*recognition* of the revolution", since without the Berlin street battle we would have no "agreed" Constitution, but at most an imposed Constitution. But the Assembly is likewise a *rejection* of the revolution, because of the way it was convoked and because of the mandate it was given by the United Diet and by the Ministry. An Assembly standing "on a revolutionary basis" does not agree, it decrees.

Thirdly. By its vote on the address the Assembly has already recognised the agreement theory and by voting against the march to the grave of those killed in the fighting it has already rejected the revolution.[61] It has rejected the revolution by "meeting" at all alongside the Frankfurt Assembly.

Herr Berends' motion has therefore been in fact already twice rejected. Its failure this time was even more inevitable because the Assembly had to express its views openly.

Since the Assembly was reactionary and since it was certain that the people could expect nothing from it, it was in the interest of the Left that the minority who voted *for* the motion should be as small as possible and should comprise only the most resolute members.

Hence there was no need for Herr *Berends* to stand on ceremony. He had to act in the most determined, the most revolutionary way. Instead of clinging to the illusion that it was and wanted to be a constituent assembly, an assembly *standing* on a revolutionary basis, he had to tell the Assembly that it had already rejected the revolution indirectly, and to invite it now to reject it openly.

But not only Berends, the speakers of the Left in general have failed to adhere to this policy, the only policy appropriate to a democratic party. They have been under the illusion that they could persuade the Assembly to make a revolutionary move. They have therefore made concessions, they have tried to soothe, they have spoken of reconciliation and they have consequently *themselves* repudiated the revolution.

It is in a very reserved manner and very wooden language that Herr *Berends* then proceeds to expatiate upon revolutions in general and the Berlin revolution in particular. In the course of his reasoning he encounters the argument that the revolution was unnecessary because already before the revolution the King[a] had conceded everything, and he replies:

"It is true that His Majesty the King conceded *many things* ... but did these concessions satisfy the people? Did we have the guarantee that this promise would become a reality? I *believe* this assurance was ... only obtained after the battle!... It is well established that such a political transformation can only come to birth and be firmly grounded in the great catastrophes of battle. On March 18 one great concession was not yet made; that is the arming of the people.... Only when the people was armed, did it feel secure against possible misunderstandings.... Struggle is *therefore* (!) certainly *a sort of natural occurrence* (!), but an inevitable occurrence ... a catastrophe in which the transformation of political life becomes a reality, a fact."

This long and confused argument, which abounds in repetitions, shows quite clearly that Herr *Berends* is completely in the dark about the results of the revolution and its necessity. The only results of the revolution known to him are the "guarantee" of the promises of the 18th, and the "arming of the people". He deduces the necessity of the revolution in a philosophical manner by once more giving a rendering of the "guarantee" in a superior style and finally by asseverating that there can be no revolution without a revolution.

The revolution was necessary, surely this means simply that it was necessary in order to obtain what we have obtained now. The necessity of the revolution is directly proportional to its results. But since Herr *Berends* is in the dark about its results, he has of course to resort to exaggerated asseverations in order to deduce the necessity of the revolution.

What were the results of the revolution? Certainly not the "guarantee" of the promises of the 18th, but rather the subversion of these promises.

The promises made on the 18th included a monarchy in which the aristocracy, the bureaucracy, the military and the clergy remained at the helm, but allowed the big bourgeoisie to exercise control by a *granted* Constitution and freedom of the press together with caution money. For the people: German flags, a German navy and compulsory military service in the army of the German Confederation instead of Prussian flags, a Prussian navy and compulsory military service in the Prussian army.

The revolution overthrew all the powers of the absolute monarchy, the aristocrats, the bureaucrats, the military and the clerics. It brought about the exclusive rule of the big bourgeoisie. It gave the people the weapon of freedom of the press without caution money, the right of association and, to some extent, the physical weapon, the musket.

---

[a] Frederick William IV.— *Ed.*

But even that is not the main result. The people that has fought on the barricades and has been victorious is entirely different from the people that on March 18 marched to the palace to be enlightened, by means of cavalry attacks, about the significance of the concessions it had received. It is able to achieve things of a quite different nature and it confronts the Government in an entirely different way. The most important achievement of the revolution is *the revolution itself*.

"As an inhabitant of Berlin I can indeed say that it has caused us *painful feelings*" (nothing more!) "... to see this struggle maligned.... I take as my starting point the words of the Prime Minister,[a] who ... declared that it was up to a great nation and all its representatives to work with *clemency towards reconciliation. I appeal to this clemency* when, as a representative of Berlin, I ask you to recognise the events of March 18 and 19. The people of Berlin has certainly on the whole acted very honourably and righteously during the whole period that has passed since the revolution. It is possible that a few excesses have occurred ... and thus I *believe* that it is *appropriate* for the Assembly to declare etc., etc."

The only thing we should like to add to this craven conclusion, which rejects the revolution, is that following such reasoning the motion deserved to be lost.

[*Neue Rheinische Zeitung* No. 16, June 16, 1848]

Cologne, June 14. The first amendment put forward in opposition to Berends' motion owed its short existence to Deputy *Brehmer*. It was a diffuse, well-meaning declaration which firstly recognised the revolution, secondly recognised the agreement theory, thirdly recognised all those who had contributed to the sudden change that had taken place, and fourthly recognised the great truth that

> No steed, no mounted knight
> Protects the lofty summits
> Where princes stand,—[b]

thus finally reducing the revolution again to a truly Prussian expression. Herr *Brehmer*, the worthy schoolmaster, wanted to please all parties, and none of them wanted to have anything to do with him. His amendment was dropped without any discussion, and Herr Brehmer retired with all the resignation of a disappointed philanthropist.

Herr *Schulze* (from Delitzsch) has mounted the rostrum. Herr Schulze, too, is an admirer of the revolution, he admires however not

---

[a] Ludolf Camphausen.— *Ed.*
[b] Words from the Prussian hymn "Heil Dir im Siegerkranz".— *Ed.*

so much the barricade fighters as the men of the morning after, those who are called the "people" as distinct from the "fighters". He desires that the "attitude of the people *after* the battle" should be especially recognised. His enthusiasm exceeded all bounds when he heard

"about the restraint and circumspection of the people when it was no longer confronted by an enemy (!) ... about the earnestness and the conciliatory spirit of the people ... about its attitude towards the dynasty ... we observed that the people was well aware that at such moments it *directly faced history itself"*!!

It is not so much the revolutionary activity of the people *during* the battle that enraptures Herr *Schulze*, as its quite non-revolutionary inactivity *after* the battle.

To recognise the magnanimity of the people after the revolution can only signify one of two things:

Either an insult to the people, for to recognise it as a merit that the people did not commit any base acts *after* its victory, is an insult to the people.

Or it means recognising that the people relaxed after the military victory, and that this gave the reaction an opportunity to rise once again.

"Combining both meanings" Herr Schulze has expressed his "admiration which turned into enthusiasm" because the people firstly behaved decently and secondly provided an opportunity for the reaction to recover its strength.

The "attitude of the people" consisted in being so busy enthusiastically "facing history itself" when it should have been making history; in the fact that for all this "attitude", "restraint", "circumspection", "profound earnestness" and "inextinguishable dedication", the people never got round to preventing the Ministers from conjuring away one part after the other of the freedom it had won; and that the people declared the revolution to be complete instead of continuing it. How differently did the Viennese act, who rapidly overwhelmed the reaction and have now won a *Constituent Imperial Diet* instead of an Agreement Assembly.[62]

Thus Herr *Schulze* (from Delitzsch) recognises the revolution on condition of not recognising it. This earned him resounding cheers.

After a short intermezzo concerning procedure, Herr *Camphausen* himself appears on the scene. He observes that according to Berends' motion "the Assembly should express its opinion and give its verdict on an *idea*". For Herr Camphausen the revolution is merely an "*idea*". He "leaves" it therefore to the Assembly to decide whether it wishes to do this. In Camphausen's view there "exist perhaps no considerable differences of opinion" about the matter under discussion, in accordance with the well-known fact that whenever two German burghers quarrel, they are always *au fond* in agreement.

"If one wants to repeat that ... we have entered a phase which *must bring about*" (that is, it has not yet brought about) "very substantial transformations ... then no one can be more in agreement with this than I."

"If, on the other hand, one intends to say that the state and the political authority have lost their legal foundation and that *the existing authority was overthrown by force* ... then I must protest against such an interpretation."

Up to now Herr Camphausen saw his principal merit in having re-tied the broken thread of legality; now he asserts that this thread has never been broken. This may be completely at variance with the facts, but the dogma of the continuity of the legal succession of power from Bodelschwingh to Camphausen cannot bother about facts.

"If one wants to say that we are on the threshold of events similar to those we know from the history of the English revolution in the seventeenth century and of the French revolution in the eighteenth, events whose upshot is the transfer of power into the hands of a dictator",

then Herr Camphausen must likewise protest.

Our thinking friend of history could of course not miss the opportunity the Berlin revolution provided for palming off those observations which the German burgher is the more eager to hear the more often he has read them in Rotteck's work.[a] The Berlin revolution must be no revolution even for the reason that otherwise it would have to produce a Cromwell or a Napoleon, and Herr Camphausen objects to this.

In the end Herr Camphausen permits his agreers "to express their *feelings* for the victims of a *fateful clash*", but he adds that in this case "many and essential aspects depend on the wording", he would therefore like to have the whole matter referred to a committee.

After another point-of-order episode, a speaker finally comes forward who knows how to pluck at people's heart-strings, because he goes to the root of the matter. This is the Reverend Pastor *Müller* of Wohlau, who supports Schulze's amendment. The pastor does "*not* want to *take up much* of the Assembly's *time*" but wishes merely to broach *one* rather *important* point".

The pastor therefore submits the following question to the Assembly.

"The motion has led us to the *moral* sphere, and if we take the motion not in its *surface*" (how does one set about to take a thing *in* its surface?) "but in its *depth*" (there

---

[a] Karl von Rotteck, *Allgemeine Geschichte vom Anfang der historischen Kenntniss bis auf unsere Zeiten.*— Ed.

is such a thing as empty depth, just as there is empty length) "we cannot help recognising, however difficult these considerations may be, that the point in question is nothing more nor less than the moral recognition of the uprising. *I therefore ask: is an uprising something moral or is it not?*"

The point at issue is not a party political question but something infinitely more important—a theological-philosophical-moral problem. The Assembly has to come to an agreement with the Crown not about a Constitution but about a system of moral philosophy. "Is an uprising something moral or not?" That is what matters. And what answer does the pastor give to the Assembly which is breathless with suspense?

"*I do not believe, however, that we are in the position here of having to solve* this high moral principle."!!

The pastor has only tried to get to the bottom of the matter in order to declare that he cannot reach the bottom.

"Many *thoughtful* men have pondered on this subject and have nevertheless not arrived at *any definite solution.* Nor shall we achieve clarity in the course of a brief debate."

The Assembly seems thunderstruck. The pastor presents a moral problem to the Assembly with great trenchancy and all the seriousness that the subject demands; he presents it and then announces that the problem cannot be solved. In this distressing situation, the agreers must have felt as if they were actually standing already "on a revolutionary basis".

But this was nothing but a simple pastoral stratagem to which the pastor resorted in order to induce the Assembly to do penance. He has moreover prepared some balm for the penitent:

"I believe that there is also a third point of view which has to be considered here. The victims of March 18 *acted in a frame of mind which makes moral judgment impossible.*"!!

The barricade fighters were *non compos mentis.*

"But if you ask me whether they were *morally competent,* my answer is a firm—'*yes!*'"

We ask: if the word of God from the countryside allows himself to be elected to the Berlin Assembly merely in order to bore the entire public by his moralising casuistry, is such an action *moral* or is it *not moral?*

Deputy *Hofer,* in his capacity of a Pomeranian peasant, protests against the whole thing.

"For who were the military? Were they not our brothers and sons? Consider well the effect it will have, when the father on the seashore" (in Wendish[63]: *po more*, i.e. Pomerania) "hears how his son has been treated here!"

However the military may have behaved and whether or not they allowed themselves to be made the tools of the most infamous treachery — it makes no difference, they were our Pomeranian boys and therefore three cheers for them!

Deputy *Schultz* of Wanzleben: Gentlemen, the people of Berlin must be recognised. Their courage was boundless. They conquered not only the fear of cannon.

"What is the fear of being pulverised by *grape-shot* compared with the *danger* of being charged with *causing a disturbance in the street* and incurring severe, perhaps even degrading punishment! The *courage* required to take up *this* struggle is so lofty that the courage needed to face the open mouth of a cannon *cannot possibly* be compared with it!"

Accordingly the Germans did not make a revolution before 1848, because they were afraid of the Police Inspector.

Minister *Schwerin* rises to declare that he will resign if Berends' motion is passed.

Elsner and *Reichenbach* speak against Schulze's amendment.

Dierschke observes that the revolution must be recognised, because "the struggle for moral freedom has not yet ended" and because it was likewise "the moral freedom which called this Assembly into being".

Jacoby demands "full recognition for the revolution with all its consequences". His was the best speech made during the entire session.

Finally, after so much morality, tedium, irresolution and reconciliation, we are pleased to see our *Hansemann* mount the rostrum. Now at last we shall hear something resolute and to the point. But no, Herr Hansemann too speaks today in a mild and mediating manner. He has his reasons, he does nothing without good reason. He sees that the Assembly wavers, that the vote is uncertain and that the proper amendment has not yet been found. He would like to have the debate adjourned.

To achieve this he summons up all his ability to speak as gently as possible. The fact is there, it is incontestable. Some, however, call it a revolution, others call it "great events". We must

"not forget that a *revolution* like that in Paris, or like the earlier one in England, has not taken place here, but what has taken place here is a *transaction* between the Crown and the people" (a strange transaction with grape-shot and rifle-bullets!). "Now precisely because in a certain sense we" (the Ministers) "do not object to the *substance of the matter*, but on the other hand the formulation has to be such that the basis of the Government on which we stand remains feasible"...

therefore the debate ought to be adjourned, so that the Ministers can take counsel.

What it must have cost our Hansemann to use such phrases and to admit that the "basis" on which the Government stands is so weak that it can be overturned by a "formulation"! His only compensation is the pleasure of being able to turn the matter again into a *question of confidence*.

Consequently, the debate was adjourned.

[*Neue Rheinische Zeitung* No. 17, June 17, 1848]

Cologne, June 14.— *Second day.*— The debate begins again with a long argument on procedure. When this has been settled

Herr *Zachariä* rises. He wants to propose an amendment designed to help the Assembly out of the predicament. The great ministerial formula has been found. It reads:

"Taking into consideration that the immense importance of the great March events — to which together with the royal consent" (which is itself a "March event", though not a "great" one) "we owe the present constitutional position — and also that the services the fighters have rendered to it" (that is to the royal consent) "are undisputed (!!) and that moreover the Assembly does not regard it as its duty to pass judgments" (the Assembly is to declare that it has no judgment!), "but *to agree with the Crown upon the Constitution,*—the Assembly passes to the agenda."

This muddled and unprincipled amendment, which pays obeisance to all sides, and in which, as Herr Zachariä flatters himself, "everybody, even Herr Berends, will find *everything that he could have possibly intended* in the well-meaning attitude in which the motion was tabled", thus this bitter-sweet pap is the "formulation" on the "basis" of which the Camphausen Government "stands" and is able to stand.

Encouraged by the success of his colleague Müller, Pastor *Sydow* of Berlin ascends into the pulpit. The moral question is on his mind. *He* will solve the question that Müller was unable to solve.

"Gentlemen, allow me at this point *immediately*" (after having already preached for half an hour) "to express what my sense of duty impels me to say: If the debate continues, then, in my opinion, no one should refrain from speaking until he has discharged his bounden duty. (Cheers.)

"Permit me to make a personal observation. *My view* of revolution is (keep to the point!) that where a revolution occurs it is merely a symptom indicating that both sides, the rulers and those they rule, are to blame. This" (this platitude, the cheapest way of disposing of the matter) "is the *higher morality* of the matter and (!) let us not anticipate the *Christian-moral judgment* of the nation." (For what purpose do the gentlemen think they are there?) (Agitation. Point of order!)

"But gentlemen," continues the imperturbable champion of the higher morality and of the not-to-be-anticipated Christian-moral judgment of the nation, "I am not of the opinion that there may not be times when, with the inevitability of a natural event, political self-defence (!) is imposed upon a nation, and ... I am of the opinion that then the *individual can participate* in it in an *entirely moral way*." (We are saved, with the help of casuistry!) "*Although it is also possible to participate in an immoral way*, that rests with his conscience."!!

The barricade fighters are not a subject to be examined by the *soi-disant* National Assembly, they ought to be heard in the confessional. Thus the matter is disposed of.

Pastor *Sydow* announces moreover that he has "courage", speaks at length about the sovereignty of the people from the standpoint of the higher morality, is three more times interrupted by impatient clamour and returns to his seat with the pleasing conviction that he has discharged his bounden duty. Now the world knows what opinion Pastor Sydow holds and what opinion he does not hold.

Herr *Plönnis* declares that the matter should be dropped. A statement qualified by so many amendments and amendments to amendments, and worn thin by so much discussion and quibbling, has after all no value. Herr Plönnis is right. But he could have rendered the Assembly no worse service than calling attention to this fact, this demonstration of cowardice on the part of so many members of both sides.

Herr *Reichensperger* from Trier:

"We are not here to construct theories and to *decree history*, we ought to *make history* as far as possible."

By no means! By accepting the substantiated agenda, the Assembly decides that on the contrary its purpose is to *unmake history*. This is indeed also a way of "making history".

"I should like to call your attention to Vergniaud's statement, that the revolution is about to devour its own children." [a]

Alas, this is not the case. On the contrary, its own children are about to devour the revolution!

Herr *Riedel* has discovered that Berends' motion "*is supposed to mean not only what is simply expressed by its words*, but that it conceals a dispute about principles". And this victim of the "higher morality" is a *geheimer Archivrat* and professor!

Another very reverend cleric approaches the platform. It is Herr

---

[a] Cf. Vergniaud's speech before the revolutionary tribunal in October 1793.— *Ed.*

Jonas, the ladies' preacher from Berlin. He really seems to have mistaken the Assembly for an audience made up of daughters of the educated élite. With all the pretentious prolixity of a true adept of Schleiermacher, he utters an endless series of the most banal commonplaces about the exceedingly important difference between revolution and reform. He was three times interrupted before completing the introduction to his sermon; at last he burst out with the grand proposition:

"Revolution is something diametrically opposed to our present religious and moral consciousness. A revolution is an act which was considered great and glorious in ancient Greece and Rome, but Christianity...." (Vehement interruptions. General confusion. Esser, Jung, Elsner, the Chairman[a] and numerous other speakers are trying to join in the discussion. At long last the popular pulpit orator can be heard again.)

"At any rate, I dispute the right of the Assembly to vote on religious and moral principles, no assembly can vote on such matters" (? what about the consistory and the synod?). "The attempt to decree or declare that the revolution is a high moral principle or anything else" (that is anything at all), "seems to me to be on a par with the Assembly attempting to assert that there is a God or that there is no God, or that there are several Gods."

There we are. The ladies' preacher has succeeded in transferring the question again to the sphere of the "higher morality", and now of course it falls only within the scope of the Protestant church councils and of the catechism manufacturers in the synod.

Thank God! At last, after all this moral fog, our *Hansemann* speaks. With this practical mind, we are quite safe from the "higher morality". Herr *Hansemann* eliminates the entire moral point of view with one disdainful remark:

"I ask, do we have leisure to indulge in such disputes about principles?"

Herr Hansemann recalls that yesterday a deputy spoke about unemployed workers. Herr Hansemann uses this observation to perform an adroit turn. He speaks of the distress of the working class, regrets their poverty and asks:

"What is the reason of the general distress? I believe ... everybody has the feeling that there is as yet no certainty that the existing state of affairs is stable, so long as our constitutional position has not yet been put in order."

Herr Hansemann now speaks from the heart. He exclaims, confidence must be restored! And the best way to restore confidence is to reject the revolution. Then the speaker for the Government, which "sees no reaction", launches into an alarming account of the importance he attaches to the friendly attitude of the reaction.

---

[a] Karl Milde.— *Ed.*

"I beseech you to promote harmony among *all classes*" (by insulting the classes that carried through the revolution!); "I beseech you to promote harmony between the people and the army; do not forget that our hope of maintaining our independence depends on the army" (! in Prussia where everyone is a soldier!); "do not forget the difficult situation in which we find ourselves, I do not have to explain this to you in greater detail, anyone *who reads the newspapers attentively*" (and surely all the gentlemen do this) "will *recognise* that the situation is difficult, *extremely difficult.* I consider it inappropriate to sow the *seeds of discord* at this moment.... Therefore, gentlemen, try to *reconcile* the parties, do not raise any question liable to *provoke our opponents,* for this is what *would certainly occur.* The adoption of the motion could have *the most deplorable consequences.*"

How the reactionaries must have smiled when they saw Hansemann, who is usually so intrepid, talking not only the Assembly but also himself into a state of alarm.

This appeal to the fear of the big bourgeois, the lawyers and the schoolmasters in the Chamber was more effective than all the sentimental phrases about the "higher morality". The question was decided. D'Ester threw himself once more into the fray to neutralise the effect, but in vain. The debate was closed and with 196 votes to 177 the Assembly passed to the agenda as substantiated by Zachariä.

Thereby the Assembly passed judgment upon itself, i.e. it admitted that it was without judgment.

Written by Engels on June 13-14, 1848

First published in the *Neue Rheinische Zeitung* Nos. 14-17, June 14-17, 1848

Printed according to the newspaper

THE POSITION OF THE PARTIES IN COLOGNE

Cologne, June 16. A few days ago we had a by-election here which clearly showed how much the position of the parties has changed since the general election.[64]

Police Superintendent Müller, substitute for Frankfurt, was elected in Gummersbach as deputy to Berlin.

Three candidates competed in the elections. The Catholic party nominated Herr *Pellmann*, the constitutional party (the Citizens' Association)[65] ran Herr *Fay*, a lawyer, and the democratic party backed Herr *Schneider II*, a barrister, and President of the (Stollwerk) Democratic Society.[66]

In the first round (there were 140 voting delegates), Herr Fay received 29 votes, Herr Pellmann 34 and Herr Schneider 52. The rest of the votes were divided.

The second round (139 votes) resulted in 14 votes for Herr Fay, 59 for Herr Pellmann and 64 for Herr Schneider. Thus, the lead of the democratic party was still steadily increasing.

Finally, in the third round (138 votes), Herr Fay did *not* receive a *single* vote. Herr Schneider obtained 55 and Herr Pellmann 75 votes. The gentlemen of the Citizens' Association had given their votes to the Catholic candidate because they feared the Stollwerk democrats.

These votes show how much public opinion here has changed. In the general elections, the democrats were everywhere in the minority. In this by-election, the democrats emerged as the by far most powerful of the three competing parties and only an unnatural coalition of the two other parties was able to defeat them.

We do not blame the Catholic party for entering into this coalition. We only stress the fact that the *constitutional party* has disappeared.

Written on June 16, 1848

Printed according to the newspaper

First published in the *Neue Rheinische Zeitung* No. 18, June 18, 1848

Published in English for the first time

THE AGREEMENT ASSEMBLY OF JUNE 15[67]

Cologne, June 17. We told you a few days ago: you deny the existence of the revolution. It will prove its existence by a second revolution.[a]

The events of June 14 are merely the first harbinger of this second revolution and already the Camphausen Government is in full dissolution. By placing itself under the protection of the people of Berlin, the Agreement Assembly has decreed a vote of confidence in them.[68] This act is a belated recognition of the March fighters. The Assembly has taken out of the hands of the Ministers the task of drawing up a Constitution and is seeking "agreement" with the people by appointing a committee which will examine all petitions and resolutions relating to the Constitution. This is a belated annulment of its declaration of incompetence.[b] The Assembly promises to begin its constitutional work by a deed: the abolition of the very basis of the old system, namely of the feudal obligations with which the land is burdened. This promises to become another night of August 4.[69]

In a word: on June 15 the Agreement Assembly repudiated its own past just as on June 9 it had repudiated the people's past. It has experienced its March 21.[70]

The Bastille, however, has not yet been stormed.

But from the East an apostle of revolution is approaching impetuously and irresistibly. He is already standing at the gates of

---

[a] See this volume, pp. 73-75.—*Ed.*
[b] Ibid., p. 72.—*Ed.*

Thorn.[a] It is the *Tsar. The Tsar will save the German revolution by centralising it.*

Written on June 17, 1848

First published in the *Neue Rheinische Zeitung* No. 18, June 18, 1848

Printed according to the newspaper

---

[a] The Polish name is Toruń.—*Ed.*

THE PRAGUE UPRISING[71]

Cologne, June 17. Another massacre similar to that of Posen[72] is being prepared in *Bohemia.* The possibility of a continued peaceful association of Bohemia and Germany has been drowned in the blood of the Czech people shed by the Austrian army.

Prince Windischgrätz had cannon mounted on the Vyshehrad and Hradshin[a] and trained on Prague. Troops were massed and a sudden attack on the Slav Congress[73] and the Czechs was being prepared.

The people discovered these preparations; they went in a body to the Prince's residence and demanded arms. The demand was rejected. Feeling began to run high and the crowds of people with and without arms were growing. Then a shot was fired from an inn opposite the commandant's palace and Princess Windischgrätz dropped, mortally wounded. The order to attack followed immediately; the grenadiers advanced, the people were driven back. But barricades were thrown up everywhere, checking the advance of the military. Cannon were brought into position and the barricades raked with grape-shot. Torrents of blood were shed. The fighting went on throughout the night of the 12th and continued on the 13th. Eventually the troops succeeded in occupying the wide streets and pressing the people back into the narrower quarters of the city where artillery could not be used.

---

[a] *Vyshehrad*—southern part of Prague with the old citadel of the same name standing on the right bank of the Vltava; *Hradshin* (the Czech name is Hradčany)—north-western part of Prague with the old castle.—*Ed.*

That is as far as our latest news goes. But in addition it is stated that many members of the Slav Congress were deported from the city under a strong escort. It would appear that the military won at least a partial victory.

However the uprising may end, a war of annihilation by the Germans against the Czechs is now the only possible outcome.

In their revolution the Germans have to atone for the sins of their whole past. They atoned for them in Italy. In Posen they have brought down upon themselves once more the curse of the whole of Poland, and to that is now added Bohemia.

The French were able to win the recognition and sympathy even of the countries to which they came as enemies. The Germans win recognition nowhere and find sympathy nowhere. Even where they adopt the role of magnanimous apostles of liberty, they are spurned with bitter scorn.

And so they deserve to be. A nation which throughout its history has allowed itself to be used as a tool of oppression against all other nations must first of all prove that it has been really revolutionised. It must prove this not merely by a few indecisive revolutions, whose only consequence is to allow the old irresolution, impotence and discord to continue in a modified form; revolutions which let a Radetzky remain in Milan, a Colomb and Steinäcker in Posen, a Windischgrätz in Prague, a Hüser in Mainz, as if nothing had changed.

A revolutionised Germany ought to have renounced her entire past, especially as far as the neighbouring nations are concerned. Together with her own freedom, she should have proclaimed the freedom of the nations hitherto suppressed by her.

And what *has* revolutionised Germany done? She has fully endorsed the old oppression of Italy, Poland, and now of Bohemia, too, by German troops. Kaunitz and Metternich have been completely vindicated.

And the Germans, after this, demand that the Czechs should trust them?

Are the Czechs to be blamed for not wanting to join a nation that oppresses and maltreats other nations, while liberating itself?

Are they to be blamed for not wanting to send their representatives to our wretched, faint-hearted "National Assembly" at Frankfurt, which is afraid of its own sovereignty?

Are they to be blamed for dissociating themselves from the impotent Austrian Government, which is in such a perplexed and helpless state that it seems to exist only in order to register the disintegration of Austria, which it is unable to prevent, or at least to give it an orderly course? A Government which is even too weak to save Prague from the guns and soldiers of a Windischgrätz?

But it is the gallant Czechs themselves who are most of all to be pitied. Whether they win or are defeated, their doom is sealed. They have been driven into the arms of the Russians by 400 years of German oppression, which is being continued now in the street-fighting waged in Prague. In the great struggle between Western and Eastern Europe, which may begin very soon, perhaps in a few weeks, the Czechs are placed by an unhappy fate on the side of the Russians, the side of despotism opposed to the revolution. The revolution will triumph and the Czechs will be the first to be crushed by it.[74]

The Germans once again bear the responsibility for the ruin of the Czech people, for it is the Germans who have betrayed them to Russia.

Written by Engels on June 17, 1848   Printed according to the newspaper

First published in the *Neue Rheinische
Zeitung* No. 18, June 18, 1848

VALDENAIRE'S ARREST—SEBALDT

Cologne. As is well known, the Berlin Agreement Assembly has deferred the debate on Wencelius' motion concerning the imprisonment of *Victor Valdenaire*, the deputy of the district of Trier. And on what grounds! Because no *law* about the immunity of people's representatives can be found in the archives of the old Prussian legislation, just as there are, of course, no people's representatives in the old lumber-room of Prussian history. Nothing is easier than on this basis subsequently to destroy all the achievements of the revolution in the interest of the state treasury. The self-evident demands, requirements and rights of the revolution are not, of course, sanctioned by a legislation whose basis has been exploded by just this revolution. From the moment there were Prussian people's representatives, the *immunity* of the Prussian people's representatives existed. Or should the continued existence of the entire Agreement Assembly be dependent on the mood of a chief of police or a law-court? By all means! *Zweiffel, Reichensperger* and the rest of the Rhenish jurists who transform every political question into procedural wrangling and who could not allow the case of Valdenaire to pass without displaying minute casuistry and gigantic servility, will be entirely safe from such a possibility.

On this occasion we would like to pose a question to Herr Reichensperger II: Has Herr Reichensperger not perhaps been appointed to become *President of the court in Cologne* after Herr Schauberg's retirement, which is supposed to take place on July 1, 1848?

Valdenaire was arrested just as he was climbing into the stage-coach to *Merzig* where the election of a *deputy for Frankfurt* was to take place. Valdenaire had secured the great majority of the votes. There is no easier method to fail an election to which one objects than to arrest the candidate! And the Government, in order to be consistent, does not summon his substitute *Gräff* in spite of his protests. Thus a population of 60,000 fallen out of favour is left unrepresented. We advise Herr Gräff to go to Berlin on his own authority.

Finally, we cannot describe the situation in Trier better than by reproducing the following *warning* issued by the high and mighty Herr *Sebaldt,* the royal *Landrat* and Chief Burgomaster of Trier:

WARNING

For several evenings in a row, unusually numerous crowds of people have shown up on the public squares and streets of the city, which have aroused the fear in nervous people that illegal demonstrations are imminent. I am not one of these nervous people, and I like it well if the street traffic moves freely. If, however, contrary to expectations, some immature persons should get the idea of misusing this traffic for knavish tricks and insulting raillery, I must urge the better part of the public to dissociate itself immediately from these elements, for serious disturbances of public order will be met by serious counter-measures and I should be very sorry if during a possible conflict the careless should come to harm rather than the guilty.

Trier, June 16, 1848   The royal *Landrat* and Chief Burgo-
                                                      master *Regierungs-Rat Sebaldt*

How kindly and patriarchally this eminent man writes!

"*He likes it well if the street traffic moves freely.*" What a pleasant liking Herr Sebaldt has!

Nervous people fear a demonstration. The dictator of Trier has the quality of not being nervous. Yet he must show his absolute authority, he must transform the chimeras of the nervous people into *official conjecture* so that he can oppose *serious* disturbances with appropriately *serious* counter-measures.

How surprisingly well the great man is able to combine seriousness and kindliness! The *better* citizens of Trier may slumber in peace under the protection of this serious, yet kindly *providence.*

Written on June 18, 1848

First published in the *Neue Rheinische Zeitung* No. 19, June 19, 1848

Printed according to the newspaper

Published in English for the first time

THE AGREEMENT ASSEMBLY SESSION
OF JUNE 17

Cologne, June 19. "Nothing learned and nothing forgotten"[a]—this saying is as valid for the Camphausen Government as it is for the Bourbons.

On June 14, the people, enraged by the agreers' repudiation of the revolution, march upon the arsenal.[b] They want a guarantee against the Assembly and they know that weapons are the best guarantee. The arsenal is taken by storm and the people arm themselves.

The storming of the arsenal, an event without immediate results, a revolution that stopped halfway, nevertheless had the effect:

1. That the trembling Assembly retracted its decision of the previous day and declared that it would place itself under the protection of the people of Berlin.

2. That it repudiated the Ministry on a vital question and rejected the Camphausen draft Constitution by a majority of 46 votes.

3. That the Ministry immediately disintegrated, that the Ministers Kanitz, Schwerin and Auerswald resigned (of these up to now only Kanitz has definitely been replaced, by Schreckenstein) and that on June 17 Herr Camphausen asked the Assembly to give him three days to replenish his decimated Ministry.

All this was accomplished by the storming of the arsenal.

And at the same time when the *effects* of this self-arming of the people become so strikingly apparent, the Government dares attack that action itself. At the same time when Assembly and Ministry acknowledge the insurrection, the participants of the insurrection are subjected to a judicial investigation, and are dealt with according

---

[a] A remark Talleyrand is supposed to have made about the Bourbons.—*Ed.*
[b] See this volume, pp. 89-90.—*Ed.*

to old-Prussian laws, slandered in the Assembly and portrayed as common thieves!

On the very same day when the trembling Assembly places itself under the protection of those who stormed the arsenal, they are described as "robbers" and "violent thieves" in decrees issued by Herr *Griesheim* (Commissioner in the Ministry of War) and Herr *Temme* (Public Prosecutor). The "liberal" Herr Temme whom the revolution brought back from exile, begins a stringent investigation of those who continue the revolution. *Korn, Löwinsohn* and *Urban* are arrested. All over Berlin, police raid after police raid is being carried out. Captain *Natzmer*, who had the sense to recognise the necessity for an immediate withdrawal from the arsenal, the man who by his peaceful retreat saved Prussia from a new revolution and the Ministers from immense danger, this man is tried by a military court which makes use of the articles of war to condemn him to death.

The members of the Agreement Assembly are likewise recovering from their fright. In their session on the 17th, they repudiate the men who stormed the arsenal just as they repudiated the barricade fighters on the 9th. The following events transpired during this session of the 17th.

Herr Camphausen explains to the Assembly that he will now reveal all facts in order that it may decide whether or not to impeach the Ministry because of the storming of the arsenal.

There was a reason, indeed, for impeaching the Ministers, not because they tolerated the storming of the arsenal, but rather because they *caused* it by circumventing one of the most significant results of the revolution: the arming of the people.

Then Herr *Griesheim*, Commissioner in the Ministry of War, rises after him. He gives a lengthy description of the weapons in the arsenal, especially of rifles "of an entirely new type of which only Prussia knows the secret", of weapons "of historical significance" and of all the other marvellous items. He describes the guarding of the arsenal: upstairs there are 250 army troops and downstairs is the civic militia. He refers to the fact that the flow of weapons to and from the arsenal, which is the main armoury of the whole Prussian state, was hardly interrupted by the March revolution.

After all these preliminary remarks with which he tried to arouse the sympathy of the agreers for the arsenal, this most interesting institution, he finally comes to the events of June 14.

The people's attention had always been drawn to the arsenal and the arms deliveries and they had been told that these weapons belonged to them.

The weapons belonged indeed to the people, first of all as national property and secondly as part of the acquired and guaranteed right of the people to bear arms.

Herr Griesheim "could state with certainty that the first shots were fired by the people against the civic militia".

This assertion is a counterpart to the "seventeen dead soldiers" of March.[75]

Herr Griesheim now relates that the people invaded the arsenal, that the civic militia retreated and that "1,100 rifles of the new type of rifle were then *stolen*, an irreplaceable loss" (!). Captain Natzmer had been talked into a "*dereliction of duty*", i.e. into retreating, and the military had withdrawn.

But now the Commissioner from the Ministry of War comes to a passage of his report which causes his old-Prussian heart to bleed: the people desecrated the sacred schrine of old Prussia. Listen:

"Thereafter *downright atrocities* began to occur in the rooms upstairs. *Theft, robbery and destruction* took place. New weapons were flung down and broken. *Antiques* of irreplaceable value, rifles inlaid with silver and ivory and artistic, hard-to-replace artillery models were destroyed. *Trophies and flags won by the blood of the people, symbols of the nation's honour*, were *torn and besmirched*!" (General indignation. Calls from all sides: Shame! Shame!)

This indignation of the old blade at the frivolity of the people is indeed laughable. The people have committed "downright atrocities" against old spiked helmets, the shakos of the army reserve and other junk "of irreplaceable value"! They have flung down the "new weapons"! What an "atrocity" such an act must represent in the eyes of a veteran lieutenant-colonel who was only allowed to admire the "new weapons" respectfully in the arsenal while his regiment had to practise with the most antiquated rifles! The people have destroyed the artillery models! Perhaps Herr Griesheim is demanding that the people are supposed to put on kid gloves before starting a revolution? But the most horrible event has yet to come—the trophies of old Prussia have been besmirched and torn!

Herr Griesheim relates an event which demonstrates that the people of Berlin showed a most correct revolutionary attitude on June 14. The people of Berlin disavowed the wars of liberation by trampling upon the flags captured at Leipzig and Waterloo.[76] The first thing the Germans have to do in their revolution is to break with their entire disgraceful past.

The old-Prussian Agreement Assembly, however, had of course to cry shame! shame! over an action in which the people for the first time confront in a revolutionary way not only their oppressors but also the glittering illusions of their own past.

In spite of all his whisker-raising indignation over such an outrage, Herr Griesheim does not, however, fail to remark that the whole matter "cost the state 50,000 talers as well as enough weapons to equip several battalions of troops".

He continues:

"It was not the desire to arm the people which caused the assault since the weapons were sold for a few groschen."

The storming of the arsenal, according to Herr Griesheim, was merely the deed of a number of thieves who stole rifles in order to sell them again for a dram of liquor. The Commissioner from the Ministry of War so far owes us an explanation why the "robbers" plundered the arsenal rather than the wealthy shops of the goldsmiths and money-changers.

"Much sympathy has been shown for the unfortunate (!) captain because he violated his duty allegedly to prevent the shedding of citizens' blood; his action has even been portrayed as commendable and deserving of thanks. Today I was even visited by a delegation which is demanding that this deed should be acknowledged by the entire fatherland as deserving of thanks. (Indignation.) It consisted of representatives of the various clubs which are under the chairmanship of Assessor Schramm. (Indignation on the Right and calls of "shame!") One thing is certain, the captain has broken the first and foremost law of the soldier: he has abandoned his post in spite of explicit instructions given him not to leave it without explicit orders. It was put to him that his withdrawal would save the throne, that all troops had left the city and the King had fled from Potsdam. (Indignation.) *He acted in exactly the same manner as the fortress commandant in 1806* who also surrendered that which had been entrusted to him without further ado instead of defending it.[77] Incidentally, the rejoinder that his withdrawal prevented the shedding of citizens' blood does not hold water. Not a hair on anybody's head would have been touched since he surrendered his post at the moment when the rest of the battalion was coming to his aid." (Shouts of "bravo" from the Right, hissing from the Left.)

Herr Griesheim has, of course, forgotten again that Captain Natzmer's restraint saved Berlin from renewed armed fighting, the Ministers from the greatest danger and the monarchy from being overthrown. Herr Griesheim, who again plays the role of lieutenant-colonel to the hilt, sees in Natzmer's act nothing but insubordination, cowardly desertion of his post and treason in the well-known old-Prussian manner of 1806. The man to whom the monarchy owes its continued existence is to be condemned to death. What a wonderful example for the entire army!

And how did the Assembly act at this tale by Herr Griesheim? It became the echo of his indignation. The Left finally protested — by hissing. The Berlin Left is generally behaving in a more and more cowardly and ambiguous manner. Where were these gentlemen, who exploited the people during the elections, on the night of June

14, when the people soon let the advantages gained slip from their grasp again, solely because of their perplexity, and when only a leader was lacking to make the victory complete? Where were Herr Berends, Herr Jung, Herr Elsner, Herr Stein, and Herr Reichenbach? They remained at home or made innocuous complaints to the Ministers. But that is not all. They do not even dare to defend the people against the calumnies and vilifications of the Government Commissioner. Not a single one of them speaks up. Not a single one wants to be responsible for the action of the people which gave them their first victory. They dare not do anything but—*hiss*. What heroism!

Written by Engels on June 19, 1848

First published in the *Neue Rheinische Zeitung* No. 20, June 20, 1848

Printed according to the newspaper

Published in English for the first time

THE STUPP AMENDMENT

Cologne, June 20. Herr *Stupp* from *Cologne* has proposed an amendment to the law concerning the *immunity of deputies* which was not discussed in the Agreement Assembly but which might not be uninteresting to his fellow citizens from Cologne. We do not want to deprive them of the undivided enjoyment of this legislative work of art.

The Amendment of Deputy Stupp

Paragraph 1. "No member of the Assembly may be called to account in any manner whatsoever either for his votes or for the words and opinions that he expresses in his capacity as deputy."

Amendment: "Delete the word 'words' in the third line."

Reason: "It suffices that a deputy may freely express his *opinion*. The expression '*words*' may also comprise slander which entitles the insulted person to sue for libel in a *civil action*. To protect the deputies from such suits seems to be contrary to the respect and honour of the Assembly."

It suffices that the deputy expresses *no opinion at all* but simply drums and votes. Why then not also delete "*opinions*" since opinions must be expressed in "words", may even be expressed in "slanderous" words, and since also slanderous opinions may be "*subsumed*" under the expression "opinions"?

Paragraph 2. "For the duration of the Assembly none of its members may be called to account or arrested for an act liable to punishment without the permission of the Assembly except when that member is caught in the act or within 24 hours thereafter. A similar permission is necessary for an arrest on account of debts."

Amendment: "Delete the final sentence: 'A similar permission is necessary for an arrest on account of debts.'"

Reason: "We are dealing here with an *infringement of the civil rights of citizens* and the ratification of such an infringement seems to me to be questionable. Though it might be greatly in the interest of the Assembly to keep some deputy in its midst, I still find respect for *civil rights* more important.

> "We must, however, bear in mind especially that we are promulgating this law not for the future, i.e. not for the members of a future Chamber, but *for us*. Let us assume that there are members among us who have to fear arrest on account of debts; it would certainly make a bad impression on our voters if we were to protect ourselves against the *legitimate* prosecution of our creditors by a law which we have passed ourselves."

Rather the other way around! It makes a bad impression upon Herr Stupp that the voters have sent members "among us" who could be arrested on account of debts. How lucky were *Mirabeau* and *Fox* not to have had to live under the legislation of Stupp. One single difficulty disconcerts Herr Stupp for a moment, it is "the interest of the Assembly to keep some deputy in its midst". The *interest of the people*—but who wants to speak of that? It is only a question of the interests of a "closed society" which wants to keep someone in its midst while the creditors would like to see him outside in gaol. Collision of two important interests! Herr Stupp could have given a more convincing version of his amendment: individuals who are embarrassed by debts may only be elected representatives of the people with the permission of their respective creditors. They may be recalled at any time by their creditors. In the final analysis, both Assembly and Government are subject to the supreme decision of the *creditors of the state*.

Second *amendment* to Paragraph 2:

> "While the Assembly is in session none of its members may be prosecuted or arrested by the authorities without the permission of the Assembly for a punishable act unless he is caught in the act."
>
> *Reason*: "The word 'Assembly' in the first line is taken to mean a corporation, and with regard to this the expression 'duration of the Assembly' seems unsuitable. I am proposing the substitution of 'while the Assembly is in session'.
>
> "It also seems more fitting to replace 'an act liable to punishment' with 'a punishable act'.
>
> "I am of the opinion that we must not exclude *civil proceedings* on account of punishable acts because we would thereby allow an infringement of *civil law*. Hence the addition 'by the authorities'.
>
> "If the addition 'or within the next 24 hours etc.' remains, the judge may arrest any deputy within 24 hours after any transgression."

The Bill assures the immunity of the deputies for the duration of the Assembly, the amendment of Herr Stupp only for "the duration of the sessions", i.e. for 6, or at most 12 hours per day. And what an ingenious justification! One can speak of the *duration of a session* but can one speak of the *duration of a corporation?*

Herr Stupp does not want *the authorities* to prosecute or arrest the deputies without the Assembly's permission. He thus takes the liberty to infringe *criminal law*. But as regards *civil proceedings*! On no account should there be an encroachment upon civil law! Long live civil law! What the state has no right to do, the private person may carry out! Civil proceedings above everything! Civil proceedings are Herr Stupp's fixed idea. Civil law is Moses and the prophets! Swear by civil law, particularly civil proceedings! People, show respect for the Holy of Holies!

There are no infringements of civil law upon public law but there are "questionable" encroachments of public law upon civil law. Why bother with a Constitution since we possess the *Code civil*[78] as well as civil courts and lawyers?

Paragraph 3. "Any criminal procedure against a member of the Assembly and any arrest is suspended for the duration of the session if the Assembly demands it."

Motion to change Paragraph 3 in the following manner:

"Any criminal procedure against a member of the Assembly and any arrest arising out of it—unless the arrest has been made by virtue of a *judicial verdict*—shall be cancelled at once if the Assembly so decides."

Reason: "It is surely not the intention to release deputies from gaol who have already been sentenced to imprisonment by a judicial verdict.

"If the amendment is passed, it will apply also to those who are in gaol on account of debts."

Could the Assembly have the treasonable intention to weaken the "force of a judicial verdict" or even to take into its midst a man who is "in gaol" on account of debts? Herr Stupp is trembling at this assault upon civil proceedings and the force of judicial verdicts. Any question of the sovereignty of the people has now been disposed of. Herr Stupp has proclaimed the *sovereignty of civil proceedings and civil law*. How cruel to snatch such a man away from civil law practice and to throw him into the *inferior* sphere of the legislative power! The sovereign people has committed this "questionable" infringement of "civil law". Herr Stupp, on the other hand, starts civil proceedings against the sovereignty of the people and public law.

Emperor Nicholas, however, may calmly turn back. Upon the first crossing of the Prussian frontier he will be met by Deputy Stupp who will hold in one hand "civil proceedings" and in the other hand a "judicial verdict". For, he will declare with appropriate solemnity: War, what is war? A questionable infringement of civil law! A questionable infringement of civil law!

Written on June 20, 1848

First published in the *Neue Rheinische Zeitung* No. 21, June 21, 1848

Printed according to the newspaper

Published in English for the first time

A NEW POLICY IN POSEN

Cologne, June 20. Once again there is a new twist to the Posen affair! After the Willisen phase with its lofty promises and enthusiastic proclamations came the Pfuel phase with shrapnel, brandings and shaved heads,[79] the phase of the blood bath and Russian barbarity. Now after the Pfuel phase comes a new phase of reconciliation!

Major *Olberg,* Chief of the General Staff at Posen and chief participant in the massacres and brandings, is suddenly transferred against his will. General *Colomb* is also transferred against his will from Posen to Königsberg. General *Pfuel* (von Höllenstein[a]) has been ordered to go to Berlin and *Oberpräsident Beurmann* has already arrived there.

Thus Posen has been completely deserted by the knights who bore lunar caustic in their coat of arms, were swinging shearing knives and bravely, from secure ambush, mowed down defenceless scythemen with shrapnel at a distance of 1,000 to 1,200 paces. The German-Jewish Polonophobes are shaking. Just like the Poles at an earlier time they find themselves betrayed by the Government.

A light has suddenly dawned upon the Camphausen Government. The danger of a Russian invasion has convinced it that it made an enormous mistake when it surrendered the Poles to the wrath of the bureaucracy and the Pomeranian army reserve. Now that it is too late, it wants to regain the sympathy of the Poles at any price!

Moreover, the entire bloody war of extermination against the Poles with all its cruelties and barbarities which will for ever form a disgraceful chapter in German history, the justifiable deadly hatred

---

[a] *Höllenstein* means "lunar caustic".—*Ed.*

of the Poles against us, the now inevitable Russian-Polish alliance against Germany, an alliance by which the enemies of the revolution will be reinforced by a brave people of 20 million, has all this happened and taken place merely in order to give Herr Camphausen the opportunity to stammer his *pater peccavi*?

Does Herr Camphausen really believe that now when he is in need of the Poles, it is possible through gentle oratory and concessions to regain former sympathies which have been drowned in blood? Does he really believe that the stigmatised hands will ever be raised in his defence or that the shaven foreheads will ever expose themselves to Russian sabres? Does he really believe that he can ever lead those who escaped Prussian shrapnel against Russian grape-shot?

And does Herr Camphausen believe that his Government can survive now that he himself has so unambiguously admitted his inability?

Written by Engels on June 20, 1848

First published in the *Neue Rheinische Zeitung* No. 21, June 21, 1848

Printed according to the newspaper

Published in English for the first time

THE DOWNFALL OF THE CAMPHAUSEN GOVERNMENT

*Cologne, June 21. 10 p.m. We received the following information from Berlin, June 20: **The Camphausen Government has fallen**; at 8 o'clock this morning Herr Camphausen returned his portfolio to the King.[a] When the Agreement Assembly met this morning after an adjournment due to the proposed changes, the President[b] read out a letter from Camphausen announcing his resignation to the Chamber because he had not succeeded in filling the ministerial vacancies. Herr Hansemann, Herr von Auerswald, Herr Bornemann, Herr von Patow, Herr Roth von Schreckenstein and Herr Schleinitz sat on the ministerial bench, Schreckenstein as newly appointed Minister of War and Schleinitz, the well-known favourite of the **Princess** of **Prussia**[c] and **Russophile**, as **Minister of Foreign Affairs**. Hansemann and von Auerswald further declared that now that the Prime Minister had resigned they were all provisional, with the exception of von Schreckenstein and Schleinitz, and would merely handle day-to-day affairs until the formation of a new Cabinet.*

The Agreement Assembly was moreover asked for an indefinite adjournment of the Chamber.

It has been decided to adjourn until next Monday.

*Our readers will not be surprised by this news. For days now we have been predicting the downfall of the Camphausen Government. And we added: Either a new revolution or a definitely reactionary Government. The attempt at a new revolution has failed. **A Russophile Government will pave the way for the Tsar.***

Written on June 21, 1848

First published in the special supplement to the *Neue Rheinische Zeitung* No. 22, June 22, 1848

Printed according to the newspaper

Published in English for the first time

---

[a] Frederick William IV.— *Ed.*
[b] Karl Milde.— *Ed.*
[c] Augusta, Marie Luise Katharina.— *Ed.*

THE DOWNFALL OF THE CAMPHAUSEN
GOVERNMENT[80]

Cologne, June 22.

> May the sun shine very clear
> Once it, too, will disappear,[a]

and the sun of March 30, tinged by the hot blood of the Poles, has also set.[81]

The Camphausen Government has covered the counter-revolution with its liberal-bourgeois cloak. The counter-revolution now feels strong enough to shake off this irksome mask.

It is possible that the Government of March 30 will be followed for a few days by some untenable Government of the Left Centre. Its real successor will be the *Government of the Prince of Prussia*. Camphausen has the honour of having given the absolutist feudal party its natural boss and himself a successor.

Why pamper the bourgeois guardians any longer?

Are the Russians not standing on the eastern frontier and the Prussian troops on the western border? Have not shrapnel and lunar caustic prepared the Poles for the Russian propaganda campaign?

Have not all steps been taken to repeat in almost all Rhenish towns the bombardment of Prague?[b]

Have not the Danish and Polish wars, and the many small clashes between the military and the people, provided the army with all the time and opportunity in the world to form itself into a brutal soldiery?

---

[a] Quotation from Ferdinand Raimund's play *Das Mädchen aus der Feenwelt oder der Bauer als Millionär*, Act II, Scene 6.—*Ed.*

[b] See this volume, pp. 91-93.—*Ed.*

Is not the bourgeoisie tired of revolution? And is there not standing in the middle of the ocean the rock upon which the counter-revolution will build its church[a]: *England*?

The Camphausen Government seeks to snatch a pennyworth of popularity,[b] to stir up public compassion by the assurance that it is making its exit from the stage of the state as a *dupe*. It certainly is a case of the deceived deceiver.[c] Since it served the big bourgeoisie, it was compelled to try to cheat the revolution out of its democratic gains; in combating democracy it was forced to ally itself with the aristocratic party and become the tool of its counter-revolutionary aims. The aristocratic party is now strong enough to throw its protector overboard. *Herr Camphausen has sown reaction as envisaged by the big bourgeoisie and he has reaped reaction as envisaged by the feudal party.* One was the well-meant intention of the man, the other his evil fate. A penny's worth of popularity for the disappointed man.

A penny's worth of popularity!

> May the sun shine very clear
> Once it, too, will disappear!

But it will rise again in the *East*.

Written on June 22, 1848   Printed according to the newspaper

First published in the *Neue Rheinische Zeitung* No. 23, June 23, 1848

---

[a] Matthew 16:18 (paraphrased).—*Ed.*
[b] Cf. Heinrich Heine, *Deutschland. Ein Wintermärchen*, Caput XXIV.—*Ed.*
[c] G. E. Lessing, *Nathan der Weise*, Act III, Scene 7.—*Ed.*

THE FIRST DEED OF THE GERMAN NATIONAL ASSEMBLY IN FRANKFURT

Cologne. The German National Assembly has at last risen to its task! It has at last made a decision of immediate practical value, it has intervened in the Austro-Italian war.[82]

And how has it intervened? Has it proclaimed Italy's independence? Has it sent a courier to Vienna with the order that Radetzky and Welden must at once withdraw behind the River Isonzo? Has it issued a congratulatory message to the Provisional Government of Milan?[83]

Not at all! It has declared that it would *regard any attack upon Trieste as a casus belli.*

This means: The German National Assembly, in cordial agreement with the Federal Diet, allows the Austrians to commit the greatest brutalities in Italy, to plunder, to murder, to pour incendiary rockets into every village and town (see under *Italy*) and then to retreat safely to neutral territory of the German Confederation! It allows the Austrians at any time to inundate Lombardy from German soil with Croats and Pandours[84] but it wants to prohibit the Italians from pursuing the beaten Austrians into their hiding-places! It permits the Austrians to use Trieste to blockade Venice and the mouths of the Piave, the Brenta, the Tagliamento; but it prohibits any hostile action of the Italians against Trieste!

The German National Assembly could not have acted with greater cowardice than it did by adopting this decision. It does not have the courage openly to sanction the Italian war. It has even less courage to prohibit the Austrian Government from conducting the war. Caught in this embarrassing situation, it passes the decision on Trieste (to top it all by acclamation, so as to still its secret fear by loud cries) which formally neither approves nor disapproves of the war against the Italian revolution but which, nevertheless, approves of it in fact.

This decision is an indirect *declaration of war on Italy*, and because it is an indirect declaration, doubly disgraceful for a nation of 40 million people like the German.

The decision of the Frankfurt Assembly will evoke a storm of protest in all Italy. If the Italians still have some pride and energy, they will answer by a bombardment of Trieste and a march on the Brenner.

But while the Frankfurt Assembly proposes, the French people disposes. Venice has appealed for French aid. After this, the French will probably soon cross the Alps and then it will not be long before we have them on the Rhine.

One deputy[a] has accused the Frankfurt Assembly of being idle. On the contrary! It has already worked so hard that we have one war in the north[b] and another one in the south and that wars in the west and east have become inevitable. We shall be in the fortunate position of having to fight simultaneously the Tsar and the French Republic, reaction and revolution. The Assembly has made sure that Russian and French, Danish and Italian soldiers will meet at St. Paul's Church in Frankfurt.[c] And it is said the Assembly has been idle!

Written by Engels on June 22, 1848

First published in the *Neue Rheinische Zeitung* No. 23, June 23, 1848

Printed according to the newspaper

Published in English for the first time

---

[a] Kohlparzer.— *Ed.*
[b] The war with Denmark over Schleswig-Holstein.— *Ed.*
[c] The meeting place of the German National Assembly.— *Ed.*

THE HANSEMANN GOVERNMENT[85]

Cologne, June 23. A new turn in the government crisis in Berlin! Our *Hansemann* has been entrusted with the formation of a Cabinet and he will drop pathetically into the arms of the Left Centre together with *Patow, Bornemann, Schleinitz* and *Schreckenstein*, the debris of the old Cabinet. Herr *Rodbertus* is supposed to participate in the new combination. He is the mediator who obtains favour and forgiveness from the Left Centre for the contrite wreckage of the Camphausen Government.

By the grace of Herr Rodbertus, our Prussian Duchâtel sees his wildest dreams coming true—he becomes Prime Minister. Camphausen's laurels did not let him rest. Now he will at last have the opportunity to prove what he is capable of when he is in a position to spread his wings unhindered. Now we will be able to admire in all their glory his gigantic financial plans and his limitless projects for the elimination of all want and misery—those plans which he used to present in such a magnificent light to his deputies. Only now is he in a position to devote to the state the entire range of his talents which he earlier displayed so brilliantly and successfully as railwayman and in other posts. And now it will begin to rain votes of confidence.

Herr Hansemann has surpassed his model. Thanks to Rodbertus' devotion he will be Prime Minister, a position never held by Duchâtel. But we warn him. Duchâtel had his reasons for always remaining ostensibly in the background. Duchâtel knew that the more or less cultured circles of the country both within and without the Chamber need a well-spoken knight of the "great debate", a Guizot or Camphausen, who on every occasion could soothe the consciences and capture the hearts of all audiences with the required arguments, philosophical deductions, statesman-like theories and other empty phrases. Duchâtel never envied his loquacious ideologists the nimbus of the Prime Minister's office. Caring for real, actual power, he considered vain glitter worthless. He knew that where *he* was, there was real power. Herr Hansemann wants to try it another way, he must know what he is doing. But we repeat, being Prime Minister is not the natural role for a Duchâtel.

We are struck with a painful feeling when we contemplate how soon Herr Hansemann must plunge from his dizzy height. For before the Hansemann Government has been formed, before it has had a single moment to enjoy its existence, it is already doomed.

"The hangman stands at the door,"[a]

reaction and the Russians are knocking and before the cock will have crowed thrice,[b] the Hansemann Government will have fallen despite Rodbertus and despite the Left Centre. Then good-bye to the Prime Minister's office, good-bye financial plans and gigantic projects for the elimination of want; the abyss will swallow them all and best wishes to Herr Hansemann when he quietly returns to his humble civil hearth and can contemplate the fact that life is but a dream.[c]

Written on June 23, 1848	Printed according to the newspaper
First published in the *Neue Rheinische Zeitung* No. 24, June 24, 1848	Published in English for the first time

---

[a] Heinrich Heine, "Ritter Olaf", Caput II.—*Ed.*
 [b] Cf. Mark 14:30.—*Ed.*
 [c] An allusion to the title of Calderón de la Barca's play *La vida es sueño* (Life Is a Dream).—*Ed.*

THE *NEUE BERLINER ZEITUNG*
ON THE CHARTISTS

Cologne, June 23. The first issue of the *Neue Berliner Zeitung* reports all sorts of curious things about England. It is nice to be original; the *Neue Berliner Zeitung* has at least the merit that it describes conditions in England in quite brand-new fashion. First of all, it says:

"O'Connor, who, indeed, seems to be a man without intelligence or principles, enjoys no esteem here at all."[a]

It is not up to us to decide whether O'Connor possesses as much intelligence and principle as the *Neue Berliner Zeitung*. This scion of ancient Irish kings, this leader of Great Britain's proletariat may in these advantages lag behind the educated Berlin newspaper. You are entirely correct, however, oh educated Berlin newspaper, in what you have to say about his reputation: O'Connor, like all revolutionaries, is held in very bad odour. He has never been able to gain the respect of all the pious people the way you have already done by your first issue. The Berlin newspaper says further:

"O'Connell said that he" (that is O'Connor) "possesses energy but no logic."

That is just splendid. The blessed Dan[b] was an honourable man; the logic of his energy consisted in pulling an annuity of 30,000 pound sterling from the pockets of his poor countrymen. The logic of O'Connor's agitation resulted only in the sale of the entire worldly possessions of this notorious Chartist.

---

[a] From an article dated "London, 15. Juni", published in the *Neue Berliner Zeitung* No. 1, June 20, 1848, supplement, p. 9.—*Ed.*
[b] Daniel O'Connell.—*Ed.*

"Mr. Jones, the second leader of the extreme faction of the Chartists, who is now being sought by the courts and who is nowhere to be found, cannot even find anyone to put up bail of 1,000 pound sterling."

That is the third piece of news from our extremely well-educated Berlin newspaper. In these three lines, it states three extreme absurdities. In the first place, bail is out of the question so long as the courts are still searching for someone. Secondly, Mr. Ernest Jones has already been in Newgate[a] for a fortnight. The educated Berlin newspaper was perhaps only invited to tea at another extremely well-educated and well-informed fellow newspaper when quite recently the entire bourgeois press of England gave expression to its brutal joy over Jones' arrest. Thirdly, Mr. Jones has indeed at last found someone who gladly offered to pay 1,000 pound sterling for him, namely none other than the unintelligent and unprincipled O'Connor himself who was, however, turned down by the courts since as a Member of Parliament he cannot put up bail.

The Berlin newspaper ends by alleging that the Chartists in the country's smaller towns frequently have fisticuffs with each other. If you had only once read an English newspaper, esteemed Berlin paper! You would have made the discovery that the Chartists have always had more fun in beating up the police than each other.

We commend the intelligent and principled *Neue Berliner Zeitung* to the special attention of our readers.

Written on June 23, 1848

First published in the *Neue Rheinische Zeitung* No. 24, June 24, 1848

Printed according to the newspaper

Published in English for the first time

---

[a] The London prison.—*Ed.*

THREAT OF THE *GERVINUS ZEITUNG*[a]

Cologne, June 24.

"There will not be *any trouble* if the prestige of the Frankfurt Assembly and its constitutional provisions keep France in check; Prussia will restore its prestige from its eastern provinces and *in doing this it may perhaps hardly shrink from the temporary loss of its Rhine Province.*" (*Gervinus Zeitung* of June 22.)

How diplomatically the Berlin correspondent of the professorial newspaper writes! Prussia will restore "its prestige *from* its eastern provinces". Where will it restore its prestige? *In* the eastern provinces? Oh no, *from* the eastern provinces. *In* the Rhine Province? Even less so, since in connection with this *restoration* of its prestige it counts "*on a temporary loss of the Rhine Province*", i.e. a temporary *loss* of its "prestige" in the Rhine Province.

Thus in *Berlin* and *Breslau.*[b]

And why will it not restore *with* its eastern province rather than *from* its eastern province the prestige it has apparently lost in Berlin and Breslau?

Russia is not the *eastern province* of Prussia, Prussia is rather the *western province* of Russia. But *from* the Prussian eastern province, the Russians will move arm in arm with the worthy Pomeranians to *Sodom* and *Gomorrah* and restore the "*prestige*" *of Prussia*, i.e. the Prussian dynasty and absolute monarchy. This "prestige" was lost on the day when absolutism was forced to push a "*written scrap of paper*", soiled by plebeian blood, between itself and *its* people, and when the Court was compelled to place itself under the protection and supervision of bourgeois grain and wool merchants.[86]

Thus the friend and saviour is to come from the East. What then is the purpose of concentrating soldiers that side of the frontier? It is from the West that the enemy is approaching and it is therefore in the West that the troops should be concentrated. A naive Berlin

---

[a] *Deutsche Zeitung* edited by Professor Gervinus.— *Ed.*
[b] Wrocław.— *Ed.*

correspondent of the *Kölnische Zeitung* does not comprehend the heroism of *Pfuel*, that upright Polonophile who accepts a mission to Petersburg without an escort of 100,000 men behind him. *Pfuel* travels to Petersburg *unafraid! Pfuel in Petersburg! Pfuel* does not hesitate to cross the Russian frontier and the German public spins yarns about Russian forces along the German frontier! The correspondent of the *Kölnische Zeitung* feels sorry for the German public. But let us return to our professorial newspaper!

If from the East the Russians rush to the aid of the Prussian dynasty, from the West the French will rush to help the German people. The "Frankfurt Assembly" may continue to debate calmly the best agenda and the best "constitutional provisions". The correspondent of the *Gervinus Zeitung* hides this opinion by the rhetorical embellishment "that the Frankfurt Assembly and its constitutional provisions" will keep France "in check". Prussia will *lose* the Rhine Province. But why should it *shrink* from such a loss? It will only be "temporary". German patriotism will march once again under Russian command against the French Babylon and also restore for good "the *prestige of Prussia*" in the Rhine Province and in all South Germany. Oh, you foreboding angel, you![a]

If Prussia does not "*shrink from the temporary loss of the Rhine Province*", the Rhine Province shrinks even less from the "*permanent*" loss of Prussian rule. If the Prussians ally themselves with the Russians, the Germans will ally themselves with the French and united they will wage the war of the West against the East, of civilisation against barbarism, of the republic against autocracy.

We want the unification of Germany. Only as the result of the disintegration of the large German monarchies, however, can the elements of this unity crystallise. They will be welded together only by the stress of war and revolution. Constitutionalism, however, will disappear of itself as soon as the *watchword of the time* is: *Autocracy or Republic*. But, the bourgeois constitutionalists exclaim indignantly, who has brought the Russians into German affairs? Who else but the democrats? Down with the democrats!—And they are right!

If we ourselves had introduced the Russian system in our country, we would have saved the Russians the trouble of doing it and we would have saved *the costs of war*.

Written on June 24, 1848   Printed according to the newspaper

First published in the *Neue Rheinische Zeitung* No. 25, June 25, 1848   Published in English for the first time

---

[a] Goethe, *Faust*, Erster Teil, "Marthens Garten".— *Ed.*

PATOW'S REDEMPTION MEMORANDUM[87]

Cologne, June 24. During the agreement session of the 20th of this [month], that fateful session during which Camphausen's sun went down and the ministerial chaos began, Herr Patow submitted a memorandum[a] which contains the chief principles according to which he intends to regulate the abolition of feudalism in the countryside.

Reading this memorandum, one cannot understand why there had not been a peasant war long ago in the old-Prussian provinces. What a mess of services, fees and dues, what a jumble of medieval names, one more fantastic than the other! Seigniory, death dues, heriot,[b] tithes on livestock, protection money, Walpurgis rent, bee dues, wax rent, commonage, tithe, liege money,[88] additional rent — all that has been in existence until today in the "best-administered state of the world" and would have continued into all eternity if the French had not made their February revolution.

Yes, most of these obligations, particularly the *most burdensome* among them, would continue into all eternity if Herr Patow were to get his way. It was exactly for this reason that Herr Patow was put in charge of this department so that he should spare the squires from the backwoods of Brandenburg, Pomerania and Silesia as much as possible and cheat the peasants as much as possible of the fruits of the revolution!

---

[a] Patow, *Promemoria, betreffend die Massregeln der Gesetzgebung, durch welche die zeitgemässe Reform der guts- und grundherrlichen Verhältnisse und die Beseitigung der noch vorhandenen Hemmungen der Landeskultur bezweckt wird.— Ed.*

[b] In the original *Besthaupt* and *Kurmede* are used, which are regional variants of the German expression for heriot.— *Ed.*

The Berlin revolution has rendered these feudal conditions impossible for all time. The peasants, as was quite natural, abolished them at once in practice. All the Government had to do was to legalise the *abolition of all feudal obligations which had in fact already been abrogated by the people's will.*

But its castles must go up in flames before the aristocracy decides upon a fourth of August.[89] The Government, itself represented in this case by an aristocrat, declares for the aristocracy; it submits to the Assembly a memorandum in which the agreers are requested now also to betray to the aristocracy the peasant revolution which broke out in all Germany in March. The Government is responsible for the consequences which the application of Patow's principles will have in the countryside.

For Herr Patow wants the peasants to pay indemnities for the abrogation of all feudal obligations, even the liege money. The only obligations which are to be abolished without compensation are those which are derived from serfdom, from the old tax system and from patrimonial jurisdiction[90] or those which are worthless to the feudal lords (how gracious!), i.e. on the whole *those* obligations which constitute the smallest part of the entire feudal burden.

On the other hand, all feudal redemption payments which have previously been fixed by contract or judgment are to be definitive. This means: the peasants, who have paid off their obligations under the reactionary, pro-aristocratic laws issued since 1816 and particularly those issued since 1840, and who have been cheated out of their property in favour of the feudal lords, first by the law and then by bribed officials, will receive no compensation.

Instead mortgage banks[91] are to be created so as to throw dust into the peasants' eyes.

If all were to go according to the wishes of Herr Patow, the feudal obligations would be just as little removed under his laws as under the old laws of 1807.[92]

The correct title of Herr Patow's essay should be: "Memorandum concerning the Preservation of Feudal Obligations for All Time by Way of Redemption."

The *Government is provoking a peasant war.* Perhaps Prussia will also *"not shrink from the temporary loss"* of *Silesia.*

Written on June 24, 1848   Printed according to the newspaper

First published in the *Neue Rheinische Zeitung* No. 25, June 25, 1848

THE DEMOCRATIC CHARACTER
OF THE UPRISING[93]

Prague. Every day brings further confirmation of our view of the Prague uprising (No. 18 of this paper[a]), and shows that the insinuations of German newspapers which alleged that the Czech party served reaction, the aristocracy, the Russians etc. were downright lies.

They only saw Count Leo Thun and his aristocrats, and failed to notice the mass of the people of Bohemia—the numerous industrial workers and the peasants. The fact that at one moment the aristocracy tried to use the Czech movement in its own interests and those of the camarilla at Innsbruck,[94] was regarded by them as evidence that the revolutionary proletariat of Prague, who, already in 1844, held full control of Prague for three days, represented the interests of the nobility and reaction in general.

All these calumnies, however, were exploded by the first decisive act of the Czech party. The uprising was so decidedly democratic that the Counts *Thun,* instead of heading it, immediately withdrew from it, and were detained by the people as Austrian hostages. It was so definitely democratic that all Czechs belonging to the aristocratic party shunned it. It was aimed as much against the Czech feudal lords as against the Austrian troops.

The Austrians attacked the people not because they were Czechs, but because they were *revolutionaries.* The military regarded the storming of Prague simply as a prelude to the storming and burning down of Vienna.

---

[a] See this volume, pp. 91-93.—*Ed.*

Thus the *Berliner Zeitungs-Halle* writes:

"*Vienna,* June 20. The deputation which the local Citizens' Committee[95] had sent to Prague has returned today. Its sole errand was to arrange for some sort of supervision of telegraphic communications, so that we should not have to wait for information 24 hours, as was often the case during the last few days. The deputation reported back to the Committee. They related dreadful things about the military rule in Prague. Words failed them to describe the horrors of a conquered, shelled and besieged city. At the peril of their lives they drove into the city from the last station before Prague by cart, and at the peril of their lives they passed through the lines of soldiers to the castle of Prague.

"Everywhere the soldiers called out to them: 'So you're here, too, you Viennese dogs! Now we've got you!' Many wanted to set upon them, even the officers were extremely rude. Finally the deputies reached the castle. Count Wallmoden took the credentials the Committee had given them, looked at the signature and said: '*Pillersdorf?* He is of no account here.' Windischgrätz treated the plebeian rabble more arrogantly than ever, saying: '*The revolution has been victorious everywhere; here we are the victors and we recognise no civilian authority.* While I was in Vienna things were quiet there. But the moment I left everything was suddenly upset.' The members of the deputation were disarmed and confined in one of the rooms of the castle. They were not allowed to leave until two days later, and their arms were not returned to them.

"This is what our deputies reported, this is how they were treated by the Tilly of Prague[96] and this is how the soldiers behaved, yet people here still act as though they believe that this is merely a fight against the Czechs. Did our deputies perhaps speak Czech? Did they not wear the uniform of the Viennese national guard? Did they not have a warrant from the Ministry and the Citizens' Committee which the Ministry had recognised as a legal authority?

"But the revolution has gone too far. Windischgrätz thinks he is the man who can stem it. The Bohemians are shot down like dogs, and when the time for the venture comes the advance against Vienna will begin. Why did Windischgrätz set Leo Thun free, the same Leo Thun who had put himself at the head of the Provisional Government in Prague and advocated the separation of Bohemia? Why, we ask, was he freed from Czech hands if his entire activity were not a game prearranged with the aristocracy in order to bring about the explosion?

"A train left Prague the day before yesterday. On it travelled German students, Viennese national guards, and families who were fleeing from Prague, for, despite the fact that tranquillity had been restored, they no longer felt at home there. At the first station the military guard posted there demanded that all the passengers without exception hand over their weapons, and when they refused the soldiers fired into the carriages at the defenceless men, women and children. Six bodies were removed from the carriages and the passengers wiped the blood of the murdered people from their faces. This was how Germans were treated by the very military whom people here would like to regard as the guardian angels of German liberty."

Written by Engels on June 24, 1848   Printed according to the newspaper

First published in the *Neue Rheinische Zeitung* No. 25, June 25, 1848

[NEWS FROM PARIS]

Cologne, June 24, 10 p.m. Letters of the 23rd from Paris have failed to arrive. A courier who has passed through Cologne has told us that when he left fighting had broken out in Paris between the people and the national guard,[97] and that he had heard heavy cannon-fire at some distance from Paris.[98]

Written on June 24, 1848

First published in the special supplement to the *Neue Rheinische Zeitung* No. 25, June 25, 1848

Printed according to the newspaper

Published in English for the first time

REICHENSPERGER

Cologne, June 25. We have the misfortune to be good prophets. What we foretold in No. 19 has come to pass.[a] Herr Reichensperger from Trier really has become President of the provincial court of justice. That is a consolation in these hard times. Guizot-Camphausen may have been overthrown, Duchâtel-Hansemann may be tottering — but the Guizot-Duchâtel system of corruption seems to be intent on striking new roots here. And what do the individuals matter, as long as the thing itself is at hand?—Incidentally, we would recommend Herr Reichensperger to read the address from Berncastel[99] in our special supplement published this morning.[b]

Written on June 25, 1848	Printed according to the newspaper
First published in the *Neue Rheinische Zeitung* No. 26, June 26, 1848	Published in English for the first time

---

[a] See this volume, p. 94.—*Ed.*

[b] "Berncastel, 18. Juni", *Neue Rheinische Zeitung* No. 25, June 25, 1848.—*Ed.*

[NEWS FROM PARIS]

Cologne, June 25, 10 p.m. Letters from Paris have again failed to arrive; the Paris newspapers which came today are those of the 23rd and in the regular course of the postal service they should have arrived already yesterday evening. In these circumstances, the only sources at our disposal are the confused and contradictory reports of Belgian newspapers and our own knowledge of Paris. Accordingly we have tried to give our readers as accurate a picture as possible of the uprising of June 23.[a]

There is no time for further comments. Tomorrow we shall publish a detailed account of our views[b] as well as a detailed report of the meeting of the Paris Chamber on June 23.

Written on June 25, 1848

First published in the special supplement to the *Neue Rheinische Zeitung* No. 26, June 26, 1848

Printed according to the newspaper

Published in English for the first time

---

[a] See next article.—*Ed.*
[b] See this volume, pp. 128 and 130-33. *Ed.*

DETAILS ABOUT THE 23rd OF JUNE

The insurrection is purely a workers' uprising. The workers' anger has burst forth against the Government and the Assembly which had disappointed their hopes, taken daily recourse to new measures which served the interests of the bourgeoisie against the workers, dissolved the Labour Commission at the Luxembourg, limited the national workshops and issued the law against gatherings.[100] The decidedly proletarian nature of the insurrection emerges from all the details.

The boulevards, the great arteries of Parisian life, became the scenes of the first gatherings. All the way from the Porte St. Denis down to the old rue du Temple was thronged with people. Workers from the national workshops declared that they would not go to Sologne to the national workshops there. Others related that they had left for that place yesterday but had waited in vain at the Barrière Fontainebleau for the travel papers and orders to start the journey which had been promised them the evening before.

Around ten o'clock the call went out for the erection of barricades. The eastern and south-eastern parts of Paris, starting with the Quartier and Faubourg Poissonnière, were quickly barricaded but, it seems, in somewhat unsystematic and desultory fashion. The rues St. Denis, St. Martin, Rambuteau, Faubourg Poissonnière and on the left bank of the Seine the approaches to the faubourgs St. Jacques and St. Marceau—the rues St. Jacques, La Harpe and La Huchette and the adjacent bridges—were more or less strongly fortified. Flags were raised on the barricades which bore the inscription: "Bread or Death!" or "*Work or Death!*"

Thus the insurrection was definitely based on the eastern part of the city which is predominantly inhabited by workers, first of all on the "*aimables faubourgs*",[a] those of Saint Jacques, Saint Marceau, Saint Antoine, du Temple, Saint Martin and Saint Denis, then on the districts between them (quartiers Saint Antoine, du Marais, Saint Martin and Saint Denis).

The erection of the barricades was followed by attacks. The guard post of the boulevard Bonne Nouvelle, which in almost every revolution is first to be seized, had been occupied by the mobile guard.[101] The post was disarmed by the people.

Soon afterwards, however, the bourgeois guard from the western parts of the city came to the rescue. It reoccupied the post. A second unit occupied the high pavement in front of the Théâtre du Gymnase which commands a large section of the boulevards. The people attempted to disarm the advanced posts, but, for the time being, neither side made use of arms.

At last the order came to capture the barricade across the boulevard at the Porte Saint Denis. The national guard, led by the Police Inspector, advanced; there were negotiations; a few shots were fired — it is not clear from which side — and the firing quickly became general.

Immediately, the guard post of Bonne Nouvelle also opened fire. A battalion of the second legion, which had occupied the boulevard Poissonnière, also advanced with loaded rifles. The people were surrounded on all sides. The national guard, firing from their advantageous and partially secure positions, caught the workers in an intense cross-fire. The workers defended themselves for half an hour. Finally, the boulevard Bonne Nouvelle and the barricades up to the Porte Saint Martin were seized. Here, too, the national guard, attacking around eleven o'clock from the direction of the Temple, had taken the barricades and occupied the approaches to the boulevard.

The heroes who stormed these barricades belonged to the bourgeoisie of the second arrondissement, which extends from the Palais Ex-Royal[102] over the entire Faubourg Montmartre. The wealthy *boutiquiers*[b] of the rues Vivienne and Richelieu and the boulevard des Italiens live here. Here, too, dwell the great bankers of the rues Laffitte and Bergère and also the merry gentlemen of private means of the chaussée d'Antin. Rothschild and Fould, Rougemont de Lowemberg and Ganneron live here. In a word, here lies the Stock Exchange, Tortoni[103] and all that is connected with or dependent on them.

---

[a] As Louis Philippe called these suburbs.— *Ed.*
[b] Shopkeepers. *Ed.*

These heroes, who were threatened first and foremost by the red republic, were also the first on the scene. It is significant that *the first barricade of June 23 was captured by those who were conquered on February 24.* They advanced three thousand men strong. Four companies, marching at the double, captured an overturned omnibus. The insurgents, meanwhile, seemed to have entrenched themselves once again at the Porte Saint Denis, for towards noon General Lamoricière had to move up with strong detachments of the mobile guard, regular troops, cavalry and two cannon in order to seize a strong barricade in conjunction with the second legion (the national guard of the 2nd arrondissement). The insurgents forced a platoon of the mobile guard to retreat.

The battle on the boulevard Saint Denis was the signal for engagements in all eastern districts of Paris. The fighting was bloody. Over 30 insurgents were killed or wounded. The enraged workers vowed to attack from all sides during the following night and to fight the "municipal guard of the republic"[104] to the death.

At eleven o'clock fighting also took place in the rue Planche-Mibray (the continuation of the rue Saint Martin towards the Seine) and one man was killed.

There were also bloody clashes in the region of the Halles, the rue Rambuteau etc. Four or five dead were left lying.

At one o'clock a fight took place in the rue du Paradis-Poissonnière. The national guard fired but the result is unknown. After a bloody clash in the Faubourg Poissonnière, two non-commissioned officers of the national guard were disarmed.

The rue Saint Denis was cleared by cavalry charges.

During the afternoon heavy fighting took place in the Faubourg Saint Jacques. Barricades in the rues Saint Jacques and La Harpe and in the Place Maubert were assaulted with varying degrees of success and *much use of grape-shot.* In the Faubourg Montmartre troops were also using cannon.

The insurgents were on the whole pushed back. The Hôtel de Ville[a] remained free. By three o'clock, the insurrection was confined to the faubourgs and the [Quartier du] Marais.

By the way, *few non-uniformed* national guardsmen (i.e. workers who do not have the money for the purchase of uniforms) were seen under arms. On the other hand, there were people among them who carried *luxury weapons,* hunting rifles etc. Men of the mounted national guards (traditionally the scions of the wealthiest families), too, had entered the ranks of the infantry on foot. On the boulevard

---

[a] Town Hall.— *Ed.*

Poissonnière, national guardsmen calmly let themselves be disarmed by the people and then took to their heels.

At five o'clock the battle was still going on when it was all of a sudden suspended by a downpour.

In some places, however, the fighting lasted until late in the evening. At nine o'clock, there was still rifle-fire in the Faubourg St. Antoine, the centre of the working-class population.

Up to then the battle had not yet been fought with the full intensity of a decisive revolution. The national guard, with the exception of the second legion, seems for the most part to have hesitated to attack the barricades. The workers, angry though they were, understandably limited themselves to the defence of their barricades.

Thus, the two parties separated in the evening after making a date for the following morning. The first day of battle resulted in no advantages for the Government. The insurgents, who had been pushed back, could reoccupy the lost positions during the night, as indeed they did. The Government, on the other hand, had two important points against it: it had fired with grape-shot and it had been unable to crush the rebellion during its first day. With grape-shot, however, and one night, not of victory but of mere truce, *rebellion ceases and revolution begins.*

Written by Engels on June 25, 1848

First published in the special supplement to the *Neue Rheinische Zeitung* No. 26, June 26, 1848

Printed according to the newspaper

Published in English for the first time

128

NEWS FROM PARIS[105]

Cologne, June 26. The news just received from Paris takes up so much space that we are obliged to omit all articles of critical comment.

Therefore only a few words to our readers. The latest news received from Paris is: *The resignation of Ledru-Rollin and Lamartine and their Ministers*; the transfer of *Cavaignac's military dictatorship* from Algiers to Paris; *Marrast the dictator in civilian clothes*; *Paris bathed in blood*; *the insurrection* growing into the *greatest revolution that has ever taken place*, into a *revolution of the proletariat against the bourgeoisie*. Three days which sufficed for the *July revolution* and the *February revolution* are insufficient for the colossal contours of this *June revolution*, but the *victory of the people is more certain than ever*. The *French bourgeoisie has dared to do what the French kings never dared—it has itself cast the die.* This *second act of the French revolution* is only the beginning of the *European tragedy*.

Written by Marx on June 26, 1848

First published in the *Neue Rheinische Zeitung* No. 27, June 27, 1848

Printed according to the newspaper

THE *NORTHERN STAR* ABOUT THE *NEUE RHEINISCHE ZEITUNG*[106]

The *Northern Star*, the organ of the English Chartists, which is edited by Feargus *O'Connor*, G. Julian *Harney* and Ernest *Jones*, contains in its latest issue an appreciation of the manner in which the *Neue Rheinische Zeitung* interprets the English people's movement and advocates democracy in general.

We thank the editors of the *Northern Star* for the friendly and genuinely democratic way in which they have mentioned our newspaper. At the same time we want to assure them that the *revolutionary Northern Star* is the only English newspaper for whose appreciation we care.

Written on June 26, 1848

First published in the *Neue Rheinische Zeitung* No. 27, June 27, 1848

Printed according to the newspaper

Published in English for the first time

THE 23rd OF JUNE

We are still finding numerous new facts about the battle of the 23rd. The available material is inexhaustible; time, however, allows us only to publish what is most important and characteristic.

The June revolution offers the spectacle of an embittered battle such as Paris and the world in general have never seen before. The fiercest fighting of all previous revolutions took place during the March days at Milan. An almost entirely unarmed population of 170,000 souls beat an army of 20,000 to 30,000 men! Yet the March days of Milan are child's play compared with the June days of Paris.

What distinguishes the June revolution from all previous revolutions is the *absence of all illusions and all enthusiasm*.

The people are not standing on the barricades as in February singing *"Mourir pour la patrie"*.[107] The workers of June 23 are fighting for their existence and the fatherland has lost all meaning for them. The *Marseillaise* and all memories of the great Revolution have disappeared. The people as well as the bourgeoisie sense that the revolution which they are experiencing will be more significant than that of 1789 or 1793.

The June revolution is the revolution of despair and is fought with silent anger and the gloomy cold-bloodedness of despair. The workers know that they are involved in a *fight to the death* and in the face of the battle's terrible seriousness, even the cheerful French *esprit* remains silent.

History offers only two other examples which show similarities with the battle that is probably still being fought in Paris at this very moment: the Roman slave war and the 1834 insurrection at Lyons. The old Lyons motto "to work while one lives or to die fighting" has also suddenly reappeared after fourteen years and has been written on the banners.

The June revolution is the first which has actually divided all society into two large hostile armed camps which are represented by Eastern Paris and Western Paris. The unanimity of the February revolution, that poetic unanimity full of dazzling delusions and beautiful lies so appropriately symbolised by that windbag and traitor Lamartine, has disappeared. Today the inexorable seriousness of reality tears up all the hypocritical promises of February 25. Today the February fighters are battling against each other, and — what has never happened before — all indifference is gone and every man who can bear arms really takes part in the fight either *in*side or *out*side the barricade.

The armies which are fighting each other in the streets of Paris are as strong as the armies which fought in the battle of the nations at Leipzig.[108] This fact alone proves the tremendous significance of the June revolution.

But let us go on to describe the battle itself.

The information which reached us yesterday led us to believe that the barricades had been constructed in somewhat haphazard fashion. The extensive reports of today prove the opposite. Never before have the defence works of the workers been constructed with so much composure and so methodically.

The city was divided into two armed camps. The dividing line ran along the north-eastern edge of the city from Montmartre down to the Porte St. Denis and from there down to the rue St. Denis across the Île de la Cité and along the rue St. Jacques up to the barrière. Everything east of that line was occupied and fortified by the workers. The bourgeoisie attacked from the western part and obtained its reinforcements from there.

Starting early in the morning, the people silently began to erect their barricades. They were higher and firmer than ever before. A colossal red flag was flying on the barricade at the entrance to the Faubourg St. Antoine.

The boulevard St. Denis was fortified very heavily. The barricades of the boulevard, the rue de Cléry, and the adjacent houses which had been transformed into regular fortresses formed a complete system of defence. Here, as we already reported yesterday, the first significant battle broke out. The people fought with indescribable defiance of death. A strong detachment of the national guard made a flanking attack upon the barricade of the rue de Cléry. Most of the barricade's defenders withdrew. Only seven men and two women, two beautiful young *grisettes*, remained at their post. One of the seven mounts the barricade carrying a flag. The others open fire. The national guard replies and the standard-bearer falls. Then a *grisette*, a tall, beautiful, neatly-dressed girl with bare arms, grasps the flag, climbs over the barricade and advances upon the national guard. The firing continues and the bourgeois members of the national guard shoot down the girl just as she has come close to their bayonets. The other *grisette* immediately jumps forward, grasps the flag, raises the head of her companion and, when she finds her dead, furiously throws stones at the national guard. She, too, falls under the bullets of the bourgeoisie. The firing gets more and more intense and comes both from the windows and the barricade. The ranks of the national guard grow thinner. Aid finally arrives and the barricade is stormed. Of the barricade's seven defenders, only one is left alive and he is disarmed and taken prisoner. The lions and stock exchange wolves of the second legion have carried out this heroic deed against the seven workers and two *grisettes*.

After the joining of the two corps and the capture of the barricade, there is a short and ominous silence. But it is soon interrupted. The courageous national guard opens up a heavy platoon-fire against the unarmed and quiet masses of people who occupy part of the boulevard. They scatter in horror. The barricades, however, were not taken. It was only when Cavaignac himself moved up with infantry and cavalry units that the boulevard up to the Porte Saint Martin was taken after long fighting and only towards three o'clock.

A number of barricades had been erected in the Faubourg Poissonnière, particularly at the corner of the Allée Lafayette, where several houses also served the insurgents as fortresses. An officer of the national guard led them. The 7th Light Infantry Regiment, the mobile guard and the national guard moved against them. The battle lasted half an hour. The troops finally won but only after they had lost about 100 dead and wounded. This engagement took place after 3 o'clock in the afternoon.

Barricades had also been erected in front of the Palace of Justice, in the rue Constantine and the adjacent streets as well as on the Saint Michel Bridge where the red flag was waving. After prolonged fighting these barricades, too, were captured.

The dictator Cavaignac ordered his artillery to take up positions along the Notre-Dame Bridge. From here he took the rue Planche-Mibray and the Cité under fire and could easily bring it [the artillery] into play against the barricades of the rue Saint Jacques.

This latter street was intersected by numerous barricades and the houses were transformed into genuine fortresses. Only artillery could be effective here and Cavaignac did not hesitate for one moment to use it. The roar of the cannon could be heard during the entire afternoon. Grape-shot swept the street. At 7 o'clock in the evening only one barricade had still to be taken. The number of dead was very large.

Cannon were also fired along the Saint Michel Bridge and the rue Saint-André des Arts. Right at the north-eastern end of the city, at the rue Château Landon where a troop detachment had dared to advance, a barricade was also battered down with cannon-balls.

During the afternoon the fighting in the north-eastern faubourgs grew in intensity. The inhabitants of the suburbs of La Villette, Pantin etc. came to the aid of the insurgents. Barricades were erected again and again in very great numbers.

In the Cité a company of the republican guard, under the pretext of wanting to fraternise with the insurgents, had crept between two barricades and then opened fire. The people fell furiously upon the traitors and beat them to the ground one by one. Barely 20 of them found a chance to escape.

The intensity of the fighting grew all along the line. Cannon were fired everywhere as long as daylight prevailed. Later on the fighting was limited to rifle-fire which continued till late into the night. At 11 o'clock the sounds of the military rally could still be heard all over Paris and at midnight there was still shooting in the direction of the Bastille. The Place de la Bastille together with all its approaches was entirely controlled by the insurgents. The centre of their power, the Faubourg Saint Antoine, was heavily fortified. Cavalry, infantry, national guard and mobile guard units stood massed along the boulevard from the rue Montmartre to the rue du Temple.

At 11 p.m. there were already over 1,000 dead and wounded.

This was the first day of the June revolution, a day unequalled in the revolutionary annals of Paris. The workers of Paris fought all alone against the armed bourgeoisie, the mobile guard, the newly organised republican guard and against regular troops of all arms. They held their own with unprecedented bravery equalled only by the likewise unprecedented brutality of their foe. One becomes forbearing towards a Hüser, a Radetzky and a Windischgrätz if one observes how the Parisian bourgeoisie participates with genuine enthusiasm in the massacres arranged by Cavaignac.

The Society of the Rights of Man[109] which had again been set up on June 11, decided in the night of the 23rd-24th to make use of the insurrection in order to advance the *red flag* and accordingly to play its part in the uprising. The Society then held a meeting, decided upon the necessary measures and appointed two permanent committees.

Written by Engels on June 27, 1848   Printed according to the newspaper

First published in the *Neue Rheinische*   Published in English for the first
Zeitung No. 28, June 28, 1848   time

THE 24th OF JUNE

Paris was occupied by the military throughout the entire night. Strong pickets were stationed in the squares and boulevards.

At four o'clock in the morning the rally was sounded. An officer and several men of the national guard went from house to house and fetched out men of their company who had failed to report voluntarily.

At the same time the roar of the cannon resumes most violently in the vicinity of the Saint Michel Bridge which forms the juncture between the insurgents on the left bank and those of the Cité. General Cavaignac who this morning has been invested with dictatorial powers, is burning with the desire to employ them against the uprising. Yesterday the artillery was used only in exceptional cases and for the most part only in the form of grape-shot. Today, however, the artillery is brought everywhere into action not only against the barricades but also against houses. Not only grape-shot is used but *cannon-balls, shells* and *Congreve rockets.*

This morning a heavy clash began in the upper part of the Faubourg Saint Denis. Near the northern railway, the insurgents occupied several barricades and a house which was under construction. The first legion of the national guard attacked without, however, gaining any advantage. It used up its ammunition and lost about fifty dead and wounded. It barely held its own position until the artillery arrived (towards 10 o'clock) and blew the house and the barricades to smithereens. The troops reoccupied the northern railway. The battle in this whole neighbourhood (called Clos Saint Lazare which the *Kölnische Zeitung* has transformed into "courtyard of Saint Lazare") continued, however, for a long time and was conducted with great bitterness. "It is a veritable massacre," writes the correspondent of a Belgian newspaper.[a] Strong barricades went up at the barrières of Rochechouart and Poissonnière. The fortification at the Allée Lafayette was also built up again and yielded only in the afternoon to cannon-balls.

The barricades in the rues Saint Martin, Rambuteau and du Grand Chantier could likewise only be captured with the aid of cannon.

The Café Cuisinier opposite the Saint Michel Bridge was destroyed by cannon-balls.

The main battle, however, took place towards three o'clock in the afternoon on the Quai aux Fleurs where the famous clothing store *La Belle Jardinière* was occupied by 600 insurgents and transformed into a fortress. Artillery and regular troops attack. A corner of the wall is smashed in. Cavaignac, who here commands the firing himself, calls on the insurgents to surrender, otherwise they will all be put to the sword. The insurgents reject this demand. The cannonade begins anew and finally incendiary rockets and shells are poured in. The house is totally destroyed, burying eighty insurgents under the rubble.

The workers also fortified themselves on all sides in the Faubourg Saint Jacques, in the neighbourhood of the Panthéon. Every house had to be besieged as in Saragossa.[110] The efforts of dictator Cavaignac to storm these houses proved so fruitless that the brutal Algerian soldier declared that he would set them on fire if the occupants refused to surrender.

In the Cité, girls were firing from windows at the troops and the civic militia. Here, too, howitzers had to be used in order to achieve any success at all.

The Eleventh Battalion of the mobile guard which attempted to join the insurgents was wiped out by the troops and the national guard. So at least goes the story.

Around noon the insurrection had definitely gained the advantage. All faubourgs, the suburbs of Les Batignolles, Montmartre, La Chapelle and La Villette, in brief, the entire outer rim of Paris from the Batignolles to the Seine as well as the greater part of the left bank of the Seine were in their hands. Here they had seized 13 cannon which they did not use. In the centre, in the Cité and in the lower part of the rue Saint Martin, they advanced towards the Hôtel de Ville which was guarded by masses of troops. Nevertheless, Bastide declared in the Chamber that within an hour the Hôtel de Ville might fall to the insurgents and the stupefaction which this piece of

---

[a] *L'Indépendance belge* No. 179, June 27, 1848, p. 3, column 2.— *Ed.*

news evoked caused the Chamber to proclaim a dictatorship and martial law. Cavaignac had hardly been endowed with his new powers when he took the most extreme and cruel measures, such as never before have been used in a civilised city, measures that even Radetzky hesitated to employ in Milan. Once again the people were too magnanimous. Had they used arson in reply to the incendiary rockets and howitzers, they would have been victorious by the evening. They had, however, no intention to use the same weapons as their opponents.

The ammunition of the insurgents consisted mostly of gun-cotton, large amounts of which were produced in the Faubourg Saint Jacques and in the Marais. A cannon-ball foundry was set up in the Place Maubert.

The Government continuously received support. Troops were rolling into Paris throughout the entire night. National guards arrived from Pontoise, Rouen, Meulan, Mantes, Amiens and Le Havre. Troops came from Orléans and artillery and sappers from Arras and Douai; a regiment came from Orléans. On the morning of the 24th, 500,000 rounds of ammunition and twelve artillery pieces arrived in the city from Vincennes. By the way, the railway workers on the northern railway have torn up the tracks between Paris and Saint Denis in order to prevent the arrival of further reinforcements.

These combined forces and that unprecedented brutality succeeded in pushing back the insurgents during the afternoon of the 24th.

The fact that not only Cavaignac but the national guard itself *wanted to burn down* the entire quarter of the Panthéon shows how savagely the national guard fought and how well it knew that it was fighting for its very survival!

Three points were designated as headquarters of the attacking troops: the Porte Saint Denis where General Lamoricière was in command, the Hôtel de Ville where General Duvivier stood with 14 battalions, and the Place de la Sorbonne whence General Damesme attacked the Faubourg Saint Jacques.

Towards noon the approaches to the Place Maubert were taken and the square itself was encircled. At one o'clock the square fell; fifty members of the mobile guard were killed there! At the same time, after an intense and persistent cannonade, the Panthéon was taken, or rather, it surrendered. The 1,500 insurgents who had entrenched themselves here capitulated, probably upon the threat of M. Cavaignac and the infuriated bourgeoisie to set fire to the entire quarter.

At the same time, the "defenders of order" advanced further and further along the boulevards and captured the barricades of the adjacent streets. At the rue du Temple, the workers were forced to retreat to the corner of the rue de la Corderie. Fighting was still going on in the rue Boucherat and also on the other side of the boulevard in the Faubourg du Temple. Single rifle shots were still being fired in the rue Saint Martin and one barricade was still holding out at the Pointe Saint Eustache.

Around 7 p.m. General Lamoricière received two national guard battalions from Amiens which he immediately used to encircle the barricades behind the Château d'Eau.[a] The Faubourg Saint Denis and also almost the entire left bank of the Seine were at that time peaceful and free. The insurgents were besieged in a part of the Marais and the Faubourg Saint Antoine. These two quarters were, however, separated by the boulevard Beaumarchais and the Saint Martin Canal behind it, and the latter could be used by the military.

General Damesme, the commander of the mobile guard, received a bullet wound in his thigh at the barricade of the rue l'Estrapade. The wound is not dangerous. Nor are the representatives Bixio and Dornès as severely injured as was at first believed.

The wound of General Bedeau is also light.

At nine o'clock the Faubourg Saint Jacques and the Faubourg Saint Marceau were as good as captured. The battle had been exceptionally fierce. General Bréa was in command there at the time.

General Duvivier at the Hôtel de Ville had less success. But even here the insurgents were pushed back.

General Lamoricière had cleared the faubourgs Poissonnière, Saint Denis and Saint Martin up to the barrières after overcoming heavy resistance. Only in the Clos Saint Lazare were the workers still holding out; they were entrenched in the Louis Philippe Hospital.

This same information was given by the President[b] to the National Assembly at 9:30 p.m. He was forced, however, to disavow his own statements several times. He admitted that heavy shooting was still going on in the Faubourg Saint Martin.

Thus the situation in the evening of the 24th was as follows:

The insurgents still held about half the terrain which they had occupied in the morning of the 23rd. This terrain consisted of the eastern part of Paris, i.e. the faubourgs St. Antoine, du Temple, St. Martin and the Marais. The Clos St. Lazare and a few barricades along the Botanical Gardens formed their outposts.

---

[a] Water Tower.—Ed.
[b] Senard.—Ed.

All the rest of Paris was in the hands of the Government.

What is most striking in this desperate battle is the savagery with which the "defenders of order" fight. They who in former times displayed such tender feelings for every drop of "citizen's blood" and who had even sentimental fits over the death of the municipal guards[111] on February 24, shoot down the workers like wild beasts. Not a word of compassion or of reconciliation and no sentimentality whatever, but violent hatred and cold fury against the insurgent workers reign in the ranks of the national guard and in the National Assembly. The bourgeoisie, fully conscious of what it is doing, conducts a war of extermination against them. The workers will wreak terrible vengeance on the bourgeoisie no matter whether it wins for the moment or is defeated at once. After a battle like that of the three June days, only *terrorism* is still possible whether it be carried out by one side or the other.

We shall end by quoting some passages from a letter written by a captain of the republican guard who describes the events of the 23rd and 24th as follows:

"I am writing to you while muskets are rattling and cannon are thundering. By about 2 o'clock we had captured three barricades at the head of the Notre-Dame Bridge. Later we moved to the rue St. Martin and marched down its entire length. When we arrived at the boulevard, we saw that it was abandoned and as empty as at 2 o'clock in the morning. We ascended the Faubourg du Temple and stopped before reaching the barracks. Two hundred paces further on there was a formidable barricade supported by several others and defended by about 2,000 people. We negotiated with them for two hours, but in vain. The artillery finally arrived towards 6 o'clock. The insurgents opened fire first.

"The cannon replied and until 9 o'clock windows and bricks were shattered by the thunder of the artillery. The firing was terrible. Blood flowed in streams while at the same time a tremendous thunderstorm was raging. The cobblestones were red with blood as far as one could see. My men are falling under the bullets of the insurgents; they defend themselves like lions. Twenty times we mount an assault and twenty times we are driven back. The number of dead is immense and the number of injured much greater still. At 9 o'clock we take the barricade with the bayonet. Today (June 24) at 3 o'clock in the morning we are still up. The cannon are thundering incessantly. The Panthéon is the centre. I am in the barracks. We guard *prisoners* who are being brought in all the time. There are many injured among them. *Some are shot out of hand.* I have lost 53 of my 112 men."

Written by Engels on June 27, 1848

First published in the *Neue Rheinische Zeitung* No. 28, June 28, 1848

Printed according to the newspaper

Published in English for the first time

THE 25th OF JUNE

Every day the intensity, violence and fury of the battle increased. The bourgeoisie became more and more ruthless towards the insurgents the more its brutality failed to lead to immediate success, the more it was itself becoming exhausted as a result of fighting, night-watches and bivouacking, and the closer it came to final victory.

The bourgeoisie declared the workers to be not ordinary enemies who have to be defeated but *enemies of society* who must be destroyed. The bourgeois spread the absurd assertion that the workers, whom they themselves had forcibly driven to revolt, were interested only in plunder, arson and murder and that they were a gang of robbers who had to be shot down like beasts in the forest. Yet, for 3 days the insurgents held a large part of the city and behaved with great restraint. Paris would have been reduced to ruins but they would have triumphed had they used the same violent means as were employed by the bourgeoisie and its mercenaries led by Cavaignac.

All the details show with what barbarism the bourgeois conducted themselves during the fighting. Disregarding for the moment the grape-shot, the shells, and the incendiary rockets which they used, it is an established fact that *they gave no quarter at most of the captured barricades.* The bourgeois massacred everyone they found there without exception. In the evening of the 24th over 50 captured insurgents were shot in the Allée de l'Observatoire without any trial. "It is a war of extermination," writes a correspondent of the *Indépendance belge*[a] which itself is a bourgeois paper. On all the

[a] "Paris, dimanche, 23 juin, 2 heures de relevée", *L'Indépendance belge* No. 179, June 27, 1848.—*Ed.*

barricades it was understood that the insurgents would be killed without exception.

When Larochejaquelein said in the National Assembly that something should be done to counteract this belief, the bourgeois would not even let him finish speaking but made such a clamour that the President had to put on his hat and suspend the session. The same kind of clamour broke out again when M. Senard himself later (see below, session of the Assembly[a]) wanted to say a few hypocritical words of mildness and reconciliation. The bourgeois did not want to hear of forbearance. Even at the risk of losing part of their property by a bombardment, they were determined to put an end once and for all to the enemies of order, to plunderers, robbers, incendiaries and communists.

Yet the bourgeois did not display any of that heroism which their journals attempted to attribute to them. From today's session of the National Assembly it is clear that the national guard was paralysed with fear at the outbreak of the insurrection. In spite of all the pompous phrases, reports from all the newspapers of the most diverse trends reveal that on the first day the national guard was very weak, that on the second and third day Cavaignac had to get them out of bed and that he had a corporal and four soldiers lead them into battle. The fanatical hatred of the bourgeois for the revolutionary workers was not capable of overcoming their natural cowardice.

The workers on the other hand fought with unequalled bravery. Although they were less and less capable of replacing their casualties and more and more pushed back by superior strength, they did not tire for one moment. Already from the morning of the 25th they must have realised that the chance of victory had decisively turned against them. Masses upon masses of new troops arrived from all regions. Large contingents of the national guard came to Paris from the outskirts and more distant towns. The regular troops who fought on the 25th numbered 40,000 more men than the normal garrison. In addition, there was the mobile guard of 20,000 to 25,000 men as well as national guard units from Paris and other towns. Moreover, there were several thousand men from the republican guard. The entire armed force which took the field against the insurrection on the 25th certainly numbered some 150,000 to 200,000 men, whereas the workers had at most a quarter of that strength, had less ammunition, no military leadership and no serviceable cannon. Yet they fought silently and desperately against colossal superior

---

[a] "Schluss der Sitzung der Nationalversammlung vom 25. Juni", *Neue Rheinische Zeitung* No. 29, June 29, 1848.—*Ed.*

strength. Masses upon masses of troops moved on the breaches in the barricades which the heavy guns had created; the workers met them without uttering a sound and fought everywhere down to the last man before they let a barricade fall into the hands of the bourgeois. On Montmartre the insurgents called out to the inhabitants: Either we shall be cut to pieces or we shall cut the others to pieces, but we will not budge. Pray God that we may win because otherwise we shall burn down all Montmartre. This threat, which was not even carried out, counts, of course, as a "despicable plan", whereas Cavaignac's shells and incendiary rockets "are skilful military measures which are admired by everyone"!

On the morning of the 25th, the insurgents occupied the following positions: the Clos Saint Lazare, the suburbs of St. Antoine and du Temple, the Marais and the Quartier Saint Antoine.

The Clos Saint Lazare (the former monastery precinct) is a large expanse of land which is partly built on and partly covered as yet only with houses in construction, streets merely laid out etc. The Northern Railway Station is situated exactly in its middle. In this quarter, which has many irregularly placed buildings and a lot of building material, the insurgents had established a mighty stronghold. Its centre was the Louis Philippe Hospital which was under construction. They had raised imposing barricades which were described by eyewitnesses as quite impregnable. Behind them was the city wall which was hemmed in and occupied by the insurgents. From there their fortifications ran to the rue Rochechouart, that is to the area of the barrières. The barrières of Montmartre were heavily defended and Montmartre itself was completely occupied by them. Forty cannon, which had been firing at them for two days, had not yet reduced them.

Once again the 40 cannon bombarded these fortifications during the entire day. At last, at 6 in the evening, the two barricades at the rue Rochechouart were taken and soon thereafter the Clos Saint Lazare also fell.

At 10 a.m. the mobile guard captured several houses on the boulevard du Temple from which the insurgents had directed their bullets into the ranks of the attackers. The "defenders of order" had advanced approximately to the boulevard des Filles du Calvaire. The insurgents, in the meantime, were driven further and further into the Faubourg du Temple. The Saint Martin Canal was seized in places and from here as well as from the boulevard, the broad and straight streets were taken under heavy artillery fire. The battle was unusually violent. The workers knew full well that here the core of their position was being attacked and they defended themselves furiously. They even recaptured barricades which they had earlier been forced to abandon. After a long battle, however, they were crushed by the superiority of numbers and weapons. One barricade after another fell. At nightfall, not only the Faubourg du Temple, but, by way of the boulevard and the canal, the approaches to the Faubourg Saint Antoine and several barricades in the faubourg had also been captured.

At the Hôtel de Ville, General Duvivier made slow but steady progress. Moving from the direction of the quays, he made a flanking attack upon the barricades of the rue Saint Antoine and, at the same time, used heavy guns against the Île St. Louis and the former Île Louvier.[112] Here, too, a very bitter battle was fought, details of which are lacking, however. All that is known is that at four o'clock the *Mairie* of the ninth arrondissement and the adjacent streets were captured, that one after another the barricades of the rue Saint Antoine were stormed and that the Damiette Bridge, which gave access to the Île Saint Louis, was taken. At nightfall, the insurgents here had everywhere been driven off and all access routes to the Place de la Bastille had been freed.

Thus the insurgents had been driven out of all parts of the city with the exception of the Faubourg Saint Antoine. This was their strongest position. The many approaches to this faubourg, which had been the real focus of all Paris insurrections, were guarded with special skill. Slanting barricades covering each other, reinforced by cross-fire from the houses, represented a terrifying objective for an attack. Storming them would have cost an infinite number of lives.

The bourgeois, or rather their mercenaries, were encamped in front of these fortifications. The national guard had done little that day. The regular troops and the mobile guard had accomplished most of the work. The national guard occupied the quiet and conquered parts of the city.

The worst conduct was displayed by the republican guard and the mobile guard. The newly organised and purged republican guard fought the workers with great animosity and thereby won its spurs as the republican municipal guard.[113]

The mobile guard, which was mostly recruited from the Paris lumpenproletariat, has already during its brief period of existence, thanks to good pay, transformed itself into the praetorian guard of whoever was in power. The organised lumpenproletariat has given battle to the unorganised working proletariat. It has, as was to be expected, placed itself at the disposal of the bourgeoisie, just as the *lazzaroni* in Naples placed themselves at the disposal of

Ferdinand.[a] Only those detachments of the mobile guard that consisted of *real* workers changed sides.

But in what a contemptible light the entire present state of affairs in Paris appears when one observes how these former beggars, vagabonds, rogues, gutter-snipes and small-time thieves of the mobile guard are being pampered, praised, rewarded and decorated when only in March and April every bourgeois described them as a ruffianly gang of robbers capable of all sorts of reprehensible acts, no longer to be tolerated. These "young heroes", these "children of Paris", whose courage is unrivalled, who climb barricades with the most dashing bravery etc., are treated that way because these ignorant barricade fighters of February now fire just as ignorantly upon the working proletariat as they had formerly fired upon soldiers, because they let themselves be bribed to massacre their brothers for thirty sous a day! Honour to these corrupt vagabonds because they have shot down the best and most revolutionary part of the Parisian workers for thirty sous a day!

The courage with which the workers have fought is truly marvellous. For three full days, 30,000 to 40,000 workers were able to hold their own against more than 80,000 soldiers and 100,000 men of the national guard, against grape-shot, shells, incendiary rockets and the glorious war experiences of generals who did not shrink from using methods employed in Algeria! They have been crushed and in large part massacred. Their dead will not be accorded the honour that was bestowed upon the dead of July and February. History, however, will assign an entirely different place to them, the martyrs of the first decisive battle of the proletariat.

Written by Engels on June 28, 1848

First published in the *Neue Rheinische Zeitung* No. 29, June 29, 1848

Printed according to the newspaper

Published in English for the first time

---

[a] See this volume, p. 25.—*Ed.*

THE JUNE REVOLUTION[114]

The workers of Paris were *overwhelmed* by superior strength, but they were not *subdued*. They have been *defeated* but their enemies are *vanquished*. The momentary triumph of brute force has been purchased with the destruction of all the delusions and illusions of the February revolution, the dissolution of the entire moderate republican party and the division of the French nation into two nations, the nation of owners and the nation of workers. The tricolour republic now displays only *one colour*, the colour of the defeated, the *colour of blood*. It has become a *red republic*.

None of the big republican figures, whether of the *National* or the *Réforme*,[115] sided with the people. In the absence of leaders and means other than rebellion itself, the people stood up to the united forces of the bourgeoisie and army longer than any French dynasty with the entire military apparatus at its disposal was ever able to stand up to any group of the bourgeoisie allied with the people. To have the people lose its last illusions and break completely with the past, it was necessary that the customary poetic trimmings of French uprisings—the enthusiastic bourgeois youth, the students of the *école polytechnique*, the tricornes—should be on the side of the suppressors. The medical students had to deny the wounded plebeians the succour of their science. Science does not exist for the plebeian who has committed the heinous, unutterable crime of fighting this time for his own existence instead of for Louis Philippe or Monsieur Marrast.

The Executive Committee,[116] that last official vestige of the February revolution, vanished like a ghost in the face of these grave events. Lamartine's fireworks have turned into the incendiary rockets of Cavaignac.

Fraternité, the brotherhood of antagonistic classes, one of which exploits the other, this *fraternité* which in February was proclaimed

Neue Rheinische Zeitung.

Organ der Demokratie.

№ 29. Köln, Donnerstag 29. Juni 1848.

Die „Neue Rheinische Zeitung" erscheint vom 1. Juni an täglich. Bestellungen für das nächste Quartal, Juli bis September, wolle man baldigst machen.

Alle Postämter Deutschlands nehmen Bestellungen an.

Für Frankreich übernehmen Abonnements Herr **G. A. Alexandre**, Nr. 28, Brandgasse in Straßburg, und 23, rue Notre Dame de Nazareth in Paris; so wie das königliche Ober-Post-Amt in Aachen. Für England die HH. **J. J. Ewer & Comp.** 72, Newgate Street in London. Für Belgien und Holland die respekt. königlichen Briefpost-Aemter und das Postbüreau zu Lüttich.

Abonnementspreis in Köln vierteljährlich 1 Thlr. 15 Sgr., in allen übrigen Orten Preußens 2 Thlr. 3 Sgr. 9 Pf. Außerhalb Preußens mit Zuschlag des fremden Zeitungsportos. Inserate: die vierspaltige Petitzeile oder deren Raum 1 Sgr. 6 Pf.

Anzeigen aller Art erlangen durch die großen Verbindungen der Zeitung die weiteste Verbreitung.

Zu Nr. 28 der „Neuen Rheinischen Zeitung" ist am 28. Juni Morgens eine außerordentliche Beilage ausgegeben und versandt worden.

Französische Republik.

** Die Pariser Arbeiter sind erdrückt worden von der Uebermacht, sie sind ihr nicht erlegen. Sie sind geschlagen, aber ihre Gegner sind besiegt. Der augenblickliche Triumph der brutalen Gewalt ist erkauft mit der Vernichtung aller Täuschungen und Einbildungen der Februar-Revolution, mit der Auflösung der ganzen alt-republikanischen Partei, mit der Zerklüftung der französischen Nation in zwei Nationen, die Nation der Besitzer und die Nation der Arbeiter. Die trikolore Republik trägt nur mehr Eine Farbe, die Farbe der Geschlagenen, die Farbe des Bluts. Sie ist zur rothen Republik geworden.

Keine republikanische Reputation, sei es vom National, sei es von der Reforme auf Seite des Volks! Ohne andre Führer, ohne andre Mittel als die Empörung selbst, widerstand es der vereinigten Bourgeoisie und Soldateska länger, als je eine französische Dynastie, mit allem militärischen Apparat versehn, einer mit dem Volk vereinigten Fraktion der Bourgeoisie widerstand. Damit die letzte Illusion des Volks verschwinde, damit gänzlich mit der Vergangenheit gebrochen werde, mußte auch die gewohnte poetische Zuthat der französischen Emeute, die enthusiastische Bourgeoisjugend, die Zöglinge der école polytechnique, die dreikrampigen Hüthe auf der Seite der Unterdrücker stehn. Die Zöglinge der medizinischen Fakultät mußten den verwundeten Plebejern die Hülfe der Wissenschaft versagen. Die Wissenschaft existirt nicht für den Plebejer, der das unsagbare, das unsägliche Verbrechen beging, sich einmal für seine eigne Existenz in die Schanze zu schlagen, statt für Louis Philippe oder für Herrn Marrast.

Der letzte offizielle Rest der Februar-Revolution, die exekutive Kommission ist vor dem Ernst der Ereignisse wie ein Nebelbild zerflossen. Lamartine's Leuchtkugeln haben sich verwandelt in die Brandraketen Cavaignac's.

Die Fraternité, die Brüderlichkeit der entgegengesetzten Klassen, von denen die eine die andere exploitirt, diese Fraternité, im Februar proklamirt, mit großen Buchstaben auf die Stirne von Paris geschrieben, auf jedes Gefängniß, auf jede Kaserne — ihr wahrer, unverfälschter, ihr prosaischer Ausdruck, das ist der — Bürgerkrieg, der Bürgerkrieg in seiner fürchterlichsten Gestalt, der Krieg der Arbeit und des Kapitals. Diese Brüderlichkeit flammte vor allen Fenstern von Paris am Abend des 25. Juni, als das Paris der Bourgeoisie illuminirte, während das Paris des Proletariats verbrannte, verblutete, verächzte.

Die Brüderlichkeit währte grade so lang, als das Interesse der Bourgeoisie mit dem Interesse des Proletariats verbrüdert war. Pedanten der alten revolutionären Ueberlieferung von 1793, socialistische Systematiker, die bei der Bourgeoisie für das Volk bettelten und denen erlaubt wurde, lange Predigten zu halten und sich so lange zu compromittiren, als der proletarische Löwe in Schlaf gelullt werden mußte, Republikaner, welche die ganze alte bürgerliche Ordnung mit Abzug des gekrönten Kopfes verlangten, dynastische Oppositionelle, denen der Zufall an die Stelle eines Ministerwechsels den Sturz einer Dynastie unterschob, Legitimisten, welche die Livrée nicht abwerfen, sondern ihren Schnitt verändern wollten, das waren die Bundesgenossen, womit das Volk seinen Februar machte. Was es in Louis Philipp instinktmäßig haßte, war nicht Louis Philippe, sondern die gekrönte Herrschaft einer Klasse, das Kapital auf dem Throne. Aber wie immer großmüthig, wähnt es seinen Feind vernichtet zu haben, nachdem es den Feind seiner Feinde, den gemeinschaftlichen Feind gestürzt hat.

Die Februarrevolution war die schöne Revolution, die Revolution der allgemeinen Sympathie, weil die Gegensätze, die in ihr gegen das Königthum eklatirten, unentwickelt, einträchtig neben einander schlummerten, weil der sociale Kampf, der ihren Hintergrund bildete, nur eine luftige Existenz gewonnen hatte, die Existenz der Phrase, des Worts. Die Junirevolution ist die häßliche Revolution, die abstoßende Revolution, weil an die Stelle der Phrase die Sache getreten ist, weil die Republik das Haupt des Ungeheuers selbst entblößte, indem sie ihm die schirmende und versteckende Krone abschlugen.

Ordnung! war der Schlachtruf Guizots! Ordnung! schrie Sebastiani, der Guizotin, als Warschau russisch wurde. Ordnung! schreit Cavaignac, das brutale Echo der französischen Nationalversammlung und der republikanischen Bourgeoisie.

Ordnung! donnerten seine Kartätschen, als sie den Leib des Proletariats zerrissen.

Keine der zahllosen Revolutionen der französischen Bourgeoisie seit 1789 war ein Attentat auf die Ordnung, denn sie ließ die Herrschaft der Klasse, sie ließ die Sklaverei der Arbeiter, sie ließ die bürgerliche Ordnung bestehen, so oft auch die politische Form dieser Herrschaft und dieser Sklaverei wechselte. Der Juni hat diese Ordnung angetastet. Wehe über den Juni!

Unter der provisorischen Regierung war es Anstand und noch mehr, es war Nothwendigkeit, den großmüthigen Arbeitern, die, wie man in tausend von offiziellen Plakaten abdrucken ließ: „Drei Monat Elend zur Verfügung der Republik bereit stellten", es war Politik und Schwärmerei zugleich, ihnen vor zu predigen, die Februarrevolution sei in ihrem eigenen Interesse gemacht und es handle sich in der Februarrevolution vor allem um die Interessen der Arbeiter. Seit der Eröffnung der Nationalversammlung — wurde man prosaisch. Es handelte sich nur noch darum, — die Arbeit auf ihre alten Bedingungen, wie der Minister Trélat sagte, zurückzuführen. Also die Arbeiter hatten sich im Februar geschlagen, um in eine industrielle Crise geworfen zu werden.

Das Geschäft der Nationalversammlung besteht darin, den Februar ungeschehen zu machen, wenigstens für die Arbeiter und sie in die alten Verhältnisse zurückzuwerfen. Aber selbst das geschah nicht, weil es so wenig in der Gewalt einer Versammlung, wie eines Königs steht, einer industriellen Krise von universellem Charakter zuzurufen: bis hierhin! Die Nationalversammlung, im brutalen Eifer zu enden mit den verdrießlichen Februarredensarten, ergriff selbst die Maßregeln nicht, die auf dem Boden der alten Verhältnisse möglich waren. Die Pariser Arbeiter von 17—25 Jahr preßt sie für die Armee oder wirft sie auf das Pflaster; die auswärtigen verweist sie aus Paris in die Sologne, ohne ihnen selbst die zum Laufpaß gehörigen Gelder auszuzahlen; den erwachsenen Parisern versichert sie provisorisch ein Gnadenbrod in militärisch organisirten Werkstätten, unter der Bedingung, daß sie an keiner Volksversammlung Theil nehmen, d. h. unter der Bedingung, daß sie aufhören Republikaner zu sein. Nicht die sentimentale Rhetorik nach dem Februar reichte aus, nicht die brutale Legislatur nach dem 15. Mai. Faktisch, praktisch mußte entschieden werden. Habt ihr Canaillen die Februarrevolution für Euch gemacht, oder für Uns? Die Bourgeoisie stellte die Frage so, daß sie den Juni beantwortet werden mußte — mit Kartätschen und Barrikaden.

Und dennoch schlägt, wie ein Volksrepräsentant am 25. Juni sagt, der Stupor die ganze Nationalversammlung. Sie ist betäubt, als Frage und Antwort das Pflaster von Paris in Blut ertränken, betäubt, die Einen, weil ihre Illusionen im Pulverdampf zerrinnen, die andern, weil sie nicht begreifen, wie das Volk es wagen kann, seine allereigensten Interessen selbstständig zu vertreten. Russisches Geld, englisches Geld, der bonapartische Adler, die Lilie, Amulette aller Art müssen dies sonderbare Ereigniß ihrem Verstande vermitteln. Beide Theile der Versammlung aber fühlen, daß eine unermeßliche Kluft sie von dem Volke trennt. Keine wagt, sich für das Volk zu erheben.

Sobald der Stupor vorüber ist, bricht die Raserei aus und mit Recht zischt die Majorität jene elenden Utopisten und Heuchler aus, die den Anachronismus begehen, noch die Phrase Fraternité, Brüderlichkeit im Mund zu führen. Es handelte sich ja eben um die Abschaffung dieser Phrase und der Illusionen, die ihr vieldeutiger Schoos verbirgt. Als Larochejaquelin, der Legitimist, der ritterliche Schwärmer gegen die Infamie eiferte, mit der man Vae victis! Weh den Besiegten! ausruft, geräth die Majorität der Versammlung in Veitstänze, als wäre sie von der Tarantel gestochen. Sie schreit Weh! über die Arbeiter, um zu verbergen, daß Niemand anders der „Besiegte" ist, als sie selbst. Entweder sie muß jetzt untergehen oder die Republik. Und darum heult sie krampfhaft: Es lebe die Republik!

Der tiefe Abgrund, der sich vor uns eröffnet hat, darf er die Demokraten irren, darf er uns wähnen lassen, die Kämpfe um die Staatsform seien inhaltlos, illusorisch, null?

Nur schwache feige Gemüther können die Frage aufwerfen. Die Kollisionen, welche aus den Bedingungen der bürgerlichen Gesellschaft selbst hervorgehen, sie müssen durchkämpft, sie können nicht wegphantasirt werden. Die beste Staatsform ist die, worin die gesellschaftlichen Gegensätze nicht verwischt, nicht gewaltsam, also nur künstlich, also nur scheinbar gefesselt werden. Die beste Staatsform ist die, worin sie zum freien Kampf und damit zur Lösung kommen.

Man wird uns fragen, ob wir keine Thräne, keinen Seufzer, kein Wort für die Opfer haben, welche vor der Wuth des Volkes fielen, für die Nationalgarde, die Mobilgarde, die republikanische Garde, die Linie?

Der Staat wird ihre Wittwen und Waisen pflegen, Dekrete werden sie verherrlichen, feierliche Leichenzüge werden ihre Reste zur Erde bestatten, die offizielle Presse wird sie unsterblich erklären, die europäische Reaktion wird ihnen huldigen vom Osten bis zum Westen.

Aber die Plebejer, vom Hunger zerrissen, von der Presse geschmäht, von den Aerzten verlassen, von den Honnetten Diebe gescholten, Brandstifter, Galeerensklaven, ihre Weiber und Kinder in noch gränzenloseres Elend gestürzt, ihre besten Lebenden über die See deportirt, — ihnen den Lorbeer um die drohend finstere Stirn zu winden, das ist das Vorrecht, das ist das Recht der demokratischen Presse.

Der 25. Juni.

* Mit jedem Tage nahm die Heftigkeit, die Erbitterung, die Wuth des Kampfes zu. Die Bourgeoisie wurde immer fanatisirter gegen die Insurgenten, je weniger ihre Brutalitäten sofort zum Ziele führten, je mehr sie selbst im Kampf, Nachtwachen und Bivouakiren ermattete, je näher sie ihrem endlichen Siege rückte.

Die Bourgeoisie erklärte die Arbeiter nicht für gewöhnliche

Westphalen.

Der Zufall spielt uns eine Beilage zu Nro. 67 des Osnabrücker Tagblattes in die Hände. Wir sind dem freundlichen Zufall für diese Artigkeit sehr verbunden.

Ein Aufruf an alle Westphalen, von Seiten des Dr. Phil. W. von Bruchhausen, Lieutenant, nimmt die ehrenwerthe Beilage ganz in Beschlag. Der Raum gestattet es uns nicht, den ganzen Aufruf wieder zu geben; wir halten es aber für unsre heilige Pflicht, wenigstens einen Theil dieses Dokumentes an die große Glocke zu bringen. „Westphalen! d. h. Hannoveraner, Braunschweiger, Lipper, Oldenburger und Preußen! An Euch alle muß ich ein ernstes Wort richten," so beginnt der Dr. Phil. W. von Bruchhausen, Lieutenant. — „Ich habe aufmerksam alle Berichte der Zeitereignisse durchstudirt; ich hatte das Glück: auf verschiedenen Wegen, die ich zum Theil verschweigen muß, von den russischen Kniffen Kenntniß zu erhalten. — Westphalen! Die sämmtlichen slavischen Völker (sie tagen jetzt in Prag), die seit langer Zeit von den Russen aufgestachelt sind, werden noch in diesem Jahre als unsre Feinde in Deutschland erscheinen. — Selbst die Bosniaken und Albanesen, die Mohamed anerkennen, und alle andern Volksstämme der europäischen Türkei werden mit im Bunde sein — — Es wird sich entscheiden, ob das Russenthum, d. h. die Lüge in Staat, Kirche und Familie auch bei uns heimisch, oder ob der Deutsche wieder frei werden wird, wie unter den karolingischen Kaisern. —

Westphalen! Ihr werdet sogleich einsehen, daß in Eurer Heimath die Hauptschlachten werden geschlagen, und die „rothe Erde" auf's Neue durch Blut wird geröthet werden. Die Südslaven (darunter die türkischen Stämme) werden jenseits des Sauerlandes auf Mainz und Köln, die Russen aber auf Paderborn und Minden vordringen.

Unter Gottes Beistand und mit Beihülfe der mit uns verbündeten Franzosen und Belgier werdet Ihr hoffentlich die Russen überwinden. Die Südwestdeutschen u. s. w. werden mit den Südslaven fertig.

Westphalen! Eure Aufgabe ist eine viel schwerere, denn die Russen werden geführt von Generälen deutscher Abkunft. „Aber werden dann die Russen bis zu uns Westphalen vordringen können?" höre ich Euch fragen. Allerdings! Denkt daran, daß noch im 15. Jahrhundert die Hussiten, d. h. die eigentlichen Böhmen, die Stadt Soest belagerten, gerufen durch einen verrätherischen Reichsfürsten. — Rußlands Pläne sind längst bekannt; ganz Deutschland wurde durch seine Spione bewacht; es hatte unter den Zeitungskorrespondenten überall seine Männer. Rußland wollte längst Deutschland erobern; einem einigen Deutschlande mit einem Kaiser an der Spitze ist es nicht gewachsen. — Westphalen! bereitet Euch zu einem ernsten Kampfe vor; noch in diesem Jahre wird Euer Sommerkorn von fremden Kriegern geschnitten werden. Schaart Euch deswegen um Preußens König; Ihr Alle, seid der Väter Sitte treu und Feinde der Lüge. Auch Friedrich Wilhelm IV. hat nie gelogen. Westphalen! Ihr vorzugsweise unter den Völkern Europa's habt Euch der Lüge fern gehalten; Ihr allein und die Bergschotten in England seid es, welche Sehergaben haben; fast in jedem Eurer Dörfer habt Ihr Jemanden, der „Vorgeschichten" sieht, der Häuser, Straßen, Leichenzüge, Festzüge und dergleichen lange vorher genau so sieht, wie diese später kommen werden. Westphalen! Ihr kennt alle Schlachtfelder, auf denen in diesem Jahre die „rothe Erde" mit Blut wird getränkt werden; Ihr wisst genau (wenn Ihr Euch dessen genau erinnert, was Eure „Spökenkiker" gesehen und vor Kurzem, vor 20 Jahren und vielleicht noch früher erzählt haben) was in jedem Dorfe passiren wird; nur der Tag des Ereignisses blieb unbekannt.

Allein auch darüber seid Ihr einigermaßen belehrt worden; Kinder und erwachsene Leute sollen in dem höhern Theile des Paderborner Landes gesehen haben, wie fremde Truppen Gerste abmäheten.

Ich wende mich daher an Euch Alle vom westphälischen Stamme! Es ist nicht allein ein Kampf um unsere Freiheit und Gesittung; es ist ein Kampf, durch den für einige Zeiten die Frage entschieden wird: Ob Europa der Barbarei verfallen und die Lüge mit allen ihren Gräueln die Oberhand behalten soll, oder ob das, was in uns Deutschen lebt, und vorzugsweise in Westphalen heimisch ist: Wahrheit in Staat, Kirche und Familie, auch in Asien sich verbreiten wird."

Dieser Aufruf ist datirt: Münster, den 5. Juni 1848, und der ehrenwerthe Herr Verfasser, der Dr. Phil. W. von Bruchhausen, Lieutenant, fügt in einem Postscriptum noch hinzu, daß der Westphälische Merkur denselben nicht habe abdrucken wollen, weil der Inhalt des Aufrufes zu aufregend sei, als daß man die Verantwortlichkeit des Abdruckes übernehmen könne.

Ohne gerade zu den „Spökenkikern" zu gehören, sehen wir uns doch veranlaßt, dieses Manifest eines der treuesten Söhne unsres guten, treuen Westphalens, als eine Perle westphälischer Literatur in unserm Feuilleton aufzubewahren.

— Die westphälische Post hat außer guten Schinken und Pumpernickeln auch die beruhigende Nachricht mitgebracht, daß die Revolution in dem komischen Fürstenthum Waldeck die besten Früchte zu tragen beginnt. Waldeck ist ruhig, Se. Durchlaucht sieht man täglich nach dem Essen mit der Meerschaumpfeife im Munde vor dem Schloßportale auf und abwandeln grüßend jeden guten Bürger.

First page of the *Neue Rheinische Zeitung* containing Marx's article "The June Revolution"

and inscribed in large letters on the façades of Paris, on every prison and every barracks—this *fraternité* found its true, unadulterated and prosaic expression in *civil war*, civil war in its most terrible aspect, the war of labour against capital. This brotherhood blazed in front of all the windows of Paris on the evening of June 25, when the Paris of the bourgeoisie held illuminations while the Paris of the proletariat was burning, bleeding, groaning in the throes of death.

This brotherhood lasted only as long as there was a fraternity of interests between the bourgeoisie and the proletariat. Pedants sticking to the old revolutionary tradition of 1793; socialist doctrinaires who begged alms for the people from the bourgeoisie and who were allowed to deliver lengthy sermons and compromise themselves so long as the proletarian lion had to be lulled to sleep; republicans who wanted to keep the old bourgeois order *in toto*, but without the crowned head; members of the dynastic opposition[117] on whom chance imposed the task of bringing about the downfall of a dynasty instead of a change of government; legitimists,[118] who did not want to cast off their livery but merely to change its style—these were the allies with whom the people had fought their February revolution. What the people instinctively hated in Louis Philippe was not Louis Philippe himself, but the crowned rule of a class, capital on the throne. But magnanimous as always, the people thought they had destroyed their enemy when they had overthrown the enemy of their enemies, their *common* enemy.

The *February revolution* was the *nice* revolution, the revolution of universal sympathies, because the contradictions which erupted in it against the monarchy were still *undeveloped* and peacefully dormant, because the social struggle which formed their background had only achieved a nebulous existence, an existence in phrases, in words. The *June revolution* is the *ugly* revolution, the nasty revolution, because the phrases have given place to the real thing, because the republic has bared the head of the monster by knocking off the crown which shielded and concealed it.

Order! was Guizot's war-cry. *Order!* shouted Sébastiani, the Guizotist, when Warsaw became Russian. *Order!* shouts Cavaignac, the brutal echo of the French National Assembly and of the republican bourgeoisie.

Order! thundered his grape-shot as it tore into the body of the proletariat.

None of the numerous revolutions of the French bourgeoisie since 1789 assailed the existing *order,* for they retained the class rule, the slavery of the workers, the *bourgeois order*, even though the political form of this rule and this slavery changed frequently. The June uprising did assail this *order*. Woe to the June uprising!

Under the *Provisional Government* it was considered good form and, moreover, a *necessity* to preach to the magnanimous workers—who, as a thousand official posters proclaimed, "*placed three months of hardship at the disposal of the republic*"—it was both politic and a sign of enthusiasm to preach to the workers that the February revolution had been carried out *in their own interests* and that the principal issue of the February revolution was the *interests of the workers*. With the *opening* of the National Assembly the speeches became more prosaic. Now it was only a matter of *leading labour back to its old conditions*, as Minister Trélat said. Thus the workers fought in February in order to be engulfed in an industrial crisis.

It is the business of the National Assembly to undo the work of February, at least as far as the workers are concerned, and to fling them back to their old conditions. But even this was not done, because it is not within the power of any assembly any more than of a king to tell a universal industrial crisis—*advance up to this point and no further*. In its crude eagerness to end the embarrassment of the February phraseology, the National Assembly did not even take the measures that were *possible* on the basis of the old conditions. Parisian workers aged 17 to 25 were either pressed into the army or thrown onto the street; those from other parts were ordered out of Paris to Sologne without even receiving the money normally due to them under such an order; adult Parisians could for the time being secure a pittance in workshops organised on military lines on condition that they did not attend any public meetings, in other words on condition that they ceased to be republicans. Neither the sentimental rhetoric which followed the February events nor the brutal legislation after May 15[119] achieved their purpose. A real, practical decision had to be taken. For whom did you make the February revolution, you rascals—for *yourselves* or for *us*? The bourgeoisie put this question in such a way that it had to be answered in June with grape-shot and barricades.

The entire National Assembly is nevertheless struck with paralysis, as one representative of the people[a] put it on June 25. Its members are stunned when question and answer make the streets of Paris flow with blood; some are stunned because their illusions are lost in the smoke of gunpowder, others because they cannot understand how the people dare stand up *on their own* for their *own vital* interests. *Russian money, British money, the Bonapartist eagle, the lily*, amulets of

---

[a] Ducoux.— *Ed.*

all kinds—this is where they sought an explanation of this strange event. *Both parts* of the Assembly feel however that a vast gulf separates them from the people. None of them dares stand up for the people.

As soon as the stupor has passed frenzy breaks out. The majority quite rightly greets with catcalls those pitiful utopians and hypocrites guilty of the anachronism of still using the term *fraternité*, brotherhood. The question at issue was precisely that of doing away with this term and with the illusions arising from its ambiguity. When the legitimist *Larochejaquelein*, the chivalrous dreamer, protested against the infamy of those who cried "*Vae victis! Woe to the vanquished!*" the majority of the deputies broke into a St. Vitus's dance as if stung by a tarantula. They shouted *woe!* to the workers in order to hide the fact that it is precisely they themselves who are the "*vanquished*". Either the Assembly must perish now, or the republic. And that is why it frantically yells—long live the republic!

Is the deep chasm which has opened at our feet to be allowed to mislead the democrats, to make us believe that the struggle over the form of the state is meaningless, illusory and futile?

Only weak, cowardly minds can pose such a question. Collisions proceeding from the very conditions of bourgeois society must be fought out to the end, they cannot be conjured out of existence. The best form of state is that in which the social contradictions are not blurred, not arbitrarily—that is merely artificially, and therefore only seemingly—kept down. The best form of state is that in which these contradictions reach a stage of open struggle in the course of which they are resolved.

We may be asked, do we not find a tear, a sigh, a word for the victims of the people's wrath, for the national guard, the mobile guard, the republican guard and the troops of the line?

The state will care for their widows and orphans, decrees extolling them will be issued, their remains will be carried to the grave in solemn procession, the official press will declare them immortal, European reaction in the East and the West will pay homage to them.

But the plebeians are tormented by hunger, abused by the press, forsaken by the doctors, called thieves, incendiaries and galley-slaves by the respectabilities; their wives and children are plunged into still greater misery and the best of those who have survived are sent overseas. It is the *right* and the *privilege of the democratic press* to place laurels on their clouded threatening brow.

Written by Marx on June 28, 1848   Printed according to the newspaper

First published in the *Neue Rheinische Zeitung* No. 29, June 29, 1848

THE *KÖLNISCHE ZEITUNG*
ON THE JUNE REVOLUTION

Cologne, June 30. If one reads the following passages from the *London Telegraph* and compares them to the babble about the Paris June revolution that emanates from the German liberals, especially Herr Brüggemann, Herr Dumont and Herr Wolfers, one will have to admit that the English bourgeois, apart from many other distinctions, surpass the *German philistines* in at least *this* regard: although they judge great events from a bourgeois point of view, they judge them as *men* and not in the manner of *gutter-snipes*.

The *Telegraph* comments in its issue No. 122:

"... And here we may be expected to say something of the origin and consequence of this terrible bloodshed.

"At once it proclaims itself a complete battle between classes."

(A kingdom for such a thought—is the mental exclamation of the august *Kölnische Zeitung* and its "Wolfers".)

"It is an insurrection of the workmen against the government they believed themselves to have created, and the classes who now support it. How the quarrel immediately originated is less easy to explain, than to detect its lasting and ever present causes. *The revolution of February* was chiefly effected by the *working classes* [...] and it was proclaimed *to have been made for their advantage*. It was a social, more than a political revolution. The masses of discontented workmen have not all of a sudden sprung, endowed with all the capabilities of soldiers, into existence; nor are their distress and their discontent the offspring merely of the events of the last four months. On Monday only we quoted the statement, perhaps exaggerated, of M. Leroux, which was made, however, in the National Assembly, and not denied [...] that there are in France 8,000,000 beggars and 4,000,000 workmen who have no secure wages. He spoke generally, and meant expressly to describe the time *before* the revolution; for his complaint was, that *since* the revolution nothing had been done to remedy that great disease. The theories of Socialism and Communism which had become rife in France, and now exercise such influence over the public mind, grew

from the terribly depressed condition of the bulk of the population under the government of Louis Philippe [...]. The main fact to be kept in view is *the distressed condition of the multitude as the great living cause of the revolution.* [...]
  ... "The National Assembly [...] speedily voted to deprive the workmen of the advantages which the politicians of the revolution [...] had so hastily and unthinkingly conferred on them. In a *social*, if not *political*, point of view, a *great reaction* was apparent, and authority was invoked, backed by a large part of France, *to put down the men who had given that authority existence* [....] That they should from such proceedings—first flattered and fed, then divided and threatened with starvation, drafted off to the country, where all the labour connections were destroyed, and a deliberate plan adopted to annihilate their power—that they should have been irritated can surprise no man; that after accomplishing one successful revolution they should have spontaneously thought they could bring about another, is not astonishing, and their chances of success against the armed force of the government, from the great length of time they have already resisted, seem greater than most people were prepared to expect. According to this view, which is confirmed by no political leaders having been detected amongst the people, and by the fact that the *ouvriers* ordered to quit Paris [...] proceeded no further than just outside the banners and then returned, *the insurrection is the consequence of a general feeling of indignation amongst the working classes and not of any political agency.* They fancy their interest is again betrayed by their *own government*, and they have taken up arms now *as they took them up in February* to fight against the *terrible distress* of which they have so long been the victims.
  " *The present battle, then, [...]*[a] *is but a continuation of the battle which took place in February* [....] *The contest is only a continuation of that struggle which pervades all Europe, more or less, for a fairer distribution of the annual produce of labour.* Put down in Paris now it probably will be; for the force which the new authority has inherited from the old authority that it displaced, is apparently overwhelming. *But, however successfully put down, it will be again and again renewed,* till government either makes a fairer distribution of the produce of labour, or, finding that impossible, retreats from the awful responsibility of attempting it and leaves it to be decided by the [...] open competition of the market.... *The real fight is for the means of comfortable subsistence*; the middle classes have been deprived of them by the politicians who undertook to guide the revolution; *they have been savaged as well as the workmen*; the strongest passions of both are now roused into mischievous activity; and, *forgetting their brotherhood, they make brutal war on each other.* The ignorant if not ill-meaning government, which seems to have no conception of its duty in this extraordinary crisis, [...] has first hurled the workmen on the middle classes, and is now *helping the middle classes to exterminate the deceived, deluded, and indignant workmen.* The principle of the Revolution, *the resolve to fight against distress and oppression*, must not be suffered to bear the blame of this great calamity, it must be thrown rather on those ignorant meddling politicians who have so aggravated all the disasters bequeathed to them by Louis Philippe."

Thus writes a *London* newspaper of the bourgeoisie about the June revolution, a newspaper which represents the principles of *Cobden*, *Bright* etc. and which after the *Times* and the *Northern Star*, the two despots of the English press, according to the *Manchester Guardian*, is the *most widely read paper in England.*

---

[a] Modified quotation. The *Telegraph* has: "The battle, then, that was raging on Friday, Saturday and Sunday."

Let us compare No. 181 of the *Kölnische Zeitung*! This remarkable newspaper transforms the *battle between two classes* into a *battle between respectable people* and *rogues*! What a worthy paper! As if the two classes did not hurl these epithets at each other. It is the same newspaper which *at first*, when rumours about the June uprising began to circulate, admitted *its total ignorance as to the nature* of the insurrection, and *then* had to get the information *from Paris* that an *important social revolution* was taking place whose scope would not be circumscribed *by one defeat*. *Finally*, strengthened by *one* defeat of the workers, it sees in the insurrection nothing but a battle between "the *enormous majority*" and a "*wild horde*" of "*cannibals, robbers and murderers*".

What was the Roman slave war? *A war between respectable people and cannibals!* Herr *Wolfers* will write Roman history and Herr *Dumont* and Herr *Brüggemann* will enlighten the *workers*, the "unfortunate ones", as to their real rights and duties and

"initiate them into *the science* which leads to order and which *forms* the true citizen"!

Long live the *science of Dumont-Brüggemann-Wolfers*, the secret science! To cite *one* example of this *secret science*: This praiseworthy triumvirate has told its gullible readers throughout two issues that General Cavaignac *wants to mine the district of St. Antoine*. The district of St. Antoine happens to be somewhat *larger than the golden city of Cologne*. The scientific triumvirate, however, that we recommend to the German National Assembly for ruling Germany, the triumvirate *Dumont-Brüggemann-Wolfers*, have overcome this difficulty; they know how to blow up the city of Cologne with one mine! Their notions of the mine which blows up the Faubourg St. Antoine correspond to the notion of the subterranean forces which undermine modern society, caused the Paris earthquake in June and spat up bloody lava from its revolutionary crater.

But dearest triumvirate! Great *Dumont-Brüggemann-Wolfers*, great personalities proclaimed by the world of advertisement! Cavaignacs of the world of advertisement! *We* modestly bowed our heads, bowed them before the greatest historical crisis that has ever broken out: the *class war between the bourgeoisie and the proletariat*. We have not created the fact, we have stated it. We have stated that one of the classes is *the conquered one* as *Cavaignac himself* says.[120] On the grave of the conquered, we have cried "*woe!*" *to the victors* and even Cavaignac shrinks from his historical responsibility! And the National Assembly charges with cowardice every member who does not openly accept the terrible historical responsibility. Did we open up the Sibylline Book for the *Germans* so that they should burn it? Do we ask the

Germans to become Englishmen when we describe the battle between the Chartists and the English bourgeoisie?

Germany, however, ungrateful Germany, you may know the *Kölnische Zeitung* and its advertisements but you do not know your greatest men, your *Wolfers*, your *Brüggemann* and your *Dumont*! How much sweat of the brain, sweat of the face and sweat of the blood has been shed in the *battle between classes*, in the battle between free men and slaves, patricians and plebeians, feudal lords and serfs, capitalists and workers! *But only because there was no Kölnische Zeitung*. But, most courageous triumvirate, if modern society produces "*criminals*", "*cannibals*", "*murderers*" and "*plunderers*" in such masses and with such energy that their insurrection shakes the basis of official society, what kind of society is this? What anarchy in alphabetical order! And you believe that you can heal the schism, that you have uplifted the actors and spectators of this terrible drama by dragging them down into a servant tragedy *à la* Kotzebue.

Among the *national guardsmen of the faubourgs St. Antoine, St. Jacques* and *St. Marceau* only *50* could be found who followed the call of the bourgeois bugle. Thus reports the Paris *Moniteur*, the official newspaper, the paper of Louis XVI, *Robespierre, Louis Philippe* and *Marrast-Cavaignac*! There is nothing simpler for the *science* which "turns" a man into a *true citizen*! The three largest faubourgs of Paris, the three most industrialised faubourgs of Paris, whose patterns made the muslins of Dacca and the velvet of Spitalfields pale and fade, are supposed to be inhabited by "cannibals", "plunderers", "robbers" and "criminals". So says *Wolfers*!

And *Wolfers* is an honourable man![a] He has bestowed honours upon the rogues by having them fight greater battles, produce greater works of art and accomplish more heroic deeds than those of Charles X, Louis Philippe, Napoleon and the spinners of Dacca and Spitalfields.

We were just now mentioning the *London Telegraph*. Yesterday our readers heard *Emil Girardin*. The working class, he says, after allowing its debtor, the February revolution, to delay paying off its debts for a month, the working class, the creditor, knocked at the debtor's house with the musket, the barricade and its own body! But *Emil Girardin*! Who is he? No anarchist! Heaven forbid! He is, however, a *republican of the coming day*, a *republican of the morrow* (*républicain du lendemain*) whereas the *Kölnische Zeitung*, the *Wolferses, Dumonts* and *Brüggemanns* are all *republicans of the day before yesterday, republicans before the republic* and *republicans of the eve* (*répub-*

---

[a] Shakespeare, *Julius Caesar*, Act III, Scene 2.—*Ed.*

licains de la veille)! Can *Emil Girardin* give evidence by the side of *Dumont?*

Admire the patriotism of the Cologne newspaper as it *gloats with malicious pleasure over the deportations and hangings.* It only wants to prove to the world, to the incredulous, stone-blind German world, that the *republic is more powerful than the monarchy* and that the republican National Assembly with Cavaignac and Marrast was able to carry out what the constitutional Chamber of Deputies with Thiers and Bugeaud was unable to do! *Vive la république!* Long live the republic! exclaims the Spartan Cologne paper at the sight of Paris, bleeding, moaning and burning. The crypto-republican! That is why this paper is suspected of being *cowardly* and *unprincipled* by a *Gervinus,* by an *Augsburg paper*[a]! The immaculate one! The Charlotte Corday of Cologne!

Please notice that *not one Paris newspaper,* not the *Moniteur,* not the *Débats* and not the *National,* speaks of "*cannibals*", "*plunderers*", "*robbers*" and "*murderers*". There is only one newspaper, the paper of *Thiers,* the man whose immorality was condemned by *Jacobus Venedey* in the *Kölnische Zeitung,* the man against whom the Cologne paper screamed at the top of its voice:

> They are not going to get it,
> Our own free German Rhine,[b]

it is Thiers' paper, the *Constitutionnel,* from which the Belgian *Indépendance* and Rhenish science embodied in *Dumont, Brüggemann* and *Wolfers* derive their knowledge!

Examine now in a critical vein these scandalous anecdotes with which the *Kölnische Zeitung* brands the oppressed, - the same newspaper which *at the outbreak of fighting* declared its complete *ignorance* of the nature of the struggle, which *during* the battle declared it to be an "*important social revolution*", and which *after* the battle calls it a boxing match between *the police and the robbers.*

They *looted!* But what did they loot? *Weapons, ammunition, surgical dressings* and the *most necessary items of food.* The robbers wrote on the window shutters: "*Mort aux voleurs!*" *Death to the robbers!*

They "*murdered like cannibals*". The cannibals did not willingly permit the *national guardsmen,* who advanced upon the barricades *behind* the regular troops, to *smash the skulls* of their *wounded,* to shoot their overwhelmed comrades and to stab their women. The cannibals who *exterminated* during a *war of extermination* as a French bourgeois

---

[a]   *Allgemeine Zeitung.—Ed.*

[b]   Nikolaus Becker, "Der deutsche Rhein".—*Ed.*

newspaper writes! They *set on fire?* Yet the *sole* incendiary torch which they hurled against the *legitimate* incendiary rockets of Cavaignac in the 8th arrondissement was a *poetic, imaginary* torch, as the *Moniteur* confirms.

"Some," says Wolfers, "held up high the programme of Barbès, Blanqui and Sobrier, the others hailed Napoleon and Henry V."

The chaste *Cologne* newspaper, which has not been pregnant either with the descendants of Napoleon or with Blanqui, declared already on the second day of the insurrection that the "fight was waged in the name of the *red republic*". What then is she babbling about *pretenders?* She is, however, as has already been intimated, an obdurate *crypto-republican*, a female Robespierre that scents pretenders everywhere, and these pretenders cause her morality to shudder.

"Almost all of them had money and several of them had considerable sums."

There were from 30,000 to 40,000 workers and "almost all of them had money" during this time of want and business slump! The money was probably *so scarce because the workers had hidden it*!

The Paris *Moniteur* has published with the greatest conscientiousness all cases where *money* was found on the insurgents. There were at most *twenty* such cases. Different newspapers and correspondents have repeated these cases and cited different sums. The *Kölnische Zeitung*, with its tried critical tact, which takes all these different reports of the *twenty* cases for so many different cases and then still adds all the cases circulated by rumours, might at best perhaps arrive at 200 cases. And that entitles the paper to state that almost all the 30,000 to 40,000 workers had money! All that has been established is that legitimist, Bonapartist and perhaps Philippist emissaries provided with money mingled or intended to mingle with the barricade fighters. M. *Payer*, that most conservative member of the National Assembly, who spent 12 hours as a prisoner among the insurgents, declares:

"*Most of them were workers who had been driven to desperation by four months of misery.* They said: *Better to die of a bullet than of starvation!*"

"*Many, very many* of the dead," affirms *Wolfers*, "bore the ominous mark with which society stigmatises crime."

That is one of the base lies, shameful calumnies and infamies which *Lamennais*, the foe of the insurgents and the man of the *National*, has stigmatised in his *Peuple constituant*—and which the always chivalrous legitimist *Larochejaquelain* has stigmatised in the National Assembly. The entire lie is based upon the quite unconfirmed assertion of *one* press-agency, which has *not been corroborated* by the *Moniteur*, that *eleven corpses* had been discovered which were marked with the letters T. F.[a] And in which revolution have the eleven corpses not been found? And which revolution will not brand with these letters eleven times 100?

Let us note that the newspapers, proclamations and illuminations of the victors testify that they starved out, drove to desperation, bayonetted, fusilladed, buried alive and deported the vanquished and desecrated their corpses. And against the conquered there are only *anecdotes,* and only anecdotes that are related by the *Constitutionnel,* reprinted by the *Indépendance* and translated into German by the *Kölnische.* There is no greater insult to truth than to try to prove it by an *anecdote,* says—*Hegel.*[b]

The women are sitting in front of the houses of Paris and scraping *lint* for dressings for the wounded, even the wounded insurgents. The editors of the *Kölnische Zeitung* pour *sulphuric acid* into their wounds.

They have denounced *us* to the bourgeois *police.* We recommend in return that the *workers,* the "*unfortunate ones*", let themselves "be enlightened as to their real rights and duties and initiated into the *science* which leads to order and which forms the true citizen", by the immortal triumvirate *Dumont-Brüggemann-Wolfers.*

Written by Engels on June 30, 1848   Printed according to the newspaper

First published in the *Neue Rheinische*   Published in English for the first
Zeitung No. 31, July 1, 1848   time

---

[a] Convict brand (*travaux forcés*: forced labour).— *Ed.*

[b] G. W. F. Hegel, *Phänomenologie des Geistes.* VI. "Der Geist", § Die Bildung und ihr Reich der Wirklichkeit.— *Ed.*

THE JUNE REVOLUTION[121]

[THE COURSE OF THE PARIS UPRISING]

[*Neue Rheinische Zeitung* No. 31, July 1, 1848]

Gradually we gain a more comprehensive view of the June revolution; fuller reports arrive, it becomes possible to distinguish facts from either hearsay or lies, and the nature of the uprising stands out with increasing clarity. The more one succeeds in grasping the interconnection of the events of the four days in June, the more is one astonished by the vast magnitude of the uprising, the heroic courage, the rapidly improvised organisation and the unanimity of the insurgents.

The workers' plan of action, which Kersausie, a friend of Raspail and a former officer, is said to have drawn up, was as follows:

The insurgents, moving in four columns, advanced concentrically towards the Hôtel de Ville.

The first column, whose base of operations was the suburbs of Montmartre, La Chapelle and La Villette, advanced southwards from the barrières of Poissonnière, Rochechouart, St. Denis and La Villette, occupied the boulevards and approached the Hôtel de Ville through the rues Montorgueil, St. Denis and St. Martin.

The second column, whose base was the faubourgs du Temple and St. Antoine, which are inhabited almost entirely by workers and protected by the St. Martin Canal, advanced towards the same centre through the rues du Temple and St. Antoine and along the quays of the northern bank of the Seine as well as through all other streets running in the same direction in this part of the city.

The third column based on the Faubourg St. Marceau advanced towards the Île de la Cité through the rue St. Victor and the quays of the southern bank of the Seine.

The fourth column, based on the Faubourg St. Jacques and the vicinity of the Medical School, advanced along the rue Saint Jacques also to the Cité. There the two columns joined, crossed to the right bank of the Seine and enveloped the Hôtel de Ville from the rear and flank.

Thus the plan, quite correctly, was based on the districts in which only workers lived. These districts form a semicircular belt, which surrounds the entire eastern half of Paris, widening out towards the east. First of all the eastern part of Paris was to be cleared of enemies, and then it was intended to move along both banks of the Seine towards the west and its centres, the Tuileries and the National Assembly.

These columns were to be supported by numerous flying squads which, operating independently alongside and between the columns, were to build barricades, occupy the smaller streets and be responsible for maintaining communications.

The operational bases were strongly fortified and skilfully transformed into formidable fortresses, e.g. the Clos St. Lazare, the Faubourg and Quartier St. Antoine and the Faubourg St. Jacques, in case it should become necessary to retreat.

If there was any flaw in this plan it was that in the beginning of the operations the western part of Paris was completely overlooked. Here there are several districts eminently suitable for armed action on both sides of the rue St. Honoré near the Halles and the Palais National, which have very narrow, winding streets inhabited mainly by workers. It was important to set up a fifth centre of the insurrection there, thus cutting off the Hôtel de Ville and at the same time holding up a considerable number of troops at this projecting strongpoint. The success of the uprising depended on the insurgents reaching the centre of Paris as quickly as possible and seizing the Hôtel de Ville. We cannot know what prevented Kersausie from organising insurgent action in this district. But it is a fact that no uprising was ever successful which did not at the outset succeed in seizing the centre of Paris adjoining the Tuileries. It suffices to mention the uprising which took place during General Lamarque's funeral[122] when the insurgents likewise got as far as the rue Montorgueil and were then driven back.

The insurgents advanced in accordance with their plan. They immediately began to separate their territory, the Paris of the workers, from the Paris of the bourgeoisie, by two main fortifications—the barricades at the Porte Saint Denis and those of the Cité. They were dislodged from the former, but were able to hold the latter. June 23, the first day, was merely a prelude. The plan of the insurgents already began to emerge clearly (and the *Neue Rheinische Zeitung* grasped it correctly at the outset, see No. 26, special supplement[a]), especially after the first skirmishes between the advanced guards which took place in the morning. The boulevard St. Martin, which crosses the line of operation of the first column, became the scene of fierce fighting, which, partly due to the nature of the terrain, ended with a victory for the forces of "order".

The approaches to the Cité were blocked on the right by a flying squad, which entrenched itself in the rue Planche-Mibray; on the left by the third and fourth columns, which occupied and fortified the three southern bridges of the Cité. Here too a very fierce battle raged. The forces of "order" succeeded in taking the St. Michel Bridge and advancing to the rue St. Jacques. They felt sure that by the evening the revolt would be suppressed.

The plan of the forces of "order" stood out even more clearly than that of the insurgents. To begin with, their plan was merely to crush the insurrection with all available means. They announced their design to the insurgents with cannon-ball and grape-shot.

But the Government believed it was dealing with an uncouth gang of common rioters acting without any plan. After clearing the main streets by the evening, the Government declared that the revolt was quelled, and the stationing of troops in the conquered districts was undertaken in an exceedingly negligent manner.

The insurgents made excellent use of this negligence by launching the great battle which followed the skirmishes of June 23. It is quite remarkable how quickly the workers mastered the plan of campaign, how well-concerted their actions were and how skilfully they used the difficult terrain. This would be quite inexplicable if in the national workshops the workers had not already been to a certain extent organised on military lines and divided into companies, so that they only needed to apply their industrial organisation to their military enterprise in order to constitute immediately a fully organised army.

On the morning of the 24th they had not only completely regained the ground they had lost, but even added new terrain to it. True, the line of boulevards up to the boulevard du Temple remained in the hands of the troops, thus cutting off the first column from the centre, but on the other hand the second column pushed forward from the Quartier St. Antoine until it almost surrounded the Hôtel de Ville. It established its headquarters in the church of St. Gervais, within 300 paces of the Hôtel de Ville. It captured the St. Merri monastery and the adjoining streets and advanced far beyond the Hôtel de Ville, so that together with the columns in the Cité it almost

[a] See this volume, pp. 124-27.—Ed.

completely encircled the Hôtel de Ville. Only one way of approach, the quays of the right bank, remained open. In the south the Faubourg St. Jacques was completely reoccupied, communication with the Cité was restored, reinforcements were sent there, and preparations were made for crossing to the right bank.

There was no time to be lost. The Hôtel de Ville, the revolutionary centre of Paris, was threatened and was bound to fall unless the most resolute measures were taken.

[*Neue Rheinische Zeitung* No. 32, July 2, 1848]

Cavaignac was appointed dictator by the terrified National Assembly. Accustomed as he was in Algeria to "energetic" action, he did not have to be told what to do.

Ten battalions promptly moved towards the Hôtel de Ville along the wide Quai de l'École. They cut off the insurgents in the Cité from the right bank, secured the safety of the Hôtel de Ville and even made it possible to attack the barricades surrounding it.

The rue Planche-Mibray, and its continuation, the rue Saint Martin, were cleared and kept permanently clear by cavalry. The Notre-Dame Bridge, which lies opposite and leads to the Cité, was swept by heavy guns, and then Cavaignac advanced directly on the Cité in order to take "energetic" measures there. The "*Belle Jardinière*", the main strongpoint of the insurgents, was first shattered by cannon and then set on fire by rockets. The rue de la Cité was also seized with the aid of gun-fire; three bridges leading to the left bank were stormed and the insurgents on the left bank were pressed back. Meanwhile, the 14 battalions deployed on the Place de Grève and the quays freed the besieged Hôtel de Ville and reduced the church of Saint Gervais from a headquarters to a lost outpost of the insurgents.

The rue St. Jacques was not only bombarded from the Cité but also attacked in the flank from the left bank. General Damesme broke through along the Luxembourg to the Sorbonne, seized the Quartier Latin and sent his columns against the Panthéon. The square in front of the Panthéon had been transformed into a formidable stronghold. The forces of "order" still faced this unassailable bulwark long after they had taken the rue St. Jacques. Gun-fire and bayonet attacks were of no avail until finally exhaustion, lack of ammunition and the threat of the bourgeois to set the place on fire compelled the 1,500 workers, who were completely hemmed in, to surrender. At about the same time, the Place Maubert fell into the hands of the forces of "order" after a long and courageous resistance, and the insurgents, deprived of their strongest positions, were forced to abandon the entire left bank of the Seine.

Meanwhile the troops and national guards stationed on the boulevards of the right bank of the Seine were likewise put into action in two directions. Lamoricière, who commanded them, had the streets of the faubourgs St. Denis and St. Martin, the boulevard du Temple and part of the rue du Temple cleared by heavy artillery and swift infantry attacks. By the evening he could boast of brilliant successes. He had cut off and partly surrounded the first column in the Clos St. Lazare; he had pushed back the second column and by advancing along the boulevards had thrust a wedge into it.

How did Cavaignac win these advantages?

First, by the vastly superior force he was able to use against the insurgents. On the 24th he had at his disposal not only the 20,000-strong Paris garrison, the 20,000 to 25,000 men of the mobile guard and the 60,000 to 80,000 available men of the national guard, but also the national guard from the whole environs of Paris and from many of the more distant towns (20,000 to 30,000 men) and in addition 20,000 to 30,000 soldiers who were called in with the utmost dispatch from the neighbouring garrisons. Even on the morning of the 24th he had well over 100,000 men at his disposal, and by the evening their numbers had increased by half. The insurgents, on the other hand, numbered 40,000 to 50,000 men at most!

Secondly, by the brutal means he used. Until then cannon had been fired in the streets of Paris only once, i.e. in Vendémiaire 1795, when Napoleon dispersed the insurgents in the rue Saint Honoré with grape-shot.[123] But no artillery, let alone shells and incendiary rockets, was ever used against barricades and against houses. The people were unprepared for this, they were unable to defend themselves, for the only counteraction they could take was to set fire to houses, but this was repugnant to their sense of what was right. Up till then the people had no idea that this brand of Algerian warfare could be used right in the centre of Paris. They therefore retreated, and their first retreat spelt their defeat.

On the 25th Cavaignac attacked with even larger forces. The insurgents were confined to a single district, the faubourgs Saint Antoine and du Temple; in addition they still held two outposts, the Clos St. Lazare and a part of the St. Antoine district up to the Damiette Bridge.

Cavaignac, who had received further reinforcements of 20,000 to 30,000 men as well as a substantial park of artillery, first attacked the isolated outposts of the insurgents, especially the Clos St. Lazare. The insurgents were entrenched here as in a fortress. After a

12-hour bombardment with cannon and mortar shells, Lamoricière finally succeeded in dislodging the insurgents and occupying the Clos St. Lazare, but not until he had mounted a flank attack from the rues Rochechouart and La Poissonnière, and had demolished the barricades by bombarding them with 40 guns on the first day and with an even greater number on the next.

Another part of his column penetrated through the Faubourg Saint Martin into the Faubourg du Temple, but was not very successful. A third section moved along the boulevards towards the Bastille, but it did not get very far either, because a number of the most formidable barricades there resisted for a long time and only succumbed after a fierce cannonade. The houses here suffered appalling destruction.

Duvivier's column advancing from the Hôtel de Ville pressed the insurgents back still further with the aid of incessant artillery fire. The church of St. Gervais was captured, a long stretch of the rue Saint Antoine well beyond the Hôtel de Ville was cleared, and several columns moving along the quay and streets running parallel to it seized the Damiette Bridge, which connected the insurgents of the St. Antoine district with those of the St. Louis and Cité islands. The Saint Antoine district was outflanked and the insurgents had no choice but to fall back into the faubourg, which they did in fierce combat with a column advancing along the quays to the mouth of the St. Martin Canal and thence along the boulevard Bourdon skirting the canal. Several insurgents who were cut off were massacred, hardly any were taken prisoner.

The St. Antoine district and the Place de la Bastille were seized in this operation. Lamoricière's column managed to occupy the whole boulevard Beaumarchais by the evening and join up with Duvivier's troops on the Place de la Bastille.

The capture of the Damiette Bridge enabled Duvivier to dislodge the insurgents from the Île St. Louis and the former Île Louvier. He did this with a commendable display of Algerian barbarity. Hardly anywhere in the city was heavy artillery used with such devastating effect as in the Île St. Louis. But what did that matter? The insurgents were either driven out or massacred and among the blood-stained ruins "order" triumphed.

One more post remained to be seized on the left bank of the Seine. The Austerlitz Bridge, which east of the St. Martin Canal links the Faubourg St. Antoine with the left bank of the Seine, was heavily barricaded and had a strong bridgehead on the left bank where it adjoins the Place Valhubert in front of the Botanical Gardens. This bridgehead, which after the fall of the Panthéon and the Place

Maubert was the last stronghold of the insurgents on the left bank, was taken after stubborn resistance.

Only their last bulwark, the Faubourg St. Antoine and a part of the Faubourg du Temple, was thus left to the insurgents on the following day, the 26th. Neither of these faubourgs is very suitable for street-fighting; the streets there are fairly wide and almost perfectly straight, offering full play for the artillery. Their western side is well protected by the St. Martin Canal, but the northern side is completely exposed. Five or six perfectly straight, wide streets run from the north right into the centre of the Faubourg Saint Antoine.

The principal fortifications were at the Place de la Bastille and in the rue Faubourg St. Antoine, the main street of the whole district. Remarkably strong barricades were set up there, built partly of big flagstones and partly of wooden beams. They were constructed in the form of an angle pointing inward in order partly to weaken the effect of the gun-fire, partly to offer a larger defensive front making cross-fire possible. Openings had been made in the fire-proof walls of the houses so that the rows of houses were connected with each other, thus enabling the insurgents to open rifle-fire on the troops or withdraw behind the barricades as circumstances demanded. The bridges and quays along the canal as well as the streets running parallel to it were also strongly fortified. In short, the two faubourgs the insurgents still held resembled a veritable fortress, in which the troops had to wage a bloody battle for every inch of ground.

On the morning of the 26th the fighting was to be resumed, but Cavaignac was not keen on sending his troops into this maze of barricades. He threatened to shell them; mortars and howitzers were brought up. A parley was held. Cavaignac meanwhile ordered the nearest houses to be mined, but this could only be done to a very limited extent, because the time was too short and because the canal covered one of the lines of attack; he also ordered internal communication to be established between the occupied houses and the adjoining houses through gaps in the fire-proof walls.

The negotiations broke down and fighting was resumed. Cavaignac ordered General Perrot to attack from the Faubourg du Temple and General Lamoricière from the Place de la Bastille. The barricades were heavily shelled from both directions. Perrot pushed forward fairly rapidly, occupied the remaining section of the Faubourg du Temple and even penetrated into the Faubourg St. Antoine at several points. Lamoricière's advance was slower. The first barricades withstood his guns, although his grenades set the first houses of the faubourg on fire. He began once more to negotiate. Watch in hand he awaited the moment when he would have the pleasure of shelling and razing to the ground the most thickly populated district of Paris. Some of the insurgents at last capitulated, while others, attacked in the flank, withdrew from the city after a short battle.

It was the end of the June barricade fighting. Skirmishes still continued outside the city, but they were of no significance. The insurgents who fled were scattered in the neighbourhood and were one by one captured by cavalry.

We have given this purely military description of the struggle to show our readers with what heroic courage, unity, discipline and military skill the Paris workers fought. For four days 40,000 of them opposed forces four times their strength, and were within a hairbreadth of victory. They almost succeeded in gaining a footing in the centre of Paris, taking the Hôtel de Ville, forming a Provisional Government and doubling their number not only by people from the captured parts of the city joining them but also from the ranks of the mobile guard, who at that time needed but a slight impetus to make them go over to their side.

German newspapers assert that this was the decisive battle between the red and the tricolour republics, between workers and bourgeois. We are convinced that this battle will decide *nothing* but the disintegration of the victors. Moreover, the whole course of events proves that, even from a purely military standpoint, the workers are bound to triumph within a fairly short space of time. If 40,000 Paris workers could achieve such tremendous things against forces four times their number, what will the whole mass of Paris workers accomplish by concerted and co-ordinated action!

Kersausie was captured and by now has probably been shot. The bourgeois can kill him, but cannot take from him the fame of having been the *first to organise street-fighting*. They can kill him, but no power on earth can prevent his techniques from being used in all future street-fighting. They can kill him, but they cannot prevent his name from going down in history as the *first commander-in-chief of barricade fighting*.

Written by Engels on June 30 and July 1,   Printed according to the newspaper
1848

First published in the *Neue Rheinische
Zeitung* Nos. 31 and 32, July 1 and 2, 1848

GERMANY'S FOREIGN POLICY[124]

Cologne, July 2. All hitherto existing rulers and their diplomats have employed their skill and efforts to set one nation against another and use one nation to subjugate another, and in this manner to perpetuate absolute rule. Germany has distinguished herself in this respect. During the last 70 years alone, she has furnished the British, in exchange for English gold, with mercenaries to be used against the North Americans fighting for their independence; when the first French revolution broke out it was the Germans again who, like a rabid pack, allowed themselves to be set upon the French; in a vicious manifesto issued by the Duke of Brunswick they threatened to raze the whole of Paris to the ground[125]; they conspired with the émigré aristocrats against the new order in France and were paid for this in the form of subsidies received from England. When the Dutch, for the first time in two hundred years, finally hit upon the sensible idea of putting an end to the mad rule of the House of Orange and establishing a republic,[126] it was the Germans again who acted as the hangmen of freedom. The Swiss, too, could tell a tale about their German neighbours, and it will be some time before the Hungarians recover from the harm which Austria, i.e. the German Imperial Court, inflicted upon them. Indeed, German mercenary troops were sent as far as Greece to prop up the little throne of dear Otto,[127] and German policemen were sent even to Portugal. Then there were the congresses after 1815, Austria's expeditions to Naples, Turin and the Romagna; the imprisonment of Ypsilanti, the German-imposed war of suppression which France waged against Spain[128]; Dom Miguel[129] and Don Carlos,[130] who were supported by Germany; the reaction in Britain had Hanoverian troops at its disposal; German influence has led to the dismemberment of Belgium and the establishment of a Thermidorian rule there; in the

very heart of Russia Germans are the mainstay of the *one* autocrat
and of the smaller ones; all Europe is flooded with sprigs of the
House of Coburg.

Poland has been plundered and dismembered and Cracow
throttled with the help of German soldiers.[131] German money and
blood have helped to enslave and impoverish Lombardy and Venice,
and directly or indirectly to stifle any movement of liberation
throughout Italy by means of bayonets, gallows, prisons and galleys.[a]
The list of sins is much longer, let us close it.

The blame for the infamies committed with the aid of Germany in
other countries falls not only on the governments but to a large
extent also on the German people. But for the delusions of the
Germans, their slavish spirit, their aptitude as mercenaries and
"benign" jailers and tools of the masters "by divine right", the
German name abroad would not be so detested, cursed and
despised, and the nations oppressed by Germany would have long
since been able to develop freely. Now that the Germans are
throwing off their own yoke, their whole foreign policy must change
too. Otherwise the fetters with which we have chained other nations
will shackle our own new freedom, which is as yet hardly more than a
presentiment. Germany will liberate herself to the extent to which
she sets free neighbouring nations.

Things are indeed beginning to look brighter. The lies and
misrepresentations which the old government organs have been so
busy spreading about Poland and Italy, the attempts at stirring up
enmity artificially, the turgid phrases proclaiming that German
honour or German power is at stake—all these formulas have lost
their magic power. The official patriotism is effective only when
these patriotic postures conceal material interests, only among a
section of the big bourgeoisie whose business depends on this official
patriotism. The reactionary party knows this and makes use of it. But
the great mass of the German middle class and the working class
understand or feel that the freedom of the neighbouring nations is
the guarantee of their own freedom. Is Austria's war against Italy's
independence or Prussia's war against the restoration of Poland
popular, or on the contrary do they not destroy the last illusions
about such "patriotic" crusades? However, neither this understanding nor this feeling is sufficient. If Germany's blood and money are
no longer to be squandered, to her own detriment, in suppressing
other nations, then we must achieve a really popular government,
and the old edifice must be razed to the ground. Only then can an

---

[a] See this volume, pp. 385-87 and 395-98.—*Ed.*

international policy of democracy take the place of the sanguinary, cowardly policy of the old, revived system. How can a democratic foreign policy be carried through while democracy at home is stifled? Meanwhile, everything possible must be done to prepare the way for the democratic system on this side and the other side of the Alps. The *Italians* have issued a number of declarations which make their friendly attitude towards Germany perfectly clear. We would mention the Manifesto of the Provisional Government at Milan[132] addressed to the German people[a] and the numerous articles written in the same vein, which are published in the Italian press. We have now received further evidence of this attitude—a private letter from the administrative committee of the newspaper *L'Alba*, published in Florence, to the editors of the *Neue Rheinische Zeitung*. It is dated June 20, and says among other things:

"We thank you sincerely for the esteem in which you hold our poor Italy.[b] Meanwhile we whole-heartedly assure you that all Italians know who really violates and attacks their liberty; they know that their most deadly enemy is not the strong and magnanimous German people, but rather their unjust, despotic, and cruel government; we assure you that every true Italian longs for the moment when he will be free to shake hands with his German brother, who, once his inalienable rights are established, will be able to defend them, to respect them himself and to secure the respect of all his brothers for them. Placing our trust in the principles to whose careful elaboration you have dedicated yourselves, we remain

Your faithful friends and brothers
(signed) *L. Alinari*"

The *Alba* is one of the few papers in Italy which firmly advocate democratic principles.

Written by Engels on July 2, 1848   Printed according to the newspaper

First published in the *Neue Rheinische Zeitung* No. 33, July 3, 1848

---

[a] *Il Governo provvisorio alla Nazione Germanica*, April 6, 1848.—*Ed.*
[b] See this volume, pp. 11-12.—*Ed.*

MARRAST AND THIERS

We have continuously drawn the attention of the readers of the *Neue Rheinische Zeitung* to the intrigues of the party of the *National*, personified by *Marrast*. We have investigated the underhanded means by which this party strives to seize the dictatorship. At the same time we have pointed out how the dictatorship of Marrast conjures up the dictatorship of Thiers.

Several facts strikingly illustrate how much the party of the *National*, due to its victory, has already succumbed to the party of Thiers which is now closely fused with the dynastic opposition.[133]

The appointment of *Carnot*, a man of the *National*, as Minister has stirred up a violent uproar in the National Assembly. *Marie's* candidature for the presidency of the National Assembly was rivalled by *Dufaure's* candidature and, as the *Débats* reports, was only approved because he was known as "the wisest and most moderate man of the old Executive Committee",[a] i.e. because he made the most concessions to the old dynastic party and because he drafted the Bill on gatherings, the continuation of the September Laws,[134] and sponsored and defended it in the National Assembly! The fact remains that "Marrast" and "Thiers" threw dice for the presidency of the National Assembly.

This does not satisfy, however, the "dynastic opposition". One of the first laws that it is preparing is a law concerning the municipal councils, a law which is directly aimed against the autocracy and influence of Marrast, the Mayor of Paris. And he will fall.

In a few days the entire National Assembly will tear itself apart. The reaction will proceed until the party of the *National* is excluded

---

[a] "Paris, 29 juillet", *Journal des Débats*, July 30, 1848.—*Ed.*

from all exercise of power. "Republic" and "dynastic opposition" will confront each other once more, but the republic will no longer win on the terms of February.

The people will no longer indulge in fancies. It will no longer "hide its revenge under a bushel" as Caussidière puts it and it will no longer "fling its wrath into the torrents of Styx".[a] *Qui vivra verra.*

Written on July 2, 1848

First published in the *Neue Rheinische Zeitung* No. 33, July 3, 1848

Printed according to the newspaper

Published in English for the first time

---

[a] From Caussidière's speech in the National Assembly on June 27, 1848 (*Neue Rheinische Zeitung* No. 31, July 1, 1848, supplement).—*Ed.*

THE AGREEMENT DEBATES

Cologne, July 2. After the tragedy the idyll, after the thunder of the Paris June days, the beating of the drums of the Berlin agreers. We had completely lost sight of the gentlemen but now we learn that at the very moment when Cavaignac shelled the Faubourg St. Antoine, Herr Camphausen gave a nostalgic farewell address and Herr Hansemann submitted the programme of the new Ministry.

First of all, we observe with pleasure that Herr Hansemann has taken our advice and has *not* become Prime Minister.[a] He has realised that it is greater to *make* Prime Ministers than to *be* one.

The new Government, in spite of the borrowed name (*prête-nom*) of Auerswald, is and remains the *Hansemann* Government. It shows itself as such by presenting itself as the Government of *Action* and of accomplishing things. Herr Auerswald has certainly no claim to be a Minister of action!

Herr Hansemann's programme is well known. We will not examine the points of his political programme since they have already provided feed for the more or less petty German newspapers. There is only one point that nobody has dared to examine. We want to make up for that omission so that Herr Hansemann should not feel neglected.

Herr Hansemann declares:

"There is at present no more effective means to revive industry and thus to eliminate the poverty of the labouring classes than to restore the weakened confidence in the preservation of law and order and to establish soon a firm constitutional monarchy. By concentrating all our efforts on this aim, *we can best counteract unemployment and poverty.*"

---

[a] See this volume, pp. 111-12.—*Ed.*

At the beginning of his programme, Herr Hansemann has already said that he proposes to submit new repressive laws for this purpose insofar as the old (police state!) legislation does not suffice.

That is plain enough. The old despotic legislation does not suffice! The abolition of the poverty of the working class is not the province of the Minister of Public Works or the Minister of Finance but of the Minister of *War!* First repressive laws, to be followed by grape-shot and bayonets—indeed, "there is no more effective means"! Perhaps Herr Schreckenstein,[a] whose mere name—according to the Westphalian address[b]—strikes terror into the agitators, wants to continue his heroic deeds of Trier[135] and become a Cavaignac on a reduced Prussian scale?

But Herr Hansemann has still other means besides the "most effective" one:

"What is *also* necessary for this purpose is to procure employment by public works projects of genuine usefulness to the country."

Herr Hansemann will thus "order still more comprehensive work for the good of *all* industrious classes of the people" than Herr Patow. But he will do this

"when the Government succeeds in removing the anxieties over the possible overthrow of the political system which are nourished by unrest and *agitation* and in *restoring* the general *confidence* necessary to obtain the required *finances*".

For the moment Herr Hansemann cannot order any public works to be started because he cannot obtain any money. He can only obtain the money when confidence is restored. But, as he himself says, when confidence is restored, the workers will be employed and the Government will no longer *need* to procure jobs for them.

Herr Hansemann's measures for the abolition of poverty are going round in a circle which is by no means vicious but rather very virtuous in a bourgeois sense. For the moment Herr Hansemann has nothing to offer the workers but the September Laws[136] and a reduced version of Cavaignac. This is indeed a Government of *Action!*

It is not our purpose to examine the recognition of the revolution in his programme. The "well-informed G-correspondent" of the *Kölnische Zeitung* has already hinted to the public how far Herr Hansemann has saved the legal basis for the benefit of the

---

[a] The name, literally translated, means "terror-stone". — *Ed.*

[b] "Adresse der Krieger und Wehrmänner des Kreises Hagen vom 19. Juni 1848" (*Neue Rheinische Zeitung* No. 25, June 25, 1848, special supplement).—*Ed.*

neighbouring journalist.[a] As regards the revolution Herr Hansemann has recognised that it is basically no revolution.

Herr Hansemann had hardly finished when Prime Minister *Auerswald* rose, for he was obliged to say something as well. He took out a written scrap of paper and read approximately the following thoughts, only not in verse:

> Gentlemen! I am happy today
> To tarry at your meeting,
> Where many a noble kindred spirit
> Lovingly howls a greeting.
> My feelings at this very moment
> Are quite beyond all measure;
> And oh! these truly blissful hours
> All my life I'll treasure![b]

We want to emphasise that we have given the most favourable interpretation to the somewhat unintelligible scrap of paper of the Prime Minister.

Herr Auerswald has hardly finished when our Hansemann jumps up again in order to prove by raising a question of confidence that he has not changed his tune. He demands that the draft address[c] be referred back to committee and says:

"The reception which this first motion will find in the Assembly will be a measure of the amount of confidence that the High Assembly has in the new Ministry."

This was really too much. Deputy *Weichsel*, no doubt a reader of the *Neue Rheinische Zeitung*, angrily rushes to the rostrum and protests emphatically against this everlasting method of the question of confidence. So far, so good. But once a German has begun to talk, it is hard to stop him, and so Herr Weichsel let himself go in a long discourse about this and that, about the revolution, the year 1807 and the year 1815, about a warm heart beating beneath a shirt and several other topics. All this he said because "he felt it necessary to get these matters off his chest". A dreadful clamour, mingled with a few bravos from the Left, forced the worthy fellow to leave the rostrum.

Herr Hansemann assured the Assembly that it was by no means the Ministry's intention to raise *frivolous questions of confidence*. It would not be worth the trouble to discuss the issue further since on

---

[a] Marx and Engels frequently use this expression when referring to Karl Brüggemann, the editor-in-chief of the *Kölnische Zeitung*.—*Ed.*

[b] Heinrich Heine, *Deutschland. Ein Wintermärchen*, Caput XII.—*Ed.*

[c] See this volume, pp. 62-63.—*Ed.*

this occasion it was not really a full question of confidence but only half a question.

There ensues debate such as seldom occurs. Everybody speaks at once and the debate wanders off into a myriad trivialities. The question of confidence, the agenda, standing orders, Polish nationality, adjournment, accompanied by bravos and clamour, all circulate for some time. At last Herr *Parrisius* observes that Herr Hansemann has put a motion on behalf of the Government, whereas the Government as such cannot put motions but can only make communications.

Herr *Hansemann* replies that it was a slip of the tongue. The motion was really no motion but merely a *request* from the Government.

The grandiose question of confidence is thus reduced to a mere "request" of the Ministers!

Herr Parrisius rushes to the rostrum from the left side, Herr Ritz from the right. At the summit they confront each other. A collision is unavoidable since neither of the two heroes wants to withdraw. At this point, the Chairman, Herr Esser, begins to speak and both heroes turn back.

Herr *Zachariä* adopts the Government's motion as his own and demands an immediate debate.

Herr Zachariä, the obedient servant of this as well as the previous Government, who had once before played the redeeming angel by just at the right moment. proposing an amendment to Berends' motion, could not find anything to say in support of his motion. What had been stated by the Finance Minister sufficed entirely.

A lengthy debate now ensues with the indispensable amendments, interruptions, table-banging, blustering and sophistries about rules of procedure. It would be asking too much of us to lead our readers through this labyrinth. We can merely point out to them some of the more charming aspects of this confusion:

1. Deputy *Waldeck* enlightens us: the address cannot be referred back to the committee since the committee no longer exists.

2. Deputy *Hüffer* elaborates: the address is not a reply to the Crown but to the Ministers. The Ministers who produced the speech from the throne no longer exist. How are we supposed to reply to someone who does not exist any more?

3. Deputy d'Ester draws the following conclusion in the form of an amendment: the Assembly wishes to drop the address.

4. The amendment is disposed of by Chairman *Esser* in the following manner: This proposal seems to be a new motion and not an amendment.

That is the whole skeleton of the debate. To this meagre skeleton, however, there adheres a mass of bloated flesh in the form of speeches by the Ministers Rodbertus and Kühlwetter, the deputies Zachariä, Reichensperger II etc.

The situation is exceedingly strange. Herr Rodbertus himself says that it is

"unprecedented in the history of parliaments that a Government resigns while the draft of an address is on the table and the debate about it is supposed to begin!"

During its first six weeks of parliamentary life, Prussia has on the whole had the good fortune of encountering events almost all of which were "unprecedented in the history of parliaments".

Herr Hansemann finds himself in the same dilemma as the Chamber. The address, ostensibly a reply to the speech from the throne by Camphausen-Hansemann, is in reality supposed to be a reply to the Hansemann-Auerswald programme. The committee which was complaisant towards Camphausen is therefore supposed to show similar complaisance towards Herr Hansemann. The difficulty is merely to convince people of the need for this demand which is "unprecedented in the history of parliaments". All means are employed. Rodbertus, the Aeolian harp of the Left Centre, murmurs the most gentle sounds. Kühlwetter makes soothing gestures in all directions: it is, of course, possible that a new examination of the draft address "might convince everybody that *no changes need now be made after all* (!) but in order to win this conviction" (!!) the draft ought to be returned once more to the committee! Finally, Herr Hansemann, who as always is bored by a long debate, cuts the knot by stating bluntly why the draft should be returned to the committee: he does not want the new changes to slip in through the back door in the form of ministerial amendments, they should rather, in the form of committee proposals, strut into the hall through a large folding-door with wide-open leaves.

The Prime Minister declares that it is necessary that

"the Government should *collaborate in a constitutional way* in the drafting of the address".

Even after much cogitation, we are unable to explain what this is supposed to mean and which Constitution Herr Auerswald has in mind, particularly since Prussia *does not have* a Constitution at all at this moment.

Only two speeches from the side of the opposition need be mentioned: those of Herr d'Ester and Herr Hüffer. Herr d'Ester successfully ridiculed Herr Hansemann's programme by using Herr

Hansemann's former disparaging remarks about abstractions, useless quarrels over principles etc. against the very abstract programme. D'Ester called upon the Government of *Action* "at last to proceed to action and to set aside questions of principle". We have already mentioned above his proposal, which was the only sensible one that was made in the course of the day.

Herr *Hüffer*, who most clearly expressed the correct point of view in relation to the address, also formulated it most clearly in relation to Herr Hansemann's request: the Government demands that we should have enough confidence in it to send the address back to the committee and it makes the continuation of its existence dependent upon such a decision. The Government, however, can only demand a vote of confidence for actions which *it carries out itself* but not for actions which *it requires of the Assembly.*

In short: Herr Hansemann demanded a vote of confidence and the Assembly, to spare Herr Hansemann unpleasantness, gave an indirect vote of censure to its address committee. Under the Government of Action the deputies will soon find out what the famous treasury-whip[a] is.

Written by Engels on July 2, 1848

First published in the *Neue Rheinische Zeitung* No. 34, July 4, 1848

Printed according to the newspaper

Published in English for the first time

---

[a] Engels uses the English term and adds a German translation in brackets.— *Ed.*

176

ARRESTS

Cologne, July 3. Up to now the Government of *Action* has only proved itself as the Ministry of the Police. Its first act was the arrest of Herr *Monecke* and Herr *Fernbach* in Berlin. Its second act was the arrest of Bombardier *Funk* in Saarlouis. Now "action" is beginning to make itself felt here in Cologne too. This morning Dr. *Gottschalk* and Lieutenant (ret.) *Anneke* were arrested. We are reserving our judgment since we are still lacking definite information about the reasons for their arrest and the manner in which it was carried out.

The workers will be sensible enough not to let themselves be provoked into creating a disturbance.

Written on July 3, 1848

First published in the *Neue Rheinische Zeitung* No. 34, July 4, 1848

Printed according to the newspaper

Published in English for the first time

ARRESTS

Cologne, July 4. We promised our readers yesterday that we would come back to the arrest of Dr. *Gottschalk* and *Anneke*. Up to now we have only been able to obtain greater details about Anneke's arrest.

Six to seven policemen entered Anneke's residence between six and seven in the morning, immediately maltreated the maid in the hall and then silently sneaked up the stairs. Three of them remained in the anteroom while four invaded the bedroom where Anneke and his wife, who is in an advanced state of pregnancy, were asleep. One of these four pillars of justice was already at this early hour somewhat unsteady, being filled with "spirit", the true fluid of life: firewater.

Anneke asked what they wanted. He should go along with them! was the laconic answer. Anneke asked that at least his sick wife should be spared and asked the gentlemen to go into the anteroom. The gentlemen of the Holy Hermandad[137] declared that they would not leave the bedroom. They urged Anneke to dress quickly and did not even permit him to speak to his wife. Once they found themselves in the anteroom, the urging turned into assault during which one of the policemen smashed a glass door. Anneke was *pushed down* the stairs. Four policemen led him off to the new gaol. Three of them remained with Frau Anneke to guard her until the arrival of the Public Prosecutor.

According to the law, there must be at least one *official of the court police* (a police inspector or similar person) present during an arrest. Why such formalities, however, since the people possess two assemblies, one in Berlin and one in Frankfurt, to represent their rights?

Half an hour later, Public Prosecutor *Hecker* and Examining Magistrate *Geiger* came to search the house.

Frau Anneke complained that the Public Prosecutor had left the arrest to police whose brutality was unconstrained by the presence of any member of the municipal authorities. Herr Hecker declared that he had given *no orders to commit brutalities*. As if Herr Hecker could order brutalities!

Frau *Anneke*: It seems that the police were sent ahead *alone* so that the authorities would not have to assume the responsibility for their brutality. Besides, the arrest was not carried out according to legal procedure since none of the police produced a warrant. One of them merely pulled a scrap of paper out of his pocket which Anneke was not allowed to read.

Herr *Hecker*: "The police were *judicially commanded* to proceed with the arrest." Does not the command of a judge also fall under the command of the law? The Public Prosecutor and the Examining Magistrate confiscated a mass of papers and pamphlets, including Frau Anneke's whole briefcase, etc. Incidentally, Examining Magistrate Geiger has been designated as *Police Superintendent*.

Anneke was interrogated for half an hour in the evening. A supposedly seditious speech that he made during the last popular assembly at the Gürzenich Hall[138] was given as the reason for his arrest. Article 102 of the *Code pénal*[139] speaks of public orations which *directly* incite to conspiracy against the Emperor and his family or which aim at disturbing the public peace by civil war, the illegal use of armed force or open vandalism and looting. The Code does not contain the Prussian "excitement of dissatisfaction". For lack of the Prussian law, Article 102 will be employed for the time being wherever its employment is a judicial impossibility.

A great show of military force accompanied the arrest. From four o'clock onwards the troops were confined to barracks. Bakers and artisans were allowed in but not let out again. Towards six o'clock the hussars moved from Deutz to Cologne and rode through the whole city. The new gaol was occupied by 300 men. For today, four new arrests have been announced, those of Jansen, Kalker, Esser and a fourth one. *Eyewitnesses* assure us that Jansen's posters, in which he urged the *workers to remain calm,* were *torn down from* the walls by the police yesterday evening. Was that done in the interest of order? Or was someone looking for a pretext to carry out carefully prepared plans in the good old city of Cologne?

Chief Public Prosecutor Zweiffel is supposed to have inquired earlier at the Provincial Court of Appeal at Arnsberg whether he should arrest Anneke on the basis of his former conviction[140] and have him transported to Jülich. The royal amnesty seems to have stood in the way of this well-meaning intention. The matter was referred to the Ministry.

Chief Public Prosecutor Zweiffel, moreover, is supposed to have declared that he would within a week put an end to March 19, the clubs, freedom of the press and other outrages that the evil year 1848 had brought to Cologne on the Rhine. Herr Zweiffel is not among the sceptics.

Is Herr Zweiffel perhaps combining the executive with the legislative power? Are the laurels of Chief Public Prosecutor supposed to cover the weak points of the people's representative? Once again we will scrutinise our much beloved stenographic reports and give the public a true picture of the work of the people's representative and Chief Public Prosecutor Zweiffel.[a]

Those are the actions of the *Government of Action,* the Government of the Left Centre, the Government of transition to an old aristocratic, old bureaucratic and old Prussian Government. As soon as Herr Hansemann has fulfilled his transitory function, he will be dismissed.

The Berlin Left, however, must realise that the old regime is willing to let it keep its small parliamentary victories and large constitutional designs as long as the old regime in the meantime is able to seize all the really important positions. It can confidently recognise the revolution of March 19 inside the Chamber provided the revolution can be disarmed outside of it.

Some fine day the Left may find that its parliamentary victory coincides with its real defeat. *Perhaps German development needs such contrasts.*

The Government of Action recognises the revolution in principle in order to carry out the counter-revolution in practice.

Written on July 4, 1848   Printed according to the newspaper

First published in the *Neue Rheinische*   Published in English for the first
Zeitung No. 35, July 5, 1848   time

---

[a] See this volume, pp. 94-95.—*Ed.*

THE AGREEMENT DEBATES

Cologne, July 4. Today we will take up the agreement session of June 28. The Assembly is confronted by a new President,[a] a new set of standing orders and new Ministers. One can therefore imagine how great is the confusion.

After lengthy preliminary debates about standing orders and other matters, Deputy *Gladbach* was finally allowed to speak. A few days ago in Spandau, the Prussian soldiery forcibly disarmed, and in some instances even arrested, on their return from Schleswig-Holstein, the members of the 6th Company of the Volunteer Corps which had been disbanded for republican sentiments. It had no legitimate reason or legal authority whatever to carry out this act. In law, the army cannot take such steps on its own initiative at all. Most of these volunteers, however, had formerly fought on the barricades of Berlin and the gentlemen of the guard had to get even with them.

Herr *Gladbach* questioned the Ministry on this act of military despotism.

The Minister of War, *Schreckenstein,* declares that he does not know anything about this matter and that he must reserve the right to demand a report on it from the appropriate authority.

Hence the people pay a Minister of War so that he does not yet know in Berlin on the 28th what steps the military took on the 25th a mere three hours from Berlin, in Spandau, and so that, right in front of his eyes, as it were, a mere three hours from Berlin, lieutenants of the guard should occupy the railway stations and seize the weapons from the armed nation (weapons which belong to the people, and

---

[a] Wilhelm Grabow.— *Ed.*

which they captured on the battlefield), without even deigning to honour the Minister of War with a report! But to be sure, Lieutenant-Colonel Schlichting who accomplished this heroic deed acted according to "instructions", which he probably receives from Potsdam, and it is probably also to Potsdam that he reports!

Tomorrow, the well-informed Minister of War pleads, tomorrow I will *perhaps* be able to give an answer!

There follows a question by Zacharias: The Ministry had promised a Bill on the civic militia. Will this Bill be based upon the principle of arming the whole nation?

The new Minister of the Interior, Herr Kühlwetter, answers: Indeed, a civic militia Bill was under consideration, but it had not yet been discussed in the Ministry, hence he could not say anything further about it.

Thus the new Ministry has been formed so precipitously and has reached so little agreement upon its guiding principles that even the burning question of the arming of the nation has not yet been debated!

A second question by Deputy *Gladbach* concerned the definitive appointing of burgomasters and other officials by the authorities hitherto empowered to do so. Since the entire prevailing administration will continue to exist only on a provisional basis, it will be able to fill the existing vacancies also only provisionally until it is determined by legislation how and by whom the different authorities are to be appointed. Nevertheless, burgomasters and other officials have been appointed definitively.

Minister *Kühlwetter* expresses his general agreement with Herr Gladbach and will allow only provisional burgomasters to be appointed.

President Grabow skilfully evades a further question by Herr *Gladbach* about the suspension of the many officials hated by those they administer; during the initial flush of revolutionary ardour a number of these officials, especially in the country, having been put to flight.

After some debates on procedure, the question of Deputy *Dierschke* concerning the Köslin address[141] and its furtherance by the governments and the rural district administrations was reached. But the deputy had completely forgotten that his question had been put on the agenda and he had failed therefore to bring along the papers necessary to substantiate his case. Thus there was nothing left for him to do but to indulge in a few general phrases about the reaction, to accept a highly unsatisfactory reply from the Minister and to be told by the President that he must surely be satisfied with it.

But he had still to put a second question: Whether or not the Ministers intended to oppose the reactionary schemes of the aristocracy and the party of the officials.

In this case, too, he seems to have forgotten the necessary papers. Once again he spouts declamatory phrases instead of quoting facts and demands nothing better from the Ministry than that it issue a proclamation against reaction.

Herr *Kühlwetter* answers, of course, that the views of lords of the manor and of officials were not his concern, only their actions were. These people had the same freedom as Herr *Dierschke*, and besides, would Herr Dierschke please cite facts. In duly dignified manner, he rejected the absurd idea of an "enactment" against reaction. Herr Dierschke then cited the fact that in his district of Ohlau the *Landrat* had stated that the National Assembly would not be unanimous until it was glued together with grape-shot, and that their deputy (Dierschke himself) had said that it would be a trifle to string up a Minister.

The Chairman deduced from this remark that Herr Dierschke was now also satisfied in regard to the second question and Herr Dierschke could not think of any objections to raise.

Herr *Hansemann*, however, is not satisfied. He accuses the speaker of having digressed from the main question. He

"leaves it to the Assembly to judge the propriety of making personal accusations against officials when proof of these accusations is not supplied at the same time".

After delivering this proud challenge and being greeted by the resounding applause of the Right and the Centre, Herr Hansemann sits down.

Deputy *Elsner* puts an urgent motion. He calls for the immediate appointment of a committee of inquiry into the situation of the spinners and weavers as well as of the entire Prussian linen manufacture.

In a brief and striking speech Herr *Elsner* tells the Assembly how the old Government had in every single case sacrificed the linen industry to dynastic and legitimist interests or rather notions. Spain, Mexico, Poland and Cracow served as proofs.[142]

Fortunately the facts were striking and affected only the old Government. Therefore no difficulties were raised by any side. The Government put itself at the disposal of the committee in advance and the motion was passed unanimously.

There follows a question by *d'Ester* concerning the shaved Poles.[143]

D'Ester declares that he does not just seek information about the fact but specifically about the measures taken by the Government against this treatment. That was the reason why he was not just addressing himself to the Minister of War but to the entire Government.

Herr *Auerswald:* If d'Ester does not want an answer to this specific case "the Government is not *interested*" in replying.

Really, the Government is not "interested" in replying to the question! What novelty! It is indeed customary to ask questions precisely in those cases in which "the Government is *not a bit interested*". Precisely *because* it is not interested in answering it, precisely for that reason, Herr Prime Minister, the Government is asked the question.

The Prime Minister, by the way, must have believed that he was not among his superiors but among his subordinates. He attempts to make the reply to the question dependent upon the interest shown not by the Assembly but by the Government.

We attribute it solely to the inexperience of President Grabow that he did not call Herr Auerswald to order for this bureaucratic arrogance.

The Prime Minister, by the way, gave the assurance that the shaving of Poles would be vigorously counteracted but that he could not reveal any details until a later date.

D'Ester is very willing to agree to a delay but wants to know the date when Auerswald intends to answer.

Herr *Auerswald*, who must be hard of hearing, replies: I believe that there is nothing in my declaration which indicates that the Ministry does not wish (!) to revert to this matter at a later date. But he cannot yet fix the date.

Behnsch and *d'Ester* moreover declare explicitly that they are also demanding further information about the fact itself.

Then follows *d'Ester*'s second question: What was the meaning of the military preparations in the Rhine Province, particularly in Cologne, and did perhaps the necessity arise to protect the frontier with France?

Herr *Schreckenstein* replies: For several months now no troops have gone to the Rhine with the exception of individual reservists. (To be sure, brave Bayard, but there were already too many troops there.) Not just Cologne but *all* fortresses are being fortified so that the fatherland should not be endangered.[a]

Thus if the troops are not drafted into the forts at Cologne where they have nothing to do and are in very poor quarters, if the artillery units do not get any rifles, if the troops do not receive bread for a

---

[a] See this volume, pp. 68-71.—*Ed.*

week in advance and if the infantry is not provided with live bullets and the artillery with grape and ball shot, the fatherland is in danger? Thus, according to Herr Schreckenstein, the fatherland is only *out of* danger when Cologne and the other big cities are *in* danger!

By the way,

"all troop movements must be left entirely to the judgment of a military person, i.e. the Minister of War, otherwise he cannot be responsible"!

Imperial Baron Roth von Schreckenstein[a] of the terror-inspiring name sounds like a young girl whose virtue is threatened rather than the Prussian *pro tempore* Bayard without fear and reproach!

When Deputy d'Ester, M.D., who truly is a dwarf by the side of the mighty Imperial Baron Roth von Schreckenstein, asks the said Schreckenstein about the meaning of one or another measure, the great Imperial Baron believes that the little M.D. wants to take away his prerogative freely to decide on the disposition of troops. In such an event he could of course no longer be responsible!

In a word, the Minister of War declares that he must not be *called to account*; otherwise he would not *be accountable* at all.

By the way, what weight does a deputy's question carry compared with the "judgment of a military person, and particularly a Minister of War"!

Although *d'Ester* declares that he is not satisfied, he nevertheless draws from Schreckenstein's answer the conclusion that the military preparations are designed to protect the French frontier.

Prime Minister *Auerswald* protests against this conclusion.

If *all* border fortresses are fortified, it stands to reason that *all* frontiers are "protected". If *all* frontiers are protected, surely the *French* frontier, too, is "protected".

Herr Auerswald admits the correctness of the premises but "rejects" the deduction "in the name of the Government".

We, on the other hand, "assume in the name" of common sense that Herr Auerswald is not merely hard of hearing.

D'Ester and *Pfahl* protest at once. *Reichenbach* declares that Neisse,[b] the most significant Silesian fortress against the East, is not being fortified at all and that it is in a most sorry plight. When he begins to give details, the Right supported by the Centre makes a terrible racket and Reichenbach is forced to leave the rostrum.

Herr *Moritz*:

"Count Reichenbach has given *no* reason for addressing the Assembly (!). I believe that I may speak for *the same reason* (!!). I consider it to be unparliamentary and

---

[a] The name, literally translated, means "terror-stone".—*Ed.*
[b] The Polish name is Nysa.—*Ed.*

unheard of in the history of parliaments to *embarrass* the Ministry in such a manner ... (great commotion), to bring up matters which should not be discussed before the public ... we have not been sent here to *endanger* the fatherland." (A terrible din ensues. Our Moritz has to get off the rostrum.)

Deputy Esser I calms the tumult by a disquisition, as thorough as it is appropriate, on Paragraph 28 of the standing orders.

Herr *Moritz* protests; he had not intended to correct a fact but merely "wanted to speak for the same reason as Count Reichenbach"! The conservative faction supports him and grants him a loud cheer, whereas the extreme Left bangs on the tables.
Auerswald:

"Is it appropriate to discuss in detail the defensive capacity of Prussia either in individual cases or as a whole?"

We note in the first place that the discussion did not deal with the defensive capacity of the state but rather with the *defencelessness* of the state. Secondly, what is inappropriate is not that the Minister of War should be reminded of his duties but rather that he should make military preparations against domestic opponents and not against external foes.

The Right is terribly bored and calls for an end to the debate. The President, in the midst of much noise, declares that the matter is settled.

Next on the agenda is a motion by *Jung*. Herr Jung deems it appropriate to be absent. What a wonderful representation of the people!

Now comes a question by Deputy *Scholz*. It reads literally as follows:

"Question to the Minister of the Interior inquiring whether he is able or inclined to supply information on the *inopportune introduction of constables in the districts.*"[144]

President: To begin with I am asking whether this question has been *understood*.

(It has not been understood and it is read once again.)

Minister *Kühlwetter*: Indeed, I do not know what information is demanded of me. I do not understand the question.

President: Is there support for the question? (It is not supported.)

Scholz: I withdraw my motion for the time being.

We, too, are "withdrawing" for today after this priceless scene which is "unheard of in the history of parliaments".

Written by Engels on July 4, 1848

First published in the *Neue Rheinische Zeitung* No. 35, July 5, 1848

Printed according to the newspaper

Published in English for the first time

LEGAL PROCEEDINGS AGAINST THE *NEUE RHEINISCHE ZEITUNG*

Cologne, July 6. We have just received the following rejoinder to the article printed in yesterday's [*Neue*] *Rheinische Zeitung* dated "Cologne, July 4" which dealt with the arrest of Dr. Gottschalk and Anneke.[a]

"I declare it to be a falsehood that I answered the complaint of Frau Anneke concerning the arrest of her husband without the presence of a member of the municipal authorities in the following manner:

"'I have given *no orders to commit brutalities.*'

"Rather, I merely remarked that I should regret it if the police had conducted themselves in an unseemly manner.

"I furthermore declare it to be a falsehood to state that I used the expression:

"'The police were *judicially commanded* to proceed with the arrest.'

"I merely observed that the arrest was effected by virtue of a warrant to appear in court issued by the Examining Magistrate.

"Under the law, such warrants are discharged by court bailiffs or agents of the armed forces. The presence of an official of the court police is nowhere prescribed.

"The defamations and insults contained in this article, directed against Chief Public Prosecutor Zweiffel and the police who carried out the arrest, will be evaluated in the legal proceedings which will be initiated on this count.

Cologne, July 5, 1848

Hecker, Public Prosecutor"

Our esteemed readers may perceive from the preceding that the *Neue Rheinische Zeitung* has gained a new contributor of great promise—the *Public Prosecutor's office.*

We have erred on a *single* point of law. During an arrest there is no need for an *"official of the court police"* but merely for an *agent of the*

---

[a] See this volume, pp. 177-79.— *Ed.*

public authority. With what careful guarantees the Code assures the safety of the person!

Incidentally, the fact that the police did not produce their warrant remains illegal. It also remains illegal that they, as we are subsequently informed, *scrutinised documents* even *before* the appearance of Herr Hecker and his companion. But above all the *brutalities*, which Herr Hecker *regretted*, remain illegal. We are amazed to see court proceedings pending not against the police but against the newspaper that has denounced their impropriety.

The *insult* could only refer to one of the policemen of whom it was said that he "*was unsteady*" at an early hour for more or less spiritual or spirituous reasons. If the investigation, however, as we do not doubt for one moment, should prove the correctness of the evidence, namely the brutalities committed by the agents of the public authority, then we believe that we shall have only acted in the interests of the gentlemen accused by us by carefully emphasising, with the complete impartiality becoming the press, the only "*extenuating circumstance*". And this affable statement of the only extenuating circumstance is transformed into an "insult" by the Public Prosecutor.

And now as to the insult or defamation of Chief Public Prosecutor *Zweiffel!*

We have simply reported, and as we have ourselves indicated in the report, we have reported *rumours*, rumours which reached us from a reliable source. The press not only has the right but the duty to keep a close watch on the conduct of the people's representatives. At the same time we pointed out that Herr Zweiffel's past parliamentary activity seems to be in line with the anti-popular remarks ascribed to him. Is it really the intention to deprive the press of the right to *judge* the parliamentary activity of a representative of the people? What then is the purpose of the press?

Or does not the press have the right to detect in the people's representative *Zweiffel* too much of the Chief Public Prosecutor and in the Chief Public Prosecutor too much of the people's representative? Why then in Belgium, France etc. the debate on incompatibilities?

As to the *constitutional usage*, one should read again how the *Constitutionnel*, the *Siècle* and the *Presse* during the reign of Louis Philippe judged the parliamentary activity of *Hébert, Plougoulm* etc. at the time when these men occupied the highest positions in the Public Prosecutor's office and at the same time served as deputies. One should read how the Belgian newspapers, particularly the strictly constitutional ones such as the *Observateur*, the *Politique* and the *Emancipation,* barely a year ago judged the parliamentary activity of M. *Bavay* when he combined in one person the office of deputy and Public Prosecutor-General.

And what was always allowed under the Guizot Ministry and the Rogier Ministry should not be allowed under a *monarchy built on the broadest democratic foundation?* A right which was not contested by any Administration of the French Restoration becomes a wrong under the *Government of Action* which recognises the *revolution in principle?*

Incidentally, the public has been able to convince itself from our special supplement of this morning just how correctly we have judged the course of events. *Rodbertus* has left the Government and *Ladenberg* has entered it. The Government of the Left Centre has *transformed* itself in a few days into a decidedly *old-Prussian reactionary Government.* The *Right* has dared a *coup d'état,*[145] and the *Left* has *withdrawn with the threats.*

And is it not palpably clear that the most recent acts in Cologne were part of the great plan of campaign of the *Government of Action?*

Just now we are being informed that the *Neue Rheinische Zeitung* has been banned from the house of detention. Do the prison rules provide for such a prohibition? Or are the politically accused condemned to the penalty of having to read exclusively the *Kölnische Zeitung?*

Written by Marx on July 6, 1848

First published in the *Neue Rheinische Zeitung* No. 37, July 7, 1848

Printed according to the newspaper

Published in English for the first time

THE BERLIN AGREEMENT DEBATES

Cologne, July 6. While ministerial crisis No. 2 continues in Berlin, we would like for the time being, in the words of Deputy *Mätze*, to return "from these tempests" to the hitherto "calm lake" of the agreement debates. Say what you like, we have spent here more than one hour of genial cheerfulness—

> Here, breeding and custom hold sway,
> And many a quiet pleasure blooms
> Amidst us to this day.[a]

It is the turn of the session of *June 30*. Right from the beginning it opens with significant and very peculiarly characteristic occurrences.

Who has not heard of the great campaign of the 57 family heads from Berg and Mark who set out to save the fatherland? Who does not know with what defiance of death this cream of conservative philistinism, forsaking wives, children and business, set out to step into the breach to give battle to the revolution in a fight to the death, in a word, to go to Berlin and present to the Ministry a petition against agitators?

These 57 paladins then also presented to the Agreement Assembly an address containing mild, reactionary pious wishes. The address is read. A few gentlemen of the Right wish also to have the signatures read. The secretary begins to read but is interrupted by shouts of "Enough, enough!"

Deputy *Berg*:

"The document which has just been read must be either a motion or a petition. If it is a motion I would like to know which member has adopted it. If it is a petition, let it be sent to the appropriate committee so that we may *no longer be bored with it.*"

---

[a] Heinrich Heine, *Deutschland. Ein Wintermärchen*, Caput XXV.— *Ed.*

This laconic answer of Herr Berg disposes of the matter. The President[a] stammers a few apologies and puts aside the address of the 57 family heads.

Thereupon rises an old friend of ours and of the Left, Deputy *Schultz* from Wanzleben:

> "The day before yesterday I withdrew my motions concerning civil marriage etc. with the explanation that my proposed Bills are to be drafted differently by me. I find in the stenographic reports that my remarks are followed by the comment: '*Laughter*.' It may be that somebody or other has laughed at my remarks, but if so, he certainly did it *without reason*." (Renewed laughter.)

Deputy Schultz from Wanzleben explains now with the most ingenuous good nature that he only wanted to do his best, that he would be happy to be taught better, that he had been convinced of the imperfections of his Bills, that he could, however, hardly move amendments to his own proposals and that he therefore considered it his duty not to "submit" his motion to the Assembly in its original form but to withdraw it for the time being.

> "I cannot find anything laughable in this and I must protest if by the word 'laughter' my judicious procedure is presented as *laughable*."

Deputy Schultz from Wanzleben fares like the Knight Tann-häuser:

> Whenever I think about this *laughter*,
> My eyes shed sudden tears.[b]

Deputy *Brill* remarks that the otherwise excellent stenographic reports lack the statement by Minister Hansemann that the programme of the present Ministry is a continuation of the speech from the throne. He remembered this particularly well because being a printer it had reminded him of the phrase "to be continued", which he used to print so often.

This frivolous treatment of the most serious subjects enrages Deputy *Ritz* exceedingly. He rushes to the rostrum and states:

> "Gentlemen, I believe that the dignity of this Assembly demands that in our speeches we refrain from relating *parables* and comparisons which are out of place here. They are also *unparliamentary*. (Considerable agitation.) I do not consider our great *hilarity* during the previous session as commensurate with the dignity of the Assembly ... in the interest of this Assembly's dignity I would recommend a certain *sobriety*."

"In the interest" of the "sobriety" recommended by Deputy Ritz we would recommend that "in the interest of the Assembly's dignity"

---

[a] Wilhelm Grabow.— *Ed.*
[b] Heinrich Heine, "Der Tannhäuser", Caput 2.— *Ed.*

Deputy Ritz should speak as little as possible because his words are always followed by "great hilarity".

It became revealed at once, however, how much the well-meaning intentions of such worthies as Herr Schultz from Wanzleben and Herr Ritz are inevitably misunderstood in this wicked world. For President *Grabow* appointed the scrutineers and among them were to be found none others than Herr Schultz from Wanzleben for the Left Centre (laughter) and Herr Brill for the Right Centre (hilarity). Concerning Herr Brill, our readers should know that this deputy who belongs to the extreme Left has seated himself in the Right Centre smack into the midst of the Upper Silesian and Pomeranian peasants where, by his popular oratorical talents, he has defeated quite a number of the reactionary party's insinuations.

Then follows the question of Herr *Behnsch* concerning the Russian Note which is supposed to have caused the withdrawal of Wrangel from Jutland.[a] *Auerswald* denies the existence of this Note despite the *Morning Chronicle* and the Russian *Bee*.[b] We believe that Herr Auerswald is right. We do not believe that Russia has sent an official "Note" to Berlin. But neither we nor Herr Auerswald can know what Nicholas sent to Potsdam.

Herr *Behnsch* also puts a question on the Note of Major Wildenbruch addressed to the Danish Government[146] according to which the Danish war was merely a feigned war and a dalliance designed to work off "superabundant patriotism".[c]

Herr *Auerswald* finds some reason for *not* answering this question.

After a boring and confused discussion about the committee of experts there occurs finally a truly interesting parliamentary scene, a scene during which a certain amount of indignation and passion victoriously rises above the stereotyped drumming of the Right. We owe this scene to Deputy *Gladbach*. The Minister of War had promised today to answer his question on the disarming and arrest of the returned volunteers.[d]

As soon as the President indicates that this subject is reached, Lieutenant-Colonel *Griesheim*, who is an old acquaintance of ours, rises and begins to speak. This bureaucratic-soldierly importunity is, however, rejected at once by a vigorous interruption.

The *President* states that under Paragraph 28 of standing orders

---

[a] See this volume, pp. 42-44.— *Ed.*

[b] A reference to the Russian periodical *Severnaya Pchela* (The Bee of the North).— *Ed.*

[c] Heinrich Heine, "Bei des Nachtwächters Ankunft zu Paris". In *Zeitgedichte.— Ed.*

[d] See this volume, pp. 180-81.— *Ed.*

assistants to Ministers may only speak with the permission of the Assembly.

Griesheim: I am here as representative of the Minister of War.

President: I have *not* been so *informed*.

Griesheim: Well, if the *gentlemen* do not want to listen to what I have to say.... (Aha! Agitation.)

"The gentlemen!" For Herr Griesheim "the gentlemen" surely ought to be the "High Assembly"! The President should have called Herr Griesheim to order because of his repeated disregard for all propriety.

The Assembly wants to listen to Herr Griesheim. First, however, Herr *Gladbach* is given the floor to amplify his question. He explains first of all that he has put the question to the Minister of War and he demands that he be present and under standing orders the Assembly has the right to demand this. The President, however, sets this aside and Mr. Gladbach, bearing in mind the urgency of the matter, goes into the substance of his question. He relates that the volunteers, after they had left their corps and returned home because of the application of military despotism, had been branded in Spandau as vagabonds "by the execrable police system that had crept out of its hiding places overnight". He relates that in Spandau they had been disarmed, detained and sent home under police orders. Herr Gladbach is the first deputy who has succeeded in relating such an ignominious deed with entirely appropriate indignation.

Herr *Griesheim* declares that this measure was taken upon the request of police headquarters in Berlin.

Herr *Gladbach* now reads the honourable discharge of one of the volunteers signed by Prince Friedrich of Schleswig-Holstein and contrasts it to the police pass, quite vagabond-like in tone, which was issued to the same volunteer "*upon ministerial decision*" in Spandau. He points to the *arrest, forced labour* and *cash fines* threatened in the police pass, gives the lie to Herr Griesheim's assertion that this measure originated with the Chief of Police by citing an official document, and asks whether perhaps there existed a special *Russian* Ministry in Spandau.

For the first time the Ministry was caught out in a direct lie. The entire Assembly becomes extremely excited.

The Minister of the Interior, Herr Kühlwetter, finally has to get up perforce and stammer a few apologies. *All that had happened* had been the disarming of 18 armed men — merely an illegal act! One could not tolerate armed bands moving through the countryside without permission — 22 volunteers who are returning home! (Without permission!)

The initial words of the Minister are received with unambiguous signs of displeasure. Even the Right is still too much under the depressing influence of the facts not to keep at least quiet. But they soon pull themselves together as they perceive how their unfortunate Minister painfully manoeuvres under the laughter and the grumbling of the Left, and greet his lame excuses with loud cheers; part of the Centre joins in and Herr Kühlwetter finally gathers enough courage to say: Not I, but my predecessor has ordered this measure, but I herewith declare that I fully approve it and should the case arise I would do the same.

The Right and the Centre reward the courage of their heroic Kühlwetter with a thundering cheer.

Gladbach, however, does not let himself be intimidated. He mounts the rostrum amidst the noise and clamour of the conservatives and asks once more: How is it possible that Herr Schreckenstein, who was the Minister already before the Spandau incident, *did not know anything about it*? How is it possible that *four* volunteers with good testimonials can endanger the security of the state? (Interruption — the gentlemen of the Centre raise points of order.) The question is not settled. How can one forcibly send these people home like vagabonds? (Interruption and noise.) I still have not received an answer to my question about the police pass. These people have been maltreated. Why does one tolerate a pack of Sunday-school heroes who to the disgrace of the capital (loud noise) have arrived armed from Wuppertal? (Noise. Cheers.)

Kühlwetter finally comes clean: this action had been taken under the pretext of a doubtful proof of identity! Thus an honourable discharge signed by the General Staff of Schleswig-Holstein is for the police bureaucrats of Herr Kühlwetter proof of identity which is "open to doubt"? What a strange bureaucracy!

Several more deputies speak against the Ministers until the President finally drops the matter and Deputy *Mätze* leads the Assembly from the tempests of this debate to the calm seas of the life of a schoolteacher where we leave them, wishing them the most beautiful idyllic joys.

We are pleased that a deputy of the Left has at long last succeeded by a well-reasoned question and resolute demeanour in forcing the Ministers to run the gauntlet and in causing a scene which recalls French and English parliamentary debates.

Written by Engels on July 6, 1848   Printed according to the newspaper

First published in the *Neue Rheinische*   Published in English for the first
Zeitung No. 37, July 7, 1848   time

194

THE GOVERNMENT OF ACTION

Cologne, July 7. We have a *new ministerial crisis.* The *Camphausen* Ministry *fell,* the *Hansemann* Ministry *faltered.* The *Government of Action* had a life-span of *a week* in spite of all the little household remedies, cosmetics, press trials, arrests, in spite of the arrogant impudence with which the bureaucracy once again reared its document-dusty head, hatching petty, brutal plots of vengeance for its dethronement. The *"Government of Action"*, composed entirely of mediocrities, was at the start of the Agreement Assembly's most recent session still so deluded as to believe in its own imperturbability.

By the end of the session[a] it was completely routed. This momentous session convinced Prime Minister von *Auerswald* that he should tender his resignation; nor did Minister von *Schreckenstein* want any longer to remain as Hansemann's train-bearer and thus the entire Ministry yesterday betook themselves to the King at Sanssouci. What was decided there we shall learn tomorrow.

Our Berlin #correspondent writes in a postscript:

"Just now the rumour is spreading that *Vincke, Pinder* and *Mevissen* have been urgently sent for to help in the formation of a new Ministry."

If this rumour is confirmed we shall *finally* have come from the Government of mediation through the Government of Action to the Government of the counter-revolution. *At last!* The very brief life-span of this ministerial counter-revolution would suffice to show to the people in full life-size these dwarfs who raise their diminutive heads at the slightest stirring of reaction.

Written by Marx on July 7, 1848Written by Marx on July 7, 1848   Printed according to the newspaper

First published in the *Neue Rheinische Zeitung* No. 39, July 9, 1848   Published in English for the first time

---

[a] July 4, 1848.— *Ed.*

THE AGREEMENT DEBATE

Cologne, July 8. Simultaneously with the news of the dissolution of the Hansemann Ministry the stenographic report about the agreement session of July 4 reached us. It was during this session that the resignation of Herr Rodbertus, the first symptom of this dissolution, was announced, and at the same time the two contradictory votes concerning the Posen committee and the exodus of the Left have greatly accelerated the Ministry's disintegration.

The announcements of the Ministers regarding the resignation of Rodbertus published in the stenographic report contain nothing new. We shall skip them.

Herr *Forstmann* rose: He had to protest against the expressions which Herr Gladbach used on June 30[a] in referring to the "deputation of the most honourable men of Rhineland and Westphalia".

Herr *Berg*: I have already a few days ago observed in connection with the standing orders that the reading of this petition is out of place here and that it bores me.[b] (Exclamation: It bores *us*!) Well then, *us*. I have spoken for myself and *several others* and the circumstance that we are being bored today by a supplementary observation does not invalidate this remark.

Herr *Tüshaus*, the expert adviser of the central section on the question of the Posen committee, gives a report. The central section proposes that a committee be formed to investigate all questions concerning the Posen affair, and leaves open the question what funds shall be put at the committee's disposal for this purpose.

---

[a] See this volume, p. 193.— *Ed.*
[b] Ibid., p. 189.— *Ed.*

Herr Wolff, Herr Müller, Herr Reichensperger II and Herr Sommer have proposed amendments which have all met with support and are down for discussion.

Herr *Tüshaus* adds to his report a few comments directed against the idea of a committee. The truth, in this case, too, was evidently to be found as always in the middle and after long and contradictory reports one would merely arrive at the conclusion that both sides were to blame. With that one would be exactly where one is at present. One should at least first ask for a detailed report by the Government and then decide what to do further.

Why did the central section select a reporter who speaks against his own report?

Herr *Reuter* explains the reasons which caused him to put the motion to appoint the committee. Finally he remarks that he had no intention of making an accusation against the Ministers and that as a jurist he knew only too well that up to now all ministerial responsibility was illusory so long as there existed no law concerning this point.

Herr *Reichensperger II* rises. He protests his boundless sympathies for Poland and hopes that the day may not be far when the German nation pays off its old debt of honour to the grandchildren of Sobieski. (As if this debt of honour had not been paid off a long time ago by the eight partitions of Poland, by shrapnel, lunar caustic and canings!)

"We must, however, also maintain the calmest circumspection since German interests must always come first."

(The German interests are, of course, to keep as much as possible of this territory.) And Herr Reichensperger is especially opposed to the appointment of a committee to investigate the evidence:

"This is a question which should be dealt with expressly by *history* or the courts."

Has Herr Reichensperger forgotten that he himself declared during the debate on the revolution that the gentlemen were here "*to make history*"?[a] He concludes with a juridical sophistry about the position of the deputies. We shall return later to the question of competence.

Now, however, Herr *Bauer* from Krotoschin,[b] himself a German Pole, rises to defend the interests of his community.

"I would like to ask the Assembly to draw a veil over the past and to occupy itself solely with the future of a people that has every right to lay claim to our sympathy."

---

[a] See this volume, p. 84.— *Ed.*

[b] The Polish name is Krotoszyn.— *Ed.*

How touching! Herr Bauer from Krotoschin is so taken up with sympathy for the future of the Polish people that he wants to "draw a veil" over its past, over the barbarities of the Prussian soldiery, the Jews and the German Poles. The matter should be dropped in the interest of the Poles themselves!

"What does one hope to gain from such depressing discussions? If you find the Germans guilty will you, therefore, be less concerned for the preservation of their nationality, and the safety of their person and their property?"

That was, indeed, a magnificent show of candour! Herr Bauer from Krotoschin admits that the Germans could possibly be wrong, but even so German nationality must be supported at the expense of the Poles!

"I am unable to perceive how digging through the rubbish of the past can produce anything beneficial for a satisfactory solution of these difficult questions."

There certainly would not be anything "beneficial" in store for the German Poles and their fervent allies. That is why they are so much opposed to it.

Herr Bauer then seeks to intimidate the Assembly: such a committee would inflame the minds of people once again, incite fanaticism anew, and might lead to a new bloody clash. These philanthropic considerations prevent Herr Bauer from voting for the committee. Nor can he vote against it since that might create the impression that his mandataries have reason to fear the committee. Thus out of consideration for the Poles he is *against* the committee and out of consideration for the Germans he is *for* it, and to maintain his perfect impartiality in this dilemma, he does not vote at all.

Bussmann of Gnesen,[a] another deputy from Posen, regards his mere presence as proof that Germans, too, live in Posen. He wants to prove statistically that there are "whole masses of Germans" who live in his region. (Interruption.) Furthermore, over two-thirds of the entire property is supposed to be in German hands.

"On the other hand I believe that I can provide the proof that we Prussians not merely *conquered* Poland *with our weapons* (!?!) in 1815 but that we have conquered it a second time by our intelligence" (of which this session offers samples) "through 33 years of peace. (Interruption. The President asks Herr Bussmann not to digress from the question.) I am not opposed to a reorganisation; but the most sensible reorganisation would be a system of local government with election of officials. Such a measure combined with the Frankfurt decisions for the protection of all nationalities would offer Poland every guarantee. I am, however, very much opposed to the line of demarcation. (Interruption. A second reprimand.) Well, if I must not digress from the subject, I am against the committee because it is useless and provocative; incidentally,

---

[a] The Polish name is Gniezno.— *Ed.*

I am not afraid of it and I shall support the committee if it comes to the point....
(Interruption: He is therefore speaking in favour of it!) No, I am speaking against it....
Gentlemen, in order that you may at least understand why the insurrection came
about I will explain to you in a few words...." (Interruption. Disagreement.)

Cieszkowski: "Don't interrupt! Let him finish speaking!"
President[a]: "I am asking the speaker again to speak strictly to the question."
Bussmann: "I have spoken out against the idea of a committee and I have nothing further to add!"

With these angry words the enraged German-Polish lord of the manor leaves the rostrum and hurries back to his seat to the ringing laughter of the Assembly.

Herr *Heyne*, the deputy from the Bromberg district, tries to save the honour of his countrymen by voting for the committee. Nevertheless, he cannot refrain either from accusing the Poles of deceit, fraud etc.

Herr *Baumstark*, also a German Pole, is likewise against the committee. The reasons are always the same.

The Poles abstain from the discussion. Only Pokrzywnicki speaks for the committee. It is well known that the Poles have all along pressed for an investigation while it now becomes apparent that the German Poles, with one exception, have all protested against it.

Herr *Pohle* is so much a Pole that he regards all Posen as part of Germany and declares the border between Germany and Poland to be a "dividing wall running through Germany".

The defenders of the committee were mostly long-winded and their arguments betrayed little acumen. Just like their opponents, they repeated themselves over and over again. Their arguments were mostly of a hostile and trivial nature and much less entertaining than the biassed protestations of the German Poles.

Tomorrow we shall come back to the attitude of the Ministers and officials in regard to this question and to the well-known question of competence.

Written by Engels on July 8, 1848   Printed according to the newspaper

First published in the *Neue Rheinische Zeitung* No. 39, July 9, 1848   Published in English for the first time

[a] Wilhelm Grabow.— *Ed.*

Cologne, July 8.[147] With great tenacity, the *Hansemann* Ministry postpones its dissolution by a few days. The Finance Minister especially seems to be too patriotic to leave the administration of the exchequer in unskilled hands. From a parliamentary point of view the Ministry was dissolved, and yet it continues to exist in fact. It seems that it has been decided in Sanssouci to make one more attempt to prolong its life. The Agreement Assembly itself, on the point of administering the death blow to the Ministry at any moment, recoils the next, frightened by its own desires, and the majority seems to surmise that if the Hansemann Ministry is not yet a Ministry to its liking, a Ministry to its liking would at the same time be a Ministry of crisis and of decision. Hence its vacillations, its inconsistencies, its wanton invectives and its sudden turns to remorse. And the *Government of Action,* with unshakeable, almost cynical equanimity, accepts this borrowed, humiliating life which at any moment may be called into question and which only feeds on the alms of weakness.

Duchâtel! Duchâtel! The inevitable demise of the Ministry, laboriously postponed by only a few days, will be as inglorious as its existence. Tomorrow's edition[a] will present to our readers a further contribution to the evaluation of this existence by our Berlin #correspondent. We can summarise the agreement session of July 7 in a few words.[b] The Assembly teases the Hansemann[c] Ministry, it takes pleasure in inflicting partial defeats upon it; the Ministry bows its head half smiling, half frowning, but at the leave-taking, the High Assembly calls after it: "*No harm meant!*" and the stoic triumvirate *Hansemann-Kühlwetter-Milde* murmurs in response: *Pas si bête! Pas si bête!*[d]

Written by Marx on July 8, 1848

First published in the special supplement to the *Neue Rheinische Zeitung* No. 39, July 9, 1848, and in the *Neue Rheinische Zeitung* No. 40, July 10, 1848

Printed according to the newspaper

Published in English for the first time

---

[a] The version printed in the *Neue Rheinische Zeitung* No. 40 has: "Today's edition".— *Ed.*

[b] For a more detailed report see this volume, pp. 216-22 and 226-31.— *Ed.*

[c] In the original a play on the words *hänseln* (to tease) and Hansemann.— *Ed.*

[d] We are not that stupid!— *Ed.*

THE AGREEMENT SESSION OF JULY 4

(SECOND ARTICLE)

Cologne, July 9. The series of articles[a] based upon authentic documents, which we started three days ago, clearly show that the appointment of an investigation committee with unrestricted powers is an urgent and necessary act of justice towards the Poles.

The old-Prussian officials, who from the outset assumed a hostile attitude towards the Poles, saw their existence threatened by the promises of reorganisation. They sensed danger in the smallest act of justice towards the Poles. Hence the fanatical fury with which, supported by the unrestrained soldiery, they fell upon the Poles, broke the conventions, maltreated the most harmless people and permitted or sanctioned the greatest infamies merely to force the Poles to a fight in which the Poles were bound to be crushed by vastly superior forces.

The Camphausen Ministry, which was not only weak, perplexed and badly informed but remained *deliberately*, on principle, inactive, allowed everything to go its own way. The most horrifying barbarities were perpetrated, and Herr Camphausen did not stir.

What reports are now available on the civil war in Posen?

On the one hand there are the biassed, slanted reports of the originators of this war: the officials and the officers, and the data based on their evidence which the Ministry can quote. The Ministry *itself* is biassed as long as it includes Herr Hansemann. These documents are biassed, but they are *official*.

On the other hand there are the facts collected by the Poles, their written complaints to the Ministry, especially the letters of Arch-

---

[a] [Ernst Dronke,] "Die preussische Pacificirung und Reorganisation Posens", *Neue Rheinische Zeitung* Nos. 38-40, July 8-10, 1848.— *Ed.*

bishop Przyluski to the Ministers.[a] These documents for the most part have no official character, but their authors are prepared to prove the truth of their statements.

The two kinds of reports totally contradict each other and the committee is supposed to investigate which side is right.

The committee, except in a few instances, can only do this by travelling to the spot in order to clear up at least the most significant points by the hearing of witnesses. If it is forbidden to do this, its entire activity becomes illusory. It may practise a certain historical-philological criticism and it may declare that one or another report is more trustworthy, but it will not be able to resolve anything.

Thus the entire importance of the committee depends on its authority to question witnesses, hence the eagerness of all the Polonophobes in the Assembly to remove this authority by all sorts of subtle and ingenious arguments, hence also the coup d'état at the end of the session.[148]

Deputy *Bloem* said in the debate on the 4th [of July]:

"Does one genuinely seek the truth if, as a few amendments want it, the truth is to be derived from documents submitted by the Government? Most certainly not! Whence did the government documents originate? For the most part from the reports of officials. Whence did the officials originate? From the old system. Have these officials vanished? Have new *Landräte* been appointed through new, popular elections? By no means. Do the officials inform us about the true mood? The old officials report today just as they did formerly. It is, therefore, apparent that a mere examination of ministerial records will lead us nowhere."

Deputy *Richter* goes even further. He sees in the behaviour of the Posen officials only the most extreme, but inevitable, result of the preservation of the old system of administration and the old officials in general. Similar conflicts between the duties and the interests of the old officials could also occur at any time in other provinces.

"Since the revolution we have had a new Ministry and even a second one but a Ministry is, of course, only the soul which has to set up a uniform organisation everywhere. In the provinces, however, the old administrative organisation has remained the same everywhere. Do you expect a different picture? One does not pour new wine into old rotten skins. Accordingly we have the most terrible complaints in the Grand Duchy. Should we not *therefore* form a committee even if only to show how very necessary it is in the other provinces as well as in Posen to replace the old organisation by a new one suited to the times and circumstances?"

Deputy *Richter* is right. After a revolution, the first necessity is to replace all civil and military officials as well as part of the judiciary,

---

[a] Leon Przyluski, ["Die Korrespondenz des Erzbischofs von Posen, Przyluski, mit dem Berliner Kabinett",] *Neue Rheinische Zeitung* Nos. 5, 7, 10, 14, 38 and 39, June 5, 7, 10 and 14, and July 8 and 9, 1848.— *Ed.*

and especially officials in the *Public Prosecutor's office.* Otherwise the best measures of the Central Authority fail through the obstinacy of subordinates. The weakness of the French Provisional Government and the weakness of the Camphausen Ministry are the bitter fruits of just such a situation.

In Prussia, however, where for forty years a thoroughly organised bureaucratic hierarchy has dominated the administration and the military with absolute force, in Prussia where that very same bureaucracy was the chief enemy that was vanquished on March 19, there the complete replacement of all civil and military officials was infinitely more urgent. The Government of mediation, of course, did not feel called upon to carry through revolutionary necessities. It had admittedly the task not to do anything and therefore left the real power for the time being in the hands of its old enemies, the bureaucrats. It "mediated" between the old bureaucracy and the new conditions. In return the bureaucracy through its "mediation" presented the Ministry with the civil war in Posen and the responsibility for barbarities such as have not occurred since the Thirty Years' War.[149]

As heir to the Camphausen Ministry, the Hansemann Ministry was forced to take over all the assets and liabilities of its testator, that is not only the majority in the Chamber but also the events and officials in Posen. Thus the Ministry had a direct interest in making the committee's investigation as illusory as possible. The speakers representing the Ministry's majority, especially the jurists, used their entire stock of casuistry and sophistry to discover a profound, principled reason for prohibiting the committee from questioning witnesses. We would stray too far afield if we allowed ourselves to be involved here in admiring the jurisprudence of a Reichensperger etc. We have to limit ourselves to bringing to light the painstaking disquisition of Minister *Kühlwetter.*

Herr *Kühlwetter,* leaving entirely aside the material question, begins with the declaration that the Government would be extremely pleased if such committees were to assist it in performing its difficult task by clarifications etc. Indeed, if Herr Reuter had not had the fortunate idea of proposing such a committee,[a] Herr Kühlwetter himself would undoubtedly have insisted upon it. One should give the committee the most far-reaching tasks (so that it may never finish its business); he entirely agreed that any scrupulous weighing of its actions was unnecessary. Let the committee include the entire past,

---

[a] See this volume, pp. 57-61.— *Ed.*

present and future of the Province of Posen in the scope of its activity; the Ministry would not scrupulously examine the committee's competence insofar as it was only a question of clarifications. One could, of course, go too far, but he would leave it up to the wisdom of the committee whether it wanted to take into its scope, for example, the question of the dismissal of the Posen officials as well.

So much for the introductory concessions of the Minister which, embellished with a few philistine declamations, were given several vigorous cheers. However the "*buts*" were to follow.

"*But* since it has been remarked that the reports about Posen cannot possibly shed accurate light because they came only from *officials*, and moreover old-time officials, I consider it to be my duty to defend an honourable profession. If it be proved true that individual officials have neglected their duty, then let us punish the individuals who neglect their duty but *officialdom* as such must never be denigrated just because a few individuals have violated their duty."

What a bold stand Herr Kühlwetter has taken! To be sure a few individual violations of duty have taken place but on the whole the officials have done their duty honourably.

And, indeed, the mass of Posen officials *have* done their "duty", their "duty to their official oath", to the entire old-Prussian system of bureaucracy and to their own interests which concur with this duty. They have fulfilled their duty by using every means to destroy the 19th of March in Posen. It is exactly for that reason, Herr Kühlwetter, that it is your "duty" to dismiss these officials *en masse*.

But Herr Kühlwetter speaks of a duty which is determined by pre-revolutionary laws, whereas here it is a matter of an entirely different duty which arises after every revolution and which consists of interpreting correctly the altered conditions and of furthering their development. To ask of the officials to replace the bureaucratic with the constitutional standpoint and to support the revolution in the same way as the new Ministers, that means, according to Herr Kühlwetter, to denigrate an honourable profession.

Herr Kühlwetter also rejects the general accusation that favouritism was shown to party chiefs and that crimes remained unpunished. Specific cases should be cited.

Does Herr Kühlwetter perhaps maintain in all seriousness that even a small part of the brutalities and atrocities committed by the Prussian soldiery, tolerated and supported by the officials and cheered by the German Poles and Jews, have been punished? Herr Kühlwetter states that he has not yet been able to examine the colossal amount of material in all its aspects. Indeed, he seems at the most to have examined it in one aspect alone.

It is now that Herr Kühlwetter takes up "the most difficult and delicate question", namely the *forms* in which the committee should transact its business. Herr Kühlwetter would have liked to have this question discussed more thoroughly, for,

"as has been rightly remarked, this question contains a question of principle, the question of the *droit d'enquête*".[a]

Herr Kühlwetter now blesses us with a longish discourse about the separation of powers in the state which surely contains much that is new for the Upper Silesian and Pomeranian peasants in the Assembly. To hear in the year of our Lord 1848 a Prussian Minister, and a "Minister of action" at that, solemnly interpreting Montesquieu from the rostrum makes a strange impression.

The separation of powers which Herr Kühlwetter and other great political philosophers regard with the deepest reverence as a sacred and inviolable principle is basically nothing but the profane industrial division of labour applied for purposes of simplification and control to the mechanism of the state. Just like all sacred, eternal and inviolable principles it is only applied as long as it suits existing conditions. Thus, for example, in a constitutional monarchy, the ruler possesses both legislative and executive power; in the Chambers, furthermore, legislative power mingles with control over executive power etc. This indispensable limitation on the division of labour in the state is expressed by political sages of the calibre of a "Minister of action" in the following manner:

"The legislative power, inasmuch as it is exercised by popular representation, has its own organs; the executive power has its own organs, and the judicial power no less so. It is *therefore* (!) inadmissible for one branch to lay claim to the organs of another unless such power has been transferred to it *by a special law*."

A divergence from the separation of powers is inadmissible "unless" it is dictated "by a special law". And the other way round: the application of the dictated separation of powers is similarly inadmissible "unless" it is dictated "by special laws"! What profundity! What revelations!

Herr Kühlwetter does not mention the case of a revolution where the separation of powers comes to an end without "a special law".

Herr Kühlwetter now argues at great length that the authority of the committee to question witnesses under oath, to summon officials etc., in short, to see with *its own eyes*, is an infringement upon the separation of powers and must be established by a special law. As

---

[a] The right of investigation.— *Ed.*

an example, the Belgian Constitution is cited, Article 40 of which expressly gives the Chambers the *droit d'enquête*.

But, Herr Kühlwetter, is there in Prussia legally and factually a separation of powers in the sense that you interpret it, i.e. in the constitutional sense? Is not the existing separation of powers the limited, trimmed one which corresponds to the *absolute*, the bureaucratic monarchy? How then can one use constitutional phrases for it before it has been reformed constitutionally? How can Prussia have an Article 40 of a Constitution as long as this Constitution itself does not yet exist at all?

Let us summarise. According to Herr Kühlwetter the appointment of a committee with unlimited authority is an infringement on the constitutional separation of powers. The constitutional separation of powers does not yet exist at all in Prussia; hence there can also be no infringement upon it.

It is supposed to be introduced, however, and according to Herr Kühlwetter it must be regarded as *already existing* during the provisional revolutionary state of affairs in which we live. If Herr Kühlwetter were right we would surely also have to presume the existence of constitutional *exceptions*! And these constitutional exceptions surely include the right of legislative bodies to carry out investigations!

But Herr Kühlwetter is by no means right. On the contrary: the provisional revolutionary state of affairs consists in the fact that the separation of powers has been provisionally *abolished* and that the legislative authority seizes executive power or that the executive authority seizes legislative power for the time being. It does not make any difference whether the revolutionary dictatorship (and it is a dictatorship no matter how feebly it is enforced) is in the hands of the Crown or of an Assembly or both. French history since 1789 provides plenty of examples of all three cases if Herr Kühlwetter wants them.

The provisional state of affairs to which Herr Kühlwetter appeals actually speaks against him. It gives the Assembly yet other attributes besides the mere right of investigation; it even empowers it, if need be, to transform itself into a *court of justice* and to judge without laws!

Had Herr Kühlwetter been able to foresee these results, he might perhaps have been more careful in speaking of the "recognition of the revolution".

But he may rest assured:

> Germany, pious nursery,
> Is not a Roman cutthroats' den,[a]

---

[a] Heinrich Heine, "Zur Beruhigung". In *Zeitgedichte.—Ed.*

and Messrs. the agreers may sit as long as they like, they will never become a "Long Parliament".[150]

We find, by the way, a significant difference when we compare the bureaucratic doctrinaire of the Government of Action with his doctrinaire predecessor, Herr Camphausen. Herr Camphausen, at any rate, possessed infinitely more originality. He almost approached Guizot whereas Herr Kühlwetter does not even reach the tiny Lord John Russell.

We have sufficiently admired the state philosophical wealth of Kühlwetter's oration. Let us now examine the purpose, the actual practical reason for this moss-covered wisdom, for this entire separation theory *à la* Montesquieu.

For Herr Kühlwetter now comes to the results of his theory. The Ministry, by way of exception, is inclined to instruct the authorities to comply with the requirements of the committee. It must, however, oppose the committee giving direct instructions to the authorities, i.e. the committee, which has no direct connection with the authorities and which has no power over them, cannot force them to convey other information to it than they consider appropriate. In addition there is the tedious routine and the endless hierarchy of appeals authorities! It is quite a pretty trick to render the committee illusory under the pretext of the separation of powers!

"It cannot be the intention to transfer to the committee the entire job of the Government!"

As if anybody intended giving the committee the right to *govern*!

"*In addition* to the committee, the Government would have to continue its inquiry into the underlying causes of dissension in Posen" (it is exactly because it has already "inquired" for such a long time without finding *out* anything that there is reason enough to exclude it now altogether from such an inquiry), "and since this purpose would be served by a double road there would often be unnecessary waste of time and effort and conflicts could hardly be avoided."

According to all hitherto existing precedents, the committee would certainly spend much "unnecessary time and effort" if it were to agree to Herr Kühlwetter's proposal for the protracted hierarchy of appeals authorities. In this way, conflicts would also occur much more easily than if the committee were to deal directly with the authorities and could immediately clear up misunderstandings as well as put down bureaucratic obduracy.

"It seems *therefore* (!) to be in the nature of things that the committee will seek to achieve its purpose in *agreement* with the Ministry and with its *constant co-operation.*"

It gets better and better! A committee which is supposed to control the Ministry is also supposed to work in agreement with it and with its constant co-operation! Herr Kühlwetter is not at all embarrassed to let it be known that he would find it desirable to have the committee under his control and not the other way round.

"If, on the other hand, the committee should want to assume an isolated position, the question must arise whether the committee wants to and is able to assume the responsibility which rests with the Government. It has already been observed with as much truth as intelligence that the inviolability of the deputies is incompatible with this responsibility."

The question is not one of administration but merely of establishing facts. The committee is to receive the authority to employ the means necessary for this purpose. That is all. It goes without saying that the committee will be responsible to the Assembly for either the neglect or the excessive use of these means.

The whole matter has as little to do with ministerial responsibility and deputies' irresponsibility as with "truth" and "intelligence".

In short, under the pretext of the separation of powers Herr Kühlwetter warmly recommends these proposals to the agreers for the solution of the conflict without, however, making a precise proposal. The Government of Action feels that it stands on uncertain ground.

We cannot go into the debate which ensued. The results of the voting are known: the defeat of the Government in the roll-call vote and the coup d'état of the Right which adopted a motion after it had already been defeated. We have already reported all that.[a] We only add that among the Rhinelanders who voted *against* giving unlimited authority to the committee we noticed the names of:

Arntz, LL. D., Bauerband, Frencken, Lensing, von Loe, Reichensperger II, Simons and last but not least our Chief Public Prosecutor *Zweiffel*.

Written by Engels on July 9, 1848

First published in the *Neue Rheinische Zeitung* No. 41, July 11, 1848

Printed according to the newspaper

Published in English for the first time

---

[a] See this volume, p. 188.— *Ed.*

LEGAL PROCEEDINGS AGAINST THE *NEUE RHEINISCHE ZEITUNG*

Cologne, July 10. Yesterday *eleven* compositors of our newspaper as well as Herr Clouth were summoned to appear as witnesses before the examining magistrate on Tuesday, July 11. It is still a question of finding the author of the incriminatory article.[a] We recall that at the time of the old *Rheinische Zeitung*, the time of the censorship and the Arnim Government, when they tried to find out who had sent in the famous "Marriage Bill",[151] there were neither house searches nor were examinations of compositors and the printshop owner resorted to. In the meantime, of course, we have experienced a revolution which had the misfortune to be recognised by Herr Hansemann.

We have to revert once again to the July 5 "*rejoinder*" of Public Prosecutor *Hecker*.[b]

In this rejoinder Herr Hecker accuses us of *lying* with respect to one or another remark which, we ascribed to him. Perhaps we have now the means at our disposal to correct the correction, but who will vouch that during this unequal battle we will not once again be answered with Paragraph 222 or Paragraph 367 of the Penal Code?

Herr *Hecker*'s *rejoinder* ends with the following words:

"The *defamations and insults* contained in this article" (dated Cologne, July 4), "directed against Chief Public Prosecutor Zweiffel and the police who carried out the arrest, will be *evaluated* in the *legal proceedings* which will be initiated on this count."

Evaluation! Have the *black-red-gold* colours been "*evaluated*" in the "legal proceedings" which were initiated by the *Kamptz* Government?[152]

---

[a] See this volume, pp. 177-79.— *Ed.*

[b] Ibid., p. 186. In the *Neue Rheinische Zeitung:* "July 6", which is a misprint.— *Ed.*

Let us consult the Penal Code.[153] Paragraph 367 reads:

"Whosoever at public places ... or in an authentic and public document, or in a printed or unprinted piece of writing which has been posted, sold or distributed, accuses someone of facts which, *if they were true*,[a] could result in the prosecution of the accused in a criminal or police court, or merely expose him to the contempt and hatred of his fellow citizens, is guilty of the offence of defamation."

Paragraph 370: "If the fact which forms the subject of the accusation should, after *due process of law*, prove to be true, then the originator of the accusation shall go free of all punishment. Only proof which is derived from a *verdict* or some other *authentic document* is regarded as *legal*."

In order to elucidate this paragraph we shall still add Paragraph 368:

"Consequently it will be *of no avail* to the originator of the accusation *to plead* in his defence that *he will undertake to provide proof*; nor can he enter *the plea* that the *documents or the facts are notorious* or that the accusations which gave rise to the prosecution were copied or extracted from foreign papers *or other printed matter*."

The imperial era with all its crafty despotism radiates from these paragraphs.

According to *ordinary* human understanding, somebody is *defamed* if he is charged with fictitious evidence. According to the *extraordinary* understanding of the Penal Code, however, he is defamed if he is charged with *real* facts that can be *proved* but not in an *exceptional* manner, not by a *verdict* or by an *official document*. Oh for the miraculous power of verdicts and official documents! Only facts which have been *judged in court*, only *officially documented* facts are *true* and *genuine* facts. Has there ever been a penal code which has more maliciously *defamed* the most ordinary common sense? Has any bureaucracy ever thrown up a similar Chinese Wall between itself and the public? Covered with the shield of this paragraph, officials and deputies are *immune* like constitutional kings. These gentlemen may *commit* as many facts as they deem proper "which will expose them to the hatred and contempt of their fellow citizens", but these facts must not be pronounced, written or printed on penalty of loss of civil rights in addition to the inevitable prison sentence and fine. Long live the freedom of the press and free speech moderated by Paragraphs 367, 368 and 370! You are arrested illegally. The press denounces this illegality. *Result:* the denunciation is "*evaluated*" in "legal proceedings" because of the "defamation" of the venerable official who has committed the illegality, unless a miracle occurs and a *verdict* has already been rendered yesterday about the illegality which he commits today.

---

[a] All italics in the quotations from the Penal Code are by Marx.— *Ed.*

No wonder that the Rhenish jurists, among them the *people's representative Zweiffel*, voted against a *Polish commission* with absolute authority! From their point of view, the Poles ought to have been sentenced to loss of their civil rights and also mandatory imprisonment and fine because of their *"defamation"* of Colomb, Steinäcker, Hirschfeld, Schleinitz, the Pomeranian army reserve and the old-Prussian police. Thus this peculiar pacification of Posen would be most gloriously crowned.

And what a contradiction it is to use these paragraphs of the Penal Code in order to label the rumour of the threat of getting rid of "March 19, the clubs and freedom of the press" a *"defamation"*![a] As if the use of Paragraphs 367, 368 and 370 of the Penal Code against political speeches and writings were not the real definitive destruction of March 19, clubs and freedom of the press! What is a club without freedom of speech? And what is freedom of speech with Paragraphs 367, 368 and 370 of the Penal Code? And what is March 19 without clubs and freedom of speech? The suppression of freedom of speech and the press in *deed*: is there a more striking proof that only *defamation* could tell fables about the *intention* of this deed? Beware of signing the address which was drawn up yesterday at the Gürzenich Hall.[154] The Public Prosecutor's office would *"appreciate"* your address by initiating *"legal proceedings"* on the count of the *"defamation"* of *Hansemann* and *Auerswald*. Or may only *Ministers* be defamed with impunity, defamed in the sense of the French Penal Code, that code of political slavery carved in such a pithy style? Do we have responsible Ministers and irresponsible policemen?

Thus it is not that the incriminatory article can be *evaluated* by the use of the paragraphs on *"defamation in a juridical sense"*, a defamation in the sense of *despotic fiction* which is an outrage to common sense. All that can thereby be evaluated are purely and simply the accomplishments of the March revolution, that is the height reached by the counter-revolution and the recklessness with which the bureaucracy may revive and enforce weapons still to be found in the arsenal of the old legislation against the new political life. This use of the calumny paragraphs in attacks upon the *people's representatives* is a marvellous method of shielding these gentlemen from criticism and of depriving the press of the protection of the jury system.

Let us now pass from the charge of *defamation* to the charge of *insult*. Here Paragraph 222 is applicable; it reads as follows:

---

[a] See this volume, p. 179.— *Ed.*

"If one or more officials from the administrative or judicial authorities *during the exercise of their official duties* or *as a result of these duties* suffer any *verbal* insults which aim at an attack upon their honour or delicacy of feeling, the person who insults them in this way shall be punished with imprisonment of from one month to two years."

When the article appeared in the *Neue Rheinische Zeitung*, Herr *Zweiffel* was acting as *people's representative in Berlin* and by no means as an *official of the judicial authorities in Cologne*. It was indeed impossible to insult him in the exercise of his official duties or as a result of these duties since he was not performing any official duties. The honour and delicacy of feeling of the gentlemen of the police, however, could only then come under the protection of this article if they had been insulted *in words* (*par parole*). We have *written*, however, and not *spoken*, and *par écrit* is not *par parole*. Thus, what is there left to do? The moral is to speak with more circumspection of the lowest of policemen than of the foremost of princes and in particular not to take liberties with the most irritable gentlemen of the Public Prosecutor's office. We remind the public once more that *similar* prosecutions have been started simultaneously in different places such as Cologne, Düsseldorf and Koblenz. What a strange method of coincidence!

Written by Marx on July 10, 1848

First published in the *Neue Rheinische Zeitung* No. 41, July 11, 1848

Printed according to the newspaper

Published in English for the first time

GERMAN FOREIGN POLICY
AND THE LATEST EVENTS IN PRAGUE

Cologne, July 11. Despite the patriotic shouting and beating of the drums of almost the entire German press, the *Neue Rheinische Zeitung* from the very first moment has sided with the Poles in Posen, the Italians in Italy, and the Czechs in Bohemia. From the very first moment we saw through the machiavellian policy which, shaking in its foundations in the interior of Germany, sought to paralyse democratic energies, to deflect attention from itself, to dig conduits for the fiery lava of the revolution and forge the weapon of suppression within the country by calling forth a narrow-minded *national hatred* which runs counter to the cosmopolitan character of the Germans, and in national wars of unheard-of atrocity and indescribable barbarity trained a brutal soldiery such as could hardly be found even in the Thirty Years' War.[155]

What deep plot it is to let the Germans under the command of their governments undertake a crusade against the freedom of Poland, Bohemia and Italy at the same moment that they are struggling with these same governments to obtain freedom at home! What an historical paradox! Gripped by revolutionary ferment, Germany seeks relief in a *war of restoration,* in a campaign *for* the consolidation of the old authority *against* which she has just revolted. Only a *war against Russia* would be a war of *revolutionary Germany,* a war by which she could cleanse herself of her past sins, could take courage, defeat her own autocrats, spread civilisation by the sacrifice of her own sons as becomes a people that is shaking off the chains of long, indolent slavery and make herself free within her borders by bringing liberation to those outside.

The more the light of publicity reveals in sharp outlines the most recent events, the more facts confirm our view of the national wars by which Germany has dishonoured her new era. As a contribution to this enlightenment we publish the following report by a *German* in Prague even though it reached us belatedly:

Prague, June 24, 1848 (delayed)

The *Deutsche Allgemeine Zeitung* of the 22nd [of this month] contains an article[a] about the assembly of Germans held in Aussig[b] on the 18th [of this month] in which speeches were made which show such ignorance of our recent events and, in part, to put it mildly, such a willingness to heap abusive accusations upon our independent press that [this] writer considers it his duty to correct these errors as far as this is now possible and to confront these thoughtless and malicious persons with the firmness of truth. It comes as a surprise when a man like "the founder of the League to Preserve German Interests in the East"[c] exclaims before an entire assembly: "There can be no talk of forgiveness so long as the battle in Prague continues and, should the victory be ours, we must make full use of it in future." What victory then have the Germans achieved and what conspiracy then has been crushed? Whoever, of course, lends credence to the correspondent of the *Deutsche Allgemeine*, who, it seems, is always only superficially informed, and whoever trusts the pathetic catchwords of "a small-time Polonophobe and Francophobe" or the articles of the perfidious *Frankfurter Journal* which seeks to incite Germans against Bohemians just as it stirred up Germans against Germans during the events in Baden, such a person will never obtain a clear view of the situation here. Everywhere in Germany the opinion seems to prevail that the battle in the streets of Prague was aimed solely at the suppression of the German element and the founding of a Slav republic. We will not even discuss the latter suspicion, for it is too naive; in regard to the former, however, not the smallest trace of a rivalry between nationalities could be observed during the fighting on the barricades. Germans and Czechs stood side by side ready for defence, and I myself frequently requested a Czech-speaking person to repeat what he had said in German, which was always done without the slightest remark. One hears it said that the outbreak of the revolution came two days too early; this would imply that there must already have been a certain degree of organisation and at least provisions made for the supply of ammunition; however, there was no trace of this either. The barricades grew out of the ground in a haphazard way wherever ten to twelve people happened to be together; incidentally, it would have been impossible to raise any more barricades, for even the smallest alleys contained three or four of them. The ammunition was mutually exchanged in the streets and was exceedingly sparse. There was no question whatsoever of a supreme command or of any other kind of command. The defenders stayed where they were being attacked and fired without direction and without command from houses and barricades. No thought of a conspiracy could have had any foundation in such an unguided and unorganised resistance, unless this is suggested by some official declaration and publication of the results of an investigation. The Government, however, does not seem to find this appropriate, for nothing has transpired from the castle that might enlighten Prague about its bloody June days. With the exception of a few, the imprisoned members of the Svornost[156] have all been released again. Other prisoners are also being released, only Count

---

[a] "Aussig, 18 Juni", *Deutsche Allgemeine Zeitung*, supplement to No. 174, June 22, 1848.— *Ed.*

[b] The Czech name is Usti.— *Ed.*

[c] Johann Wuttke.— *Ed.*

Buquoy, Villány and a few others are still under arrest, and one fine morning we will perhaps read a poster on the walls of Prague according to which it was all based on a misunderstanding. The operations of the commanding general do not suggest protection of Germans against Czechs either; for in that case, instead of winning the German population to his side by explaining the situation to them, storming the barricades and protecting the life and property of the "loyal" inhabitants of the city, he evacuates the Old City, moves to the left bank of the Moldau[a] and shoots down Czechs and Germans alike; for the bombs and bullets that flew into the Old City could not possibly seek out only Czechs, they mowed people down without looking at the cockade. How can one rationally deduce a Slav conspiracy when the Government up to now has been unable or unwilling to give any clarification?

Dr. Göschen, a citizen of Leipzig, has drawn up a letter of thanks to Prince von Windischgrätz, to which the general should not ascribe too much importance as an expression of the popular voice. Citizen Göschen is one of those circumspect liberals who suddenly turned liberal after the February days; he was the initiator of a letter of confidence to the Saxon Government concerning the electoral law while the whole of Saxony cried out in indignation, for one-sixth of her inhabitants, especially some of her more able citizens, thereby lost their first civil right, the right to vote; he is one of those who spoke out emphatically in the German League against the admission of German non-Saxons to the election in Saxony and—listen to the double-dealing—who shortly afterwards in the name of his club promised to the League of the non-Saxon German citizens who reside in Saxony complete co-operation in the election of a deputy of its own for Frankfurt. In short, to characterise him in a word: he is the founder of the German League. This man has addressed a letter of thanks to the Austrian general and thanked him for the protection which he allegedly bestowed upon the entire German fatherland. I believe that I have shown that the events do not as yet prove at all to what extent, if any, Prince von Windischgrätz has deserved well of the German fatherland. Only the result of the investigation will determine that. We will, therefore, leave the "high courage, the bold enterprise and firm endurance" of the general to the judgment of history. As for the expression "cowardly assassination" in regard to the death of the Princess[b] we will only mention that it has by no means been proved that that bullet was intended for the Princess who had enjoyed the undivided respect of all Prague. If it should be the case, however, the murderer will not escape his punishment, and the grief of the Prince was surely no greater than that of the mother who saw her nineteen-year-old daughter, also an innocent victim, carried off with a shattered skull. I am in complete agreement with Citizen Göschen concerning the passage in the address which speaks of "brave bands that fought so gallantly under your leadership", for if he had been able to observe, as I did, the warlike vehemence with which these "brave bands" rushed upon the defenceless crowd in the Zeltner Lane on Monday at noon, he would have found his expressions much too weak. Much as it hurts my military vanity, I have to admit that I myself, peacefully strolling among a group of women and children near the temple, allowed thirty to forty royal and imperial grenadiers to put myself to flight together with these people and so effectively that I had to leave my entire baggage, i.e. my hat, in the hands of the victors, for I considered it unnecessary to wait for the beatings, which were being administered to the crowd behind me, to reach me as well. I had the opportunity, nevertheless, to observe that six hours later at the Zeltner Lane barricade these same royal and imperial grenadiers thought it proper to fire for half an hour with canister-shot and six-pounders at this barricade which was defended by at most

---

[a] The Czech name is Vltava.— *Ed.*
[b] Maria Eleonora Windischgrätz.— *Ed.*

twenty men, and then not to take it, however, until it was abandoned by its defenders around midnight. There was no hand-to-hand fighting except in a few instances where the superior strength was on the side of the grenadiers. To judge by the devastation of the houses, the Graben and the Neue Allee were largely cleared by artillery, and I leave it open whether or not it takes great defiance of death to clear a broad avenue of a hundred barely armed defenders with canister-shot.

Concerning the most recent speech by Dr. Stradal from Teplitz[a] according to which "the Prague newspapers are acting for foreign interests", that is presumably Russian, I declare in the name of the independent press of Prague that this comment is either an abundance of ignorance or an infamous calumny whose absurdity has been and will be sufficiently proved by the attitude of our newspapers. Prague's free press has never defended any other goal than the preservation of Bohemia's independence and the equal rights of both nationalities. It knows, however, very well that German reaction is seeking to rouse a narrow-minded nationalism just as in Posen and in Italy, partly *in order to suppress the revolution in the interior of Germany* and partly to *train the soldiery for civil war.*

Written on July 11, 1848

First published in the *Neue Rheinische Zeitung* No. 42, July 12, 1848

Printed according to the newspaper

Published in English for the first time

---

[a] The Czech name is Teplice.— *Ed.*

THE AGREEMENT DEBATES OF JULY 7

Cologne, July 12. It was not until late last night that we received the report about the agreement session of July 7. The stenographic reports, which usually arrived here not more than 24 hours after the epistolary reports, are constantly arriving later instead of earlier.

How easily this delay could be remedied is demonstrated by the speed with which the French and English newspapers carry the reports of their legislative assemblies. The sessions of the English Parliament often last until four o'clock in the morning and yet four hours later the stenographic report of the session is printed in *The Times* and distributed to all parts of London. The French Chamber, which seldom began its sessions before one o'clock, terminated them between five and six and yet already around seven o'clock the *Moniteur* had to deliver a copy of the deliberations taken down in shorthand to all Paris newspaper offices. Why cannot the praiseworthy *Staats-Anzeiger* get ready just as quickly?

Let us now turn to the session of the 7th, the session during which the Hansemann Ministry was teased. We shall pass over the protests which were submitted immediately at the start, d'Ester's motion concerning the repeal of the decision adopted towards the end of the session of the 4th [a] (this motion remained on the agenda) and several other motions which were on the agenda. We shall begin right away with the questions and the disagreeable motions which today were raining down upon the Ministry.

Herr *Philipps* was the first to speak. He asked the Ministry what measures had been taken to protect our borders against Russia.

---

[a] See this volume, p. 207.— *Ed.*

Herr *Auerswald*: I do not consider this question suitable for an answer in this Assembly.

We very readily believe Herr Auerswald. The only reply that he could possibly give would be "*None*", or, if you want to be precise: the transfer of several regiments from the Russian frontier to the Rhine. The only thing that surprises us is that the Assembly allowed this amusing reply of Herr Auerswald, this appeal to the *car tel est notre bon plaisir*,[a] to pass, without much ado, with merely some hissing and cheering.

Herr *Borries* proposes that the graduated income tax of the lowest tax level should be remitted for the last six months of 1848 and that all coercive measures to collect the arrears for the first six months at the same level should be discontinued immediately.

The motion goes to the relevant committee.

Herr *Hansemann* rises and declares that such financial matters ought to be very thoroughly examined. One could, incidentally, wait the more readily as next week he proposes to table several financial Bills among which will be one referring to the graduated income tax.

Herr *Krause* asks the Minister of Finance whether it would be possible to replace the milling and slaughter taxes as well as the graduated income tax with an income tax by the beginning of 1849.

Herr *Hansemann* has to get up again and declare irritably that he had already stated that he will table the financial Bills next week.

But his ordeal is not yet over. Only now Herr *Grebel* rises and submits a lengthy motion every word of which must be a stab through Herr Hansemann's heart:

Considering that it was by no means sufficient to motivate the prospective compulsory loan by merely asserting that the treasury and finances were exhausted;

Considering that for the debate on the compulsory loan itself (against which Herr Grebel protests as long as a Constitution is not in force which fulfils all promises) an examination of all books and records of the state budget was necessary, Herr Grebel submits:

that a committee be appointed which will inspect all books and records concerning the administration of the finances and the treasury since 1840 and report on the matter.

But even worse than Herr Grebel's motion are his arguments in support of it. He mentions the many rumours about the squandering and unlawful spending of the state treasury that alarm public

---

[a] Because this is our will (the closing phrase of royal edicts introduced by Louis XI).— *Ed.*

opinion. In the interest of the people, he demands to know where all the money has gone that it has paid during 30 years of peace. He declares that the Assembly could not vote a single penny as long as such an explanation is not given. The compulsory loan has created an enormous sensation. The compulsory loan condemns the entire hitherto existing financial administration. The compulsory loan is the penultimate step towards the bankruptcy of the state. The compulsory loan surprised us all the more since we were accustomed to hear constantly that the financial situation was excellent and that the state treasury would make unnecessary any loan even in the case of an important war. Herr Hansemann himself had estimated at the United Diet that the state funds must amount to at least 30 million. This, of course, was only to be expected since not only were the same high taxes paid as during the war years, but the amount of the taxes was constantly increasing.

Then, suddenly, there came the news of the intended compulsory loan and with that, with this painful disappointment, confidence sank at once to zero.

The only means of restoring confidence was the immediate, unreserved explanation of the financial situation of the state.

Herr Hansemann, to be sure, had attempted to sweeten the bitter pill of his communication on the compulsory loan by a humorous address; but he had nevertheless to admit that a compulsory loan would produce an unpleasant impression.

Herr *Hansemann* answers: It goes without saying that if the Ministry requests money, it will also give all the necessary information as to how the money that has so far been raised was spent. You should wait until I submit the financial Bills which I have already mentioned twice. As to the rumours, it is incorrect that the state treasury contained enormous sums and that they have been reduced during recent years. It is natural that an excellent financial position should have been transformed into a critical one, considering the recent years of distress and the current political crisis which goes hand in hand with unprecedented economic stagnation.

"It has been stated that the compulsory loan will be a precursor of the state's bankruptcy. No, gentlemen, it *must* not be that. On the contrary, it *must* serve the *invigoration of credit.*"

(It *must*, it *must*, as if the effect of the compulsory loan upon credit depends upon the pious wishes of Herr Hansemann!) How unfounded these apprehensions are is shown by the rise of the government securities. Gentlemen, wait for the financial Bills which I am herewith promising you for the fourth time.

(Hence the credit of the Prussian state is in such bad shape that no capitalist will advance money even at usurious rates of interest and Herr Hansemann sees no other alternative than the compulsory loan, the last resort of bankrupt states. And all the while Herr Hansemann speaks of rising state credit because the government stocks have laboriously crept upward by two to three per cent to the same extent that March 18 has receded! And how the stocks will tumble when the compulsory loan is put into effect!)

Herr *Behnsch* urges the appointment of the proposed financial investigation committee.

Herr *Schramm*: The relief of want from state funds was not worth mentioning and if freedom has cost *us* money, it has up to now certainly not cost the *Government* anything. On the contrary, the Government has rather spent money in order that freedom may not advance to its present state.

Herr *Mätze*: In addition to our knowledge that there was nothing left in the state treasury, we are now being informed that it has been empty for a long time. This piece of news is new proof of the need to appoint a committee.

Herr *Hansemann* has to get up once more:

> "I have never said that there is nothing and that there has not been anything in the state treasury. On the contrary, I declare that the state treasury has significantly increased during the past six to seven years."

(Compare Herr Hansemann's memorandum to the United Diet with the speech from the throne and now we shall all the less know where we stand.)

Cieszkowski: I am in favour of Grebel's motion because Herr Hansemann keeps making us promises and yet every time when financial matters come up for debate, he refers us to elucidations that *he* will make in the near future but that are never given. This dilatoriness is the more incomprehensible as Herr Hansemann has now been a Minister for over three months.

Herr *Milde*, the Minister of Trade, at last comes to the aid of his hard pressed colleague. He implores the Assembly not to appoint the committee. He promises the greatest frankness on the part of the Ministry. He protests that it will be given a detailed account of the state of affairs. But now the Government should be left alone, for at the moment it is busy steering the ship of state out of the difficulties in which it finds itself at present. The Assembly will surely lend a helping hand. (Cheers.)

Herr *Baumstark*, too, attempts to some extent to come to Herr Hansemann's aid. The Minister of Finance, however, could not have found a worse and more tactless defender:

"It would be a *bad* Minister of Finance who attempted to conceal the financial situation, and if a Minister of Finance says that he will make the necessary submissions we must either consider him an *honest man or the contrary* (!!!). (Commotion.) Gentlemen, I have not insulted anybody. I have said if *a* Minister of Finance, not if *the* Minister of Finance (!!!)."

Reichenbach: What has happened to the wonderful days of the great debates, of questions of principle and of confidence? In those days Herr Hansemann longed for nothing more than to be able to enter the fray and now, when he has the opportunity to do so, and in his own field at that, he is evasive! Indeed, the Ministers keep making promises and establishing principles for the sole purpose of violating them a few hours later. (Commotion.)

Herr *Hansemann* waits to see whether anyone will rise to defend him, but there is no one to speak for him. At last he sees with horror that Deputy Baumstark is rising and in order to prevent him from labelling him once again as an "honest man", he quickly takes the floor himself.

We expect the tormented Lion Duchâtel, pricked by needles and tugged by the whole opposition, to rise to his full stature, to crush his opponents, in short, to ask for a *vote of confidence in the Government.* Alas, there is nothing left of his original firmness and daring, and the old greatness has all melted away just like the state treasury during the hard times! The great financier stands bent, broken and misunderstood; things have come to such a pass that he has to give *reasons*! And what reasons, to boot!

"Anybody who concerns himself with financial affairs and the many *figures* (!!) which occur in them, knows that a thorough discussion of financial matters is not possible on the occasion of a question, that the problems of taxation are so comprehensive that legislative assemblies have spent days and even weeks debating them" (Herr Hansemann thinks of his brilliant speeches in the erstwhile United Diet).

But who is demanding a thorough discussion? What has been requested of Herr Hansemann first of all has been an answer, a simple yes or no, concerning the question of taxes. Furthermore, he has been asked for his approval of a committee to investigate the administration of the state treasury etc. up to now. When he refused both, reference was made to the contrast between his former promises and his present reticence.

The committee should start its work immediately precisely because it takes time "to discuss financial affairs and the many figures which occur in them".

"I had good reasons, by the way, for not raising financial matters at an earlier date since I believed that it would be better for the country's position if I waited a little longer. I had hoped that the peace of the country and with it the state credit would somewhat increase. I do not want to see these hopes disappointed and it is my conviction that I *did well not to table these Bills at an earlier date.*"

What disclosures! Herr Hansemann's financial Bills which were supposed to shore up the state credit are of such a nature that they are a threat to the state credit!

Herr Hansemann deemed it better to keep the financial situation of the country a secret for the time being!

If the state finds itself in such a situation, it is irresponsible of Herr Hansemann to make such a vague statement instead of immediately presenting the state of the finances frankly and, by letting the facts speak for themselves, vanquish all doubts and rumours. In the English Parliament, such a tactless utterance would immediately be followed by a vote of no confidence.

Herr *Siebert*:

"Up to now we have done nothing. All important questions, as soon as they matured for solution, were broken off and pushed aside. We have not yet made a single decision which contained anything in its *entirety*, we have not completed anything. Shall we once more proceed in this fashion today and postpone answering the question merely on the basis of promises? Who can guarantee that the *Ministry will remain at the helm for another week?*"

Herr *Parrisius* moves an amendment according to which Herr Hansemann is called upon to present within a fortnight the necessary documents on the administration of the finances and the treasury from the year 1840 to an auditing committee of 16 members to be elected immediately. Herr Parrisius explains that this is a special mandate from his electorate: they want to know what has happened to the state funds which had amounted to over 40 million in 1840.

Surely this amendment, which is stronger than the original motion, will sting the weary Duchâtel into action! Surely he will now put the question of confidence in the Government!

On the contrary! Herr Hansemann who *opposed* the motion has no objections whatsoever to this amendment with its insulting time limit! He merely observes that the matter will require an astonishing amount of time and expresses his sympathy for the unfortunate members of the committee who will have to take on this laborious task.

There follows a debate about the voting during which a few more unpleasant comments are made concerning Herr Hansemann. Then the vote is taken, the various motivated and unmotivated demands to proceed to the order of the day are rejected and the Parrisius amendment, which is supported by Herr Grebel, is almost unanimously adopted.

Herr Hansemann escaped a decisive defeat only by his lack of resistance and the self-abnegation with which he accepted Parrisius' insult. Bent, broken and destroyed he sat on his bench like a defoliated tree that arouses the compassion of even the most cruel mockery. Let us remember the words of the poet:

> It ill beseems the sons
> Of Germany to mock the fallen
> Great with heartless puns![a]

The second half of the session will be reported tomorrow.

Written by Engels on July 12, 1848

First published in the *Neue Rheinische Zeitung* No. 44, July 14, 1848

Printed according to the newspaper

Published in English for the first time

---

[a] Heinrich Heine, "Der Tambourmajor". In *Zeitgedichte*.—*Ed.*

HERR FORSTMANN ON THE STATE CREDIT

Cologne, July 13. During the agreement session of the 7th [of this month], Herr *Forstmann* knocked down all doubts of the unprincipled Left concerning the imperturbability of the Prussian state credit by the following irrefutable argument:

"Please decide whether the confidence in Prussia's finances sank to zero when yesterday on the Stock Exchange a $3^{1}/_{2}$ per cent government security stood at 72 per cent while the rate of discount was $5^{1}/_{2}$ per cent."

One can see that Herr Forstmann is no more a speculator on the Stock Exchange than he is an economist. If Herr Forstmann's hypothesis that the price of government securities stands always in an inverse relationship to the price of money were correct, then the quotations of the Prussian $3^{1}/_{2}$ per cent securities would indeed be unusually favourable. In that case, with a discount rate of $5^{1}/_{2}$ per cent, they should be listed not at 72 per cent but only at $63^{7}/_{11}$. But who has told Herr Forstmann that this inverse relationship exists at every particular moment of a business slump and not as an average over 5 to 10 years.

On what does the price of money depend? It depends on the relationship of supply and demand at a given time and upon the currently existing scarcity or abundance of money. On what does the scarcity or abundance of money depend? It depends on the state of industry at the particular time and on the stagnation or prosperity of commerce in general.

On what does the price of government securities depend? It depends likewise on the relationship of supply and demand at the time. But on what does this relationship depend? It depends on many circumstances, which in Germany, in particular, are extremely complicated.

State credit is of decisive importance in France, England, Spain and in general in those countries whose government securities are traded on the *world market*. State credit plays a secondary role in Prussia and the smaller German states whose securities are quoted only on the small local exchanges. Here most government securities are not used for speculation but for the safe investment of capital and to secure a fixed *rent*. Only a disproportionately small part reaches the stock exchanges and is traded. Almost the entire national debt is in the hands of small pensioners, widows and orphans, boards of guardians, etc. A fall of the exchange quotations due to the decrease of the state credit is an additional reason for this type of state creditors *not* to sell their stocks. The interest is just enough for them to get by. If they sell these stocks at a heavy loss, they are ruined. The small number of securities which circulates on the few small local exchanges cannot, of course, be subject to the enormous and rapid fluctuations of supply and demand, of rise and fall like the enormous mass of French, Spanish etc. securities which are mainly designed for speculation and are traded on all the world's great stock exchanges in large quantities.

Hence it happens only rarely in Prussia that capitalists, through lack of money, are forced to sell their bonds at any price and thereby push down the exchange prices, while in Paris, Amsterdam etc. that is an everyday occurrence, which particularly after the February revolution affected the incredibly rapid fall of the French government securities much more than the diminished state credit.

In addition, fictitious purchases (*marchés à terme*),[157] which make up the bulk of the stock exchange transactions in Paris, Amsterdam etc., are *prohibited* in Prussia.

This entirely different commercial position of the Prussian securities based on local exchanges and the French, English, Spanish etc. securities which are traded on the world market, explains the fact that the prices of the Prussian securities do not reflect the most minute political complications of their state in anything like the measure in which this is the case with French etc. securities, that the state credit has not by a long shot the decisive and rapid influence on the market price of the Prussian stocks that it has upon the securities of other states.

In the measure in which Prussia and the small German states are pulled into the maelstrom of European politics and in which the domination of the bourgeoisie is developing, in the same measure government securities, just like landed property, will lose this patriarchal, inalienable character, will be drawn into circulation, become an ordinary, frequently exchanged article of commerce, and perhaps even be allowed to lay claim to a modest existence on the world market.

Let us draw from these facts the following conclusions:

Firstly: It is not contested that the market price of government securities will *on average over a lengthy period* rise everywhere in the same ratio as the rate of interest falls and vice versa, given that the state credit remains unchanged.

Secondly: In France, England etc. this ratio prevails even during shorter periods because there the speculators own the largest part of the government securities and because, due to shortage of money, people are frequently compelled to sell and this governs the daily ratio between the exchange price and the rate of interest. Hence, this ratio often really prevails even at a particular moment.

Thirdly: In Prussia, on the other hand, this ratio exists only on average over relatively long periods because the amount of disposable government securities is small and the stock exchange business is limited; because sales due to shortage of money, which actually govern this relation, occur only rarely; because the prices of securities at these local stock exchanges are primarily determined by local influences whereas the price of money is determined by the influence of the world market.

Fourthly: If thus Herr Forstmann wants to draw conclusions for the Prussian state credit from the ratio of the price of money to the market price of the government securities, he only proves his total ignorance of these relations. The quotation of 72 for the $3^1/_2$ per cent stocks, with a discount rate of $5^1/_2$ per cent, demonstrates *nothing in favour of* the Prussian state credit, and the compulsory loan speaks *entirely against* it.

Written on July 13, 1848

First published in the *Neue Rheinische Zeitung* No. 44, July 14, 1848

Printed according to the newspaper

Published in English for the first time

THE AGREEMENT DEBATES

Cologne, July 14. Today we come to the second half of the agreement session of the 7th [of this month]. After the debate about the financial committee, which was so painful for Herr Hansemann, there occurred yet another series of small woes for the ministerial gentlemen. It was a day of urgent motions and questions, of attacks on and embarrassment for the Ministry.

Deputy *Wander* proposed that any official who orders the unjust arrest of a citizen should be obliged to make full reparation and besides should be jailed for a period four times as long as the person he arrested.

The motion, as not urgent, is sent to the relevant committee.

Minister of Justice *Märker* declares that the adoption of this motion would not only fail to strengthen the legislation hitherto in force against officials who carry out unlawful arrests, but that it would actually weaken this legislation. (Cheers.)

The Minister of Justice only forgot to observe that according to the laws hitherto in force, particularly the old Prussian Law, it is *hardly possible* for an official to arrest anybody *unlawfully*. The most arbitrary arrest may be justified by the paragraphs of the most time-honoured Prussian Law.

We want to call attention, by the way, to the most unparliamentary method which the Ministers have fallen into the habit of using. They wait until a motion *is referred* to the relevant committee or section and then they still continue to discuss it. They are then certain that *nobody* can *answer* them. Thus Herr Hansemann acted in the case of Herr Borries' motion [a] and now Herr Märker follows suit.

---

[a] See this volume, p. 217.— *Ed.*

Ministers trying to get away with such parliamentary improprieties in England and France would have been called to order very differently. But not in Berlin!

Herr *Schulze* (from Delitzsch): A motion to request the Government *at once* to hand over to the Assembly for debate in committee the already completed or soon to be completed constitutional Bills.

This motion again contained an indirect reproof of the Government for its negligence or intentional delay in submitting Bills to supplement the Constitution. The reproof was the more painful as during that same morning two Bills had been submitted, including the Bill on the civic militia. Thus, had the Prime Minister shown any energy, he would have decisively rejected this motion. But instead he makes only a few general remarks about the Government's desire to meet all just wishes of the Assembly in every possible way and the motion is adopted by a large majority.

Herr *Besser* asks the Minister of War about the absence of service regulations. The Prussian army is the only one which lacks such regulations. Hence there exist in all army units down to company and squadron level the greatest differences of opinion about the most important service matters, particularly about the rights and duties of the various ranks. There exist, to be sure, thousands of orders, ordinances and instructions but they are worse than useless precisely because of their countless number, their confusion and the contradictions which prevail in them. Besides, every such official document is mixed up and rendered unrecognisable by as many different corollaries, elucidations, marginal notes and notes to the marginal notes as there are intermediate authorities through which it passes. This confusion naturally works to the advantage of the superior in all kinds of arbitrary acts whereas the subordinate only reaps the disadvantage of it. The subordinate, therefore, knows no rights but only duties. There used to be service regulations called the pigskin regulations, but they were *taken away from those individuals who had a copy of them* during the 1820s. Since then *no subordinate* may cite them *to his advantage* whereas the *higher* authorities are allowed to cite them constantly *against* the subordinates! It is the same with the service regulations of the guard corps which are never communicated to the army or made accessible to subordinates who are nevertheless punished under them! The staff officers and generals naturally only profit from this confusion which allows them to exercise the most extreme arbitrariness and the harshest tyranny. The subaltern officers, non-commissioned officers and soldiers, however, suffer under it and it is in their interest that Herr Besser questions General Schreckenstein.

How Herr *Schreckenstein* must have been astonished when he had to listen to this lengthy "quill-driving"—to use a popular term from the year 1813! What, the Prussian army does not have service regulations? What absurdity! Honestly, the Prussian army has the best, and at the same time the shortest, regulation in the world consisting of only two words: "*Obey orders!*" If a soldier of this "unbeaten" army is cuffed, kicked and struck with rifle-butts, if he has his beard or nose pulled by a lieutenant not yet of age and just escaped from officers' training school, and if he should complain, it is: "*Obey orders!*" If a tipsy major after dinner and for his special amusement marches his battalion into a swamp up to the waist, and there lines them up in square formations, and a subordinate dares to complain, it is: "*Obey orders!*" If officers are forbidden to visit one or another café and they take the liberty to comment, it is: "*Obey orders!*" This is the best service regulation, for it fits every occasion.

Of all the Ministers, Herr *Schreckenstein* is the only one who has not yet lost heart. This soldier who served under Napoleon, who for thirty-three years has practised the senseless Prussian spit and polish and has heard many a bullet whistle, will certainly not be afraid of agreers and questioners, particularly not when the great "Obey orders!" is in danger!

Gentlemen, he says, I am bound to know better. I ought to know what changes have to be made. It is here a question of tearing down, and tearing down must not be allowed to prevail since rebuilding is very difficult. The military organisation has been created by Scharnhorst, Gneisenau, Boyen and Grolmann, it comprises 600,000 armed and tactically trained citizens and offers a secure future to every citizen as long as there is discipline. I shall maintain it and that is all I have to say.

Herr *Besser*: Herr Schreckenstein has not answered the question at all. It seems evident, however, from his remarks that he believes service regulations would slacken discipline!

Herr *Schreckenstein*: I have already stated that I will do what is expedient for the army and benefits the *service*.

Herr *Behnsch*: We can at least demand that the Minister answers yes or no or declares that he does not wish to reply. Up to now we have only heard evasive phrases.

Herr *Schreckenstein*, annoyed: I do not consider it in the interest of the *service* to discuss this question any further.

The service, always the service! Herr Schreckenstein believes that he is still the commander of a division and that he is speaking to his officer corps. He imagines that as Minister of War, too, he only needs be concerned with the service and not with the legal relations between the individual ranks of the army, least of all with the relations of the army to the state as a whole and its citizens! We are still living under Bodelschwingh; the spirit of the old Boyen seems to prevail unbroken at the Ministry of War.

Herr *Piegsa* asks about the maltreatment of Poles at *Mielzyn* on June 7.

Herr *Auerswald* declares that he must first wait for full reports.

Thus *an entire month* of 31 days after the event Herr Auerswald is not yet fully informed! What a wonderful administration!

Herr *Behnsch* asks Herr Hansemann as to whether at the presentation of the budget he will give a survey of the administration of the *Seehandlung* [158] since 1820 and of the state treasury since 1840.

Herr *Hansemann* declares amidst resounding laughter that he will be able to reply in a week's time.

Herr *Behnsch* once again inquires about government support of emigration.

Herr *Kühlwetter* replies that this is a German affair and refers Herr Behnsch to Archduke John.

Herr *Grebel* asks Herr Schreckenstein about the officials of the Military Administration who are simultaneously officers of the army reserve and who do active service during the army reserve exercises thereby depriving other officers of the army reserve of the opportunity to perfect their training. He moves that these officials be released from service in the army reserve.

Herr *Schreckenstein* declares that he will do his duty and even take the matter into consideration.

Herr *Feldhaus* asks Herr Schreckenstein about the soldiers who lost their lives on the march from Posen to Glogau[a] on June 18 and the measures taken to punish this barbarity.

Herr *Schreckenstein*: The matter has taken place. The report of the regimental commander has been submitted. The report of the General Command which arranged the stages of the march is still lacking. I cannot yet say, therefore, whether the order of march was transgressed. Besides, we are in this case passing judgment on a staff officer and such judgments are painful. It is to be hoped that the "High General Assembly" (!!!) will wait until the reports have arrived.

Herr Schreckenstein does not consider this barbarity a barbarity, he merely asks whether the major in question has "*obeyed orders*". What does it matter if 18 soldiers die miserably like so many heads of cattle on a country road so long as *orders* are *obeyed*!

---

[a] The Polish name is Głogów.— *Ed.*

Herr *Behnsch* who had asked the same question as Herr Feldhaus says: I withdraw my question which has now become superfluous but I demand that the Minister of War fixes a day on which he will answer. Three weeks have already passed since this incident and the reports could have been here long ago.

Herr *Schreckenstein:* We have not wasted a moment; the reports from the General Command were requested immediately.

The *President*[a] wants to skip over the matter.

Herr *Behnsch*: I am only asking the Minister of War to give an answer and to fix a day.

President: Would Herr Schreckenstein....

Herr *Schreckenstein*: It is not yet possible to surmise when that will be.

Herr *Gladbach*: Paragraph 28 of standing orders lays the obligation upon Ministers to fix a day. I also insist upon it.

President: I am asking the Minister once again.

Herr *Schreckenstein*: I cannot fix a specific day.

Herr *Gladbach*: I insist upon my demand.

Herr *Temme*: I am of the same opinion.

President: Would the Minister of War perhaps in a fortnight....

Herr *Schreckenstein*: That could very well be. I shall answer as soon as I know whether or not orders have been obeyed.

President: All right then, in a fortnight.

This is how the Minister of War carries out "his duty" to the Assembly!

Herr *Gladbach* has yet another question, directed to the Minister of the Interior concerning the suspension of unpopular officials and the merely temporary, provisional filling of vacancies.

Herr *Kühlwetter*'s answers are most unsatisfactory and further remarks of Herr Gladbach are drowned after brave resistance by the muttering, shouting and hissing of the Right which is at last moved to fury by so much insolence.

A motion by Herr *Berends* to place the army reserve, which has been called up for domestic service, under the command of the civic militia is not recognised as urgent and is thereupon withdrawn. Thereafter a pleasant conversation begins about all sorts of subtleties linked to the Posen committee. The storm of questions and urgent motions has passed and the last conciliatory sounds of the famous session of July 7 fade away like the soft whispering of zephyr and the pleasant murmuring of a meadow brook. Herr Hansemann returns

---

[a] Wilhelm Grabow.— *Ed.*

home with the consolation that the blustering and table-banging of the Right has woven a few flowers into his crown of thorns, and Herr Schreckenstein smugly twirls his moustache and murmurs: "Obey orders!"

Written by Engels on July 14, 1848

First published in the *Neue Rheinische Zeitung* No. 45, July 15, 1848

Printed according to the newspaper

Published in English for the first time

THE DEBATE ON JACOBY'S MOTION[159]

[*Neue Rheinische Zeitung* No. 48, July 18, 1848]

Cologne, July 17. Again a "great debate", to use an expression of Herr Camphausen, has taken place, a debate which lasted two full days.

The substance of the debate is well known—the reservations the Government advanced regarding the immediate validity of the decisions passed by the National Assembly and Jacoby's motion asserting the Assembly's right to pass legally binding decisions without having to await anyone's consent, and at the same time objecting to the resolution on the Central Authority.[160]

That a debate on this subject was possible at all may seem incomprehensible to other nations. But we live in a land of oaks and lime-trees[a] where nothing should surprise us.

The people send their representatives to Frankfurt with the mandate that the Assembly assume sovereign power over the whole of Germany and all her governments, and, by virtue of the sovereignty the people have vested in the Assembly, adopt a Constitution for Germany.

Instead of immediately proclaiming its sovereignty over the separate states and the Federal Diet,[161] the Assembly timidly avoids any question relating to this subject and maintains an irresolute and vacillating attitude.

Finally it is confronted with a decisive issue—the appointment of a provisional Central Authority. Seemingly independent, but in fact guided by the governments with the help of Gagern, the Assembly elects as Imperial Regent a man whom these governments had in advance designated for this post.[b]

---

[a] Heinrich Heine, "Zur Beruhigung". In *Zeitgedichte.—Ed.*
[b] Archduke John of Austria.—*Ed.*

The Federal Diet recognises the election, pretending, as it were, that only its confirmation makes the election valid.

Reservations are nevertheless made by Hanover and even by Prussia, and it is the Prussian reservation that has caused the debate of the 11th and 12th.

This time, therefore, it is not so much the fault of the Chamber in Berlin[a] that the debates are vague and hazy. The irresolute, weak-kneed, ineffectual Frankfurt National Assembly itself is to blame for the fact that its decisions can only be described as so much twaddle.

Jacoby introduces his motion briefly and with his usual precision. He makes things very difficult for the speakers of the Left, because he says everything that can be said about the motion if one is to avoid enlarging upon the origin of the Central Authority, whose history is so discreditable to the National Assembly.

In fact, the deputies of the Left who follow him advance hardly any new arguments, while those of the Right fare much worse—they lapse either into sheer twaddle or juridical hair-splitting. Both sides endlessly repeat themselves.

Deputy *Schneider* has the honour of first presenting the case for the Right to the Assembly.

He begins with the grand argument that the motion is self-contradictory. On the one hand, the motion recognises the sovereignty of the National Assembly, on the other hand, it calls upon the Agreement Chamber to censure the National Assembly, thus placing itself above it. Any individual could express his disapproval but not the Chamber.

This subtle argument, of which the Right seems to be very proud seeing that it recurs in all the speeches of its deputies, advances an entirely new theory. According to this theory, the Chamber has fewer rights with regard to the National Assembly than an individual.

This first grand argument is followed by a republican one. Germany consists for the most part of constitutional monarchies, and must therefore be headed by a constitutional, irresponsible authority and not by a republican, responsible one. This argument was rebutted on the second day by Herr *Stein*, who said that Germany, under her federal constitution, had always been a republic, indeed a very edifying republic.

"We have been given a mandate," says Herr Schneider, "to agree on a constitutional monarchy, and those in Frankfurt have been given a similar mandate, i.e. to agree with the German governments on a Constitution for Germany."

---

[a] The Prussian National Assembly.— *Ed.*

The reaction indulges in wishful thinking. When, by order of the so-called Preparliament[162]—an assembly having no valid mandate—the trembling Federal Diet convened the German National Assembly, there was no question at the time of any agreement; the National Assembly was then considered to be a sovereign power. But now things have changed. The June events in Paris have revived the hopes of both the big bourgeoisie and the supporters of the overthrown system. Every squire from the backwoods hopes to see the old rule of the whip re-established, and a clamour for "an agreed German Constitution" is already arising from the Imperial Court at Innsbruck to the ancestral castle of Henry LXXII. The Frankfurt Assembly has no one but itself to blame for this.

"In electing a constitutional supreme head the National Assembly has therefore acted according to its mandate. But it has also acted in accordance with the will of the people; the great majority want a constitutional monarchy. Indeed, had the National Assembly come to a different decision, I would have regarded it as a misfortune. Not because I am *against the republic*; in *principle* I admit that the republic—and I have quite definitely made up my mind about it—*is the most perfect and most noble form of state*, but in reality we are still very far from it. We cannot have the form unless we have the spirit. We cannot have a republic while we lack *republicans*, that is to say, noble minds capable, at all times, with a clear conscience and noble selflessness, and not only in a fit of enthusiasm, of subordinating their own interests to the common interest."

Can anyone ask for better proof of the virtues represented in the Berlin Chamber than these noble and modest words of Deputy Schneider? Surely, if any doubt still existed about the fitness of the Germans to set up a republic, it must have completely vanished in face of these examples of true civic virtue, of the noble and most modest self-sacrifice of our Cincinnatus-Schneider! Let Cincinnatus pluck up courage and have faith in himself and the numerous noble citizens of Germany who likewise regard the republic as the most noble form of state but consider themselves bad republicans—they are ripe for the republic, they would endure the republic with the same heroic equanimity with which they have endured the absolute monarchy. The republic of worthies would be the happiest republic that ever existed—a republic without Brutus and Catiline, without Marat and upheavals like those of June, it would be a republic of well-fed virtue and solvent morality.[a]

How mistaken is Cincinnatus-Schneider when he exclaims:

"A republican mentality cannot be formed under absolutism; it is not possible to create a republican spirit *offhand*, we must first educate our children and grandchildren in this way. At present I would regard a republic as the greatest

---

[a] Modified quotation from Heinrich Heine's "Anno 1829". In *Romanzen.*— *Ed.*

calamity, for it would be anarchy under the desecrated name of republic, despotism under the cloak of liberty."

On the contrary, as Herr *Vogt* (from Giessen) said in the National Assembly, the Germans are republicans *by nature*, and to educate his children in the republican spirit Cincinnatus-Schneider could do no better than bring them up in the old German tradition of propriety, modesty and God-fearing piety, the plain and honest way in which he himself grew up. Not anarchy and despotism, but those cosy beer-swilling proceedings, in which Cincinnatus-Schneider excels, would be brought to the highest perfection in the republic of worthies. Far removed from all the atrocities and crimes which defiled the First French Republic, unstained by blood, and detesting the red flag, the republic of worthies would make possible something hitherto unattainable: it would enable every respectable burgher to lead a quiet, peaceful life marked by godliness and propriety. Who knows, the republic of worthies might even revive the guilds together with all the amusing trials of non-guild artisans. This republic of worthies is by no means a fanciful dream; it is a reality existing in Bremen, Hamburg, Lübeck and Frankfurt, and even in some parts of Switzerland. But its existence is everywhere threatened by the contemporary storms, which bid fair to engulf it everywhere.

Therefore rise up, Cincinnatus-Schneider, leave your plough and turnip field, your beer and agreement policy, mount your steed and save the threatened republic, *your* republic, the *republic of worthies!*

[*Neue Rheinische Zeitung* No. 49, July 19, 1848]

Cologne, July 18. Herr Waldeck takes the floor after Herr Schneider, in support of the motion.

"The present position of the Prussian state is surely quite without precedent, and one *really* cannot conceal the fact that it is also *somewhat* precarious."

This beginning is likewise somewhat precarious. We get the impression that we are still listening to Deputy Schneider:

"It must be said that Prussia was destined to exercise hegemony in Germany."

This is the same old-Prussian illusion, the cherished dream of merging Germany in Prussia and of declaring Berlin the German Paris. Herr Waldeck, it is true, sees this cherished hope dwindling, but he hankers after it with painful feelings, and he blames both the previous and the present Government for the fact that Prussia is not at the head of Germany.

Unfortunately the fine days have passed when the Customs Union [163] paved the way for Prussian hegemony in Germany, days when provincial patriots could believe that "the Brandenburg stock has determined the fate of Germany for 200 years" and will continue to do so in the future, the fine days when the disintegrating Germany of the Federal Diet could regard even the Prussian bureaucratic strait jacket as a last means of maintaining some sort of cohesion.

"The Federal Diet, on which public opinion has passed judgment long since, is disappearing and suddenly the Constituent National Assembly in Frankfurt emerges before the eyes of an *astonished world!*"

The "world" was naturally "astonished" when it saw *this* Constituent National Assembly. One need only read the French, English and Italian newspapers to understand this.

Herr Waldeck then explains at some length that he is against the idea of a German emperor and gives up his place on the rostrum to Herr Reichensperger II.

Herr *Reichensperger II* declares the supporters of Jacoby's motion to be republicans and desires them to state their aims as candidly as did the republicans in Frankfurt. Then he too asserts that Germany is not yet in possession of the

"full measure of civic and political virtues which have been described by a great political scientist[a] as the essential precondition for a republic".

If Reichensperger, the patriot, says this, Germany must be in a bad way!

Herr Reichensperger continues, the Government has made no reservations (!) but merely expressed wishes. There was reason enough for this and I also hope that the National Assembly will not always ignore the opinions of governments when making decisions. It is outside our competence to lay down the sphere of competence of the Frankfurt National Assembly; the National Assembly itself has refused to advance theories concerning its own competence; it has acted in a practical manner when necessity has demanded action.

In other words, at the time when the Frankfurt Assembly was omnipotent, it failed during the revolutionary agitation to settle the inevitable conflict with the German governments with one decisive stroke. It has preferred to postpone the decision and to fight small skirmishes with one or another Government over each individual resolution, skirmishes which weaken the Assembly the further it recedes from the time of the revolution and the more it compromises itself in the eyes of the people by its feeble actions. And

---

[a] Montesquieu.— *Ed.*

in this respect, Herr Reichensperger is quite right: it is not worth our while to come to the aid of an Assembly which has forsaken itself!

But it is touching when Herr Reichensperger says:

"It is therefore *unstatesmanlike* to discuss such questions of competence; what matters is simply to solve practical questions as they arise."

It is indeed "unstatesmanlike" to dispose of these "practical questions" once and for all by means of a forceful decision; it is "unstatesmanlike" if, in the face of reactionary attempts to halt the movement, the revolutionary mandate were asserted, a mandate which every Assembly that has come into being as a result of barricade fighting possesses. Cromwell, Mirabeau, Danton, Napoleon and the entire English and French revolutions were indeed exceedingly "unstatesmanlike", but Bassermann, Biedermann, Eisenmann, Wiedenmann and Dahlmann behave in a very "statesmanlike" manner! "Statesmen" disappear altogether when a revolution takes place, and the revolution must be temporarily dormant for "statesmen" to re-emerge, and, moreover, statesmen of the caliber of Herr Reichensperger II, the deputy for the Kempen district.

"If you depart from this system, it will be difficult to avoid conflicts with the German National Assembly and with the governments of individual [German] states; at any rate you will unfortunately promote discord and, as a result of discord, anarchy will raise its head and nothing will then save us from civil war. Civil war, however, marks the beginning of still greater misfortune.... It is not out of the question that people may in that case say—order has been restored in Germany, by our Eastern and Western friends!"

Herr Reichensperger may be right. If the Assembly engages in a discussion of competence, it may give rise to clashes, possibly leading to a civil war and intervention by the French and the Russians. If the Assembly does not discuss this, however, and, in fact, it has not done so, a civil war is even more certain. The conflicts which, at the beginning of the revolution, were still fairly simple, every day become more involved, and the longer the decision is delayed, the more difficult and the more bloody will be the solution.

A country like Germany, which is forced to work its way up from indescribable fragmentation to unity, which, if it does not want to perish, needs the more stringent revolutionary centralisation, the more divided it has been up to now, a country which contains twenty Vendées,[164] which is sandwiched between the two most powerful and most centralised states of the Continent and surrounded by numerous small neighbours, with whom it is on strained terms, if not at war—such a country cannot, in the present period of universal revolution, avoid *either civil war or war with other countries*. These wars, which we will certainly have to face, will be the more perilous and devastating, the more irresolute is the conduct of the people and its leaders and the longer the decision is postponed. If Herr Reichensperger's "statesmen" remain at the helm, we might witness another Thirty Years' War.[165] But, fortunately, the force of events, the German people, the Emperor of Russia and the French people also have a say in the matter.

[*Neue Rheinische Zeitung* No. 53, July 23, 1848]

Cologne, July 22. Current events, Bills, armistice proposals etc. at last allow us once more to return to our beloved agreement debates. On the rostrum we see Deputy von *Berg* from Jülich, a man in whom we are interested for two reasons; first, because he is a Rhinelander, and second, because he is a ministerialist of very recent date.

Herr Berg has several reasons for opposing Jacoby's motion. The first is this:

"The first part of the motion, which requires us to express our disapproval of a decision made by the German Parliament, this first part is nothing but a protest made in the name of a minority against a legal majority. It is nothing but an attempt by a party which has been *defeated within* a legislative body *to obtain support from outside*; it is an attempt whose consequences are *bound to lead to civil war*."

Mr. Cobden, with his motion to abolish the Corn Laws, also belonged to the minority in the House of Commons from 1840 to 1845. He belonged to "a party which" had "been defeated within a legislative body". What did he do? He sought "support from outside". He did not simply state his disapproval of parliamentary decisions, he went much further; he set up and organised the Anti-Corn Law League[166] and the Anti-Corn Law press, in short, the whole enormous agitation against the Corn Laws. According to Herr Berg, this was an attempt that was "bound to lead to civil war".

The minority in the erstwhile United Diet likewise sought "support from outside". Herr Camphausen, Herr Hansemann and Herr Milde had no scruples whatever over this. The facts that stand as proof of this are well known. It is obvious that the consequences of their conduct, according to Herr Berg, were "bound to lead to civil war". They led not to civil war, however, but to the Ministry.

We could cite a hundred more such examples.

The minority in a legislative body, if it does not want to bring about civil war, must not, therefore, seek support from outside. But what then does "from outside" mean? It means the constituents, i.e. the people who *create* the legislative body. If one is no longer supposed to obtain "support" by influencing these constituents, where is one to gain support?

Are the speeches of Hansemann, Reichensperger, von Berg and so on, delivered merely for the benefit of the Assembly or also for the public, to whom they are presented in stenographic reports? Are not these speeches likewise means by which this "party within a legislative body" seeks, or *hopes*, to obtain "support from outside"?

In short, Herr Berg's principle would lead to the abolition of all political propaganda. For propaganda is simply the practical application of the immunity of advocates of freedom of the press and of freedom of association, i.e. of freedoms which legally exist in Prussia. Whether these freedoms lead to civil war or not is not our concern. It is sufficient that they exist, and we shall see where it "leads", if they continue to be infringed.

"Gentlemen, these efforts of the minority to find strength and recognition outside the legislative authority did not begin today or yesterday, they date from the first day of the German uprising. The minority expressed its objections and left the Preparliament, and the result was civil war."

First, as regards Jacoby's motion, there is no question of a "minority objecting and leaving".

Secondly, "the efforts of the minority to find recognition outside the legislative authority" did, it is true, "not begin today or yesterday", for they date from the moment when legislative authorities and minorities came into being.

Thirdly, it is not the fact that the minority expressed its objections and left the Preparliament which led to civil war, but Herr Mittermaier's "moral conviction" that Hecker, Fickler and their associates were traitors to their country, and the measures which the Government of Baden consequently took and which were dictated by the most abject fear.[167]

The civil war argument, which is, of course, apt to throw the German burgher into a dreadful state of alarm, is followed by the argument about the absence of a mandate.

"We have been elected by our constituents in order to establish a Constitution in Prussia; the same constituents have sent other citizens to Frankfurt, to set up a Central Authority there. It cannot be denied that the constituent who gives the mandate is certainly entitled to approve or disapprove the mandatary's actions, but the constituents have not authorised us to speak on their behalf in this respect."

This weighty argument has been greatly admired by the legal experts and legal dilettanti in the Assembly. We have no mandate!

Nevertheless, two minutes later, the same Herr Berg asserts that the Frankfurt Assembly was "convoked in order to create the future Constitution of Germany, in concert with the German governments", and it is to be hoped that the Prussian Government will *not*, in this case, ratify it without consulting the Agreement Assembly or the Chamber which is to be elected under the new Constitution. The Ministry has nevertheless immediately informed the Assembly of its recognition of the Imperial Regent,[a] as well as of its reservations, thereby inviting the Assembly to pronounce its decision.

It is therefore precisely the point of view expressed by Herr Berg, his own speech and Herr Auerswald's information which lead to the conclusion that the Assembly certainly has a mandate to deal with the Frankfurt resolutions.

We have no mandate! Hence, if the Frankfurt Assembly reintroduces censorship, if it sends Bavarian and Austrian troops to Prussia to support the Crown in a conflict between the Chamber and the Crown, then Herr Berg has "no mandate"!

What mandate has Herr Berg? Literally only this: "to agree with the Crown upon the Constitution". By no means has he, therefore, a mandate to put down parliamentary questions, and to agree to laws on immunity, on the civic militia, on redemption and to all other laws not mentioned in the Constitution. This is what reactionaries daily assert. Berg himself says:

"Every step beyond this mandate is a breach of faith, it is an abandonment of the mandate or even a betrayal!"

Nevertheless, under the force of necessity, Herr Berg and the entire Assembly constantly abandon their mandate. The Assembly must do so due to the revolutionary, or rather, at present, reactionary, provisional state of affairs. Because of this provisional state, everything serving to safeguard the achievements of the March revolution falls within the competence of the Assembly and if it can achieve this by exerting moral influence on the Frankfurt Assembly, then the Agreement Chamber is not only entitled, but even obliged, to do so.

Then follows the Rhenish-Prussian argument, which is of special importance for us Rhinelanders, because it shows how we are represented in Berlin.

"We Rhinelanders and Westphalians and the inhabitants of other provinces as well have *absolutely* no bond with Prussia other than the fact that we have *come under the jurisdiction of the Prussian Crown*. If we dissolve this bond, the state disintegrates. I do not understand at all, and I believe most deputies from my province do not

---

[a] Archduke John of Austria.— *Ed.*

understand either, what benefit a Berlin republic would be to us. We might prefer rather a republic in Cologne."

We shall not discuss at all the idle speculations about what we "might prefer" if Prussia is turned into a "Berlin republic", nor the new theory about the conditions of existence of the Prussian state etc. As Rhinelanders, we simply protest against the statement that "we have come under the jurisdiction of the Prussian Crown". On the contrary the "Prussian Crown" has come *to us*.

The next speaker against the motion is Herr *Simons* from Elberfeld. He repeats everything that Herr Berg has said.

He is followed by a speaker from the Left and then by Herr *Zachariä*. Zachariä repeats everything that Herr Simons has said.

Deputy *Duncker* repeats everything that Herr Zachariä has said, but he also adds a few other things, or he expresses what has been said before in such an extreme way, that we find it advisable to deal briefly with his speech.

"Do we, the Constituent Assembly of 16 million Germans, reinforce the authority of the German Central Government and the authority of the German Parliament in the minds of the people by thus censuring the Constituent Assembly of all Germans? Do we not thereby undermine the willing obedience which the individual nationalities must [accord] it, if it is to work for Germany's unity?"

According to Herr Duncker, the authority of the Central Government and the National Assembly and this "willing obedience" exist; the obedience consists in the *people* submitting blindly to this authority, whereas the individual *governments* make *reservations* and, when it suits them, refuse to obey.

"What is the point of making theoretical statements in our time, when the force of fact is so immense?"

Recognition of the sovereignty of the Frankfurt Assembly by the representatives "of 16 million Germans" is thus merely a "theoretical statement"!?

"If, in future, a resolution passed in Frankfurt were to be *regarded* by the Government and Parliament of Prussia as impossible and impracticable, would there then be any possibility of carrying through such a resolution?"

Hence, the mere opinions, the *views* held by the Prussian Government and Parliament are supposed to be capable of making the resolutions of the National Assembly *impossible*.

"Today, we may say whatever we like, but the Frankfurt resolutions could not be carried through, if the entire Prussian people, if two-fifths of Germany, refused to submit to them."

Here we have again all the old Prussian arrogance, the Berlin national patriotism in all its old glory, with the pigtail and crooked stick of old Fritz.[a] It is true, we are only a minority, only two-fifths (and not even that) but we will certainly show the majority that *we* are masters in Germany, that we are Prussians!

We do not advise the gentlemen of the Right to provoke a conflict of this kind between "two-fifths" and "three-fifths". The numerical balance may prove to be quite different, and many a province may remember that it has been German from time immemorial, but that it has been Prussian for only thirty years.

Herr Duncker has a remedy, however. Those in Frankfurt must, along with us, "pass only those resolutions that express the reasonable collective will, the true opinion of the public, so that they can be approved by the moral consciousness of the nation", i.e. resolutions after Deputy Duncker's own heart.

> "If we, and those in Frankfurt, pass such resolutions then we are, and they are, sovereign, otherwise we are not sovereign, even if we decree it ten times over."

After this profound definition of sovereignty, which is in keeping with his moral consciousness, Herr Duncker heaves a sigh: "In any case, this belongs to the future", and thus concludes his speech.

Lack of space and time prevents us from discussing the speeches of the Left made on the same day. Nevertheless, even from the speeches of the Right presented here, our readers will have realised that Herr Parrisius was not entirely mistaken when he moved the adjournment because "the temperature in the hall has risen so high that it is impossible to maintain *absolute clarity of thought*"!

[*Neue Rheinische Zeitung* No. 55, July 25, 1848]

Cologne, July 24. A few days ago, when the pressure of world events caused us to interrupt our account of the debate, a neighbouring journalist[b] was kind enough to carry on the report in our stead. He has already drawn the attention of the public to "the profusion of penetrating thoughts and bright ideas" and to "the fine and healthy feeling for true freedom" displayed by "the speakers of the majority", and especially by our incomparable Baumstark, "during this great debate, which lasted two days".[c]

We must bring our report of the debate to a hasty close, but cannot refrain from presenting a few examples from the "profusion"

---

[a] King Frederick II of Prussia.— *Ed.*

[b] Karl Brüggemann.— *Ed.*

[c] "Köln, 20. Juli. Die Debatte über den Jacobyschen Antrag", *Kölnische Zeitung* No. 203, July 21, 1848.— *Ed.*

of "penetrating thoughts and bright ideas" expressed by the Right.

Deputy *Abegg* opened the second day of the debate[a] with a threat to the Assembly: to get to the bottom of this motion, one would have to repeat all the Frankfurt debates in their entirety—and the High Assembly is obviously not entitled to do this! Their constituents "with their practical tact and practical sense" would never approve of this! Incidentally, what is to become of German unity, if (now follows a particularly "penetrating thought") people "do *not simply* confine themselves to making *reservations*", but express their "firm approval or disapproval of the Frankfurt resolutions". In this case nothing remains but "purely formal submissiveness"!

Of course, "purely formal submissiveness" can be evaded by "reservations" and, if need be, even directly denied—that cannot harm German unity; but to approve or disapprove of these resolutions and to judge them with regard to their style, logic or usefulness—that's the limit!

Herr *Abegg* concludes with the observation that it was for the Frankfurt Assembly, and *not* the Berlin Assembly, to comment upon the reservations presented to the Assembly in Berlin, *not* that in Frankfurt. One ought not to anticipate the Frankfurt deputies as this would surely be an insult to them!

The gentlemen in Berlin are not competent to express an opinion on statements made by their own Ministers.

Let us skip the idols of the small people, such as *Baltzer, Kämpf* and *Gräff*, and make haste to hear the hero of the day, the incomparable *Baumstark*.

Deputy *Baumstark* declares that he would never pronounce himself incompetent, unless he is forced to admit no knowledge of the matter in hand—and surely eight weeks of debate cannot leave one with no knowledge of the matter?

Consequently, Deputy Baumstark is *competent*. Namely, in the following manner:

"I ask whether, as a result of the wisdom we have shown so far, we are fully entitled" (i.e. competent) "to confront an Assembly, which has attracted
general interest in Germany,
and the admiration of the whole of Europe,
thanks to its noble-mindedness,
its high intelligence
and its moral political standpoint,
that is thanks to everything that has made the name of Germany great and glorious throughout history? I *submit* to it" (i.e. I declare myself *incompetent*) "and wish that the Assembly, sensing the truth (!!), would likewise submit" (i.e. declare itself *incompetent*)!

[a] July 12, 1848.— *Ed.*

"Gentlemen," continues the "competent" Deputy Baumstark, "it was stated at yesterday's session that there has been talk of a republic etc. which is unphilosophical. But it cannot possibly be unphilosophical to describe the responsibility of the person who heads the state, as a characteristic feature of the republic, in the democratic sense. Gentlemen, it is certain that all political philosophers, from *Plato down to Dahlmann*" (Deputy Baumstark could indeed not go further "down"), "have expressed this view, and we must not contradict this more than a thousand-year-old truth (!) and historical fact, without very special reasons, which have yet to be adduced."

Herr Baumstark thinks, therefore, that sometimes there can be "very special reasons" to contradict even "historical facts". Indeed, the gentlemen of the Right usually have no scruples in this respect.

Herr Baumstark, moreover, declares himself once again *incompetent*, by pushing the competence on to the shoulders of "all political philosophers, from Plato down to Dahlmann". Herr Baumstark, of course, does not belong to this category of political philosophers.

"Let us consider this political edifice! *One* Chamber and a responsible Imperial Regent, and this on the basis of the present electoral law! Further examination will show that it is against all *common sense.*"

Then Herr Baumstark makes the following penetrating pronouncement which, even on the closest examination, will not be against all "common sense".

"Gentlemen, a republic requires two things, popular opinion and leading personalities. If we make a closer examination of our German popular opinion, we shall find that it contains very little about *this* republic (namely that of the Imperial Regent previously mentioned).

Thus, Herr Baumstark once more declares himself *incompetent*, and this time, in his place, it is *popular opinion* that is competent to judge the republic. Popular opinion, therefore, has more "knowledge" about the matter than Deputy Baumstark.

At last, however, the speaker proves that there are also matters about which he has some "knowledge", and first and foremost among these is popular sovereignty.

"Gentlemen, history—I have to return to this—proves that *we have had popular sovereignty since time immemorial*, but it has assumed different forms under different conditions."

Then follows a series of "extremely penetrating thoughts and bright ideas" about Brandenburg-Prussian history and popular sovereignty causing the neighbouring journalist to forget all worldly sufferings in a fit of constitutional ecstasy and doctrinaire bliss.

"When the Great Elector[a] disregarded, and *indeed* (!) crushed" (to "crush" something is certainly the best way of disregarding it), "the decaying elements of the

---

[a] Frederick William of Brandenburg.— *Ed.*

estates, which were infected with the poison of French demoralisation" (the right of the first night had in fact been gradually buried by the "French demoralised" civilisation!), "he was generally acclaimed by the people, deeply imbued with the moral feeling that this gave strength to the German, and especially the Prussian, political edifice."

One has to admire the "deep moral feeling" of the Brandenburg philistines of the seventeenth century who, profoundly moved by their profits, acclaimed the Elector when he attacked their enemies, the feudal lords, and sold privileges to the philistines—but one has to admire even more the "common sense" and "bright ideas" of Herr Baumstark, who regards this acclamation as an expression of "popular sovereignty"!

"At that time, everybody, without exception, paid homage to the absolute monarchy" (since otherwise he would have been flogged) "and the Great Frederick would never have achieved such importance had he not been supported by *genuine* popular sovereignty."

The popular sovereignty of flogging, serfdom and soccage services is, for Herr Baumstark, *genuine* popular sovereignty. An artless admission!

From genuine popular sovereignty, Herr Baumstark now goes on to consider *false* popular sovereignties.

"But there followed a different period, that of constitutional monarchy."

This is then proved by a long "constitutional rigmarole" in which, to cut a long story short, he asserts that, from 1811 to 1847, the people of Prussia called continuously for a Constitution, and never for a Republic (!). This is naturally followed by the remark that "the people has turned away in indignation" from the recent republican insurrection in Southern Germany.

From this it follows quite naturally that the second kind of popular sovereignty (although it is no longer the "genuine" one) is the "constitutional sovereignty proper".

"This is the kind of popular sovereignty which divides political power between the King and the people, it is *divided* popular sovereignty" (let the "political philosophers, from Plato down to Dahlmann", tell us what this is supposed to mean), "which the people must receive *unimpaired* and *unconditionally* (!!), but without depriving the King of any of his constitutional power" (what laws define this power in Prussia since the 19th March?). "This point is quite clear" (especially in Deputy Baumstark's mind); "the concept has been determined by the history of the constitutional system and no one can still entertain any doubts about it" (it is only when one reads Deputy Baumstark's speech that, unfortunately, "doubts" arise again).

Finally "there is a third kind of popular sovereignty, the democratic-republican kind, which is supposed to rest on the so-called broadest basis. What an unfortunate expression is *'broadest basis'!*"

Then Herr Baumstark "raises a word" against this broadest basis. This basis leads to the decline of countries, to barbarism! We have no Cato, who could give the republic a moral foundation. Herr Baumstark then begins to blow Montesquieu's old horn of republican virtue—a horn which has long been out of tune and full of dents—and to blow it so loudly that the neighbouring journalist,[a] in transports of admiration, chimes in likewise and, to the astonishment of all Europe, demonstrates brilliantly that it is "precisely republican virtue ... which leads to constitutionalism"! Meanwhile, Herr Baumstark changes his tune and also comes to constitutionalism but through the *absence* of republican virtue. The reader can imagine the splendid effect of this duet when, after a series of the most heart-rendingly discordant notes, the two voices finally unite to produce the conciliatory chord of constitutionalism.

After a lengthy argument, Herr Baumstark comes to the conclusion that the Ministers have actually made "no *real* reservation" at all, but merely "a *slight* reservation concerning the future" and, in the end, he finds himself on the broadest basis, since he considers only a *democratic* and constitutional state to be Germany's salvation. He is so "overwhelmed by the prospect of Germany's future" that he gives vent to his feelings by crying:

"Cheers, three cheers for the popular-constitutional, hereditary German monarchy!"

He was indeed quite right when he said—this unfortunate broadest basis!

Several speakers from both sides then take the floor but, after Deputy Baumstark, we dare not present them to our readers. We shall just mention Deputy *Wachsmuth's* declaration that his principal tenet is the point made by the noble Stein: The will of free men is the unshakeable support of every throne.

"That strikes right to the core of the matter!" exclaims our enraptured neighbouring journalist. "Nowhere does the will of free men prosper more than in the shelter of the unshakeable throne, and nowhere does the throne rest more securely than on the intelligent love of free men!"[b]

---

[a] Karl Brüggemann.— *Ed.*

[b] "Köln, 20. Juli. Die Debatte über den Jacobyschen Antrag", *Kölnische Zeitung* No. 203, July 21, 1848.— *Ed.*

Indeed, the "profusion of penetrating thoughts and bright ideas" and the "healthy feeling for true freedom" displayed by the speakers of the majority in this debate are far from matching the depth and penetration of the thoughts of the neighbouring journalist!

Written by Engels between July 17 and 24, 1848

Printed according to the newspaper

First published in the *Neue Rheinische Zeitung* Nos. 48, 49, 53 and 55, July 18, 19, 23 and 25, 1848

Published in full in English for the first time

THE SUPPRESSION OF THE CLUBS
IN STUTTGART AND HEIDELBERG

Cologne, July 19.

> My Germany got drunk with toasts,
> You, you believed them all,
> And every black-red-golden tassel
> As well as each pipe-bowl![a]

And that, upright German, has indeed been your fate once again. You believe you have made a revolution? Deception! You believe that you have overcome the police state? Deception! You believe that you possess freedom of association, freedom of the press, the arming of the people and other beautiful slogans which were bandied about on the March barricades? Deception, nothing but deception!

> But when the blissful glow wore off,
> Beloved friend, you stood bewildered.[b]

Bewildered about your indirectly chosen, so-called National Assemblies,[168] bewildered about the renewed expulsions of German citizens from German cities, bewildered about the tyranny of the sabre in Mainz, Trier, Aachen, Mannheim, Ulm, and Prague, bewildered about the arrests and political trials in Berlin, Cologne, Düsseldorf, Breslau[c] etc.

But there was one thing left to you, upright German, the clubs! You were able to attend the clubs and to complain to the public about the political swindles of the last few months. You could pour out your heavy heart to like-minded fellow citizens and find consolation in the words of like-minded, equally oppressed patriots!

---

[a] Heinrich Heine, "An Georg Herwegh". In *Zeitgedichte.—Ed.*
[b] Ibid.—*Ed.*
[c] Wrocław.—*Ed.*

But now even this has come to an end. The clubs are incompatible with the preservation of "order". In order that "confidence may be restored" it is urgently necessary to put an end to the subversive activities of the clubs.

Yesterday we related that the *Württemberg* Government downright *prohibited* the Democratic District Association in Stuttgart by a royal ordinance.[a] One does not even bother any longer to haul the leaders of the clubs before a court but instead falls back upon the old police measures. Yes, the gentlemen *Harpprecht, Duvernoy* and *Maucler* who countersigned this ordinance go even further: they prescribe extra-legal penalties for the violators of this prohibition, penalties of up to one-year imprisonment. They devise penal laws, without the Chambers' approval, and exceptional penal laws at that, merely "on the strength of Paragraph 89 of the Constitution".

It is no better in *Baden.* Today we report the prohibition of the Democratic Student Union in Heidelberg.[b] There, generally, the right of association is not so openly contested except in the case of the *students,* on the strength of the old, long abolished special laws of the Federal Diet,[169] the students are threatened by the penalties prescribed by these invalid laws.

We shall now probably have to expect the suppression of our clubs next.

We have a National Assembly in Frankfurt so that the governments may take such measures in complete safety without incurring the wrath of public opinion. This Assembly will, of course, pass over these police measures to the agenda just as lightly as over the revolution in Mainz.[c]

Thus it is not in order to achieve anything in the Assembly but merely in order to force the majority of the Assembly to proclaim once again before all Germany its alliance with reaction that we call upon the deputies of the extreme Left in Frankfurt to propose:

That the originators of these measures, particularly Herr Harpprecht, Herr Duvernoy, Herr Maucler and Herr Mathy, *be impeached* for violating the fundamental rights of the German people.

Written by Engels on July 19, 1848

First published in the *Neue Rheinische Zeitung* No. 50, July 20, 1848

Printed according to the newspaper

Published in English for the first time

---

[a] "Stuttgart, 15. Juli", *Neue Rheinische Zeitung* No. 49, July 19, 1848.— *Ed.*

[b] "Heidelberg, 17. Juli", *Neue Rheinische Zeitung* No. 50, July 20, 1848.— *Ed.*

[c] See this volume, pp. 17-19.— *Ed.*

THE PRUSSIAN PRESS BILL[170]

Cologne, July 19. We had thought that today we might be able to amuse our readers once again with the agreement debates, in particular to present to them the brilliant speech of Deputy Baumstark,[a] but events prevent us from doing so.

Charity begins at home. When the existence of the press is threatened, even Deputy Baumstark is abandoned.

Herr Hansemann has submitted to the Agreement Assembly a provisional press law. The paternal solicitude of Herr Hansemann for the press calls for immediate consideration.

In former times the *Code Napoléon* was beautified by the most edifying headings of the Prussian Law. Now, after the revolution, this has been changed: now, the Prussian Law is enriched by the most fragrant blossoms of the Code and the September Laws. Duchâtel, of course, is no Bodelschwingh.

We have already several days ago given the main points of the press Bill.[b] No sooner had a defamation trial given us the chance to prove that Articles 367 and 368 of the *Code pénal* stand in starkest contradiction to freedom of the press,[c] than Herr Hansemann proposes not only to extend them to the entire kingdom but also to make them three times worse. We rediscover in the new draft all that has already become dear and valued to us by practical experience:

---

[a] See the end of the article "The Debate on Jacoby's Motion", July 24, 1848 (this volume, pp. 242-47).— *Ed.*

[b] "Berlin, 14. Juli (Pressgesetz)", *Neue Rheinische Zeitung* No. 47, July 17, 1848.— *Ed.*

[c] See this volume, pp. 209-10.— *Ed.*

We find it prohibited—on pain of imprisonment from three months to three years—to make a charge against anybody which would make him punishable by law or merely "expose him to public contempt". We find it prohibited to demonstrate the truth of the matter in any other way than by a "valid legal document", in short, we rediscover the most classical monuments of the Napoleonic despotism over the press.

Indeed, Herr Hansemann keeps his promise to let the old provinces share in the advantages of Rhenish legislation!

Paragraph 10 of the Bill tops all these regulations: in the case of calumny directed at *state officials* in respect to the exercise of their official duties, the ordinary punishment may be *increased by half*.

If an official in the exercise or on the occasion (*à l'occasion*) of the exercise of his duties is *insulted in words* (*outrage par parole*), the punishment under Article 222 of the Penal Code is a prison sentence of from one month to two years. Despite the benevolent efforts of the Public Prosecutor's office, this article has hitherto not been used against the press, and for very good reasons. In order to remedy this situation, Herr Hansemann has transformed this article into the above-mentioned Paragraph 10. In the first place, "on the occasion" is transformed into the more convenient "in *respect* to the exercise of their duties". Secondly, the troublesome *par parole* is changed to *par écrit*. In the third place, the penalty is trebled.

From the day when this Bill becomes law, Prussian officials may relax. If Herr Pfuel brands Polish hands and ears with lunar caustic and the press publishes it—four and a half months to four and a half years imprisonment! If citizens are inadvertently thrown into prison even though it is known that they are not the right ones and the press communicates this fact—four and a half months to four and a half years imprisonment! If *Landräte* turn themselves into *commis voyageurs* for reaction and collectors of signatures for royalist addresses and the press unmasks these gentlemen—four and a half months to four and a half years imprisonment!

From the day when this Bill becomes law, officials, may with impunity carry out any arbitrary act, any tyrannical and any unlawful act. They may calmly administer beatings or order them, arrest and detain people without a hearing; the press, the only effective control, has been rendered ineffective. On the day when this Bill becomes law, the bureaucracy may celebrate a festival: it will have become mightier, less restrained and stronger than it was in the pre-March period.

Indeed, what remains of freedom of the press if that which *deserves* public contempt can no longer be held up to public contempt?

According to the laws hitherto in force the press could at least adduce facts to back up its general assertions and accusations. This will now come to an end. The press will no longer *report*, it will be allowed merely to *speak* in general *phrases* so that well-meaning people from Herr Hansemann down all the way to the beer-parlour politicians will have the right to say that the press is merely *reviling* and is not *proving* anything! Precisely for this reason the press is being prohibited from offering proofs!

We recommend, by the way, that Herr Hansemann make the following addition to his well-meaning draft. He should also declare it punishable to expose the officials to public ridicule besides penalising their exposure to public contempt. This omission might otherwise be painfully regretted.

We will not go in detail into the paragraphs dealing with obscenity or the regulations concerning confiscations etc. They surpass the *crème* of the press legislation of Louis Philippe and the Restoration. We do want to mention just one regulation: under Paragraph 21, the Public Prosecutor may request the confiscation not only of materials already printed but even of a *manuscript* which has only just been *handed over for printing*, if its contents condone a crime or offence that is liable to official prosecution! What a wide field of activity for philanthropic prosecutors! What a charming diversion to be able to go at any time to newspaper offices and demand to be shown for examination any "manuscript which has just been handed over for printing" since it might just be possible that it condoned a crime or offence!

Compared with this, how odd seems the solemn paragraph of the draft Constitution and of the "Fundamental Rights of the German Nation" which reads: *The censorship can never again be restored!*

Written by Marx on July 19, 1848   Printed according to the newspaper

First published in the *Neue Rheinische Zeitung* No. 50, July 20, 1848

THE *FAEDRELAND* ON THE ARMISTICE
WITH DENMARK[171]

Cologne, July 20. In order that the fatherland may see for itself that the so-called revolution with its National Assembly, Imperial Regent[a] etc. accomplished nothing more than a thorough revival of the famous Holy Roman Empire of the German nation,[172] we reprint the following article from the Danish *Faedreland.* It is to be hoped that the article will suffice to prove to even the most trusting friends of the established order that forty million Germans have once again been duped by two million Danes with the assistance of English mediation and Russian threats just as happened all the time under the "constant augmenters of the Empire".[b]

The *Faedreland,* Minister Orla Lehmann's own newspaper, speaks about the armistice as follows[c]:

"If one looks at the armistice solely from the vantage point of our own hopes and wishes one cannot, of course, be satisfied with it; if one assumes that the Government had the choice between this armistice and the prospect of expelling the Germans from Schleswig with Swedish and Norwegian aid, forcing them to recognise Denmark's right to settle the affairs of this duchy in conjunction with its inhabitants—then, indeed, one would have to admit that the Government has acted irresponsibly by agreeing to the armistice. This choice, however, did not exist. One has to assume that both England and Russia, the two great powers which have the most direct interest in this controversy and its settlement, have demanded the conclusion of an armistice as a condition for their future sympathy and mediation; that the Swedish-Norwegian Government has likewise demanded that an attempt at a peaceful arrangement be made before it decides to render any effective aid and that it will give such aid only with the delimitation set out at the very beginning, namely that such aid must not serve a reconquest of Schleswig but merely the defence of Jutland and the

---

[a] Archduke John of Austria.— *Ed.*
[b] Part of the title of the Holy Roman Emperors.— *Ed.*
[c] No. 179 of July 13, 1848.— *Ed.*

islands. Thus the alternative was as follows: on the one hand the gain of a respite so as to await the course of events abroad and to complete the political and military organisation at home; on the other hand the prospect of desperate single combat against superior strength; even if our army, which is half as strong as the federal army, were to have launched an assault upon the advantageous positions of the enemy, it would have been as good as impossible to achieve victory but the fight could well have led to the occupation of the entire peninsula by the Germans after the withdrawal of the Swedish-Norwegian forces; a combat which would at best have led to dearly bought, useless victories and at worst held out the prospect of the exhaustion of all our defence forces and a humiliating peace."

The Danish newspaper then proceeds to defend the conditions of the armistice as advantageous to Denmark. It describes as groundless the fear that the resumption of war would occur during the winter when the German troops could cross the ice to Fünen and Alsen.[a] The Germans would be as incapable as the Danes of sustaining a winter campaign in such a climate whereas the advantages of a three-month truce would be very great for both Denmark and the loyal population of Schleswig. If no peace was concluded within the three months, the armistice would be automatically prolonged until spring. The paper continues:

"The lifting of the blockade and the freeing of the prisoners will be approved; the return of the seized ships, however, may perhaps have aroused the dissatisfaction of certain individuals. It must be remembered that the capture of German ships was rather a means of coercion to deter the Germans from crossing our frontier, and had by no means the purpose of enriching ourselves by the acquisition of foreign private property; moreover, the value of these ships is not nearly so great as some would like to believe. If these ships were to come under the hammer during the present stagnation both in our own and in European trade generally, they would *at the very most* fetch $1^1/_2$ *million*, i.e. the cost of the war for two months. And in exchange for these ships we obtain the evacuation of both duchies by the Germans as well as compensation for the goods requisitioned in Jutland. Thus the means of coercion we have used has fulfilled its purpose and its now being halted is quite in order. It seems to us that *the evacuation of three counties by a superior army* which we had no prospect of evicting by our own strength makes up tenfold for the small advantage that the state might have derived from the sale of the seized ships."

Paragraph 7 is described as the most questionable one. It is supposed to prescribe the continuation of the special Government for the duchies which in fact means a continuation of "Schleswig-Holsteinism". The King of Denmark is supposed to be bound to the *notables* of Schleswig-Holstein for the selection of the two members of the Provisional Government and it would be quite difficult to find one who is not a "Schleswig-Holsteinian". In return, however, the "entire insurrection" is expressly disavowed, all decisions of the

---

[a] The Danish names are Fyn and Als.— *Ed.*

Provisional Government are annulled and the *status quo ante* March 17 is restored.

"Thus we have examined the most essential conditions of the armistice from a Danish point of view. Now, for a change, let us try to take the German point of view.

"All that Germany is demanding is the release of the ships and the lifting of the blockade.

"It gives up the following:

"Firstly, *the duchies,* occupied by an army which up to now has suffered no defeat and is strong enough to maintain its positions against an army twice as strong as the one which has confronted it up to now;

"Secondly, *Schleswig's admission to the Confederation,* which was solemnly announced by the Federal Diet and confirmed by the National Assembly's admission of the deputies from Schleswig;

"Thirdly, the *Provisional Government,* which it recognised as legitimate and with which it negotiated in that capacity;

"Fourthly, the *Schleswig-Holstein party,* whose demands, which were supported by the whole of Germany, have not been ratified but referred to the decision of non-German powers;

"Fifthly, the Augustenburg pretenders,[a] to whom the King of Prussia had personally pledged his support but who are not mentioned at all in the armistice, and who have been assured of neither amnesty nor asylum;

"Finally, *the costs caused by the war,* which are borne in part by the duchies and in part by the Confederation, but *which will be refunded insofar as they were borne by Denmark proper.*

"It seems to us that our overwhelmingly strong enemies have much more to find fault with in this armistice than we, the small, despised nation."

Schleswig has had the incomprehensible desire to become German. It is quite in order that it should be punished for that and that it should be left in the lurch by Germany.

Tomorrow we shall carry the text of the armistice.[b]

Written by Engels on July 20, 1848   Printed according to the newspaper

First published in the *Neue Rheinische Zeitung* No. 51, July 21, 1848   Published in English for the first time

---

[a] Duke Christian August and Prince Frederick of Schleswig-Holstein.— *Ed.*
[b] See this volume, pp. 266-69.— *Ed.*

THE CIVIC MILITIA BILL

[*Neue Rheinische Zeitung* No. 51, July 21, 1848]

Cologne, July 20. *The civic militia is disbanded,* that is the *chief paragraph* of the Bill on the establishment of a civic militia, even though this paragraph appears at the very end of it as Paragraph 121, in the modest form:

"By the establishment of the civic militia under this law, all armed units, which at present either belong to or exist side by side with the civic militia, are herewith disbanded."

The disbandment of the units which do not belong directly to the civic militia has started without much ado. The disbandment of the civic militia itself can only be brought about under the pretext of *reorganising* it.

Legislative propriety necessitated the inclusion of the conventional constitutional phrase in Paragraph 1:

"It is the *function* of the civic militia to *protect constitutional freedom* and lawful order."

In order to live up to the "*nature of this function*", however, the civic militia may neither think nor speak of public affairs nor consult or decide about them (Paragraph 1), neither assemble nor arm (Paragraph 6), nor show any sign of life except by permission of the superior authorities. It is not that the civic militia "protects" the Constitution from the authorities but rather the authorities protect the Constitution from the civic militia. Thus the civic militia has to "obey" blindly the "demands of the authorities" (Paragraph 4) and to abstain from all interference "in the activities of communal, administrative or judicial authorities", and must also abstain from all arguments. If it "refuses" to obey passively, the *Regierungspräsident* may *"suspend it from service"* for four weeks (Paragraph 4). If it should moreover arouse the royal displeasure, a "royal decree" may order "its *suspension*" for "six months", or even "disbandment"; thereupon it *shall* be re-formed only after six months have passed (Paragraph 3). Thus there "shall exist a civic militia in every community of the kingdom" (Paragraph 2), that is insofar as the *Regierungspräsident* or the King does not find it necessary to order the exact opposite in every community. Whereas matters of state are not within the "competence" of the civic militia, the civic militia, on the contrary, is "within the competence of the Minister of the Interior", i.e. the *Police Minister* who is its natural superior and who "by the nature of his function" is the faithful Eckart of "constitutional freedom" (Paragraph 5). Insofar as the civic militia is not ordered by the *Regierungspräsident* and the other officials "to protect constitutional freedom", i.e. to carry out the judgment of the authorities, i.e. to be commandeered for *service*, its specific life's work is to implement a set of *service regulations* designed by a royal *colonel*. This set of service regulations is its Magna Carta[173] for whose protection and execution it was, so to speak, created. Long live the *service regulations!* Finally, enrolment in the civic militia provides the occasion to make every Prussian "after completion of his 24th and before the completion of his 50th year of life" swear the following *oath*:

"I swear loyalty and obedience to the King, the Constitution and the laws of the kingdom."

The poor Constitution! How cramped, bashful, civilly modest and with what submissive attitude it stands between the King and the law. First there is the royalist oath, the oath of the dear faithful ones, then the constitutional oath and finally an oath which does not make any sense at all unless it be a legitimist one indicating that besides the laws derived from the Constitution there are still other laws which originate from royal authority. And now the good citizen belongs from head to foot to the "competence of the Ministry of the Interior".

This worthy fellow has received weapons and uniform on condition that he first of all relinquish his primary political rights, the right of association, etc. He fulfils his task to protect "constitutional freedom", according to the "nature of the function", by blindly carrying out the orders of the authorities, by exchanging the usual civil liberty which was tolerated even under the absolute monarchy for the passive, automatic and disinterested obedience of the soldier. A fine school, as Herr Schneider said in the Agreement

Assembly,[a] to bring up the republicans of the future! What has become of our *citizen?* A hybrid between a Prussian policeman and an English constable! Yet for all his losses he is consoled by the set of *service regulations* and the knowledge that he is obeying orders. Would it not be more original to dissolve the nation in the army rather than to dissolve the army in the nation?

This *transformation of constitutional phrases into Prussian facts* is a truly bizarre spectacle.

If Prussianism condescends to become constitutional, constitutionalism ought surely to take the trouble to become Prussian. Poor constitutionalism! Worthy Germans! They have been moaning for so long that the *"most solemn"* promises were not fulfilled. Soon they will have only *one* fear, the fear of seeing the fulfilment of these solemn promises! The nation is punished *par où il a péché.*[b] You have demanded *freedom of the press?* You will be *punished* by freedom of the press, and you will get censorship without censors, censorship by the Public Prosecutor's office, censorship by a law that discovers in the "nature of the function" of the press that it must be concerned with everything except the authorities, the infallible authorities, the censorship of prison sentences and fines. As the hart panteth after the water brooks, so you are to pant after the good old much-maligned and much-misunderstood censor, the last of the Romans under whose ascetic providence you led such a comfortable and safe life.

You demanded a *people's militia?* You will get a set of *service regulations.* You will be put at the disposal of the authorities. You will get military drill and schooling in passive obedience until your eyes water.

Prussian acumen has found out that every new constitutional institution offers the most interesting opportunity for new penal laws, new rules, new punishments, new supervision, new chicanery and new bureaucracy.

Still more constitutional demands! Still more constitutional demands! exclaims the Government of Action. We have an *act* for every demand!

Demand: Every citizen must be armed to protect "constitutional freedom".

Answer: From now on every citizen comes under the competence of the Ministry of the Interior.

---

[a] See this volume, pp. 233-35.— *Ed.*
[b] By its sins.— *Ed.*

It would be easier to recognise the Greeks in the shape of the animals into which Circe transformed them than to recognise the constitutional institutions in the fantastic images into which they have been transfigured by *Prussianism* and its *Government of Action.*

The *Prussian reorganisation of Poland* is followed by *the Prussian reorganisation of the civic militia!*

[*Neue Rheinische Zeitung* No. 52, July 22, 1848]

Cologne, July 21. We have seen that the "general stipulations" of the *civic militia* Bill amount to the following: the civic militia has ceased to exist. We shall touch very briefly upon yet some other sections of the Bill to distil from them the spirit of the "Government of Action", and here, too, we have to be selective in handling the raw materials of the pseudonymous institute. A great number of paragraphs presuppose new community and district regulations, a new administrative division of the monarchy etc., all creatures that conduct their hidden lives, as is well known, in the secret-pregnant womb of the Government of Action. Why then has the Government of Action issued the Bill on the reorganisation of the civic militia before the promised Bills on the community and district regulations etc.?

In Section III we find two service lists: the list of the respectable people serving in the civic militia and the list of citizens who are supported from public funds (Paragraph 14 [and Paragraph 16]). The host of officials, of course, is not included among the people who are supported from public funds. It is generally known that in Prussia these officials constitute the productive class proper. The poor, however, like the slaves in ancient Rome, "are only to be called up under extraordinary circumstances". If because of their civil dependence the poor are as little qualified to protect "constitutional freedom" as the *lazzaroni* in Naples,[174] do they deserve to occupy a subordinate position in this new institute of passive obedience?

Apart from the poor, we find a far more important distinction between the *solvent* and *insolvent* people on the active list of the militia.

But first another observation. Under Paragraph 53:

"Throughout the country, the civic militia must wear the same simple uniform prescribed by the King. The uniform must not be of such a kind that it gives occasion for confusion with the army."

Of course! The clothing must be of such a kind that the army is distinct from the civic militia and the civic militia from the people, and that no confusion can occur on such occasions as hand-to-hand combat, shooting and similar war manoeuvres. The *service* uniform *as such* is, however, as indispensable as the *service* list and the *service* regulations. It is precisely the *service* uniform which is the livery of freedom. This livery causes a significant rise in the cost of equipping a civic militiaman and the increased cost of this equipment gives the welcome excuse for creating an infinite abyss between *bourgeois* and *proletarian* members of the civic militia.

Listen to this:

Paragraph 57: "Every member of the civic militia must pay *out of his own pocket* for uniform (in case one is required), service badges and weapons. The community, however, is obliged to provide these items at its expense in the quantities required for the equipment of *soldiers on duty who cannot pay the costs from their own means*."

Paragraph 59: "The community retains the right of possession of the items of equipment that it has supplied and *it can keep these in special stores when not in service use*."

Thus, all those who cannot equip themselves militarily from top to toe, and that is the great majority of the Prussian population, the entire working class and a large part of the middle class, are *all* legally *disarmed* "except during the period of service", whereas the *bourgeois* section of the civic militia remains at all times in possession of its weapons and uniforms. Since in the guise of the "community" the same bourgeoisie "can keep in special stores the items of equipment that it has supplied", it is not only in possession of its *own* weapons but, in addition, is in possession of the weapons of the proletariat of the civic militia, and it "*can*" and "*will*" refuse to hand out these weapons even for "*service use*" if political collisions occur which are not to its liking. Thus the political privilege of capital has been restored in its most inconspicuous but most effective and decisive form. Capital has the privilege of possessing arms as opposed to those who own little, just as medieval feudal barons over against their serfs.

In order that this privilege should operate in its full exclusiveness, Paragraph 56 states that

"in the countryside and in towns of less than 5,000 inhabitants it suffices to arm civic militiamen with pikes or swords, and with this kind of armament only a *service badge* to be determined by the colonel need be worn in place of a uniform".

In all towns of *more than* 5,000 inhabitants the *uniform* must enlarge the *property qualification*, which alone enables a man to bear arms, and with it increase the numbers of the proletariat in the civic militia. Just as this proletariat, that is the largest part of the population, have uniforms and weapons only *on loan,* so they have the *right to bear arms* in general only *on loan;* their existence as servicemen is only on loan and—*beati possidentes,* blessed are the propertied! The moral uneasiness with which a *borrowed garb* envelops an individual, particularly in the case of soldiers where the borrowed uniform flits successively from one body to another, this moral uneasiness is, of course, the first requisite for Romans called upon "to protect constitutional freedom". By contrast, however, will not the proud self-esteem of the *solvent* civic militia grow, and what more can be desired?

And even these stipulations, which render the right to bear arms illusory for the greater part of the population, are encased in still more novel and more restrictive stipulations, in the interests of the propertied section of the population, the privileged capitalists.

For the community needs to have in stock merely enough items of equipment required by that part of the insolvent servicemen "who are on active service". Under Paragraph 15, the conditions for "active service" are as follows:

"In all communities where the total number of men currently available for service exceeds the 20th part of the population, the representatives of the community have the right to limit the personnel on active service to that part of the population. If they make use of this authorisation, they must lay down a service roster in such a way that all men currently available for service take their turn in due course. At every turn, however, not more than a third may leave at any one time; and all age groups must be called up at the same time in proportion to the available number of civic militiamen contained in each group."

And now one should try to calculate for what tiny fraction of the proletariat of the civic militia and the total population these items of equipment are *really* provided by the community?

In yesterday's article we observed how the *Government of Action* is reorganising the constitutional institution of the civic militia along the lines of the old-Prussian, bureaucratic state. Only today we see it at the height of its mission and observe how it is forming this institution of the civic militia along the lines of the July revolution and Louis Philippe and in the spirit of the epoch which crowns capital and pays homage

> With drums and trumpets
> To its youthful splendour.[a]

---

[a] Modified quotation from Heinrich Heine's poem "Berg-Idylle". In *Die Harzreise.—Ed.*

A few words to the Hansemann-Kühlwetter-Milde Government. A few days ago a circular letter against the intrigues of the reaction was sent by Herr Kühlwetter to every *Regierungspräsident*. What has led to this phenomenon?

The Government of Action intends to establish the rule of the bourgeoisie by simultaneously reaching a compromise with the old police and feudal state. While it is engaged in this dual and contradictory task, it sees that the rule of the bourgeoisie, which has still to be set up, and the existing Government itself are constantly outflanked by the absolutist and feudal reaction—and it is bound to succumb. The bourgeoisie cannot achieve domination without previously gaining the support of the people as a whole, and hence without acting more or less democratically.

But attempting to combine the Restoration period with the July period, and causing the bourgeoisie, which is still grappling with absolutism, feudalism, the country squires, and the rule of the military and the bureaucracy, already at this stage to exclude the people, and to subjugate and bypass it, is tantamount to attempting to square the circle. This is a historical problem which will frustrate the efforts even of a Government of Action, even of the Hansemann-Kühlwetter-Milde triumvirate.

[*Neue Rheinische Zeitung* No. 54, July 24, 1848]

Cologne, July 23. The section of the *civic militia Bill* which deals with the "*election and appointment of superiors*" is a genuine *labyrinth* of *electoral methods*. We want to play Ariadne and give the modern Theseus, the praiseworthy civic militia, the thread that will guide him through the labyrinth. The modern Theseus, however, will be as ungrateful as the ancient one and, having killed the Minotaur, will treacherously abandon his Ariadne, the press, upon the rock of Naxos.

Let us number the different passages of the labyrinth.

Passage One. Direct elections.

Paragraph 42. "The leaders of the civic militia up to and including captains, are elected by the civic militiamen on *active service*."

Side passage. "The civic militiamen on active service" constitute only a small part of the really "able-bodied" personnel. Compare Paragraph 15 [a] and our article of the day before yesterday.

---

[a] The *Neue Rheinische Zeitung* has "Paragraph 25", evidently a misprint.— *Ed.*

Thus the "direct" elections, too, are only so-called direct elections.
Passage Two. Indirect elections.

Paragraph 48. "The battalion's major is elected with an absolute majority of
votes by the captains, platoon leaders and corporals of the respective companies."

Passage Three. Combination of indirect elections with royal appointment.

Paragraph 49. "The *colonel* is appointed by the *King* from a list of three
candidates elected by the leaders of the respective battalions down to and including
the platoon leaders."

*Passage Four. Combination of indirect elections with appointment by the
commanders.*

Paragraph 50. "The respective commanders will appoint adjutants from among
the platoon leaders, battalion clerks from among the corporals and battalion
drum-majors from among the drummers."

Passage Five. Direct appointment by bureaucratic means.

Paragraph 50. "The sergeant and the clerk of a company are appointed by the
captain, the sergeant-major and the clerk of a squadron by a cavalry captain and the
corporal by the platoon leader."

Thus if these electoral methods begin with adulterated direct
elections, they end with the unadulterated cessation of *all* elections,
namely with the discretion of the captains, cavalry captains and
platoon leaders. *Finis coronat opus.*[a] This labyrinth has its apex, its
point.

The crystals—ranging from the effulgent colonel to the insignificant corporal—which are precipitated in this complicated chemical
process, settle for six years.

Paragraph 51. "Elections and appointments of leaders are made for *six* years."

It is hard to understand why after such precautionary measures
the Government of Action needed to commit another gaffe by
shouting in the face of the civic militia, in the "general regulations":
You are to be transformed from a *political* into a purely *police*
institution and you are to be reorganised as a nursery for *old-Prussian
drill.* Why take away the illusion?

The *royal* appointment is so like a *canonisation* that in the section on
"*Civic Militia Courts*" we find no courts for "*colonels*" but only courts
for ranks up to *major.* How could a royal colonel possibly commit a
crime?

In contrast, the mere existence as a militiaman is to such an extent
a *profanation* of the citizen, that a word from his superior officers, a

---

[a] The end crowns the work.— *Ed.*

word from the infallible royal colonel, or even from the first chap
that comes along who has been appointed sergeant by the captain or
corporal by the platoon leader, is enough to rob the militiaman of his
personal freedom for 24 hours and to have him arrested.

Paragraph 81. "Every superior may reprimand his *subordinate* while on service; he
can even *order* his *immediate arrest and imprisonment for 24 hours* if the subordinate is
guilty of drunkenness while on duty or *some other* gross violation of *service regulations.*"

The superior, of course, decides *what* constitutes *some other* gross
violation of service regulations and the *subordinate* has to obey orders.

Thus if the citizen at the very beginning of the Bill matures
towards the "nature of his function", the "protection of constitutional freedom", by ceasing to be what according to Aristotle is the
function of man—a *"zoon politikon"*, a "political animal" [a]—he only
completes his calling by surrendering his freedom as a citizen to the
discretion of a colonel or a corporal.

The *"Government of Action"* seems to subscribe to some peculiar
oriental-mystical notions, to a sort of *Moloch cult.* To protect the
"constitutional freedom" of *Regierungspräsidenten,* burgomasters,
police superintendents, chiefs of police and police inspectors,
officials of the public prosecution, presidents or directors of
law-courts, examining magistrates, justices of the peace, village
mayors, Ministers, clergymen, military personnel on active service,
frontier, customs, tax, forestry and postal officials, superintendents
and warders of all kinds of penal institutions, the executive security
officers and of the people under 25 and over 50 years of age—all of
them persons who according to Paragraphs 9, 10, and 11 do not
belong to the civic militia—to protect the "constitutional freedom"
of this élite of the nation, the rest of the nation must let its
constitutional freedom and even personal freedom die a bloody
sacrificial death upon the altar of the fatherland. *Pends-toi,Figaro! Tu
n'aurais pas inventé cela!*[b]

It is hardly necessary to mention that the section dealing with
penalties has been worked out with voluptuous thoroughness. The
entire institution, in accordance with "the nature of its function", is,
of course, to be purely a penalty for the desire of the praiseworthy
citizenry to have a Constitution and a civic militia. We merely observe
that in addition to the *legally* determined criminal cases, the *service
regulations,* the Magna Carta of the civic militia, devised by the *royal
colonel* in consultation with the major and with the permission of the

---

[a] Aristotle, *Politica,* I, 1, 9.— *Ed.*

[b] Hang yourself, Figaro, you would not have thought of that! (Modified quotation
from Beaumarchais' *La folle journée, ou le mariage de Figaro,* Act V, Scene 8.) — *Ed.*

apocryphal "district representation", give rise to a new specimen collection of penalties (see Paragraph 82 and the subsequent paragraphs). It goes without saying that *fines* can be substituted for *imprisonment* so that the difference between the *solvent* and *insolvent* members of the civic militia, i.e. the difference between the *bourgeoisie* and the *proletariat* of the civic militia invented by the "Government of Action", may enjoy penal sanction.

The *exempt judiciary*, which the Government of Action had by and large to give up in the Constitution, is smuggled back again into the civic militia. All disciplinary offences of the men and corporals of the civic militia are within the competence of company courts consisting of two platoon leaders, two corporals and three civic militiamen (Paragraph 87). All disciplinary offences of "leaders of companies belonging to the battalion, from platoon leaders up to and including majors", are under the jurisdiction of battalion courts consisting of two captains, two platoon leaders and three corporals (Paragraph 88). For the major there is a specially exempt judiciary since the same Paragraph 88 prescribes that "if the investigation concerns a major, the battalion court will be joined by two majors serving as members of the court". Finally, a colonel, as has already been mentioned, is *exempt* from any court.

The admirable Bill ends with the following paragraph:

(Paragraph 123.) "The rules concerning the participation of the civic militia in the defence of the fatherland in case of war and its armament, equipment and provisioning to be carried out then are reserved for the law on the organisation of the army."

In other words: *the old army reserve continues to exist side by side with the reorganised civic militia.*

Does not the *Government of Action* deserve to be *impeached* just because of this Bill and the projected armistice with Denmark?

Written on July 20-23, 1848

First published in the *Neue Rheinische Zeitung* Nos. 51, 52 and 54, July 21, 22 and 24, 1848

Printed according to the newspaper

Published in English for the first time

THE ARMISTICE WITH DENMARK [175]

Cologne, July 21. As our readers know, we have always regarded the Danish war with great equanimity. We have joined neither in the blatant bluster of the nationalists, nor in the well-worn tune of the sham enthusiasm for sea-girt Schleswig-Holstein.[a] We knew our country too well, we knew what it means to rely on Germany.

Events have fully borne out our views. The unimpeded capture of Schleswig by the Danes, the recapture of the country and the march to Jutland, the retreat to the Schlei, the repeated capture of the duchy up to Königsau [b]—this utterly incomprehensible conduct of the war from first to last has shown the Schleswigers what sort of protection they can expect from the revolutionary, great, strong, united etc. Germany, from the supposedly sovereign nation of forty-five million. However, in order that they lose all desire to become German, and that the "Danish yoke" appear infinitely more desirable to them than "German liberty", Prussia, in the name of the German Confederation,[176] has negotiated the armistice of which we print today a word-for-word translation.

Hitherto it has been the custom, when signing an armistice, for the two armies to maintain their positions, or at most a narrow neutral strip was interposed between them. Under this armistice, the first result of the "prowess of Prussian arms", the victorious Prussians withdraw over 20 miles, from Kolding to this side of Lauenburg, whereas the defeated Danes maintain their positions at Kolding and

---

[a] Engels paraphrases the first words of a song which was written by Matthäus Friedrich Chemnitz in 1844.—*Ed.*

[b] The Danish name is Kongeaa.—*Ed.*

relinquish only Alsen.[a] Furthermore, in the event of the armistice being called off, the Danes are to advance to the positions they held on June 24, in other words they are to occupy a six to seven miles wide stretch of North Schleswig without firing a shot—a stretch from which they were *twice* driven out—whereas the Germans are allowed to advance only to Apenrade[b] and its environs. Thus "the honour of German arms is preserved" and North Schleswig, exhausted because it was deluged with troops four times, is promised a possible fifth and sixth invasion.

But that is not all. A part of Schleswig is to be occupied by Danish troops even during the armistice. Under Clause 8, Schleswig is to be occupied by regiments recruited in the duchy, i.e. partly by soldiers from Schleswig who took part in the movement, and partly by soldiers who at that time were stationed in Denmark and fought in the ranks of the Danish army against the Provisional Government. They are commanded by Danish officers and are in every respect *Danish* troops. That is how the Danish papers, too, size up the situation.

The *Faedreland* of July 13 writes:

"The presence in the duchy of *loyal* troops from Schleswig will undoubtedly substantially harden popular feeling which, now that the country has experienced the misfortunes of war, will forcefully turn against those who are the cause of these misfortunes."

On top of that we have the movement in Schleswig-Holstein. The Danes call it a *riot*, and the Prussians *treat* it *as a riot.* The Provisional Government, which has been recognised by Prussia and the German Confederation, is mercilessly sacrificed; all laws, decrees etc., issued after Schleswig became independent, are abrogated; on the other hand, the repealed Danish laws have again come into force. In short, the reply concerning *Wildenbruch's* famous Note, a reply which Herr Auerswald refused to give,[c] can be found here in Clause 7 of the proposed armistice. Everything that was revolutionary in the movement is ruthlessly destroyed, and the Government created by the revolution is to be replaced by a legitimate administration nominated by three legitimate monarchs. The troops of Holstein and Schleswig are again to be *commanded by Danes and thrashed by Danes*; the ships of Holstein and Schleswig are to remain "*Dansk-Eiendom*"[d] as before, despite the latest order of the Provisional Government.

---

[a] The Danish name is Als.— *Ed.*
[b] The Danish name is Aabenraa.— *Ed.*
[c] See this volume, p. 191.— *Ed.*
[d] "Danish property."— *Ed.*

The new Government which they intend to set up puts the finishing touch to all this. The *Faedreland*[a] declares:

"Though in the limited electoral district from which the Danish-elected members of the new Government are to be chosen we shall probably not find the combination of energy, talent, intelligence and experience which Prussia will dispose of when making her selection", this is not decisive. "The members of the Government must of course be elected from among the population of the duchies, but no one prevents us giving them secretaries and assistants *born* and *residing in other parts of the country*. In selecting these secretaries and administrative advisers one can be guided by considerations of fitness and talent without regard to local considerations, and it is likely that these men will exert a great influence on the spirit and trend of the administration. Indeed, it is to be hoped that even *high-ranking Danish officials* will accept such a post, though its official status may be inferior. Every true Dane will consider such a post an honour under the present circumstances."

This semi-official paper thus promises the duchies that they will be swamped not only with Danish troops but also with Danish civil servants. A partly Danish Government will take up its residence in Rendsburg on the officially recognised territory of the German Confederation.

These are the advantages which the armistice brings Schleswig. The advantages for Germany are just as great. The admission of Schleswig to the German Confederation is not mentioned at all. On the contrary, the decision of the Confederation is *flatly repudiated* by the composition of the new Government. The German Confederation chooses the members for Holstein, and the King of Denmark chooses those *for Schleswig*. Schleswig is therefore under Danish, and not German, jurisdiction.

Germany would have rendered a real service in this Danish war if she had compelled Denmark to abolish the Sound tax, a form of old feudal robbery.[177] The German seaports, hard hit by the blockade and the seizure of their ships, would have willingly borne the burden even longer if it led to the abolition of the Sound tax. The governments also made it known everywhere that the abolition of this tax must at any rate be brought about. And what came of all this boastfulness? Britain and Russia want the tax kept, and of course Germany obediently acquiesces.

It goes without saying that in exchange for the return of the ships, the goods requisitioned in Jutland have to be refunded, on the principle that Germany is rich enough to pay for her glory.

These are the advantages which the Hansemann Ministry offers to the German nation in this draft armistice. These are the fruits of a war waged for three months against a small nation of a million and a

---

[a] No. 180, July 14, 1848.— *Ed.*

half. That is the result of all the boasting by our national papers, our formidable Dane-haters!

It is said that the armistice will not be concluded. General Wrangel, encouraged by Beseler, has definitely refused to sign it, despite repeated requests by Count Pourtalès, who brought him Auerswald's order to sign it, and despite numerous reminders that it was his duty as a Prussian general to do so. Wrangel stated that he is above all subordinated to the German Central Authority, and the latter will not approve of the armistice unless the armies maintain their present positions and the Provisional Government remains in office until the peace is concluded.

Thus the Prussian project will probably not be carried out, but it is nevertheless interesting as a demonstration of how Prussia, when she takes over the reins, defends Germany's honour and interests.

Written by Engels on July 21, 1848   Printed according to the newspaper

First published in the *Neue Rheinische Zeitung* No. 52, July 22, 1848

THE ARMISTICE "NEGOTIATIONS"

The armistice has still neither been signed nor definitively rejected. Reports both from Wrangel's headquarters and from Copenhagen continually contradict one another. All that is certain is that Wrangel initially refused to sign, that Mr. Reedtz returned to Copenhagen with this refusal and that as a result fresh troops were embarked for Jutland from the 15th July onwards. The *Börsen-Halle* says[a] that on receiving the news of another three-day cease-fire the English and Swedish ambassadors,[b] together with Mr. Reedtz, left Copenhagen for Kolding. They are said to be joining General Neumann, who has been sent there from Berlin, in an attempt to overcome Wrangel's opposition.

All this news reaches us via Copenhagen, while from Berlin and from Wrangel's headquarters we hear nothing but empty rumours. Our present constitutional right of access to information is in this sense no different from the old mystery-mongering. We read of the things which concern us most closely in the newspapers of countries furthest away from us.

According to a letter in the *Faedreland* the Jutes have reacted fairly peacefully to the German invasion.

Written by Engels on or about July 23, 1848

First published in the *Neue Rheinische Zeitung* No. 54, July 24, 1848

Printed according to the newspaper

Published in English for the first time

---

[a] "Kopenhagen, den 19. Juli", *Börsen-Halle* No. 11224, July 21, 1848.— *Ed.*
[b] Henry Wynn and Elias Lagerheim.— *Ed.*

THE *CONCORDIA* OF TURIN

Cologne, July 23. We have recently mentioned the newspaper *L'Alba* which appears in Florence and which has held out its fraternal hand to us across the Alps.[a] It was to be expected that another journal, *La Concordia* in Turin, a newspaper of opposite colours, should declare itself in an opposite, though by no means hostile, manner. In a former issue *La Concordia* expressed the opinion that the *Neue Rheinische Zeitung* backs any group as long as it is "*oppressed*".[b] The paper was led to this not very sensible invention by our judgment of the events in Prague and our sympathy for the democratic forces against the reactionary Windischgrätz and Co.[c] Perhaps the Turin journal has become more enlightened in the meantime about the so-called *Czech* movement.

Lately, however, *La Concordia*[d] felt induced to devote a more or less doctrinaire article to the *Nuova Gazzetta Renana*.[e] It has read in our newspaper the programme for the Workers' Congress[178] which is to be convened in Berlin and the eight points which are to be discussed by the workers are disturbing it to a significant degree.

After faithfully translating the whole, it begins a sort of criticism with the following words:

"There is much that is true and just in these proposals, but the *Concordia* would betray its mission if it did not raise its voice against the errors of the socialists."

---

[a] See this volume, p. 167.—*Ed.*
[b] *La Concordia* No. 161, July 7, 1848.—*Ed.*
[c] See this volume, pp. 91-93 and 119-20.—*Ed.*
[d] *La Concordia* No. 168, July 15, 1848.—*Ed.*
[e] *Neue Rheinische Zeitung.*—*Ed.*

We on our part protest against the "error" of the *Concordia* which consists in mistaking the programme issued by the respective commission for the Workers' Congress, and which we merely reported, for *our own*. We are nevertheless ready to enter upon a discussion on political economy with the *Concordia* as soon as its programme offers something more than a few well-known philanthropic phrases and picked-up free trade dogmas.

Written on July 23, 1848

First published in the *Neue Rheinische Zeitung* No. 55, July 25, 1848

Printed according to the newspaper

Published in English for the first time

THE AGREEMENT DEBATES ON THE DISTRICT ESTATES

(AGREEMENT SESSION OF JULY 18)

Cologne, July 25. Among the many confused, purposeless and purely personal documents and negotiations that occur at the beginning of each session, we want to stress today two points.

The first one is the declaration by ex-Minister *Rodbertus*, submitted in writing to the President and repeated from the rostrum: It is true that he had put his name down as a speaker *against* Jacoby's motion[a] but, for all that, had wanted to speak *only* against its first part, which disapproves of the Frankfurt decision, and *at the same time against* the respective *declaration of the Ministry* made on July 4. As is known, the debate was broken off before Herr Rodbertus had the opportunity to speak.

The second point is a declaration by Herr *Brodowski* in the name of all Polish deputies made with regard to any possible declaration of the German-Polish delegates: He did not recognise the legality of the incorporation of a part of Posen into the German Confederation on the grounds of the treaties of 1815 and the declaration of the Provincial Estates, provoked by the King, *against* its admission into the Confederation.[179]

"I do not know of a subsequent *legal way* because *the nation has not yet been consulted on it.*"

Then follows the final debate on the address. As is known, the address was rejected amid shouts of the Left: "Twice repeated question of confidence!" and general laughter.

Now it was the turn of the committee's report dealing with the motion of 94 deputies to rescind the authority of the District Estates to levy taxes.

---

[a] See this volume, p. 232.—*Ed.*

11*

We are going into this matter deliberately. It makes us recall once again a piece of genuine old-Prussian legislation, and the mounting reaction more and more holds up this legislation to us as a faultless model, while the Government of Action, not wanting to represent the Government of transition, becomes every day more of an unabashed eulogist for the Bodelschwingh Ministry.

By a series of laws, all of which are of more recent date than 1840, the District Estates have been authorised to decide upon taxes with binding effect for the inhabitants of the districts.

These District Estates are a marvellous example of old-Prussian "representation". All the large landowning peasants of the district send *three* deputies. As a rule, every town sends *one*; but *every squire is a member of the District Estates by virtue of his birth*. Not at all represented are the workers and part of the petty bourgeoisie in the towns, and the small proprietors and non-established inhabitants in the countryside, who together form the overwhelming majority. These non-represented classes are nevertheless taxed by the deputies, namely by the gentlemen who are "members of the District Estates by virtue of their birth"; how and for which purposes we shall see presently.

These District Estates, who moreover are entitled to dispose quite independently of the district assets, are in decisions on taxation bound by the permission either of the *Oberpräsident* or of the King, and additionally, when they are divided and one estate votes in a different way, by the decision of the Minister of the Interior. One can see how cunningly the old Prussianism knew how to preserve the "vested rights" of the big landowners, but at the same time also the right of superintendence of the bureaucracy.

The fact that the right of superintendence of the bureaucracy exists only in order to prevent any encroachment by the District Estates on the rights of the officialdom and not in order to protect the inhabitants of the district, particularly those who are not represented at all, from encroachments by the District Estates, has been expressly recognised by the report of the central commission.

The report closes with the motion to rescind the laws which entitle the District Estates to levy taxes.

Herr *Bucher*, who gave the report, speaks to the motion. Precisely those decisions of the District Estates which most oppressed and embittered the non-represented ones, had been singled out by the local governments for confirmation.

"It is precisely a curse of the police state, which in principle has been abolished but which in fact unfortunately continues to exist to this day, that the higher the standing of an official or authority in this hierarchy of mandarins, the more they feel that they are able also to understand such detailed measures although they are that much further removed from local needs."

The proposal was the more commendable since it was not constructive but merely *destructive*.

"It cannot be denied that up to now the Assembly has *not* been *fortunate* in its attempts at *productive* activity ... it might be advisable, therefore, to devote ourselves for the time being more to *destructive* activity."

The speaker suggests accordingly that especially the reactionary laws issued since 1815 should be abolished.

This was too much. The reporter had not only denounced old Prussianism, bureaucracy and the District Estates, he had even cast an ironic side-glance at the products of the agreement debates so far. Here was a favourable opportunity for the Ministry. In any case, even out of consideration for the Court, it could not admit that only the laws issued by the present King[a] would be rescinded.

Herr *Kühlwetter* therefore rises.

"The District Estates are constituted in such a way that their constitution will undoubtedly be changed because"—the whole business of estates altogether contradicts the principle of equality before the law? On the contrary! Merely "because now every squire is still a member of the District Estates by virtue of his birth, a town, however, no matter *how many manors* it may contain, is entitled to send only one deputy to the District Estates and the rural communities are represented by only three deputies".

Let us take a look at the hidden plans of the Government of Action. The estate system had to be abolished in the central national representation, that could not be avoided. In the smaller areas of representation, however, that is in the local districts (perhaps also in the provinces?), the attempt will be made to *preserve the representation by estates* by doing away with only the most egregious advantages of the squirearchy over the burghers and peasants. That Herr Kühlwetter's explanation cannot be interpreted in any other way emerges from the fact that the report of the central commission directly refers to the application of the principle of equality before the law in the district representation. Herr Kühlwetter, however, passes over this point in deepest silence.

Herr Kühlwetter has no objection to the *content* of the motion. He is merely asking whether it is necessary to give validity to the motion by "way of legislation".

"The danger that the District Estates may abuse their right to tax is *surely not so great*.... The Government's right of supervision is *by no means so illusory* as has been presented; it has *always* been exercised conscientiously and in that way 'the lowest class of tax payers has been relieved from contributions as much as possible'."

_____

[a] Frederick William IV.— *Ed.*

Of course! Herr Kühlwetter was a bureaucrat under Bodelschwingh and even at the risk of compromising the entire Government of Action he has to defend the past heroic deeds of the Bodelschwingh bureaucracy. We notice that Herr Hansemann was absent when his colleague Kühlwetter made him fraternise so much with Herr Bodelschwingh.

Herr Kühlwetter declares that he has already instructed all the local governments not to confirm any more taxation by the District Estates until further notice, and with that the purpose is surely achieved.

Herr *Jentzsch* spoils the Minister's game by observing that it is the District Estates' custom to assess the turnpike tolls, which benefit the manorial estates most, in accordance with the *principles of the graduated tax from which the estates of the aristocracy are entirely exempted.*

Herr *Kühlwetter* and Herr *von Wangenheim*, who is an interested party, attempt to defend the District Estates. In particular von Wangenheim, a Justice of the Court of Appeal, District Estate of Saatzig, delivers a long eulogy on this laudable institution.

Deputy *Moritz*, however, again thwarts the effect. What good is Herr Kühlwetter's instruction? If the Ministry should one day have to resign, the local governments would disregard the instruction. If we have laws as bad as these, I cannot see why we should not rescind them. And as far as the denied abuses are concerned,

"not only have the District Estates abused their authority to levy taxes by showing *personal favouritism*, by deciding upon expenditures which were not for the common good of the district, but they have even decided upon highway construction in the interest of certain individuals, of a privileged class.... The district town of Ruppin was to be connected to the railway line Hamburg-Berlin. Instead of letting the highway pass through the town of Wusterhausen, the *local Government refused* to let this highway run through this small, impoverished town—even though this town declared that it would pay the additional cost from its own funds—and on the contrary decided that the highway was to run through *three estates of one and the same lord of the manor*"!!

Herr *Reichenbach* calls attention to the fact that the Ministry's instruction has no effect whatsoever upon the district assets which are entirely at the disposal of the District Estates.

The *Minister* replies with a few lame phrases.

Herr *Bucher* declares that in his opinion the Minister is by no means *entitled* to issue instructions, which *in effect rescind* existing laws. Only by legislation could an improvement be brought about.

Herr Kühlwetter stammers yet a few more incoherent words to defend himself, and then a vote is taken.

The Assembly adopts the motion of the central commission whereby the laws authorising the District Estates to levy taxes and dispose of the district assets are rescinded, with the addendum:

"decisions of the District Estates taken on the basis of these decrees notwithstanding".

It is obvious that the "acts" of the Government of Action consist of police-type attempts at reaction and parliamentary defeats.

(To be continued) [a]

Written by Engels on July 25, 1848

First published in the *Neue Rheinische Zeitung* No. 56, July 26, 1848

Printed according to the newspaper

Published in English for the first time

---

[a] See Engels' article "The Agreement Debate about the Valdenaire Affair" (pp. 301-04 of this volume).—*Ed.*

THE BILL ON THE COMPULSORY LOAN AND ITS MOTIVATION [180]

[*Neue Rheinische Zeitung* No. 56, July 26, 1848]

Cologne, July 25. A notorious rogue of London's blessed district of St. Giles appeared before the Assizes. He was accused of having relieved the chest of a notorious City miser of £2,000.

"Gentlemen of the jury," began the accused, "I will not lay claim to your patience for very long. Since my defence will be of an economical nature, I shall use words economically. I have taken £2,000 from Mr. Cripps. Nothing is more certain than that. I have, however, only taken from a private person in order to give to the public. What happened to the £2,000? Did I perhaps keep them egoistically? Search my pockets. I will sell you my soul for a farthing if you are able to find one penny. You will find the £2,000 at the tailor's, the shopkeeper's,[a] the restaurateur's etc. Thus what have I done? I have taken '*idle* sums of money which' could be retrieved from the grave, in which avarice kept them, '*only by a compulsory loan*' and '*put them into circulation*'. I was an agent of circulation and circulation is the foremost requirement for national wealth. Gentlemen, you are Englishmen! You are economists! You will surely not condemn a benefactor of the nation!"

The economist of St. Giles resides in Van Diemen's Land[b] and has the opportunity to think about the blind ingratitude of his fellow countrymen.

He did not live in vain, however. His principles form the basis of *Hansemann's compulsory loan*.

Explaining the *motives* for this measure, Herr Hansemann states that "the admissibility of the compulsory loan rests upon the well-founded supposition that a major portion of the available cash lies *idle* in the possession of private individuals in *small and large sums* and *can be put into circulation only by a compulsory loan*".

---

[a] This word is in English in the German original.— *Ed.*
[b] Now Tasmania. From 1803 to 1854 a British penal colony.—*Ed.*

When you *consume* a capital, you bring it into circulation. If you do not bring it into circulation, the state will *consume* it in order to bring it into circulation.

A cotton manufacturer employs 100 workers, for example. He pays to each of them 9 silver groschen daily. Thus every day 900 silver groschen, i.e. 30 talers, migrate from his pocket into the pockets of the workers and from there into the pockets of the *epiciers*,[a] landlords, shoemakers, tailors etc. This migration of the 30 talers is known as their *circulation*. From the moment when the manufacturer can sell his cotton material only at a loss or not at all, he ceases to produce and to employ his workers, and with the cessation of production the migration of the 30 talers, i.e. their *circulation*, ceases. We shall create circulation by force! exclaims Hansemann. Why does the manufacturer let his money lie *idle*? Why does he not let it circulate? When the weather is fine, many people circulate in the open air. Hansemann drives the people outside and forces them to circulate so as to create fine weather. What a great weather-maker!

The ministerial and commercial crisis robs the capital of bourgeois society of its interest. The state helps society to its legs by taking away its capital as well.

In his book on *Circulation*[b] the Jew *Pinto*, the famous eighteenth-century stock exchange speculator, recommends speculating in stocks. He states that although speculation does not produce circulation, it promotes circulation, that is the migration of wealth from one pocket into another. Hansemann is transforming the exchequer into a wheel of fortune upon which the property of the citizens circulates. Hansemann-Pinto!

In his *"preamble"* for the "Bill on the Compulsory Loan", Hansemann is encountering one great difficulty. Why has the *voluntary loan* not produced the required sums?

The "unreserved confidence" which the present Government enjoys is well known. Also well known is the rapturous patriotism of the big bourgeoisie whose main complaint is that a few agitators have the insolence not to share its confidence. The loyalty declarations from all the provinces are well known. But "for a' that and a' that",[c] Hansemann is compelled to transform the poetic voluntary loan into the prosaic compulsory loan!

For example, in the district of Düsseldorf, aristocrats have

---

[a] Grocers.—*Ed.*

[b] Isaac Pinto, *Traité de la circulation et du crédit.—Ed.*

[c] Quoted from Ferdinand Freiligrath's translation ("Trotz alledem!") of Robert Burns' poem "For a' that and a' that".—*Ed.*

contributed 4,000 talers and officers 900 talers, and where does more confidence reign than among the aristocrats and officers of the district of Düsseldorf? We will not even mention the contributions of the princes of the Royal House.

But let Hansemann explain this phenomenon to us.

"Up to now *voluntary* contributions have come in slowly. This is *probably* to be ascribed *less to a lack of confidence* in our state of affairs than to the *uncertainty* about the *real needs* of the state, since people seem to believe it permissible to wait and see *if and to what extent the monetary resources of the nation might be drawn upon.* On this *circumstance* rests the hope that everybody will contribute *voluntarily* according to his ability once the *duty to contribute* has been demonstrated to be an *imperative necessity.*"

The state, finding itself in dire need, appeals to patriotism. It politely asks patriotism to deposit 15 million talers on the altar of the fatherland, and moreover not as a gift but only as a voluntary *loan.* One possesses the greatest confidence in the state but turns a deaf ear towards its cry for help! Unfortunately one finds oneself in such a state of "*uncertainty*" about the "*real needs* of the state" that one decides after the greatest spiritual torment not to give the state *anything* for the time being. One has, indeed, the greatest confidence in the state authority, and the honourable state authority claims that the state needs 15 million talers. It is certainly due to confidence that one does not trust the assertions of the state authority and rather views its clamour for 15 million as a mere frivolity.

There is a famous story about a stout-hearted *Pennsylvanian* who never lent a dollar to his friends. He had such confidence in their orderly mode of life, and he gave such credit to their business that to the day of his death he never gained the "certainty" that they were in "real need" of a dollar. He regarded their impetuous demands as rather a test of his confidence, and the confidence of this man was unshakeable.

The Prussian state authority found the entire state inhabited by Pennsylvanians.

Herr Hansemann, however, explains this strange economic phenomenon by yet another peculiar "*circumstance*".

The people did not contribute voluntarily "because they believed it permissible to wait and see *if and to what extent their monetary resources might be drawn upon*". In other words: nobody paid voluntarily because everybody waited to see *if and to what extent* he would be *forced* to pay. What circumspect patriotism! What most canny confidence! It is upon this "*circumstance*", namely that behind the blue-eyed, sanguine voluntary loan there stands now the sinister, hypochondriacal compulsory loan, that Herr Hansemann "rests his *hope* that everybody will contribute *voluntarily* according to his ability". By now even the most obdurate doubter must have lost his uncertainty and must have gained the conviction that the state authority is really serious about its need for money. The entire misfortune, as we have seen, lay just in this embarrassing uncertainty. If you do not give, it will be taken from you, and the taking will cause both you and us inconvenience. We hope, therefore, that your confidence will lose some of its exaggerated character and will express itself in well-ringing talers instead of hollow-sounding phrases. *Est-ce clair?*[a]

Much as Herr Hansemann is basing his "*hopes*" upon this "*circumstance*", he has nevertheless himself become infected by the brooding temperament of his *Pennsylvanians* and he feels induced to look around for yet stronger *incentives* to confidence. The confidence indeed exists but it does not want to reveal itself. It needs *incentives* to drive it out of its latent state.

"In order to create an even stronger motive" (than the prospect of the compulsory loan) "for voluntary participation, however, Paragraph 1 projects an interest rate of $3^1/_3$ per cent for the loan, and a date" (October 1) "is left open up to which voluntary loans are to be accepted at 5 per cent."

Thus Herr Hansemann puts a *premium* of $1^2/_3$ per cent upon voluntary loans, and now, to be sure, patriotism will flow freely, coffers will jump open and the golden flood of confidence will stream into the exchequer.

Herr Hansemann naturally finds it "just" to pay the big shots $1^2/_3$ per cent more than he is paying the little people who will part with their essentials only under duress. In addition they will have to bear the *cost of the appeal* as punishment for their less comfortable circumstances.

Thus the biblical saying is realised. For whosoever hath, to him shall be given; but whosoever hath not, from him shall be taken away even that he hath.[b]

[*Neue Rheinische Zeitung* No. 60, July 30, 1848]

Cologne, July 29. Just as Peel once invented a "sliding scale" [181] for the duty on corn, Hansemann-Pinto has invented one for involuntary patriotism.

"A progressive scale will be employed for the obligatory contributions," our Hansemann says in his preamble, "since the ability to supply money obviously rises in *arithmetical* progression with the amount of a person's wealth."

---

[a] Is that clear?—*Ed.*
[b] Matthew 13:12.—*Ed.*

The ability to supply money rises with wealth. In other words: the more money one has at one's disposal the more money one has to dispose of. So far, it is undoubtedly correct. The fact, however, that the ability to supply money rises only in *arithmetical* progression even if the various amounts of wealth are in *geometrical* proportion is a discovery by Hansemann which is bound to earn him greater fame with posterity than Malthus gained by the statement that food supply grows only in arithmetical progression whereas population grows in geometrical progression.[a]

Thus, for example, if different amounts of wealth are to each other as

1, 2, 4, 8, 16, 32, 64, 128, 256, 512,

then, according to Herr Hansemann's discovery, the ability to supply money grows in the ratio of

1, 2, 3, 4, 5, 6, 7, 8, 9, 10.

In spite of the apparent growth of the obligatory contribution, the ability to supply money, according to our economist, decreases to the same degree that wealth increases.

In a short story by Cervantes[b] we find the chief Spanish financier in a lunatic asylum. This man had discovered that the Spanish national debt would vanish as soon as

"the Cortes approve a law that all vassals of His Majesty between the ages of 14 and 60 are obliged to fast on bread and water for one day during each month, and that on a day freely to be chosen and decided. The monetary value of the fruits, vegetables, meat dishes, fish, wines, eggs and beans which would otherwise have been consumed on that day would be delivered to His Majesty, without holding back one penny on pain of punishment for perjury".

Hansemann shortens the procedure. He calls upon all his Spaniards who possess an annual income of 400 talers to find one day in the year on which they can do without 20 talers. According to the sliding scale, he has asked the small fry to refrain from just about all consumption for 40 days. If they cannot find the 20 talers between August and September, a bailiff will look for them in October in accordance with the words: seek and ye shall find.[c]

Let us further examine the "*preamble*" which the Prussian Necker reveals to us.

"Any income," he instructs us, "derived from industry in the widest sense of the word, that is irrespective of whether it is subject to a business tax, as is the case with

---

[a] [Th. R. Malthus,] *An Essay on the Principle of Population,* pp. 25-26.— *Ed.*
[b] Cervantes, *Novelas ejemplares: Coloquio de los perros.—Ed.*
[c] Matthew 7:7; Luke 11:9.—*Ed.*

doctors, lawyers etc., can only be taken into consideration *after the subtraction of the operating expenditures* including any interest to be paid on debts, *since the net income can only be found in this way*. For *the same reason the working capital* must be disregarded if the loan contribution which is calculated from *income exceeds that calculated from the working capital*."

Nous marchons de surprise en surprise.[a] The *income* can only be taken into consideration *after the subtraction of the working capital* since the compulsory loan can and ought to be nothing but an extraordinary form of *income tax*. And the operating costs belong as little to the income of an industrialist as the stem and root of a tree belong to its fruits. Hence *for the reason* that only the income is to be taxed and not the working capital, it is precisely the working capital that is taxed and not the income if this first method seems more profitable to the exchequer. Thus it is a matter of complete indifference to Herr Hansemann "in which way the *net* income is found". He is looking for "the way in which the *greatest* income is found" for the exchequer.

Herr Hansemann who lays hands on the working capital itself can be compared to a savage who cuts down a tree in order to seize hold of its fruits.

"Thus if" (Art. 9 of the Bill) "the loan contribution to be calculated from the working capital is greater than the tenfold amount of the income, the first method of estimation will be employed", that is one "will resort to" the "working capital" itself.

Hence the exchequer may base its demands upon wealth rather than income whenever it chooses.

The people demands inspection of the mysterious Prussian exchequer. The Government of Action answers this tactless demand by reserving the right to make a thorough inspection of the ledgers of all merchants and an inventory of the wealth of everybody. The constitutional era in Prussia opens not with the control of the finances of the state by the people but rather by letting the state control the wealth of the people so as to open the door to the most brazen intervention of the bureaucracy into civil intercourse and private relationships. In Belgium, too, the state has had recourse to a compulsory loan, but there it modestly limited itself to tax records and mortgage deeds, i.e. to available public documents. The Government of Action on the other hand introduces the Spartanism of the Prussian army into the Prussian national economy.

Hansemann, to be sure, attempts in his "preamble" to appease the citizen by all sorts of mild phrases and friendly persuasion.

---

[a] We go from one surprise to another.—*Ed.*

"The distribution of the loan," he whispers to him, "will be based upon *self-assessment.*" All "recrimination" is to be avoided.

"*Not even* a *summary* listing of the individual parts of one's property will be required.... The district commission set up to *examine self-assessments* will call for appropriate contributions by way of *amicable* exhortations, and only if this method should be unsuccessful will it estimate the amount. The citizen can *appeal* against this decision to a regional commission etc."

Self-assessment! Not even a *summary* listing of the individual parts of one's property! Amicable exhortations! Appeal!

Tell me, what more do you want?[a]

Let us start at the end, with the *appeal.*

Article 16 lays down:

"The collection will be carried out at the fixed dates *irrespective of any appeals made* with the proviso of repayment if the appeal is found justified."

Thus first comes the *execution,* the appeal notwithstanding, and afterwards the justification, the execution notwithstanding!

There is more to come!

"The costs" which are caused by the appeal "shall be borne by the appellant if his appeal is totally *or partially* rejected and if need be will be collected by executive action" (Art. 19).

Anybody who is familiar with the economic impossibility of an exact estimate of wealth will realise at first sight that an appeal can *always* be *partially* rejected and that the appellant will always be the loser. No matter what the nature of the appeal, a fine is its inseparable shadow. Let us have every respect for the appeal!

Let us return from the appeal, the end, to the beginning, the *self-assessment.*

Herr Hansemann does not appear to be afraid that his Spartans will assess themselves too heavily.

Under Art. 13

"voluntary declarations of the persons obliged to contribute are the *foundation* of the distribution of the loan".

Herr Hansemann's architecture is such that one cannot deduce the further outline of his structure from its foundation.

Or rather the "voluntary declaration" which, in the form of a "statement", is "to be filed with officials appointed by the Finance

---

[a] Modified quotation from Heinrich Heine, "Du hast Diamanten und Perlen". In *Die Heimkehr.— Ed.*

Minister or by the regional administration on his behalf", this foundation is now substantiated more thoroughly. Under Art. 14

"one or more commissions will be formed to examine the filed declarations; their presidents and other members to the number of not less than five are *to be appointed by the Finance Minister or an authority acting on his behalf*".

Thus the *appointment* made by the Finance Minister or the authority acting on his behalf forms the *foundation* proper of the examination.

If the self-assessment varies from the "*estimate*" made by the district or town commission appointed by the Finance Minister, the "self-assessor" is called upon to give an *explanation* (Art. 15). He may give an explanation or not, it all depends whether it "*suffices*" for the commission appointed by the Finance Minister. If it does not suffice,

"it is the duty of the commission to determine the contribution by its *own assessment* and to *inform* the contributories thereof".

First the contributory assesses himself and informs the official thereof. Then the official makes an assessment and informs the contributory thereof. What has become of the "self-assessment"? The foundation has foundered. Whereas the self-assessment only gives rise to a serious "examination" of the contributory, the assessment by a stranger turns at once into execution. For Art. 16 decrees:

"The transactions of the district (town) commissions are to be filed with the regional administration which will *forthwith* compile the lists of the bond amounts and pass them on to the respective collectors for collection—if necessary by way of execution — under the regulations governing the collection of [...] taxes."

We have already seen that all is not "roses" with the appeals. The appeals path hides still other thorns.

Firstly: The regional commission which examines the appeals consists of deputies who are elected by the delegates etc. elected under the law of April 8, 1848.

But the compulsory loan divides the entire state into two hostile camps, the camp of the obstructionists and the camp of the men of good will against whose rendered or proffered contributions no objections have been raised by the district commission. The deputies may only be elected from the camp of the men of good will (Art. 17).

Secondly: "A commissioner appointed by the Finance Minister will preside; an official may be attached to him for his assistance" (Art. 18).

Thirdly: "The regional commission is authorised to *order* special appraisal of *property or incomes* and for this purpose is entitled to *draw up inventories* or *order the inspection of commercial ledgers*. If these measures do not suffice, the appellant may be required to swear an affidavit" [Art. 19].

Thus, whoever refuses to accept without reservation the "assessment" of the officials appointed by the Finance Minister, may, as a penalty, have to reveal all his financial affairs to two bureaucrats and 15 competitors. Thorny path of appeal! Thus Hansemann only mocks his public when he says in his preamble:

"The distribution of the loan is based upon self-assessment. In order to make sure that this is *in no way offensive, not even a summary listing of the individual parts of one's property will be required*."

Not even the penalty for "perjury" of Cervantes' project designer is lacking in the project of the Minister of action.

Instead of tormenting himself with his sham arguments, our Hansemann would have done better to join the character in the comedy who says:

"How can you expect me to pay old debts and enter upon new ones *unless you lend me money?*" [a]

At this moment, however, when Prussia, attending to her particularist interests, is seeking to commit a treachery against Germany and to rebel against the Central Authority, it is the *duty of every patriot* to refuse to contribute a single penny voluntarily to the compulsory loan. Only by persistent deprivation of nourishment can Prussia be forced to surrender to Germany.

Written on July 25 and 29, 1848   Printed according to the newspaper

First published in the *Neue Rheinische*   Published in English for the first
Zeitung Nos. 56 and 60, July 26 and 30,   time
1848

---

[a] Cervantes, *Novelas ejemplares: Coloquio de los perros.—Ed.*

ARMISTICE NEGOTIATIONS WITH DENMARK
BROKEN OFF

Cologne, July 27. We have just received letters from *Copenhagen* according to which the *armistice negotiations have really been broken off.* On July 21, the Swedish and British ambassadors,[a] with the rest of the diplomats who had gone to the headquarters, returned to Copenhagen *without having achieved their object.* Although General Neumann brought General Wrangel a *definite order* from the King of Prussia[b] to sign the armistice and although the armistice had already been ratified on the Prussian and Danish sides, *Wrangel's refusal was as definite* and instead he set new conditions which were firmly rejected by the Danes. It is said that he did not even grant the foreign diplomats an audience. The Danes were particularly opposed to Wrangel's stipulation that final consent *was up to the Imperial Regent.*[c]

It is therefore solely thanks to General Wrangel's firm stand that Germany has this time been saved from one of the most ignominious treaties that history has ever known.

Written by Engels on July 27, 1848

First published in the *Neue Rheinische Zeitung* No. 58, July 28, 1848

Printed according to the newspaper

Published in English for the first time

---

[a] Elias Lagerheim and Henry Wynn.— *Ed.*
[b] Frederick William IV.— *Ed.*
[c] Archduke John of Austria.— *Ed.*

THE DISSOLUTION OF THE DEMOCRATIC
ASSOCIATIONS IN BADEN

Cologne, July 27. The reactionary police measures against the right of association follow each other in rapid succession. First it was the Democratic Association in Stuttgart that was abolished, then it was the turn of the Association in Heidelberg.[a] Success made the gentlemen of the reaction bold; now the Baden Government has banned all democratic associations in Baden.

All this occurs at the same moment when the *soi-disant* National Assembly in Frankfurt is occupied with the task of securing for all time the right of association as one of the "fundamental rights of the German people".

The primary condition for the right of free association must be that no association and no society can be dissolved or prohibited by the police, that such measures can only be taken after a court sentence has established the illegality of the association or of its actions and purposes and the originators of these actions have been punished.

This method, of course, is much too protracted for the disciplinarian impatience of Herr *Mathy*. Just as it was too much trouble for him first to obtain a warrant of arrest or at least to have himself appointed as a special constable, before, in virtue of the policeman in his nature, he arrested Fickler[182] as a "traitor to his country", just so contemptible and impractical the judicial and legal path appears to him now.

The motives for this new police violence are most edifying. The associations had allegedly affiliated to an organisation of democratic

---

[a] See this volume, pp. 248-49.—*Ed.*

associations for all of Germany which had originated at the Democratic Congress in Frankfurt.[183] This Congress is alleged to have

"set as its goal the establishment of a democratic republic" (as if that were prohibited!) "and what is meant by the means by which this goal is to be reached is shown by, among other things, sympathies for the rebels expressed in those resolutions" (since when are "sympathies" unlawful "means"?), "as well as by the fact that the Central Committee of these associations even refused to grant any further recognition to the German National Assembly and called for the formal separation of the minority for the purpose of forming a new Assembly by unlawful means".[a]

There follow the resolutions of the Congress concerning the organisation of the democratic party.

Thus, according to Herr Mathy, the associations of Baden are to be held responsible for the resolutions of the Central Committee even if they do *not carry* them *out*. For if these associations, following the request of the Frankfurt Committee, had really issued an address to the Left in the National Assembly urging its withdrawal, Herr Mathy would not have failed to announce this. Whether or not the request concerned is illegal is for the courts and not for Herr Mathy to decide. And to declare illegal the organisation of the party into districts, congresses and central committees, one has really to be Herr Mathy! And are not the constitutional and reactionary associations[184] organising themselves according to this model?

Well, of course!

It "appears inadmissible and pernicious to undermine the basis of the constitution and thus to shake the entire state edifice by the force of the associations".

The right of association, Herr Mathy, exists just so that one may "undermine" the constitution with impunity, provided, of course, one does it legally! And if the power of the associations is greater than that of the state, so much the worse for the state!

We are calling once more upon the National Assembly to indict Herr Mathy at once if it does not want to lose all prestige.

Written by Engels on July 27, 1848

First published in the *Neue Rheinische Zeitung* No. 58, July 28, 1848

Printed according to the newspaper

Published in English for the first time

---

[a] Quoted from the article "Karlsruhe, 23. Juli. Ernst der Regierung, die Aufhebung der demokratischen Vereine betreffend", *Deutsche Zeitung* No. 206, July 26, 1848.— *Ed.*

THE BILL PROPOSING THE ABOLITION
OF FEUDAL OBLIGATIONS[185]

Cologne, July 29. If any Rhinelander should have forgotten what he owes to the "foreign rule", to the "yoke of the Corsican tyrant", he ought to read the Bill providing for the abolition without compensation of various obligations and dues. The Bill has been submitted by Herr Hansemann in this year of grace 1848 "for the consideration" of his agreers.[186] Seigniory, allodification rent, death dues, heriot,[a] protection money, legal dues and fines, signet money, tithes on live-stock, bees etc.— what a strange, what a barbaric ring these absurd terms have for our ears, which have been civilised by the French Revolution's destruction of feudalism and by the *Code Napoléon.* How incomprehensible to us is this farrago of medieval dues and taxes, this collection of musty junk from an antediluvian age.

Nevertheless, put off thy shoes from off thy feet, German patriot, for the place whereon thou standest is holy ground. These barbarities are the last remnants of Christian-German glory, the last links of the historical chain which connects you with your illustrious ancestors all the way back to the forests of the Cherusci. The musty air, the feudal mire which we find here in their classic unadulterated form are the very own products of our fatherland, and every true German should exclaim with the poet:

> For oh, this is the wind of home
> on my cheeks and caressing my hand!
> And all this country highway dirt
> is the dirt of my fatherland![b]

---

[a] In the original *Besthaupt* and *Kurmede* are used, which are regional variants of the German expression for heriot.— *Ed.*

[b] Heinrich Heine, *Deutschland. Ein Wintermärchen,* Caput VIII. The English translation is taken from Heinrich Heine, *Germany. A Winter's Tale,* L. B. Fischer, New York, 1944.— *Ed.*

Reading the Bill, it seems at first glance that our Minister of Agriculture Herr *Gierke*, on the orders of Herr Hansemann, has brought off a terrifically "bold stroke",[a] has done away with the Middle Ages by a stroke of the pen, and of course quite gratuitously.

But when one looks at the Bill's *motivation*, one discovers that it sets out straight away to prove that in fact *no* feudal obligations *whatever* ought to be abolished without compensation, that is to say, it starts with a bold assertion which directly contradicts the "bold stroke".

The Minister's practical timidity now manoeuvres warily and prudently between these two bold postures. On the left "the general welfare" and the "demands of the spirit of our time"; on the right the "established rights of the lords of the manor"; in the middle the "praiseworthy idea of a freer development of rural relations" represented by Herr Gierke's shamefaced embarrassment—what a picture!

In short, Herr Gierke fully recognises that feudal obligations in general ought to be abolished only against compensation. Thus the most onerous, the most widespread, the principal obligations are to *continue* or, seeing that the peasants have in fact already done away with them, they are to be *reimposed*.

But, Herr Gierke observes,

if, nevertheless, particular relations, whose intrinsic justification is insufficient or whose continued existence is incompatible with the demands of the spirit of our time and the general welfare, are abolished *without compensation*, then the persons affected by this should appreciate that they are making a few sacrifices not only for the good of all but also in their own well-understood interests, in order that relations between those who have claims and those who have duties shall be peaceful and friendly, thereby helping landed property generally to maintain the political status which befits it for the good of the whole".

The revolution in the countryside consisted in the actual abolition of all feudal obligations. The Government of Action, which recognises the revolution, recognises it in the countryside by destroying it surreptitiously. It is quite impossible to restore the old *status quo* completely; the peasants would promptly kill their feudal lords—even Herr Gierke realises that. An impressive list of insignificant feudal obligations existing only in a few places are therefore abolished, but the principal feudal obligation, simply epitomised in the term *compulsory labour*, is reintroduced.

---

[a] The expression *ein kühner Griff* (a bold stroke) was first used by Karl Mathy and Heinrich von Gagern in the Frankfurt National Assembly in 1848 and quickly became popular.— *Ed.*

As a result of all the rights that are to be abolished, the aristocracy will sacrifice less than 50,000 talers a year, but will thereby save several million. Indeed the Minister hopes that they will thus placate the peasants and even gain their votes at future parliamentary elections. This would really be a very good deal, provided Herr Gierke does not miscalculate.

In this way the objections of the peasants would be removed, and so would those of the aristocrats, insofar as they correctly understand their position. There remains the Chamber, the scruples of the legal and radical pettifoggers. The distinction between obligations that are to be abolished and those that are to be retained—which is simply the distinction between practically worthless obligations and very valuable obligations—must be based as regards the Chamber on some semblance of legal and economic justification. Herr Gierke must prove that the obligations to be abolished 1. have an insufficient inner justification, 2. are incompatible with the general welfare, 3. are incompatible with the demands of the spirit of our time, and 4. that their abolition is fundamentally no infringement of property rights, no expropriation without compensation.

In order to prove the insufficient justification of these dues and services Herr Gierke delves into the darkest recesses of feudal law. He invokes the entire, "originally very slow development of the Germanic states over a period of a thousand years". But what use is that to Herr Gierke? The deeper he digs, the more he stirs up the stagnant mire of feudal law, the more does that feudal law prove that the obligations in question have, not an insufficient justification, but from the feudal point of view, a very solid justification. The hapless Minister merely causes general amusement when he tries his hardest to induce feudal law to make oracular pronouncements in the style of modern civil law, or to make the feudal lord of the twelfth century think and judge like a bourgeois of the nineteenth century.

Herr Gierke fortunately has inherited Herr von Patow's principle that everything emanating from feudal sovereignty and serfdom is to be abolished without payment, but everything else is to be abolished only against payment of compensation.[a] But does Herr Gierke really think that special perspicacity is required in order to show that all and every obligation subject to repeal "emanates from feudal sovereignty"?

It is hardly necessary to add that for the sake of consistency Herr

---

[a] See this volume, pp. 117-18.— *Ed.*

Gierke constantly insinuates modern legal concepts into feudal legal regulations, and in an extremity he always invokes them. But if Herr Gierke evaluates some of these obligations in terms of the modern ideas of law, then it is incomprehensible why the same should not be done with all obligations. In that case, however, compulsory labour service, faced with the freedom of the individual and of property, would certainly come off badly.

Herr Gierke fares even worse when he advances the argument of public welfare and the demands of the spirit of our time in support of his differentiations. Surely it is self-evident that if these insignificant obligations impede the public welfare and are incompatible with the demands of the spirit of our time, then this applies in still greater measure to such obligations as labour service, the corvée, liege money[187] etc. Or does Herr Gierke consider that the right to pluck the peasants' *geese* (Clause 1, No. 14) is out of date, but the right to pluck the *peasants themselves* is not?

Then follows the demonstration that the abolition of those particular obligations does not infringe any property rights. Of course, only spurious arguments can be adduced to prove such a glaring falsehood; it can indeed only be done by reckoning up these rights to show the squires how worthless they are for them, though this, obviously, can be proved only approximately. And so Herr Gierke sedulously reckons up all the 18 sections of Clause 1, and does not notice that, to the extent in which he succeeds in proving the given *obligations* to be worthless, he also succeeds in proving *his proposed legislation to be worthless.* Virtuous Herr Gierke! How it pains us to have to destroy his fond delusions and obliterate his Archimedean-feudalist diagrams.

But there is another difficulty. Both in previous commutations of the obligations now to be abolished and in all other commutations, the peasants were flagrantly cheated in favour of the aristocracy by corrupt commissions. The peasants now demand the revision of all commutation agreements concluded under the previous Government, and they are quite justified in doing so.

But Herr Gierke will have nothing to do with this, since "formal right and law are opposed" to it; such an attitude is altogether opposed to any progress, since every new law nullifies some old formal right and law.

"The consequences of this, it can confidently be predicted, will be that, in order to secure advantages to those under obligations by means that run counter to the eternal legal principles" (revolutions, too, run counter to the eternal legal principles), "*incalculable damage* must be done to a very large section of landed property in the state, and hence (!) to the state itself."

Herr Gierke now proves with staggering thoroughness that such a procedure

"would call in question and undermine the entire legal framework of landed property and this together with numerous lawsuits and the great expenditure involved would cause great damage to landed property, which is the principal foundation of national welfare"; that it "would be an encroachment on the legal principles underlying the validity of contracts, an attack on the most indubitable contractual relations, the consequences of which would shake all confidence in the stability of civil law, thereby constituting a grave menace to the whole of commercial intercourse"!!!

Herr Gierke thus sees in this an infringement of the rights of property, which would undermine all legal principles. Why is the abolition of the obligations under discussion without compensation not an infringement? These are not merely indubitable contractual relations, but claims that were invariably met and not contested since time immemorial, whereas the demand for revision concerns contracts that are by no means uncontested, since the bribery and swindling are notorious, and can be proved in many cases.

It cannot be denied that, though the abolished obligations are quite insignificant, Herr Gierke, by abolishing them, secures "advantages to those under obligation by means that run counter to the eternal legal principles" and this is "directly opposed to formal right and law"; he "undermines the entire legal framework of landed property" and attacks the very foundation of the "most indubitable" rights.

Really, Herr Gierke, was it worth while to go to all this trouble and commit such a grievous sin in order to achieve such paltry results?

Herr Gierke does indeed *attack property*—that is quite indisputable—but it is feudal property he attacks, not modern, bourgeois property. By destroying feudal property he *strengthens* bourgeois property which arises on the ruins of feudal property. The only reason he does not want the commutation agreements revised is because by means of these agreements feudal property relations were converted into *bourgeois* ones, and consequently he cannot revise them without at the same time formally infringing bourgeois property. Bourgeois property is, of course, as sacred and inviolable as feudal property is vulnerable and—depending on the requirements and courage of the Ministers—violable.

What in brief is the significance of this lengthy law?

It is the most striking proof that the German revolution of 1848 is merely a *parody of the French revolution of 1789*.

On August 4, 1789, three weeks after the storming of the Bastille, the French people, in a *single* day, got the better of the feudal obligations.[188]

On July 11, 1848, four months after the March barricades, the feudal obligations got the better of the German people. *Teste Gierke cum Hansemanno.*[a]

The French bourgeoisie of 1789 never left its allies, the peasants, in the lurch. It knew that the abolition of feudalism in the countryside and the creation of a free, landowning peasant class was the basis of its rule.

The German bourgeoisie of 1848 unhesitatingly betrays the peasants, who are its *natural allies*, flesh of its own flesh, and without whom it cannot stand up to the aristocracy.

The perpetuation of feudal rights and their endorsement in the form of the (illusory) commutations — such is the result of the German revolution of 1848. That is much ado about nothing.

Written by Marx on July 29, 1848   Printed according to the newspaper

First published in the *Neue Rheinische Zeitung* No. 60, July 30, 1848

---

[a] Testified by Gierke and Hansemann.—*Ed.*

296

THE *KÖLNISCHE ZEITUNG* ON THE STATE
OF AFFAIRS IN ENGLAND[189]

Cologne, July 31.

"Where is it possible in England to discover *any trace of hatred* against the class which *in France is called the bourgeoisie?* This hatred was *at one time* directed against the aristocracy, which by means of its corn monopoly imposed a heavy and unjust tax on industry. The bourgeois *in England enjoys no privileges*, he depends on his own diligence; in France under Louis Philippe he depended on monopolies, on privileges."[a]

This great, this scholarly, this veracious proposition can be found in Herr Wolfers' leading article in the always well-informed *Kölnische Zeitung*.

It is indeed strange. England has the most numerous, the most concentrated, the most classic proletariat, a proletariat which every five or six years is decimated by the crushing misery of a commercial crisis, by hunger and typhus; a proletariat which for half its life is redundant to industry and unemployed. One man in every ten in England is a pauper, and one pauper in every three is an inmate in one of the Poor Law Bastilles.[190] The annual cost of poor-relief in England almost equals the entire expenditure of the Prussian state. Poverty and pauperism have been openly declared in England to be necessary elements of the present industrial system and the national wealth. Yet, despite this, where in England is there any trace of hatred against the bourgeoisie?

There is no other country in the world where, with the huge growth of the proletariat, the contradiction between proletariat and

---

[a] "Köln, 28. Juli. Die europäische Revolution und die Handelsfreiheit", *Kölnische Zeitung* No. 211, July 29, 1848.— *Ed.*

bourgeoisie has reached such a high level as in England; no other country presents such glaring contrasts between extreme poverty and immense wealth—yet where is there any trace of hatred against the bourgeoisie?

Obviously, the associations of workers, set up secretly before 1825 and openly after 1825,[191] associations not for just *one* day against a *single* manufacturer, but permanent associations directed against entire groups of manufacturers, workers' associations of entire industries, entire towns, finally associations uniting large numbers of workers throughout England, all these associations and their numerous fights against the manufacturers, the strikes, which led to acts of violence, revengeful destructions, arson, armed attacks and assassinations—all these actions just prove the love of the proletariat for the bourgeoisie.

The entire struggle of the workers against the manufacturers over the last eighty years, a struggle which, beginning with machine wrecking, has developed through associations, through isolated attacks on the person and property of the manufacturers and on the few workers who were loyal to them, through bigger and smaller rebellions, through the insurrections of 1839 and 1842,[192] has become the most advanced class struggle the world has seen. The class war of the Chartists, the organised party of the proletariat, against the organised political power of the bourgeoisie, has not yet led to those terrible bloody clashes which took place during the June uprising in Paris, but it is waged by a far larger number of people with much greater tenacity and on a much larger territory—this social civil war is of course regarded by the *Kölnische Zeitung* and its Wolfers as nothing but a long demonstration of the love of the English proletariat for its bourgeois employers.

Not so long ago it was fashionable to present England as the classic land of social contradictions and struggles, and to declare that France, compared with England's so-called unnatural situation, was a happy land with her Citizen King, her bourgeois parliamentary warriors and her upright workers, who always fought so bravely for the bourgeoisie. It was not so long ago that the *Kölnische Zeitung* kept harping on this well-worn tune and saw in the English class struggles a reason for warning Germany against protectionism and the "unnatural" hothouse industry to which it gives rise. But the June days have changed everything. The horrors of the June battles have scared the *Kölnische Zeitung*, and the millions of Chartists in London, Manchester and Glasgow vanish into thin air in face of the forty thousand Paris insurgents.

France has become the classic country as regards hatred of the bourgeoisie and, according to the present assertions of the *Kölnische Zeitung*, this has been the case since 1830. How strange. For the last ten years English agitators, received with acclamation by the entire proletariat, have untiringly preached fervent hatred of the bourgeoisie at meetings and in pamphlets and journals, whereas the French working-class and socialist literature has always advocated reconciliation with the bourgeoisie on the grounds that the class antagonisms in France were far less developed than in England. The men at whose very name the *Kölnische Zeitung* makes the triple sign of the cross, men like Louis Blanc, Cabet, Caussidière and Ledru-Rollin, have, for many years before and after the February revolution, preached peace with the bourgeoisie, and they generally did it *de la meilleure foi du monde.*[a] Let the *Kölnische Zeitung* look through any of the writings of these people, or through the *Réforme*, the *Populaire*, or even the working-class journals published during the last few years like the *Union*, the *Ruche populaire* and the *Fraternité*—though it should be sufficient to mention two works which everybody knows, Louis Blanc's entire *Histoire de dix ans*, especially the last part, and his *Histoire de la révolution française* in two volumes.

But the *Kölnische Zeitung* is not content with merely *asserting* as a fact that no hatred exists in England against "the class which in France is called the *bourgeoisie*" (in England too, our well-informed colleague, cf. the *Northern Star* for the last two years)—it also explains *why* this must be so.

Peel saved the English bourgeoisie from this hatred by repealing the monopolies and establishing Free Trade.

"The bourgeois in England enjoys no privileges, no monopolies; in France he depended on monopolies.... It was Peel's measures that saved England from the most appalling upheaval."

By doing away with the monopoly of the *aristocracy*, Peel saved the *bourgeoisie* from the threatening hatred of the proletariat, according to the amazing logic of the *Kölnische Zeitung*.

"The English people, we say: the *English people* day by day increasingly realise that only from *Free Trade* can they expect a solution of the vital problems bearing on all their present afflictions and apprehensions, a solution which was recently attempted amid streams of blood.... We must not forget that the first notions of Free Trade came from the *English people*."

The English people! But the "English *people*" have been fighting the Free Traders since 1839 at all their meetings and in the press,

---

[a] In good faith.— *Ed.*

and compelled them, when the Anti-Corn Law League[193] was at the height of its fame, to hold their meetings in *secret* and to admit only persons who had a ticket. The people with bitter irony compared the practice of the Free Traders[a] with their fine words, and fully identified the bourgeois with the Free Trader. Sometimes the English people were even forced temporarily to seek the support of the aristocracy, the monopolists, against the bourgeoisie, e.g. in their fight for the ten-hour day.[194] And we are asked to believe that the people who were so well able to drive the Free Traders off the rostrum at *public* meetings, that it was these "English *people*" who originally conceived the ideas of Free Trade! The *Kölnische Zeitung*, in its artless simplicity, not only repeats mechanically the illusions of the big capitalists of Manchester and Leeds, but lends a gullible ear to their deliberate lies.

"The bourgeois in England enjoys no privileges, no monopolies." But in France things are different:

"The worker for a long time regarded the bourgeois as the monopolist who imposed a tax of 60 per cent on the poor farmer for the iron of his plough, who made extortionate profits on his coal, who exposed the vine-growers throughout France to death from starvation, who added 20, 40, 50 per cent to the price of everything he sold them...."

The only "monopoly" which the worthy *Kölnische Zeitung* knows is the *customs* monopoly, i.e. the monopoly which only *appears* to affect the workers, but actually falls on the bourgeoisie, on all industrialists, who do not profit from tariff-protection. The *Kölnische Zeitung* knows only a local, legally created monopoly, the monopoly which was attacked by the Free Traders from Adam Smith to Cobden.

But the *monopoly of capital*, which comes into being without the aid of legislation and often exists despite it, this monopoly is not recognised by the gentlemen of the *Kölnische Zeitung*. Yet it is this monopoly which directly and ruthlessly weighs upon the workers and causes the struggle between the proletariat and the bourgeoisie. Precisely this monopoly is the *specifically modern* monopoly, which produces the modern class contradictions, and the solution of just these contradictions is the specific task of the nineteenth century.

But this *monopoly of capital* becomes more powerful, more comprehensive, and more threatening *in proportion as the other small and localised monopolies disappear.*

The freer competition becomes as a result of the abolition of all "monopolies", the more rapidly is capital concentrated in the hands

---

[a] Here and below these two words are given in English in the German original.— *Ed.*

of the industrial barons, the more rapidly does the petty bourgeoisie become ruined and the faster does the industry of England, the country of capital's monopoly, subjugate the neighbouring countries. If the "monopolies" of the French, German and Italian bourgeoisie were abolished, Germany, France and Italy would be reduced to proletarians compared with the all-absorbing English bourgeoisie. The pressure which the individual English bourgeois exerts on the individual English proletarian would then be matched by the pressure exerted by the English bourgeoisie as a whole on Germany, France and Italy, and it is especially the petty bourgeoisie of these countries which would suffer.

These are such commonplace ideas that today they can no longer be expounded without causing offence — to anyone but the learned gentlemen of the *Kölnische Zeitung*.

These profound thinkers see in Free Trade the only means by which France can be saved from a devastating war between the workers and the bourgeois.

To reduce the bourgeoisie of a country to the level of the proletariat is indeed a means of solving class contradictions which is worthy of the *Kölnische Zeitung*.

Written by Engels on July 31, 1848   Printed according to the newspaper

First published in the *Neue Rheinische Zeitung* No. 62, August 1, 1848

THE AGREEMENT DEBATE
ABOUT THE VALDENAIRE AFFAIR

Cologne, August 1. Once again we have to catch up with a couple of agreement sessions.

During the session of July 18 the motion calling for the summoning of Deputy Valdenaire was discussed.[a] The central section called for its adoption. Three Rhenish jurists spoke against it.

First there was Herr *Simons* of Elberfeld, a former Public Prosecutor. Herr Simons was apparently under the impression that he was still in the Assizes or in the police court. He demeaned himself like a Public Prosecutor by making a formal plea against Herr Valdenaire and for the judicature. He said: The matter has been placed before the indictment board and will be quickly decided there. Valdenaire will either be freed or referred to the Assizes. If the latter should occur

"it would be exceedingly desirable that the whole case is not then pulled apart so that judgment is not delayed".

As far as Herr Simons is concerned, the interests of the judicature, i.e. the convenience of the indictment board, the Public Prosecutor and the Court of Assizes, carry much more weight than the interest of freedom and the immunity of the people's representatives.

Herr Simons then throws suspicion first upon Valdenaire's defence witnesses and afterwards upon Valdenaire himself. He declares that the Assembly "would not be deprived of any talent" by

---

[a] See this volume, pp. 94-95.—*Ed.*

his absence. He then proceeds to pronounce him unfit to sit in the Assembly as long as he is not completely cleared of every suspicion of having plotted against the Government or rebelled against the armed forces. As far as talent is concerned, one could, according to Herr Simons' logic, arrest nine-tenths of the praiseworthy Assembly just·as well as Herr Valdenaire and still not deprive it of any talent whatever. As far as the second argument is concerned, it does indeed redound to Herr Simons' honour that he has never hatched any "plots" against absolutism nor been guilty of "rebellion against the public authority" on the March barricades.

After Valdenaire's substitute, Herr *Gräff*, had irrefutably proved that neither was there the slightest suspicion against Valdenaire nor had the action in question been unlawful (since it consisted in having helped the *legally constituted civic militia*, which was occupying the barricades of Trier with the *approval of the Municipal Council* in the execution of its functions), Herr Bauerband rises to support the Public Prosecutor's office.

Herr *Bauerband* also has a very weighty scruple:

"Would not the summoning of Valdenaire prejudice the future judgment of the jury?"

Profoundly thoughtful doubts which are made still more insoluble by the simple remark of Herr *Borchardt*: Whether the *non-summoning* of Valdenaire would not likewise prejudice the jury? The dilemma is really so profound that a thinker of even greater mental force than Herr Bauerband might spend years trying in vain to resolve it. There is perhaps only *one* man in the entire Assembly who has enough strength to solve the riddle: Deputy *Baumstark.*[a]

Herr Bauerband continues to plead for a while in an extremely verbose and confused manner. Herr *Borchardt* answers him briefly. After him, Herr *Stupp* gets up in order to say also so much against Valdenaire that he "had in every respect nothing (!) to add" to the speeches of Simons and Bauerband. All this is, of course, enough reason for him to continue speaking until he is interrupted by shouts calling for the closure of the debate. Herr Reichensperger II and Herr Wencelius speak briefly in favour of Valdenaire and, as we know, the Assembly decides to summon him. Herr Valdenaire has played a trick on the Assembly by not obeying the summons.

Herr *Borchardt* puts the following motion: In order to prevent the impending executions of the death penalty before the Assembly has given its decision on Herr Lisiecki's motion which advocates the

---

[a] The name, literally translated, means as strong as a tree, i.e. very strong.— *Ed.*

abolition of capital punishment, a decision should be made on this motion within a week.

Herr *Ritz* is of the opinion that such a precipitous procedure would not be *parliamentary*.

Herr *Brill*: If we shall in the near future, as I certainly hope, abolish the death penalty it would certainly be very *unparliamentary* to decapitate somebody in the meantime.

The President would like to terminate the discussion but the popular Herr *Baumstark* has already mounted the rostrum. Casting fiery glances and his face flushed with noble indignation, he exclaims:

"Gentlemen, permit me to say a *serious word!* The subject here in question is not of the kind that should be treated lightly from this rostrum by referring to decapitation as an unparliamentary matter!" (The Right, which looks upon decapitation as the height of parliamentarism, bursts into tempestuous shouts of bravo.) "It is a subject of the greatest, most serious significance" (it is well known that Herr Baumstark says this of every topic he discusses). "Other parliaments ... the greatest men of legislation and science" (i.e. "all political philosophers, from Plato down to Dahlmann") "have occupied themselves with this problem for 200 to 300 years" (each of them?) "and if you want us to be blamed for having passed over such an important question with such levity...." (Bravo!) "Nothing but my conscience impels me ... but the question is too serious ... *surely, one more week* will not make any difference!"

Because the subject is of the greatest, most serious significance the serious words of the noble Deputy Baumstark become the rashest frivolity. Is there, indeed, greater frivolity than Herr Baumstark's apparent intention to discuss the abolition of capital punishment for the next 200 to 300 years and in the meantime to let decapitations continue at a smart pace? "Surely, one more week will not make any difference" and the heads which will roll during this time will not make any difference either!

Incidentally, the Prime Minister[a] declares that it is not intended to carry out death sentences for the time being.

After Herr Schulze from Delitzsch has expressed a few ingenious scruples concerning rules of procedure, Borchardt's motion is rejected. On the other hand, an amendment by Herr Nethe, which recommends greater dispatch to the central commission, is adopted.

Deputy *Hildenhagen* proposes the following motion: Until the relevant Bill has been submitted, the President should terminate every session with the following solemn pronouncement:

"We, however, are of the opinion that the Ministry should work most zealously on the submission of the new municipal laws."

---

[a] Rudolf von Auerswald.— *Ed.*

This edifying proposal was unfortunately not designed for our bourgeois times.

We are not Romans, we smoke tobacco.[a]

The attempt to carve from the raw material of President Grabow the classical figure of an Appius Claudius and to apply the solemn *Ceterum censeo*[b] to the municipal legislation failed under "huge mirth".

After Deputy *Bredt* of Barmen has asked the Minister of Trade three fairly mildly-worded questions on the unification of all Germany into a customs union and into a maritime league with navigation duties, and finally on provisional protective tariffs, and after he has received similarly mild, but also rather unsatisfactory answers to his questions from Herr *Milde*, Herr *Gladbach* is the last speaker of the session. Herr *Schütze* of Lissa[c] had intended to move that he be called to order because of his vigorous language during the debate over the disarming of the volunteers.[d] He decided, however, to withdraw his motion. Herr Gladbach, however, quite unceremoniously challenged the brave Schütze and the entire Right and to the great annoyance of the hidebound Prussians related the amusing anecdote of a Prussian lieutenant who, having fallen asleep on his horse, rode into the midst of the volunteers. These troops greeted the officer with the song "Sleep, Baby, Sleep" and for this offence they were to be court-martialled! Herr Schütze stammered a few words which were as indignant as incoherent and the session was terminated.

Written by Engels on August 1, 1848

First published in the *Neue Rheinische Zeitung* No. 63, August 2, 1848

Printed according to the newspaper

Published in English for the first time

---

[a] Heinrich Heine, "Zur Beruhigung". In *Zeitgedichte.—Ed.*

[b] "*Ceterum censeo, Carthaginem esse delendam*" (As for the rest, Carthage must be destroyed)—the words with which Cato the Elder usually concluded every speech in the Senate (from 157 B. C. onwards).—*Ed.*

[c] The Polish name is Leszno.—*Ed.*

[d] See this volume, pp. 180-81 and 191-93.—*Ed.*

305

THE MILAN BULLETIN

In yesterday's issue of this newspaper we published the victory bulletin of the Provisional Government in Milan and then went on to mention the conflicting victory bulletins from Bolzano in the Augsburg newspaper[a] and from Trieste.[b]

We held the *first* of these to be the more credible because the information contained in the bulletin that reached us direct from Milan was simultaneously confirmed by reports from two different cities in Switzerland—Zurich and Basle—which have numerous commercial and close geographical links with Milan. But in evaluating the information we had to give special weight to the fact that the Austrian reports of victory were dated earlier and spoke of the battle on July 23, whereas the Milan bulletin dealt with the events of the 24th and the early hours of the 25th.[195] Because of this combination of circumstances we did not doubt that the Italian victory had actually taken place. The Austrians, moreover, had already previously published reports of victories, for example of a victory at Curtatone[196] which later turned out to have been an Austrian defeat, and furthermore it was none other than the Augsburg paper that had acclaimed this alleged victory.[c] A comparison of the reports of both sides shows that the Italians really did win a victory, but that this victory was wrenched from them by the advance of fresh Austrian troops. If anything could have led us

---

[a] i.e. the *Allgemeine Zeitung.—Ed.*

[b] "Mailand, 25. Juli", "Mailand, 26. Juli", *Neue Rheinische Zeitung* No. 62, August 1, 1848.—*Ed.*

[c] The *Allgemeine Zeitung* No. 155 (special supplement), June 3, 1848, p. 4, and No. 156, June 4, 1848, pp. 2486-2487.—*Ed.*

12*

astray, it would have been that ambitious but totally incompetent individual *Charles Albert*, about whom we have already repeatedly expressed our opinion. Despite all the bad qualities of this "sword of Italy", the possibility still existed that at least one of his generals, favoured by such uncommonly advantageous positions, might have possessed the military skill to claim the victory for the Italian colours. Reality shows that this has not happened. And therewith Charles Albert's fate is sealed. Even his present throne, not to mention the visionary one of the whole of Italy, must shortly collapse. As victor, he could have looked forward to gratifying his ambition for a while; vanquished, he will very soon be tossed to one side as a useless tool by the Italians themselves. After many bloody sacrifices, Italy will surely triumph and show that it has no need of that wretched individual the King of Sardinia to achieve its freedom and national independence.

Written by Engels on August 1, 1848   Printed according to the newspaper

First published in the *Neue Rheinische*   Published in English for the first
Zeitung No. 62, August 2, 1848   time

THE RUSSIAN NOTE[197]

Cologne, August 1. Russian diplomacy has invaded Germany for the time being not with an army, but with a Note in the form of a circular to all Russian Embassies. This Note found its first lodgings in the official organ of the German Imperial Administration at Frankfurt[a] and it was soon also well received at other official and unofficial newspapers. The more extraordinary it is that Mr. Nesselrode, the Russian Foreign Minister, should indulge in this sort of public statecraft, the more important it is to subject this action to a closer inspection.

During the happy period preceding 1848, German censorship saw to it that no word could be printed which might incur the displeasure of the Russian Government, not even under the heading of Greece or Turkey.

Since the evil March days, however, this convenient expedient is unfortunately no longer available. Nesselrode therefore becomes a journalist.

According to him it is the "German press, whose hatred for Russia seemed for a moment suspended", which with respect to the Russian "security measures" along the frontier had seen fit to make the "most unfounded assumptions and commentaries". After this restrained introduction there follow stronger words which read:

"The German press is daily spreading the most absurd rumours and the most malicious calumnies against us."

---

[a] "Die russische Note", *Frankfurter Oberpostamts-Zeitung* No. 210 (second supplement), July 28, 1848.—*Ed.*

Soon, however, there is talk of "raving declamations", "madmen" and "perfidious malevolence".

At the next press trial, a German Public Prosecutor may well use the Russian Note in his evidence as an authenticated document.

And why is the German, especially the "democratic" press to be attacked, and if possible, to be destroyed? Because it misjudges the Russian Emperor's "benevolent as well as unselfish sentiments" and his "openly peaceful intentions"!

"Has Germany ever had to complain about us?" asks Nesselrode on behalf of his ruler.[a] "During the entire time when the Continent had to endure the oppressive rule of a conqueror, Russia shed her blood *to help* Germany *preserve her integrity and independence*. The Russian territory had long been liberated when Russia still continued to follow her German allies to all the battlefields of Europe, and to assist them."

In spite of her numerous and well-paid agents, Russia is labouring under the gravest delusion if she thinks that in the year 1848 she can arouse sympathies by evoking the memory of the so-called wars of liberation. And are we to believe that Russia shed her blood for us Germans?

Apart from the fact that before 1812 Russia "supported" Germany's "integrity and independence" by an open alliance and secret treaties with Napoleon, she was later sufficiently indemnified for her so-called aid by robbery and pillage. Her aid was for the princes who were allied to her, her assistance, in spite of the Proclamation of Kalisch,[198] for the representatives of absolutism, "by the grace of God", against a ruler who had emerged from the revolution. The Holy Alliance and its unholy works, the bandit congresses of Carlsbad, Laibach, Verona etc.,[199] the Russian-German persecutions of every enlightened word, as a matter of fact all politics since 1815 which were guided by Russia ought indeed to have impressed upon our memories a profound sense of gratitude. The House of Romanov, along with its diplomats, may rest assured; we will never forget *this* debt. As for Russia's aid during the years 1814 and 1815, we would sooner be susceptible to any other feeling than that of gratitude for that aid paid for with English subsidies.

The reasons are obvious for discerning minds. If Napoleon had remained victor in Germany, he would have removed at least three dozen beloved "fathers of their people" with his well-known energetic formula. French legislation and administration would have created a solid base for German unity and spared us 33 years of humiliation and the tyranny of the Federal Diet which is, of course,

---

[a] Nicholas I.— *Ed.*

highly praised by Mr. Nesselrode. A few Napoleonic decrees would have completely destroyed the entire medieval chaos: the compulsory labour services and tithes, exemptions and privileges, the entire feudal and patriarchal systems which still torment us from end to end of our fatherlands. The rest of Germany would long since have reached the level which the left bank of the Rhine reached soon after the first French revolution; we would have neither Uckermark grandees nor a Pomeranian Vendée[200] and we would no longer have to inhale the stuffy air of the "historical" and "Christian-Germanic" swamps.

Russia, however, is magnanimous. Even if no gratitude is expressed, the Emperor retains as much as ever his old "benevolent as well as unselfish sentiments" towards us. Yes, "in spite of insults and challenges the attempt to change our" (Russia's) "sentiments has not been successful".

These sentiments manifest themselves for the time being in a "passive and watchful method", a method in which Russia has undeniably achieved great virtuosity. She knows how to wait until the appropriate moment seems to have arrived. Notwithstanding the colossal troop movements which have taken place in Russia since March, Mr. Nesselrode is so naive as to try to make us believe that the Russian troops "remained immobile within their cantonments". The Russian Government remains animated by sentiments of "peace and reconciliation" in spite of the classical: "Gentlemen, saddle your horses!",[a] in spite of the confidential outpouring of heart and bile against the German people by Abramowicz, Chief of Police in Warsaw, and in spite of or rather because of the threatening and successful Notes from Petersburg. Russia perseveres in her "openly peaceful and defensive attitude". In the Nesselrode circular, Russia is portrayed as patience personified and as a pious, much-maligned and insulted innocence.

We want to enumerate some of Germany's crimes against Russia which are listed in the Note: 1. "hostile mood", and 2. "fever of change in the whole of Germany". Such a "hostile" mood towards so much benevolence on the part of the Tsar! How grievous this must be for the paternal heart of our dear brother-in-law. And to top it all, this execrable disease called "fever of change"! This is actually the first, albeit in this case the second, dreadfulness. From time to time Russia bestows another kind of disease upon us: the cholera. Be that as it may! Not only is this "fever of change" contagious but it often

---

[a] Nicholas I is reported to have addressed these words to his officers after being informed that the February 1848 revolution had taken place in France.— Ed.

reaches such a virulent intensification that highly-placed personages are easily compelled to make hasty departures for England![a] Was the "German fever of change" perhaps one of the reasons for dissuading Russia from an invasion in March and April? The third crime: The Preparliament of Frankfurt[201] has represented war against Russia as a necessity of the time. The same has happened in associations and newspapers and is all the more unpardonable since according to the clauses of the Holy Alliance and the later treaties between Russia, Austria and Prussia, we Germans are only supposed to shed our blood in the interest of the princes and not in our own interest. 4. There has been talk in Germany of reconstituting old Poland within her true borders of 1772.[202] The knout over you and then off to Siberia! But no, when Nesselrode wrote his circular, he had not yet heard of the Frankfurt Parliament's vote on the question of incorporating Posen. Parliament has atoned for our sins and a mild, forgiving smile now howers upon the lips of the Tsar. The 5th crime of Germany: "Her regrettable war against a Nordic monarchy." In view of the success of the menacing Note from Russia, the rapid retreat of the German army ordered by Potsdam and the declaration issued by the Prussian Ambassador in Copenhagen on the motives and purposes of the war,[203] Germany deserved a milder punishment for her impertinence than would have been admissible without these circumstances. 6. "Open advocacy of a defensive and offensive alliance between Germany and France." Lastly, 7. "The reception given to the Polish refugees, their free trips on the railways and the insurrection in the Posen region."

If the diplomats and similar persons had not received the gift of language "so as to conceal their thoughts"[b] both Nesselrode and brother-in-law Nicholas would have embraced us with shouts of joy and thanked us ardently for having lured so many Poles from France, England, Belgium etc. to the Posen region and for having made it easy for them to be transported there only to have them mowed down by grape-shot and shrapnel, branded with lunar caustic, slaughtered, sent off with shorn heads etc., and, on the other hand, to exterminate them in Cracow by a treacherous bombardment, if possible completely.

And Russia, faced with these seven mortal sins of Germany, has nevertheless remained on the defensive and not taken the offensive? Yes, that's how it is, and it is for this reason that the Russian diplomat

---

[a] An allusion to the flight of the Prince of Prussia to England during the March revolution.— *Ed.*

[b] Words attributed to Talleyrand.— *Ed.*

is asking the world to admire the love of peace and the moderation of his Emperor.

The Russian Emperor's rule of procedure "from which he has so far not deviated for one moment", according to Mr. Nesselrode,

"is not to interfere in any way in the internal affairs of countries which want to change their organisation; on the contrary, to allow these nations complete freedom to effect the political and social experiments which they want to undertake without let or hindrance on his part, and not to attack any power which has not attacked him. On the other hand, he is determined to repel any encroachment upon his own internal security and to make sure that if the territorial balance of power is anywhere destroyed or altered, that will not be done at the expense of our own legitimate interests."

The Russian Note forgets to add the illustrative examples. After the July revolution the Emperor assembled an army along the western frontier so as, allied with his faithful followers in Germany, to give practical proof to the French how he would allow the nations "complete freedom to effect their political and social experiments". The fact that he was disturbed in his rule of procedure was not his fault but that of the Polish revolution of 1830[204] which gave his plans a different direction. Soon thereafter, we saw the same procedure with respect to Spain and Portugal. The evidence is his open and secret support of Don Carlos and Dom Miguel. When at the end of 1842 the King of Prussia wanted to issue a sort of constitution according to the estates principle, on the most comfortable "historical" basis, which had played such an admirable role with respect to the Patents of 1847,[205] it was, of course, Nicholas who would not tolerate it and thus cheated us "Christian Germans" out of the joy of having these Patents for several years. He did all this, as Nesselrode says, because Russia never interferes in the internal organisation of a country. We hardly need to mention Cracow.[206] Let us merely recall the most recent sample of the imperial "rule of procedure": the Wallachians overthrow the old Government and replace it provisionally by a new one. They want to transform the entire old system and create an organisation patterned after those of civilised nations. "So as now to let them effect their political and social experiments in complete freedom" a Russian army corps invades the country.[207]

After that anybody can guess the nature of the application of this "rule of procedure" to Germany. But the Russian Note makes our own deduction unnecessary. It reads:

"So long as the *Confederation*, no matter what *new forms* it may assume, leaves the neighbouring states untouched, and does not seek to expand its territorial limits by force or try to assert its lawful authority beyond the *limits* set by the *treaties*, the Emperor will also *respect* its *internal* independence."

The second passage which refers to the same subject reads still more clearly:

"If Germany should actually succeed in solving her organisational problem without detriment to her internal calm, and without the new forms impressed on her nationality being of a kind which endanger the tranquillity of other states, we shall sincerely congratulate ourselves on that for the same reasons which made us hope for her strength and unity under her previous political forms."

But the following passage sounds most clear and removes any possible doubt; here the circular speaks of Russia's incessant efforts to recommend and preserve harmony and unity in Germany:

"*Of course, we are not referring to that material unity of which a democracy addicted to a levelling and aggrandising process is dreaming today,* and which, if it could realise its ambitious theories as it interprets them, would inevitably sooner or later plunge Germany into a state of war with all adjacent states, but rather to the *moral unity,* that sincere conformity of views and intentions in all political questions which the *German Confederation* had to negotiate in external affairs.

"Our policy had only one aim: *to preserve this unity* and to strengthen the bonds which link the German governments with each other.

"That which we wanted in those days, we still desire today."

As one can see from the preceding passage, the Russian Government most willingly allows us *moral* unity, only no *material* unity, no replacement of the present Federal Diet by a central authority, not the mere semblance of central authority, but a genuine and seriously effective central authority based on popular sovereignty. What magnanimity!

"That which we wanted in those days" (before February 1848), "we still desire today."

That is the only phrase of the Russian Note which nobody will call in question. But we should like to tell Mr. Nesselrode that desire and fulfilment are still two separate things.

The Germans now know exactly where they stand as far as Russia is concerned. As long as the old system, painted over with new, modern colours, persists, or if one obediently moves back again to the Russian and "historical" track after having strayed from it in a "moment of intoxication and exultation", Russia will remain "openly peaceful".

The internal conditions of Russia, the raging cholera, the partial insurrections in individual districts, the revolution plotted in Petersburg which was, however, prevented just in time, the conspiracy inside the citadel of Warsaw, the volcanic soil of the Kingdom of Poland,[208] all these are at any rate circumstances which have contributed to the Tsar's benevolent as well as "unselfish sentiments" towards Germany.

But of much greater influence upon the "passive and watchful method" of the Russian Government was undoubtedly the course of events in Germany proper up to the present.

Could Nicholas in person have taken better care of his affairs and carried out his intentions sooner than has up to now been done in Berlin-Potsdam, in Innsbruck, in Vienna and Prague, in Frankfurt and in Hanover and in almost every other cosy corner of our fatherland, now again filled with Russian moral unity? Have not (lunar caustic) Pfuel, Colomb and the shrapnel general[a] in Posen and Windischgrätz in Prague worked so well as to enrapture the Tsar's heart? Did not Windischgrätz receive a brilliant letter of commendation from Nicholas via Potsdam from the hands of young Mr. Meyendorf? And do the gentlemen Hansemann-Milde-Schreckenstein in Berlin and the Radowitzes, Schmerlings and Lichnowskis in Frankfurt leave anything to be desired as far as Russia is concerned? Must not the *Bieder-* and *Basser*dom[b] in the Frankfurt Parliament form a soothing balm for many a pain of the most recent past? In such circumstances Russian diplomacy did not need any armies to invade Germany. It is perfectly right to be content with the "passive and watchful method", and the just discussed Note!

Written on August 1, 1848   Printed according to the newspaper

First published in the *Neue Rheinische Zeitung* No. 64, August 3, 1848

---

[a] Alexander Adolf von Hirschfeld.—*Ed.*

[b] An allusion to the deputies Biedermann and Bassermann; the German word *Biederkeit* means "respectability".—*Ed.*

314

MISCELLANEOUS[209]

Very shortly a Bill on defamation along entirely new lines will be laid before the Chamber. Our criticism of the article of the *Code Napoléon* in connection with Hecker's suit against the *Neue Rheinische Zeitung* was evidently only too well founded.[a]

Written by Marx on August 2, 1848

First published in the *Neue Rheinische Zeitung* No. 64, August 3, 1848

Printed according to the newspaper

Published in English for the first time

---

[a] See this volume, pp. 208-11.—*Ed.*

315

BAKUNIN[210]

In number 36, of this paper, we communicated a rumour circulating in Paris, according to which George Sand was stated to be possessed of papers which placed the Russian refugee, Bakunin, in the position of an agent of the Emperor Nicholas.[a] We gave publicity to this statement, because it was communicated to us simultaneously by two correspondents wholly unconnected with each other. By so doing, we only accomplished the duty of the public press, which has severely to watch public characters. And, at the same time we gave to Mr. Bakunin an opportunity of silencing suspicions thrown upon him in certain Paris circles. We reprinted also from the *Allgemeine Oder Zeitung* Mr. Bakunin's declaration, and his letter addressed to George Sand, without waiting for his request.[b] We publish now a literal translation of a letter addressed to the Editor of the *New Rhenish Gazette*, by George Sand, which perfectly settles this affair.[c]

To the editor
Sir,
Under the date line Paris, July 3, you have published the following article (there follows a translation of the relevant item) in your newspaper. The facts conveyed by your correspondent are entirely false and do not have even the slightest semblance of truth. I have never had the smallest scrap of evidence in support of the imputations you seek to make against Mr. Bakunin, who was banished from France by the dethroned King.[d] I have therefore never had any warrant for the slightest doubt about the sincerity of Mr. Bakunin's character and the honesty of his views.

Yours etc.
George Sand

---

[a] "Bakunin", *Neue Rheinische Zeitung* No. 36, July 6, 1848.—*Ed.*
[b] "Bakunin. Erklärung", *Neue Rheinische Zeitung* No. 46 (supplement), July 16, 1848.—*Ed.*
[c] This passage is given in Marx's own translation as printed in *The Morning Advertiser*, September 2, 1853.—*Ed.*
[d] Louis Philippe.—*Ed.*

P.S. I appeal to your honour and your conscience to publish this letter immediately in your newspaper.

La Châtre (Dept. Indre), July 20, 1848

Written by Marx on August 2, 1848

First published in the *Neue Rheinische Zeitung* No. 64, August 3, 1848

Printed according to the newspaper

Published in English for the first time

THE HANSEMANN GOVERNMENT
AND THE OLD-PRUSSIAN CRIMINAL BILL

Cologne, August 3. We have already often said that the Hansemann Government extols the Bodelschwingh Ministry in every possible way.[a] After the recognition of the revolution follows the recognition of the old-Prussian state of affairs. That's the way of the world.[b]

That Herr Hansemann, however, would achieve *such* virtuosity that he even praises *those* deeds of such gentlemen as Bodelschwingh, Savigny and consorts which he used to combat with the greatest vehemence in his days as Rhenish deputy to the Provincial Diet, that is a triumph with which the Potsdam camarilla had certainly not counted. And yet! Please read the following article of the latest *Preussische Staats-Anzeiger*[c]:

Berlin, August 1. The most recent issue of the journal of the Ministry of Justice reported in its "unofficial part" statistical observations about the death penalty as well as a survey of death sentences passed and confirmed between the years 1826 and 1843 (inclusive) with the exception of sentences passed in the so-called demagogical investigations. This work was undertaken with the utilisation of documents of the Ministry of Justice and, because of the importance of the issue, should claim the special attention of the reader in this respect. According to the survey, in the aforementioned period of time:

1. In the Rhine Province	189	death sentences were passed,				6	confirmed
2. In the other provinces	237	"	"	"	"	94	"

altogether 426 death sentences were passed, 100 confirmed, of which, however, four were not carried out because of flight or death of the criminals.

If the Bill on the new Penal Code of 1847 had been in force during that period there would have been:

1. In the Rhine Province only	53	death sentences passed,				5	confirmed
2. In the other provinces only	134	"	"	"	76	"

altogether 187 death sentences passed, 81 confirmed, provided that the same principles were applied to the confirmation as heretofore. Thus, the death penalty would not have been imposed on 237 criminals who were

---

[a] See this volume, p. 274.—*Ed.*
[b] Modified quotation from Goethe's *Faust*, Erster Teil, "Garten".— *Ed.*
[c] "Berlin, 1. August", *Preussischer Staats-Anzeiger* No. 90, August 2, 1848.— *Ed.*

sentenced to death under the existing laws. Nor would the death penalty have been carried out on 19 executed criminals.

According to the survey, there were annually on the average:

1. In the Rhine Province $10^9/_{18}$ death sentences passed and $^6/_{18}$ confirmed
2. In the other provinces 13 " " " " $5^4/_{18}$ "

If, however, the Bill had been in force at the time, there would have been annually on the average:

1. In the Rhine Province only $2^{17}/_{18}$ death sentences passed and $^5/_{18}$ confirmed
2. In the other provinces only $7^7/_{18}$ " " " " $4^4/_{18}$ "

And now admire the mildness, the excellence and the glory of the Royal Prussian Criminal Bill of 1847! Perhaps as much as one entire death sentence less would have been carried out in the Rhine Province in 18 years! What advantages!

But the innumerable defendants who would have been deprived of a jury and sentenced and jailed by royal justices, the disgraceful corporal punishments which here on the Rhine would have been carried out with old-Prussian rods, here, where we freed ourselves of the rod forty years ago; the dirty proceedings consequent upon the crimes against morals, unknown to the Code, which would have been conjured up again by the depraved haemorrhoidal imagination of the knights of the Prussian Law; the most inexorable confusion of juridical concepts, and finally the innumerable political trials consequent upon the despotic and insidious regulations of that contemptible patchwork, in a word, the *Prussianising* of the entire Rhine Province; do the Rhenish renegades in Berlin really believe that we would forget all this on the account of *one* fallen head?

It is clear: Herr Hansemann, through his agent in the judicial branch, Herr Märker, wants to carry through that which was beyond Bodelschwingh. He really wants now to bring into force the thoroughly hated old-Prussian criminal Bill.

At the same time we learn that the jury system will only be introduced in Berlin, and even there only on an experimental basis.

Thus: not the introduction of Rhenish law to the old-Prussians but the introduction of old-Prussian law to the Rhinelanders is the great result, the tremendous "achievement" of the March revolution! *Rien que ça.*[a]

Written on August 3, 1848   Printed according to the newspaper

First published in the *Neue Rheinische Zeitung* No. 65, August 4, 1848   Published in English for the first time

---

[a] Nothing but that.— *Ed.*

THE *KÖLNISCHE ZEITUNG*
ON THE COMPULSORY LOAN

Cologne, August 3. Number 215 of the *Kölnische Zeitung* carries the following appeal to Rhenish patriotism:

"As we have just been reliably informed, up to today, about 210,000 talers in contributions to the voluntary loan, partly in cash and partly by subscription, have been received here in the city of Cologne. It is to be expected that persons who up to now have not contributed to this government loan will recognise and fulfil their duty as citizens within the next ten days, *the more so* since their own advantage is bound to counsel them to lend their money at 5 per cent interest *before* August 10—rather than at $3^1/_3$ per cent after that date. It is particularly necessary that the rural inhabitants, who up to now have not yet contributed to the loan in the right proportion, should not miss this deadline. *Otherwise compulsion would have to be used where patriotism and correct insight are lacking.*"

A total of $1^2/_3$ per cent premium has been placed upon the patriotism of the taxpayers and yet "for a' that and a' that"[a] patriotism persists in its latent condition! *C'est inconcevable.*[b] A difference of $1^2/_3$ per cent! Can patriotism resist this ringing argument of $1^2/_3$ per cent?

It is our duty to explain this wonderful phenomenon to our beloved fellow newspaper.

By what means does the Prussian state want to pay not 5, but only $3^1/_3$ per cent? By new taxes. And if the usual taxes are not enough, as is to be expected, by a new compulsory loan. And by what means compulsory loan No. II? By compulsory loan No. III. And by what means compulsory loan No. III? By *bankruptcy.* Thus patriotism

---

[a] Quoted from Ferdinand Freiligrath's translation ("Trotz alledem!") of Robert Burns' poem "For a' that and a' that".—*Ed.*

[b] This is incomprehensible.—*Ed.*

commands that the road which the Prussian Government has entered upon must be barricaded in every possible way, not by talers but by protests.

Prussia, moreover, is already enjoying an extra debt of 10 million talers for the Hunnish war in Posen. Thus a voluntary loan of fifteen million talers would only be a bill of indemnity for the intrigues of the secret cabinet in Potsdam[211] which, against the orders of the weak cabinet at Berlin, conducted this war in the interests of the Russians and the reaction. The junker counter-revolution condescends sufficiently to appeal to the purse of the townsmen and peasants who afterwards must pay for its heroic deeds. And the hard-hearted "rural inhabitants" resist such condescension? The "Government of Action", moreover, demands money for the *constabulary business* and you do not possess the "correct insight" into the blessings of the constabulary which has been brought from England to Prussia? The "Government of Action" wants to gag you and you refuse to give it the money for the gags? What a strange lack of insight!

The Government of Action needs money to make the particular interests of the Uckermark prevail against German unity. And the rural inhabitants of the administrative district of Cologne are deluded enough not to want to bear the costs for the defence of Uckermark-Pomeranian nationality in spite of the premium of $1^2/_3$ per cent? What has become of patriotism?

Finally, our patriotic fellow newspaper which threatens "*execution*" forgets in its ardour that the compulsory loan has not yet been voted by the Agreement Assembly[a] and the ministerial Bills have the same force of law as editorials of the *Kölnische Zeitung*.

Written on August 3, 1848

First published in the *Neue Rheinische Zeitung* No. 65, August 4, 1848

Printed according to the newspaper

Published in English for the first time

---

[a] The Prussian National Assembly.— *Ed.*

PROUDHON'S SPEECH AGAINST THIERS

Paris, August 3. The day before yesterday we were able to render Proudhon's speech only piecemeal.[212] We will now enter upon a thorough discussion of it.[a] M. Proudhon starts with the explanation that the February revolution was nothing but the emergence of socialism which attempted to assert itself in all the following events and phases of this revolution.

"You want to finish with socialism. Oh well, just watch. I will lend you a helping hand. The success of socialism does not by any means depend upon a single man; the present battle is by no means a battle between myself and M. Thiers, but between labour and privilege."

M. Proudhon demonstrates instead that M. Thiers has only attacked and slandered his private life.

"If we proceed on that level, I would suggest to M. Thiers: let us both go to confession! You confess your sins, and I will confess mine!"

The point at issue was the revolution. The financial committee regarded the revolution as a fortuitous event, as a surprise, whereas he, Proudhon, had taken it seriously. In the year 93 property had paid its debt to the republic by paying a third of taxes. The revolution of 48 must remain in a "proportional relationship". In the year 93 the foes had been despotism and foreign countries. In the year 48, pauperism was the foe. "What is this *droit au travail*", this right to work?

---

[a] "Paris, 31. Juli...—National-Versammlung", *Neue Rheinische Zeitung* No. 64, August 3, 1848, pp. 3-4.—*Ed.*

"If the demand for labour were greater than the supply there would be no need for any promises on the part of the state. This, however, is not the case. Consumption is very low. The stores are full of goods and the poor are naked! And yet which country has a greater propensity to consume than France? If instead of 10 million, we were given 100, i.e. 75 francs per head and per day, we certainly would know how to consume it." (Hilarity in the Chamber.)

The rate of interest is supposed to be the basic cause of the people's ruin. The creation of a national bank of two milliards which would lend its money without interest and grant the free use of the land and of houses would bring immense advantages. (Vigorous interruptions.)

"If we stick to *this* (laughter), if the fetishism of money were supplanted by the realism of gratification (renewed laughter), then there would exist the guarantee of labour. Let the duties on the instruments of labour be abolished and you are saved. Those who maintain the opposite, may they be called Girondists or Montagnards, are no socialists and no republicans (Oh! Oh!).... Either property will smash the republic or the republic will smash property." (Calls of: enough!)

M. Proudhon now becomes enmeshed in a lengthy discourse about the significance of interest and how the rate of interest could be reduced to zero. M. Proudhon stands on weak grounds as long as he maintains this economic point of view even though he creates an immense scandal in this bourgeois Chamber. But whenever, excited by just this scandal, he adopts the proletarian point of view, the Chamber seems to go into nervous convulsions.

"Gentlemen, my ideas are different from yours. I represent a different point of view from yours! The liquidation of the old society began on February 24 with the fight between the bourgeoisie and the working class. This liquidation will be accomplished either by violent or by peaceful means. All will depend upon the discernment of the bourgeoisie and its greater or lesser resistance."

M. Proudhon now proceeds to elaborate his idea of "the abolition of property". He does not intend to abolish property all at once but only gradually. It is for this reason that he had stated in his journal[a] that *rent of land was a voluntary gift of the earth* which the state must gradually abolish.

"I have thus on the one hand explained the meaning of the February revolution to the bourgeoisie; I have given notice to property so that it may hold itself ready for liquidation and so that the property owners may be held responsible for their refusal."

A thunderous roar arises from several sides: responsible in what way?

---

[a] *Le Représentant du Peuple. Journal quotidien des travailleurs.*— Ed.

"By that I mean if the property owners will not liquidate voluntarily, we will carry through this liquidation."

Several voices: Who are we?

Other voices: Send him to the lunatic asylum at Charenton. (Tremendous excitement; a proper storm accompanied by thunder and the roaring of wind.)

"If I say we, I identify myself with the proletariat and you with the bourgeoisie."

M. Proudhon then enters upon the specification of his tax system and he becomes once again "scientific". This "science" which has always been Proudhon's weakness becomes his strength in this narrow-minded Chamber by giving him the boldness to combat with his pure, genuine "science" the defiled financial science of M. Thiers. M. Thiers has proved his practical financial discernment. During his administration, the state treasury decreased while his personal fortune increased.

When the Chamber paid little attention to Proudhon's further arguments, he declared bluntly that he would continue speaking for at least $^3/_4$ of an hour. When the majority of the Chamber was thereupon getting ready to leave he proceeded once again to direct attacks upon property.

"By the February revolution alone you have abolished property!"

One could almost say that terror kept the people glued to their seats every time that Proudhon said anything against property.

"By recognising in the Constitution the right to work, you have proclaimed the recognition of the abolition of property."

Larochejaquelein asks whether one has the right to steal. Other deputies do not want to let M. Proudhon continue.

"You cannot destroy the consequences of the *faits accomplis*" (accomplished facts). "If debtors and tenants are still paying, they are doing so of their own free will." (Tremendous uproar. The President calls the speaker to order: Everybody is obliged to pay his debts.)

"I am not saying that the liabilities have been repealed but those who are trying to defend them here are destroying the revolution...."

"What are we, representatives? Nothing. Nothing at all. The power which gave us power lacked principle and basis. Our entire authority is force, despotism and the might of the stronger. (New eruption of the storm.) Universal suffrage is an accident and in order that it may gain significance, it must be preceded by organisation. We are not ruled by law or justice. We are ruled by force, necessity, providence.... April 16th, May 15th, June 23rd, 24th and 25th are facts, nothing more than facts, which are legitimised by history. We can do today whatever we want to. We are the stronger ones. Let us not speak therefore of rebels. Rebels are those who have no other right than that of superior might but will not recognise this right for others. I know that my motion will not be accepted. But you are in a position where you can only escape death by accepting my motion. It is a question of credits and labour. Confidence will never return, nay, it is impossible for it to return...." (Horrible!) "For all that you might say that you are trying to create a respectable, moderate republic, capital does not dare to show itself under a republic which has to hold demonstrations in favour of the workers. While capital is thus waiting for us so as to liquidate us, we are waiting for capital so as to liquidate it. February 24 has proclaimed the right to work. If you eliminate this right from the Constitution, you proclaim the right to insurrection.

"Place yourselves for ever under the protection of bayonets, prolong the state of siege for ever: capital will still be afraid and socialism will keep its eyes on it."

The readers of the *Kölnische Zeitung* know M. Proudhon of yore. M. Proudhon, who, according to the reasoning of the agenda, has attacked morality, religion, family and property, was not so long ago still the acclaimed hero of the *Kölnische Zeitung*. Proudhon's "so-called social-economic system" was thoroughly glorified in articles from correspondents in Paris, in feuilletons and in lengthy treatises. All social reforms were to proceed from Proudhon's determination of value. The story of how the *Kölnische Zeitung* made this dangerous acquaintance does not belong here. But how strange! The very newspaper which in those days looked upon Proudhon as a saviour, now cannot find enough invective to label him and his "lying party" as corrupters of society. Is M. Proudhon no longer M. Proudhon?

What we were attacking in M. Proudhon's theory was the "utopian science" by which he wanted to settle the antagonism between capital and labour, between proletariat and bourgeoisie.[a] We shall come back to this point. His whole system of banking and his entire exchange of products is nothing but a petty-bourgeois illusion. Now, when to realise this pale illusion he is compelled to speak as a democrat in the face of the whole bourgeois Chamber and is expressing this antagonism in harsh terms, the Chamber cries of offence against morality and property.

Written on August 3, 1848

First published in the *Neue Rheinische Zeitung* No. 66, August 5, 1848

Printed according to the newspaper

Published in English for the first time

---

[a] See Karl Marx, *The Poverty of Philosophy. Answer to the "Philosophy of Poverty" by M. Proudhon.*—*Ed.*

DR. GOTTSCHALK

Cologne, August 4. Dr. Gottschalk had his three first interrogations published in the *Zeitung des Arbeiter-Vereines zu Köln*. As a punishment, the warders he has had up to now have been removed and a new gaoler appointed in the person of warder *Schröder*.[a]

"The latter was not willing to take over his duties without an exact inventory," writes the local workers' paper, "and so Dr. Gottschalk and his cell were searched again, customs-style. Although nothing suspicious was found, a much closer watch than before is being kept on him."[b]

Public proceedings in the Rhine Province are a sheer illusion as long as they are supplemented by *"Spanish Inquisition proceedings"*.[213] In order to appreciate Gottschalk's arrest, one should read the *Gervinus Zeitung*.[c] The forceful intervention of the Public Prosecutor, it says, has *restored confidence once more*. On the other hand, the approaching festivities[d] are diverting the attention of the frivolous citizens of Cologne from all thought of politics. And these same citizens of Cologne, to whom the Government has handed over Gottschalk and the Cathedral festivities, these same ungrateful citizens, the *Gervinus Zeitung* exclaims, forget all these good deeds of the Prussian Government as soon as it stammers the first word about a compulsory loan!

---

[a] "Die Beiden Verhöre des Herren Dr. Gottschalk" and "Der dritte Verhör des Dr. Gottschalk" (*Zeitung des Arbeiter-Vereines zu Köln* Nos. 16 and 18, July 20 and 27, 1848).—*Ed.*

[b] "Köln", ibid., No. 20, August 3, 1848.—*Ed.*

[c] *Deutsche Zeitung.—Ed.*

[d] Celebration of the 600th anniversary of the Cologne Cathedral in August 1848.—*Ed.*

The arrest of Gottschalk and Anneke, the press trials, and so on, have restored *confidence*. In the city, confidence is the basis of *public credit*. Therefore lend the Prussian Government money, a great deal of money, and it will lock up even more people, stage even more press trials, manufacture even more confidence. More arrests, more press trials, more reaction from the Government. But in honest exchange—mark this well—more money, more and more money from the citizens!

We advise the Prussian Government in its financial difficulties to take refuge in a measure tried and tested under Louis XIV and Louis XV. Let it sell *Lettres de cachet! Lettres de cachet! Lettres de cachet!*[214] as a means of restoring confidence and filling up the Prussian treasury!

Written on August 4, 1848

First published in the *Neue Rheinische Zeitung* No. 66, August 5, 1848

Printed according to the newspaper

Published in English for the first time

DEBATE ABOUT THE EXISTING REDEMPTION LEGISLATION

Cologne, August 4. The Berlin Assembly from time to time unearthes all sorts of old-Prussian dirt and just now when the black-white knighthood becomes daily more insolent, such revelations come in very handy.

The session of July 21st dealt again with the feudal obligations. Following a deputy's motion, the central section proposed that the pending negotiations or court hearings on redemptions and the division of common property be suspended either by the authorities or on application by one of the interested parties.

Deputy *Dierschke* examined the mode of redemption existing up to now. He explained, to begin with, how the method of redemption itself already takes advantage of the peasant:

"Compensation for corvée" (compulsory labour),[a] "for instance, has been fixed in a very partial manner. It has not been taken into account that the wages for corvée, which in former centuries were stipulated at 1 or 2 silver groschen, corresponded to the *then prevailing prices* of natural produce and the conditions of the times, and that they represented, therefore, an appropriate equivalent for work done, so that neither the lords of the manor nor the serfs should have a preponderant advantage. A free labourer, however, must now be paid 5 to 6 instead of 2 silver groschen per day. If now one of the interested partners of a service relationship requests redemption he will have to pay, after first converting corvée days into substitute days, a differential amount of at least 3 silver groschen per day, which will amount to a yearly rent (based upon 50 days) of 4 to 5 talers. The poor peasant cannot afford such payments since he often possesses barely a quarter of a morgen[b] of land and cannot find sufficient opportunity for work elsewhere."

---

[a] Dierschke used the word *Robotdienste* (corvée). Engels has inserted *Frondienste* (compulsory labour) in brackets.— *Ed.*

[b] An old German land measure, varying in different localities between 0.25 and 1.23 hectares.— *Ed.*

This passage of Herr Dierschke's speech leads to all sorts of observations about the famous enlightened legislation of 1807-11,[215] none of which made it appear in a very favourable light.

First of all, it is evident from this that the compulsory labour services (especially those in Silesia of which Herr Dierschke is speaking) are certainly not a rent or fee which is paid in kind, they are not a compensation for the use of the land; despite Herr Patow and Herr Gierke they are nothing but an "outcome of seigniory and serfdom" and hence ought to be *abolished without compensation* according to the very *own principles* of these great statesmen.

Wherein consisted the obligation of the peasant? In placing himself at the disposal of the lord of the manor during certain days of the year or for certain specified duties. But certainly not gratuitously. He received a wage for this which originally completely equalled the daily wage of free labour. Thus the advantage of the landlord consisted not in the gratuitous or merely cheaper labour of the peasant but in the fact that he had labourers at his disposal for the usual wage whenever he needed them without being obliged to employ them when he did not need them. The advantage to the landlord did not consist in the monetary value of the service in kind but rather in its *compulsory* nature. It did not consist in the economic disadvantage but rather in the *constraint* of the peasant. And this obligation is not supposed to be an "outcome of seigniory and serfdom"!

If Patow, Gierke and Co. want to be consistent, there is no doubt that in accordance with their original character, these labour services must be abolished *without compensation*.

But what is the situation if we take their *present* nature into account?

For centuries the compulsory services remained the same and so did the wages for these services. But the price of food increased and so did the wages for free labour. The compulsory service, which at the beginning brought equal economic advantage to both parties and often even resulted in well-paid work during the peasant's idle days, gradually became, to use the language of Herr Gierke, an "actual charge on his land" and a direct monetary gain for the gracious landlord. To the certainty that he will always have a sufficient number of labourers at his disposal, he could now add a hefty cut which he made in the wages of these workers. By means of a consistent, century-old trickery the peasants were cheated of a steadily growing part of their wage so that they finally received only a third or a quarter of it. Let us assume that a farmstead is obliged to supply only *one* worker for only 50 days a year and that the daily wage has increased on the average by only 2 silver groschen for the past 300 years. Then the gracious landlord will have earned a full 1,000 talers off this *one* worker. The interest on 500 talers over 300 years at 5 per cent will be 7,500 talers. Altogether he will have made 8,500 talers off *one* worker, and that according to an estimate which does not take into account half the actual position!

What deduction can be made from all this? A rent ought to be paid not by the peasant to the gracious lord but by the gracious lord to the peasant, that is not by the farmstead to the manor, but by the manor to the farmstead.

The Prussian liberals of 1848, however, do not judge like this. On the contrary, the Prussian judicial conscience declares that it is not the nobleman who must indemnify the peasant but the peasant who must pay compensation to the nobleman for the difference between statute wages and free wages. It is exactly *because* the peasant has been cheated out of the wage difference for so long by his gracious lord that he has now to indemnify his gracious lord for the cheating. For whosoever hath, to him shall be given; but whosoever hath not, from him shall be taken away even that he hath.[a]

The difference in wages is therefore calculated and the annual amount is regarded as rent of land. It flows in this form into the pockets of the gracious lords. If the peasant wants to redeem it, it will be capitalised at 4 per cent (not even at 5 per cent) and this capital, which is 25 times the amount of the rent, will have to be paid off. It is obvious that the peasant is being dealt with in a thoroughly businesslike fashion. Our foregoing estimate of the aristocracy's profits was thus entirely justified.

The upshot is that peasants often have to pay from 4 to 5 talers rent for a quarter of a morgen of bad land whereas one morgen of good land free from corvée can be had for three talers rent per annum!

The redemption can also be achieved by surrendering a piece of land of the same value as the capital sum that is outstanding. Only the more prosperous peasants, of course, can do this. In that case, the lord of the manor gets a piece of land as premium for the skill and persistence with which he and his ancestors have defrauded the peasants.

That is the theory of redemption. It corroborates entirely what has taken place in all other countries where feudalism has gradually been abolished, in particular in England and Scotland: the transformation of feudal into bourgeois property and of seigniory

---

[a] Matthew 13:12.— *Ed.*

into capital means in every case a new crass defrauding of the bondsman to the advantage of the feudal lord. The bondsman must *purchase* his freedom every time and he must buy it dearly. The bourgeois state acts according to the principle: only death is gratuitous.

The theory of redemption, however, proves even more.

As Deputy *Dane* observes, the inevitable result of these enormous demands upon the peasants is that they fall into the hands of usurers. Usury is the inevitable companion of a class of *free* small peasants as has been demonstrated in France, the Palatinate and the Rhine Province. The Prussian science of redemption managed to let the small peasantry of the old provinces partake of the joys of being squeezed by usurers even before they were freed. The Prussian Government, in general, has always had a knack for subjecting the oppressed classes to the pressure of feudal and of modern bourgeois conditions at the same time, thus making the yoke twice as heavy.

One has to add to this another matter, to which Deputy *Dane* also calls attention: the tremendous costs which mount in proportion to the negligence and inaptness of the commissioner who is paid by the term.

"The town of Lichtenau in Westphalia paid 17,000 talers for 12,000 morgen and *this has not yet covered the costs* (!!)."

Even more telling proof is provided by the practice of redemption. The land commissioners, continues Herr Dierschke, i.e. the officials who prepare the redemption,

"appear in three capacities. First, they appear as *examining officials*. In this capacity they interrogate the parties, determine the factual basis of the redemption and calculate the amount of compensation. They often carry out their task in a very one-sided manner and often do not take into account the existing legal conditions for in part they lack legal knowledge. Furthermore, they appear in part as *experts* and *witnesses* by themselves autonomically appraising the value of the redeemable objects. In the end they give their *testimony* which almost amounts to a decision since the general commission must as a rule rely on their opinions which are derived from local conditions.

"Finally there is the fact that the land commissioners do not enjoy the confidence of the rural population because they often put the parties at a disadvantage by letting them wait for hours while they *eat with relish at the table of the landlord*" (who is himself a party) "whereby they particularly arouse the mistrust of the parties against themselves.[216] When after a waiting period of three hours, the threshing gardeners are finally admitted, the land commissioners often roar at them and brusquely reject their rejoinders. Here I can speak from my own experience because I assisted the interested party of peasants in my capacity as attorney-at-law in cases involving redemptions. The dictatorial power of the land commissioners must therefore be removed. The combination of the threefold capacity as examining magistrate, witness and judge in *one and the same* person cannot be justified either."

Deputy *Moritz* defends the land commissioners. Herr *Dierschke* answers: I can state that there are very many among them who disregard the interests of the peasants. I myself have even called for the investigation of some of them and I can give proof of this if demanded.

Minister *Gierke,* of course, appears again as defender of the old-Prussian system and the institutions which have emerged from it. The land commissioners must, of course, also be praised again:

"I must leave it to the judgment of the Assembly, however, to decide whether it is just to use this rostrum to make accusations which *lack all proof and are entirely unsubstantiated!*"

And Herr Dierschke is offering proofs!

Since, however, his Excellency Gierke seems to be of the opinion that notorious facts can be knocked down by ministerial assertions, we shall shortly submit a few "proofs" which will show that Herr Dierschke, far from exaggerating, has not by a long way condemned the conduct of the land commissioners sufficiently strongly.

So much for the debate. The amendments submitted were so numerous that the report accompanied by them had to be referred back to the central section. Thus the definitive decision of the Assembly has yet to be made.

Among these amendments, there is one by Herr *Moritz* which calls attention to a further edifying measure of the old Government. He proposes the cessation of all negotiations concerning mill dues.

For when in the year 1810 it was decided to abolish the feudal prerogatives and banalities,[217] a commission was appointed simultaneously to compensate the millers for the fact that they were now exposed to free competition. This was already a paradoxical decision. Were the guild masters compensated for the abolition of their privileges? But there are special circumstances in this case. The mills paid extraordinary dues for the enjoyment of feudal prerogatives and banalities. Instead of simply abolishing these, they were given a compensation and the dues were continued. The form is paradoxical but there remains at least a *semblance* of justice in this case.

It so happens, however, that in the provinces added since 1815, the mill dues have been kept, the feudal prerogatives and banalities have been abolished and yet *no compensation* has been given. This is old-Prussian equality before the law. The industrial law, to be sure, abolishes all business taxes but under the trade regulations of 1845 and the law on compensation all mill dues are in case of doubt to be regarded not as business taxes but as *land taxes*. Innumerable law cases have resulted from this jumble and these violations of the law. The law-courts have contradicted each other in their sentences and even the Supreme Court has pronounced the most contradictory judgments. Just what was formerly regarded by the ex-legislative power as "land tax" emerges from a case cited by Herr Moritz: a mill in Saxony to which belongs, except for the mill buildings, only the water power but not the land, is burdened with a "land tax" of *four wispels*[a] of grain!

Indeed, say what you like, Prussia has always been the most wisely, most justly and best administered state!

Written by Engels on August 4, 1848	Printed according to the newspaper
First published in the *Neue Rheinische Zeitung* No. 67, August 6, 1848	Published in English for the first time

---

[a] Prior to 1872 a grain measure in Germany; in Prussia it was equal to 1,319 litres (approximately 36 bushels).— *Ed.*

THE "MODEL STATE" OF BELGIUM

Cologne, August 6. Let us once again cast a glance upon Belgium, our constitutional *"model state"*, the monarchical El Dorado with the broadest *democratic* basis, the university of the Berlin statesmen and the pride of the *Kölnische Zeitung*.

Let us look, to begin with, at the economic conditions of which the much-praised political constitution only forms the gilded frame.

The Belgian *Moniteur*—Belgium has her *Moniteur*—carries the following piece of news about Leopold's greatest vassal: *pauperism*.[a]

In the province of		1	inhabitant	out	of	receives	support
"	*Luxembourg*	1	inhabitant	out	of	69	receives	support
"	*Namur*	1	"	"	"	17	"	"
"	*Antwerp*	1	"	"	"	16	"	"
"	*Liége*	1	"	"	"	7	"	"
"	*Limburg*	1	"	"	"	7	"	"
"	*Hainaut*	1	"	"	"	6	"	"
"	*Eastern Flanders*	1	"	"	"	5	"	"
"	*Brabant*	1	"	"	"	4	"	"
"	*Western Flanders*	1	"	"	"	3	"	"

This growth of pauperism will necessarily be followed by a further increase in pauperism. All individuals who maintain an independent existence lose their civil equilibrium as a result of the assistance tax with which these poor fellow citizens burden them and they too plunge into the abyss of public charity. Pauperism creates pauperism

---

[a] "Emigration aux Etats-Unis de l'Amérique du Nord", *Le Moniteur belge* No. 212, July 30, 1848, p. 2074.—*Ed.*

at an increasing rate. To the same extent, however, that pauperism increases, *crime* increases and the life source of the nation itself, the *youth*, is demoralised.

The years 1845, 1846 and 1847 offer sad documents on that score.[a]

The number of young boys and girls under 18 years of age who were in judicial confinement:

	1845	1846	1847
Boys	2,146	4,607	7,283
Girls	429	1,279	2,069
Sum:	2,575	5,886	9,352

Sum total: 17,813

Thus starting with 1845 there is an approximately annual doubling of the number of juvenile delinquents *under* 18 years of age. According to this ratio, Belgium would have 74,816 juvenile delinquents in the year 1850 and 2,393,312 in the year 1855, i.e. more than the number of young people under 18 years of age she has and more than half her population. By 1856 all Belgium would be in gaol, the unborn children included. Could the monarchy hope for a *broader* democratic basis? *Equality* prevails in gaol.

Both types of Morison pill have been tried in vain on the national economy: on the one hand free trade and on the other hand protective tariffs. Pauperism in Flanders was born under the system of free trade, it grew and became stronger under the protective tariffs against foreign linen goods and linen yarn.

Thus while pauperism and crime grow among the proletariat, the bourgeoisie's sources of income are drying up as the recently published comparative tabulation of the Belgian foreign trade during the first six months of the years 1846, 1847 and 1848 proves.

With the exception of arms and nail factories, which have been exceptionally favoured by circumstances, the cloth factories which maintain their ancient renown and the zinc production which compared to overall production is insignificant, the whole of Belgian industry is in a condition of decay or stagnation.

With a few exceptions, there is a considerable decrease in the *export* of the products of the Belgian mines and metalworks.

---

[a] The data on juvenile delinquency are taken from: Edouard Ducpétiaux, *Mémoire sur l'organisation des écoles de réforme*, pp. 4-5.—*Ed.*

We quote a few examples[a]:

	First six months 1847	First six months 1848
Coal (in metric tons)	869,000	549,000
Pig iron	56,000	35,000
Cast iron wares	463	172
Iron, rails	3,489	13
Wrought iron wares	556	434
Nails	3,210	3,618
Total:	932,718	588,237

Thus the total decrease of these three types of articles for the first six months of 1848 amounts to 344,481 tons which is somewhat more than $1/3$.

We come to the linen industry.

	First six months 1846	First six months 1847	First six months 1848
Linen yarn [in kilograms]	1,017,000	623,000	306,000
Linen fabric	1,483,000	1,230,000	681,000
Total:	2,500,000	1,853,000	987,000

The decrease of the first six months of 1847 compared with those of 1846 amounted to 657,000 kilograms, the decrease in 1848 compared with that in 1846 amounts to 1,613,000 kilograms or 64 per cent.

The export of books, crystal ware and window glass has decreased enormously. So has the export of raw and dressed flax, tow, tree bark and manufactured tobacco.

The spreading pauperism, the unprecedented hold that crime has over young people, and the systematic deterioration of Belgian industry form the material basis of the following constitutional gaieties: The pro-government journal *Indépendance* numbers over 4,000 subscribers as it never grows tired of proclaiming. The aged *Mellinet*, the only general who saved Belgian honour, is confined to quarters and in a few days will appear before the Assizes in Antwerp.[b] The lawyer *Rolin* from Ghent, who conspires against

[a] The figures are quoted from "Exportations.—Marchandises belges", *Le Moniteur belge* No. 213, July 31, 1848, pp. 2085-2087.—*Ed.*
[b] See this volume, pp. 404-06.—*Ed.*

Leopold in the interest of the Orange family and conspires against his later allies, the Belgian liberals, in the interest of Leopold of Coburg, this Rolin, the double apostate, has obtained the portfolio of Public Works. The ex-pedlar Cha-a-azal, *Fransquillon*,[a] Baron and Minister of War, swings his large sabre and saves the European equilibrium. The *Observateur* has augmented the programme of the September Day Celebrations[218] by a new amusement: a procession, an *Ommeganck General*, in honour of the *Doudou* of Mons, the *Houplala* of Antwerp and the *Mannequin Pisse* of Brussels. The *Observateur*, the journal of the great *Verhaegen*, is perfectly in earnest. Finally, what compensates for Belgium's suffering is the fact that it has risen to become the university of Berlin's Montesquieus—of a Stupp, a Grimm, a Hansemann and a Baumstark—and that it enjoys the admiration of the *Kölnische Zeitung*. Oh happy Belgium!

Written by Marx on August 6, 1848

First published in the *Neue Rheinische Zeitung* No. 68, August 7, 1848

Printed according to the newspaper

Published in English for the first time

---

[a] A Belgian name for an admirer of everything French.— *Ed.*

THE FRANKFURT ASSEMBLY DEBATES
THE POLISH QUESTION[219]

[*Neue Rheinische Zeitung* No. 70, August 9, 1848]

Cologne, August 7. The Frankfurt Assembly, whose debates even during the most excited moments were conducted in a truly German spirit of geniality, at last pulled itself together when the Posen question came up. On this question, the ground for which had been prepared by Prussian shrapnel and the docile resolutions of the Federal Diet, the Assembly had to pass a clear-cut resolution. No middle course was possible; it had either to save Germany's honour or to blot it once again. The Assembly acted as we had expected; it sanctioned the seven partitions of Poland, and shifted the disgrace of 1772, 1794 and 1815 from the shoulders of the German princes to its own shoulders.[220]

The Frankfurt Assembly, moreover, declared that the seven partitions of Poland were benefactions wasted on the Poles. Had not the forcible intrusion of the Jewish-German race lifted Poland to a level of culture and a stage of science which that country had previously never dreamed of? Deluded, ungrateful Poles! If your country had not been partitioned you would have had to ask this favour yourselves of the Frankfurt Assembly.

Pastor Bonavita Blank of the Paradise monastery near Schaffhausen trained magpies and starlings to fly in and out. He had cut away the lower part of their bill so that they were unable to get their own food and could only receive it from his hands. The philistines who from a distance saw the birds alight on the Reverend's shoulders and seem to be friendly with him, admired his great culture and learning. His biographer says that the birds *loved their benefactor*.[a]

---

[a] [F. G. Benkert,] *Joseph Bonavita Blank's ... kurze Lebens-Beschreibung.—Ed.*

Yet the fettered, maimed, branded Poles refuse to love their Prussian benefactors!

We could not give a better description of the benefactions which Prussia bestowed on the Poles than that provided by the report which the learned historiographer Herr *Stenzel* submitted on behalf of the Committee for International Law, a report which forms the basis of the debate.

The report, entirely in the style of the conventional diplomatic documents, first recounts how the Grand Duchy of Posen was set up in 1815 by "incorporation" and "merging". Then follow the promises which at the same time Frederick William III made to the inhabitants of Posen, i.e. the safeguarding of their nationality, language and religion, the appointment of a native governor, and participation in the famous Prussian Constitution.[221]

The extent to which these promises were kept is well known. The freedom of communication between the three fragments of Poland, to which the Congress of Vienna could the more easily agree the less feasible it was, was of course never put into effect.

The make-up of the population is then examined. Herr Stenzel calculates that 790,000 Poles, 420,000 Germans and about 80,000 Jews lived in the Grand Duchy in 1843, making a total of almost 1,300,000.

Herr Stenzel's statement is challenged by the Poles, notably by Archbishop Przyluski,[a] according to whom there are considerably more than 800,000 Poles, and, if one deducts the Jews, officials and soldiers, hardly 250,000 Germans, living in Posen.

Let us, however, accept Herr Stenzel's figures. For our purposes it is quite sufficient. To avoid all further discussion, let us concede that there are 420,000 Germans living in Posen. Who are these Germans, who by the inclusion of the Jews have been brought up to half a million?

The Slavs are a predominantly agricultural people with little aptitude for urban trades in the form in which up to now they were feasible in the Slav countries. The first crude stage of commerce, when it was still mere hawking, was left to *Jewish* pedlars. With the growth of culture and population the need for urban trades and urban concentration made itself felt, and *Germans* moved into the Slav countries. The Germans, who after all had their heyday in the philistinism [*Kleinbürgerei*] of the imperial cities of the Middle Ages, in the sluggish inland trade conducted in caravan style, in a restricted

---

    [a] Leon Przyluski, ["Die Korrespondenz des Erzbischofs von Posen, Przyluski, mit dem Berliner Kabinett",] *Neue Rheinische Zeitung* Nos. 5, 7, 10, 14, 38 and 39, June 5, 7, 10 and 14, and July 8 and 9, 1848.—*Ed.*

maritime trade, and in the handicraft workshops of the fourteenth and fifteenth centuries organised on guild lines—the Germans demonstrated their vocation as the philistines of world history by the very fact that they still to this day form the core of the petty bourgeoisie throughout Eastern and Northern Europe and even in America. Many, often most of the craftsmen, shopkeepers and small middlemen in Petersburg, Moscow, Warsaw and Cracow, in Stockholm and Copenhagen, in Pest, Odessa and Jassy, in New York and Philadelphia are Germans or of German extraction. All these cities have districts where only German is spoken, and some of them, for example Pest, are almost entirely German.

This German immigration, particularly into the Slav countries, went on almost uninterruptedly since the twelfth and thirteenth centuries. Moreover, from time to time since the Reformation, as a result of the persecution of various sects large groups of Germans were forced to migrate to Poland, where they received a friendly welcome. In other Slav countries, such as Bohemia and Moravia, the Slav population was decimated by German wars of conquest, whereas the German population increased as a result of invasion.

The position is clearest in Poland. The German philistines living there for centuries never regarded themselves as politically belonging to Germany any more than did the Germans in North America; just as the "French colony" in Berlin and the 15,000 Frenchmen in Montevideo do not regard themselves as belonging to France. As far as that was possible during the days of decentralisation in the seventeenth and eighteenth centuries, they became Poles, German-speaking Poles, who had long since renounced all ties with the mother country.

But the Germans brought to Poland culture, education and science, commerce and trades.—True, they brought retail trade and guild crafts; by their consumption and the limited intercourse which they established they stimulated production to some extent. Up to 1772 Poland as a whole was not particularly well known for her high standard of education and science, and the same applies to Austrian and Russian Poland since then; of the Prussian part we shall speak later. On the other hand, the Germans in Poland prevented the formation of Polish towns with a Polish bourgeoisie. By their distinct language, their separateness from the Polish population, their numerous different privileges and urban judicial systems, they impeded centralisation, that most potent of political means by which a country achieves rapid development. Almost every town had its own law; indeed towns with a mixed population had, and often still have, different laws for Germans, Poles and Jews. The German Poles remained at the lowest stage of industrial development; they did not accumulate large capitals; they were neither able to establish large-scale industry nor control any extensive system of commerce. The Englishman Cockerill had to come to Warsaw for industry to strike root in Poland. The entire activity of the German Poles was restricted to retail trade, the handicrafts and at most the corn trade and manufacture (weaving etc.) on the smallest scale. In considering the merits of the German Poles it should not be forgotten also that they imported German philistinism and German petty-bourgeois narrow-mindedness into Poland, and that they combined the worst qualities of both nations without acquiring their good ones.

Herr Stenzel seeks to enlist the sympathy of the Germans for the German Poles:

"When the kings ... especially in the seventeenth century, became increasingly powerless and were no longer able to protect the native Polish peasants against the severest oppression by the nobles, the German villages and towns, too, declined, and many of them became the property of the nobility. Only the larger royal cities kept some of their old liberties" (read: privileges).

Does Herr Stenzel perhaps demand that the Poles should have protected the "Germans" (i.e. German Poles, who are moreover also "natives") better than themselves? Surely it is obvious that foreigners who immigrate into any country must expect to share the good and bad with the indigenous inhabitants.

Let us pass now to the blessings for which the Poles are indebted to the Prussian Government in particular.

Frederick II seized the Netze district[a] in 1772, and in the following year the Bromberg canal was built, which made inland navigation between the Oder and Weichsel[b] possible.

"The region, which for centuries was an object of dispute between Poland and Pomerania, and which was largely desolate as a result of countless devastations and because of vast swamps, was now brought under cultivation and populated by numerous colonists."

Thus, the first partition of Poland was no robbery. Frederick II merely seized an area which "for centuries was an object of dispute". But since when has there no longer existed an independent Pomerania which *could* have disputed this region? For how many centuries were in fact the rights of Poland to this region no longer challenged? And in general, what meaning has this rusted and rotten

---

[a] After the name of the River Netze (the Polish name is Noteć).— *Ed.*
[b] The Polish name is Vistula.—*Ed.*

theory of "disputes" and "claims", which, in the seventeenth and eighteenth centuries, served the purpose of covering up the naked commercial interests and the policy of rounding off one's lands? What meaning can it have in 1848 when the bottom has been knocked out of all "historical justice" and "injustice"?

Incidentally, Herr Stenzel ought to bear in mind that according to this junk-heap doctrine the Rhine borders between France and Germany have been "an object of dispute for millennia", and that Poland could assert her claims to suzerainty over the province of Prussia and even over Pomerania.

In short, the Netze district became part of Prussia and hence ceased to be "an object of dispute". Frederick II had it colonised by Germans, and so the "*Netze brethren*", who received such praise in connection with the Posen affair, came into being. The state-promoted Germanisation began in 1773.

"*According to all reliable information*, all the Jews in the Grand Duchy are Germans and *want* to be Germans.... The religious toleration which used to prevail in Poland and the possession of certain qualities which were lacking in the Poles, enabled the Jews in the course of centuries to develop activities which penetrated deep into Polish life" (namely into Polish purses). "As a rule they have a thorough command of both languages, although they, and their children from the earliest years, speak *German* at home."

The unexpected sympathy and recognition which Polish Jews have lately received in Germany has found official expression in this passage. Maligned wherever the influence of the Leipzig fair extends as the very incarnation of haggling, avarice and sordidness, they have suddenly become German brethren; with tears of joy the honest German presses them to his bosom, and Herr Stenzel lays claim to them on behalf of the German nation as Germans who *want* to remain Germans.

Indeed, why should not Polish Jews be genuine Germans? Do not "they, and their children from the earliest years, speak German at home"? And what German at that!

Incidentally, we would point out to Herr Stenzel that he might just as well lay claim to the whole of Europe, one half of America, and even part of Asia. German, as everyone knows, is the universal language of the Jews. In New York and Constantinople, in St. Petersburg and Paris "the Jews, and their children from the earliest years, speak German at home", and some of them even a more classical German than the Posen Jews, the "kindred" allies of the "Netze brethren."

The report goes on to present the national relations in terms that are as vague as possible and as favourable as possible to the alleged half a million Germans consisting of German Poles, "Netze brethren", and Jews. It says that German peasants own more land than the Polish peasants (we shall see how this has come to pass), and that since the first partition of Poland enmity between Poles and Germans, especially Prussians, reached its highest degree.

"By the introduction of its exceptionally rigidly regulated political and administrative orders" (what excellent style!) "and their strict enforcement, Prussia in particular seriously disturbed the old customs and traditional institutions of the Poles."

Not only the Poles but also the other Prussians, and especially we from the Rhine, can tell a tale about the "rigidly regulated" and "strictly enforced" measures of the worthy Prussian bureaucracy, measures which "*disturbed*" not only the old customs and traditional institutions, but also the *entire social* life, industrial and agricultural production, commerce, mining, in short all social relations without exception. It is, however, not to the bureaucracy of 1807-48 that Herr Stenzel refers here but to that of 1772-1806, to the officials of the most genuine, dyed-in-the-wool Prussianism, whose baseness, corruptibility, cupidity and brutality were clearly evident in the treacherous acts of 1806.[222] These officials are supposed to have protected the Polish peasants against the nobles and received in return nothing but ingratitude; of course the officials ought to have understood "that nothing, not even the good things granted or imposed, can compensate for the loss of national sovereignty".

We too know the way in which quite recently the Prussian officials used "to grant or impose everything". What Rhinelander, who had dealings with recently imported old-Prussian officials, did not have an opportunity to admire their inimitable, impertinent obtrusiveness, their impudent meddlesomeness, their overriding insolence and combination of narrow-mindedness and infallibility. True, among us, in most cases, these old-Prussian gentry soon lost some of their roughness for they had at their disposal no "Netze brethren", no secret inquisition, no Prussian law and no floggings which last deficiency even brought some of them to an early grave. We do not have to be told what havoc they wrought in Poland, where they could indulge in floggings and secret inquisitions to their heart's content.

In short, the arbitrary Prussian rule won such popularity that "already after the battle of Jena, the hatred of the Poles found vent in a general uprising and the ejection of the Prussian officials". This, for the time being, put an end to the bureaucratic rule.

But in 1815 it returned in a somewhat modified form. The "best", "reformed", "educated", "incorruptible" officialdom tried its hand at dealing with these refractory Poles.

"The founding of the Grand Duchy of Posen, too, was not conducive to the establishment of cordial relations, since ... at that time the King of Prussia could not possibly agree to have any single province set up as an entirely independent unit, thus turning his state, as it were, into a federal state."

Thus according to Herr Stenzel, the King of Prussia could "not possibly agree" to keep his own promises and the treaties of Vienna! [223]

"When, in 1830, the sympathies which the Polish nobility showed for the Warsaw uprising caused anxiety, and after systematic efforts were subsequently made by means of various arrangements (!)—notably by buying up the Polish landed estates, dividing them and handing them over to the Germans—gradually to eliminate the Polish nobility altogether, the latter's resentment against Prussia increased."

"By means of various arrangements"! By prohibiting Poles from buying land brought under the hammer, and similar measures, which Herr Stenzel covers with the cloak of charity.

What would Rhinelanders say if among us, too, the Prussian Government were to prohibit Rhinelanders from buying land put up for sale by order of the court. Sufficient pretexts could easily be found, namely: in order to amalgamate the population of the old and new provinces; in order that the natives of the old provinces could share in the blessings of parcellation and of the Rhenish laws; in order that Rhinelanders be induced to emigrate to the old provinces and implant their industries there as well, and so on. There are enough reasons to bestow Prussian "colonists" on us too. How would we look upon people who bought our land for next to nothing while competition was excluded, and who did it moreover with the support of the Government; people who were thrust upon us for the express purpose of accustoming us to the intoxicating motto "With God for King and Fatherland" [a]?

After all we are Germans, we speak the same language as the people in the old provinces. Yet in Posen those colonists were sent methodically, with relentless persistence, to the domains, the forests and the divided estates of the Polish nobility in order to oust the native Poles and their language from their own country and to set up a truly Prussian province, which would surpass even Pomerania in black-and-white fanaticism.

In order that the Prussian peasants in Poland should not be left without their natural masters, they were sent the flower of Prussian knighthood, men like *Tresckow* and *Lüttichau*, who also bought landed estates for next to nothing, and with the aid of government

---

[a] These words are taken from the decree on the establishment of an army reserve issued by Frederick William III on March 17, 1813.— *Ed.*

loans. In fact, after the Polish uprising of 1846,[224] a joint-stock company was formed in Berlin, which enjoyed the gracious protection of the highest personages in the land, and whose purpose was to buy up Polish estates for German knights. The poor starvelings from among the Brandenburg and Pomeranian aristocracy foresaw that trials instituted against the Poles would ruin numerous big Polish landowners, whose estates would shortly be sold off dirt-cheap. This was a real godsend for many a debt-ridden Don Ranudo from the Uckermark. A fine estate for next to nothing, Polish peasants who could be thrashed, and what is more, a good service rendered to King and Fatherland—what brilliant prospects!

Thus arose the third German immigration into Poland, Prussian peasants and Prussian noblemen settled throughout Posen with the declared intention, supported by the Government, not of Germanising, but of *Pomeranising* Posen. The German Poles had the excuse of having contributed in some measure to the promotion of commerce, the "Netze brethren" could boast that they had reclaimed a few bogs, but this last Prussian invasion had no excuse whatever. Even parcellation was not consistently carried through, the Prussian aristocrats following hard on the heels of the Prussian peasants.

[*Neue Rheinische Zeitung* No. 73, August 12, 1848]

Cologne, August 11. In the first article we have examined the "historical foundation" of Stenzel's report insofar as he deals with the situation in Posen before the revolution. Today we proceed to Herr Stenzel's history of the revolution and counter-revolution in Posen.

"The German people, who at all times is filled with compassion for all the unfortunate" (so long as this compassion costs nothing), "always deeply felt how greatly its princes wronged the Poles."

Indeed, "deeply felt" within the calm German heart, where the feelings are so "deeply" embedded that they never manifest themselves in action. Indeed, there was "compassion", expressed by a few alms in 1831 and by dinners and balls in aid of the Poles, so long as it was a matter of dancing and drinking champagne for the benefit of the Poles, and of singing "Poland is not yet lost!" [a] But when were the Germans prone to do something really decisive, to make a real sacrifice!

---

[a] The words are from the Polish national anthem.— *Ed.*

"The Germans honestly and fraternally proffered their hand to expiate the wrongs their princes had perpetrated."

Indeed, if it were possible to "expiate" anything with sentimental phrases and dull tub-thumping, then the Germans would emerge as the purest people in the annals of history.

"Just at the moment, however, when the Poles shook hands" (that is, took the fraternally proffered hand) "the interests and aims of the two nations already diverged. The Poles' only thought was for the restoration of their old state at least within the boundaries that existed before the first partition of 1772."

Surely, only the unreasoning, confused, haphazard enthusiasm, which from time immemorial has been a principal adornment of the German national character, could have caused the Germans to be surprised by the Polish demands. The Germans wanted to *"expiate"* the injustice the Poles had suffered. What started this injustice? To say nothing of earlier treacheries, it certainly started with the first partition of Poland in 1772. How could this be "expiated"? Of course, only by restoration of the *status quo* existing *before* 1772, or at least by the Germans returning to the Poles what *they* had robbed them of since 1772. But this was against the interests of the Germans? Well, if we speak of interests, then it can no longer be a question of sentimentalities like "expiation" etc.; here the language of cold, unfeeling practice should be used, and we should be spared rhetorical flourishes and expressions of magnanimity.

Moreover, firstly, the Poles did not at all *"only* think" of the restoration of the Poland of 1772. In any case what the Poles did *"think"* is hardly our concern. For the time being they *demanded* only the reorganisation of the *whole* of Posen and mentioned other eventualities only in case of a German-Polish war against Russia.

Secondly, "the interests and aims of the two nations diverged" only insofar as the "interests and aims" of revolutionary Germany in the field of international relations remained exactly the same as those of the old, absolutist Germany. If Germany's "interest and aim" is an alliance with Russia, or at least peace with Russia at any price, then of course everything in Poland must remain as it was hitherto. We shall see later, however, to what extent the *real* interests of Germany are identical with those of Poland.

Then follows a lengthy, confused and muddled passage, in which Herr Stenzel expatiates on the fact that the German Poles were right when they wanted to do justice to Poland, but at the same time to remain Prussians and Germans. Of course it is of no concern to Herr Stenzel that the "when" excludes the "but" and the "but" the "when".

Next comes an equally lengthy and confused historical account, in which Herr Stenzel goes into detail in an attempt to prove that, owing to the "diverging interests and aims of the two nations" and the ensuing mutual enmity which was steadily growing, a bloody clash was *unavoidable*. The Germans adhered to the *"national"* interests, the Poles merely to the *"territorial"* interests. In other words, the Germans demanded that the Grand Duchy should be divided according to nationalities, the Poles wanted the whole of their old territory.

This is again not true. The Poles asked for reorganisation but at the same time stated that they were quite willing to relinquish the frontier districts with a mixed population where the majority are Germans and *want* to join Germany. The inhabitants, however, should not be declared German or Polish by the Prussian *officials* at will, but according to their *own* wishes.

Herr Stenzel goes on to assert that Willisen's mission was of course bound to fail because of the (alleged, but nowhere existing) resistance of the Poles to the cession of the predominantly German districts. Herr Stenzel was able to examine the statements of Willisen about the Poles and those of the Poles about Willisen. These *published* statements prove the opposite. But this happens if "one is a man who", as Herr Stenzel says, "has studied history for many years and deems it his duty never to utter an untruth and never to conceal what is true".

With the same truthfulness which never conceals what is true, Herr Stenzel easily passes over the cannibalism perpetrated in Posen, the base and perfidious violation of the Convention of Jaroslawiec,[225] the massacres of Trzemeszno, Miloslaw and Wreschen,[a] the destructive fury of a brutal soldiery worthy of the Thirty Years' War,[226] and does not say a word about it.

Now Herr Stenzel comes to the four partitions of Poland recently effected by the Prussian Government. First the Netze district and four other districts were torn away (April 14); to this were added certain parts of other districts. This territory with a total population of 593,390 was incorporated in the German Confederation on April 22. Then the city and fortress of Posen together with the remainder of the left bank of the Warta were also included, making an additional 273,500 persons and bringing the combined population of these lands to *double* the number of Germans living in the whole of Posen even according to *Prussian* estimates. This was effected by an Order in Council on April 26,[b] and already on May 2 they were

---

[a] The Polish name is Września.— *Ed.*
[b] The *Neue Rheinische Zeitung* has "April 29", evidently a misprint.— *Ed.*

admitted to the German Confederation. Now Herr Stenzel pleads
with the Assembly that it is absolutely essential for Posen to remain in
German hands, that Posen is an important, powerful fortress, with a
population of over 20,000 Germans (most of them Polish Jews) who
own two-thirds of all the landed property etc. That Posen is situated
in the midst of a purely Polish territory, that it was forcibly
Germanised, and that Polish Jews are not Germans, does not make
the slightest difference to men who "never utter an untruth and
never suppress what is true", to historians of Herr Stenzel's
calibre.

In short, Posen, for military reasons, should not be relinquished.
As though it were not possible to raze the fortress, which, according
to Willisen, is one of the greatest strategic blunders, and to fortify
Breslau [a] instead. But ten million (incidentally this is again not
true—barely five million) have been invested, and it is of course
more advantageous to retain this precious work of art and 20 to 30
square miles of Polish land into the bargain.

With the "city and fortress" of Posen in one's hands, it will be all
the easier to seize still more.

"But to keep the fortress it will be necessary to secure its approaches from Glogau,
Küstrin and Thorn[b] as well as a fortified area facing the east" (it need be only 1,000
to 2,000 paces wide, like that of Maestricht facing Belgium and Limburg). "This,"
continues Herr Stenzel with a smile of satisfaction, "will at the same time ensure
undisturbed possession of the Bromberg canal; but numerous areas with a
predominantly Polish population will have to be incorporated into the German
Confederation."

It was for all these reasons that lunar caustic Pfuel, the well-known
philanthropist, carried through two new partitions of Poland, thus
meeting all the desires of Herr Stenzel and incorporating three-
fourths of the Grand Duchy into Germany. Herr Stenzel is the more
grateful for this procedure, since the revival of Louis XIV's
chambers of reunion [227] with augmented powers must evidently have
demonstrated to this historian that the Germans have learned to
apply the lessons of history.

According to Herr Stenzel, the Poles ought to find consolation in
the fact that their share of the land is more fertile than the
incorporated territory, that there is considerably less landed
property in their part than in that of the Germans and that "no
unbiassed person will deny that the lot of the Polish peasant under a
German Government will be far more tolerable than that of the

---

[a] The Polish name is Wrocław.—Ed.
[b] The Polish names are Głogów, Kostrzyn and Toruń.—Ed.

German peasant under a Polish Government"! History provides some curious examples of this.

Finally, Herr Stenzel tells the Poles that even the small part left to them will enable them, by practising all the civic virtues,

"to befittingly prepare themselves for the moment, which at present is still shrouded in the mists of the future, and which, quite pardonably, they are trying—perhaps too impatiently—to precipitate. One of their most judicious fellow citizens exclaimed very pertinently. 'There is a crown which is also worthy of your ambition, it is the *civic crown*!' A German would perhaps add: It does not shine, but it is solid!"

"It is solid!" But even more "solid" are the real reasons for the last four partitions of Poland by the Prussian Government.

You worthy German—do you believe that the partitions were undertaken in order to deliver your German brothers from Polish rule; to ensure that the fortress of Posen serves as a bulwark protecting you from any attack; to safeguard the roads of Küstrin, Glogau and Bromberg,[a] and the Netze canal? What a delusion! You have been shamefully deceived. The sole reason for the recent partitions of Poland was to *replenish the Prussian treasury*.

The earlier partitions of Poland [b] up to 1815 were annexations of territory by force of arms; the partitions of 1848 are *robbery*.

And now, worthy German, see how you have been deceived! After the third partition of Poland the estates of the Polish *starosten* [c] and those of the Catholic clergy were confiscated by Frederick William II in favour of the state. As the Declaration of Appropriation issued on July [d] 28, 1796, says, the estates of the church in particular constituted "a *very considerable* part of landed property as a whole". The new domains were either managed on the King's account or leased, and they were so extensive that 34 crown-land offices and 21 forestry divisions had to be set up for their administration. Each of these crown-land offices was responsible for a large number of villages; for example, altogether 636 villages came under the ten offices of the Bromberg district, and 127 were administered by the Mogilno crown-land office.

In 1796, moreover, Frederick William II confiscated the estates and woodlands of the convent at Owinsk and sold them to the merchant von Tresckow (forefather of the brave Prussian troop leader in the last heroic war[e]). These estates comprised 24 villages

---

[a] The Polish name is Bydgoszcz.— *Ed.*
[b] In 1795.— *Ed.*
[c] *Starosten*— formerly a nobleman in Poland who held a fief of the Crown.— *Ed.*
[d] The *Neue Rheinische Zeitung* has "March".— *Ed.*
[e] An ironic allusion to the war against Denmark over Schleswig-Holstein.— *Ed.*

with flour mills and 20,000 morgen[a] of forest land, worth at least 1,000,000 talers.

Furthermore, the crown-land offices of Krotoschin, Rozdrazewo, Orpiszewo and Adelnau,[b] worth at least two million talers, were in 1819 made over to the Prince of Thurn und Taxis to compensate him for the post-office privileges in several provinces which had become part of Prussia.

Frederick William II took over all these estates on the pretext that he could administer them better. Nevertheless, these estates, the property of the Polish nation, were given away, ceded or sold, and the proceeds flowed into the *Prussian* treasury.

The crown lands in Gnesen, Skorzencin and Trzemeszno were broken up and sold.

Thus 27 crown-land offices and forestry divisions, to a value of *twenty million talers* at the very least, still remain in the hands of the Prussian Government. We are prepared to prove, map in hand, that all these domains and forests—with very few exceptions, if any at all—are located in the incorporated part of Posen. To prevent this rich treasure from reverting to the Polish nation it had to be absorbed into the German Confederation, and since it could not go to the German Confederation, the German Confederation had to come to it, and three-fourths of Posen were incorporated.

That is the true reason for the four famous partitions of Poland within two months. Neither the protests of this or that nationality nor alleged strategic reasons were decisive—the frontier was determined solely by the position of the domains, and the rapacity of the Prussian Government.

While German citizens were shedding bitter tears over the invented sufferings of their poor brothers in Posen, while they were waxing enthusiastic about the safety of the Eastern Marches of Germany, and while they allowed themselves to be infuriated against the Poles by false reports about Polish barbarities, the Prussian Government acted on the quiet, and feathered its nest. This German enthusiasm without rhyme or reason merely served to disguise the dirtiest deed in modern history.

That, worthy German, is how you are treated by your responsible Ministers!

Actually however you ought to have known this beforehand. Whenever Herr Hansemann has a hand in something, it is never

---

[a] An old German land measure, varying in different localities between 0.25 and 1.23 hectares.—*Ed.*

[b] The Polish name is Odolanów.— *Ed.*

a matter of German nationality, military necessity or suchlike empty phrases, but always a matter of cash payment and of net profit.

[*Neue Rheinische Zeitung* No. 81, August 20, 1848]

Cologne, August 19. We have examined in detail Herr Stenzel's report, which forms the basis of the debate. We have shown that he falsifies both the earlier and the more recent history of Poland and of the Germans in Poland, that he confuses the whole issue, and that Stenzel the historian is not only guilty of deliberate falsification but also of gross ignorance.

Before dealing with the debate itself we must take another look at the Polish question.

The problem of Posen taken by itself is quite meaningless and insoluble. It is a fragment of the Polish problem and can only be solved in connection with and as a part of it. Only when Poland exists again will it be possible to determine the borders between Germany and Poland.

But can and will Poland exist again? This was denied during the debate.

A French historian has said: *Il y a des peuples nécessaires*—there are *necessary nations*. The Polish nation is undoubtedly one of the necessary nations of the nineteenth century.

But for no one is Poland's national existence more necessary than for us Germans.

What is the main support of the reactionary forces in Europe since 1815, and to some extent even since the first French revolution? It is the Russian-Prussian-Austrian *Holy Alliance*. And what holds the Holy Alliance together? The *partition of Poland*, from which all the three allies have profited.

The tearing asunder of Poland by the three powers is the tie which links them together; the robbery they jointly committed makes them support one another.

From the moment the first robbery of Polish territory was committed Germany became dependent on Russia. Russia ordered Prussia and Austria to remain absolute monarchies, and Prussia and Austria had to obey. The efforts to gain control—efforts which were in any case feeble and timid, especially on the part of the Prussian bourgeoisie—failed entirely because of the impossibility of breaking away from Russia, and because of the support which Russia offered the feudalist-absolutist class in Prussia.

Moreover, as soon as the allies attempted to introduce the first oppressive measures the Poles not only rose to fight for their independence, but simultaneously came out in *revolutionary* action against their own internal social conditions.

The partition of Poland was effected through a pact between the big feudal aristocracy of Poland and the three partitioning powers. It was not an advance, as the ex-poet Herr Jordan maintains, it was the last means the big aristocracy had to protect itself against a revolution, it was thoroughly reactionary.

Already the first partition led quite naturally to an alliance of the other classes, i.e. the nobles, the townspeople and to some extent the peasants, both against the oppressors of Poland and against the big Polish aristocracy. The Constitution of 1791 [228] shows that already then the Poles clearly understood that their independence in foreign affairs was inseparable from the overthrow of the aristocracy and from the agrarian reform within the country.

The big agrarian countries between the Baltic and the Black seas can free themselves from patriarchal feudal barbarism only by an agrarian revolution, which turns the peasants who are serfs or liable to compulsory labour into free landowners, a revolution which would be similar to the French revolution of 1789 in the countryside. It is to the credit of the Polish nation that it was the first of all its agricultural neighbours to proclaim this. The first attempted reform was the Constitution of 1791; during the uprising of 1830 Lelewel declared an agrarian revolution to be the only means of saving the country, but the Diet recognised this too late; during the insurrections of 1846 and 1848 the agrarian revolution was openly proclaimed.

From the day of their subjugation the Poles came out with revolutionary demands, thereby committing their oppressors still more strongly to a counter-revolutionary course. They compelled their oppressors to maintain the patriarchal feudal structure not only in Poland but in all their other countries as well. The struggle for the independence of Poland, particularly since the Cracow uprising of 1846, is at the same time a struggle of *agrarian democracy*—the only form of democracy possible in Eastern Europe—against *patriarchal feudal absolutism.*

So long, therefore, as we help to subjugate Poland, so long as we keep part of Poland fettered to Germany, we shall remain fettered to Russia and to the Russian policy, and shall be unable to eradicate patriarchal feudal absolutism in Germany. The creation of a democratic Poland is a primary condition for the creation of a democratic Germany.

But the restoration of Poland and the settlement of her frontiers with Germany is not only necessary, it is the most easily solvable of all the political problems which have arisen in Eastern Europe since the revolution. The struggle for independence of the diverse nationalities jumbled together south of the Carpathians is much more complicated and will lead to far more bloodshed, confusion and civil wars than the Polish struggle for independence and the establishment of the border line between Germany and Poland.

Needless to say, it is not a question of restoring a bogus Poland, but of restoring the state upon a viable foundation. Poland must have at least the dimensions of 1772, she must comprise not only the territories but also the estuaries of her big rivers and at least a large seaboard on the Baltic.

The Germans could have secured all this for Poland and at the same time protected their own interests and their honour, if after the revolution they had had the courage, for their own sake, arms in hand, to demand that Russia relinquish Poland. Owing to the commingling of Germans and Poles in the border regions and especially along the coast, it goes without saying that both parties would have had to make some concessions to one another, some Germans becoming Polish and some Poles German, and this would have created no difficulties.

After the indecisive German revolution, however, the courage for so resolute an action was lacking. It is all very well to make florid speeches about the liberation of Poland and to welcome passing Poles at railway stations, offering them the most ardent sympathies of the German people (to whom had these sympathies not been offered?); but to start a war with Russia, to endanger the European balance of power and, to cap all, hand over some scraps of the annexed territory — only one who does not know the Germans could expect that.

And what would a war with Russia have meant? A war with Russia would have meant a complete, open and effective break with the whole of our disgraceful past, the real liberation and unification of Germany, and the establishment of democracy on the ruins of feudalism and on the wreckage of the short-lived bourgeois dream of power. War with Russia would have been the only possible way of vindicating our honour and our interests with regard to our Slav neighbours, and especially the Poles.

But we were philistines and have remained philistines. We made several dozen small and big revolutions, at which we ourselves took fright even before they were accomplished. We talked big, but carried nothing through. The revolution narrowed our mental horizon instead of broadening it. All problems were approached from the standpoint of the most timid, most narrow-minded, most illiberal philistinism, to the detriment, of course, of our real interests. From the standpoint of this petty philistinism, the great question of Poland's liberation was therefore reduced to the paltry slogan calling for reorganisation of a part of the Province of Posen, while our enthusiasm for the Poles turned into shrapnel and lunar caustic.

War with Russia, we repeat, was the only possible means of upholding Germany's honour and Germany's interests. We shrank from it and the inevitable happened—the reactionary soldiery, beaten in Berlin, raised their head again in Posen; under the pretext of saving Germany's honour and national integrity they raised the banner of counter-revolution and crushed our allies, the revolutionary Poles—and for a moment the hoodwinked Germans exultantly applauded their victorious enemies. The new partition of Poland was accomplished, and only the sanction of the German National Assembly was still missing.

The Frankfurt Assembly still had a chance to mend matters: it should have excluded the whole of Posen from the German Confederation and left the border question open until it could be discussed with a restored Poland *d'égal à égal*.

But that would be asking too much of our professors, lawyers and pastors who sit in the Frankfurt National Assembly. The temptation was too great. These peaceful burghers, who had never fired a rifle, were, by simply rising or remaining seated, to conquer for Germany a country of 500 square miles and to incorporate 800,000 "Netze brethren", German Poles, Jews and Poles, even though this was to be done at the expense of the honour and of the real, lasting interests of Germany—what a temptation! They succumbed to it, they endorsed the partition of Poland.

What the motives were, we shall see tomorrow.

[*Neue Rheinische Zeitung* No. 82, August 22, 1848]

Cologne, August 21. We shall leave aside the preliminary question as to whether the deputies from Posen should take part in the discussion and voting and proceed at once to the debate on the main question.

Herr *Stenzel*, the reporter, opened the debate with an appallingly confused and verbose speech. He poses as a historian and a conscientious man, he speaks of fortresses and field-works, of heaven and hell, of sympathies and German hearts. He goes back to the eleventh century to prove that the Polish nobility has always oppressed the peasants. He uses a few meagre facts from Polish history as an excuse for an unending stream of the most insipid commonplaces about nobility, peasants, towns, benefactions of the absolute monarchy etc. He defends the partition of Poland in a clumsy and self-conscious manner; he explains the provisions of the Constitution of May 3, 1791, in such a completely muddled way that those members not already familiar with it now know even less about it. He is just about to turn to the Grand Duchy of Warsaw when he is interrupted by the exclamation: "This is too much!" and by the President.

Thrown into complete confusion, the great historian continues with the following touching words:

"I shall be brief. The question is—what are we to do? This question is quite natural" (!literally). "The nobility wants to restore the Empire. It asserts that it is democratic. I do not doubt that this is meant in honesty. However, gentlemen, it is quite natural (!) for certain estates to cherish great illusions. I believe completely in their sincerity, but when princes and counts must join the people, I do not know how the merging is to come about" (why should that concern Herr Stenzel!). "In Poland it is impossible" etc.

Herr Stenzel speaks as if in Poland there were no difference at all between nobility and aristocracy. Lelewel's *Histoire de Pologne*, which he himself quotes, Mieroslawski's *Débat entre la révolution et la contrerévolution en Pologne* and a great many other recent publications could disabuse the "man who has studied history for many years". Most of the "princes and counts" mentioned by Herr Stenzel are precisely those against whom Polish democracy is fighting.

Therefore, Herr Stenzel thinks, the nobility with its illusions should be dropped and a Poland for the peasants set up (by incorporating one Polish district after another into Germany).

"You should, on the contrary, hold out your hands to the poor peasants so that these can rise up and perhaps (!) succeed in establishing a free Poland, and not only in establishing it but also in maintaining it. That, gentlemen, is the main thing!"

Elated with victory, the historian leaves the rostrum accompanied by exultant shouts of "Bravo!", "Excellent!" from the national twaddlers of the Centre groups.[229] To describe the new partition of Poland as a blessing for the Polish peasants, this astonishingly absurd turn of events was of course bound to bring tears of emotion to the eyes of the genial and philanthropic mass in the Centre of the Assembly!

Next comes Herr *Goeden* from *Krotoszyn*, a German Pole of the first water. He is followed by Herr *Senff* from *Inowroclaw*, a fine example of a "Netze brother", devoid of guile. He put his name down as a speaker against the motion tabled by the committee but spoke for the motion and, as a result of this trick, a speaker against the motion lost his turn.

The way the "Netze brethren" behave here is the most ludicrous comedy one can imagine and shows once again what a genuine Prussian is capable of. We all know that the profit-hungry Jewish-Prussian small fry from Posen, who fought against the Poles, acted in close unity with the bureaucracy, the royal Prussian officers and the Brandenburg and Pomeranian squirearchy, in short with all who were reactionary and old-Prussian. The betrayal of Poland was the first insurrection of the counter-revolution, and no one was more counter-revolutionary than the "Netze brethren".

Now let us here in Frankfurt take a look at these rabidly Prussophile schoolmasters and officials with their "God for King and Fatherland",[a] who call their counter-revolutionary betrayal of Polish democracy a revolution, a real and genuine revolution in the name of the sovereign "Netze brotherhood", who trample historical rights under foot and over the allegedly dead Poland exclaim: "Right is on the side of the living!"[b]

But that's how the Prussian behaves: on the Spree by "the grace of God", on the Warta the sovereign people; on the Spree mob riots, on the Warta the revolution; on the Spree "historical right which does not have no date",[c] on the Warta the right of the living facts which date from yesterday—but for all that his faithful Prussian heart is devoid of guile, is honest and upright!

Let us hear Herr Goeden.

"This is the second time that we are having to defend a cause which is so important and so momentous for our country that, had it not of itself turned out (!) to be entirely right as far as we are concerned, it *would have been necessary to make it so* (!!). Our right is rooted not so much in the past as in the *fast beating pulse*" (and especially in beatings with the butt-end) "*of the present.*"

"As a result of the" (Prussian) "occupation, the Polish peasants and townspeople found themselves in a state of security and well-being which they had never known previously." (Especially not since the time of the Polish-Prussian wars and the partitions of Poland.)

"The infringement of justice implied in the partition of Poland is completely expiated by the humane attitude of your" (the German) "people" (and in particular by the floggings ordered by Prussian officials, "by its diligent work" (on Polish land which has been stolen and given away), "and in April of this year also by its *blood!*"

The blood of Herr Goeden from Krotoszyn!

"The *revolution* is our right and we are here on the strength of it!"

"The proof that we have been legally incorporated into Germany does not consist of parchment documents, turned yellow with age; we have not been acquired through

---

[a] These words are taken from the decree on the establishment of an army reserve issued by Frederick William III on March 17, 1813.—*Ed.*

[b] Modified quotation from Schiller's "An die Freunde".—*Ed.*

[c] This ungrammatical phrase occurred in a speech of the Right-wing Deputy Lichnowski (see this volume, p. 369).—*Ed.*

marriage, inheritance, purchase or exchange; we are Germans, and belong to our fatherland because *a sovereign will* which is rational and just impels us, a will which is based on our geographical position, our language and customs, our numbers (!), our property, but above all on our German way of thinking and our love of our fatherland."

"Our rights are so secure and rest so firmly in the *modern concept of the world*, that one does not even need a German heart to be compelled to recognise this!"

Long live the "sovereign will" of the Prussian-Jewish "Netze brotherhood", a will which rests in the "modern concept of the world", relies on the shrapnel "revolution" and is rooted in the "fast beating pulse" of the present, with its martial law! Long live the German nationalism of the bureaucrats' salaries in Posen, of the plunder of church and state property and of loans *à la* Flottwell!

The oratorical knight of superior rights is followed by the impertinent "Netze brother". Even Stenzel's motion is still too polite towards the Poles for Herr Senff of Inowroclaw; he therefore proposes a somewhat ruder wording. With the same impudence with which he used this pretext to put his name down as a speaker against the motion, he now declares that to debar the Posen deputies from voting was a disgraceful injustice.

"I believe that the deputies from Posen are *especially* competent to take part in the voting, for it is the most important rights of those who have sent us here which are at issue."

Herr Senff then talks about Poland's history since the first partition, elaborating it with a series of deliberate falsifications and gross lies so that, in comparison, Herr Stenzel is a pitiable dabbler. Everything that is tolerable in Posen owes its inception to the Prussian Government and the "Netze brethren".

"The Grand Duchy of Warsaw was set up. The Prussian officials were replaced by Polish officials and, in 1814, hardly a trace remained of the benefits these provinces derived from Prussian rule."

Herr Senff is quite right. "No trace remained" of serfdom or of the cash contributions that Polish districts had to pay to Prussian educational institutions, e.g. the University of Halle, or of the extortions and brutalities perpetrated by Prussian officials who did not speak Polish. But Poland was not yet lost[a] for, thanks to Russia, Prussia began to thrive once more and Posen was again incorporated into Prussia.

"From that time on, the Prussian Government renewed its efforts to improve conditions in the Province of Posen."

---

[a] The words are from the Polish national anthem.—*Ed.*

Those who want to know more about this should read Flottwell's memorandum of 1841.[a] Up to 1830, the Government did *nothing* at all. Flottwell found only *four* miles of highway in the whole Grand Duchy! Shall we enumerate Flottwell's benefactions? Herr Flottwell, a cunning bureaucrat, sought to bribe the Poles by building roads, opening up rivers, draining marshes etc.; but he bribed them not with the money of the Prussian Government, but *with their own money.* All those improvements were, in the main, carried through with the aid of private and district resources and, though the Government occasionally contributed some money, this was only a small fraction of the amount it extracted from the province as taxes and revenues from the Polish state and church domains. The Poles, moreover, are indebted to Herr Flottwell not only for the continuing suspension (since 1826) of district council elections, but especially for the gradual expropriation of Polish landowners as a result of the Government buying up the auctioned estates of noblemen and reselling them only to loyal Germans (Order in Council of 1833). The last benefaction of Flottwell's administration was the improvement of the educational system. But this too was a measure designed to further Prussianisation. Prussian teachers were to Prussianise the young noblemen and future Catholic priests in the secondary schools, and the peasants in the primary schools. In an unguarded outburst, Herr Wallach, the *Regierungspräsident* of the Bromberg administrative district, has divulged the purpose of these educational establishments. He writes to Herr Beurmann, the *Oberpräsident,* that the *Polish language* is one of the *chief obstacles* to the dissemination of education and well-being among the rural population. This is indeed quite true if the teacher does not speak Polish.

Incidentally, it was again the Poles themselves who paid for these schools. For, first of all, the majority, including the most important institutes, which did not, however, directly serve the goal of Prussianisation, were founded and endowed by private contributions or by the Provincial Estates and, secondly, even the schools designed to Prussianise the population were maintained out of the revenues of monasteries secularised on March 31, 1833, and only 21,000 talers a year, for ten years, were granted by the treasury.

Herr Flottwell admits, moreover, that all reforms were initiated by the Poles. The fact that the greatest benefactions of the Prussian Government consisted in the collection of large revenues and taxes

---

[a] "Denkschrift des Oberpräsidenten Herrn Flottwell, ueber die Verwaltung des Gros-Herzogthum Posen, vom Dezember 1830 bis zum Beginn des Jahres 1841."—*Ed.*

and in enlisting young men into the Prussian military service, is passed over in silence by Herr Flottwell, just as it is by Herr Senff.

In short, all the benefactions of the Prussian Government simply amount to the provision of posts for Prussian non-commissioned officers in Posen, be it as drill-master, schoolmaster, policeman or tax-collector.

We cannot discuss in detail the other unfounded accusations which Herr Senff levels against the Poles, nor his false statistical data. It is sufficient to say that the purpose of Herr Senff's speeches is simply to make the Assembly detest the Poles.

Herr *Robert Blum* follows. As usual, he delivers what is called a *profound* oration, i.e. an oration which contains more opinion than reason and more rhetoric than opinion, and which, incidentally, as a piece of rhetoric—as we have to admit—produces no greater effect than the "modern concept of the world" of Herr Goeden from Krotoszyn. Poland is the rampart against Nordic barbarism ... if the Poles have vices it is the fault of their oppressors ... old Gagern declares that the partition of Poland is the nightmare that weighs on our time ... the Poles warmly love their fatherland and, in this respect, we might take a leaf out of their book ... danger is imminent from Russia ... if the red republic were victorious in Paris and desired to liberate the Poles by force of arms, what then, gentlemen?... Let us not be prejudiced etc., etc.

We are sorry for Herr Blum, but when all these fine observations are divested of their rhetorical flourishes, nothing remains but the most vapid political hot air, be it political hot air on a grand scale and in high style—as we gladly admit. Even when Herr Blum asserts that, to be consistent, the National Assembly must act in Schleswig, Bohemia, the Italian Tyrol, the Russian Baltic provinces and Alsace according to the same principle as in Posen, the argument is justified only with regard to the stupid lies about nationality and the convenient inconsistency of the majority. When, again, he asserts that, if Germany wants to behave decently, she can conduct negotiations on Posen only with an already existing Poland, we shall not deny this, but merely observe that this argument—the only weighty one of his speech—had been advanced hundreds of times before by the Poles themselves and in a much more convincing way, whereas Herr Blum, with great "restraint and indulgent moderation", shoots it quite ineffectively, like a blunt rhetorical arrow, at the callous breast of the majority.

Herr Blum is right when he says that shrapnel is no argument, but he is wrong—and he knows it—when he tries impartially to take a "moderate" superior standpoint. Herr Blum may not clearly understand the Polish question, but that is his own fault. He is in a sorry plight however, first, when he hopes to prevail upon the majority to demand even a report from the Central Authority, and secondly, when he imagines he will gain anything by virtue of a report furnished by the Ministers of this Central Authority, who, on August 6, submitted so disgracefully to the Prussian desire for sovereignty.[230] To sit with the "extreme Left" one must first of all entirely discard indulgent moderation and refrain from attempts to secure anything, however small, from the majority.

Whenever the Polish question is debated, almost the entire Left indulges, as usual, in declamation or even in extravagant rhapsody, without discussing the facts and the actual content of the question. Yet, with regard to this question in particular, there is ample material available and the facts are extremely convincing. But this requires that one really studies the problem, and one can of course save oneself the trouble, since, having passed through the purgatory of the election, one is no longer accountable to anybody.

We shall return to the few exceptions to this rule in the course of the debate. Tomorrow we shall say a few words to Herr Wilhelm Jordan, who is no exception, but who this time, in the literal sense and for definite reasons, follows the multitude.

[*Neue Rheinische Zeitung* No. 86, August 26, 1848]

Cologne, August 25. At last, thank God, we leave the low sandy plain of vapid political hot air and enter the more elevated Alpine regions of great debate. At last we mount the cloud-covered peak where eagles nest, where man finds himself face to face with the gods and looks down disdainfully on the diminutive rabble that far, far below grapples with the few arguments at the disposal of the ordinary human intellect. At last, after the skirmishes of a Blum with a Stenzel, a Goeden, a Senff of Inowroclaw, the great battle begins, during which Ariostian heroes scatter the splintered arrows of their mind all over the battlefield.

The ranks of the combatants open reverentially and Herr *Wilhelm Jordan* of Berlin advances with drawn sword.

Who is Herr Wilhelm Jordan of Berlin?

In the heyday of German men of letters, Herr Wilhelm Jordan of Berlin was one such in Königsberg. Semi-legal meetings were held in the Böttchershöfchen. Herr Wilhelm Jordan went to one, read a poem of his—"Der Schiffer und sein Gott" [The Skipper and His God]—and was expelled. Herr Wilhelm Jordan of Berlin went to Berlin. Certain student meetings were held there. Herr Wilhelm Jordan recited a poem—"Der Schiffer und sein Gott"—and was expelled. Herr Wilhelm Jordan of Berlin went to Leipzig. There, too, some innocuous meetings were held. Herr Wilhelm Jordan recited a poem—"Der Schiffer und sein Gott"—and was expelled.

Herr Wilhelm Jordan, moreover, published several of his writings: a poem "Glocke und Kanone" [Bell and Cannon]; a collection of Lithuanian folk-songs, including some of his own manufacture, in particular songs of Poland written by himself; translations of George Sand's works; a periodical, the incomprehensible "comprehended world"[a] etc.—all this in the service of the renowned Herr Otto Wigand, who has not yet got on so far as his French original, M. Pagnerre; furthermore, he published a translation of Lelewel's *Histoire de Pologne*, with an introduction full of enthusiasm for Poland etc.

The revolution came. *En un lugar de la Mancha, cuyo nombre no quiero acordarme*[b]—in a locality in the German Mancha, in Brandenburg, where Don Quixotes still thrive, a locality the name of which I do not like to remember, Herr Wilhelm Jordan of Berlin proposed himself as candidate for the German National Assembly. The peasants of the district were amiably constitutional men. Herr Wilhelm Jordan delivered several impressive speeches, full of the most constitutional amiability. The delighted peasants elected the great man as their deputy. As soon as he arrived in Frankfurt, the noble "irresponsible" man took his seat on the "extreme" Left and voted with the republicans. The peasants who, as electors, have produced this parliamentary Don Quixote, send him a vote of no confidence, reminding him of his promises and recalling him. But Herr Wilhelm Jordan considers that his word is as little binding as that of a king and at every opportunity continues to sound his "bell and cannon" in the Assembly.

Each time Herr Wilhelm Jordan mounted the pulpit of St. Paul's Church,[c] he in fact recited only a poem—"Der Schiffer und sein Gott"—but this does not mean that he therefore deserves to be expelled.

---

[a] *Die begriffene Welt. Blätter für wissenschaftliche Unterhaltung.—Ed.*

[b] "At a certain village of *La Mancha*, which I shall not name"—the words with which Cervantes' *Don Quixote* begins.—*Ed.*

[c] The meeting place of the German National Assembly in Frankfurt.—*Ed.*

Let us listen to the great Wilhelm Jordan's latest ringing of the bell and the most recent roar of his cannon about Poland.

"On the contrary I believe that we must raise ourselves to the *world-historical standpoint*, from which the Posen affair has to be examined in terms of its significance as an episode in the great Polish drama."

The powerful Herr Wilhelm Jordan has, with one move, raised us high above the clouds to the lofty, snow-capped Chimborazo of the "world-historical standpoint" and unfolds an infinite prospect before us.

But, to begin with, he remains for a moment in the commonplace sphere of "special" deliberation, and with much success at that. Here are a few examples:

"It" (the Netze district) "later, as a result of the Treaty of Warsaw" (i.e. the first partition), "came under Prussian rule and has since remained in Prussia, if one leaves out of accout the short interlude of the Duchy of Warsaw."

Herr Jordan speaks here of the Netze district as *distinct* from the rest of Posen. What source does he use here, this knight of the world-historical standpoint, the ·expert in Polish history, the translator of Lelewel? None other than the speech of Herr Senff of Inowroclaw! He sticks so closely to this source, that he quite forgets that, in 1794, the other, Polish part of Posen "came under Prussian rule and, if one leaves out of account the short interlude of the Duchy of Warsaw, has since remained in Prussia". But the "Netze brother" Senff never mentioned this, and the "world-historical standpoint" consequently knows merely that the administrative district of Posen "came under Prussian rule" only in 1815.

"Furthermore, from time *immemorial*, the western districts of Birnbaum, Meseritz, Bomst and Fraustadt[a] have been German as regards the overwhelming majority of their inhabitants—you can see this even from the *names* of these towns."

And the district of Międzychód, Herr Jordan, was "from time immemorial Polish", as regards the overwhelming majority of its inhabitants—you can see this even from the name, can't you, Herr Jordan?

The district of Międzychód is nothing but the district of Birnbaum. Międzychód is the Polish name of the town.

What backing will these etymological chambers of reunion of the "world-historical standpoint" of the "comprehended world" obtain from the Christian-German Herr *Leo*! Not to mention the fact that Mailand, Lüttich, Genf, Kopenhagen[b] have been "German from

---

[a] The Polish names are Międzychód, Międzyrzecz, Babimost, Wschowa.—*Ed.*
[b] The German names for Milan, Liége, Geneva and Copenhagen.—*Ed.*

time immemorial, as you can see even from their names". Does not the "world-historical standpoint" also deduce the immemorial Germanity of Haimons-Eichicht, Welsch-Leyden, Jenau and Kaltenfelde "even from their names"? True, he will have trouble finding these primevally German names on the map and when he learns that they denote Le Quesnoi, Lyons, Genoa and Campo Freddo, he will only have Herr Leo, who manufactured them, to thank for his embarrassment.

What will the world-historical standpoint say, if presently the French claim Cologne, Coblence, Mayence and Francfort as primevally French territory? Woe then to the world-historical standpoint!

But let us dwell no longer on these *petites misères de la vie humaine*,[a] they also befall greater men. Let us follow Herr Wilhelm Jordan of Berlin, as he soars to higher spheres. He says of the Poles that one

"likes them more the further away one is from them and the less one knows about them, and one likes them less the closer one gets to them". Hence the reason for "this affection is not some superior quality of the Polish character but rather a certain *cosmopolitan idealism*".

But how does the world-historical standpoint explain that the peoples of the world do not "like" a certain nation, either when they are "at a great distance from it" or when they "get closer" to it, and that, with rare concurrence, they despise, exploit, deride and spurn this nation? This is the *German* nation.

The world-historical standpoint will say, this is due to "*cosmopolitan materialism*", thus extricating himself.

Quite untroubled by such petty objections, however, the world-historical eagle on his mighty pinions soars higher and higher, until he reaches the pure ether of the idea that exists in itself and for itself, and gives vent to the following heroic world-historical Hegelian hymn:

"Even if one vindicates history, which in the course of its necessary progress inexorably crushes with its iron heel a nation that is no longer strong enough to maintain its position among equal nations, it would nevertheless be inhuman and barbaric to feel no sympathy when one observes the long suffering of such a people, and I am far from harbouring such callous thoughts." (God will not fail to reward you for this, noble Jordan!) "But it is one thing to be moved by a tragedy, and quite another to attempt to undo this tragedy. It is precisely the fact that the hero succumbs to iron necessity that turns his fate into *true tragedy* and, trying to interfere with the course of destiny and out of human considerations attempting to stay the revolving wheels of history and turn them back once more, is to expose oneself to the danger of being crushed by them. The desire to restore Poland simply because her ruin justly fills us with sorrow, is, to my mind, imbecile sentimentality!"

---

[a] Small mishaps of life.— *Ed.*

What an abundance of ideas! What profound wisdom! What stirring language! Thus speaks the world-historical standpoint, once he has corrected the shorthand reports of his speeches.

The Poles have the choice; if they want to stage a "true tragedy" they have to submit humbly to being destroyed by the iron heel and the revolving wheels of history and say to Nicholas: Thy will be done! If, however, they want to rebel and, for a change, try to use the "iron heel of history" to crush their oppressors, then there is no "true tragedy", and Herr Wilhelm Jordan of Berlin can no longer take any interest in them. Thus speaks the world-historical standpoint whose aesthetic knowledge stems from Professor Rosenkranz.

What was the inexorable, the iron necessity which has temporarily destroyed Poland? It was the decline of the noblemen's democracy based on serfdom, that is the development of a big aristocracy *within* the nobility. This was a step forward, as it was the only way out of the antiquated noblemen's democracy. What was the result? The iron heel of history, i.e. the three Eastern autocrats, crushed Poland. The aristocracy was compelled to enter into an alliance with foreign states, in order to cope with the noblemen's democracy. The Polish aristocracy until recently, and partially even up to the present, remained the faithful ally of Poland's oppressors.

What is the reason for the inexorable, the iron necessity for Poland's liberation? It is the fact that the rule of the aristocracy in Poland, which has continued, since 1815, at least in Posen and Galicia, and to some extent even in Russian Poland, is today just as antiquated and hollow as was the democracy of the lower nobility in 1772. It is the fact that the establishment of a form of agrarian democracy has become vital to Poland, not only politically but also socially; the fact that agriculture, the source of existence of the Polish people, will be ruined, if the peasants who are serfs or liable to labour services, do not become free landowners, and the fact that an agrarian revolution cannot possibly be carried through without simultaneously winning a national existence and taking possession of the Baltic coast and the estuaries of the Polish rivers.

And Herr Jordan of Berlin calls this attempting to stay the revolving wheels of history and trying to turn them back once more!

It is true that the old Poland of the *noblemen's* democracy died and was buried long since, and only Herr Jordan can expect that anyone wants to nullify the "true tragedy" of this Poland, but the "hero" of this tragedy has produced a strapping son, and many a foppish

Berlin literary man may indeed shudder at the thought of making his closer acquaintance. This son, who is still only preparing to act out *his* drama and to put his shoulder to the "revolving wheels of history", but who is bound to achieve success, this son is the Poland of the *peasant* democracy.

Some stale literary flourishes, a little imitated contempt of the world—which in Hegel was a sign of audacity, but becomes a cheap and nonsensical platitude in Herr Jordan—in short a sample of the bell and cannon, "sound and fury"[a] expressed in inadequate sentences and, in addition, incredible confusion and ignorance of quite ordinary historical circumstances—this is what the world-historical standpoint amounts to.

Long live the world-historical standpoint and its comprehended world!

[*Neue Rheinische Zeitung* No. 90, August 31, 1848]

Cologne, August 26. The second day of battle provides an even grander picture than the first. True, we miss Herr Wilhelm Jordan of Berlin, whose lips captivated the hearts of all who heard him, but let us be modest, a Radowitz, Wartensleben, Kerst and Rodomont-Lichnowski are not to be despised.

Herr *Radowitz* mounts the rostrum first. The speech of the leader of the Right is short, firm and calculated. No more declamation than necessary. Wrong premises, but concise rapid conclusions based on these premises. An appeal to the *fear* of the Right. Cold-blooded certainty of success which banks on the cowardice of the majority. Profound contempt for the entire Assembly, for the Right as well as the Left. These are the outlines of the short speech delivered by Herr Radowitz, and we understand very well the effect these few icy and unostentatious words were bound to produce in an assembly used to hearing the most pompous and shallow rhetorical exercises. Herr Wilhelm Jordan of Berlin would have been delighted, if with his entire "comprehended" and not comprehended world of images he had produced a tenth of the effect Herr Radowitz produced with his short and, basically, also quite superficial speech.

Herr Radowitz is not a man of "character", not a steadfast worthy, but he is a person with clear-cut, distinct traits; one needs only to read one of his speeches to know him thoroughly.

---

[a] Goethe, *Faust*, Erster Teil, "Marthens Garten".— *Ed.*

We have never coveted the honour of being an organ of any particular group of the parliamentary Left. On the contrary, because of the various different elements from which the democratic party has been formed in Germany, we have considered it essential to keep an especially close watch on the democrats. In view of the lack of energy, of decision, of talent and of knowledge we have encountered among the leaders, with a few exceptions, of all parties, we are pleased that Herr Radowitz is at least a worthy *opponent*.

Herr Radowitz is followed by Herr Schuselka. In spite of all previous warnings, he nevertheless makes a touching appeal to the heart. An immensely long-winded discourse, interspersed with a few historical arguments and occasionally some Austrian common sense. On the whole, it has a wearisome effect.

Herr Schuselka has gone to Vienna, having been elected a member of the Imperial Diet which meets in that city. This is the right place for him. If in Frankfurt he sat on the Left, there he will find himself in the Centre. If in Frankfurt he had some influence, his first speech in Vienna will prove a failure. This is the fate of all literary and philosophical great pot-house politicians, who use the revolution only to improve their own position—if for a moment they are placed on really revolutionary ground, they disappear at once.

The *ci-devant* Count *von Wartensleben* follows. Herr Wartensleben steps forth as a portly, honest man overflowing with benevolence, who tells anecdotes about his march as a member of the army reserve to the Polish frontier in 1830, he then turns into Sancho Panza and speaks in proverbs to the Poles, e.g. a bird in the hand is worth two in the bush, and, at the same time, he quite innocently manages to slip in the following perfidious remark:

"What is the reason that even Polish officials were not prepared to take over the reorganisation of the part that was to be ceded? I fear they are themselves afraid, they feel that they are not yet advanced enough to be able to organise the population in an orderly manner, and consequently merely pretend that it is Polish patriotism which prevents them from making even the initial preparations for a happy resurrection!"

In other words, the Poles have, for eighty years, been continuously fighting and sacrificing their lives and property for a cause which they themselves regard as impossible and absurd.

In conclusion Herr Wartensleben is in agreement with Herr Radowitz.

Mr. Janiszewski from Posen, a member of the Posen National Committee, mounts the rostrum.

Mr. Janiszewski's speech is the first piece of truly parliamentary eloquence to be delivered from the rostrum of St. Paul's Church. At last we hear a speaker who does not simply try to win the approval of the hall, but whose language is marked by true dynamic passion, and who, for this reason, produces an effect quite different from that produced by any of the preceding speakers. Blum's appeal to the conscience of the Assembly, Jordan's cheap bombast, Radowitz's cold logic, Schuselka's genial prolixity, all, without exception, sink into insignificance by the side of this Pole who fights for the existence of his nation and demands the restoration of his legitimate rights. Janiszewski speaks in an impassioned and forceful way, but without declamation. He merely reports facts with the justified indignation, without which a correct description of such facts is impossible and which is doubly justified after the shameless misrepresentations made earlier in the debate. His speech, which in fact constitutes the core of the debate, refutes all earlier attacks against the Poles, makes amends for the mistakes of the supporters of the Poles, leads the debate back to the only real and just basis, and deprives speakers of the Right who are to follow of the most high-sounding arguments in advance.

"You have swallowed the Poles, but, by God, you shall not digest them!"[231]

This striking summary of Janiszewski's speech will endure, as will also the pride with which he replies to the begging speeches of the supporters of the Poles:

"I do not come to you as a beggar, I come relying on my legitimate right; I do not ask for sympathy but only for justice."

Mr. Janiszewski is followed by Herr Kerst, a head-master from Posen. The Pole fighting for the existence and the social and political freedom of his people is followed by a Prussian schoolmaster who has immigrated to Posen and is fighting for his salary. The fine passionate indignation of the oppressed is followed by the trite impudence of the bureaucrat who lives on oppression.

The partition of Poland "which today is called a disgrace" was at the time "a *quite ordinary event*".

"The right of peoples to separate according to nationality is a brand-new right recognised nowhere.... It is only *actual possession* which matters in politics."

These are a few of the pithy expressions on which Herr Kerst bases his arguments. They are followed by the most clumsy contradictions:

"As a result of the acquisition of Posen, a piece of land has been incorporated into Germany which is indeed predominantly Polish", and a little later: "As far as the Polish part of Posen is concerned, it has not asked to be joined to Germany and, as far as I know, you, gentlemen, do not intend to admit this part against its will!"

In this connection he gives statistical data about the population ratio, data which correspond to the famous survey of the "Netze brethren", according to which only those are regarded as Poles who do not speak any German, and all those are deemed Germans who speak a little broken German. Finally comes a most artificial calculation, by which he proves that the minority that voted *for* joining Germany, when the vote was taken in the Posen Provincial Diet—a minority of 17 to 26—was really a majority.

"It is true that under the Provincial Law there must be a majority of $^2/_3$ to pass resolutions. Now, it is true that 17 is not quite $^2/_3$ of 26, but the missing fraction is so small that over such a serious question it cannot really be taken into consideration."!!

Thus, if the minority is $^2/_3$ of the majority, then it is "under the Provincial Law" a majority! The old Prussians will greatly honour Herr Kerst for this discovery.— But in fact the position is this—in order to make an *application,* $^2/_3$ must vote for it. Admission into the German Confederation was such an application. Application for admission was therefore only legal if $^2/_3$ of the Assembly, i.e. $^2/_3$ of the 43 who took part in the division, voted for it. But, instead, almost $^2/_3$ voted against it. But what does it matter? For 17 is almost "$^2/_3$ of 43"!

It is not surprising that the Poles are not so well "educated" as are the citizens of the "*Staat der Intelligenz*"[a] if this intelligent state sends them teachers who are such expert arithmeticians.

Herr *Clemens* from Bonn makes the correct observation that the Prussian Government was not interested in the Germanisation of Posen but in its *Prussianisation*, and compares the attempts to Prussianise Posen with similar attempts in the Rhineland.

Herr *Ostendorf* of Soest, the son of red soil,[b] reads from a compendium of political platitudes and twaddle, he indulges in possibilities, probabilities and conjectures, jumping from one subject to another, from Herr Jordan to the French, from the red republic to the redskins of North America, and puts the Poles on a par with them, and the "Netze brethren" on a par with the Yankees. An audacious comparison worthy of the red soil! Imagine Herr Kerst, Herr Senff and Herr Goeden as backwoodsmen in a log hut with shotgun and spade—what a priceless comedy!

Herr *Franz Schmidt* from Löwenberg mounts the rostrum. He speaks calmly and unostentatiously. This is all the more commendable since Herr Schmidt belongs to a profession which is usually

---

[a] See G. W. F. Hegel, *Vorlesungen über die Geschichte der Philosophie. Vorrede, gesprochen zu Heidelberg den 28sten Oktober 1816*, note.—*Ed.*

[b] Westphalia.—*Ed.*

excessively fond of declamation, i.e. the German Catholic priest-
hood. Herr Schmidt's speech, after that of Janiszewski, is certainly
the best of the whole debate, because it is the most convincing and
best informed. Herr Schmidt demonstrates that the committee's
display of learning (the content of which we have already examined[a])
hides abysmal ignorance of actual conditions. Herr Schmidt, who has
lived for many years in the Grand Duchy of Posen, shows that even
with regard to this small district, which he knows in great detail, the
committee has made the crudest blunders. He shows that the
committee has failed to give the Assembly adequate information
about any of the decisive questions and has even called upon the
Assembly to make decisions at random without any factual data or
any knowledge of the matter. He demands in the first place
information about the actual state of affairs. He proves that the
proposals of the committee are incompatible with their premises. He
quotes Flottwell's memorandum and calls upon Flottwell, who is also
present as a deputy, to make a statement should the document not be
genuine. He finally makes public the fact that the "Netze brethren"
came to Gagern and, by false news about an alleged uprising in
Posen, tried to persuade him to bring the debate to a rapid close.
True, Gagern denied this, but Herr Kerst has loudly boasted of it.

The majority has taken revenge on Herr Schmidt for his bold
speech by seeing to it that the speech was falsified in the stenographic
reports. Herr Schmidt himself three times rectified the nonsense
inserted in one passage, but it was nevertheless printed. Table-
banging against Schlöffel,[b] crude violence against Brentano[232] and
falsification against Schmidt—the gentlemen of the Right are indeed
subtle critics!

Herr Lichnowski concludes the sitting, but we shall save this friend
of ours for the next article; one should not act precipitately when
dealing with a speaker of Herr Lichnowski's calibre!

[*Neue Rheinische Zeitung* No. 91, September 1, 1848]

Cologne, August 31. The *bel-homme* of the Assembly, the German
Bayard, the knight without fear and without reproach, the ex-Prince
(Paragraph 6 of the Fundamental Rights[233]) von *Lichnowski* mounts
the rostrum with chivalrously courteous propriety and a self-satisfied
smile. With the pure accents of a Prussian lieutenant and with

---

[a] See this volume, pp. 337-49.—*Ed.*
[b] Ibid., p. 18.— *Ed.*

disdainful nonchalance, he divests himself of the few disconnected thoughts he has to communicate to the Assembly.

The handsome knight is definitely a necessary element in this debate. If there is anyone to whom Herr Goeden, Herr Senff and Herr Kerst have still not demonstrated the worth of the German Poles sufficiently clearly, the example of the knight Lichnowski will show him what a disgusting phenomenon—despite the comely figure—is the Prussianised Slav. Herr Lichnowski and the German Poles are kindred spirits; by his mere appearance on the rostrum, Herr Lichnowski makes the dossier more complete. The *slachcic*[a] from Upper Silesia who has been transformed into a Prussian squire from the backwoods provides a living example of what the loving Prussian Government intends to do with the nobility of Posen. Herr Lichnowski, despite all his protestations, is not a German, he is a "reorganised" Pole; he does not speak German, he speaks Prussian.

Herr *Lichnowski* begins with the assertion that he feels the most chivalrous sympathy for the Poles, he pays compliments to Mr. Janiszewski, he upholds the Poles' claim to "the great poetry of martyrdom", and then he suddenly makes an about turn and asks: Why has this sympathy waned? Because "the Poles fought in the first line at the barricades" in all insurrections and revolutions! This is indeed a crime that will no longer be committed once the Poles are "reorganised". Incidentally, we can give Herr Lichnowski the reassuring information that even among the "Polish emigrants" and even among the Polish nobility in exile who, according to Herr Lichnowski, have sunk so low, there are people who have remained entirely uncontaminated by any contact with the barricades.

Now follows an amusing scene.

Lichnowski: "The gentlemen of the Left, who trample under foot documents that have turned yellow with age, have, in a conspicuous way, evoked historical rights. There is no justification for stressing one date as against another in the interest of the Polish cause. With regard to historical right there does not exist no date."[b] (Loud laughter on the Left.)

"With regard to historical right there does not exist no date." (Loud laughter on the Left.)

President: "Gentlemen, allow the speaker to finish the sentence, do not interrupt him."

Lichnowski: "Historical right does not have no date." (Laughter on the Left.)

President: "Please do not interrupt the speaker, silence, please!" (Agitation.)

Lichnowski: "As regards historical right, no date exists" (cheers and hilarity on the Left) "which could vindicate a greater degree of right than any earlier date!"

---

[a] A Polish nobleman.— *Ed.*

[b] This ungrammatical phrase of Lichnowski's is used several times by Engels in this series of articles.— *Ed.*

Were we not justified in saying that the noble knight speaks not German, but Prussian?

The historical right which "does not have no date" encounters a formidable adversary in our noble paladin.

"If we go further back into history, we find" (in Posen) "many districts which were Silesian and German; if we go back still further, we reach the time when Leipzig and Dresden were built by Slavs, and we then arrive at Tacitus, and God only knows, where the gentlemen would lead us if we were to broach this subject."

The world must be in a bad way. The estates of the Prussian knights must be mortgaged beyond redemption, the pressure of their Jewish creditors must have become formidable, their promissory notes must be coming due for payment in rapid succession, public auction, imprisonment, dismissal from service owing to thoughtlessly incurred debts—all these horrors of extreme pecuniary distress must threaten the Prussian knights with inevitable ruin, for things to have come to such a pass that a Lichnowski attacks the same historical right in whose defence he won his spurs at Don Carlos' round table.[234]

True, only God knows whither the bailiffs would convey the lean knights[a] if we were to broach the subject of the historical right governing debts! Yet, are these debts not their best quality and the only one that can serve the Prussian paladins as an excuse?

The *bel-homme* then comes to his subject and observes that, when speaking to the German Poles, one should not "paint a vague picture of a remote and obscure future Poland" (!); he thinks the Poles would not be satisfied with Posen:

"If I had the *honour* to be a Pole, I would every morning and every evening ponder on the re-establishment of the old Polish kingdom."

But since Herr Lichnowski does not "have the honour", since he is merely a reorganised Pole of Upper Silesia [*Wasserpolack*],[235] he ponders on quite different and less patriotic matters "every morning and every evening."

"To be frank, I must say that a few hundred thousand Poles must become Germans, which, to tell the truth, would not, under the present conditions, be a misfortune for them either."

On the contrary, how nice it would be if the Prussian Government laid out a new plantation to grow still more of the wood from which the Lichnowskis are made.

---

[a] "The lean knights" (*die magere Ritterschaft*) is from Heinrich Heine's poem *Deutschland. Ein Wintermärchen*, Caput VIII.— *Ed.*

The moustache-twirling knight continues to talk for some time in the same pleasantly nonchalant manner, which is in the main intended for the ladies in the gallery, but is still good enough for the Assembly as well, and then concludes:

"I have nothing more to say. It is now up to you to decide whether to absorb five hundred thousand Germans or to turn them away ... but in that case, you will cross out the poem of our old national bard: 'As far as the German language rings, and God in Heaven his poem sings.'[a] Strike out this poem!"

It is indeed bad that, when old Arndt wrote his poem, he did not think of the Polish Jews and their German. But fortunately, we have our Upper Silesian paladin. Who is not aware of the nobility's old obligations to the Jews, obligations that have become respectable in the course of centuries? What the old plebeian omitted, Lichnowski, the knight, remembers.

As far as a Polish Jew jabbers of German a spate,
Lends at high interest, falsifies money and weight

—that is the extent of Herr Lichnowski's fatherland!

[*Neue Rheinische Zeitung* No. 93, September 3, 1848]

Cologne, September 2. The third day of the debate revealed a general weariness. The same arguments are repeated without any improvement and the stenographic report would have been dull enough to send one to sleep if the first honourable speaker, Citizen *Arnold Ruge*, had not produced his rich stock of new reasons. Citizen Ruge moreover [knows] his merits better than anyone else. He promises:

"I will apply *all* the *passion* I possess and *all* my *knowledge*."

He tables a motion; this is, however, not an ordinary motion, not a motion in general, but the only correct motion, the *true* motion, the absolute motion:

"*There is nothing else that can be proposed and that is admissible.* One can choose to do something else, gentlemen, for man is able to deviate from the correct path. By deviating from what is right, man shows that he has free will ... but what is right does not thereby cease to be right. In our case, my motion represents the *only right thing* that can be done."

---

[a] From Ernst Moritz Arndt's poem "Des Deutschen Vaterland".— *Ed.*

(In this case therefore, Citizen Ruge sacrifices his "free will" to what is "right".)

Let us closer examine the passion, the knowledge and the only right thing of Citizen Ruge.

"The destruction of Poland is a shameful injustice because it has stifled the remarkable development of a nation that had rendered great services to the European family of nations and in a resplendent way had developed chivalry, one of the aspects of medieval life. The republic of nobles was prevented by despotism from bringing about its own internal (!) abolition, which would have been possible by means of the Constitution that had been prepared during the revolutionary period."

The people in Southern France were, in the Middle Ages, no closer to the people in Northern France than the Poles are now to the Russians. In the Middle Ages, the Southern French, commonly called Provençals, achieved not only a "remarkable development", they even led European development. They were the first modern nation to have a literary language. Their poetry was regarded by all Romance peoples, and even by the Germans and the English, as a model unequalled at the time. They vied with the Castilians, the Northern Frenchmen and the English Normans in the perfection of feudal chivalry and were equal to the Italians in industry and commerce. They did not only develop "one aspect of medieval life" "in a resplendent way", they even produced a flash of the ancient Hellenic culture in the darkest Middle Ages. The people from Southern France have, therefore, rendered not only great, but immeasurable "services to the European family of nations". Nevertheless, like the Poles, they were first partitioned between Northern France and England and later completely subjugated by the Northern French. From the wars against the Albigenses[236] to Louis XI, the Northern French — who were culturally just as inferior to their Southern neighbours as the Russians to the Poles — waged continuous wars of conquest against the Southern French and, finally, conquered the whole country. The Southern French "republic of nobles" (this designation is quite correct for its heyday) "was prevented by despotism" (Louis XI) "from bringing about its own internal abolition", which would have been certainly no less possible there, owing to the rise of the middle class in the towns, than it would have been in the Polish case by means of the Constitution of 1791.

The Southern French fought against their oppressors for centuries — but historical development was inexorable. After a struggle lasting three centuries, their beautiful language was reduced to a patois and they themselves were turned into Frenchmen. Northern French despotism ruled over Southern

France for three hundred years and, only then, did the Northern French make amends for their oppressive rule — by destroying the last vestiges of Southern French independence. The Constituent Assembly divided up the independent provinces, and it was the iron fist of the Convention that first turned the inhabitants of Southern France into *Frenchmen* and, in reparation for their nationality, gave them democracy. What Citizen Ruge says about the Poles is, however, quite literally a fitting description of the three hundred years of oppression:

> "Russia's despotism has not liberated the Poles; the annihilation of the Polish nobility and the exile of so many noble families from Poland has not established democracy or humane conditions of life in Russia."

But the subjugation of Southern France by the Northern French has never been called "shameful injustice". What is the reason, Citizen Ruge? Either the subjugation of Southern France is a shameful injustice, or the subjugation of Poland is not a shameful injustice. It is up to Citizen Ruge to decide.

What is the difference between the Poles and the people of Southern France? Why was Southern France like inert ballast taken in tow by the Frenchmen from the North, even as far as the total obliteration of its nationality, whereas the Poles have every prospect of finding themselves very soon in the van of all Slav nationalities?

As a result of social conditions which we cannot explain in detail here, Southern France became the reactionary section of France. Its opposition to Northern France very soon became opposition to the progressive classes in the whole of France. It became the principal support of feudalism and has remained the backbone of the French counter-revolution up to now.

Poland, on the other hand, became a revolutionary part of Russia, Austria and Prussia, as a result of social conditions which we examined earlier (No. 81).[a] Its opposition to its oppressors was, at the same time, opposition to the big aristocracy in Poland itself. Even the nobility, which was in part still feudal, supported the democratic-agrarian revolution with quite unprecedented selflessness. Poland had already become the focus of East-European democracy, when Germany was still floundering in the ideology of the most insipid constitutionalism and high-flown philosophy.

This, and not the resplendent development of chivalry which belongs to the past, guarantees the restoration of Poland and makes it inevitable.

---

[a] See this volume, pp. 350-53.— *Ed.*

Articles from the *Neue Rheinische Zeitung*

But Herr Ruge has also a second reason for the necessity of an independent Poland within the "European family of nations".

"The violence which has been done to the Poles has scattered them throughout Europe and they are everywhere giving vent to their anger over the injustice they suffered ... the Polish spirit has been humanised and purified in France and in Germany (!?): the Polish emigration constitutes *propagation of freedom*" (No. 1). "The Slavs have become capable of entering the great European family of nations" (the "family" is unavoidable!) "for ... their emigration has become the true *apostolate of freedom*" (No. 2). "The entire Russian army (!!) has been infected with modern ideas by the Poles, these *apostles of freedom*" (No. 3.). "I respect the forthright conviction of the Poles, which they have demonstrated throughout Europe, to make *propaganda* for *freedom* with all their might" (No. 4). "Throughout the annals of history they will be honoured for being *pioneers*" (No. 5), "*wherever they have acted as pioneers* (!!!).... The Poles are the *element of freedom*" (No. 6), "which has been tossed into Slavdom; they have *led* the Slav Congress in Prague [237] towards *freedom*" (No. 7), "they have been active in France, Russia and Germany. The Poles consequently constitute an effective element in present-day culture as well, they are effective, and because they are effective, because they are necessary, they are by no means dead."

Citizen Ruge has to prove that the Poles are, first, necessary, and second, not dead. He does this by saying: "Because they are necessary, they are by no means dead."

If one removes a few words—Poles, element, freedom, propaganda, culture, apostolate—from the above lengthy passage, in which one and the same idea is repeated seven times, one can see what remains of the whole bombastic statement.

Citizen Ruge has to prove that the restoration of Poland is necessary. He proves this in the following way: The Poles are not dead, on the contrary they are very much alive, they are effective, they are the apostles of freedom in the whole of Europe. What is the reason for this? The violence, the shameful injustice perpetrated on them, has scattered them all over Europe, where they gave vent to their anger over the injustice they suffered, to their just revolutionary anger. This anger has been "purified" during their exile, and this purified anger has enabled them to become apostles of freedom and has placed them "first at the barricades". What follows from this? Wipe out the shameful injustice, the violence done, restore Poland, and the "anger" ceases, in can no longer be purified, the Poles go home and cease to be "apostles of freedom". If it was only the "anger over the injustice they suffered" that turned the Poles into revolutionaries, then the removal of the injustice will turn them into reactionaries. If the only thing that keeps the Poles alive is reaction to oppression, then remove oppression and they will be dead.

Citizen Ruge therefore proves the exact opposite of what he wants to prove. His arguments show that, in the interest of freedom and of the European family of nations, Poland must *not be re-established.*

Incidentally, the fact that, when discussing Poland, Citizen Ruge mentions only the emigrants and sees only emigrants at the barricades, throws a strange light on his "knowledge". We certainly do not want to hurt the feelings of the Polish emigrants, who have proved their energy and courage on the battlefield and during eighteen years of conspiratorial activity in the interests of Poland. But we cannot deny that those who are well acquainted with the Polish emigrants know that they are far from being as apostolically freedom-loving and as keen on barricade fighting as they are depicted by Citizen Ruge who, in good faith, repeats ex-Prince Lichnowski's assertions. The Polish emigrants have steadfastly persevered, have endured much and have worked hard for the restoration of Poland. But have the Poles within Poland done less, have they not braved greater dangers, have they not risked incarceration in Moabit and Spielberg, the knout and Siberian mines, Galician butcheries [238] and Prussian shrapnel? But all this does not exist for Herr Ruge. He has not noticed either that the Poles who did not emigrate, have absorbed much more of the general European culture and have understood the needs of Poland, where they have lived all the time, much better than almost all the emigrants apart from Lelewel and Mieroslawski. All intelligent thinking which exists in Poland, or to use Ruge's expression, which "has come to the Poles and upon the Poles", is attributed by Citizen Ruge to their stay abroad. In No. [81][a] we have shown that the Poles did not have to go either to the French political dreamers — who failed in February, thanks to their own phrases — or to the profound German ideologists — who have not yet been able to find an opportunity to fail — in the quest for an understanding of their country's needs; and that Poland itself was the best school to gain an understanding of what Poland needs. It is the great merit of the Poles that they were the first to realise and to propagate the fact that, for all Slav nations, the only possible form of liberation is agrarian democracy and not, as Citizen Ruge imagines, that the Poles "introduced into Poland and Russia" general phrases, such as "the great idea of political freedom, which matured in France, and even (!) the philosophy which emerged in Germany" (and in which Herr Ruge was submerged).

After this speech by Citizen Ruge, the Poles can exclaim: God protect us from our friends and we will protect ourselves from our enemies! But it has always been the greatest misfortune of the Poles

---

[a] See this volume, pp. 350-53.— *Ed.*

that their non-Polish friends defend them with the worst possible arguments.

It certainly speaks in favour of the Left in Frankfurt that, apart from a few exceptions, the deputies of the Left were perfectly delighted with Citizen Ruge's speech on Poland, a speech which contained the following passage:

"Whether we have in mind democratic monarchy, democratised monarchy (!) or pure democracy, let us not quarrel about this; *on the whole we want the same thing*—freedom, national freedom, and rule of the people!"

Are we expected to be enthusiastic about a Left that allows itself to be carried away when someone says that it wants "on the whole the same thing" as the Right, as Herr Radowitz, Herr Lichnowski, Herr Vincke and all the other fat or lean knights? A Left whose head has been turned with rapture and which forgets everything as soon as it hears a few empty slogans, such as "national freedom" and "rule of the people"?

But let us leave the Left and return to Citizen Ruge.

"So far, no revolution that swept the world was greater than the revolution of 1848."

"As regards its principles, it is the most humane revolution" for these principles have arisen as a result of the glossing over of the most contradictory interests.

"It is the most humane revolution as regards its decrees and proclamations", for they represent a compendium of philanthropical fantasies and sentimental phrases about fraternity produced by all the feather-heads of Europe.

"It is the most humane revolution as regards its actuality", that is the massacres and barbarities in Posen, the murderous incendiarism of Radetzky, the ferocious cruelties committed in Paris by the victors of June, the butcheries in Cracow and Prague, the rule of brutal soldiery everywhere—in short, all the outrages which constitute the "actuality" of this revolution today, September 1, 1848, and which have spilled more blood in four months than was spilled in 1793 and 1794 taken together.

The "humane" Citizen Ruge!

[*Neue Rheinische Zeitung* No. 96, September 7, 1848]

Cologne, September 6. We have followed the historical investigations about the necessity of the existence of Poland undertaken by the "humane" Citizen Ruge. Citizen Ruge has spoken so far about the bad past, the period of despotism, he has edited the *events* of *irrationalism*; he comes now to the present, to the glorious year 1848, to the revolution, he is now on his home ground, he now edits the "*rationale* of events".[239]

"How can the emancipation of Poland be brought about? It can be brought about by agreements in which the two great civilised nations of Europe participate; they, together with Germany, a liberated Germany, are *therefore* bound to form a new Triple Alliance, for they think the same way and, *on the whole*, want the same thing."

Here, in *one* bold passage, we have the whole rationale of events in foreign policy—alliance between Germany, France and Britain, all three of whom "think the same way and, on the whole, want the same thing", a new Rütli Federation[240] concluded by the three modern Swiss—Cavaignac, Leiningen and John Russell! It is true that France and Germany, with God's help, have meanwhile again retrogressed so far that as regards general political principles their governments "think" more or less "the same way" as official circles in Britain, that stable counter-revolutionary rock surrounded by the sea.

But the countries do not only "think" the same way, they "also, on the whole, want the same thing". Germany wants Schleswig, and Britain does not want to cede it to her; Germany wants protective tariffs, and Britain wants free trade; Germany wants unity, and Britain wants to see her disunited; Germany wants to be independent, and Britain seeks to subjugate her industrially—but what does that matter? "On the whole" they nevertheless want "the same thing"! And as to France, France issues tariff laws directed against Germany and France's Minister Bastide sneers at schoolmaster Raumer, who represents Germany there—hence it is obvious that France "on the whole" wants "the same thing" as Germany! Indeed, Britain and France prove in the most striking manner that they want the same thing as Germany, by threatening her with war, Britain on account of Schleswig and France on account of Lombardy!

Citizen Ruge is ideologically naive enough to believe that nations which have certain political ideas in common, would, just for that reason, conclude an alliance. Altogether, Citizen Ruge's political palette has only two colours—black and white, slavery and freedom. The world for him is divided into two great camps—into civilised nations and barbarians, freemen and serfs. The boundary line of freedom, which six months ago was situated on the other side of the Rhine, now coincides with the Russian frontier, and this advance is called the revolution of 1848. It is in this confused manner that the present movement is reflected in Citizen Ruge's head. That is how he translates the battle-cry of those who fought at the barricades in February and March into Pomeranian.[a]

If we translate it from the Pomeranian back into German, we find that the three civilised nations, the three free peoples, are those where bourgeois rule exists in various forms and at various stages of development, whereas the "slaves and serfs" are peoples ruled by patriarchal and feudal absolutism. For Arnold Ruge, the *farouche*[b] republican and democrat, freedom denotes the most ordinary "insipid" liberalism, the rule of the bourgeoisie, with perhaps some quasi-democratic forms—so that is the poodle's core![c]

Citizen Ruge argues that France, Britain and Germany must of course be allies, because the bourgeoisie rules in these countries. And if the objective interests of the three countries are diametrically opposed to one another, if free trade with Germany and France is an indispensable condition for the existence of the British bourgeoisie, if protective tariffs against Britain are an indispensable condition for the existence of the French and German bourgeoisie, if, in many respects, similar relations obtain between Germany and France, and if this Triple Alliance amounted, in practice, to the industrial subjugation of France and Germany?—"Narrow-minded egoism, mean mercenary minds," mutters Ruge, the Pomeranian thinker, into his blond beard.

Herr Jordan spoke of the tragic irony of universal history. Citizen Ruge is a striking example of this. He, like the rest of the more or less ideological Left, sees his most cherished pet fantasies, his greatest mental efforts, wrecked by the class whom he represents. His philanthropically cosmopolitan project is wrecked by mean mercenary minds and he himself must, unknowingly and unintentionally, represent precisely these mercenary minds in a more or less ideologically distorted fashion. The ideologist proposes, the shopkeeper disposes. Tragic irony of universal history!

Citizen Ruge then says that France "has declared that, though the treaties of 1815 [241] have been torn up, she is nevertheless willing to recognise the territorial division as it exists at present". "This is quite right" for Citizen Ruge has found something in Lamartine's manifesto,[242] which so far nobody tried to find there—that is the

---

    [a] Paraphrase from Heinrich Heine who spoke about Ruge as a man who knew "how to translate Hegel into Pomeranian".—*Ed.*
    [b] Fierce, wild.—*Ed.*
    [c] "The poodle's core" (*des Pudels Kern*)—Goethe, *Faust*, Erster Teil, "Studierzimmer".—*Ed.*

basis of a new international right. He explains this in the following way:

"The new *historical* (!) right" (No. 1) "must proceed from this relationship with France. Historical right is the *right of nations*" (! No. 2). "In the case we are discussing (?), it is the new *international right*" (! No. 3). "This is the only correct interpretation of *historical right*" (!No. 4). "Any other interpretation of *historical right*" (!No. 5) "is absurd. There is no other *international right*" (!No. 6). *"Historical right"* (No. 7) "is the right" (at last!) "which is *brought about by history* and *sanctioned by time,* since it" (which?) "annuls and tears up hitherto existing treaties and replaces them by new ones."

In *short,* historical right — edits the rationale of events!

Thus it is written, word for word, in the acts of the apostles of German unity, i.e. the stenographic reports of Frankfurt, page 1186, column one—and people complain that the *Neue Rheinische Zeitung* criticises Herr Ruge by means of exclamation marks! But this dizzy gyrating dance of historical right and international right was, of course, bound to stun the worthy members of the Left, as they were bound to be filled with admiration when the philosopher from Pomerania called out to them with unshakeable certainty: "Historical right is the right which is brought about by history and sanctioned by time" etc.

"History" has indeed always "brought about" the exact opposite of what had been "sanctioned by time", and the sanction of "time" has always consisted in overturning that which had been "brought about by history".

Citizen Ruge then tables the "only correct and admissible" motion:

"To instruct the Central Authority, in concert with Britain and France, to prepare a congress for the restoration of a free and independent Poland; all powers concerned are to be invited to send their envoys to this congress."

What upright, honest views! Lord John Russell and Eugène Cavaignac are to restore Poland. The English and French bourgeoisie are to threaten Russia with war so as to bring about the liberation of Poland, which at present is a matter of complete indifference to them! At this time of general confusion and disarray, when the effect of every piece of reassuring news causing shares to rise by $^1/_8$ per cent is nullified by six disturbing blows, when industry is struggling against creeping bankruptcy, when commerce is stagnant, when the unemployed proletariat has to be supported by enormous sums of money to prevent it from taking a last desperate stand—at this moment, can the bourgeoisie of the three civilised nations be expected to create an additional difficulty? And what a difficulty! A war with Russia, which has been the closest ally of Britain since February! War with Russia, a war which, as everybody knows, would spell the downfall of the German and French bourgeoisie! To what advantage? None at all. This is indeed more than Pomeranian ingenuousness! But Citizen Ruge is absolutely confident that a "peaceful solution" of the Polish question is possible. This is getting better and better! And why? Because the point now is:

> "What the treaties of Vienna *want* must now be put into practice and really carried out.... The treaties of Vienna wanted to maintain the right of *all* nations against the *great* French nation ... they wanted the restoration of the German nation."

Now it becomes clear why Herr Ruge "on the whole wants the same thing" as the Right. The Right also wants the treaties of Vienna carried out.

The treaties of Vienna are the epitome of the great victory of reactionary Europe over revolutionary France. They are the classic form in which European reaction ruled for fifteen years during the Restoration period. They restore legitimacy, monarchy by divine right, feudal aristocracy, clerical rule, and patriarchal jurisdiction and administration. But since victory was won with the help of the English, German, Italian, Spanish and especially the French *bourgeoisie*, concessions had also to be made to the bourgeoisie. While the sovereigns, aristocrats, priests and bureaucrats divided the rich spoils among themselves, the bourgeoisie was put off with promissory notes drawn on the future, which were not honoured and which nobody had any intention of honouring. Instead of examining the real practical content of the treaties of Vienna, Herr Ruge assumes that these empty promises are their true content, and that reactionary practice is merely an improper misinterpretation!

One must indeed be an astonishingly good-natured person to believe, after 33 years, after the revolutions of 1830 and 1848, that these promissory notes will still be paid and to imagine that the sentimental phrases in which the illusory promises of Vienna are wrapped up have still any meaning in the year 1848.

Citizen Ruge appears as the Don Quixote of the treaties of Vienna.

Finally, Citizen Ruge reveals a great secret to the Assembly — it is only the fact that the treaties of 1815 were broken in Cracow in 1846 which caused the revolutions of 1848. Let this be a warning to all despots!

To sum up, Citizen Ruge has not changed in any way since we last met him in the field of literature. He still uses the same phrases which he had learned by heart and repeated ever since he worked as the door-keeper of German philosophy at the *Hallischen* and *Deutschen Jahrbücher*; there is still the same confusion, the same jumble of views, the same lack of ideas, the same gift of presenting the most banal and nonsensical ideas in a pompous manner, the same lack of "knowledge", and, in particular, the same pretensions to the approbation of the German philistine, who has never heard the like in his life.

Here we conclude our summary of the debate on Poland. To expect us to deal with Herr Löw from Posen and the other great intellects that follow, is asking too much.

The debate as a whole leaves a sad impression. So many long speeches and so little content, so little knowledge of the subject and so little talent! The worst debate in the previous or the present French Chamber or in the British House of Commons contains more intelligence, more expert knowledge and more real content than this discussion, which lasted for three days and dealt with one of the most interesting subjects of modern politics. *Everything* could have been made of it, and the National Assembly simply turned it into political twaddle.

There has indeed never and nowhere been an assembly like this!

The results are well known.[243] Three-quarters of Posen has been conquered but it has been conquered not by force, or "German industry" or the "plough", but by political twaddle, false statistics and timorous decisions.

"You have swallowed the Poles, but, by God, you shall not digest them!"[a]

Written by Engels between August 7 and September 6, 1848

First published in the *Neue Rheinische Zeitung* Nos. 70, 73, 81, 82, 86, 90, 91, 93 and 96, August 9, 12, 20, 22, 26 and 31, September 1, 3 and 7, 1848

Printed according to the newspaper

Published in full in English for the first time

---

[a] See this volume, p. 366.— *Ed.*

THE DANISH ARMISTICE AND HANSEMANN

Cologne, August 10. We draw our readers' attention to our article on *Denmark*.[a] The Danish newspapers have furnished us with some quite new disclosures about the behaviour of the "Government of Action" in the armistice affair.[b] So, in one way or another, Herr Hansemann's secret transgressions are coming to light after all.

Written by Engels on August 10, 1848

First published in the *Neue Rheinische Zeitung* No. 72, August 11, 1848

Printed according to the newspaper

Published in English for the first time

---

[a] See "Kopenhagen, 5. August", *Neue Rheinische Zeitung* No. 72, August 11, 1848.— *Ed.*

[b] See this volume, pp. 266-70 and 287.— *Ed.*

THE GERMAN CITIZENSHIP AND THE PRUSSIAN POLICE

Cologne, August 11. It is well known how the Prussian army paid homage to German unity on August 6.[244] The *Prussian police* must not lag behind the Prussian army. Never have there been in its opinion more *German foreigners* or *foreign Germans* in Prussia than since an indivisible German National Assembly, a German Imperial Regent[a] and a German Imperial Government have been meeting in Frankfurt.

Herr *Geiger*, acting Police Superintendent, whose accession to the throne was greeted by us earlier[b] with misgivings, seems to have received the special order to purge Cologne of German *foreigners* and to tolerate only Prussian *subjects* within the walls of the old imperial city. If he is consistent, who will save a person's right of domicile except the police, the army, the bureaucracy and the natives? Herr Geiger himself will not be missing among these "*last of the Mohicans*".

We shall report at a later time about the conflicts the editor-in-chief of the *Neue Rheinische Zeitung*, Karl Marx, had with regard to the Prussian right of citizenship.[c] Today we are dealing with Herr *Karl Schapper*, a contributor and proof-reader of the *Neue Rheinische Zeitung*.

Herr Schapper has received an invitation to visit the Police Inspector of his district this morning. The Police Inspector informed him that due to an order of Herr Geiger, he would have to leave Cologne and the Prussian state by tomorrow because he is a

---

[a] Archduke John of Austria.— *Ed.*
[b] See this volume, p. 178.— *Ed.*
[c] Ibid., pp. 407-10.— *Ed.*

foreigner. The Inspector informed him at the same time that he would extend the period by a week out of courtesy.

Herr Schapper is not only a German but he is also a *citizen of Nassau* and he is equipped with a Nassau passport *in optima forma.*[a] Herr Schapper resides at Cologne with his wife and three children. His crime consists of being a member of the Democratic Society and the Workers' Association[245] as well as being the proof-reader of the *Neue Rheinische Zeitung.* These are, of course, three crimes all at once.

"*Every German possesses the general German citizenship,*" reads the first paragraph of the German Fundamental Rights[246] which has already been approved. Herr Geiger seems to interpret this in such a way that every German has the right to be expelled from 37 German states. Besides the legislation of the National Assembly, there is now Geiger's legislation!

For Herr *Hansemann,* however, the Minister of action, we have a piece of advice: he may use police methods against deputies at his own discretion, but there is no playing around with the press. It can open the book of the bourgeois past and

> If you are after a little amusement,
> You may go dancing, but I'll play the tune[b]—

no matter how many *Geigers* may threaten with their *violins.*[c]

Written on August 11, 1848	Printed according to the newspaper
First published in the *Neue Rheinische Zeitung* No. 73, August 12, 1848	Published in English for the first time

---

[a] In all formality.— *Ed.*

[b] Mozart, *The Marriage of Figaro,* English version by Edward. J. Dent, Oxford University Press, London, 1937, Act I, Cavatina Figaro.— *Ed.*

[c] Play on the words Geiger—the name of the Police Superintendent of Cologne—which literally translated means "violinist", and *violine* (derived from the French word *violon* meaning both "violin" and "prison").— *Ed.*

THE ITALIAN LIBERATION STRUGGLE
AND THE CAUSE OF ITS PRESENT FAILURE [247]

With the same celerity with which they were expelled from Lombardy in March, the Austrians have now returned in triumph and have already entered Milan.

The Italian people spared no sacrifice. They were prepared at the cost of life and property to complete the work they had begun and win their national independence.

But this courage, enthusiasm and readiness to make sacrifices were nowhere matched by those who stood at the helm. Overtly or covertly, they did everything to use the means at their disposal, not for the liberation of the country from the harsh Austrian tyranny, but to paralyse the popular forces and, in effect, to restore the old conditions as soon as possible.

The Pope,[a] who was worked on more and more every day and won over by the Austrian and Jesuitical politicians, put all the obstacles in the way of the Mamiani Ministry which he, in conjunction with the "Blacks"[b] and the "Black-Yellows",[c] could find. The Ministry itself delivered highly patriotic speeches in both Chambers, but did not have the energy to carry out its good intentions.

The Government of Tuscany distinguished itself by fine words, but even fewer deeds. But the arch-enemy of Italian liberty among the native princes was and remains Charles Albert. The Italians should have repeated and borne in mind every hour of the day the saying: "Heaven protect us from our friends, we will protect ourselves from our enemies!" They hardly needed to fear Ferdinand

---

[a] Pius IX.— Ed.
[b] An allusion to the Jesuits.— Ed.
[c] An allusion to the Austrians, whose colours were black and yellow.— Ed.

of Bourbon, he was unmasked long ago. Charles Albert, on the other hand, let himself be acclaimed everywhere as "*la spada d'Italia*" (the sword of Italy) and the hero whose rapier was Italy's best guarantee of freedom and independence.

His emissaries went to all parts of Northern Italy portraying him as the only man who could and would save the country. To enable him to do this, however, it was necessary to set up a North Italian kingdom. Only this could give him the power required not only to oppose the Austrians but to drive them out of Italy. The ambition which had previously made him join forces with the Carbonari,[248] whom he afterwards betrayed, this ambition became more inflamed than ever and made him dream of a plenitude of power and magnificence before which the splendour of all the other Italian princes would very soon pale. He thought that he could appropriate the entire popular movement of 1848 and use it in the interests of his own miserable self. Filled with hatred and distrust of all truly liberal men, he surrounded himself with people more or less loyal to absolutism and inclined to encourage his royal ambitions. He placed at the head of the army generals whose intellectual superiority and political views he did not have to fear, but who neither enjoyed the confidence of the soldiers nor possessed the talent required to wage a successful war. He pompously called himself the "liberator" of Italy while making it a condition that those who were to be liberated accept his yoke. Seldom was a man so favoured by circumstances as he was. His greed, his desire to possess a great deal and if possible everything led in the end to his losing all that he had gained. So long as there was no firm decision that Lombardy would join Piedmont, so long as the possibility of a republican form of government still existed, he remained in his entrenchments and did not move against the Austrians, although they were relatively weak at the time. He let Radetzky, d'Aspre, Welden, and others seize the towns and fortresses of the Venetian provinces one by one and did not stir a finger. Only when Venice sought the refuge of his crown did he deign to give his help. The same applies to Parma and Modena. Radetzky meanwhile had mustered strength and made all preparations for an attack which, in view of the incompetence and blindness of Charles Albert and his generals, led to a decisive victory. The outcome is well known. Henceforth Italians can and will no longer entrust their liberation to a prince or king. On the contrary, in order to save themselves they must completely discard this useless "*spada d'Italia*" as quickly as possible. If they had done this earlier, and had superannuated the King with his system and all the hangers-on, and had formed a democratic union, it is likely that by now there would have been no more Austrians in Italy. Instead, the Italians not only bore all the hardships of a war waged with fury and barbarity by their enemies and suffered the heaviest sacrifices in vain, but were left defenceless to the thirst for vengeance of the Metternich-Austrian reactionaries and their soldiery. Anyone reading Radetzky's manifestos to the people of Lombardy and Welden's manifestos to the Roman legations will understand that to the Italians Attila and his Hun hordes would have appeared merciful angels. The reaction and restoration have triumphed. The Duke of Modena,[a] called "*il carnefice*" (the hangman), who loaned the Austrians 1,200,000 florins for war purposes, has returned as well. The people, in their magnanimity, have so often made a stick for their own back, that it is time they got wiser and learned something from their enemies. Although, during his previous reign, the Duke had imprisoned, hanged and shot thousands of people for their political convictions, the Modenese let him depart unmolested. Now he has returned to discharge his sanguinary princely office with redoubled zeal.

The reaction and restoration have triumphed, but only for a time. The people are so deeply imbued with the revolutionary spirit that they cannot be held in check for long. Milan, Brescia and other towns showed in March what this spirit is capable of. The excessive suffering inflicted upon them will lead to a new rising. By taking into account the bitter experience of the past months, Italy will be able to avoid new delusions and to secure her independence under a single democratic banner.

Written by Engels on August 11, 1848   Printed according to the newspaper

First published in the *Neue Rheinische Zeitung* No. 73, August 12, 1848

---

[a] Francis V.— *Ed.*

388

CHARLES ALBERT'S BETRAYAL

The newspapers of Turin, Genoa etc. are loudly complaining that the cause of Italy's freedom and independence has been betrayed by him and by those who up to the very last moment were repeatedly swearing under oath that they would win or die for Italy. What was earlier uttered only by a small handful of men—that Charles Albert is a traitor—is now loudly repeated day after day by the mass of the people and by all those newspapers that have not completely sold out to the perfidious King of Sardinia. This insight will later bear its fruit; this time, however, it has come too late. Since the battles of Goito and Mozambano [249] it became more and more clear to many people as the days went by that the Sardinian was either plotting a betrayal or was totally incapable of carrying out the task that he has undertaken. He lapsed into complete inactivity and whatever was done was against all the rules of common sense, of politics and of the art of war. For a long time now many questions have been obtruding themselves on the public's attention. Some of the answers to these questions have in fact already been given, and others will shortly come to light. Who, for example, constantly obstructed the arrangements for the arming of the whole people? Who distributed and dispersed the Italian army over so many points and neglected to form a reserve-line, with the result that every defeat was bound to lead to ruin? Why did Charles Albert not advance on Vicenza? Why did the army in Valleggio lack bread? Why did the Modenese desert? How did it happen that the Lombardian volunteers did not find a single cannon on the banks of the Mincio? How was it that the cartridges distributed during the battle to several Piedmontese corps could not be used because the bullets were too big? And lastly: how could Charles Albert, who had long since decided to retreat, still order the destruction of a large number of houses in the suburbs of Milan, to the value of 30 million lire? There is only one answer to these questions, unless we are prepared to assume the most lamentable and incredible incompetence, and that is that Charles Albert behaved just as treacherously and perfidiously in the year 1848 as he did in the year 1821, when he shamelessly betrayed his fellow conspirators and helped to deliver them up to the hangman's rope, to the galleys and to banishment.[250]

Written by Engels on August 16, 1848

First published in the *Neue Rheinische Zeitung* No. 77-78, August 17, 1848

Printed according to the newspaper

Published in English for the first time

THE ATTEMPT TO EXPEL SCHAPPER

Cologne, August 18.

"We demand a universal German right of domicile and full freedom of movement throughout the German fatherland."

So said His Majesty Frederick William IV in his charter of March 18.[251]

But the King proposes and Herr Geiger disposes. Herr Geiger, acting Police Superintendent of Cologne, is insisting on the expulsion of Herr Karl Schapper on the pretext that Herr Schapper is a citizen of *Nassau* and moreover a German *in partibus infidelium.*[a]

Yesterday a police-sergeant pushed his way into Frau Schapper's bedroom and deposited the following letter, which we reproduce exactly as it was written. What might appear to be incorrectness is perhaps nothing more than a *Prussian* protest against *German* grammar.

Herr Schapper,

I am instructed to inform you that the Police Superintendent still continues to insist that you should leave the city, should you however have any objection to raise against the laws then please lodge an appeal immediately with the Police Inspector, to be sent to him immediately.

Cologne 17/8. 48

Quetting
Police-Sergeant

---

[a] Beyond the realm of reality (literally "in the country of infidels")—an addition to the title of Catholic bishops appointed to a purely nominal diocese in non-Christian countries.— *Ed.*

Thereupon, Herr Schapper addressed the following note to the Police Inspector:

Dear Sir,

Under the date of the 11th of this month you signified to me that I must leave the city of Cologne within a week, in accordance with the decision of Herr Geiger, Police Superintendent. I had already lodged a protest against the decision on that occasion. You have now communicated to me through a police-sergeant that the said expulsion order still stands but that I may appeal against it. This I am now doing and I base my case on the following reasons.

1) As early as *March 18,* 1848, the day *before* the March revolution, the King of Prussia issued a charter calling on all German states to observe a universal German right of domicile and admit the freedom of movement. No Prussian authority ought to refuse the citizens of another German state what the King of Prussia has demanded for citizens of the Prussian state. The charter of March 18 either has no meaning at all or it implies the abolition of all earlier provisions for the expulsion of non-Prussian German citizens.

2) On July 21 of this year the German National Assembly at Frankfurt adopted Paragraph 2, Article 1, of the German Fundamental Rights[252] in a form which expressly forbids all expulsions of Germans from German cities or states. It says:

"Every German has the right to *sojourn and make his domicile,* acquire real estate etc., etc. ... pursue any type of employment *in any part of the territory of the Empire....*

"The conditions of sojourn and domicile will be laid down for the whole of Germany ... by a law of domicile issued by the imperial authority. Until such a time as these laws of the Empire are proclaimed, the exercise of the said rights is open to every German in every German state *under the same conditions as apply to the citizens of the state in question.*

"No German state may make any distinction in connection with civil, penal or adjective law between its own citizens and the citizens of any other German state whereby the latter, as foreigners, are treated at a disadvantage."

According to this paragraph I have the right, until the proclamation of the relevant laws of the Empire, to sojourn or domicile in Cologne, a town situated on the territory of the German Empire, and gain my livelihood as a proof-reader under the same conditions as the citizens of the Prussian state. But citizens of the Prussian state can only be expelled from Cologne, under the existing laws, if they have no means of subsistence. I have not been accused of lacking these and if I were I could at any time prove the contrary, since my salary as proof-reader on the *Neue Rheinische Zeitung* is sufficient to guarantee myself and my family a decent standard of living.

It is not valid to object that the relevant paragraph of the Fundamental Rights has not yet been promulgated. It has all along been the practice of administrative authorities in all constitutional states to suspend the execution of regulations such as the right of expulsion and other restrictions on personal freedom when a resolution abolishing these regulations has been passed by the appropriate Legislative Assembly and only awaits formal promulgation.

We are here dealing, then, with a resolution of the National Assembly which abolishes the powers of expulsion and a royal charter which recognises this resolution in advance. Consequently I believe that I am fully within my rights when I declare that I protest against the expulsion order, which was not even communicated to me in writing or accompanied by a statement of reasons, as an illegal act and that I will only yield to force.

Sir, I would ask you to be so kind as to lodge this protest with the appropriate authorities and to forward the decision to me as soon as possible, for if it is ignored I will appeal immediately to the royal *Regierungspräsident* or the Ministry of the Interior and in the last instance to the Berlin Constituent Assembly and the German National Assembly.

Cologne, August 17, 1848

(signed) *Karl Schapper*

The "*cathedral of German unity*", in which the solemn speeches that our great political architects made for three days running culminate, has, as its foundation stone the expulsion of a *citizen of Nassau from Cologne* on the Rhine.

Written on August 18, 1848

First published in the *Neue Rheinische Zeitung* No. 80, August 19, 1848

Printed according to the newspaper

Published in English for the first time

GEIGER AND SCHAPPER

Cologne, August 22. At the request of Police Superintendent Geiger (from Koblenz), Herr Schapper has been ordered to leave Cologne, since he is not a Prussian subject but a citizen of Nassau. The Workers' Association, of which Herr Schapper is an active member, feels compelled to make this cause its own and to protest against the arbitrary expulsion of Herr Schapper. Last Friday the protest was handed over to Herr Dolleschall in the absence of Herr Geiger. Since Herr Dolleschall declared that he knew nothing of the affair, the deputation appointed to deliver the protest was postponed to the following Tuesday, August 22, so as to be able to speak to Herr Geiger himself. Today Herr Geiger received the deputation with the declaration that the matter was no longer in his hands but that following an article in the *Neue Rheinische Zeitung*[a] the Ministry had asked him, Geiger, for a detailed report on the affair. The report had been sent off today; it was therefore no longer within his powers either to carry out or to countermand the expulsion of Schapper. One member of the deputation believed he understood Herr Geiger to say that Herr Schapper's expulsion order emanated from the Ministry, whereupon Herr Geiger vehemently assured the deputation on his most sacred word of honour that it was *he* who had taken the initiative in this measure. He referred first of all to his special knowledge of the law, since he had earlier been an examining magistrate; but that was not the only reason.

"I believe that I have acted not only as Police Superintendent, but also in accordance with the dictates of reason: *I* have acted as *I myself*."

---

[a] See this volume, pp. 383-84.— *Ed.*

He knew full well, he added, that everything he said would be reprinted in the *Neue Rheinische Zeitung* and given a special interpretation, but that did not worry him: "*I* have acted as *I myself.*" Another member of the deputation pointed out to him that if Herr Geiger had acted as "*I myself*", then this "*I*" was surely none other than the "*I*" of the Police Superintendent and it was of course possible that this "*I*" was in accordance with the dictates of reason. But the Workers' Association also had an "I", the "I" of 6,000 workers, and this "I" probably carried just as much weight as Herr Geiger's "I" and was likewise in accordance with the dictates of reason. The Workers' Association, he added, protested against a measure that went against all existing laws and the Frankfurt National Assembly. The first member of the deputation demanded that Herr Geiger at least disavow the measure; Herr Geiger refused, and gave the deputation the assurance that for his part, until the Minister gave a reply, Herr Schapper could stay undisturbed in Cologne. Herr Geiger also refused to give an explanation as to how his report had been drawn up. Has Herr Geiger taken different decisions from Herr Gagern and is a citizen of Nassau not a German citizen, who is entitled to settle in any of the 34 German fatherlands?

Written on August 22, 1848

First published in the *Neue Rheinische Zeitung* No. 84, August 24, 1848

Printed according to the newspaper

Published in English for the first time

THE *KÖLNISCHE ZEITUNG* ABOUT ITALY

Cologne, August 26. Yesterday we were condemned to having to listen to the political hot air of a writer of belles-lettres, Herr Wilhelm Jordan of Berlin, who lectured from the world-historical standpoint.[a] Fate is pursuing us relentlessly. A similar lot befalls us today: the main achievement of March consists in the belles-lettres writers having monopolised political life.

Herr *Levin Schücking* of Münster, the fourth or fifth wheel on the advertising wagon of Herr Dumont, has published an article in the *Kölnische Zeitung* on "our policy in Italy".[b]

And what does "my friend Levin with the eerie eyes"[c] have to say?

"There has never been a *more propitious* moment for Germany than the present one to place its policy vis-à-vis Italy upon a healthy basis which promises to endure for centuries. We have gloriously" (!by the betrayal of Charles Albert) "wiped off the disgrace with which our flags were besmirched by a people that in times of fortune easily becomes overweening. At the head of a matchless army, worthy of admiration not only in victory and battle but also for its patience and endurance, *barba bianca*, the *White-Beard*, planted Germany's glorious (!?) double-headed eagle on the battlements of the *rebellious* town where more than six hundred years ago the imperial *Red-Beard* hoisted the same banner as a *symbol of Germany's sovereignty over Italy. This sovereignty still belongs to us today.*"

Thus speaks Herr Levin Schücking of the *Kölnische Zeitung*.

In those days when Radetzky's Croats and Pandours were driven out of Milan by an unarmed people after a five-day battle, in those

---

[a] See this volume, pp. 359-64.— *Ed.*
[b] "Unsere Politik in Italien", *Kölnische Zeitung* No. 238, August 26, 1848.— *Ed.*
[c] From Ferdinand Freiligrath's poem "Die Rose".— *Ed.*

days when the "army worthy of admiration" which had been routed at Goito withdrew to Verona, in those days the political lyre of "my friend Levin with the eerie eyes" was silent! But ever since the reinforced Austrian army achieved an undeserved victory because of the equally cowardly and clumsy betrayal of Charles Albert, a betrayal which we predicted innumerable times, ever since then the neighbouring journalists have been reappearing on the scene, ever since then they have been trumpeting about the "wiped-off disgrace", risking parallels between Frederick Barbarossa and Radetzky Barbabianca and reducing heroic Milan, which made the most glorious revolution of 1848, to a mere "rebellious town". Ever since then "sovereignty over Italy" belongs to us Germans, to whom otherwise nothing ever belongs.

"Our flags"! The black-and-yellow rags of the Metternich reaction which are being trodden under foot in Vienna, those are the flags of Herr Schücking of the *Kölnische Zeitung!*

"Germany's glorious double-headed eagle"! That selfsame heraldic monster which had its feathers plucked by the armed revolution at Jemappes, Fleurus, Millesimo, Rivoli, Neuwied, Marengo, Hohenlinden, Ulm, Austerlitz and Wagram [253] happens to be the "glorious" Cerberus of Herr Schücking of the *Kölnische Zeitung.*

When the Austrians were beaten, they were separatists [*Sonderbündler*] [254] and practically traitors to their country. Ever since Charles Albert was caught in the trap and they have moved to the Ticino, they have become "Germans" and it is "*we*" who have accomplished all this. We have no objections to the *Kölnische Zeitung* having achieved the victories of Volta and Custozza and conquered Milan [255], but then it will also have to assume the responsibility for the — to it — very well known brutalities and infamies of that barbarian army "whose patience and endurance are worthy of admiration", just as it also assumed in former times the responsibility for the Galician slaughter. [256]

"This sovereignty still belongs to us today. Italy and Germany are nations around which nature and history have after all formed a bond. They belong together providentially, being related like science and art, thought and sentiment."

Just like Herr Brüggemann and Herr Schücking!

And it is exactly for that reason that the Germans and Italians have constantly fought each other for 2,000 years. It is exactly for that reason that the Italians shook off German oppression again and again. It is exactly for that reason that German blood has so often reddened the streets of Milan. All this was done to prove that Germany and Italy "belong together providentially".

It is exactly because Italy and Germany "are related" that Radetzky and Welden have allowed the burning and plundering of all Venetian towns!

My friend Levin with the eerie eyes now demands that we surrender Lombardy up to the River Etsch[a] because the people does not want us even if a few poor "*cittadini*"[b] (the learned Herr Schücking thus refers to the *contadini*, peasants) received the Austrians jubilantly. But if we conduct ourselves as "a free people",

"then it [the Italian people] will gladly offer us its hand in order to let *us* guide it along a path which it cannot enter upon by itself, the path to freedom".

Indeed! Italy which won for herself freedom of the press, a jury system and a Constitution before Germany had awakened from the laziest slumber; Italy which at Palermo fought the first revolution of this year [257]; Italy which without weapons conquered the "matchless" Austrians at Milan, that Italy cannot enter upon the path to freedom without being guided by Germany, which means by a Radetzky! Of course, if it takes a Frankfurt Assembly, a meaningless central power, 39 separatist leagues [*Sonderbünde*] and the *Kölnische Zeitung* to walk the path of freedom....

Enough of that! So as to make sure that the Italians "will let themselves be guided towards freedom" by the Germans, Herr Schücking retains Italian Tyrol and Venetia for the enfeoffment of an Austrian archduke and he sends

"2,000 South German imperial troops to Rome so that Christ's vicar may restore order in his own domain".

But unfortunately

The French and Russians own the land,
The English rule the sea;
But we in dream's ethereal realm
Hold sovereign mastery.

Our unity is perfect there,
Our might beyond dispute.
The other folk in solid earth
Have meanwhile taken root.[c]

And up there in the ethereal realm of dreams we also possess "sovereignty over Italy". Nobody knows this better than Herr Schücking. After he has developed this worthy policy of sovereignty for the benefit of the German Empire, he closes with a sigh:

---

[a] The Italian name is Adige.— *Ed.*
[b] Citizens.— *Ed.*
[c] Heinrich Heine, *Deutschland. Ein Wintermärchen*, Caput VII.— *Ed.*

"A policy which is great, high-minded and worthy of a power like that of the German Empire has unfortunately always been regarded by us as fantastic *and thus it will probably be for a long time to come!*"

We recommend Herr Schücking as door-keeper and frontier guard of German honour upon the summit of the Stilfser Ridge. From up there the vigorous literary supplement of the *Kölnische Zeitung* may survey Italy and make certain that not one iota of "Germany's sovereignty over Italy" will be lost. Only then can Germany sleep calmly.

Written by Engels on August 26, 1848

First published in the *Neue Rheinische Zeitung* No. 87, August 27, 1848

Printed according to the newspaper

Published in English for the first time

THE *ZEITUNGS-HALLE* ON THE RHINE PROVINCE [258]

Cologne, August 26. The *Berliner Zeitungs-Halle* contains the following article [a]:

"We recently had occasion to mention that the time has come when the spirit which for so long has held together the old political entities is gradually vanishing. As regards Austria, hardly anyone will call this in question, but in Prussia, too, the signs of the times confirming our observation are becoming daily more manifest, and we cannot turn a blind eye to them. There is at present only one interest capable of tying its various provinces to the Prussian state, namely that of developing liberal political institutions and jointly establishing and promoting a new and free mode of social relations. Silesia, which is making vigorous advances on the road to political and social progress, will hardly be happy in Prussia unless Prussia as a state is entirely adequate to these aspirations. As regards the Province of Saxony we know only too well that ever since its incorporation into the Prussian state it has resented it at heart. And as to the Rhine Province, surely everybody will still remember the threats which the Rhenish deputies made here prior to March 18, and thus helped to precipitate the turn of events. There is a growing spirit of alienation in this province. New evidence of this is provided in a now rather widely distributed leaflet which contains no mention of the publisher or place of publication."

The leaflet referred to by the *Zeitungs-Halle* is presumably known to all our readers.

What must please us is the view—which is at last advanced by at least *one* of the inhabitants of Berlin—that Berlin does not play the role of Paris as far as either Germany or the Rhineland in particular is concerned. Berlin is beginning to realise that it cannot govern us, cannot acquire the authority befitting a capital city. Berlin has amply proved its incompetence during the indecisive March revolution,

---

[a] "Das Rheinlands Herz zu Preussen", *Berliner Zeitungs-Halle* No. 194, August 24, 1848.— *Ed.*

during the storming of the arsenal and during the recent disturbances.[259] To the irresolution displayed by the people of Berlin is added a complete lack of talent in all parties. Since February the whole movement has not produced a single man in Berlin capable of leading his party. The spirit in this capital of the "spirit" is indeed very willing but just as weak as the flesh. The Berliners even had to import their Hansemann, their Camphausen and their Milde from the Rhine or Silesia. Far from being a German Paris, Berlin is not even a Prussian Vienna. It is not a metropolis, it is a "seat of the Court".

It is, however, noteworthy that even in Berlin people are coming to the conclusion, long widespread in the Rhineland, that German unity can come about *only as a result of the disintegration* of the German so-called great powers. We have never concealed our views on this point. We are not enraptured with either the past or present glory of Germany, with either the wars of independence[260] or the "glorious victories of German arms" in Lombardy and Schleswig. But if Germany is ever to achieve anything she must unite, she must become *one* state not only in word but in deed. And to bring this about it is necessary above all that there should be "neither an Austria nor a Prussia".[a]

Incidentally, "the spirit" which "for so long held together" us and the old Prussian provinces was a very palpable, crude spirit; it was the spirit of 15,000 bayonets and a number of cannon. It was not for nothing that a military colony of *Wasserpolacken*[261] and Kashubians was set up here on the Rhine, and that our young men had to serve in guards regiments in Berlin. This was done not in order to reconcile us with the other provinces, but to stir up hatred between the provinces and to exploit the national enmity between the Germans and Slavs, and the regional hatred of every petty German province against all the neighbouring provinces, in the interests of patriarchal feudal despotism. *Divide et impera!*

It is indeed time to put an end to the fictitious role assigned to the Berliners by "the provinces", i.e. by the junkerdom of the Uckermark and Further Pomerania, in their panic-stricken declarations, a role which the Berliners promptly accepted. Berlin is not and will never become the seat of the revolution, the capital of democracy. Only the imagination of the knights of Brandenburg, terrified at the prospect of bankruptcy, the debtor's prison and the lamp-post, could ascribe to Berlin such a role, and only the coquettish vanity of the Berliners could believe that Berlin rep-

---

[a] From Ernst Moritz Arndt's poem "Der Freudenklang".— *Ed.*

resented the provinces. We acknowledge the March revolution, but only for what it really was. Its greatest shortcoming is that it has not revolutionised the *Berliners.*

The *Zeitungs-Halle* believes that the disintegrating Prussian state can be cemented by means of liberal institutions. On the contrary. The more liberal the institutions are, the more will the heterogeneous elements be at liberty to separate, and the clearer will become the necessity of dissociation and the more evident the incompetence of the politicians of all parties in Berlin.

We repeat, the Rhine Province by no means objects to remaining within *Germany,* together with the old Prussian provinces, but trying to compel it to remain for ever within Prussia, whether it be an absolutist, a constitutional or a democratic Prussia, means making Germany's unity impossible, perhaps means even losing for Germany — we express the general attitude of the people — a large and beautiful territory by attempting to keep it for Prussia.

Written by Engels on August 26, 1848   Printed according to the newspaper

First published in the *Neue Rheinische Zeitung* No. 87, August 27, 1848

MEDIATION AND INTERVENTION.
RADETZKY AND CAVAIGNAC [262]

The armistice [263] concluded as the result of Charles Albert's treachery will expire in about three weeks (on September 21). France and Britain have offered to act as mediators. The *Spectateur républicain*, Cavaignac's paper, writes that Austria has not yet stated whether she will accept or decline the offer. France's dictator is getting annoyed over the discourtesy of the Austrians and threatens armed intervention if by a given date the Viennese Cabinet does not reply, or rejects mediation. Will Austria allow a Cavaignac to prescribe the peace terms to her, especially now after the victory over democracy in Vienna [264] and over the Italian "rebels"? Austria understands perfectly well that the French bourgeoisie wants "peace at any price", that the freedom or bondage of the Italians is altogether a matter of complete indifference to the bourgeoisie and that it will agree to anything so long as it is not openly humiliated and thus reluctantly compelled to draw the sword. It is said that Radetzky will pay a short visit to Vienna in order to say the decisive word about mediation. He does not have to travel to Vienna to do that. His policy has now prevailed, and his opinion will be none the less weighty for his remaining in Milan. If Austria were to accept the basis for peace proposed by Britain and France, she would do so not because she is afraid of Cavaignac's intervention but for much more pressing and compelling reasons.

The Italians were just as much deluded by the March events as the Germans. The former believed that foreign rule at any rate was now at an end; the latter thought that the old system was buried for good and all. On the contrary, the foreign rule in Italy is worse than ever, and in Germany the old system has recovered from the few blows it sustained in March and it acts with greater ferocity and vindictiveness than ever before.

The Italians are now making the mistake of expecting salvation from the present Government of France. Only the fall of this Government could save them. The Italians are further mistaken in regarding the liberation of their country as possible while democracy in France, Germany and other countries continues to lose ground. Reaction, to whose blows Italy has succumbed, is not merely an Italian phenomenon, it is a European phenomenon. Italy alone cannot possibly free herself from the grip of this reaction, least of all by appealing to the French bourgeoisie, which is the real pillar of reaction in Europe as a whole.

Before reaction can be destroyed in Italy and Germany, it must be routed in France. A democratic social republic must first be proclaimed in France and the French proletariat must first subjugate its bourgeoisie before a lasting victory of democracy is conceivable in Italy, Germany, Poland, Hungary and other countries.

Written by Engels on August 31, 1848

First published in the *Neue Rheinische Zeitung* No. 91, September 1, 1848

Printed according to the newspaper

THE ANTWERP DEATH SENTENCES [265]

Cologne, September 2. Belgium, the model constitutional state, has produced a further brilliant proof of the excellence of her institutions. *Seventeen death sentences* resulting from the ridiculous Risquons-Tout affair [266]! Seventeen death sentences to avenge the humiliation inflicted upon the prudish Belgian nation by a few imprudent men, a few hopeful fools,[a] who attempted to raise a small corner of the constitutional cloak! Seventeen death sentences — what savagery!

The Risquons-Tout affair is well known. Belgian workers in Paris joined forces to attempt a republican invasion of their country. Belgian democrats came from Brussels to support the venture. Ledru-Rollin assisted as much as he could. Lamartine, the "noble-minded" traitor, who was as ready with fine words and ignoble deeds for foreign as for French democrats—Lamartine, who prides himself on having conspired with the anarchists, like a lightning-conductor with the lightning — Lamartine at first supported the Belgian Legion the better to be able later to betray it. The Legion set out. Delescluze, Commissioner of the Department du Nord, *sold* the first column to Belgian railway officials; the train in which it travelled was treacherously hauled into Belgian territory right into the midst of the Belgian bayonets. The second column was led by *three Belgian spies* (we were told this by a member of the Paris Provisional Government, and the course of events confirms it), and these treacherous leaders brought it into a forest on Belgian territory, where an ambush of loaded guns was waiting for it. The column was shot to pieces and most of its members were captured.

This tiny episode of the 1848 revolution—an episode which assumed a farcical aspect as a result of the many betrayals and the magnitude ascribed to it in Belgium—served the Brussels judiciary as

---

[a] *Hoffnungsvolle Toren* (hopeful fools)— from Goethe's poem "Prometheus".— *Ed.*

a canvas on which to embroider the most colossal plot that was ever devised. Old General Mellinet, the liberator of Antwerp, Tedesco and Ballin, in short the most resolute and most active democrats of Brussels, Liége and Ghent, were implicated. M. Bavay would even have M. Jottrand of Brussels dragged into it, had not the latter known things and possessed documents whose publication would greatly compromise the entire Belgian Government, the wise Leopold included.

Why were these democrats arrested, why were these most monstrous proceedings started against men who had as little to do with the whole affair as the jurymen who faced them? It was meant to scare the Belgian bourgeoisie and, under cover of this scare, to collect the excessive taxes and compulsory loans, which are the cement of the glorious Belgian political edifice, and the payments on which were rather behindhand.

In short, the accused were arraigned before the Antwerp jury, the élite of the Flemish faro-playing fraternity, who lack both the *élan* of French political dedication and the cool assurance of magnificent English materialism, i.e. before those dried-cod merchants who spend their whole life vegetating in philistine utilitarianism, in the most short-sighted and timid profiteering. The great Bavay knew his men and appealed to their fear.

Indeed, had anyone ever seen a republican in Antwerp? Now thirty-two of the monsters faced the terrified men of Antwerp, and the trembling jury in concert with the wise bench consigned seventeen of the accused to the tender mercies of Article 86 and others of the *Code pénal*, i.e. the death sentence.

Mock trials were also held during the Reign of Terror in 1793, and convictions based on other facts than those officially stated did occur, but even the fanatical Fouquier-Tinville did not conduct a trial so distinguished by clumsy barefaced lies and blind partisan hatred. Moreover, is Belgium in the grip of a civil war and are the armies of half Europe assembled at her frontiers conspiring with the rebels, as was the case in France in 1793? Is the country in danger? Has a crack appeared in the crown? On the contrary, no one intends to subjugate Belgium, and the wise Leopold still drives every day without an escort from Laeken to Brussels and from Brussels to Laeken.

What has the 81-year-old Mellinet done to be sentenced to death by jury and judges? The old soldier of the French Republic saved the last spark of Belgian honour in 1831. He liberated Antwerp and in return Antwerp condemns him to death! His only sin is that he defended his old friend Becker against the insinuations of the Belgian official press and did not change his friendly attitude towards Becker even when the latter was plotting in Paris. Mellinet was in no way connected with the plot. And because of this he is without further ado sentenced to death.

As to Ballin, he was a friend of Mellinet's, often visited him, and was seen in the company of Tedesco in a coffee-house. Reason enough to sentence him to death.

And finally Tedesco. Had he not visited the German Workers' Association,[267] did he not associate with people on whom the Belgian police had planted stage daggers? Had he not been seen with Ballin in a coffee-house? The case was established—Tedesco had provoked the great battle of Risquons-Tout—to the scaffold with him!

And so with the others.

We are proud of being able to call many of these "conspirators", sentenced to death only because they are democrats, our friends. If the venal Belgian press slings mud at them, then we, at least, want to vindicate their honour before the face of German democracy; if their country disowns them, we want to acclaim them.

When the President of the Court pronounced the death sentence on them, they passionately exclaimed: "Long live the republic!" Throughout the whole procedure and the reading of the sentence they behaved with truly revolutionary steadfastness.

And now listen to what the wretched Belgian press has to say:

"The verdict," writes the *Journal d'Anvers*, "has caused no more of a sensation in the city than the entire trial, which aroused hardly any interest. Only among the working classes" (read: the lumpenproletariat) "can one find sentiments hostile to the paladins of the republic; the rest of the population hardly took any notice of it. The attempt to bring about a revolution does not cease to appear absurd to them even after the death sentence, which, in any case, no one believes will be executed."

To be sure, if the citizens of Antwerp were afforded the interesting spectacle of watching the guillotining of seventeen republicans headed by old Mellinet, their liberator, then they would certainly have taken notice of the trial.

The savagery of the Belgian Government, the Belgian jury and law-courts lies precisely in the fact that they play with death sentences.

The *Libéral Liégeois* says: "The Government wanted to show its *strength*, but it has merely demonstrated its *savagery*."

But then that has always been the lot of the Flemish nation.

Written by Engels on September 2, 1848

First published in the *Neue Rheinische Zeitung* No. 93, September 3, 1848

Printed according to the newspaper

THE CONFLICT BETWEEN MARX
AND PRUSSIAN CITIZENSHIP [268]

Cologne, September 4. As has already been mentioned earlier,[a] Karl Marx, the editor-in-chief of the *Neue Rheinische Zeitung*, has become involved in a conflict with Prussian citizenship. This affair is a new example of the way in which the attempt is made to conjure away the promises of March. How the matter stands emerges from the following document that Marx has sent to the Minister of the Interior, Herr Kühlwetter:

Dear Minister,

Permit me to protest against a decision of the local royal administration which affects me personally.

I left my homeland, Rhenish Prussia, during the year 1843 in order to settle for the time being in Paris. In 1844 I learned that the royal *Oberpräsidium* in Koblenz had sent to the respective border police authorities an order to arrest me because of my writings. This piece of news was also published in the censured Berlin newspapers.

From that moment on, I regarded myself as a political refugee. Later on, in January 1845, I was expelled from France at the direct instigation of the then Prussian Government and settled in Belgium.

Since here too the Prussian Government applied to the Belgian Ministry for my expulsion, I was finally forced to relinquish Prussian nationality. I had to use this last expedient in order to escape these persecutions. The best proof that I only asked for permission to emigrate in self-defence is the fact that I did not accept citizenship in

---

[a] See this volume, p. 383.— *Ed.*

any other state even though it was offered to me by members of the Provisional Government in France after the February revolution.

After the March revolution, I returned to my homeland and applied for citizenship in Cologne in the month of April. It was readily granted to me by the local City Council. Under the law of December 31, 1842, the matter was sent for confirmation to the royal administration. I then received from the local acting Police Superintendent, Herr Geiger, a communication which reads as follows:

"Dear Sir,

"I am herewith informing you that in view of your position up to now the royal administration has for the present not used in your favour Paragraph 5 of the law of December 31, 1842, which authorises it to bestow the status of a Prussian subject upon a foreigner. You are therefore still to be regarded as a foreigner. (Paragraphs 15 and 16 of the cited law.)

Cologne, August 3, 1848
acting Police Superintendent
(signed) Geiger

To
Dr. Marx, Esquire,
No. 2678."

I regard the decision of the royal administration as unlawful on the following grounds:

Under the decision of the Federal Diet of March 30 of this year, political refugees, too, may vote for and be elected to the German National Assembly provided they return to Germany and declare that they want to resume their German citizenship.[269]

The decision of the Preparliament,[270] which it is true does not have a direct legal force but nevertheless sets the standard of the prospects and promises which were held out to the German people immediately after the revolution, accords the right to vote and to be elected even to all those political refugees who became *citizens abroad* but want to resume their German citizenship.

In any case, the decision of the Federal Diet and the electoral regulations of the Camphausen Government which are based upon it, are legally valid in Prussia.

Since I declared clearly enough my intention to resume my German citizenship by virtue of my application to obtain the right to reside in Cologne, it is an established fact that I had the right to vote for and to be elected to the German National Assembly. Thus I at least possess citizenship rights in the German Empire.

If, however, I possess the greatest right which a German can

Passport used by Karl Marx in 1848 and 1849

Passport used by Karl Marx in 1848 and 1849

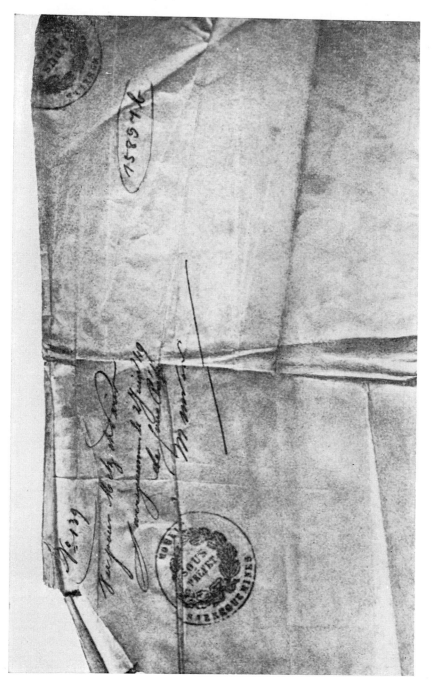

Passport used by Karl Marx in 1848 and 1849

possess, so much less reason is there for refusing me the lesser right of *Prussian* citizenship.

The royal administration at Cologne refers to the law of December 31, 1842. This law, taken together with the above-mentioned decision of the Federal Diet, also speaks in my favour.

Under Paragraph 15, 1 and 3, a subject loses his Prussian citizenship if he asks to be relieved of it or if he has resided abroad for ten years. After the revolution many political refugees who had been abroad for more than ten years returned home and so had lost their rights as Prussians under Paragraph 15 of the above-mentioned law as much as I have. Some of them, Herr J. Venedey, for example, even sit in the German National Assembly. Thus, if they wanted to, the Prussian "police authorities" (Paragraph 5 of the law) could likewise refuse Prussian citizenship to these German legislators!

Finally, I deem it to be thoroughly improper that the local royal administration or Police Superintendent Geiger uses the word "subject" in the notice sent to me, considering that both the former and the present Ministry have barred this designation from all official documents and speak instead only of citizens. It is equally improper, disregarding for the moment my right to Prussian citizenship, to label me, a citizen of the German Empire, as a "foreigner".

Furthermore, if the royal administration "in view of my position up to now" refuses to confirm my Prussian citizenship, it cannot refer to my material circumstances since, even according to the text of the law of December 31, 1842, only the City Council of Cologne could decide this issue and has done so in my favour. Thus it can only refer to my activities as editor-in-chief of the *Neue Rheinische Zeitung* and that means in view of my democratic attitude and my opposition to the present Government. But even if the local district administration or the Ministry of the Interior in Berlin should have the authority, which I deny, to withhold from me my Prussian citizenship because this is a special case which comes under the decision of the Federal Diet of March 30, such tendentious reasons could only be employed in the old police state, not however by revolutionary Prussia and her responsible Government.

Finally, I must mention that Police Superintendent Müller, upon my comment that I could not transfer my family from Trier to Cologne under these uncertain circumstances, assured me that there would be no objections to my renaturalisation.

For all of these reasons I demand that you, Herr Minister, instruct the local royal district administration to confirm my right (request) to

take up residence which was approved by the local City Council, and
thereby to restore my Prussian citizenship to me.

Please, Herr Minister, accept the assurances of my perfect esteem.

Cologne, August 22, 1848

Karl Marx

First published in the *Neue Rheinische
Zeitung* No. 94, September 5, 1848

Printed according to the newspaper

Published in English for the first
time

THE DANISH ARMISTICE[271]

Cologne, September 7.

"What will become of Germany if she is no longer led by Prussia, if Prussia's armies no longer protect Germany's honour, if Prussia's strength and influence as a great power perish in the fanciful might of an imaginary German Central Authority!"

Thus boasts the Prussian party, the party of the heroes "with God for King and Fatherland",[a] the counter-revolutionary knighthood of Further Pomerania and the Uckermark.

Well, Prussia *has* led, Prussia has protected Germany's honour, in Schleswig-Holstein.

And what was the result? After a series of easy, inglorious victories over a weak enemy, after a warfare which was paralysed by the most pusillanimous diplomacy, after the most disgraceful retreats before a *beaten* army, finally, an armistice which is so dishonourable for Germany that even a *Prussian* general[b] found reason not to sign it.

The hostilities and negotiations began anew. The Imperial Regent[c] authorised the Prussian Government to conclude an armistice. This authorisation *had not been countersigned by any of the Imperial Ministers* and it did not therefore possess *any validity whatsoever*. It recognised the first armistice, but with the following modifications: 1. Even before the conclusion of the armistice, the members of the new Government of Schleswig-Holstein "are to be agreed upon in such a manner that the permanency and the salutary

---

[a] From Frederick William III's decree on the formation of an army reserve, issued on March 17, 1813.— *Ed.*

[b] Wrangel.— *Ed.*

[c] Archduke John of Austria.— *Ed.*

effectiveness of the new Government appear safeguarded". 2. All the laws and decrees of the Provisional Government issued before the conclusion of the armistice are to retain full validity. 3. All the troops that remain behind in Schleswig-Holstein are to remain under the command of the German commander-in-chief.

If one compares this directive with the stipulations of the first Prussian-Danish project, then its purpose becomes quite evident. It certainly does not secure all that victorious Germany could have demanded, but by making quite a few concessions for form's sake, it saves many matters in effect.

The first stipulation was intended to guarantee that within the new Government the Schleswig-Holstein (German) influence would retain predominance over the Danish. And what does Prussia do? It agrees that Karl *Moltke*, the *head of the Danish party* in Schleswig-Holstein, becomes the head of the new Government and that Denmark obtains *three* votes in the Government against *two* for Schleswig-Holstein.

The second stipulation was supposed to accomplish the recognition although not of the Provisional Government itself which had been recognised by the Federal Diet, but of its activity up to now. Its decisions were to be maintained. And what does Prussia do? Under the pretext that Denmark, too, will drop its illusory decisions issued from Copenhagen for the duchies, and which never acquired even the shadow of legal force except upon the Island of Alsen,[a] under this pretext, counter-revolutionary Prussia agrees to nullify all decisions of the Provisional Government.

The third stipulation finally was to bring about the provisional recognition of the unity of the duchies and their incorporation into Germany. By placing all troops remaining in Schleswig and Holstein under the German commander-in-chief, it was supposed to thwart the attempt of the Danes to smuggle the Schleswigers serving in the Danish army back into Schleswig. And Prussia? Prussia agrees to separate the Schleswig troops from the Holstein troops, to remove them from the supreme command of the German general and to put them simply at the disposal of the new Government which is $3/5$th Danish.

Besides, Prussia was only authorised to conclude an armistice of three months (Article 1 of the original draft) but concluded one of seven months on its own authority, i.e. it granted a truce to the Danes during the winter months when the chief weapon of the Danes, their fleet, became useless for a blockade of the German and Schleswig

---

[a] The Danish name is Als.— *Ed.*

coasts and during a time when the cold would have enabled the Germans to cross the ice of the Little Belt, to conquer Fünen [a] and to limit Denmark to Zealand.

In short, Prussia has spurned its authority in respect of all three points. And then why not? After all, it *had not been countersigned!* And did not Herr Camphausen, the Prussian envoy to the Central Authority, state point-blank in his communication of September 2 to "His Excellency"(!!) Herr Heckscher that on the basis of that authority the Prussian Government

"considered itself empowered *to negotiate without any restrictions*"?

But that is not all. The Imperial Regent sends "his" Under-Secretary of State Max Gagern to Berlin and from there to Schleswig in order to supervise the negotiations. He sends along with him an authorisation which once again is *not countersigned.* Herr Gagern—we do not know how he was treated in Berlin—arrives in the duchies. The Prussian negotiators are in Malmö. He is not told anything. The ratifications are exchanged in Lübeck. Herr Gagern is informed that this has taken place and that he can now calmly go home again. Naturally there is nothing left to do for the unfortunate Gagern with his not countersigned authorisation but to return to Frankfurt and to bemoan the shabby role which he has played.

Thus the glorious armistice was born which ties the Germans' hands during the most favourable time for war, which dissolves the revolutionary Government and democratic Constituent Assembly of Schleswig-Holstein, which destroys all decrees of this Government — a Government that the Federal Diet had recognised — which delivers the duchies to a Danish Government led by the hated Moltke, which pulls the Schleswig troops out of their regiments, withdraws them from the German supreme command and delivers them up to the Danish Government that may dissolve them at its discretion, which forces the German troops to withdraw from Königsau [b] to Hanover and Mecklenburg and which delivers Lauenburg into the hands of the old reactionary Danish Government.*

Not just Schleswig-Holstein, but all Germany, with the exception of old parts of Prussia, is enraged about this ignominious armistice.

---

* This trick was accomplished in the following way: the old Government was dissolved. Thereupon Denmark re-elected the first, Prussia the second and both of them together the third member of the old Government.— *Note by Engels.*

[a] The Danish name is Fyn.— *Ed.*
[b] The Danish name is Kongeaa.— *Ed.*

The Imperial Government, to be sure, trembled at first upon being informed about it by Herr Camphausen but in the end it shouldered the responsibility for it after all. What else could it have done? Herr Camphausen seems to have threatened and official Prussia is still a power for the cowardly counter-revolutionary Imperial Government. But now it was the turn of the National Assembly. Its approval was necessary, and edifying as this Assembly is, "His Excellency" Herr Heckscher was nevertheless ashamed to come forward with this official document. He read it aloud to the accompaniment of a thousand bows and the most humble pleas for calm and moderation. The result was a general outburst. Even the Right Centre, indeed a part of the Right and Herr *Dahlmann* himself flew into the most violent fit of anger. The committees were ordered to report within 24 hours. In view of this report, it was decided to discontinue immediately the retreat of the troops. No decision has yet been taken concerning the armistice itself.

The National Assembly for once has finally passed an energetic resolution even though the Government declared that it would resign, if the resolution is carried. This resolution is not the cancellation but a *breach* of the armistice. In the duchies it will create not only excitement but open opposition to the execution of the armistice and to the new Government and it will bring about new complications.

But we have little hope that the Assembly will repudiate the armistice. Herr Radowitz only needs to obtain nine votes from the Centre and he has a majority. And should he not be able to do that during the few days when the matter rests?

If the Assembly decides to uphold the armistice, we shall have the proclamation of a republic and civil war in Schleswig-Holstein, the subjugation of the Central Authority by Prussia, the universal contempt of all Europe for the Central Authority and the Assembly and yet just enough complications as will suffice to crush any future Imperial Government under unsolvable difficulties.

If it decides to discard the armistice, we shall have another European war, a rupture between Prussia and Germany, new revolutions, the disintegration of Prussia and the *genuine unification of Germany.* The Assembly should not let itself be intimidated: at least two-thirds of Prussia supports Germany.

But will the representatives of the bourgeoisie at Frankfurt not rather swallow any insult and will they not rather place themselves under Prussian servitude than risk a European revolutionary war and expose themselves to new storms which would endanger their own class rule in Germany?

We believe that they will. Their cowardly bourgeois nature is too powerful. We do *not* have enough confidence in the Frankfurt Assembly to believe that it will redeem in Schleswig-Holstein Germany's honour which it has already sacrificed in Poland.

Written by Engels on September 7, 1848

First published in the *Neue Rheinische Zeitung* No. 97, September 8, 1848

Printed according to the newspaper

Published in English for the first time

EDITORIAL NOTE ACCOMPANYING THE ARTICLE "THE FINANCIAL PROJECT OF THE LEFT" [272]

We find it hard to understand that deputies on the Left submit financial plans for the procurement of the necessary funds to a Ministry that they intend to overthrow. The principal and in Herr Hansemann's case perhaps the only means of overthrowing a Ministry is precisely the *refusal* of funds. If at least some reforms had been included in the financial plan—but no, its aim is to spare the Government the hated measure of a compulsory loan. But what could be better for the opposition than the Ministry making itself hated?

Written by Engels on September 8, 1848

First published in the *Neue Rheinische Zeitung* No. 98, September 9, 1848

Printed according to the newspaper

Published in English for the first time

THE FALL OF THE GOVERNMENT
OF ACTION

Cologne, September 8, 10 p. m. The Government of Action has fallen. After it had "stumbled" several times, it was only able to stay in office by insolence. Finally, the constantly rising pretensions of the Government revealed the secret of its existence to the Assembly.

In yesterday's session of the Agreement Assembly **Stein's motion**[273] was debated. The motion reads:

> "It was the urgent duty of the Government to issue without more ado the decree which was approved on August 9 to pacify the country and avoid a break with the Assembly."

The Government declared that it would not consider any attempt at whitewashing or mediation.

The Left declared that it would walk out if the Assembly were to drop its resolution of August 9.

After a meaningless speech by the Prime Minister,[a] Deputy *Unruh* introduced the following amendment at yesterday's session:

> "Taking into account that the resolutions of August 9 do not constitute any investigation into attitudes or any constraint of conscience, but that they merely intend to bring about the agreement between the people and the army which is necessary in a constitutional state and that it is their purpose to avoid reactionary endeavours as well as further conflicts between the citizens who belong to the army and those who are civilians",

the Assembly declares

> **"that the Government does not possess the confidence of the country if it hesitates any further to issue to the army a decree which corresponds to the resolution of August 9."**

---

[a] Rudolf von Auerswald.— *Ed.*

This amendment of the **Left Centre** was opposed by a second one from the **Right Centre** advanced by Deputy Tamnau.

It reads:

> "The National Assembly wishes to make the following declaration: by its resolution of August 9 of this year, the National Assembly intended to bring about a decree to the commanders of the army similar to the one promulgated by the Ministries of Finance and of the Interior to the *Regierungspräsidenten* on July 15. It does not intend to oblige the officers of the army to set forth their political views or to prescribe to the Minister of War the text of the decree. **It regards such a decree, in which the officers of the army are warned against reactionary and republican endeavours, as necessary in the interest of civil peace and for the advancement of the new constitutional state system.**"

After the debate had gone on for some time, the "noble" *Schreckenstein* declared on behalf of the Government that he **agreed** with the **Tamnau** amendment. And this after the proud protestation that it would not accept any mediation!

After the debate had continued again for some time and after even Herr *Milde* had warned the Assembly not to become a **revolutionary National Convention** (Herr Milde's fear is entirely superfluous!) a vote is taken with an enormous throng of people pressing towards the meeting hall:

The result of the division:

The **Unruh amendment** was **rejected** by 320 votes to 38.

The **Tamnau amendment** was **rejected** by 210 votes to 156.

The Stein motion was adopted by 219 votes to 152. The majority against the Ministers:

67 votes.

One of our Berlin correspondents reports:

Today the excitement in the city was great. Thousands of people surrounded the meeting house of the Assembly, so that, when the President read the quite loyal address of the civic militia, Herr Reichensperger moved that the Assembly shift its sessions to another town since Berlin was endangered.

Indescribable rejoicing broke out when news of the Government's defeat became known to the assembled crowd, and when the deputies of the Left came out, they were accompanied as far as Unter den Linden by incessant "*Vivats!*" But when Deputy Stein (the mover of today's vote) was caught sight of, the enthusiasm reached its climax. Several men from the people immediately lifted him upon their shoulders and carried him thus in a triumphal procession to his hotel in the Taubenstrasse. Thousands of people joined this procession and to the accompaniment of endless hurrahs the masses rolled across the Opera House Square. Never before has such an expression of joy been seen here. The greater the previous anxiety about success, the more surprising the brilliant victory.

Against the Government voted: the Left, the Left Centre (the Rodbertus-Berg party) and the Centre (Unruh, Duncker, Kosch). The President[a] voted for the Government on all three issues. According to this, a Waldeck-Rodbertus Government will enjoy an absolute majority.

Thus in a few days we shall have the pleasure of seeing the author of the compulsory loan, the Minister of action, *"His Excellency"* Herr Hansemann, pass through here in order to return to his "bourgeois[b] past" and to reflect on Duchâtel and Pinto.

Camphausen fell respectably. Herr Hansemann who brought about Camphausen's fall by his intrigues, Herr Hansemann has met with a very sad end! Poor Hansemann-Pinto!

Written by Engels on September 8, 1848

First published in the special supplement to the *Neue Rheinische Zeitung* No. 98, September 9, 1848

Printed according to the newspaper

Published in English for the first time

---

[a] Wilhelm Grabow.— *Ed.*
[b] In the original *bürgerlich,* which can mean "civil" or "bourgeois".— *Ed.*

HIS SUCCESSORS

Cologne, September 9. So the prospect is held out of a Waldeck-Rodbertus Ministry. We do not believe it. The King[a] will hardly submit to these gentlemen's demands, especially since his journey to Cologne.[274] Consequently there is no other choice than Radowitz and Vincke, an open break with the Assembly, an open break with the revolution—and there is no need to say what will follow next.

Written by Engels on September 9, 1848

First published in the *Neue Rheinische Zeitung* No. 99, September 10, 1848

Printed according to the newspaper

Published in English for the first time

---

[a] Frederick William IV.— *Ed.*

THE DANISH-PRUSSIAN ARMISTICE [275]

Cologne, September 9. Again we revert to the Danish armistice—we are given time to do this owing to the thoroughness of the National Assembly, which, instead of taking prompt and energetic decisions and *compelling* the appointment of new Ministers, allows the committees to deliberate in the most leisurely manner and leaves the solution of the government crisis to God—a thoroughness which barely conceals "our dear friends' lack of courage".[a]

The war in Italy was always unpopular with the democratic party, and has for a long time been unpopular even with the democrats of Vienna. The storm of public indignation over the war of extermination in Posen could be staved off only for a few weeks by means of falsifications and lies on the part of the Prussian Government. The street-fighting in Prague,[b] despite all the efforts of the national press, aroused sympathy among the people only for the defeated, but not for the victors. The war in Schleswig-Holstein, however, from the outset was popular also among the *people*. What is the reason?

Whereas in Italy, Posen and Prague the Germans *were fighting against the revolution,* in Schleswig-Holstein they *were supporting it.* The Danish war is the first *revolutionary war* waged by Germany. We therefore *advocated* a resolute conduct of the Danish war from the very beginning, but this does not denote the slightest kinship with the sea-girt bourgeois beer-garden enthusiasm.

It is a sad thing for Germany that her first revolutionary war is the most ridiculous war ever waged.

---

[a] Heinrich Heine, *Deutschland. Ein Wintermärchen*, Caput XIX.— *Ed.*
[b] See this volume, pp. 91-93 and 119-20.— *Ed.*

Let us come to the point. The Danish nation is in commercial, industrial, political and literary matters completely dependent on Germany. It is well known that the real capital of Denmark is not Copenhagen but Hamburg; that for a whole year the Danish Government copied all the United Diet experiments conducted by the Prussian Government which expired on the barricades; that Denmark obtains all her literary as well as material sustenance via Germany, and that apart from Holberg, Danish literature is a poor imitation of that of Germany.

Impotent though Germany has been from time immemorial, she has the satisfaction of knowing that the Scandinavian nations, and especially Denmark, have fallen under her sway, and that compared with *them* she is even revolutionary and progressive.

Do you require proofs? Then read the polemics carried on by the Scandinavian nations against each other ever since the concept of Scandinavianism arose. Scandinavianism is enthusiasm for the brutal, sordid, piratical, Old Norse national traits, for that deep-rooted inner life which is unable to express its exuberant ideas and sentiments in words, but can express them only in deeds, namely in rudeness towards women, perpetual drunkenness and wild berserk frenzy alternating with tearful sentimentality.

Scandinavianism and the theory of kinship with sea-girt Schleswig-Holstein[a] appeared simultaneously in the territories of the King of Denmark. The two concepts are correlated; they evoked each other and were in conflict with each other, thereby asserting their existence.

Scandinavianism was the form taken by the Danes' appeals for Swedish and Norwegian support. But as always happens with the Christian-Teutonic nation, a dispute immediately arose as to who was the genuine Christian-Teuton, the true Scandinavian. The Swede contended that the Dane had become "Germanised" and had degenerated, the Norwegian said the same of the Swede and the Dane, and the Icelander of all three. Obviously, the more primitive a nation is, the more closely its customs and way of life resemble those of the Old Norse people, the more "Scandinavian" it must be.

Morgenbladet from Christiania[b] for November 18, 1846, is lying in front of us. This charming sheet contains the following amusing passages in an article on Scandinavianism.

---

[a] A paraphrase of the first words of a song written in 1844 by Matthäus Friedrich Chemnitz.— *Ed.*

[b] Now called Oslo.— *Ed.*

After stating that the whole concept of Scandinavianism is nothing but an attempt by the Danes to create a movement in their own interest, the paper writes about the Danes:

"What have these gay, vivacious people in common with the ancient, gloomy and melancholy world of warriors (*med den gamle, alvorlige og vemodsfulde Kjämpeverden*)? How can this nation, which—as even a Danish writer admits—has a docile and gentle disposition, believe itself to be spiritually related to the tough, lusty and vigorous men of a past age? And how can these people with their soft southern accent imagine that they speak a northern tongue? Although the main trait of our nation and the Swedes, like that of the ancient Northerners, is that our feelings are kept hidden in the *innermost* part of the soul, and not given *outward* expression, nevertheless these sentimental and affectionate people, who can so easily be astonished, moved and swayed and who wear their hearts upon their sleeves, nevertheless these people believe that they are of a northern cast and that they are akin to the two other Scandinavian nations!"

Morgenbladet attributes the degeneration of the Danes to their association with Germany and the spread of German traits in Denmark. The Germans have indeed

"lost their most sacred asset, their national character; but feeble and insipid though the German nation is, there is another nation still more feeble and insipid, namely the Danes. While the German language is being ousted in Alsace, Vaud and on the Slav border" (!! the services of the "Netze brethren" still remained unnoticed at the time) "it has made enormous progress along the Danish border."

The Danes, we are told, now had to oppose their nationality to the Germans and for this purpose they invented Scandinavianism. The Danes were unable to resist,

"for the Danish nation, as we have said before, was *essentially Germanised*, although it did not adopt the German language. The writer of these lines has seen it admitted even in a Danish paper that the *Danish* nation *does not differ essentially from the German nation*."

Thus *Morgenbladet*.

Of course, it cannot be denied that the Danes are a more or less civilised nation. Unfortunate Danes!

By the same right under which France took Flanders, Lorraine and Alsace, and will sooner or later take Belgium—by that same right Germany takes over Schleswig; it is the right of civilisation as against barbarism, of progress as against stability. Even if the agreements were in Denmark's favour—which is very doubtful—this right carries more weight than all the agreements, for it is the right of historical evolution.

So long as the Schleswig-Holstein movement remained a purely legal philistine agitation of a civic and peaceful nature it evoked enthusiasm only among well-meaning petty bourgeois. When, before the outbreak of the February revolution, the present King of

Denmark[a] at his accession promised a liberal Constitution for all his territories, envisaging the same number of deputies for the duchies as for Denmark, and the duchies were opposed to this, the petty-bourgeois parochial nature of the Schleswig-Holstein movement became distastefully conspicuous. The issue, at that time, was not so much union with Germany—did a Germany exist at that time?—as separation from Denmark and establishment of a small independent parochial state.

But then came the revolution, which gave the movement a different character. The Schleswig-Holstein party was forced either to attempt a revolution or to perish. It quite correctly chose the revolution. The Danish promises, which were very favourable before the revolution, were quite inadequate after the revolution; union with Germany—formerly an empty phrase—now acquired meaning. Germany made a revolution and as usual Denmark copied it on a small provincial scale.

The Schleswig-Holstein revolution and the Provisional Government to which it gave rise behaved at first still in a rather philistine way, but the war soon compelled them to adopt a democratic course. This Government, whose members are all moderate liberal worthies, formerly kindred spirits of Welcker, Gagern and Camphausen, has given Schleswig-Holstein laws which are more democratic than those of any other German state. The Kiel Provincial Assembly is the only German assembly based not only on universal suffrage but on direct elections. The draft Constitution which the Government submitted to it was the most democratic Constitution ever drawn up in the German language. As a result of the revolutionary war, Schleswig-Holstein, which had always trailed behind Germany in political matters, suddenly acquired more progressive institutions than all the rest of Germany.

The war we are waging in Schleswig-Holstein is therefore a truly revolutionary war.

And who, from the outset, supported Denmark? The three most counter-revolutionary powers in Europe—*Russia, England* and the *Prussian Government.* As long as it was possible the Prussian Government merely *pretended* to be waging a *war*—this is evidenced by Wildenbruch's Note,[276] by the alacrity with which the Prussian Government, on the representations of England and Russia, ordered the withdrawal from Jutland, and finally by the two armistice agreements. Prussia, England and Russia are the three powers which have greater reason than anyone else to fear the German revolution

---

[a] Frederick VII.— *Ed.*

and its first result—German unity: Prussia because she would thereby cease to exist, England because it would deprive her of the possibility of exploiting the German market, and Russia because it would spell the advance of democracy not only to the Vistula but even as far as the Dvina and the Dnieper. Prussia, England and Russia have conspired against Schleswig-Holstein, against Germany and against the revolution.

The war that may now arise from the decisions taken at Frankfurt would be a war waged by Germany against Prussia, England and Russia. This is just the kind of war that the flagging German movement needs—a war against the three great counter-revolutionary powers, a war which would *really* cause Prussia to merge into Germany, which would make an alliance with Poland an indispensable necessity and would lead to the immediate liberation of Italy; a war which would be directed against Germany's old counter-revolutionary allies of 1792-1815, a war which would "imperil the fatherland" and for that very reason save it by making the victory of *Germany* dependent on the victory of democracy.

The bourgeois and the junkers at Frankfurt should not deceive themselves — if they decide to reject the armistice they will be setting the seal to their own downfall, just as the Girondists did during the first revolution when they took part in the events of August 10 and voted for the death of the ex-King,[a] thereby preparing their own downfall on May 31.[277] If, on the other hand, they accept the armistice, they will still be sealing their own downfall: they will be placing themselves under the jurisdiction of Prussia and cease to have any say in things. It is up to them to choose.

The news of Hansemann's downfall probably reached Frankfurt before the vote was taken. This may influence the vote significantly, especially since it is expected that a Government of Waldeck and Rodbertus will follow who, as we know, recognise the sovereignty of the National Assembly.

The future will show. But we repeat—Germany's honour is in bad hands!

Written by Engels on September 9, 1848   Printed according to the newspaper

First published in the *Neue Rheinische Zeitung* No. 99, September 10, 1848

---

[a] Louis XVI.— *Ed.*

426

ARRESTS

Cologne, September 11. We are addressing the following request for information to whichever gentlemen in the Public Prosecutor's department it may concern:

Is it true that at 8 o'clock yesterday evening Herr Salget and Herr Blum Jr., from Cologne, who had already formed a workers' association in Cassel, were arrested in Wesseling, by the Burgomaster Herr von Geier, on the instigation of the parson? They had intended to form a workers' association[a] in Wesseling too, but were arrested before they had even spoken a word in public and before the meeting had begun.

Is it true that the only reason for this arrest, which did in fact take place, was the pastor's denunciation that the two gentlemen wanted (!) to stir up the workers?

Assuming that this is how matters stand, will the Public Prosecutor take steps to deal with this outrageous infringement of the law or—in expectation of the Radowitz Ministry and of the speedy abolition of the right of free association—will he give Herr von Geier a vote of thanks?

Written by Engels on September 11, 1848

First published in the *Neue Rheinische Zeitung* No. 100, September 12, 1848

Printed according to the newspaper

Published in English for the first time

---

[a] See also this volume, pp. 579-80.— *Ed.*

THE CRISIS AND THE COUNTER-REVOLUTION [278]

[*Neue Rheinische Zeitung* No. 100, September 12, 1848]

Cologne, September 11. Anyone reading the reports from Berlin printed below can judge for himself whether we predicted the course of the government crisis correctly. The Ministers resigned; it seems that the camarilla did not approve of the Government's plan to dissolve the Agreement Assembly and to use martial law and guns in order to remain in office. The junkers from the Uckermark are thirsting for a conflict with the people and a repetition of the Parisian June scenes in the streets of Berlin, but they will never fight for the Hansemann Government, they will fight for a **Government of the Prince of Prussia.** The choice will fall on *Radowitz, Vincke* and similar reliable men who keep aloof from the Berlin Assembly and are in no way committed to it. The Government of the Prince of Prussia which is to be bestowed on us will comprise the cream of the Prussian and Westphalian knights associated for form's sake with a few bourgeois worthies from the extreme Right, such as Beckerath and his like, to whom will be assigned the conduct of the prosaic commercial side of the business of state. Meanwhile hundreds of rumours are being spread, Waldeck or Rodbertus is perhaps summoned, and public opinion is misled, while at the same time military preparations are being made to come out openly at the appropriate moment.

We are facing a decisive struggle. The simultaneous crises at Frankfurt and Berlin and the latest decisions of the two Assemblies compel the counter-revolution to wage its last fight. If the counter-revolution in Berlin dares to spurn the constitutional principle of majority rule, if it confronts the 219 members of the majority with twice as many guns, if it dares to defy the majority not only in Berlin but also in Frankfurt by presenting to them a Government which is quite unacceptable to either of the two Assemblies — **if it thus provokes a civil war between Prussia and Germany, then the democrats know what they have to do.**

[*Neue Rheinische Zeitung* No. 101, September 13, 1848]

Cologne, September 12. Although already by midday we may receive news of the definite formation of a new Government as described by us yesterday and confirmed from other quarters, the government crisis in Berlin continues. There are only two solutions to this crisis:

Either a Waldeck Government, recognition of the authority of the German National Assembly and recognition of popular sovereignty;

Or a Radowitz-Vincke Government, dissolution of the Berlin Assembly, abolition of the revolutionary gains, a sham constitutionalism or even the United Diet.

Don't let us shut our eyes to the fact that the conflict which has broken out in Berlin is a conflict not between the agreers and the Ministers, but between the Assembly, which for the first time acts as a *Constituent* Assembly, and the *Crown*.

The point is whether or not the latter will have the courage to dissolve the Assembly.

But has the Crown the right to dissolve the Assembly?

True, in constitutional states the Crown in case of disputes has the right to dissolve the legislative chambers convened on the basis of the Constitution and to appeal to the people by means of new elections.

Is the Berlin Assembly a constitutional, legislative chamber?

It is not. It has been convened "to come to an agreement with the Crown on the Prussian Constitution", it has been convened not on the basis of a Constitution, but on that of a *revolution*. It received its mandate by no means from the Crown or from the Ministers answerable to the Crown, but from those who elected it and from the Assembly itself. The Assembly was sovereign as the legitimate expression of the revolution, and the mandate which Herr Camphausen jointly with the United Diet prepared for it in the shape of the electoral law of April 8 was nothing but a *pious wish*, in regard to which the Assembly had to decide.

At first the Assembly more or less accepted the theory of agreement. It realised that in doing so it had been cheated by the Ministers and the camarilla. At last it performed a sovereign act, acting for a moment as a constituent assembly and no longer as an Assembly of Agreement.

Being the sovereign Assembly of *Prussia*, it had a perfect right to do this.

A sovereign assembly, however, cannot be dissolved by anybody, and cannot be given orders by anybody.

Even as a mere Agreement Assembly, even according to Herr Camphausen's own theory, it has *equal status* with the Crown. Both parties *conclude* a political treaty, both parties have an equal share of sovereignty—that is the theory of April 8, the Camphausen-Hansemann theory, the *official* theory recognised by the Crown itself.

If the Assembly and the Crown have *equal rights, then the Crown has no right to dissolve the Assembly.*

Otherwise, to be consistent, the Assembly would also have the *right to depose the King.*

The dissolution of the Assembly would therefore be a *coup d'état.* And how people reply to a coup d'état was demonstrated on July 29, 1830, and February 24, 1848.[a]

One may say the Crown could appeal again to the same voters. But who does not know that *today* the voters would elect an entirely different assembly, an assembly which would treat the Crown with much less ceremony?

Everyone knows that after the dissolution of this Assembly it will only be possible to appeal to *voters of an entirely different kind* from those of April 8, that the only elections possible will be elections carried through under the tyranny of the sword.

Let us have no illusions.

If the Assembly wins and succeeds in setting up a Left Government, then the power of the Crown existing *alongside* the Assembly is broken, then the King is merely a paid servant of the people and we return again to the morning of March 19—provided the Waldeck Government does not betray us, as did many a Government before it.

If the Crown wins and succeeds in setting up a Government of the Prince of Prussia, then the Assembly will be dissolved, the right of association abolished, the press muzzled, an electoral law based on property qualifications introduced, and, as we have already mentioned, even the United Diet may be reinvoked—and all this will be done under cover of a military dictatorship, guns and bayonets.

---

[a] The reference is to the overthrow of Charles X in July 1830 and of Louis Philippe in February 1848.— *Ed.*

Which of the two sides will win depends on the attitude of the people, especially that of the democratic party. It is up to the democrats to choose.

We have again the situation of July 25. Will they dare to issue the decrees being devised in Potsdam? Will the people be provoked to make the leap from July 26 to February 24 in a *single* day?[279]

The will to do it is certainly there, but what about the courage!

[*Neue Rheinische Zeitung* No. 102, September 14, 1848]

Cologne, September 13. The crisis in Berlin has advanced a step further. *The conflict with the Crown,* which yesterday could still be described as inevitable, *has actually taken place.*

Our readers will find below the King's reply to the resignation of the Ministers.[280] By this letter the Crown itself comes to the fore, sides with the Ministers and opposes the Assembly.

It goes even further—it forms a Government outside the Assembly, it nominates *Beckerath,* who represents the extreme Right at Frankfurt and who, as everyone knows, will never be able to count on the support of the majority in Berlin.

The King's message is countersigned by Herr *Auerswald.* Let Herr Auerswald, if he can, justify the fact that he thus uses the Crown to cover up his ignominious retreat, that at one and the same time he tries to hide behind the constitutional principle as far as the Chamber is concerned and tramples on the constitutional principle by *compromising the Crown and invoking the republic.*

Constitutional principle! shout the Ministers. Constitutional principle! shouts the Right. Constitutional principle! faintly echoes the *Kölnische Zeitung.*

"Constitutional principle!" Are these gentlemen really so foolish as to believe that it is possible to extricate the German people from the storms of 1848, and from the imminent threat of collapse of all traditional institutions, by means of the Montesquieu-Delolme worm-eaten theory of division of powers, by means of worn-out phrases and long exploded fictions!

"Constitutional principle!" But the very gentlemen who want to save the constitutional principle at all costs should realise first of all that at a provisional stage it can only be saved by energetic action.

"Constitutional principle!" But the vote of the Berlin Assembly, the clashes between Potsdam and Frankfurt, the disturbances, the reactionary attempts, the provocations of the brutal soldiery—has all this not shown long ago that despite all the empty talk we *are* still on a *revolutionary basis,* and the pretence that we have already reached the basis of an *established,* complete constitutional monarchy only leads to collisions, which have already brought the "constitutional principle" to the brink of the abyss?

Every provisional political set-up following a revolution requires a dictatorship, and an energetic dictatorship at that. From the very beginning we blamed Camphausen for not having acted in a dictatorial manner, for not having immediately smashed up and removed the remains of the old institutions. While thus Herr Camphausen indulged in constitutional dreaming, the defeated party strengthened its positions within the bureaucracy and in the army, and occasionally even risked an open fight. The Assembly was convened for the purpose of agreeing on the terms of the Constitution. It existed as an equal party alongside the Crown. Two equal powers in a provisional situation! It was this division of powers with the aid of which Herr Camphausen sought "to save freedom"—it was this very division of powers in a provisional situation that was bound to lead to conflicts. The Crown served as a cover for the counter-revolutionary aristocratic, military and bureaucratic camarilla. The bourgeoisie stood behind the majority of the Assembly. The Government tried to mediate. Too weak to act resolutely on behalf of the bourgeoisie and the peasants and overthrow the power of the nobility, the bureaucracy and the army chiefs at one blow, too unskilled to avoid always harming the bourgeoisie by its financial measures, the Government merely succeeded in compromising itself in the eyes of all the parties and bringing about the very clash it sought to avoid.

In any unconstituted state of affairs it is solely the *salut public,* the public welfare, and not this or that principle that is the decisive factor. The only way in which the Government could avoid a conflict between the Assembly and the Crown lay in recognising the public welfare as the sole principle, even at the risk of the Government *itself* coming into conflict with the Crown. But it preferred "not to compromise" itself in Potsdam. It never hesitated to employ public welfare measures (*mesures de salut public*), dictatorial measures, against the democratic forces. What else was the application of the old laws to political crimes, even after Herr Märker had recognised that these articles of the Prussian Law ought to be repealed? What else were the wholesale arrests in all parts of the kingdom?

But the Government carefully refrained from intervening against the counter-revolution in the name of public welfare.

It was this half-heartedness of the Government in face of the counter-revolution, which became more menacing with every day, that compelled the Assembly *itself to dictate* measures of public welfare. If the Crown represented by the Ministers was too weak, then the Assembly itself had to intervene. It did so by passing the resolution of August 9. It did so in a form still rather mild, by merely warning the Ministers. The Ministers took no notice of it.[281]

Indeed, how could they have agreed to it? The resolution of August 9 flouted the constitutional principle, it is an encroachment of the legislative power on the executive power, it destroys the division of powers and their mutual control, which are essential in the interests of freedom, it turns the Assembly of Agreement into a *National Convention.*

There follows a running fire of threats, a vociferous appeal to the fears of the petty bourgeois and the prospect of a reign of terror with guillotines, progressive taxes, confiscations and the red flag.

To compare the Berlin Assembly with the Convention. What irony!

But these gentlemen were not altogether wrong. If the Government continues in the way it has been doing, we shall have a Convention before long—not merely for Prussia, but for Germany as a whole—a Convention which will have to use all means to cope with the civil war in our twenty Vendées and with the inevitable war with Russia. At present, however, we merely have a parody of the Constituent Assembly.[282]

But how have the Ministers who invoke the constitutional principle upheld this principle?

On August 9, they calmly allowed the Assembly to break up in the belief that the Ministers would carry out the resolution. They had no intention of making known to the Assembly their refusal to do so, and still less of resigning their office.

They ruminated on the matter for a whole month and finally, when threatened with a number of parliamentary questions, they curtly informed the Assembly that it was self-evident that they would not put the resolution into effect.

When the Assembly thereupon instructs the Ministers, nevertheless, to put the resolution into effect, they take refuge behind the Crown, and cause a rupture between the Crown and the Assembly, thus invoking the republic.

And these gentlemen still talk about the constitutional principle!

To sum up:

The inevitable conflict between two powers having equal rights in a provisional situation has broken out. The Ministry was unable to govern with sufficient energy; it has failed to take the necessary measures of public welfare. The Assembly has merely performed its duty in demanding that the Ministry do its duty. The Ministry declares this to be an encroachment upon the rights of the Crown and discredits the Crown at the very moment of its resignation. The Crown and the Assembly confront each other. The "agreement" has led to separation, to conflict. It is possible that arms will decide the issue.

The side that has the greater courage and consistency will win.

[*Neue Rheinische Zeitung* No. 104, September 16, 1848]

Cologne, September 15. The government crisis has once again entered a new phase, due, not to the arrival and vain efforts of the impossible Herr Beckerath, but to the *army revolt in Potsdam and Nauen.*[283] The conflict between democracy and aristocracy has broken out even *within the guard regiments.* The soldiers consider that the resolution carried by the Assembly on the 7th liberates them from the tyranny of their officers; they cheer the Assembly and send letters of thanks to it.

This has wrenched the sword from the hands of the counter-revolutionaries. They will not dare now to dissolve the Assembly, and since this cannot be attempted, they will have to give in, carry out the resolution of the Assembly and form a Waldeck Ministry.

It is quite possible that the soldiers in revolt at Potsdam will save us a revolution.

Written by Marx on September 11, 12, 13 and 15, 1848

First published in the *Neue Rheinische Zeitung* Nos. 100, 101, 102 and 104, September 12, 13, 14 and 16, 1848

Printed according to the newspaper

ARMY ORDER, ELECTION CANDIDATES,
SEMI-OFFICIAL COMMENTS ON PRUSSIAN AMBIGUITY

We have received Danish newspapers up to September 9. An army order of September 4 gives the following instructions: General *Krogh* takes over command in Jutland, headquarters Viborg. For the duration of the armistice the garrison in Alsen[a] has a special command. The corps in the field is quartered as far as possible in its recruiting areas and is therefore spread across Jutland and the islands. Forty to fifty men per company remain under arms, the rest will be sent home on leave, and the brigade commanders are instructed to inspect their troops frequently and prepare for a new campaign. However, since the King[b] wants to make a personal inspection of the troops before they go on leave, these decisions will not be carried out until further orders. It is also unlikely that they will be, for as the postscript of the *Faedreland* announced on the 9th, news of the decision passed by the National Assembly about suspending the withdrawal has just reached Copenhagen in private letters.

The Danes can rely fairly firmly on the troops recruited in North Schleswig, this is evident from the fact that it was precisely these sections of the army that were moved to the vicinity of the Schleswig frontier or Alsen.

The liberal party in Copenhagen has put forward its list of candidates for the approaching elections. The representatives of the middle class, the editors of the *Faedreland* and other "men of the people" of the "constitutional monarchy established on a democratic

---

[a] The Danish name is Als.— *Ed.*
[b] Frederick VII.— *Ed.*

basis" (note how thoroughly the Danes have plagiarised the Germans) have met to draw up the list. It consists of a bank manager, a director of a life-insurance institution, two schoolmasters, an attorney, a lieutenant-colonel, a naval officer, two artisans and a "*disvacheur*" (!). It can be seen what sort of intellectual forces are at the disposal of the "*Hovedstad*".[a]

The Prussian Government is unfortunate. In the Danish affair too it has managed to give Prussia a reputation for ambiguity which almost verges on treason against both sides. This ambiguity has always been a well-known feature of Prussian policy; we need only think of the "Great" Elector's[b] betrayal of Poland when he suddenly went over to Sweden, of the Basle Peace, of 1805 and more recently of the ambiguity through which the Ministry enticed Poland into the trap.[284] And now, in the Danish affair, the Prussian Government has abused the interests of the German people and not even earned a word of thanks from Denmark. Let us listen to what the *Faedreland* says:

"According to the note of the Prussian Prime Minister Auerswald (to the Provisional Government in Rendsburg), which we publish below, it is plain that Prussia is playing a very ambiguous role. In the first place it is extremely surprising that the Prussian Government should have any dealings at all with the rebel Government in the duchies. Furthermore, Herr Auerswald has in more than one respect completely twisted the meaning of the terms of the armistice. Although the armistice was in no way intended to furnish any basis for a final peace, Herr Auerswald nonetheless claims that through it conditions are being prepared that will bring about a favourable final solution. He talks further of the significance of the terms whereby the federal troops are to remain in Schleswig and the Schleswig-Holstein army corps is to continue at its present strength, even though the armistice stipulates that the Schleswig and the Holstein troops should be separated and the federal troops remain in Altona. Lastly, he puts forward a similar falsehood when he says that the legal situation in the duchies is to continue on its present basis, whereas the armistice says that the decrees issued since March 17 both by the King of Denmark and by the Provisional Government should be repealed. As regards the Central Authority, it has shown such a lack of firmness towards the Assembly in its negotiations over Limburg[285] that from that side one can really expect anything."

Written by Engels on September 14, 1848	Printed according to the newspaper
First published in the *Neue Rheinische Zeitung* No. 103, September 15, 1848	Published in English for the first time

---

[a] Capital.— *Ed.*
[b] Frederick William.— *Ed.*

FREEDOM OF DEBATE IN BERLIN[286]

Cologne, September 16. Ever since the beginning of the crisis the counter-revolutionary press keeps alleging that the deliberations of the Berlin Assembly are not free from interference. In particular, the well-known correspondent "G" of the *Kölnische Zeitung*, who also discharges his duties only "temporarily pending the appointment of a successor",[287] refers with obvious fear to the "8,000 to 10,000 strong-arm men" in the Kastanienwäldchen who "morally" support their friends of the Left. The *Vossische*, *Spenersche* and other newspapers have set up a similar wail, and on the 7th of this month Herr Reichensperger has even tabled a motion frankly demanding that the Assembly be removed from Berlin (to Charlottenburg perhaps?).

The *Berliner Zeitungs-Halle* publishes a long article[a] in which it tries to refute these accusations. It declares that the large majority obtained by the Left was by no means inconsistent with the former irresolute attitude of the Assembly. It can be shown, it says,

"that the voting of the 7th[b] could have taken place *without conflicting* with the former attitude even of those members who previously voted always for the Government, that it was indeed from their point of view in perfect harmony with their former position...." The members who came over from the Centre parties "had laboured under a delusion; they *imagined* that the Ministers carried out the will of the people; they had taken the endeavours of the Ministers to restore law and order for an expression of their own will, i.e. that of the majority of deputies, and had not *realised* that the Ministers could accede to the popular will only when it did not run counter to the will of the Crown, but not when it was opposed to it".

---

[a] "Berlin, 14. September", *Berliner Zeitungs-Halle* No. 213, September 15, 1848.— *Ed.*

[b] September 7, 1848.— *Ed.*

Thus the *Zeitungs-Halle* "explains" the striking phenomenon of the sudden change in the attitude of so many deputies by ascribing it to the notions and delusions of these deputies. The thing could not be presented in a more innocent way.

The paper admits, however, that intimidations did occur. But, it says,

"if outside influences did have any effect, it was only that they partially counterbalanced the ministerial misrepresentations and artful temptation, thus enabling the many weak and irresolute deputies to follow their *natural vital instinct*...."

The reasons which induced the *Zeitungs-Halle* thus morally to justify the vacillating members of the Centre parties in the eyes of the public are obvious. The article is written for these gentlemen of the Centre parties rather than for the general public. For us, however, these reasons do not exist, since we are privileged to speak plainly, and since we support the representatives of a party only as long and insofar as they act in a *revolutionary* manner.

Why should we not say it? The Centre parties certainly were intimidated by the masses on September 7[a]; we leave it open whether their fear was well founded or not.

The right of the democratic popular masses, by their presence, to exert a moral influence on the attitude of constituent assemblies is an old revolutionary right of the people which could not be dispensed with in all stormy periods ever since the English and French revolutions. History owes to this right almost all the energetic steps taken by such assemblies. The only reason why people dwelling on the "legal basis" and the timorous and philistine friends of "freedom of debate" lament about this right, is that they do not want any energetic decisions at all.

"Freedom of debate"—there is no emptier phrase than this. The "freedom of debate" is, on the one hand, impaired by the freedom of the press, by the freedom of assembly and of speech, and by the right of the people to take up arms. It is impaired by the existing state power in the hands of the Crown and its Ministers—the army, the police and the so-called independent judges, who depend, however, on every promotion and every political change.

The freedom of debate is always a phrase denoting simply independence of all influences that are not recognised in law. It is only the recognised influences, such as bribery, promotion, private interests and fear of a dissolution of the Assembly, that make the debates really "free". In times of revolution, however, this phrase

---

[a] See this volume, pp. 417-19.— *Ed.*

Articles from the *Neue Rheinische Zeitung*

becomes entirely meaningless. When two forces, two parties in arms confront each other, when a fight may start at any moment, the deputies have only this choice:

Either they place themselves *under the protection of the people*, in which case they will put up occasionally with a small lecture;

Or they place themselves *under the protection of the Crown*, move to some small town, deliberate under the protection of bayonets and guns or even a state of siege, in which case they will raise no objections when the Crown and the bayonets dictate their decisions to them.

Intimidation by the unarmed people or intimidation by an armed soldiery—that is the choice before the Assembly.

The French Constituent Assembly transferred its sessions from Versailles to Paris. It would be quite in character with the German revolution if the Assembly of Agreement were to move from Berlin to Charlottenburg.

Written on September 16, 1848 Printed according to the newspaper

First published in the *Neue Rheinische Zeitung* No. 105, September 17, 1848

RATIFICATION OF THE ARMISTICE[288]

Cologne, September 19. The German National Assembly has ratified the armistice. We were not mistaken: "Germany's honour has fallen into bad hands."[a]

The vote was taken amidst uproar and complete darkness, when the benches of the deputies were thronged with strangers, diplomats etc. A majority of two forced the Assembly to vote simultaneously on two entirely different questions. The armistice was carried, Schleswig-Holstein sacrificed, "Germany's honour" trampled under foot and the *merging of Germany in Prussia* decided by a majority of 21 votes.

On no other issue has there been such a clear expression of public opinion. On no other issue have the gentlemen of the Right so openly admitted that they uphold a cause which is *indefensible*. In no other issue were Germany's interests so indubitable and so obvious as in this. The National Assembly has made its decision—it has pronounced the *death sentence* upon itself and upon the so-called Central Authority created by it. If Germany had a Cromwell it would not be long before he would say: "You are no Parliament.... Depart, I say.... In the name of God,—go!"[b]

There is talk of the impending withdrawal of the Left. If it had courage, this poor derided Left, which has been attacked with fists by the majority and in addition called to order by the noble Gagern! Never has a minority been so insolently and consistently maltreated

---

[a] See this volume, p. 425.— *Ed.*

[b] The words Cromwell used when dissolving the Rump Parliament on April 20, 1653.— *Ed.*

as has been the Frankfurt Left by the noble Gagern and his 250 champions of the majority. If only it had courage!

Lack of courage is ruining the entire German movement. The counter-revolution just as much as the revolutionary party lacks the courage for decisive blows. All Germans, whether on the Right or on the Left, know now that the present movement must lead to terrible clashes, to bloody battles, fought either to suppress it or to carry it through. But instead of courageously facing these unavoidable battles, instead of fighting them out with a few rapid and decisive blows, the two parties—the party of the counter-revolution and that of the movement—virtually conspire to put them off as long as possible. It is due to this constant resort to petty expedients, to trivial concessions and palliatives, to these attempts at mediation, that the unbearable and uncertain political situation has led everywhere to numerous isolated uprisings, which can only be liquidated by bloodshed and the curtailment of rights already won. It is this fear of struggle that gives rise to thousands of minor clashes making the year 1848 exceptionally sanguinary and so complicating the position of the contending parties that in the end the struggle is bound to become the more violent and destructive. But "our dear friends' lack of courage"![a]

The crucial struggle for Germany's centralisation and democratic organisation cannot possibly be avoided. Every day brings it nearer despite all attempts to gloss over it and compromise. The complex situation in Vienna, Berlin and Frankfurt demands a decision, and if everything should fail because of German timidity and indecision, we shall be saved by France. The consequences of the June victory are now taking shape in Paris—the royalists are getting the better of Cavaignac and his "pure republicans" in the National Assembly, in the press and in the clubs; a general uprising is threatening to break out in the legitimist South; Cavaignac has to resort to Ledru-Rollin's revolutionary remedies, i.e. to departmental commissioners invested with extraordinary powers; it was with the greatest difficulty that he managed to defend himself and his Government in Parliament last Saturday. Another such division, and Thiers, Barrot and company, the men in whose interests the June victory was won, will possess a majority, Cavaignac will be thrown into the arms of the red republic, and the struggle for the republic's existence will begin.

If Germany's irresoluteness should persist, this new phase of the French revolution will also be a signal for a fresh outbreak of open

---

[a] Heinrich Heine, *Deutschland. Ein Wintermärchen*, Caput XIX.— *Ed.*

struggle in Germany, a struggle which we hope will take us a little further and will at least free Germany from the traditional fetters of her past.

Written by Engels on September 19, 1848

First published in the *Neue Rheinische Zeitung* No. 107, September 20, 1848

Printed according to the newspaper

THE UPRISING IN FRANKFURT[289]

[*Neue Rheinische Zeitung* No. 107 (supplement),
September 20, 1848]

Cologne, September 19, 7 p.m. The German-Danish armistice has raised a storm. A sanguinary revolt has begun in Frankfurt. The workers of Frankfurt, Offenbach and Hanau, and the peasants of the surrounding districts, are defending with their lives Germany's honour betrayed by the National Assembly to a Prussian Government which has ignominiously resigned.

The outcome of the struggle is still uncertain. Until yesterday evening the soldiers apparently made little progress. In Frankfurt, apart from the Zeil and perhaps a few other streets and squares, artillery is of little use, and cavalry of almost no use at all. In this respect the people are in an advantageous position. Citizens of Hanau, armed with weapons from the arsenal they had stormed, have come to their assistance, as have also peasants from numerous villages in the vicinity. Yesterday evening the military probably numbered about 10,000 men and very little artillery. Large reinforcements of peasants must have arrived during the night, and considerably smaller ones of soldiers, the immediate vicinity being denuded of troops. The revolutionary temper of the peasants in the Odenwald, Nassau and the Electorate of Hesse precluded further withdrawals; it is likely that communications have been interrupted. If today the insurgents are still holding out, then the whole of the Odenwald, Nassau, the Electorate of Hesse and Rhenish Hesse will take up arms, the entire population between Fulda, Koblenz, Mannheim and Aschaffenburg will be in arms, and there are insufficient troops available to crush the uprising. And who will answer for Mainz, Mannheim, Marburg, Cassel and Wiesbaden—towns in which hatred of the brutal soldiery has reached its highest pitch as a result of the bloody excesses of the so-called federal troops? Who will answer for the peasants on the Rhine, who can easily prevent troops being sent along the river?

We admit, nevertheless, that we have little hope of the courageous insurgents being able to win the day. Frankfurt is too small a town, the number of troops is disproportionately large, and the well-known counter-revolutionary sentiments of the local petty bourgeoisie are too great to allow us to be very hopeful.

But even if the insurgents are defeated, this will settle nothing. The counter-revolution will become arrogant, it will enslave us for a time by introducing martial law, by suppressing freedom of the press, and banning the clubs and public meetings; but before long the crowing of the Gallic cock[a] will announce the hour of liberation, the hour of revenge.

[*Neue Rheinische Zeitung* No. 108, September 21, 1848]

Cologne, September 20. The news from Frankfurt is beginning to gradually confirm our fears of yesterday. It seems certain that the insurgents have been ejected from Frankfurt, and that now they are holding only Sachsenhausen, where they are said to be strongly entrenched. A state of siege has been declared in Frankfurt; anyone caught carrying weapons or resisting the "federal authority" is to be court-martialled.

Thus the gentlemen in St. Paul's Church are now on an equal footing with their colleagues in Paris. They can now at their leisure and under the rule of martial law reduce the fundamental rights of the German people to a "minimum".

The railway line to Mainz is torn up in many places, and the post arrives either late or not at all.

It appears that artillery decided the outcome of the fight in the wide streets and enabled the army to attack the fighters on the barricades from the rear. Additional factors were the zeal with which the petty bourgeois of Frankfurt opened their houses to the soldiers, thus giving them every advantage in the street-fighting, and the superior strength of the troops, swiftly brought up by rail, over the peasant contingents, which arrived showly on foot.

But even if the fight has not been renewed in Frankfurt itself, it certainly does not mean that the uprising has been crushed. The

---

[a] Heinrich Heine, "Kahldorf über den Adel, in Briefen an den Grafen M. von Moltke". Einleitung.— *Ed.*

angry peasants are not likely to put their weapons down forthwith. Though they may not be able to break up the National Assembly, they still have enough at home that has to be cleared away. The storm that was repelled outside St. Paul's Church can spread to six or eight petty princely residences and to hundreds of manorial estates. The peasant war begun this spring will not come to an end until its goal, the liberation of the peasants from feudalism, has been achieved.

What is the reason for the persistent victory of "order" throughout Europe and for the numerous recurrent defeats of the revolutionary party from Naples, Prague and Paris to Milan, Vienna and Frankfurt?

It is because all parties know that the struggle impending in all civilised countries is quite different from, infinitely more significant than, all previous revolutions; in Vienna and Paris, in Berlin and Frankfurt, in London and Milan the point at issue is the *overthrow of the political rule of the bourgeoisie*, an upheaval whose immediate consequences are enough to terrify all portly, stockjobbing bourgeois.

Is there a revolutionary centre anywhere in the world where the red flag, the battle emblem of the united proletariat of Europe, has not been found flying on the barricades during the last five months?

In Frankfurt, too, the fight against the Parliament of the combined landowners and bourgeois was waged under the red flag.

The reason for all these defeats is that every uprising that now takes place is a direct threat to the political existence of the bourgeoisie, and an indirect threat to its social existence. The people, mostly unarmed, have to fight not only the organised power of the bureaucratic and military state which the bourgeoisie has taken over, they have to fight the armed bourgeoisie itself. The people, who are unorganised and poorly armed, are confronted by all the other social classes, who are well organised and fully armed. That is the reason why up to now the people have been defeated and will continue to be defeated until their opponents are weakened either through dissension, or because the army is engaged in war—or until some important event impels the people to begin a desperate fight and demoralises their opponents.

Such a great event is impending in France.

Hence we need not give up hope, even though during the last four months the barricades everywhere have been defeated by grape-shot. On the contrary, every victory of our opponents was at the same time a defeat for them, for it divided them and, ultimately, gave control not to the conservative party that was victorious in

February and March, but in each case to *the* party that had been *overthrown* in February and March. Only for a short time did the victory won in Paris in June establish the rule of the petty bourgeoisie, the *pure* republicans; hardly three months have passed and the big bourgeoisie, the constitutional party, is threatening to overthrow Cavaignac and drive the "pure ones" into the arms of the "reds". This will happen in Frankfurt too — the victory will benefit, not the respectable gentlemen from the Centre parties, but those of the *Right.* The bourgeoisie will have to give pride of place to the gentlemen representing the military, bureaucratic and junker state and will very soon taste the bitter fruits of its victory.

May these bitter fruits do it good! Meanwhile we shall await the moment when the hour of liberation for Europe will have struck in Paris.

Written by Engels on September 19 and 20, 1848

First published in the supplement to the *Neue Rheinische Zeitung* No. 107 and in No. 108, September 20 and 21, 1848

Printed according to the newspaper

THE *FAEDRELAND* ON THE ARMISTICE

Cologne, September 21. It is common knowledge that the so-called National Assembly in Frankfurt approved of the armistice on Prussia's assurance that the Danish Government has *officially given notice* of its readiness to agree to *modifications.*

It is well known, however, what intrigues went on during the voting on the preliminary question. The intrigues over the main question took place *outside* the Assembly.

Listen to what the *Faedreland* of September 16 says:

After explaining the disadvantages of the armistice that was actually signed as compared with the first draft, the newspaper comes to the advantages for Denmark. England and Russia would intervene if the war broke out again; German unity, held together with difficulty by the Danish war, would immediately disintegrate; the population of Jutland could be trained as an army reserve and the army doubled in size:

"and 60,000 troops on the narrow peninsula, backed up by the fleet, are a *Dannevirke* which big, united Germany would think twice about storming".

"But whatever the terms of the armistice, it is plain that once it is signed, ratified and guaranteed, it would be irresponsible if we neglected to fulfil its terms, or tolerated their infringement by our enemies. There is no question of our Government doing such a thing, there can and must be no doubts about this, and for this reason it would be wrong to get alarmed at all the rumours hawked around in Schleswig-Holstein publications about changes in the terms *once they have been accepted.* We are fully aware that Prussian generals and officials and the Germans in general, with a few honourable exceptions, do not take their commitments and their vows, their *bona fides* so very seriously; we are quite ready to believe that General Wrangel had the effrontery to put proposals to the Danish Commissioner, Mr. Reedtz, suggesting a breach of the terms in order to make them more acceptable to his friends in Schleswig-Holstein; we are quite ready to believe that both the Frankfurt Assembly and the Prussian Ministry consider it quite in order to urge us to agree to arbitrary changes in a matter that has already been signed and sealed in due form. But we also believe that the worst thing our Government could do would be to permit them to alter even one jot or tittle of the treaty, for then "German honesty" would have no qualms about trampling the whole thing under foot. If Karl Moltke cannot find any co-regents, since it has been laid down how these are to be appointed, the Danish Government can proceed to choose two whose agreement is certain in advance, and it is then *up to Prussia to find two of its own.* If the people of Schleswig-Holstein are not willing to obey, it is *up to Prussia to force* them to. And if on the last appointed date, that is tomorrow, September 17, there is anything essential missing in the execution of the treaty after we for our part have conscientiously fulfilled all our obligations, then it is *up to the Danish Government* to set a final deadline, and if this also expires without any further developments, then it is the *right and duty of the Danish Government to move the army to Schleswig and have it occupied.* We will then see what Europe has to say and what guarantees and obligations actually mean. We certainly have no need to fear the consequences; whatever they are, it is easier to endure them than to disgrace ourselves in our own eyes and in the eyes of the whole world, than to allow ourselves to be treated as the bondsman (*Trael*) of German arrogance and German dishonesty.

"We are pleased to say that as we lay down our pen we can give the *positive assurance* **that as far as Danish Government is concerned any modification** of the armistice convention which has been concluded *is out of the question.*

Thus the semi-official organ of the Danish Cabinet.

And now? Who is the deceiver now, who the deceived, who the deceived deceiver[a]?

Written by Engels on September 21, 1848

First published in the *Neue Rheinische Zeitung* No. 109, September 22, 1848

Printed according to the newspaper

Published in English for the first time

---

[a] G. E. Lessing, *Nathan der Weise*, Act III, Scene 7.— *Ed.*

448

THE GOVERNMENT
OF THE COUNTER-REVOLUTION

Cologne, September 22. It has happened after all! The Government of the Prince of Prussia is in being and the counter-revolution intends to risk the final decisive blow.[290]

Read the following letter by a deputy:

"*Berlin*, September 20, 10 p.m. We have just learned beyond doubt that an entirely *counter-revolutionary Government* has been formed, namely" (then follows the list of Ministers which we gave yesterday in accordance with the special edition of the *Zeitungs-Halle*). "At tomorrow's session this same Government will read out a royal message wherein the *prospect of the disbandment of the Assembly* will be held out. The result of this is a *declaration of permanence* which will probably lead to a new and very bloody *revolution*. All parties of the National Assembly are consulting permanently in their usual premises. The population is very excited. Wrangel has held a military review today. Everything seems to be in question!"

It has happened after all! The Crown seeks the protection of the Uckermark grandees and the Uckermark grandees oppose the revolutionary movement of the year 1848. The Don Quixotes of Further Pomerania, these old warriors and debt-encumbered landed proprietors, will finally have their opportunity to cleanse their rusty blades in the blood of the agitators.[291] The guards, crowned with the cheap glory of Schleswig, are supposed to strike the decisive blow against the revolution which intrudes upon the rights of the Crown, which wants to prohibit the officers from plotting secretly and which intends, by the implacable hand of Hansemann's financial measures, to take a terribly "bold dip"[a] into the already limp purse of the Brandenburg junkers. The guards will take revenge for the

---

[a] An expression first used by Karl Mathy and Heinrich von Gagern in the Frankfurt National Assembly in 1848; it became quickly popular.— *Ed.*

humiliation of March 18, disperse the Berlin Assembly and the officers will ride down Unter den Linden over the corpses of the revolutionaries.

Go on! Forward with God for King and Fatherland![a]

Written on September 22, 1848

Printed according to the newspaper

First published in the *Neue Rheinische Zeitung* No. 110, September 23, 1848

Published in English for the first time

---

[a] From Frederick William III's decree on the formation of an army reserve issued on March 17, 1813.— *Ed.*

[THE COLOGNE COMMITTEE OF PUBLIC SAFETY][292]

Cologne, September 23. As already announced in this newspaper, the Committee of Public Safety has notified the authorities here that it has undertaken 1) to co-operate in the preservation of peace and 2) to watch over the gains of the revolution.[a] Herr von Wittgenstein has passed on this news to Public Prosecutor Hecker just as he received it, together with an official request to investigate whether the Committee's plans in any way constitute a punishable offence.

Poor Herr Hecker! Already overburdened with the duties of his office, he now has also to take over the capacity for judging from the administrative officials!!!

Written about September 23, 1848

First published in the supplement to the *Neue Rheinische Zeitung* No. 112, September 26, 1848

Printed according to the newspaper

Published in English for the first time

---

[a] See this volume, pp. 586-87.— *Ed.*

[PUBLIC PROSECUTOR HECKER QUESTIONS PEOPLE WHO HAD ATTENDED THE WORRINGEN MEETING]

Cologne, September 24. The Public Prosecutor, Herr Hecker, is the most harassed man in Cologne. For several days now he has been personally questioning witnesses in an attempt to find out what sort of sins against the Holy Spirit of penal law were committed at the public meeting at Worringen.[293] Up to now the results of his inquiries are said to have been extremely meagre, 1) because nothing illegal happened and 2) because it is unlikely that witnesses still remember what each individual said and especially in what context he said it. As regards 2), we think it better to refer Herr Hecker to the band of disguised policemen and *mouchards* who were wandering around the meadow taking notes in shorthand. But there again, if some of these pillars of the state are unable to give any evidence, we should not be surprised. One of them in particular was so drunk even at midday that he made his way in tears from one bar to the next gratefully accepting the drinks offered him and telling people "in confidence" that it is true he was here as a spy, but apart from this he was a decent fellow.

Written on September 24, 1848, or later

First published in the supplement to the *Neue Rheinische Zeitung* No. 112, September 26, 1848

Printed according to the newspaper

Published in English for the first time

[COUNTER-REVOLUTION IN COLOGNE]

Cologne, September 25. Scarcely had the official news of the formation of the counter-revolutionary Government[a] reached the Rhine when the Public Prosecutor's office here suddenly developed not only an almighty appetite for arrests but a zeal for activity such as was not encountered even in the old police state.

The counter-revolutionary campaign started this morning. Its heroes have won victories in some fields and suffered defeats in others—a fate that has befallen even greater generals. The intention was to lead away a few dozen Cologne democrats as early morning spoils and to delight the local wailers[294] over their breakfasts with the news. However, part of the prey was wrested from these gentlemen. For example, *Wachter*, captain of the 9th Company of the civic militia, was snatched by the people from the clutches of the Holy Hermandad.[295] Six guardians of the law forced their way into the house of our fellow citizen *Moll*. The crowd that quickly gathered around the house and its threatening attitude caused two of these gentlemen to flee into the attic and a third into the cellar. Unfortunately the house has only one exit. Moll acceded to the wishes of these terrified gentlemen and asked the people to allow the brigade of six men to withdraw in safety.

Becker and *Schapper*, on the other hand, were led off to gaol in the early hours of the morning. There are reports that in addition to Bürgers several other members of the editorial staff of our newspaper are on the proscribed list and that attempts have been made to arrest them.

---

[a] See this volume, pp. 448-49.—*Ed.*

If these gentlemen go ahead with their plans, it will soon be a mystery how the editorial work of our newspaper is to be carried out. But we believe we can declare that all the manoeuvres directed against us will fail in their main aim and that our readers will continue as usual to receive the newspaper regularly. It is merely a question of who will first lose their sense of humour: the gentlemen from the Public Prosecutor's office or the editors of the *Neue Rheinische Zeitung*.

We would add that even now some policemen etc. are on their way to Mülheim to punish several hated democrats there with arrest and imprisonment.

Written on September 25, 1848

First published in the *Neue Rheinische Zeitung* No. 112, September 26, 1848

Printed according to the newspaper

Published in English for the first time

[AN ATTEMPT TO ARREST MOLL]

Cologne, 11 a. m. This morning a detachment of the 29th Regiment was sent into the Kranz to carry out Moll's arrest. The soldiers were driven back and with the aid of the workers Moll got away safely.

Written on September 25, 1848

First published in the *Neue Rheinische Zeitung* No. 113, September 27, 1848

Printed according to the newspaper

Published in English for the first time

[STATE OF SIEGE IN COLOGNE]²⁹⁶

Cologne, September 26. Today we are also omitting the synopsis. We are hurrying to print the paper. We are being informed by a reliable source that the city will be placed in a state of siege within an hour or two, that the civic militia will be dissolved and disarmed, that the *Neue Rheinische Zeitung*, the *Neue Kölnische Zeitung*, the *Arbeiter-Zeitung* and the *Wächter am Rhein* will be suspended, that courts martial will be instituted and that all the rights gained in March are to be suppressed. It is reported that the civic militia is not inclined to let itself be disarmed.

Written on September 26, 1848

First published in the *Neue Rheinische Zeitung* No. 113, September 27, 1848

Printed according to the newspaper

Published in English for the first time

[EDITORIAL STATEMENT CONCERNING
THE REAPPEARANCE OF THE *NEUE RHEINISCHE
ZEITUNG*]

Due to the interest shown, particularly in *Cologne,* for the preservation of the *Neue Rheinische Zeitung,* we have been able to overcome the *financial* difficulties brought about by the state of siege and to let the paper reappear. The editorial board remains the same. *Ferdinand Freiligrath* has newly joined it.

Karl Marx
Editor-in-Chief of the *Neue Rheinische Zeitung*

Written by Marx on October 11, 1848

First published in the *Neue Rheinische Zeitung* No. 114, October 12, 1848

Printed according to the newspaper

Published in English for the first time

REVOLUTION IN VIENNA[297]

Cologne, October 11. In its *first* issue (for June 1) the *Neue Rheinische Zeitung* wrote of a revolution (on May 25) in Vienna. Today, when we resume publication for the *first* time after the break caused by the declaration of a state of siege in Cologne, we bring news of the much more important Viennese revolution of October 6 and 7. Detailed reports on the events in Vienna compel us today to omit all analytical articles. Only a few words of comment, therefore, on the revolution in Vienna. Our readers will see from the reports of our Vienna correspondent[a] that the bourgeoisie's distrust of the working class threatens, if not to wreck the revolution, at least to hamper its development. However that may be, the repercussions of this revolution in Hungary, Italy and Germany foiled the entire plan of campaign devised by the counter-revolution. The flight from Vienna of the Emperor and of the Czech deputies[298] compels the Viennese bourgeoisie to continue the fight unless it is prepared to surrender unconditionally. The Frankfurt Assembly, which is just now engaged in presenting us Germans with

a national gaol
and a common whip,[b]

has been rudely awakened from its day-dreaming by the events in Vienna, and the Government at Berlin is beginning to doubt the efficacy of the *state of siege* as a panacea. The state of siege, like the revolution, is making a round-the-world tour. A large-scale experiment has just been made to impose a state of siege on a whole

---

[a] Müller-Tellering.— *Ed.*
[b] Heinrich Heine, "Der Tannhäuser", Caput 3.—*Ed.*

country, Hungary. This attempt has called forth a revolution in Vienna instead of a counter-revolution in Hungary. The state of siege will not recover from this setback. Its reputation has been permanently ruined. By an irony of fate, simultaneously with Jellachich, *Cavaignac*, the hero of the state of siege in the West, has been singled out for attack by all the factions who were saved in June by his grape-shot. Only by resolutely going over to the revolution will he be able to hold out for some time.

Following the latest news from Vienna, we publish several reports sent on October 5, because they reflect the hopes and fears current in Vienna about the fate of Hungary.

Written by Marx on October 11, 1848   Printed according to the newspaper

First published in the *Neue Rheinische Zeitung* No. 114, October 12, 1848

THE LATEST NEWS FROM THE "MODEL STATE"

Brussels, October 8. *La Nation* yesterday led off with the following article about two members of the editorial staff of the *Neue Rheinische Zeitung*, Herr Frederick Engels and Herr Ernst Dronke:

"The expulsions are succeeding one another and are unfortunately all too similar. While we are still awaiting a few words of explanation about the expulsion of Herr Adam, a similar measure is taken against two German citizens who were foolish enough to rely on the protection which the Belgian Constitution grants every foreigner. Yes, this protection exists in the wording of the Constitution; until a few days ago it even beamed down from one of the façades of that charming little constitutional monument with which the courtyard of the Palais de Nation was graced; but as soon as the intoxication of the national holidays[299] is over, the liberals who rule over us hurriedly stuff away the slogans with which they so gallantly regaled the inquisitive citizens of the city and the provinces. Brussels has returned to normal and the police is fulfilling exactly as before its lofty mission of compensating by its brutal manners for the generosity of our ill-advised constitutional theories.

"Herr Engels and Herr Dronke had been staying in our city for a few days. Both members of the editorial staff of a democratic journal, the *Neue Rheinische Zeitung*, they left Cologne to avoid the consequences of warrants issued for their arrest because of a few speeches made at public meetings. They made their way to Belgium not in order to abuse that Belgian hospitality which on account of its rarity can be so valuable, but only to wait for the money they needed to continue their journey to Paris. The unhappy events that occurred in Cologne *after their departure* strengthened them in their intention. The Prussian Government has been blessed with good fortune since it followed the Belgian example and set out on the broad constitutional path—after finding a general[a] who decreed a state of siege and the suspension of the press à la Cavaignac, it also managed to find a public prosecutor-general[b] who agreed to employ the concept of moral complicity à la Hébert and à la de Bavay. But Herr Engels and Herr Dronke had forgotten that though the traveller proposes the police disposes.

---

[a] Kaiser.— *Ed.*
[b] Zweiffel.— *Ed.*

"Scarcely had the news of their arrival in Brussels the day before yesterday become public when an inspector with his retinue turned up in their hotel. They were having their dinner. The inspector took them to the Town Hall and from there to the prison of the Petits-Carmes, whence after an hour or two they were transported in a sealed carriage to the Southern Railway Station. The police were merely using their powers in relation to "vagabonds" and, as it happened, the papers of our political refugees were not in order. It is true that they had on them a safe-conduct issued by the Cologne authorities stating that they were members of the civic militia of that city; moreover as a result of their stay in Brussels before March, they had friends who could prove their identity. But the police, *only too well informed about them*, preferred to treat them as vagabonds before any proof to the contrary could be obtained.

"If this is obstinacy, at least it is not blind obstinacy.

"Judging from the way in which the arrests are at present taking place, we believe that this article will probably have its sequels in future issues, unless the friends of liberty of all countries become convinced that it is better 'to refrain under all circumstances from dropping in on us during their travels through this world'."

It is clear from this that the Belgian Government is increasingly learning to recognise its position. The Belgians gradually become policemen for all their neighbours, and are overjoyed when they are complimented on their quiet and submissive behaviour. Nevertheless, there is something ridiculous about the good Belgian policeman. Even the earnest *Times* only jestingly acknowledged the Belgian desire to please. Recently it advised the Belgian nation, after it had got rid of all the clubs, to turn itself into one big club with the motto: "*Ne risquez rien!*"[a]

It goes without saying that the official Belgian press, in its cretinism, also reprinted this piece of flattery and welcomed it jubilantly. The fact that in its very first issue the *Neue Rheinische Zeitung* quite properly ridiculed any illusions about the Belgian "model" state makes it easier to understand, moreover, why the Belgian Government meted out such brutal treatment to two members of the *Neue Rheinische Zeitung*'s editorial staff.[b]

The Belgian press itself reveals to us how the Belgian Government seeks to perpetuate these illusions. The following report is printed word for word in the *Messager de Gand*:

"We now know of what this Germany consists that cherishes such great admiration for us. This Germany consists of Herr *Wolfers* from Louvain, whom M. Rogier pays to produce enthusiastic articles about Belgium in German for the *Kölnische Zeitung*. In view of the search for all possible ways to economise, it seems to us that we could easily abolish the fund of admiration which we are paying to all the journalists in Europe. In Brussels, in the provinces, in Paris, in London and even as far as Bucharest we are buying their compliments at a very high price. Savings in this field could add up to a

---

[a] "London, Monday, October 2, 1848", *The Times* No. 19383, October 2, 1848.— *Ed.*

[b] "Brüssel, 30. Mai", *Neue Rheinische Zeitung* No. 1, June 1, 1848.— *Ed.*

sum not to be despised. In London, for example, the Belgian who writes admiring articles about Belgium for the *Times* and for the *Daily News*[a] has to be paid out of the 80,000 francs allocated to our embassy. As soon as the Prince Ligne is installed we shall have to pay for the admiration of a Roman journalist as well."

Are these revelations not delightful? But I have not finished yet. *La Nation* carries the following small item in its issue of October 10.

"We have often noticed that the 'private correspondent's' column in the *Indépendance*, dated Frankfurt and Berlin, is as like the articles in the *Kölnische Zeitung* (to which Wolfers contributes) as two drops of dirty water. This newspaper does not appear on Sundays; and the *Indépendance*, too, has no private correspondent's column on Mondays."

We need not add much. To show its gratitude to the *Indépendance* for copying its German news from the *Kölnische Zeitung*, the *Kölnische Zeitung* in turn obtains its views on Belgium and France from the *Indépendance*.

But as everyone knows, the *Indépendance* is the organ of the same M. Rogier who buys admiration for Belgium, who had the Belgian patriots of 1830, and the eighty-year-old General Mellinet, condemned to death[b] and who has political refugees conveyed across the frontier in sealed carriages.

Written between October 8 and 11, 1848

First published in the supplement to the *Neue Rheinische Zeitung* No. 114, October 12, 1848

Printed according to the newspaper

Published in English for the first time

---

[a] The *Neue Rheinische Zeitung* has "*New England*".— *Ed.*
[b] See this volume, pp. 405-06.— *Ed.*

THE "REVOLUTION OF COLOGNE"[300]

Cologne, October 12. The *Kölnische Zeitung* tells us that the "revolution of Cologne" of September 25 was a Shrovetide farce and the *Kölnische Zeitung* is right.[a] The "Garrison Headquarters of Cologne" plays Cavaignac on September 26. And the *Kölnische Zeitung* admires the wisdom and moderation of the "Garrison Headquarters of Cologne". Who, however, is more comical—the workers who practised barricade building on September 25, or the Cavaignac who most solemnly proclaimed a state of siege on September 26, suspended the newspapers, disarmed the civic militia and prohibited the associations?

The poor *Kölnische Zeitung!* The Cavaignac of the "revolution of Cologne" cannot be an inch taller than the "revolution of Cologne" itself. The poor *Kölnische Zeitung!* It must regard the "revolution" as a joke and has to take seriously the "Cavaignac" of this merry revolution. What a vexatious, ungrateful and contradictory topic!

We will not waste a word on the competence of the Garrison Headquarters. D'Ester has exhausted that subject.[301] We regard, moreover, the Garrison Headquarters as a subordinate tool. The real authors of this peculiar tragedy were the "*loyal citizens*", the *Dumonts* and their associates. Thus it was no wonder that Herr Dumont had the address against d'Ester, Borchardt and Kyll disseminated by his newspapers.[302] What these "loyal ones" had to defend was not the action of the Garrison Headquarters but their own action.

---

[a] "Köln, 29. September. Die Barrikaden in Köln", *Kölnische Zeitung* No. 268, September 30, 1848.— *Ed.*

The event at Cologne wandered through the Sahara Desert of the German press in the form given to it by the *Journal des Débats* of Cologne. That is sufficient reason to revert to it.

Moll, one of the most popular leaders of the Workers' Association,[303] was to have been arrested. Schapper and Becker had already been arrested. A *Monday* had been selected for the execution of this measure, a day on which, as is well known, the majority of workers are not working. Thus it must have been known beforehand that the arrests might arouse a great deal of ferment among the workers and that they might even give rise to violent resistance. It was a strange accident that these arrests were planned to take place on a Monday! It was the more easy to foresee the excitement since on the occasion of Stein's Army Order, after Wrangel's proclamation[304] and Pfuel's appointment as Prime Minister, a decisive counter-revolutionary blow and thus a revolution emanating from Berlin was expected at any moment. The workers, therefore, had to regard the arrests not as legal but as *political* measures. They viewed the Public Prosecutor's office only as a counter-revolutionary authority. They believed that it was the intention to rob them of their leaders on the eve of important events. They decided to prevent Moll's arrest at all costs and they left the scene of action only after they had accomplished their purpose. The barricades were not built until the workers, who had assembled on the Altenmarkt, learned that the army was advancing to attack from all sides. They were not attacked; hence they did not have to defend themselves either. They had learned, moreover, that no important news at all had arrived from Berlin. Hence they withdrew after they had spent the greater part of the night waiting in vain for the enemy.

Nothing is more ridiculous, therefore, than the reproach of cowardice which has been levelled against the workers of Cologne.

One has reproached them on yet other scores in order to justify the state of siege and to fashion the events in Cologne into a small June revolution. Their actual plan is supposed to have been the looting of the good city of Cologne. This accusation is based upon the alleged looting of *one* drapery shop. As if not every city has its contingent of thieves who naturally take advantage of days of public excitement. Or does one mean by looting the plundering of gunsmith's shops? If this is the case, the Cologne Public Prosecutor's office should be sent to Berlin to prepare the case against the March revolution. Without the looted gunsmith's shops, we would perhaps never have had the satisfaction of witnessing the transformation of Herr Hansemann into a bank President and of Herr Müller into a Secretary of State.

But enough of the workers of Cologne. Let us discuss the so-called *democrats*. What do the *Kölnische Zeitung*, the *Deutsche Zeitung*, the Augsburg *Allgemeine Zeitung* and whatever the other "loyal" papers may be called, accuse them of?

The heroic Brüggemanns, Bassermanns etc. demanded blood and the tender-hearted democrats have out of *cowardice* not allowed the blood to flow.

The facts are simply these: the democrats declared to the workers in the Kranz (on the Altenmarkt), in the Eiser Hall[305] and upon the barricades that they did not want a "*putsch*" under any circumstances. At this moment, however, when no large issue would drive the entire people into combat, and any rising would be bound to fail, such a rising would be the more senseless since tremendous events might occur within the next few days and one would thus render oneself unfit to fight *before* the day of decision. Once the Government in Berlin dares a counter-revolution, the day will have arrived for the people to dare a revolution. The judicial investigation will confirm our statement. Instead of standing in "nocturnal darkness" in front of the barricades with "folded arms and ominous glances" and "contemplating the future of their people",[a] the gentlemen of the *Kölnische Zeitung* would have done better to stand on the barricades haranguing the deluded crowd with their words of wisdom. What good is wisdom *post festum*[b]?

On the occasion of the events in Cologne, the respectable press reserved its worst treatment for the civic militia. Let us distinguish. That the civic militia refused to degrade itself by becoming the docile servant of the police, was its duty. That it turned over its weapons voluntarily can only be excused by one fact: the liberal section of it knew that the illiberal section would jubilantly take the opportunity to rid itself of the weapons. Partial resistance, however, would have been useless.

The "revolution of Cologne" has had *one* result. It has revealed the existence of a phalanx of more than 2,000 saints whose "satiated virtue and solvent morale"[c] leads a "free life"[d] only in a state of siege. Perhaps one day the occasion will arise to write an "*acta sanctorum*", the biographies of these saints. Our readers will then find out how

---

[a] "Köln, 29. September. Die Barrikaden in Köln", *Kölnische Zeitung* No. 268, September 30, 1848.— *Ed.*

[b] After the event.— *Ed.*

[c] Heinrich Heine, "Anno 1829" (modified).— *Ed.*

[d] Schiller, *Die Räuber*, Act IV, Scene 5.— *Ed.*

the "treasures" are obtained that neither "moths nor rust" doth corrupt[a] and they will learn in which way the economic background of the "loyal way of thinking" is acquired.

Written by Marx on October 12, 1848   Printed according to the newspaper

First published in the *Neue Rheinische Zeitung* No. 115, October 13, 1848

---

[a] Matthew 6:20.— *Ed.*

THE PFUEL GOVERNMENT

Cologne, October 13. When the *Camphausen* Government fell we said:

"The Camphausen Government has covered the counter-revolution with its liberal-bourgeois cloak. The counter-revolution now feels strong enough to shake off this irksome mask. It is possible that the Government of March 30 will be followed for a few days by some untenable Government of the *Left Centre* (Hansemann). Its real successor will be the *Government of the Prince of Prussia.*" (*Neue Rheinische Zeitung* No. 23, June 23.)[a]

And in fact the Government of *Pfuel* (of *Neufchâtel*) followed the *Hansemann* Government.

The Pfuel Government handles constitutional phrases in the same way as the Frankfurt Central Authority treats "German unification". If we compare the *corpus delicti*, the real body of the Government, with its echo, its constitutional declarations, appeasings, mediations and agreements in the Berlin Assembly, we can only use Falstaff's phrase:

"*Lord, lord, how subject we old men are to this vice of lying!*"[b]

The Pfuel Government can only be followed by a *Government of the revolution*.

Written by Marx on October 13, 1848

First published in the *Neue Rheinische Zeitung* No. 116, October 14, 1848

Printed according to the newspaper

Published in English for the first time

---

[a] See this volume, p. 107.— *Ed.*
[b] Shakespeare, *King Henry IV*, Part Two, Act III, Scene 2.— *Ed.*

THIERS' SPEECH
CONCERNING A GENERAL MORTGAGE BANK
WITH A LEGAL RATE

M. Thiers is publishing in the *Constitutionnel* a pamphlet about *Property*.[306] We shall take up this classically written triviality more thoroughly as soon as the publication has appeared in its entirety. M. Thiers has suddenly discontinued it. For the time being it is enough for us to observe that the "great" *Belgian* newspapers, the *Observateur* and the *Indépendance*, rave about M. Thiers' work. Today we shall follow up for a moment the speech dealing with mortgage debentures[307] which M. Thiers delivered on October 10 in the French National Assembly, a speech which according to the Belgian *Indépendance* has dealt the *"coup de grâce"* to paper money. But M. Thiers is also, as the *Indépendance* says, an orator who handles political, financial and social questions equally well.

This speech interests us only because it illustrates the tactic of the knights of the old state of affairs, a tactic with which they correctly confront the Don Quixotes of the new state of affairs.

If you demand a partial reform of the industrial and commercial conditions as was done by M. Turck whom Thiers was answering, they will confront you with the concatenation and interaction of the organisation as a whole. If you demand the transformation of the organisation as a whole, then you are destructive, revolutionary, unscrupulous, utopian and you overlook *partial* reforms. Hence the result: leave everything as it is.

M. Turck for example wants to make it easier for the peasants to turn their landed property to account by means of official mortgage banks. He wants to bring their property into circulation without it having to pass through the hands of usurers. For in France, as generally in the countries where the land is divided into lots, the power of the feudal lords has been transformed into the power of the capitalists and the feudal obligations of the peasants have been transformed into bourgeois mortgage obligations.

What does M. Thiers reply to begin with?

If you want to help the peasant by means of public banks you will encroach upon the small tradesman. You cannot aid one without hurting the other.

Consequently we have to transform the *entire system of credit*?

By no means! That is a utopia. Thus M. Turck is dismissed without ceremony.

The small tradesman for whom M. Thiers cares so tenderly is the *big* Bank of France.

The competition of paper bills for two thousand million mortgages would ruin its monopoly and dividends and perhaps still something more.[a] Behind M. Thiers' argument therefore stands Rothschild in the background.

Let us take up another of M. Thiers' arguments. The mortgage proposal, M. Thiers states, does not actually concern *agriculture* at all.

M. Thiers remarks that it lies in the "*nature*" of things that landed property can be put into circulation only under onerous conditions, that it can be turned to account only with difficulty and that capital shuns it, so to speak. For, he says, it yields only a small profit. But on the other hand, M. Thiers cannot deny that it lies in the "nature" of modern industrial organisation that all industries, hence agriculture as well, only prosper if their products and their instruments can easily be turned to account, put into circulation and mobilised. This is not the case with land. *Hence* the conclusion would be: *agriculture cannot prosper within the existing civilised conditions.* Therefore the existing conditions must be changed and M. Turck's proposal is a small, even if inconsistent, beginning. By no means! exclaims M. Thiers. "Nature", i.e. the present social conditions, condemns agriculture to its present state. The present social conditions are "*nature*", i.e. they are unalterable. The assertion of their immutability is, of course, the most irrefutable proof against proposals for any change. If "monarchy" is nature then any republican attempt is a rebellion against nature. According to M. Thiers, it is also obvious that landed property *naturally* always yields the same small profits whether the capital is advanced to the landowner at 3 per cent by the state or at 10 per cent by the usurer. Thus it is by virtue of "nature".

---

[a] Marx uses the English words "something more".— *Ed.*

By identifying industrial profit with the rent yielded by agriculture, M. Thiers also makes an assertion which plainly contradicts the present social conditions which he calls "nature".

Whereas industrial profit in general falls constantly, rent of land, i.e. the value of the soil, rises constantly. Thus M. Thiers ought to explain the phenomenon that the peasant is constantly becoming more impoverished in spite of it. Of course, he does not want to discuss that subject.

Furthermore Thiers' comments on the *difference* between French and English agriculture are really of a remarkable superficiality.

Thiers instructs us that the entire difference consists of the *land tax*. We pay a very high land tax, the Englishmen none. Apart from the inaccuracy of the latter assertion, M. Thiers certainly knows that in England agriculture is burdened with the poor-rate as well as a mass of other taxes which do not exist in France. M. Thiers' argument is used in its inverted meaning by English adherents of small-scale agriculture. Do you know, they ask, why English corn is more expensive than the French? Because we pay a *rent* and a high rent at that, something that the French do not do since on the average they are not tenants but small proprietors. Therefore, long live small property!

It takes the entire insolent triviality of Thiers to reduce the English concentration of [ownership of] land, the instrument of labour, whereby the use of machinery and the division of labour is made possible on a large scale in agriculture, and the interaction of English industry and English trade with agriculture—to reduce all these highly complex relations to the meaningless phrase that the English pay no *land tax*.

We shall contrast M. Thiers' opinion that the present mortgage procedure in France is a matter of indifference to agriculture with the opinion of the greatest French agricultural chemist. *Dombasle* has proved conclusively that French agriculture will become an impossibility if the present mortgage system in France continues to develop according to "*nature*".[a]

What insolent shallowness it takes anyway to assert that landed property relations are immaterial to agriculture, in other words that the social relations under which production takes place are immaterial to production!

By the way, there is hardly any need to add that M. Thiers, who

---

[a] C.-J.-A. Mathieu de Dombasle, *Annales agricoles de Roville, ou mélanges d'agriculture, d'économie rurale, et de législation agricole.*— *Ed.*

wants to retain credits for the big capitalists, cannot give any credit to the small ones. It is precisely the credit of the big capitalists which spells lack of credit for the small ones. We deny, to be sure, that within the present system it is possible to aid the small landed proprietors by some clever financial trick. Thiers, however, had to maintain this view since he regards the present world as the best of all possible worlds.

In regard to this part of Thiers' speech we want to make just one further observation: by opposing the mobilisation of landed property and on the other hand praising English conditions, he forgets that it is exactly in England that agriculture possesses in the highest degree *the* advantage of being run like a factory and that the rent of land, i.e. landed property, is a movable, transferable security quoted on the Stock Exchange just like any other. Factory-type agriculture, i.e. the management of agriculture in the manner of big industry, on its part requires the mobilisation and exchangeability of landed property with commercial facility.

The second part of M. Thiers' speech consists of attacks on *paper money* in general. He labels the issuing of paper money on the whole as *counterfeiting*. He reveals to us the great truth that if one throws too large a quantity of the means of circulation, i.e. money, on the market, one devalues money itself and thus cheats doubly: the individual and the state. Allegedly this is especially the case with mortgage banks.

All these discoveries can be found in the worst *catechisms* of political economy.

Let us distinguish. It is clear that we do not increase production, i.e. real wealth, by arbitrarily increasing money, be it paper or metal currency. We do not double our tricks in a card game by doubling the chips.

On the other hand it is just as clear that if production is inhibited by a lack of chips, of means of exchange, of money, every increase of the means of exchange, every decrease in the difficulty of obtaining the means of exchange, implies at the same time an *increase in production*. Bills of exchange, banks etc. owe their origin to these needs of production. In this way mortgage banks can lead to the improvement of agriculture.

M. Thiers, however, does not fight for metal currency as opposed to paper money. He has speculated too much on the Stock Exchange to be swayed by the prejudices of the old mercantilists. What he opposes is the regulation of credit by society as represented by the state as against the regulation of credit by monopoly. Thus Turck's proposal for a general mortgage bank whose bills would have a legal rate of exchange was the beginning of a regulation of credit in the general interest of society, even though this proposal in isolation means little.

Written by Marx on October 13, 1848

Printed according to the newspaper

First published in the *Neue Rheinische Zeitung* No. 116, October 14, 1848

Published in English for the first time

THE *FRANKFURTER OBERPOSTAMTS-ZEITUNG* AND THE VIENNESE REVOLUTION

Cologne, October 18.

"A peculiar destiny seems to hold sway over Germany. When one believes that one has reached the point where it is possible to help with the reconstruction of the common fatherland, when one *raises one's eyes gratefully towards heaven for this blessing,* then the thunderclouds which are still hanging over Europe, discharge new and mighty claps and make *the hands tremble* which have dedicated themselves to the drawing up of a Constitution for Germany. We have just experienced such a thunderclap again in *Vienna.*"

Thus complains the *Frankfurter Oberpostamts-Zeitung,* the *Moniteur* of the Imperial Administration. This worthy paper, whose recent editor[a] appeared on the list of Guizot's paid creatures, took itself *au sérieux* for a moment. The Central Authority with its parliamentary framework, the Council of Frankfurt, appeared to it as a serious power. Instead of issuing their counter-revolutionary orders directly to their subjects, the 38 German governments let the Central Authority in Frankfurt issue to them the order to carry out their own decisions. Everything was running smoothly just as at the time of the Direct Commission of Mainz.[308] The Central Authority was able to imagine that it was a power and its *Moniteur* was able to imagine that it was a *Moniteur.* It sang "Now thank ye all our God, your hands raised up to heaven".

And now we "experience" a thunderclap from Vienna. The "*hands*" of our Lycurguses "*tremble*" in spite of the army in spiked helmets which are so many lightning-conductors of the revolution; in spite of the decrees which declare criticism of black-red-golden

---

[a] Karl Peter Berly.— *Ed.*

persons and *gesta*[a] to be a criminal offence[309]; and in spite of the strong language of those gigantic figures, Schmerling, Mohl and Gagern. The revolutionary monster roars anew — and in Frankfurt they "*tremble*". The *Frankfurter Oberpostamts-Zeitung* is frightened out of its thanksgiving prayer. It tragically grumbles at its iron fate.

In Paris the party of Thiers is in control, in Berlin the Pfuel Government with Wrangels in all the provinces; in Frankfurt a central gendarmerie; in all Germany a more or less hidden state of siege; Italy pacified by the gentle Ferdinand and Radetzky; after the annihilation of the Magyars Jellachich, the commander of Hungary, proclaiming together with Windischgrätz "Croatian freedom and order" in Vienna; in Bucharest the revolution drowned in blood; the Danube principalities blessed by the good deeds of the Russian regime; in England all the Chartist leaders arrested and deported; Ireland too starved to be able to move — tell me, what more do you want?[b]

The Viennese revolution has not yet won. Its first summer lightning suffices, however, to illuminate all the positions of the counter-revolution in Europe and thus to render inevitable a universal fight to the death.

The counter-revolution is not yet destroyed but it has made *a fool* of itself. With the hero *Jellachich* all its heroes are transformed into comical figures, and with *Fuad Effendi's* proclamation after the blood bath of Bucharest,[310] all proclamations of the friends of "constitutional freedom and order", from the proclamations of the Imperial Diet down to the most insignificant statement of the wailers, are parodied to death.

Tomorrow we shall discuss at length the immediate situation in Vienna and the Austrian situation in general.

Written by Marx on October 18, 1848

First published in the *Neue Rheinische Zeitung* No. 120, October 19, 1848

Printed according to the newspaper

Published in English for the first time

---

[a] Deeds.— *Ed.*
[b] From Heinrich Heine's poem "Du hast Diamanten und Perlen". In *Die Heimkehr.— Ed.*

474

REPLY OF THE KING OF PRUSSIA
TO THE DELEGATION OF THE NATIONAL ASSEMBLY

Cologne, October 18. The King is consistent at any rate. His Majesty never contradicts himself. On the occasion of the festival celebrating the building of Cologne's cathedral, he told the delegation of the Frankfurt National Assembly:

"Gentlemen, I fully understand the significance of your Assembly. I realise very well how important your Assembly is!" The voice of His Majesty then assumed a very solemn and biting tone: "But please do not forget that there are still sovereigns in Germany"—at this point His Majesty placed his hand upon his heart and spoke with uncommon emphasis—"and do not forget that I am one of them!"

A similar reply was also given to the delegation of the Berlin Assembly when it visited His Majesty at Bellevue Castle on October 15[a] in order to congratulate him. The King said:

"We are in the process of constructing an edifice which is to last for centuries. But, gentlemen, I would like to call your attention to one matter. We still possess an hereditary authority *by the grace of God*"—these words were spoken by the King with great emphasis—"which is surely envied in many places and which is still endowed with full powers. It is the only foundation upon which that edifice can be constructed if it is to last for as long as I have indicated."

The King is consistent. He would always have been consistent had it not been for the unfortunate fact that the March days interposed that fateful scrap of paper between His Majesty and his people.[311]

At this moment, His Majesty, just as he did before the March days, seems again to believe in Slavdom's "*legs of iron*"[b]. Perhaps the

---

[a] Birthday of Frederick William IV.— *Ed.*
[b] Cf. Daniel 2:33.— *Ed.*

people in Vienna will turn out to be the magician who will transform the iron into clay.

Written by Marx on October 18, 1848

First published in the *Neue Rheinische Zeitung* No. 120, October 19, 1848

Printed according to the newspaper

Published in English for the first time

REPLY OF FREDERICK WILLIAM IV
TO THE DELEGATION OF THE CIVIC MILITIA

Cologne, October 18. *Frederick William IV* replied to *Rimpler,* the commander of the civic militia of Berlin, in response to the latter's congratulations on the occasion of October 15[a]:

"I know that a heroic and brave people is also a *loyal* one. But do not forget *that you obtained the weapons from me* and that I demand that you stand up dutifully for the preservation of order, law and freedom."

Constitutional kings are *not responsible,* on the understanding that they are *not answerable,* in the constitutional sense, of course. Their actions, their words, their countenances do not belong to them, they belong to the *responsible Ministers.*

Hansemann, for example, on the occasion of his exit, had the King say that he considered the execution of Stein's Army Order[312] incompatible with constitutional monarchy. *Pfuel* carried it out, that is in the parliamentary sense. Hansemann was compromised, in the constitutional sense. The King had not contradicted himself, because he had not spoken, always in the constitutional sense.

Thus the above declaration of the King is nothing but a *ministerial* declaration and as such is subject to criticism.

If *Pfuel* claims that the King has created the civic militia on his own accord, then he claims that the King is the *originator* of the *March revolution* which is nonsense, even in the constitutional sense.

Apart from this.

After God had created the world and the kings by the grace of God, he relinquished the smaller industry to human beings. Even *"weapons"* and lieutenants' uniforms are manufactured by profane

---

[a] Birthday of Frederick William IV.— *Ed.*

methods and the profane method of manufacturing does not create from nothing as the heavenly industry does. It needs raw materials, the tools of labour and wages, all items which are summed up by the unpretentious term: *production costs.* These production costs are defrayed for the state by *taxes* and the taxes are raised by the *work of the nation.* Thus in an *economic* sense it remains an enigma how any king can *give* anything to a nation. First of all, the people have to produce weapons and give the weapons to the king, in order to obtain weapons from the king. In all cases, the king can only give what is given to him. That is the position in an *economic sense.* It so happens, however, that *constitutional* kings arise exactly at those moments when people find the clue to this *economic secret.* Therefore the initial causes for the overthrow of the kings by the grace of God have always been *questions of taxation.* It is the same in Prussia. Even the *immaterial* goods, the privileges, which the nations allowed the kings to *grant* to them, were not only bestowed by them upon the kings in the first place but in order to get them back the people always had to pay *in cash*—in blood and ringing coin. Trace, for example, *English* history since the eleventh century and you will be able to calculate pretty accurately how many crushed skulls and how many pound sterling every constitutional privilege cost. Herr Pfuel apparently wants to take us back to the good old times of the *Davenant Economic Chart.*[a] In this chart concerning English production we read among other items:

Section 1. *Productive workers:* kings, officers, lords, country clergymen etc.

Section 2. *Unproductive workers:* sailors, peasants, weavers, spinners etc.

According to this chart section 1 produces and section 2 receives. It is in this sense that Herr Pfuel says the king gives.

Pfuel's declaration shows what one expects in Berlin from the hero of "Croatian order and freedom".[b]

The most recent incidents in Berlin remind one of the conflicts in Vienna on August 23 between the civic militia and the people, conflicts which were also provoked by the camarilla. *That August 23 was followed by October 5.*[313]

Written by Marx on October 18, 1848   Printed according to the newspaper

First published in the *Neue Rheinische Zeitung* No. 121, October 20, 1848   Published in English for the first time

---

[a] [Ch. Davenant,] *An Essay upon the Probable Methods of making a People Gainers in the Ballance of Trade,* pp. 23, 50.—*Ed.*

[b] Jellachich.— *Ed.*

THE *RÉFORME* ON THE JUNE INSURRECTION

Paris. When on June 29 the *Neue Rheinische Zeitung* was the only European newspaper, with the exception of the English *Northern Star*, which had the courage and the discernment to give a true appreciation of the June revolution,[a] it was not refuted but denounced.

The facts have subsequently confirmed our interpretation even for the weakest eye as long as interest has not entirely destroyed the eyesight.

At that time the *French* press, too, disgraced itself. The resolute Paris newspapers were suppressed. The *Réforme,* the only radical newspaper which Cavaignac allowed to continue to exist, stammered excuses for the magnanimous June fighters and begged the victor to treat the conquered with some humanity as an act of charity. The beggar, of course, was not listened to. It took first the complete course of the June victory, the months-long diatribes of the provincial newspapers which were not fettered by the state of siege and the obvious resurrection of the Thiers party[314] to bring the *Réforme* to its senses.

On the occasion of the amnesty project of the extreme Left, it remarked in its issue of October 18:

"The people did not punish anybody when they descended from the barricades. The people! In those days it was the ruler, the sovereign and the victor. One kissed its feet and hands, saluted its tunic and acclaimed its noble sentiments. And rightly so. It was magnanimous.

"Today the people has its children and brothers in the dungeons, on the galleys and before courts martial. After hunger had exhausted its patience, after it had seen a

---

[a] See this volume, pp. 144 and 147-49.—*Ed.*

whole crowd of ambitious people whom it had picked out of the gutter, calmly walk by and ascend to palaces, after it had for three long months put its trust in the republic, it finally lost its head in the midst of its starving children and slowly dying fathers and plunged into battle.

"It has paid dearly. Its sons have dropped under a hail of bullets and those who remained were divided into two parts. One part was thrown to the courts martial, the other was packed up for deportation without investigation, without the right of defence and without a verdict! This method is strange for any land, even for the land of the Kabyles.

"Never during its twenty years' existence did the monarchy dare to do anything similar.

"In those days the journals that speculate in dynasties arrived inebriated by the corpses' smell, boldly and immediately ready to insult the dead" (cf. the *Kölnische Zeitung* of June 29) "spewing forth calumnies of odious malice, drawing and quartering the honour of the people before the judicial investigation and dragging the vanquished, the dead and the living, before special courts. They denounced them to the destructive fury of the national guard and the army and turned themselves into agents for the hangmen and servants of the pillory. These lackeys of insane desires for vengeance invented crimes; they exacerbated our misfortune and they perfected the insult and the lie!" (Cf. the *Neue Rheinische Zeitung* of July 1 concerning the French *Constitutionnel*, the Belgian *Indépendance* and the *Kölnische Zeitung*.[a])

"The *Constitutionnel* openly displayed gruesome mutilations and despicable atrocities. It knew very well that it was *lying* but that suited its business and its politics, and being businessman and diplomatist all at the same time, it sold 'by the crime' as elsewhere one sells 'by the yard'. This beautiful speculation had to end some time or other. The contradictions poured out: not a single name of a galley convict could be found in the documents of the courts martial or the bulletins of transportation. There were no longer any means to degrade the despair, and one kept silence, having cashed in on the profit."

Written by Marx about October 20, 1848

First published in the *Neue Rheinische Zeitung* No. 123, October 22, 1848

Printed according to the newspaper

Published in English for the first time

---

[a] See this volume, pp. 150-56.—*Ed.*

ENGLISH-FRENCH MEDIATION IN ITALY

Cologne, October 21. The *English-French mediation in Italy has been given up.* The death's head of diplomacy grins after every revolution and particularly after the reactions which follow every revolution. Diplomacy hides itself in its perfumed charnel-house as often as the thunder of a new revolution rumbles. The *Viennese revolution* has blown away French-English diplomacy.

Palmerston has admitted his impotence and so has *Bastide.* The Viennese revolution, as they explain, has put an end to the boring correspondence of these gentlemen. Bastide has officially notified of this fact Marquis *Ricci,* the Sardinian envoy.

When the latter asked "whether France would under certain circumstances take up arms in favour of Sardinia"[a] the *farouche* republican Bastide (of the *National*) made a curtsy once, twice, thrice and sang:

> Put trust in me and help yourselves
> Then God will help you, brothers.[b]

France, he said, abides by the principle of *non-intervention,* that same principle which was fought by *Bastide* and the other gentlemen of the *National* for years during Guizot's times.

The "*respectable*" French Republic would have made a deadly fool of itself in regard to this *Italian* question were it not above all disgrace since the portentous June.

Rien pour la gloire![c] say the friends of business in all circumstances. *Rien pour la gloire!* is the motto of the virtuous, the moderate, the

---

[a] "Question italienne. Dernière phase de la médiation anglo-française (Communication)", *La Presse* No. 4499, October 19, 1848.— *Ed.*

[b] Heinrich Heine, *Deutschland. Ein Wintermärchen,* Caput XII.— *Ed.*

[c] Mere honour is worth nothing.—*Ed.*

decent, the sedate, the respectable, in a word, the bourgeois republic. *Rien pour la gloire!*

Lamartine was the imaginary picture which the bourgeois republic had of itself, the exuberant, fantastic, visionary conception which it had formed of itself, the dream of its own splendour. It is quite remarkable what one can imagine! As Aeolus unleashed all the winds from his bag, so Lamartine set free all spirits of the air, all the phrases of the bourgeois republic, and he blew them towards the east and the west, empty words of the fraternity of all nations, of the impending emancipation of all the nations by France and of France's sacrifice for all the nations.

He did—*nothing*.

It was *Cavaignac* who undertook to supply the deeds corresponding to Lamartine's phrases and *Bastide*, his outward turned organ.

They calmly allowed the shocking scenes in Naples, the shocking scenes in Messina and the shocking scenes in the Milan region to take place before their very eyes.[315]

And so that not the least bit of doubt should remain as to the fact that the same *class* as well as the same foreign policy prevail in the "*respectable*" republic as under the constitutional monarchy, under Cavaignac as well as under Louis Philippe, in case of strife between nations, one has recourse to the old and eternally new means, the *entente cordiale* with England,[316] with the England of Palmerston and with the England of the counter-revolutionary bourgeoisie.

History could not, however, omit the *climax*, the point. *Bastide*, an editor of the *National*, had to grasp England's hand frantically. And the *entente cordiale* has been the main trump which the poor Anglophobe *National* played off against Guizot all life long.

On the gravestone of the "respectable" republic; will be inscribed: *Bastide-Palmerston.*

But even Guizot's *entente cordiale* has been surpassed by the "respectable" republicans. The officers of the French fleet let themselves be treated to a banquet by the Neapolitan officers and cheered the health of the *King of Naples, the idiotic tiger* Ferdinand, on the still smoking ruins of Messina. Above their heads, however, the phrases of *Lamartine* were evaporating.

Written by Marx on October 21, 1848

First published in the *Neue Rheinische Zeitung* No. 123, October 22, 1848

Printed according to the newspaper

Published in English for the first time

THE "MODEL CONSTITUTIONAL STATE"

Cologne, October 21. We always revert again, and always with renewed satisfaction, to Belgium, our *"model constitutional state".*

We proved in a previous number of our newspaper that *"pauperism"* is *"Leopold's greatest vassal".* We showed that if the *crimes* of just the boys and girls under 18 years of age were to continue to develop spontaneously at the same ratio as in 1845-47, "by 1856 all Belgium would be in gaol, the unborn children included". We proved in the same article that the drying up of Belgium's industrial sources of income keeps in step with the growth of pauperism and crime (No. 68 of the *Neue Rheinische Zeitung*).[a]

Today we will look at the *financial* situation of the *"model state".*

	Francs
The regular budget of 1848	119,000,000
The first compulsory loan	12,000,000
The second compulsory loan	25,000,000
Banknotes with a fixed rate of exchange	12,000,000
Total sum:	168,000,000
In addition banknotes with a fixed rate of exchange guaranteed by the state	40,000,000
Total:	208,000,000

---

[a] See this volume, pp. 333-36.—*Ed.*

Belgium, so Rogier tells us, stands like a rock amid world-historic tempests, but is not affected by them. It stands on the bed-rock of its broad institutions. The 208,000,000 francs are the prosaic translation of the miraculous power of those model institutions. Constitutional Belgium will not be brought down by revolutionary development. It will perish ignominiously through *bankruptcy*.

The *liberal* Belgian Government, the Rogier Government, like all liberal governments, is nothing but a Government of capitalists, bankers and the big bourgeoisie. We shall see right away how in spite of growing pauperism and declining industry, it does not disdain the most cunning means to exploit ever anew the entire nation for the benefit of the bank barons.

The second loan listed in the above compilation, has been chiefly wrested from the Parliament by the assurance that *government bonds* were to be redeemed. These government bonds had been issued under the Catholic *de Theux* Government by the Catholic Finance Minister *Malou*. These were the government bonds issued against voluntary loans made to the state by a few financial barons. They constituted the main theme, the inexhaustible theme of the howling diatribes which our Rogier and his liberal accomplices directed against the de Theux Government.

And what does the liberal Government proceed to do? It announces in the *Moniteur*—Belgium has its *Moniteur*—a new issue of government bonds at 5 per cent.

What shamelessness to issue government bonds after a compulsory loan of 25,000,000 francs has been obtained surreptitiously solely under the pretext that the so much maligned government bonds issued by Malou were to be redeemed! But that is not all.

The government bonds are issued at 5 per cent. Belgian securities, which are also guaranteed by the state, yield an interest of 7 and 8 per cent. Who then will put his money into government bonds? And besides, the situation of the country in general and the compulsory loans have left few who are able to make voluntary loans to the state.

What then is the purpose of this new issue of government bonds?

The *banks* have not yet been able by far to put into circulation all the notes with a legally fixed rate of exchange which the liberal Government had authorised them to issue. There are in their portfolios still several million of these useless securities which naturally yield nothing as long as they remain hermetically sealed in the portfolios. Is there a better way of putting these securities into circulation than to give them to the state in exchange for government bonds which yield 5 per cent?

Thus the bank draws 5 per cent on several million scraps of paper which have not cost it anything and which only have an exchange value at all because the state has given them an exchange value. The taxable Belgian masses will find in the next budget a deficit of an additional several hundred thousand francs which they will be in duty bound to raise, all for the benefit of the poor bank.

Is it surprising that the Belgian financial barons find the constitutional monarchy more lucrative than the republic? The Catholic Government cherished and protected primarily the *holiest*, i.e. the *material*, interests of the landlords. The liberal Government looks with equally tender care after the interests of the landlords, the financial barons and the court lackeys. Is it any wonder that under its skilful direction these so-called parties, which equally voraciously pounce upon the national wealth, or rather in the case of Belgium, upon the national poverty, and which on such occasions sometimes quarrel amongst themselves, now, fully reconciled, fall into each other's arms and form only one big party: the "*national party*"?

Written by Marx on October 21, 1848   Printed according to the newspaper

First published in the *Neue Rheinische*   Published in English for the first
Zeitung No. 123, October 22, 1848   time

PUBLIC PROSECUTOR "HECKER"
AND THE *NEUE RHEINISCHE ZEITUNG*[317]

Cologne, October 28. No. 116 of the *Neue Rheinische Zeitung* carried *in the feuilleton section*, i.e. outside the political part of the newspaper, *"A Word to the German People"* signed *"Hecker"*. This *"historical document"* was printed by a number of German newspapers *before* the *Neue Rheinische Zeitung* printed it. Other German newspapers, Rhenish-Prussian and old-Prussian not excluded, carried it later. Even the *Kölnische Zeitung* possessed enough historical sense to print the proclamation of Struve and likewise that of Fuad Effendi.[318]

We do not know whether the laurels of the republican Hecker did not let Public Prosecutor Hecker sleep in peace. Was the astonished world to learn that the German revolution had been twice beaten by the flight of the republican Hecker to New York and the presence of the Public Prosecutor Hecker in Cologne? It cannot be denied. Posterity will see in these two giant figures the dramatic synopsis of the contradictions of the modern movement. A future *Goethe* will unite them in a *Faust*. We shall leave it to him to which Hecker he wants to assign the role of Faust and to which that of Wagner.

In short. The fantastic farewell address of the republican Hecker was followed by the no less fantastic case of Public Prosecutor Hecker.

Or are we mistaken? Does Hecker, the Public Prosecutor, believe that *"the word to the German people"* is the product of the *Neue Rheinische Zeitung* itself, that this newspaper with its inventive maliciousness has signed its own proclamation "Hecker" in order to make the German people believe that Hecker, the Public Prosecutor, is emigrating to New York, that Hecker, the Public Prosecutor, proclaims the German republic, that Hecker, the Public Prosecutor, officially sanctions pious revolutionary wishes?

Such a trick was credible because the document reproduced in the supplement to No. 116 of the *Neue Rheinische Zeitung* is not signed *Friedrich* Hecker but *tout bonnement* "Hecker". A Hecker without flourishes, a simple Hecker! And does not Germany possess a twofold Hecker?

And who of the two is the "simple Hecker"? In any case, this simplicity remains ambiguous and, in our opinion, embarrassing for the *Neue Rheinische Zeitung*.

Be that as it may, Herr Hecker, the Public Prosecutor, apparently viewed the *"word to the German people"* as a *product* of the *Neue Rheinische Zeitung*. He saw in it a *direct appeal to overthrow the Government,* high treason in its most developed form or at the very least complicity in high treason which according to the *Code pénal*[319] constitutes "simple" high treason.

Thus Herr Hecker requested the examining magistrate to *"assume"* not that the undersigned responsible publisher,[a] but that the editor-in-chief, *Karl Marx,* is guilty of high treason. But to "assume" somebody *guilty of high treason* means in other words to put him into prison for the time being and to punish him until further notice with detention pending investigation. We are dealing here with the "imposition" of solitary confinement. The examining magistrate refused to do this. Once Herr Hecker has conceived of an idea, he pursues his idea. To "constitute" the editor-in-chief of the *Neue Rheinische Zeitung* became a *fixed idea* for him just as the name of "Hecker" underneath the "farewell address" was for him *fictitious.* Hence he turned to the Council Chamber. The Council Chamber declined. He went from the Council Chamber to the Senate of Appeal. The Senate of Appeal refused to become involved. Herr Hecker, the Public Prosecutor, however, did not give up his fixed idea to "constitute", always in the above sense, the editor-in-chief of the *Neue Rheinische Zeitung, Karl Marx.* As one can see, the ideas of the Public Prosecutor's office are not speculative ideas in the Hegelian sense. They are ideas in the Kantian sense, notions of *"practical"* reason.

Karl Marx could never be directly "accused" of high treason, even if the printing of revolutionary facts or proclamations constituted a newspaper guilty of high treason. In the first place, one had to charge *the one* who had *signed* the newspaper, especially in this case, where the document in question appeared *in the feuilleton section.* What else could one do? One idea leads to another. One could cite *Karl Marx,* under Article 60 of the *Code pénal,* as an

---

[a] Korff.— *Ed.*

accomplice to the crime allegedly committed by the responsible publisher. One can also cite him, if one wants to, as an accomplice of that declaration even if it was printed in the *Kölnische Zeitung*. Hence *Karl Marx* received a summons from the examining magistrate. He appeared and his evidence was taken down. The compositors were, as far as we know, summoned as witnesses, the proof-reader was summoned as a witness and the owner of the printshop was summoned as a witness. Finally, though, the *responsible publisher* was invited as a *witness*. We do not understand the last summons.

Is the alleged author supposed to bear witness against his accomplice?

So that nothing is omitted from our narrative: a police raid was conducted against the office of the *Neue Rheinische Zeitung*.

Hecker, the Public Prosecutor, has surpassed Hecker, the republican. The one accomplishes rebellious facts and issues rebellious proclamations. The other, despite every reluctance, erases facts from the memoirs of contemporary history, from the *newspapers*. He makes what has happened not to have happened. If the "bad press" reports revolutionary facts and proclamations, it commits twofold high treason. It is a moral accomplice since it only reports the rebellious facts because it is inwardly titillated by them. It is an accomplice in the ordinary juridical sense; by reporting, it disseminates, and by disseminating, it turns itself into a tool of the rebellion. It will, therefore, be "constituted" on both counts and will thus enjoy the *fruits* of the "constitution". The "good press", by contrast, will have the monopoly to report or not to report, to falsify or not to falsify revolutionary documents and facts. *Radetzky* has made use of this theory by prohibiting the Milanese newspapers to report the Viennese facts and proclamations. The *Milanese Newspaper*,[a] on the other hand, reported in place of the great Viennese "revolution" a small Viennese riot especially composed by Radetzky. It is rumoured that an insurrection has nonetheless broken out in Milan.

Herr Hecker, the Public Prosecutor, is, as everybody knows, a *contributor* to the *Neue Rheinische Zeitung*.[b] As our contributor we forgive him much except the sin against the unholy "spirit" of our newspaper. And he commits this sin by transforming, with a lack of critical faculty unheard of in a contributor to the *Neue Rheinische Zeitung*, the proclamation of Hecker the fugitive into the proclamation of the *Neue Rheinische Zeitung*. Friedrich Hecker adopts a

---

[a] *Gazzetta di Milano.—Ed.*
[b] See this volume, p. 186.—*Ed.*

passionate attitude and the *Neue Rheinische Zeitung* a *critical* attitude towards the movement. Friedrich Hecker expects everything from the magic influence of single *personalities*. We expect everything from the collisions which arise from the economic *conditions*. Friedrich Hecker travels to the United States in order to study the "republic". The *Neue Rheinische Zeitung* finds that the grandiose class struggles which are taking place in the *French Republic* are more interesting subjects of study than those in a republic in which in the west class struggles do not yet exist and in the east move only within the old quiet English forms. For Friedrich Hecker social questions are consequences of political struggles, for the *Neue Rheinische Zeitung* political struggles are merely the manifestations of social collisions. Friedrich Hecker could be a good tricolour republican. The actual opposition of the *Neue Rheinische Zeitung* only begins with the tricolour republic.

How, for example, could the *Neue Rheinische Zeitung*, without completely repudiating its past, have called upon the German people to

"rally around the men who hold high the banner of popular sovereignty and who guard it faithfully, the men of the extreme Left in Frankfurt am Main; join firmly by word and deed the brave leaders of the republican rising".

We have repeatedly declared that we are not a "parliamentary" newspaper and that we do not hesitate, therefore, from time to time to draw the wrath of even the extreme Left of Berlin and Frankfurt upon our heads. We have called upon the gentlemen of Frankfurt to join the people, we have never called upon the people to join the gentlemen of Frankfurt. And "the brave leaders of the republican rising", where are they and who are they? Hecker is, as is well known, in America, Struve is in prison. Is it *Herwegh?* The editors of the *Neue Rheinische Zeitung*, in particular Karl Marx, have at public meetings decisively opposed Herwegh's initiative[320] in Paris without fearing the ill favour of the excited masses. They were, therefore, duly mistrusted at that time (compare the *Deutsche Volkszeitung*[321] among others) by *utopians* who mistook themselves for *revolutionaries*. Are we supposed to join the people of the opposite opinion now that events have repeatedly confirmed our predictions?

But let us be just. Herr Hecker, the Public Prosecutor, is still a young contributor to our newspaper. The novice in politics just as the novice in natural science resembles that painter who knows only two colours, white and black, or, if you prefer, black-white and red. The finer differences within each *espèce* reveal themselves only to the skilled and experienced eye. And besides, was Herr Hecker not dominated by the fixed idea to *"constitute"* Karl Marx, the editor-in-chief of the *Neue Rheinische Zeitung,* a fixed idea which melted in the purgatory neither of the Investigating Court, nor of the Council Chamber, nor of the Senate of Appeal; hence it must be a fire-proof fixed idea.

The greatest achievement of the March revolution is unquestionably, to use the words of Brutus Bassermann, the "rule of the most noble and best" and their rapid rise on the scale of power. We hope therefore that the merits of Public Prosecutor *Hecker,* our esteemed contributor, will also carry him to the heights of the state's Olympus, as the snow-white doves which were harnessed to the chariot of Aphrodite, carried her with lightning speed to Olympus. As everybody knows, our Government is constitutional. Pfuel is full of enthusiasm for constitutionalism. It is the custom in constitutional states to pay close attention to the recommendations of opposition newspapers. We are therefore moving on constitutional grounds when we advise the Government to *award* to our Hecker the vacant position of *Chief Public Prosecutor* of Düsseldorf. Public Prosecutor *Ammon* of Düsseldorf, who, as far as we know, has not yet earned a life-saving medal for his services to the fatherland, will not hesitate for one moment to dictate reverential silence to his own possible claims in view of the higher merits. If, however, Herr *Heimsoeth* should become Minister of Justice, as we hope he will, we will recommend Herr Hecker as *Attorney General.* We expect still bigger things for Herr Hecker. Herr Hecker is still young. And as the Russians say: the Tsar is great, God is greater still, but the *Tsar is still young.*

Written by Marx on October 28, 1848

First published in the *Neue Rheinische Zeitung* No. 129, October 29, 1848

Printed according to the newspaper

Published in English for the first time

"APPEAL OF THE DEMOCRATIC CONGRESS
TO THE GERMAN PEOPLE"[322]

Cologne, November 2. We give below the appeal of the "Democratic Congress"[323]:

TO THE GERMAN PEOPLE!

During long humiliating years, the German people groaned under the yoke of despotism. The bloody deeds of Vienna and Berlin justified the hope that its freedom and unity would be realised at one blow. The diabolical cunning of an execrable reaction balked this development, thus cheating the heroic people of the fruits of its grandiose insurrection. Vienna, a main bulwark of German freedom, finds itself at the moment in the greatest danger. Sacrificed by the intrigues of a still powerful camarilla, it was to be delivered again to the fetters of despotism. But its noble population rose as one man and opposes the armed hordes of its oppressors resolute unto death. The cause of Vienna is the cause of Germany and the cause of freedom. With the fall of Vienna, the old tyranny will raise its banner higher than ever, Vienna's victory would mean its destruction. It is up to us, German brothers, not to allow Vienna's freedom to perish and not to sacrifice it to the fortune of war of barbaric hordes. It is the most sacred duty of the German governments to rush to the aid of their hard pressed sister city with all their influence. It is, however, at the same time also the most sacred duty of the German people—in the interest of its freedom and in the interest of its self-preservation—to make every sacrifice for the salvation of Vienna. The German people must never draw upon itself the humiliation of blunt indifference when the most precious things, when everything is at stake. Therefore we ask you, brothers, to contribute, each according to his strength, to save Vienna from perdition. What we are doing for Vienna, we are doing for Germany. It is up to you to help! The men whom you have sent to Frankfurt in order to establish freedom have rejected the request to help Vienna with derision. It is up to you now to act! With your powerful and unshakeable energy, demand from your governments that they submit to your majority and save the German cause and the cause of freedom in Vienna. Hurry! You are the power, your will is law! Arise, ye men of freedom, arise in all German lands and wherever else the thought of freedom and humanity inflames noble hearts! Arise, before it is too late! Save the freedom of Vienna. Save the freedom of Germany. The present generation will admire you, posterity will reward you with immortal glory!

October 29, 1848

The Democratic Congress in Berlin

In this appeal lack of revolutionary energy is replaced by sermonising, wailing and ranting[324] behind which hides the most decided lack of thought and passion.

Just a few samples!

The appeal expected of the Vienna and Berlin March revolutions "the realisation of the unity and freedom" of the German people *"at one blow"*. In other words: the appeal dreamed of *"one blow"* which would render the *"development"* of the German people towards "unity and freedom" superfluous.

Immediately thereafter, however, the fantastic "one blow" which replaces the development is transformed into a *"development"* which was *balked* by the reaction. A phrase which reduces itself to nothing!

We are disregarding the monotonous repetition of the basic theme: Vienna is in danger and with Vienna Germany's freedom. Help Vienna and you will help yourselves! This thought has not been given flesh and blood. This *one* phrase is wrapped around itself so many times until it has been extended into a piece of oratory. We merely observe that artificial, insincere ranting always lapses into this clumsy rhetoric.

"It is up to us, German brothers, not to allow Vienna's freedom to perish and not to sacrifice it to the fortune of war of barbaric hordes."

And how are we to do this?

First of all, by an appeal to the sense of duty of the *"German governments"*. *C'est incroyable!*[a]

"It is the *most sacred duty of the German governments* to rush to the aid of their hard pressed sister city with all their influence."

Is the Prussian Government supposed to send Wrangel or Colomb or the Prince of Prussia against Auersperg, Jellachich and Windischgrätz? Did the *"Democratic"* Congress have the right to assume for one moment this childish and conservative attitude to the German governments? Did it have the right to separate for one moment the cause and the "most sacred interests" of the German governments from the cause and the interests of "Croatian order and freedom"? The governments will smile in self-satisfaction at this virginal enthusiasm.

---

[a] That is incredible!—*Ed.*

Articles from the *Neue Rheinische Zeitung*

And the people?

The people are exhorted in general "to make every sacrifice for the salvation of Vienna". Fine! The "people", however, expect particular demands of the Democratic Congress. Whoever demands everything, demands nothing and obtains nothing. Thus the *particular* demand, the whole point is:

"With your powerful and unshakeable energy, *demand* from *your governments* that they submit to your majority and save the German cause and the cause of freedom in Vienna. Hurry! You are the power, your will is law! Arise!"

Let us assume that great popular demonstrations succeed in compelling the governments to take steps in a semi-official way for the salvation of Vienna; we would be blessed with a second edition of "Stein's Army Order". The very idea of using the present "German governments" as "saviours of freedom"—as if in carrying out *imperial punitive measures* they were not fulfilling their true calling and their "most sacred duties" as the Gabriels of "constitutional freedom". The "Democratic Congress" had to be silent about the German governments or it had to reveal unsparingly their conspiracy with Olmütz[a] and Petersburg.

Even though the appeal recommends *"speed"* and there is indeed no time to lose, the humanistic phraseology carries it beyond the borders of Germany and beyond every geographical boundary into the cosmopolitan, misty land of "noble hearts" in general.

"Hurry! Arise, ye men of freedom, arise in all German lands and *wherever else* the thought of freedom and humanity inflames noble hearts!"

We do not doubt that there are such "hearts" even in Lapland. In Germany and *wherever else!* By evaporating into this pure and indefinite phrase the "appeal" has gained its true expression.

It remains unforgivable that the "Democratic Congress" counter-signed such a document. Neither will "the present generation admire it for this" nor will "posterity reward it with immortal glory".

Let us hope that the people, in spite of the "appeal of the Democratic Congress", will awaken from its lethargy and that it will aid the Viennese in the only way it is still able to do at this moment, by defeating the counter-revolution at home.

Written by Marx on November 2, 1848   Printed according to the newspaper

First published in the *Neue Rheinische Zeitung* No. 133, November 3, 1848

---

[a] The Austrian Emperor and his Ministers fled to Olmütz (Olomouc) during the uprising in Vienna.— *Ed.*

THE PARIS *RÉFORME* ON THE SITUATION
IN FRANCE[325]

Cologne, November 2. Even *before* the June uprising we repeatedly exposed the illusions of the republicans who cling to the traditions of 1793, the republicans of the *Réforme* (of "Paris"). The June revolution and the movement to which it gave rise are compelling the utopian republicans gradually to open their eyes.

A leading article in the *Réforme* for October 29 reveals the struggle going on within the party between its old delusions and the new facts.

The *Réforme* says:

"In our country the fights waged to seize the reins of government have long been *class wars,* struggles of the bourgeoisie and the people against the nobility when the First Republic came into being; the sacrifices of the armed people without, and rule of the bourgeoisie within during the Empire; the attempts to restore feudalism under the older branch of the Bourbons; finally, in 1830, the triumph and rule of the bourgeoisie—that is our history."

The *Réforme* adds with a sigh:

"We certainly regret that we have to speak of *classes,* of ungodly and hateful divergences, but these divergences exist and we cannot overlook this fact."

That is to say: up to now the *Réforme* in its republican optimism saw only *"citoyens",* but it has been so hard pressed by history that the splitting up of the *"citoyens"* into *"bourgeois"* and *"prolétaires"* can no longer be dismissed by any effort of imagination.

The *Réforme* continues:

"The despotism of the bourgeoisie was broken in February. What did the people demand? Justice for all and equality. That was its primary slogan, its primary desire. The wishes of the bourgeoisie, whose eyes had been opened by the flash of lightning, were at first the same as those of the people."

The *Réforme* still judges the February revolution by the speeches made during that month. The despotism of the bourgeoisie, far from having been broken during the February revolution, was completed by it. The Crown, the last feudal halo, which concealed the rule of the bourgeoisie, was cast aside. The rule of capital emerged undisguised. Bourgeoisie and proletariat fought against a common enemy during the February revolution. As soon as the common enemy was eliminated, the two hostile classes held the field of battle alone and the decisive struggle between them was bound to begin. People may ask, why did the bourgeoisie fall back into royalism, if the February revolution brought bourgeois rule to its completion? The explanation is quite simple. The bourgeoisie would have liked to return to the period when it ruled without being responsible for its rule; when a puppet authority standing between the bourgeoisie and the people had to act for it and to serve it as a cloak. A period when it had, as it were, a crowned scapegoat, which the proletariat hit whenever it aimed at the bourgeoisie, and against which the bourgeoisie could join forces with the proletariat whenever that scapegoat became troublesome and attempted to establish itself as an authority in its own right. The bourgeoisie could use the King as a kind of lightning-conductor protecting it from the people, and the people as a lightning-conductor protecting it from the King.

Since the illusions, some of them hypocritical, some honestly held, which became widespread immediately after the defeat of Louis Philippe, are mistakenly accepted by the *Réforme* as facts, the developments *following* those days in February appear to it as a series of errors, awkward accidents, that a great man adequate to the needs of the moment could have avoided. As though Lamartine, that delusive light, had not been the true man of the moment!

The *Réforme* bemoans the fact that the true man, the great man, has not yet appeared, and the situation gets worse every day.

"On the one hand the industrial and commercial crisis grows; on the other hand hatred grows and all strive towards contradictory goals. Those who were oppressed before February 24 seek their ideal of happiness and freedom in the conception of an entirely new society. The only concern of those who governed under the monarchy is to regain their realm in order to exploit it with redoubled harshness."

Now what is the attitude of the *Réforme* towards these sharply antagonistic classes? Does it realise even vaguely that class contradictions and class struggle will disappear only with the disappearance of classes?

No. Just now it admitted that class contradictions exist. But class contradictions are based on economic foundations, on the existing mode of material production and the conditions of commerce resulting from it. The *Réforme* knows no better way of changing and abolishing these contradictions than to disregard their real basis, that is these very material conditions, and to withdraw into the hazy blue heaven of republican ideology, in other words, into the poetic February period, from which it was violently ejected by the June events. It writes:

"The saddest aspect of these internal dissensions is the obliteration, the loss of patriotic, national sentiments,"

i.e. of just that patriotic and national enthusiasm which enabled both classes to veil their distinct interests, their conditions of life. When they did that in 1789, their real contradictions were not yet developed. What at that time was an adequate expression of the real position, is today merely an escape from the existing situation. What had substance then, is today just a relic.

"France," concludes the *Réforme*, "evidently suffers from a deep-seated malady, but it is curable. It is caused by a confusion of ideas and morals, by a neglect of justice and equality in social relations, and by depravity resulting from egoistical teaching. The means for reorganisation must be sought in this sphere. Instead people have recourse to material means."

The *Réforme* presents the whole case as a matter of "conscience", and moral twaddle is then used as a means to solve everything. The antithesis of bourgeoisie and proletariat accordingly derives from the ideas of these two classes. And where do these ideas derive from? From the social relations. And where do these relations derive from? From the material, economic conditions of life of the hostile classes. According to the *Réforme*, if the two classes are *no longer conscious* of their real position and their real contradictions, and become intoxicated with the opium of the "patriotic" sentiments and phrases of 1793, then their difficulties will be solved. What an admission of helplessness!

Written by Marx on November 2, 1848   Printed according to the newspaper

First published in the *Neue Rheinische Zeitung* No. 133, November 3, 1848

[THE VIENNESE REVOLUTION AND THE *KÖLNISCHE ZEITUNG*]

Cologne, November 3. Our readers have never indulged in utopian hopes in regard to *Vienna. After* the June revolution, we believed in *every baseness* of the **bourgeoisie**. We said immediately in the *first* issue of the *Neue Rheinische Zeitung* when it reappeared after the state of siege: "The bourgeoisie's distrust of the working class threatens, if not to *wreck* the revolution, at least to *hamper* its development. However that may be, the repercussions of this revolution in Hungary, Italy and Germany foiled the entire plan of campaign devised by the counter-revolution."[a]

We would therefore *not be surprised* by a defeat of Vienna. We would only find ourselves called upon to break off any negotiation with the *bourgeoisie* which measures freedom by the *freedom to trade* and we would without conciliation and without accommodation oppose the miserable German middle class which gladly relinquishes its own rule on condition that it may continue to trade *without a fight.* The English and French bourgeoisie is ambitious; the infamy of the German bourgeoisie would be confirmed by Vienna's defeat.

Thus: at no time have we vouched for the victory of the Viennese. Their *defeat* would not come as a surprise to us. It would only *convince* us that no peace with the *bourgeoisie* is possible, not even for the period of transition, and that the people must remain indifferent in the battles between the bourgeoisie and the Government and must wait for their victories or defeats in order to exploit them. Once again: our readers have only to consult our back issues in order to satisfy themselves that neither the victory nor the defeat of the Viennese can surprise us.

---

[a] See this volume, p. 457.—*Ed.*

What does surprise us, however, is the latest special edition of the *Kölnische Zeitung*. Does the Government deliberately spread false rumours about Vienna in order to calm the excitement in Berlin and the provinces? Does *Dumont pay* the Prussian *state telegraph* so that *he,* Dumont, receives news from the "Berlin" and "Breslau" morning papers which do not reach the "bad press"? And whence did Dumont get his "telegraphic dispatch" this morning, which we did not receive? Has *Birk* from Trier, a mere cipher who has replaced Wittgenstein, been engaged as editor by Dumont? We do not believe it. For even a Brüggemann, a Wolfers, a Schwanbeck, all that is still no *Birk.* We doubt that Dumont has engaged *such* a nonentity.

Today at 6 p. m., *Dumont,* who lied away the February and March revolutions, carries among his first reports once again a "telegraphic" report according to which Vienna has surrendered to the "Wendish itch", the "Windischgrätz".[a]

It is possible. But the possibilities of the once *blood-dripping* "Brüggemann",[326] the ex-correspondent of *the old Rheinische Zeitung,* this worthy whose *views* always go hand in hand with the "*exchange value*" of views in general, his possibilities are based upon the *Preussische Staats-Anzeiger* and the *Breslauer Zeitung.* The tales of "*Brüggemann*" or of the *Kölnische Zeitung* concerning the *February, March* and *October* revolutions will offer their peculiar contribution to history.

Now we shall give the reports which report nothing.[327]

Written by Marx on November 3, 1848

First published in the second supplement to the *Neue Rheinische Zeitung* No. 133, November 3, 1848

Printed according to the newspaper

Published in English for the first time

---

[a] A play on the words *wendische Krätze*—Wendish itch—and the name Windischgrätz.— *Ed.*

THE LATEST NEWS FROM VIENNA, BERLIN AND PARIS[328]

Cologne, November 4. *The outlook brightens.*
There is no direct news yet from *Vienna.* But even according to the official *Prussian newspapers,* it is clear that *Vienna* has not surrendered and that *Windischgrätz* deliberately or as a result of a *misunderstanding* issued to the world a *false telegram.* The "good" press, like an orthodox, multilingual echo, willingly repeated the message although it tried hard to mask its malicious glee behind hypocritical mournful phrases. Stripped of all their fantastic and self-contradictory trash, the reports from Silesia and Berlin bring out the following facts. By October 29 the imperial bandits had obtained control only of a few suburbs. The reports received up till now do *not* show that they have gained a foothold in Vienna itself. The whole story of Vienna's surrender boils down to a few *treasonable proclamations of the Vienna Town Council.* The advanced guard of the Hungarian army attacked Windischgrätz on October 30, and *was said* to have been driven back. On October 31 Windischgrätz resumed the bombardment of Vienna—without result. His army is now between the Viennese and the over 80,000-strong Hungarian army. Windischgrätz's infamous manifestos evoked uprisings or at least very threatening movements in all provinces. Even the Czech fanatics in Prague, the neophytes of the Slovanská Lípa,[329] have awakened from their wild dreams and declared *for Vienna* against the imperial Schinderhannes.[a] *Never* before has the counter-revolution dared to proclaim its plans with such foolish brazenness. Even at *Olmütz,*[b] that

---

[a] Jack the Skinner, a name given to Johann Bückler, a German robber chief.— *Ed.*
[b] The Czech name is Olomouc.— *Ed.*

Austrian Koblenz,[330] the crowned idiot[a] can feel the ground shaking beneath his feet. The fact that the troops are led by the world-famed *Sipehsalar*[b] *Jellachich*—whose name is so great that "*at the flash of his sabre the frightened moon hides behind the clouds*" and "the roar of cannon" always "points the way" in which he must hurriedly decamp—leaves no doubt that the people of Hungary and Vienna

> Horsewhip that scum into the Danube River,
> Go castigate that overweening rabble,
> Those starveling beggars, all so tired of living,
> That horde of miscreants, rogues and vagabonds,
> Croatian riff-raff, abject peasant hirelings,
> That vomit, spewed up by a glutted homeland
> For desperate ventures and for *certain doom.*

Later reports will give appalling details of the crimes perpetrated by Croats and other knights of "law and order and constitutional freedom". The European bourgeoisie ensconced in stock exchanges and other convenient observation posts loudly acclaims the gory spectacle; the same wretched bourgeoisie that broke into screams of moral indignation because of a few harsh acts of popular justice and with a thousand voices unanimously anathemised the "murderers" of honest Latour and noble Lichnowski.

The *Poles*, avenging the Galician murders,[331] are once more advancing at the head of the liberators of Vienna, just as they march at the head of the Italian people and everywhere act as high-minded *generals of the revolution.* Three cheers for the *Poles!*

The *Berlin camarilla*, intoxicated with the blood of Vienna, blinded by the pillars of smoke rising from the burning suburbs, stunned by the Croats' and haiduks' shouts of victory, has dropped its cloak. "Peace has been restored in Berlin." *Nous verrons.*[c]

Finally, from *Paris* come the first subterranean rumbles announcing the earthquake that will bury the respectable republic under its own ruins.

The outlook brightens.

Written by Marx on November 4, 1848   Printed according to the newspaper

First published in the *Neue Rheinische Zeitung* No. 135, November 5, 1848

---

[a] Ferdinand I.—*Ed.*
[b] Commander-in-chief.—*Ed.*
[c] We shall see.—*Ed.*

500

OUR BOURGEOISIE AND DR. NÜCKEL

Cologne, November 4. The news of the victory of the Croats and Wends in Vienna so enraptured our Cologne bourgeoisie that they celebrated with bottles of champagne and through Dr. *Nückel* proposed the following fundamental motion at the evening session of the Town Council on November 3:

"That the Town Council is not obliged to give the workers work. That this is nothing but relief and that the daily wages of workers employed by the city should consequently be fixed at a lower rate than the daily wages of workers employed by private masters."

An additional reason given by Dr. *Nückel* was that it was necessary by means of this differential to stem the rush of workers to municipal employment.

Herr *Böker* managed with difficulty to get this question adjourned.

Dr. *Nückel* has proclaimed the dogma of the local bourgeoisie. For this, the workers owe Dr. Nückel their heartfelt thanks.

It was quite consistent that our men of property, who so joyfully welcomed the declaration of a *state of siege in Cologne*, celebrated the *bombardment of Vienna* and the *restoration of Croatian freedom* as a victory, just as they had celebrated the refined cruelty of the June victors.

Written by Marx on November 4, 1848

First published in the *Neue Rheinische Zeitung* No. 135, November 5, 1848

Printed according to the newspaper

Published in English for the first time

NEWS FROM VIENNA

Cologne, November 5. *Letters and newspapers from Vienna failed to arrive.* The newspapers from *Breslau*[a] which we have received, the *Allgemeine Oderzeitung*, the *Schlesische Zeitung* and the *Breslauer Zeitung*, contain, properly speaking, *nothing*.

Several *Berlin morning* papers of November 3 carry the following news item, one newspaper having received it from *Hietzing*, the others from *Vienna*:

"*The city of Vienna is entirely occupied by imperial troops.*"

The *Kölnische Zeitung* prints this report, which it received from Breslau and which "*is described as reliable*", and it confirms this report by a "telegram" from Berlin, which "in itself" is of course reliable.

Let us leave aside the anonymous note from Breslau[b] and proceed to the *telegram* printed in big letters in the *Kölnische Zeitung*.[c]

The telegram was dispatched from Vienna at noon on November 1.

The letter to Dumont, if he received the news in writing, was sent at 8 *a.m.* on November 3, with the Berlin mail.

On the *evening* of November 3, this news was circulating merely as a rumour throughout Berlin, and the newspapers of November 4 published on the evening of November 3 *deny it*.

---

[a] Wrocław.—*Ed.*

[b] "Breslau, 2. Nov." and "Berlin, 3. Nov.", *Kölnische Zeitung* No. 299 (second edition), November 5, 1848.— *Ed.*

[c] *Kölnische Zeitung* No. 299 (second edition), November 5, 1848, p. 1.— *Ed.*

Hence we have no news from Vienna. Dumont, who reported the burning and capture of Vienna since October 6, could by way of exception have got hold of the right fact on one day in the month.

Written by Marx on November 5, 1848

First published in the second edition of the *Neue Rheinische Zeitung* No. 135, November 5, 1848

Printed according to the newspaper

Published in English for the first time

THE VICTORY OF THE COUNTER-REVOLUTION
IN VIENNA[332]

Cologne, November 6. *Croatian freedom and order won the day* and celebrated this victory with arson, rape, looting and other atrocities. *Vienna is in the hands of Windischgrätz, Jellachich and Auersperg.* Hecatombs of human victims are sacrificed on the grave of the aged traitor Latour.

The gloomy forecasts of our Vienna correspondent[a] have come true, and by now he himself may have become a victim of the butchery.

For a while we hoped Vienna could be liberated by Hungarian reinforcements, and we are still in the dark regarding the movements of the Hungarian army.

Treachery of every kind prepared the way for Vienna's fall. The entire history of the *Imperial Diet* and the *Town Council* since October 6 is a tale of continuous treachery. Who are the people represented in the Imperial Diet and the Town Council?

The *bourgeoisie.*

A part of the Viennese *national guard* openly sided with the camarilla from the very beginning of the October revolution. Towards the end of the October revolution another part of the national guard in collusion with the imperial bandits fought against the proletariat and the Academic Legion.[333] To which strata do these groups of the national guard belong?

To the *bourgeoisie.*

---

[a] [Eduard von Müller-Tellering], "Wien, 21. October", *Neue Rheinische Zeitung* No. 127, October 27, 1848.— *Ed.*

The bourgeoisie in *France*, however, *headed* the counter-revolution only after it had broken down all obstacles to the rule of its own class. The bourgeoisie in *Germany* meekly joins the *retinue* of the absolute monarchy and of feudalism before securing even the first conditions of existence necessary for its own civic freedom and its rule. In France it played the part of a tyrant and made its own counter-revolution. In Germany it acts like a slave and carries out the counter-revolution for its own tyrants. In France it won its victory in order to humble the people. In Germany it humbled itself to prevent the victory of the people. History presents no more *shameful and pitiful spectacle* than that of the *German bourgeoisie*.

Who fled from Vienna in large numbers leaving their wealth to be watched over by the magnanimous people, the people whom, in reward for their watchman's duties, they maligned while away and whose massacre they witnessed on their return?

The *bourgeoisie*.

Whose innermost secrets were revealed by the thermometer which dropped whenever the people of Vienna showed signs of life, and rose whenever the people were in the throes of death? Who used the runic language of the *stock exchange quotations*?

The *bourgeoisie*.

The "German National Assembly" and its "Central Authority" have betrayed Vienna. Whom do they represent?

Mainly the *bourgeoisie*.

The victory of "Croatian order and freedom" in Vienna depended on the victory of the "respectable" republic in Paris. Who won the day in June?

The *bourgeoisie*.

European counter-revolution began its orgies with its victory in Paris.

In February and March armed force was beaten everywhere. Why? Because it represented only the *governments*. After June it was everywhere victorious because the *bourgeoisie* everywhere had come to a secret understanding with it, while retaining official leadership of the revolutionary movement and introducing all those half measures which by the very nature of things were bound to miscarry.

The national fanaticism of the Czechs was the most powerful instrument of the Viennese camarilla. *The allies are already at loggerheads*. In this issue our readers will find the protest of the Prague delegation against the insolent rudeness with which it was greeted in Olmütz.[a]

---

[a] The Czech name is Olomouc.— *Ed.*

This is the *first symptom of the struggle which will break out between the Slav party and its hero Jellachich on the one hand, and the party of nothing but the camarilla, which stands above all nationality, and its hero Windischgrätz on the other.* Moreover the German peasants in Austria are not yet pacified. Their voice will be loudly heard above the caterwauling of the Austrian nationalities. And from a third quarter the voice of the Tsar, the friend of the people,[a] reaches as far as Pest; his executioners are waiting for the word of command in the Danube principalities.

Finally, the last decision of the German National Assembly at Frankfurt, which incorporates German Austria into the German Empire, should lead to a gigantic conflict, unless the German Central Authority and the German National Assembly see it as their task to enter the arena in order to be hissed off the stage by the European public. For all their pious resignation the struggle in Austria will assume gigantic dimensions such as world history has never yet witnessed.

The second act of the drama has just been performed in *Vienna*, its first act having been staged in Paris under the title of *The June Days.* In Paris the mobile guard,[334] in Vienna "Croats"—in both cases *lazzaroni*, lumpenproletariat hired and armed—were used against the working and thinking proletarians. We shall soon see the third act performed in *Berlin*.

Assuming that *arms* will enable the counter-revolution to establish itself in the whole of Europe, *money* would then kill it in the whole of Europe. European *bankruptcy, national bankruptcy* would be the fate nullifying the victory. Bayonets crumble like tinder when they come into contact with the salient "economic" facts.

But developments will not wait for the expiry of the bills of exchange drawn by the European states on European society. The crushing counterblow of the June revolution will be struck in *Paris.* With the victory of the "red republic" in Paris, *armies* will be rushed from the *interior* of their countries to the frontiers and across them, and the *real strength* of the fighting parties will become evident. We shall then remember this June and this October and we too shall exclaim:

Vae victis!

The purposeless massacres perpetrated since the June and October events, the tedious offering of sacrifices since February and March, the very cannibalism of the counter-revolution will convince

---

[a] Nicholas I.—*Ed.*

the nations that there is only *one means* by which the murderous death agonies of the old society and the bloody birth throes of the new society can be *shortened,* simplified and concentrated—and that is by *revolutionary terror.*

Written by Marx on November 6, 1848

Printed according to the newspaper

First published in the *Neue Rheinische Zeitung* No. 136, November 7, 1848

Frederick Engels

FROM PARIS TO BERNE [335]

Written at the end of October and in November 1848

First published in the *Neue Zeit*, Bd. I, Nos. 1 and 2, 1898-99

Printed according to the manuscript

Published in English for the first time

Map sketched by Engels, showing his route from Auxerre to Le Locle

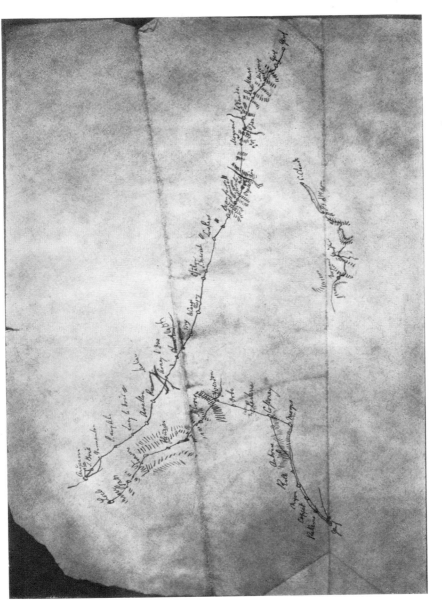

Map sketched by Engels, showing his route from Auxerre to Le Locle

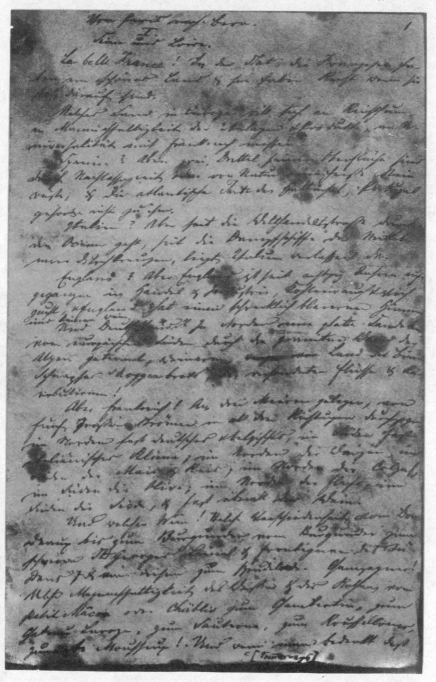

First page of Engels' travel notes "From Paris to Berne"

I

SEINE AND LOIRE

La belle France! The French certainly have a beautiful country and they are right to be proud of it.

What country in Europe can compare with France in wealth, in the variety of its gifts of nature and products, in its universality?

Spain? But neglect or nature has turned two-thirds of its area into a hot, stony desert, and the Atlantic side of the peninsula, Portugal, does not belong to it.

Italy? But ever since world trade has been routed across the ocean, ever since steamships have plied the Mediterranean, Italy has lain isolated.

England? But for the last eighty years England has been reduced to trade and industry, coal-smoke and cattle-raising, and England has a fearfully leaden sky, and no wine.

And Germany? In the north, a flat, sandy plain, cut off from Southern Europe by the granite wall of the Alps, poor in wine, a land of beer, schnaps and rye bread, ot rivers and revolutions that have dried up!

But France! Washed by three seas, traversed in three directions by five great rivers, in the north an almost German and Belgian climate, in the south almost Italian; wheat in the north, maize and rice in the south; *colza*[a] in the north, olives in the south; flax in the north, silk in the south, and wine nearly everywhere.

And what wine! What a diversity, from Bordeaux to Burgundy, from Burgundy to the heavy St. Georges, Lünel and Frontignan of the south, and from that to sparkling champagne! What variety of white and of red, from Petit Mâcon or Chablis to Chambertin, Château Larose, Sauterne, Roussillon and Ai Mousseux! And

---

[a] Rape.— *Ed.*

furthermore each of these wines intoxicates in its own way, with a few bottles one can experience every intermediate state from a Musard quadrille to the *Marseillaise,* from the exultation of the cancan to the tempestuous fever heat of revolution, and then finally with a bottle of champagne one can again drift into the merriest carnival mood in the world!

And only France has a Paris, a city in which European civilisation has its finest flowering, in which all the nerve-fibres of European history unite and from which emanate at measured intervals those electric shocks which can shake a whole world; a city whose population combines a passion for pleasure with a passion for historical action like no other people, whose populace know how to live like the most refined Epicurean of Athens and to die like the most intrepid Spartan, Alcibiades and Leonidas in *one* person; a city which really is, as Louis Blanc[a] says, the heart and mind of the world.

If one looks across Paris from a high point in the city or from Montmartre or the terrace of Saint-Cloud, if one strolls through its environs, one concludes that France knows what it possesses in Paris, that France has been prodigal of its best in tenderly fostering Paris. Like an odalisque on a glittering, bronze-coloured divan, this proud city lies beside the warm, vine-covered hills of the winding Seine valley. Where in the whole world is there a view like that from the two Versailles railways down over the green valley with its countless villages and little towns, and where are there such delightfully situated, such smartly and trimly constructed, such tastefully laid-out villages and little towns as Suresnes, Saint-Cloud, Sèvres, Montmorency, Enghien and countless others? By whichever gate one may leave, though one choose one's route at random, everywhere one encounters the same fine surroundings, the same taste in the use of the topography, the same elegance and cleanliness. And yet again it is only the Queen of Cities itself which has created this splendid setting for itself.

But of course you need a France as well, to make a Paris, and only when one has become acquainted with the abundant wealth of this magnificent country does one understand how this radiant, sumptuous, incomparable Paris could come about. One does not understand it, of course, if one comes from the north, speeding by train across the plains of Flanders and Artois and the hills of Picardy

---

[a] Evidently a slip of the pen for the words quoted are taken from a draft address to the Government of the French Republic submitted by Auguste Blanqui in March 1848.— *Ed.*

with neither forest nor vineyard. There one sees only corn-fields and pasture, whose uniformity is interrupted only by marshy river valleys and distant scrubby hills; and only when one enters within range of the atmosphere of Paris, at Pontoise, does one see something of "beautiful France". One begins to understand Paris a little more if one approaches the capital through the fertile vales of Lorraine, the vine-garlanded chalk hills of Champagne and along the beautiful Marne valley; one understands it better still if one travels through Normandy, now following and now cutting across the meanders of the Seine on the railway from Rouen to Paris. The Seine seems to exhale the air of Paris right down to its mouth; the villages, the towns, the hills, everything reminds one of the countryside near Paris, except that everything becomes finer, more sumptuous, more tasteful as one approaches the centre of France. But I did not fully understand how Paris was possible until I went along the Loire and from there turned across the hills to the vineyard valleys of Burgundy.

I had known Paris in the last two years of the monarchy, when the bourgeoisie was revelling in the full enjoyment of its dominance, when trade and industry were faring passably, when the bourgeois and petty-bourgeois youth still had money for its pleasures and for squandering it away, and when even some of the workers were still well enough placed to be able to participate in the general high spirits and light-heartedness. I had seen Paris again in March and April, in that brief intoxication of the republican honeymoon, when the workers, optimistic fools[a] that they were, cheerfully and without any hesitation "decided to endure three months of misery"[b] for the republic's sake, when they ate dry bread and potatoes by day and when evening came, planted liberty-trees along the boulevards, let off fire-crackers and sang the *Marseillaise* for all they were worth, and when the bourgeoisie, hiding in their houses all day, attempted to appease the wrath of the people with coloured lanterns. I returned — much against my will, by Hecker! — in October. Between the Paris of those days and now there lay the 15th May and the 25th June, there lay the most fearful struggle the world had ever seen, there lay a sea of blood and fifteen thousand dead. Cavaignac's shells had blown Paris's irrepressible gaiety sky-high; the sound of the *Marseillaise* and the *Chant du départ* had ceased, only the bourgeoisie was still humming its *Mourir pour la patrie*[336] between its teeth; the workers, who had neither bread nor arms, ground their

---

[a] *Hoffnungsvolle Toren* (optimistic fools) from Goethe's poem "Prometheus".— *Ed.*

[b] See this volume, p. 148.— *Ed.*

teeth in suppressed resentment; in the school of the state of siege, the exuberant republic had very soon become respectable, tame, well-behaved, and moderate (*sage et modérée*). But Paris was dead, it was no longer Paris. On the boulevards, no one but the bourgeoisie and police spies; the dance-halls and theatres deserted; the *gamins* engulfed in mobile guard jackets, bought for 30 sous a day by the respectable republic, and the stupider they became the more the bourgeoisie celebrated them — in brief, it was the Paris of 1847 again, but without the spirit, without the life, without the fire and the ferment which the workers brought to everything in those days. Paris was dead, and this beautiful corpse was all the more uncanny for being so beautiful.

I could endure it no longer in this dead Paris. I had to leave it, no matter whither. So first of all to Switzerland. I had not much money, that meant going on foot. Nor was I set on taking the shortest route; one does not readily part from France.

Thus one fine morning I set out and without any fixed plan marched due south. I lost my way among the villages once I had left the city's outskirts behind me; there was nothing strange in that. Eventually I found myself on the highroad to Lyons. I followed it for some distance, leaving it from time to time to climb the hills. From the top one has splendid views up and down the Seine, to Paris and to Fontainebleau. One sees the river meandering far, far away in the broad valley, vineyards on the hills on both sides, further away the blue hills beyond which flows the Marne.

But I did not wish to enter Burgundy by so direct a route; I wanted to reach the Loire first. So on the second day I left the highroad and went over the hills towards Orléans. I lost my way among the villages again of course, as my only guides were the sun and the peasants, cut off from the whole world and unable to tell right from left. I spent the night in some village whose name I was never able to make out in the peasant patois, fifteen leagues from Paris, on the watershed between Seine and Loire.

This watershed is formed by a broad ridge which extends from south-east to north-west. On either side it is intersected by numerous valleys, watered by small streams or rivers. Up on the wind-swept summit only corn, buckwheat, clover and vegetables do well; but vines grow everywhere on the valley sides. The eastward-facing slopes are nearly all covered with great masses of those limestone rocks which the English geologists call bolderstones[a] and which one

---

[a] This form of the English word is used in the manuscript.— *Ed.*

often finds in secondary and tertiary hill-country. The huge blue
rocks, between which green shrubs and saplings grow, provide a
pleasant contrast to the meadows of the valley and the vineyards of
the opposite slope.

Gradually I came down into one of these little river valleys and
followed it for a while. Eventually I came upon a highway with
people on it from whom I was able to discover where in fact I was. I
was not far from Malesherbes, midway between Orléans and Paris.
Orléans itself lay too far to the west for my purpose; Nevers was my
next goal, and so I once more went up over the nearest hill, heading
due south. A very pretty view from the top: the pleasant little town of
Malesherbes between wooded hills, numerous villages on the slopes,
and up on a hill-top Castle Châteaubriand. And what was even more
to my liking: opposite, on the far side of a narrow ravine, a departmental road leading due south.

There are three kinds of road in France: the state roads, formerly
called royal roads, now national, fine broad highways connecting the
most important towns with each other. These national roads, which
in the region of Paris are not merely excellently made but true
luxury roads, magnificent elm-lined avenues sixty feet wide and
more, and paved in the middle, become poorer, narrower and less
tree-lined the further one proceeds from Paris and the less
important the road is. In some places they are then so bad that they
are scarcely passable for pedestrians after two hours of moderate
rain. The second class consists of the departmental roads, providing
secondary communications, financed from departmental funds,
narrower and less resplendent than the national roads. The third
class, finally, is made up of the major vicinal routes (*chemins de grande
communication*), maintained from canton resources, narrow unas-
suming roads, but in some places in better condition than the bigger highways.

I struck uphill straight across country in the direction of my
departmental road and found to my extreme delight that it went due
south in an absolutely straight line. Villages and inns were few and
far between; after marching for several hours I eventually came
upon a large farm where I was served most hospitably with some
refreshments, for which I drew some grotesque faces on a piece of
paper for the farmer's children and declared with all gravity: this
one was a speaking likeness of General Cavaignac and that one of
Louis Napoleon, these of Armand Marrast, Ledru-Rollin etc. The
farm-folk stared at these distorted faces in great awe, thanked me in
their delight and at once fixed these strikingly life-like portraits on
the wall. These good people also told me that I was on the road from

Malesherbes to Châteauneuf on the Loire, to which I had still some twelve leagues to go.

I trampled through Puiseaux and another small town whose name I have forgotten, and late in the evening arrived in Bellegarde, an attractive fair-sized place, where I spent the night. The route over the plateau, which incidentally here produces wine in many places, was rather monotonous.

Next morning I set off for Châteauneuf, another five leagues, and from there along the Loire on the national road from Orléans to Nevers.

> Under almond trees in blossom
> On the verdant banks of Loire,
> To lie dreaming, oh how pleasant,
> Of the place I found my love[a]—

so sings many an enthusiastic German youth and many a tender Teutonic maiden in the melting words of Helmina von Chezy and the molten melody of Carl Maria von Weber. But anyone who goes looking for almond trees and gentle, sweet romance on the Loire, as was the fashion in Dresden back in the twenties, is the victim of the kind of appalling delusion which is really permissible only in Germany amongst congenital bluestockings of the third generation.

From Châteauneuf via les Bordes to Dampierre one scarcely catches a glimpse of this romantic Loire. The road goes over the hill-tops at a distance of two or three leagues from the river, and only rarely does one see the water of the Loire glinting in the sun far away. The district is rich in wine, cereals and fruit; down by the river there are luxuriant pastures; the view of the valley, which has no woods and is surrounded only by undulating hills, is however rather monotonous.

In the middle of the road, near some farm-houses, I came across a caravan of four men, three women and several children, accompanied by three heavily-laden donkey-carts, cooking their midday-meal at a big fire on the open highway. I stopped for a moment: I was not mistaken, they were speaking German, in the broadest South German dialect. I spoke to them; they were delighted to hear their native tongue in the middle of France. They were as it happened from the Strasbourg area of Alsace, and travelled into the interior of France in this way every summer, earning their keep by basket-weaving. When I asked whether this gave them enough to live on,

---

[a] Carl Maria von Weber's opera *Euryanthe* (libretto by Helmina von Chezy), Act I, Scene 2.— *Ed.*

they said: "Hardly, if we had to buy everything; mostly we're begging." Slowly, another man, of advanced age, crawled out of one of the donkey-carts, in which he had a complete bed. There was something very gypsy-like about the whole band with the ill-assorted garments they had scrounged. For all that they had an easy-going air about them and chattered interminably to me about their journeys, and in the middle of the merriest gossiping the mother and the daughter, a gentle, blue-eyed creature, almost came to pulling each other's tousled red hair. I couldn't but admire the irrepressible force with which the easy-going and emotional German character would come out, even from beneath the most gypsy-like pattern of life and attire; I wished them good day and continued my journey, accompanied for some distance by one of the gypsies, who before eating permitted himself the pleasure of an amble on the sharp-boned crupper of a lean donkey.

That evening I reached Dampierre, a small village not far from the Loire. Here the Government was employing three or four hundred workers from Paris, the remnants of the former national work-shops,[337] to build a dyke to prevent flooding. They were workers of every kind, goldsmiths, butchers, cobblers, carpenters, right down to the rag-and-bone man of the Paris boulevards. I found some twenty of them at the inn where I spent the night. A hefty butcher, who had already been promoted to a kind of supervisory position, spoke of the undertaking with great enthusiasm: they were earning between 30 and 100 sous a day, according to how they worked, it was easy to make 40 to 60 sous, if one showed any aptitude. He wanted to enrol me in his brigade there and then; I would soon get into the swing and certainly be earning 50 sous a day by the second week, I could make my fortune, and there was enough work for another six months at least. I would not have minded exchanging my pen for a spade for a month or two for a change; but I had no papers, and that would have landed me in a nice pickle.

These workers from Paris had not lost any of their old gaiety. They pursued their work, ten hours a day, amid laughter and jokes, entertained themselves in their leisure hours with outrageous pranks and in the evenings amused themselves by *"déniaising"*[a] the peasant girls. But apart from this they were quite demoralised as a result of being isolated in a small village. Not a trace of concern with the interests of their class, and with current political issues which touch the workers so closely. They appeared not to read any papers any more. Their political activity went no further than giving nicknames;

---

[a] Initiating, seducing.— *Ed.*

one of them, a big, strong lout, they called Caussidière, another, a bad worker and utter drunkard, responded to the name of Guizot, etc. The exhausting work, their relatively good living conditions and especially the separation from Paris and transfer to a remote, quiet corner of France had reduced their horizon remarkably. They were already on the point of turning into rustics, and they had only been there for two months.

The next morning I reached Gien and thus at last the Loire valley itself. Gien is a little town with crooked streets, a fine embankment and a bridge over the Loire, which here barely equals the Main at Frankfurt in breadth. It is altogether very shallow and full of sandbanks. ·

From Gien to Briare the road goes along the valley at a distance of about a quarter of a mile [a] from the Loire. It proceeds in a south-easterly direction, and the country gradually assumes a southerly character. The avenue is lined with elms, ashes, acacias or chestnuts; the valley floor comprises luxuriant pastures and fertile fields, amongst whose stubble a second harvest of the richest clover was sprouting, and which are bordered by long lines of poplars; on the other side of the Loire, in the hazy distance, a line of hills, on this side, right by the highroad, a second chain of hillocks, planted with vines in its entirety. The valley of the Loire is not at all strikingly beautiful or romantic here, as people tend to say it is, but it does create a most agreeable impression; all this rich vegetation testifies to the mild climate without which it could not flourish. Even in the most fertile areas of Germany I have nowhere found plants growing in such profusion as on the road between Gien and Briare.

Before I leave the Loire, a few words as to the inhabitants of the area I passed through and their way of life.

The villages within four or five hours travel from Paris cannot be taken as the measure for villages in the rest of France. Their disposition, the architecture of the houses, the mores of the inhabitants are far too much dominated by the spirit of the great metropolis from which they live. Only at a distance of ten leagues from Paris, in remote upland areas, does the countryside proper begin, does one see real farm-houses. A characteristic of the whole region as far as the Loire and into Burgundy is that the peasant-farmer conceals the entrance to his house as far as possible from the highroad. In the upland areas every farmyard is surrounded by a wall; one enters by a gate and then in the yard itself

---

[a] Engels uses the German word *Meile*, a linear measure which at that time differed in length in different German states but can be regarded as roughly $4\frac{1}{2}$ miles.— *Ed.*

one must look for the door to the house which is usually situated towards the rear. In this area, where most of the peasants have cows and horses, the farm-houses are fairly big; on the Loire, on the other hand, where there is much market-gardening and even well-to-do peasants own few cattle or none at all and cattle-raising is a separate branch of husbandry left to the larger landowners or tenant farmers, the farm-houses become smaller and smaller, often so small that one cannot conceive how there is room within for a peasant family with its equipment and stores. But here too the entrance is on the side facing away from the road, and in the villages the public houses and shops are almost alone in having doors facing the street.

The peasants of this area for the most part enjoy a really good life, despite their poverty. The wine, at least in the valleys, is mostly their own produce, good and cheap (this year two or three sous a bottle), the bread is everywhere, except in the highest places, good, wheaten bread and there is in addition excellent cheese and magnificent fruit, which people in France eat of course always with the bread. Like all country-people they eat little meat, but a lot of milk, vegetable soups and in general a vegetable diet of outstanding quality. The living standard of the French peasant between the Seine and the Loire is three times higher than that of the North-German peasant, even if he is significantly better off.

These peasants are good-natured, hospitable, light-hearted folk, helpful and obliging to the stranger in every possible way, and even when speaking the broadest patois, still true, courteous Frenchmen. Despite their exceedingly highly developed sense of property towards the land which their fathers won from the nobility and the clergy, they still possess many of the patriarchal virtues, especially in the villages set back from the main roads.

But peasants will be peasants, and the conditions of life of the peasants do not for one moment cease to assert themselves. Despite all the private virtues of the French peasant, despite the more advanced conditions of life he enjoys in comparison with the peasant to the east of the Rhine, the peasant in France, as in Germany, is a barbarian in the midst of civilisation.

The isolation of the peasant in a remote village with a rather small population which changes only with the generations, the hard, monotonous work, which ties him more than any serfdom to the soil and which remains always the same from father to son, the stability and monotony of all his conditions of life, the restricted circumstances in which the family becomes the most important, most decisive social relationship for him — all this reduces the peasant's horizon to the narrowest bounds which are possible in modern society. The great movements of history pass him by, from time to time sweep him along with them,but he has no inkling of the nature of the motive force of these movements, of their origin and their goal.

In the Middle Ages and in the seventeenth and eighteenth centuries there was alongside the movement of the middle class in the towns a peasant movement, which, however, constantly put up reactionary demands and,without producing any significant results for the peasants themselves, only succeeded in assisting the towns in their struggles for emancipation.

In the first French revolution the peasants acted in a revolutionary manner just so long as was required by their most immediate, most tangible private interests; until they had secured the right of ownership to their land which had hitherto been farmed on a feudal basis, until feudal relations were irrevocably abolished and the foreign armies ejected from their district. Once this was achieved, they turned with all the fury of blind avarice against the movement of the big towns which they failed to understand, and especially against the movement in Paris. Countless proclamations by the Committee of Public Safety, countless decrees by the Convention, above all those concerning the maximum and the profiteers,[338] mobile columns and travelling guillotines had to be directed against the obdurate peasants. And yet no class benefited more from the Terror which drove out the foreign armies and put down the civil war than these same peasants.

When Napoleon overthrew the bourgeois regime of the Directory, restored calm, consolidated the new property relations of the peasants and sanctioned them in his *Code civil* and drove the foreign armies ever further from the frontiers, the peasants rallied to him with enthusiasm and became his chief support. For the French peasant is nationalistic to a fanatical degree; la France has come to mean a great deal to him now that he has become hereditary proprietor of a piece of France; foreigners he only knows in the form of devastating invading armies which inflict a maximum of damage on him. Hence the French peasant's unbounded nationalism, hence his equally unbounded hatred of *l'étranger*. Hence the passion with which he went to war in 1814 and 1815.

When the Bourbons returned in 1815, when the exiled aristocracy once more raised claims to the landed property they had lost in the revolution, the peasants saw all their revolutionary conquests threatened. Hence their hatred of Bourbon rule and their jubilation

---

[a] Of 1830.— *Ed.*

when the July revolution[a] restored to them security of possession and the tricolour.

From the July revolution onwards, the peasants' participation in the general interests of their country came once more to an end. Their wishes had been fulfilled, the land they owned was no longer threatened, at the village *Mairie* the same flag was once more flying which had meant victory to them and their fathers for a quarter of a century.

But as always the fruits they enjoyed from their victory were few. The bourgeoisie began at once to exploit its rural allies to the utmost extent. The fruits of fragmentation and of the divisibility of the land, the impoverishment of the peasants and the mortgaging of their land, had already begun to ripen under the Restoration; after 1830 their manifestations became ever more widespread and ever more menacing. But the pressure which big capital exerted on the peasant remained for him simply a private relationship between himself and his creditor; he did not see and could not see that these private relationships, which were becoming increasingly widespread and increasingly the rule, were gradually developing into a class relationship between the class of big capitalists and that of small landowners. It was not the same situation as it had been with feudal burdens, whose origin had been long since forgotten, whose significance had long since fallen into oblivion, which were no longer payment for services rendered, and which had long ago become nothing but a burden oppressing one party. In the present case, with a mortgage debt, the peasant or at least his father has had the money paid out to him in solid five-franc pieces; the debt-certificate and the mortgage-repayment book remind him if necessary of the origin of the burden; the interest he has to pay, even the oppressive, constantly renewed subsidiary payments to the usurer are modern, bourgeois liabilities which apply in similar form to all debtors; the oppression operates in a quite modern, up-to-date guise, and the peasant is bled white and ruined in accordance with precisely the same principles of law which alone guarantee him his property. His own *code civil*, his modern-day bible, becomes a rod for his own back. The peasant can see no class relationship in the usurious mortgage terms, he cannot demand their abolition without simultaneously endangering his own property. The pressure of usury, instead of propelling him into the movement, utterly confuses him. The only way in which he can imagine relief is in a reduction of taxes.

When, in February of this year, a revolution took place in which the proletariat appeared for the first time with demands of its own, the peasants showed not the faintest comprehension. If the republic had any meaning for them, it was merely: reduction of taxes and maybe occasionally something about national honour, war of conquest and the Rhine frontier. But when on the morning after Louis Philippe's fall the war between the proletariat and bourgeoisie broke out in Paris, when the stagnation of trade and industry had repercussions in the countryside and the peasant's produce, already devalued in a year of good harvests, fell yet further in price and became unsaleable, when to crown it all the battle of June spread fear and terror to the furthermost corners of France, a universal cry of the most fanatical fury arose amongst the peasants against revolutionary Paris and the eternally dissatisfied Parisians. Of course! For what did the stubborn, narrow-minded peasant know of proletariat and bourgeoisie, of a democratic social republic, of the organisation of labour, of matters whose fundamental conditions and causes could never exist within the narrow confines of his village! And when occasionally, through the murky channels of the bourgeois journals, he acquired a vague notion of what was at issue in Paris, when the bourgeoisie had tossed him the great slogan they aimed against the workers of Paris: *ce sont les partageux*, they are people who want to share all property and all the land, the peasants' indignation knew no bounds, their cry of fury was redoubled. I have spoken to hundreds of peasants in the most diverse regions of France, and all were in the grip of this fanatical hatred of Paris and especially the workers of Paris. "I wish that cursed Paris would be blown sky-high during the day tomorrow"—and that was the most charitable of benedictions. It goes without saying that the peasants' age-old contempt for town-dwellers was merely increased and vindicated by this year's events. The peasants, the countryside must save France; the countryside produces everything, the towns live off our corn, dress in our flax and our wool, we must restore the proper order of things; we peasants must take charge of affairs ourselves—this was the eternal refrain that sounded, more or less clearly, more or less deliberately, through all the peasants' confused talk.

And how do they hope to save France, how do they hope to take charge of affairs themselves? By electing Louis Napoleon Bonaparte as President of the Republic, a great name borne by a confused, vain, diminutive fool! Every peasant I spoke to was just as enthusiastic about Louis Napoleon as he was full of hatred for Paris. These two passions and the most unthinking, bovine amazement at the whole European upheaval are the sum total of the French peasant's politics. And the peasants have over six million votes, more than two-thirds of all the votes in the elections in France.

It is true that the Provisional Government did not manage to bind the interests of the peasants to the revolution; with the increase of 45 centimes in the land tax, which chiefly hit the peasants, it made an unforgivable, irreparable mistake. But even if it had won over the peasants to the revolution for a few months, they would have deserted it in the summer. The present attitude of the peasants towards the revolution of 1848 is not the consequence of any mistakes or chance blunders; it is in the nature of things, it is based upon the conditions of life, the social position of the small landowner. The French proletariat, before it enforces its demands, will first have to put down a general peasants' war, a war which even the writing-off of all mortgage debts can only postpone for a short time.

One must have spent a fortnight in the almost exclusive company of peasants, peasants from the most diverse regions, one must have had the opportunity of encountering everywhere this same obtuse narrow-mindedness, this same total ignorance of all urban, industrial and commercial conditions, this same blindness in politics, this same wildly uninformed surmising about everything beyond the village, this same application of the standards of peasant life to the mightiest factors of history — in short, one must have come to know the French peasant especially in 1848 in order to experience the utterly disheartening effect which this refractory stupidity engenders.

II

BURGUNDY

Briare is a quaint little old town at the mouth of the canal which joins the Loire to the Seine. Here I took stock of the route and decided it would be better to go to Switzerland via Auxerre instead of via Nevers. I therefore left the Loire and turned across the hills towards Burgundy.

The fertility of the Loire valley declines gradually but fairly slowly. One climbs imperceptibly, and only five or six miles from Briare, in the region of Saint-Sauveur and Saint-Fargeau, does one reach the beginnings of the forested, cattle-raising uplands. The ridge between the Yonne and the Loire is higher even here, and the whole of this western part of the Department of the Yonne is generally fairly hilly.

It was in the region of Toucy, six leagues from Auxerre, that I first heard the peculiar, naively-broad dialect of Burgundy, a patois which here and throughout Burgundy proper remains pleasant and attractive, whereas in the higher regions of the Franche Comté it takes on a ponderous, clumsy, almost didactic tone. It is like the naive dialect of Austria, which gradually changes into the coarse Upper Bavarian. In a remarkably un-French way the Burgundian patois constantly stresses the syllable preceding that which takes the main emphasis in good French, it turns iambic French into trochaic and in so doing strangely distorts the subtle accentuation which the educated Frenchman manages to impart to his speech. But, as I said, in Burgundy proper, it continues to sound rather nice and from the lips of a pretty girl even charming: *Mais, mâ foi, monsieur, je vous demande ûn peu....*[a]

---

[a] But indeed, sir, I ask you ... (the accents indicate the syllables stressed in the Burgundian patois).—*Ed.*

If one can draw comparisons, the Burgundian is on the whole the Austrian of France. Naive, good-natured, confiding in the highest degree, having a great deal of native wit within their familiar social surroundings, full of naively odd ideas about everything that transcends them, comically clumsy in unfamiliar circumstances, for ever indestructibly good-humoured — in this these good people are almost one and all alike. The amiable, good-hearted Burgundian peasant is the first one forgives for his complete political vacuity and his starry-eyed enthusiasm for Louis Napoleon.

Incidentally, the Burgundians undeniably have a stronger admixture of German blood than the French who live further to the west; their hair and complexion are lighter, their physique a little bigger, especially in the women, there is already a marked decrease in that sharp critical intelligence and incisive wit, in place of which there is a more straightforward sense of humour and sometimes a faint touch of geniality. But the gaiety of the French is still markedly to the fore, and in carefree light-heartedness the Burgundian is second to none.

The hilly western part of the Department of the Yonne derives its living chiefly from cattle-raising. But Frenchmen everywhere are poor cattle-farmers, and these Burgundian cattle appear thin and small. However alongside cattle-raising a great deal of corn is grown and fine wheaten bread is eaten everywhere.

The farm-houses here also begin to resemble those in Germany; they are again larger and combine dwelling, barn and stables under one roof; but here too the door is still mostly sideways from the road or turned completely away from it.

On the long descent that takes one down to Auxerre, I saw the first Burgundy vines, for the most part still weighed down with the fantastically rich grape-harvest of 1848. On many vines the leaves were almost completely concealed by grapes.

Auxerre is a small, rugged township, rather unimpressive from within, with a pretty embankment by the Yonne and in places the beginnings of those boulevards which no French departmental capital can be without. In normal times it must indeed be quiet and dead, and the Prefect of the Yonne cannot have needed to spend much on organising the obligatory balls and dinners which under Louis Philippe he had to offer to the local notabilities. But now Auxerre was full of life, such as only occurs once a year. If Citizen Denjoy, the representative of the people who got so worked up in the National Assembly because the premises where the democratic social banquet in Toulouse took place were decorated in red, if this worthy Citizen Denjoy had accompanied me to Auxerre, he would have thrown a fit in sheer horror. It was not just one hall here but the whole town which was decorated in red. And what a red! The walls and staircases of the houses, the blouses and shirts of the people were coloured with the most unambiguous, the most blatant blood-red; dark-red streams filled even the gutters and bespattered the paving stones, and a sinister-looking blackish, foaming-red liquid was being carried about the streets in great tubs by sinister bearded men. The red republic with all its horrors appeared to be holding sway, the guillotine, the steam guillotine appeared to be working continuously, the *buveurs de sang*,[a] of which such fearful tales are recounted in the *Journal des Débats*, were obviously celebrating their cannibalistic orgies here. But the red republic of Auxerre was most innocent, it was the red republic of the Burgundian wine-harvest, and the drinkers of blood who consume the noblest produce of this red republic with such intense pleasure, are none other than the most respectable republicans, the bourgeoisie, big and small, of Paris. And in this context that honourable Citizen Denjoy also has a certain weakness for things red, despite the best intentions.

If only one could have had one's pockets full of money in that red republic! The 1848 harvest was so infinitely rich that not enough barrels could be found to take all the wine. And what is more, of such quality — better than '46, perhaps even better than '34! The peasants came pouring in from all sides to buy up what was still left of the '47 at bargain prices — at 2 francs per cask of 140 litres of good wine; cart after cart came in by every gate with empty barrels, and yet they could not cope. I saw with my own eyes a wine-merchant in Auxerre pouring out several barrels of '47, quite good wine, into the street, simply in order to accommodate the new wine, which offered very different prospects to the speculator of course. I was assured that this wine-merchant had poured away as many as forty large barrels (*fûts*) in this way in a few weeks.

Having consumed several pints of both the old and the new, I crossed the Yonne in the direction of the hills on the right bank. The highroad follows the valley; however I took the old, shorter road across the hills. The sky was overcast, the weather gloomy, I was myself rather tired, and I therefore spent the night in the first village, a few kilometres from Auxerre.

Next morning I set out very early in the most magnificent sunshine imaginable. The route passed with never a break between vineyards over a fairly high ridge. But on top, I was rewarded for the exertion of the climb by a most splendid panorama. Before me, the

---

[a] Drinkers of blood.— *Ed.*

hilly downward slope all the way to the Yonne, then the green valley of the Yonne, rich in meadows and planted with poplars, with its many villages and farms; beyond it the grey stone Auxerre, nestling against the scarp on the far side; villages everywhere, and everywhere, as far as the eye could see, vines, nothing but vines, and the most brilliant warm sunshine, attenuated only in the distance by a touch of autumn in the air, beating down over this great cauldron in which the August sun brews one of the noblest of wines.

I do not know what the reason is for the peculiar charm of these French landscapes which are not distinguished by any particularly attractive contours. It is of course not this detail or that, it is the whole, the ensemble, which invests them with the stamp of satisfaction such as is rarely found elsewhere. The Rhine and the Moselle have more beautiful combinations of crags, Switzerland has greater contrasts, Italy a fuller palette of colours, but no country has regions that make up so harmonious an ensemble as France. It is with an extraordinary inner peace that the eye roves from the broad, luxuriant meadows of the valley to the hills which are covered with vines of equal luxuriance right to their summits, and to the countless villages and towns rising from the foliage of the fruit-trees. There is nowhere a piece of bare ground, nowhere a discordant patch of infertility, or a harsh outcrop of rock with walls inaccessible to vegetation. Everywhere flora in profusion, a fine, rich green just taking on a shade of autumnal bronze, set off by the brilliance of a sun which even halfway through October still burns hotly enough for not a single grape to be left unripe on the vine.

I went a little further and a second, equally fine view unfolded before me. Far below, in a narrower bowl in the hills, lay Saint-Bris, a small township that likewise earned its livelihood entirely from the vine. The same components as before, but more closely huddled together. Pastures and gardens down in the valley round the little town, vineyards all round about on the slopes of the bowl, only on the north side ploughed fields or fields and meadows of green clover growing on the stubble. Down in the streets of Saint-Bris the same bustle as in Auxerre; everywhere barrels and wine-presses, and all the inhabitants busy amidst laughter and jokes with pressing the grape-juice, pumping it into the barrels or carrying it through the streets in great vats. Amongst it all, a market was being held; in the broader streets peasant carts were halted with vegetables, corn and other field produce; the peasants with their white Phrygian caps and the peasant women with their Madras handkerchiefs round their heads thronged gossiping, shouting, laughing amongst the vintners;

and the little town of Saint-Bris presented a picture of such lively
bustle that one could believe one was in a big city.

Past Saint-Bris my way took me once more up a hill by a long
ascent. But I climbed this hill with especial pleasure. Everybody was
still occupied with the grape-harvest here, and a grape-harvest in
Burgundy has a merriness about it of a different order to one in the
Rhineland even. At every step I found the gayest company, the
sweetest grapes and the prettiest girls; for here, where there is a
small town always within three hours travel, where the population
has a great deal of contact with the outside world by virtue of their
trade in wine, here a certain degree of sophistication prevails, and no
one assumes this sophistication more rapidly than the womenfolk,
for they derive the most immediate and striking benefits from it. No
French townswoman dreams of singing

> If I were as pretty
> As the girls who're country-bred,
> I'd wear a yellow straw hat
> With a rose-red ribbon tied.[a]

On the contrary, she knows only too well that it is to the town, to
the absence of arduous labour, to civilisation and its hundred aids to
cleanliness and arts of toilery that she owes the perfecting of her
charms; she knows that even if country girls have not already
inherited that coarse-boned build from their parents which the
Frenchman so abhors and which is the pride of the Germanic race,
country girls — as a result of exacting farm labour in the most
burning sunshine and the heaviest rain alike, the difficulties in the
way of keeping clean, the absence of any aids to physical culture, and
their admittedly venerable but no less ungainly and tasteless
attire—will mostly end up as ungainly, waddling scarecrows,
comically dolled up in garish colours. Tastes vary; our German
compatriots mostly prefer the farmer's daughter, and they are
perhaps right to do so: all due respect for the kicks—similar to those
of a trooper—and especially the fists of a strapping dairymaid; all
honour to the grass-green and fiery-red check gown that embraces
her mighty waist; hats off to that impeccably flat expanse that
reaches from the back of her neck down to her heels and gives her
from behind the appearance of a board covered with brightly
coloured calico! But tastes vary, and so that portion of my fellow
citizens which differs from me, though being no less worthy of
respect for that, must forgive me if the cleanly-washed, smoothly-
combed, slimly-built Burgundian women from Saint-Bris and

---

[a] Goethe, "Kriegserklärung" (modified).—*Ed.*

Vermenton made a pleasanter impression on me than those earthily dirty, tousled, young Molossian buffaloes between the Seine and the Loire who gape at one as though struck dumb if one rolls a cigarette, and take to their heels screaming if one asks them the way in good French.

It will therefore readily be believed that I spent more time lying in the grass with the vintners and their girls, eating grapes, drinking wine, chatting and laughing, than marching up the hill, and that it would have taken me no longer to have climbed the Blocksberg or even the Jungfrau than this insignificant ridge. The more so since one can eat one's fill of grapes sixty times over each day and has thus the best of excuses at each vineyard to establish contact with these constantly laughing and obliging people of both sexes. But everything must come to an end, and this hill was no exception. It was already afternoon when I descended the far side into the delightful valley of the Cure, a small tributary of the Yonne, to the little town of Vermenton, which has an even finer setting than Saint-Bris.

Not far beyond Vermenton, this attractive region comes to an end. One gradually approaches the higher ridge of the Faucillon which divides the basins of the Seine, the Rhône and the Loire. From Vermenton one climbs for several hours and crosses a broad infertile plateau, where rye, oats and buckwheat largely take the place of wheat.[a]

---

[a] At this point the following note is written in an unknown hand: "[The manuscript breaks off here.]"— Ed.

APPENDICES

RECEIPTS OF THE CENTRAL AUTHORITY OF THE COMMUNIST LEAGUE FOR MONEY RECEIVED AND PAID OUT[339]

I

April 2, 1848

Communist League
Workers of all countries, unite!

The Central Authority certifies that it has received the sum of twenty-five francs (f. c.[a]) from its member Karl Marx.

Paris, April 2, 1848

For the Central Authority
K. Marx
Engels
Henry Bauer
Joseph Moll

II

Communist League
Workers of all countries, unite!

The Central Authority has received an advance of seventy-four francs 20 centimes from its member Marx, which is hereby confirmed.

Paris, April 2, 1848

For the Central Authority
Engels
Bauer
J. Moll

---

[a] *Fidei-commissum.*—*Ed.*

III

Communist League
Workers of all countries, unite!

League member Friedrich Crüger acknowledges that he has received the sum of twenty-five francs as an advance from the Central Authority and he promises to repay this sum as soon as possible to the League.

Paris, April 2, 1848

Friedrich Crüger

First published in *Der Bund der Kommunisten. Dokumente und Materialen,* Bd. 1, 1836-1849, Berlin, 1970

Printed according to the manuscripts

Published in English for the first time

TO ALL WORKERS OF GERMANY[340]

BROTHERS AND WORKERS!

If we do not want once again to be the most deceived of all, and do not want for a long series of years to be exploited, despised and downtrodden by a handful of men, then we must not lose a moment, we must not remain inactive for a single minute.

Isolated, as we have been hitherto, we are weak although we number millions. United and organised, on the other hand, we shall constitute an irresistible force. Therefore, brothers, everywhere in towns and villages form workers' associations in which our conditions are discussed, measures proposed to change our present situation, representatives from the working class to the German Parliament nominated and elected, and all other steps taken that are necessary for safeguarding our interests. Furthermore, all workers' associations in Germany must as quickly as possible enter into and keep in contact with one another.

We propose that for the time being you choose *Mainz* as the centre for all the workers' associations and that you enter into correspondence with the undersigned Executive Committee so that we can agree on a common plan and as soon as possible definitively decide the seat of the Central Committee etc. at a meeting of delegates of all the associations.

We expect letters *without postage pre-paid,* just as for our part we shall write to the associations *without pre-payment.*

Mainz, April 5, 1848

The Workers' Educational Association in Mainz
On behalf of the Executive Committee

Speaker	Writer
Wallau	**Cluss**

Address: Secretariat of the Workers' Educational Association in Mainz, c/o Herr *Adolf Cluss*, Mainz, Franziskanergasse No. 156$^{1}/_{2}$.

First published in the *Deutsche Volkszeitung* No. 8, April 8, 1848, the *Mannheimer Abend-Zeitung* No. 100, April 10, 1848, and in the supplement to the *Seeblätter* No. 89, April 13, 1848

Printed according to the *Deutsche Volkszeitung*

Published in English for the first time

MARX'S APPLICATION
FOR PRUSSIAN CITIZENSHIP [341]

To the police authorities in Cologne

I have the honour herewith to request you to prevail upon the relevant Department to grant me citizenship in the city of Cologne. I was born on May 5, 1818, in Trier, studied at the local gymnasium and at the universities of Bonn and Berlin. In 1842 and 1843 I lived in Cologne as editor of the now defunct *Rheinische Zeitung.* When that newspaper ceased to exist I went abroad and relinquished my Prussian citizenship. After the events which took place recently, I returned to my country and now I intend to settle with my family in Cologne.[a]

Cologne, April 13, 1848

Yours faithfully,
Dr. Karl Marx

Address: Apostelstrasse 7

First published in the *Zeitschrift für Geschichtswissenschaft* No. 3, 1968

Printed according to the manuscript

Published in English for the first time

---

[a] The following version of the last sentence is given in the rough draft of this letter: "Following an invitation to take part in the editing of a newspaper that is to be founded in Cologne, I have now returned to my country, and intend to settle with my family in Cologne."—*Ed.*

538

ACCOUNT OF A STATEMENT MADE BY KARL MARX
TO THE COLOGNE POLICE INSPECTOR

The petitioner, the politically unreliable *Dr. Karl Marx,* was born in Trier on May 5, 1818, lived in Cologne in 1842-43, worked as editor of the *Rheinische Zeitung,* subsequently he went abroad and from there he obtained the enclosed permission to emigrate, which was issued by his home town Trier,[342] and has therefore lost his Prussian citizenship.

According to his statement he is working on a book on economics which he intends to publish and he proposes to live partly on the proceeds of his writings and partly the personal property of his wife,[a] who, together with their three children,[b] is still staying in Trier.

The stamp attached to the application has been cancelled and is duly enclosed herewith.

Cologne, April 19, 1848

Hünermund,
Police Inspector

First published in the *Zeitschrift für Geschichtswissenschaft* No. 3, 1968

Printed according to the manuscript

Published in English for the first time

---

[a] Jenny Marx.— *Ed.*
[b] Their daughters Jenny and Laura and their son Edgar.— *Ed.*

PROSPECTUS FOR THE FOUNDING
OF THE *NEUE RHEINISCHE ZEITUNG*[343]

A new spirit has broken through in Germany. It has overthrown the old regime, it has doomed the old world to destruction. It demands a new society, a new life.

It is the spirit of the *people*. The people has taken sovereign power, the people that does not want any division, any class rule, which regards its component parts as co-operating members of one great body. It is its will that is to guide its life, regulate its work, create its well-being.

The first task for this will is to create the forms in which it can deploy its strength safe from oppression or falsification. These are the forms of *democracy*. Already the people is preparing to elect a double representation[a] from which it expects the establishment of its rights, the division of the state powers and the guarantee of order, in short, a new Constitution.

This is great, difficult work, even though only preparatory. The overthrown power will resist it, personal interest will not voluntarily submit to the demands of the whole. Democracy must stand its ground in the struggle against both these enemies of an order which serves the will of the whole, and whose purpose is the good of the whole: it will have on its side the experience of the past and the needs of the present.

The immediate aim of the *Neue Rheinische Zeitung* is to co-operate vigorously in this immediate public work. For the time being its chief task will be a thorough examination of the questions which relate to the constitution of Germany and Prussia in conjunction with the same or similar questions which occupy people abroad. It will not close its columns to any tendencies except those stemming from

---

[a] A reference to the election of the Prussian and the German National Assemblies.— *Ed.*

absolutism or particular interests, it will not represent any particular party within the democracy, it will not proceed according to any preconceived theory and will not prematurely reject any view, even if it has not yet found general sympathy.

But if the political formation of the fatherland is the most immediate of the great tasks which the German nation is determined to solve, it is by no means the greatest and by far not the most difficult task. Political democracy is merely the means to achieve thoroughgoing changes in civil society. All wishes, all demands are directed to this end. The worst sufferings of unemployment, of deprivation, of misery weigh on the great majority of the nation, in particular the working class. The general demand, the general longing is to abolish a condition in which the existence of the whole is dependent on the carelessness of the governing, on the accidental insight or short-sighted egoism of private individuals, a condition which indeed still lacks guiding principles and general institutions, without which there can be no free activity, no security of earning a living, no true enjoyment of life. Everywhere, in agriculture, in industry, in commerce, in education etc., there is a recognised need for the most important reforms. The nation demands a free, happy life in free, happy work.

Between the will and the deed, between decision and execution, there is, however, a great distance, a hard road. Difficulties of every kind stand in the way. Not only malevolence, but incompetence, even more, will have to be overcome. Here every ounce of energy is required to overcome ignorance, narrow-minded particularism, and monopolistic aspirations; it is necessary to subordinate the conflicting interests, due to occupation and locality, to a common order which establishes and maintains the well-being of the whole, to organise work, intercourse and consumption according to the conditions of life of a great nation which strives to promote the well-being of the whole and of every individual not by war and exploitation but by peaceful exchange and united co-operation.

It is in this field, however, that the least thorough preparations have been made; here, where the need became general before the insight did, it is above all the press which is qualified to bring the existing circumstances to public notice, to examine the conditions for change, to discuss the means of reform, to help educate public opinion, to give a salutary direction to the will of the whole. This, then, is also the task of the *Neue Rheinische Zeitung*, on which it will concentrate its efforts more and more, in the measure in which political discussions retreat into the background.

No special justification is needed for the choice of the city of Cologne as the seat of such an enterprise. Cologne, the capital of the Rhine Province, the capital of all West Germany, as perhaps no other place in Germany, offers a suitable locality and the resources required for the publication of a great newspaper. Cologne can also confidently look forward to any change in the conditions of work and intercourse which is at the same time an improvement, and apart from the patriotism of its inhabitants, their local interest alone would make them sympathetic towards any reforms contributing to the well-being of the nation.

While, therefore, the prospects for the success of the *Neue Rheinische Zeitung* can in every respect be said to be most favourable, there arises the question of the financial resources which must be raised to cover the costs in the initial period, so long as the number of subscribers and advertisements have not yet made the enterprise secure. For this purpose a capital of 30,000 talers is required, half of which is to be regarded as a reserve fund. This capital is to be raised through a limited joint-stock company.

It will be divided into 600 shares of fifty talers each, and the payment will be in such instalments as to enable the less affluent also to promote the enterprise by their participation.

Lists for the subscription of shares are open at:

Herr W. Clouth, at St. Agatha No. 12

"   Wolff & Kapferer, Hochstrasse No. 55

"   Max Kemmerich, St. Katharinen 2 B

"   Esch & Henn, Kleine Sandkaul No. 1.

Please send applications from outside Cologne to:

Dr. Daniels, Mittelstrasse No. 2,

Cologne, April 1848.

By "provisional agreement" of the first shareholders, the following conditions have been added to those announced above:

1) As soon as 200 shares are subscribed, a general meeting of shareholders will be called to agree upon the Rules of the company. The latter thereupon comes into operation.

2) The management of the editorial office and the engagement of contributors and correspondents will be the responsibility of Herr Heinrich Bürgers.

Written by Heinrich Bürgers in April 1848

First published in the *Westphälisches Dampfboot* No. 12, May 17, 1848

Printed according to the journal

Published in English for the first time

MINUTES OF THE MEETING OF THE COLOGNE COMMUNITY OF THE COMMUNIST LEAGUE[344]

MEETING OF MAY 11, 1848

President Marx asks Gottschalk what his opinion or his decision is in regard to the League: what attitude towards the League he, Gottschalk, now intends to adopt.

Gottschalk states that he repeats his resignation already submitted, since the transformation undergone by the present conditions required also a recasting of the Rules of the League, and under the existing Rules his personal freedom was in jeopardy; he states, however, that in all cases where the League might call upon his energies he would when the occasion arises do everything in his power.

H. Bürgers, President
Jos. Moll, Secretary

First published in: Marx/Engels, *Gesamtausgabe*, Abt. 1, Bd. 7, 1935

Printed according to the manuscript

Published in English for the first time

ARTICLES OF THE *NEUE RHEINISCHE ZEITUNG* COMPANY[345]

Article 1

From today for a period of five years, a limited joint-stock company is formed for the purpose of publishing a daily newspaper under the title *Neue Rheinische Zeitung. Organ der Demokratie.*

Article 2

As a business the company carries the name H. Korff & Co., and a change of the latter shall have no effect on the continued existence of the company.

Article 3

The premises of the newspaper office in Cologne at any given time shall be the address of the company.

Article 4

The capital of the company, which is fixed at 30,000 Prussian talers, will be raised by 600 shares of 50 talers each, and shareholders shall at once proceed to form the company.

Article 5

Payment of shares is made, if necessary, in instalments of between 5 and 10 per cent which are called on the order of the managers[a] of the company announced by two insertions in the company's newspaper.

Article 6

If a shareholder does not pay a demanded instalment within the specified time, the company has the right either to declare forfeited the rights arising from the subscription, and from any payments already made, or to take him to court to force him to comply with contract.

Article 7

Interim receipts will be issued against payment of instalments, which on completion of payment are exchanged against shares.,

Article 8

Interim receipts and shares are signed by the company managers.

Article 9

Shares bear serial numbers, are registered and, like the interim receipts, are transferable.

Article 10

The transfer of shares and interim receipts is performed by a declaration to that effect, signed by both the transferor and the transferee, and if fifty shares are already issued in the name of the transferee, only by permission of the managers, and in this case the company reserves the right to acquire the shares presented for transfer, for the purpose of amortisation.

---

[a] In the original the word *Gerant* is used, which means the person who is legally responsible for the management of the newspaper and also the responsible publisher of the newspaper. In the article this word is rendered as "manager". In ensuing documents, where the other aspects seem to be predominant, the term "responsible publisher" is used.—*Ed.*

Statut

der

„Neuen Rheinischen Zeitungs-Gesellschaft."

---

§ 1.

Es bildet sich eine Kommandite-Aktien-Gesellschaft von heute ab auf die Dauer von fünf Jahren, welche den Zweck hat, ein Tageblatt unter dem Titel: „Neue Rheinische Zeitung, Organ der Demokratie" herausgegeben.

§ 2.

Als Firma führt die Gesellschaft den Namen H. Korff & Comp. und hat die Aenderung derselben auf das Fortbestehen der Gesellschaft keinen Einfluß.

§ 3.

Das jedesmalige Lokal der Zeitungs-Expedition in Cöln ist das Domizil der Gesellschaft.

§ 4.

Das Kapital der Gesellschaft, welches auf 30,000 Thaler Pr. Cour. festgesetzt ist, wird durch 600 Aktien, jede zu 50 Thaler zusammengebracht und treten Comparenten als Gesellschaft sofort zusammen.

§ 5.

Die Einzahlung der Aetien-Beträge erfolgt nach Bedürfniß in Raten von 5 bis 10 pCt., die Einforderung derselben geschieht gemäß Bestimmung der Geranten der Gesellschaft durch zweimalige Bekanntmachung in der Zeitung der Gesellschaft.

§ 6.

Zahlt ein Aktionair einen eingeforderten Einschuß nicht

Articles of the *Neue Rheinische Zeitung* Company

Article 11

Every shareholder shares in the gains and losses of the company in proportion to the number of his shares, but is answerable for its liabilities only with the amount of his share.

Article 12

Every shareholder living elsewhere is obliged to choose an address in Cologne; failing that, the address of the company is regarded as such.

Article 13

The heirs or assigns of a shareholder can in no circumstances apply for affixation of seals, form an opposition, demand an inventory or licitation, even if there are among them minors or other disqualified persons; they must content themselves with the annual balance-sheet and the dividends as they are fixed for the other shareholders.

Article 14

The company is represented by a manager (Hermann Korff) and two co-managers (Louis Schulz and Stephan Adolph Naut), whose shares are called in for the period of their management.

Article 15

The manager assumes legal liability for the content of the newspaper, handles the commercial business of the company, the publication of the newspaper, the editing of advertisements and checking of proofs. The commercial direction is in his hands with the co-operation and control of the two co-managers.

As emolument for their trouble the manager and co-managers receive a percentage of the income from subscriptions after deducting postage and stamp duty: 5 per cent of the first thousand subscriptions, 4 per cent of the next thousand, 3 per cent of the third thousand, 2 per cent of the fourth and thereafter 1 per cent of every thousand. The manager receives one-fifth of this amount, the two co-managers two-fifths each. In addition, the manager receives an annual salary of 800 talers. To be valid, all bills and promissory notes require the signatures of the manager and the two co-managers.

Article 16

The managers are expressly forbidden to participate, either directly or indirectly, in any similar enterprise.

Article 17

The salaried manager cannot allow a substitute to represent him without the permission of the co-managers, whereas the latter may do so any time they like on their own responsibility.

Article 18

The retirement of one or more of the managers either through death or termination of the employment does not entail the dissolution of the company and does not affect this agreement in any way. In such a case those who remain in office must in the first week after the demise or termination of employment call a general meeting to decide on the filling of the vacancy.

Article 19

After one year has passed, the manager is allowed to leave the company, giving three months notice. Likewise, the two co-managers are entitled by unanimous decision and with the co-operation of the general meeting to give three months notice to the manager. The co-managers are entitled to leave at any time, giving three months notice.

Article 20

The managers must contact a bank in the usual commercial manner and transfer to it, at interest, all cash which is not for immediate use or necessary for the current expenses of the week, so as to be able to use it at any time it may be needed. Repayments by the bank must be receipted over the signature of the manager and the two co-managers.

Article 21

The general meeting of shareholders elects annually a Supervisory Board consisting of seven members which superintends the conduct of business.

Article 22

Every member of the Supervisory Board is entitled to resign from his position if he has announced his intention in writing six weeks before. If the position of a member of the Board falls vacant, the Supervisory Board nominates a substitute who keeps his position until it is definitively filled by the general meeting.

Article 23

The Supervisory Board takes all decisions by majority vote in the presence of at least five members. If the voting is equal, the chairman has the casting vote.

Article 24

Minutes are taken of all proceedings and decisions and are signed by the Supervisory Board members present.

Article 25

The Supervisory Board meets regularly once a month; at the invitation of the chairman as often as he deems necessary, or if two members or one of the managers demand it.

Article 26

The Supervisory Board stands by the managers as controlling committee, checks the books and shares record at any time, either directly or through an authorised shareholder or non-shareholder, inspects the cash and the balance-sheet.

Article 27

The members of the Supervisory Board receive neither salary nor a premium for their trouble.

Article 28

Every year in the month of February a general meeting is held, the first of these in the year 1849. Extraordinary general meetings may be called as often as the Supervisory Board deems necessary, or if one of the managers or 20 members of the company who own at least 40 shares demand it.

Article 29

The invitation to ordinary or extraordinary general meetings is extended twice through the company's newspaper, to extraordinary ones with a brief indication of the agenda. Ordinary general meetings are called by the Supervisory Board, extraordinary ones by the latter or by one of the managers.

Article 30

The general meeting consists of all shareholders whose shareholdings have been entered in the company's register for at least six weeks. Registration is effected for the first time by signing the company contract, later upon written demand with the company. The holder of one share has one vote, of four shares two votes, of ten shares three votes, of fifteen shares four votes, of twenty and more shares five votes. Absentees can be represented by shareholders, but these can never combine more than ten votes in one person. Written authority for representation of absent shareholders must be submitted to the Supervisory Board for inspection on the day of the general meeting at the latest.

Article 31

All decisions are taken by an absolute majority; if voting is equal, the chairman has the casting vote. All elections, however, are made by simple majority. If two or more persons receive equal votes, the election is decided by lot.

Article 32

Elections are always held by secret ballot, but decisions only when holders of at least 50 shares demand it.

Article 33

In case of a secret ballot the chairman appoints two scrutineers and distributes the ballot papers which carry on the reverse side the number of votes and his signature. Every authorised representative can cast a separate ballot paper for each shareholder he represents, in addition to his own.

Article 34

Regular items for the agenda of the general meeting are:
a) Managers' report on last year's business;
b) Supervisory Board's report on the audit of the accounts;
c) decisions on any criticism raised by the Supervisory Board against the accounts, and endorsement;
d) election of members of the Supervisory Board;
e) decision on matters referred to the general meeting by the Supervisory Board, the managers, or individual shareholders.

Article 35

Special motions by individual shareholders must be received by the managers at the latest a week before the general meeting, otherwise they are entitled to defer the decision to the next general meeting.

Article 36

Minutes of the proceedings of the general meeting are taken by a shareholder appointed by the chairman; to be valid, they must be signed by the chairman, the Supervisory Board members present, and at least two other shareholders.

Article 37

The managers draw up a balance-sheet annually on 1st December and together with the receipts pass it on for auditing to the Supervisory Board at the latest on 20th January. The Board must present it to the ordinary general meeting together with its report.

Article 38

During the last days before the general meeting the balance-sheet and receipts must be available to all shareholders for inspection in the business premises of the company.

Article 39

If at the closing of the annual accounts after deduction of interest a net surplus is shown, then 1) all contracted royalties are settled, and

2) ten per cent is put to a reserve fund for unexpected losses and improvements of the newspaper and for extraordinary expenditures, and 3) the remaining sum is distributed as dividends among the shareholders.

Article 40

The use of the reserve fund, which must not exceed the sum of 10,000 talers, is decided by the general meeting upon the motions of the Supervisory Board and the managers.

Article 41

The managers announce by two insertions in the company's newspaper where the interest and dividends can be collected annually commencing on 1st March.

Article 42

Interest and dividends which have not been collected within two years from the pay-day announced, or collection of which has not been notified by any person within the specified period, become the property of the company.

Article 43

The company is automatically dissolved before the expiry of the period specified in Article 1 if losses occur which exhaust four-fifths of the subscribed share capital.

Article 44

In all these cases the managers must call an extraordinary meeting which shall decide on the manner in which the company is to be liquidated.

Article 45

Changes of Articles can be decided at a general meeting by a majority of three-quarters of the voters present or represented if their general content was indicated in the notice.

Article 46

Disputes between the company and shareholders shall be settled by arbitration.

Printed by W. Clouth in Cologne

First published as a separate leaflet in July 1848

Printed according to the leaflet

Published in English for the first time

LEGAL INVESTIGATION
AGAINST THE *NEUE RHEINISCHE ZEITUNG*

Cologne, July 7. The responsible publisher[a] of the *Neue Rheinische Zeitung,* Korff, and its editor-in-chief, Karl Marx, were interrogated yesterday at the office of the examining magistrate, both of them being accused of insulting or libelling the Chief Public Prosecutor, Herr Zweiffel, and the policemen who arrested Anneke. The interrogation began at 4 o'clock. After its conclusion, at about 6 o'clock, the examining magistrate and Public Prosecutor *Hecker* accompanied the accused to the office of the editorial board, where with the aid of a police inspector a search of the premises took place in order to discover the manuscript and thus the author of the inculpated article.[b] There was found a note in an unknown handwriting but it was not a copy of the inculpated article. This note was added to the dossier of the indictment against *Marx and consorts.* In view of this last expression, it seems that it is intended to institute proceedings against the editorial board *en masse* although the responsible publisher, Korff, who alone appends his signature to the newspaper, undertakes, of course, also the legal responsibility for it.

First published in the *Neue Rheinische Zeitung* No. 38, July 8, 1848

Printed according to the newspaper

Published in English for the first time

---

[a] *Gerant.* See footnote on p. 544.—*Ed.*
[b] See this volume, pp. 177-79.—*Ed.*

LEGAL PROCEEDINGS
AGAINST THE *NEUE RHEINISCHE ZEITUNG*

Cologne, July 22. This morning the editor-in-chief of the *Neue Rheinische Zeitung*, Karl Marx, was again summoned before the examining magistrate to be interrogated on account of the incriminated article on the arrest of Herr Anneke. This time the summons did not include the responsible publisher of the newspaper, Herr Korff.

First published in the *Neue Rheinische Zeitung* No. 53, July 23, 1848

Printed according to the newspaper

Published in English for the first time

REPORT OF THE SPEECHES
MADE BY MARX AND ENGELS
AT THE GENERAL MEETING
OF THE DEMOCRATIC SOCIETY IN COLOGNE
ON AUGUST 4, 1848[346]

[...] Hereupon Dr. *Marx*, editor-in-chief of the *Neue Rheinische Zeitung*, examines the principles of Herr Weitling, pronounced at the meeting of the Democratic Society held a fortnight ago,[a] and in a pithy and fairly long speech seeks to prove, on the grounds of the historical development of the revolutions that have taken place during the last few centuries, that the separation of political and social interests assumed by Weitling is as unthinkable as their direct opposition, that, rather, the political and social interests must interpenetrate. The claim that social development retards political development was also incorrect; unfortunately, in respect of social development we Germans had only now arrived at the point which the French had already reached in the year 1789; the present contradictions could only be resolved by sharply defining them and emphasising the interests of the individual classes; only in this way that is by using intellectual weapons, can an amicable settlement be achieved. The disregard of the position of the various strata of the population to one another, the refusal to make reciprocal concessions and wrong notions about class relations have led to the bloody outcome in Paris. The dictatorship which Weitling proposed as the most desirable constitutional form is, for similar reasons, regarded by Marx as impractical and quite unfeasible, since power cannot be attained by a single class; the intention to carry on a dictatorship in accordance with a system devised by a single brain, deserves to be called nonsensical. On the contrary, the governing power, just as the Provisional Government in Paris, must consist of the most heteroge-

---

[a] On July 21, 1848.—*Ed.*

neous elements, which by means of an exchange of views have to agree on the most appropriate mode of administration.

Herr *Engels* reports on the Government's rejection of the application for citizenship of Dr. Marx.[a] As the latter was a Rhineland Prussian by birth, and as since the March revolution all political refugees have had their citizenship restored to them, this interpretation of citizenship involved injustice and breach of faith; he would thereby be regarded as a foreigner who could be expelled at any time.

First published in the newspaper *Der Wächter am Rhein*, 2. Dutzend, No. 1, August 23, 1848

Printed according to the newspaper

Published in English for the first time

---

[a] See this volume, pp. 407-10.—*Ed.*

ANNOUNCEMENT OF THE CONVOCATION OF THE RHENISH DISTRICT CONGRESS OF DEMOCRATIC ASSOCIATIONS[347]

Cologne, August 4. In accordance with the decision of the Democratic Congress in Frankfurt, which resolved that Cologne should be the seat of the Executive for the Prussian Rhine Province and authorised the democratic associations there to convene a district congress for organising the democratic party in the province, the Central Committee of the associations here[348] invites all democratically-minded associations in the Rhine Province to appoint delegates to this congress, which will take place here on Sunday, August 13. The delegates must report their arrival in the upstairs hall of the Stollwerk premises.

The Central Committee
of the three democratic associations in Cologne

Schneider II, Marx
(For the Democratic Society)

Moll, Schapper   **Becker, Schützendorf**
(For the Workers' Association) (For the Association for Workers
and Employers

At a moment when reaction, operating under the name of itinerant "constitutional" congresses, is reviewing and concentrating its forces throughout the state, democrats do not need any more exhaustive exposition of the necessity for an energetic counter-attack. They merely have to make use of the same freedoms which the Association "With God for King and Fatherland"[a] and its branch associations enjoy.

First published in the *Neue Rheinische Zeitung* No. 66, August 5, 1848

Printed according to the newspaper

Published in English for the first time

---

[a] Words from the decree of Frederick William III issued on March 17, 1813, announcing the setting up of the army reserve.— *Ed.*

THE LEGAL PROCEEDINGS
AGAINST THE *NEUE RHEINISCHE ZEITUNG*

Cologne, August 4. Our entanglement with the office of the Public Prosecutor continues to take its course. Last Monday the responsible publisher *Korff* was again summoned before the examining magistrate and yesterday two of our editors, Dronke and Engels, were cited as *witnesses*. Dronke is away at present; Engels appeared but was not interrogated on oath, since it is supposed that the note recently confiscated in our office[a] is in his handwriting and it is possible, therefore, that he, too, will be involved in the indictment.

It is clear that the prosecution is not satisfied with the manager functioning as the responsible publisher. The editor-in-chief has to be implicated, the author of the article in question has to be discovered, the editors — *any one* of whom could be the author of the article in question — have to be made to give evidence *against one another*, indeed, if possible, *against themselves*.

First published in the *Neue Rheinische Zeitung* No. 66, August 5, 1848

Printed according to the newspaper

Published in English for the first time

---

[a] See this volume, p. 554.—*Ed.*

KARL MARX TO POLICE SUPERINTENDENT GEIGER[349]

To Police Superintendent *Geiger*
Here.

Sir, I inform you that I have immediately appealed[a] to the Ministry of the Interior against the paper drawn up by you[b] and that I continue to regard myself as before as a citizen of the German Empire.

Cologne, August 5, 1848

Editor-in-Chief of the *Neue Rheinische Zeitung* Dr. *Karl Marx*

First published in the *Zeitschrift für Geschichtswissenschaft* No. 3, 1968

Printed according to the manuscript

Published in English for the first time

---

[a] See this volume, pp. 407-10.— *Ed.*
[b] Ibid., p. 408.— *Ed.*

FROM THE MINUTES OF THE GENERAL MEETING OF THE DEMOCRATIC SOCIETY IN COLOGNE HELD ON AUGUST 11, 1848

After the minutes of the preceding general meeting had been read and approved at the request of acting President Marx, Herr *Wolff* read out the protest to the German National Assembly against the partition of Poland,[a] which was joyfully greeted and adopted with acclamation.

Herr *Rittinghausen* gave many reasons vindicating Herr Marx's right to citizenship recently contested by the Prussian Government.[b] He considered that the best thing would be, by means of a deputation tomorrow, to make the Government reverse this illegal and altogether ridiculous action, and if the Government is unwilling to do that, to send a protest at such behaviour directly to the Minister. The protest was read and adopted, and in the event of the refusal of citizenship for Marx not being withdrawn people will be invited to sign the protest this evening.

Herr *Marx* dwelt in more detail on the grounds proving the injustice of the measures adopted against him, and the applause of the whole meeting testified to the force of his arguments. The circumstance on account of which the Government refused him the right of citizenship really lies in the fact that previously attempts had been made in vain to win him over to the side of the Government.

Herr *Engels* reported a new vexatious police measure against Schapper by which the latter is threatened with deportation.[c] He described the intervention of the police and especially stressed that in any case Schapper as a citizen of Nassau has the right to be

---

[a] See this volume, pp. 564-65.—*Ed.*
[b] Ibid., pp. 407-10.—*Ed.*
[c] Ibid., pp. 383-84.—*Ed.*

regarded as a German and as such, by the decision of the Frankfurt National Assembly, is entitled to reside in any of the 38 German states.

Rittinghausen, Schneider and Bürgers were elected as delegates to put the case of Marx and Schapper before the *Regierungspräsident* and the Police Superintendent and try to effect a reversal of the decisions in question.

Deputy *Gladbach*, whose appearance was greeted with stormy applause, explained at length that salvation should not be expected to come either from the Berlin Assembly or from the Frankfurt Assembly.

Herr *Engels* stressed that it was Gladbach who had always distinguished himself by his liberal outlook and audacity and especially by his vigorous protest against the way the Schleswig-Holsteiners were dealt with in Spandau.[a] Thereupon three cheers were given for Herr Gladbach.

First published in the newspaper *Der Wächter am Rhein*, 2. Dutzend, No. 2, August 25, 1848

Printed according to the newspaper

Published in English for the first time

---

[a] See this volume, pp. 180-81 and 192-93.—*Ed.*

PROTEST OF THE DEMOCRATIC SOCIETY
IN COLOGNE AGAINST THE INCORPORATION
OF POSEN IN THE GERMAN CONFEDERATION[350]

Cologne, August 12. The *Democratic Society* of Cologne has submitted the following protest to the National Assembly:

To the High National Assembly!

The Democratic Society of Cologne, considering
1. that Germany, which is engaged in a struggle for freedom, does not desire to oppress other nationalities but to promote their efforts for freedom and independence;
2. that the liberation of Poland is a vital question for Germany;
3. that Poland has in fact been repeatedly robbed of its freedom and national independence by three despots;
4. that since 1792 all attacks upon Poland and all partitions of Poland have always been aimed by reaction against the freedom of the whole of Europe, and, on the other hand, whenever a liberation of the peoples took place there was insistence also on the restoration of Poland;
5. that even the Committee of Fifty,[351] in the name of the German people, indignantly rejected any share in the outrage committed against Poland and clearly proclaimed the duty of the German people to co-operate in the restoration of an independent Poland;
6. that after the March revolution even the King of Prussia, compelled by the force of public opinion, solemnly assented to the reorganisation of Posen;
7. that despite that the National Assembly in Frankfurt, which, it is true, arose from indirect elections, in its sitting of July 27, 1848, voted for the incorporation of three-quarters of the Grand Duchy of Posen in the as yet non-existent German Empire and thereby incurred the guilt of a new partition of

Poland and the flouting of liberty in the same way as did the Vienna Congress and the German Federal Diet;

8. that nevertheless the healthy part of the German people will not and cannot take any part in oppressing the Polish nation for the benefit of reaction and in the interests of a number of Prussian bureaucrats, landowners and hucksterers;

resolves in its sitting today:

to make a formal protest against the decision adopted by the German National Assembly on July 27, 1848, in regard to the Grand Duchy of Posen and herewith to lay before Germany, Poland and the whole of Europe its vigorous objections to this incorporation which is solely of advantage to the reactionary party in Prussia, Russia and Austria.

On behalf of the *Democratic Society,*
The Committee

First published in the *Neue Rheinische Zeitung* No. 74, August 13, 1848

Printed according to the newspaper

Published in English for the first time

THE LEGAL INVESTIGATION
AGAINST THE *NEUE RHEINISCHE ZEITUNG*

Cologne, August 12. The interesting relations between our news-paper and the Public Prosecutor's office continue to take their course. Yesterday one of our editors, Ernst Dronke, was again sum-moned to appear before the examining magistrate as a witness. There was no interrogation on oath since information had been received that, on the evening after Anneke's arrest, Dronke had visited Anneke's wife and obtained there particulars about the arrest. When the witness asked against whom the indictment was being made, an explanation of the term "Marx and consorts" was given to the effect that it was merely possible that the responsible publisher Korff would be indicted whereas they intended to indict the editor-in-chief, Karl Marx, as the supposed author of the incrimi-nated article.

Incidentally, Dronke stated that he did not consider himself bound to tell the truth, since as editor it was possible he might be implicated in the authorship of the article and he would not testify against himself.

First published in the *Neue Rheinische Zeitung* No. 74, August 13, 1848

Printed according to the newspaper

Published in English for the first time

RECORD OF ENGELS' SPEECH AT THE PUBLIC MEETING OF THE FIRST CONGRESS OF RHENISH DEMOCRATS HELD AT COLOGNE ON AUGUST 13, 1848

FROM A NEWSPAPER REPORT

Engels from Cologne: A characteristic feature of the Rhineland is hatred of Prussian officialdom and dyed-in-the-wool Prussianism; it is to be hoped that this attitude will endure.

First published in the *Neue Rheinische Zeitung* No. 101, September 13, 1848

Printed according to the newspaper

Published in English for the first time

NOTE IN THE *NEUE RHEINISCHE ZEITUNG* ON MARX'S DEPARTURE FOR VIENNA

Cologne, August 24. The editor-in-chief of the *Neue Rheinische Zeitung*, Karl Marx, yesterday went to Vienna for a few days.[352]

First published in the *Neue Rheinische Zeitung* No. 85, August 25, 1848

Printed according to the newspaper

Published in English for the first time

FROM A NEWSPAPER ITEM
LISTING THE NAMES OF VISITORS
WHO HAD JUST ARRIVED IN VIENNA

New Arrivals
August 27

Herr Steriol Damesa, merchant, from Semlin.— Baroness Beust, wife of the royal and imperial cavalry captain from Tarnow.— Herr Anton Feuerstein, merchant, from Schwarzenberg.— Herr Carl Marx, Ph. D., from Paris.[353]— Messrs. Alex. Kusa and Basil. Ghika, men of private means, from England.[a]

First published in the *Wiener Zeitung* No. 236, August 30, 1848

Printed according to the newspaper

Published in English for the first time

---

[a] There follows a list of other persons who had arrived in Vienna that day.— *Ed.*

NEWSPAPER REPORTS OF MARX'S SPEECH
IN THE VIENNA DEMOCRATIC ASSOCIATION
ON AUGUST 28, 1848

[*Neue Rheinische Zeitung* No. 94, September 5, 1848]

Vienna, August 29. At yesterday's meeting of the Democratic Association it was discussed whether the Association should approach the Emperor or the Imperial Diet so as to bring about the downfall of Minister Schwarzer or rather the fall of the entire Doblhoff Ministry. Herr Julius Fröbel and Herr Marx were present as guests and both took part in the debate from different standpoints.

Herr Julius Fröbel was of the opinion that the Association should approach the Emperor, whereas Herr Marx maintained that the democratic principle was to be found in the Imperial Diet. No one here is surprised that the Berlin "theoretical" so-called democrats in practice seek to "reach agreement" with the sovereigns.

[*Der Radikale* No. 64, August 31, 1848]

Vienna, August 30. The meeting of the Democratic Association on the 28th of this month is one of the most interesting and important events in our current history. Among the guests present we mention the well-known political writer *Julius Fröbel* and the editor of the *Neue Rheinische Zeitung,* Herr *Karl Marx*; both of them have become important on account of their particular fate. As writers, too, they occupy a definite position which is of importance for Germany....

Herr *Marx* was of the opinion that it was a matter of indifference *who* was Minister, for here too—as in Paris—it was now a question of the struggle between the bourgeoisie and the proletariat. His speech was very witty, trenchant and instructive....

[*Wiener Zeitung* No. 252 (supplement), September 17, 1848]

... in a Viennese Association, where a debate about the dismissal of the Ministers was in progress, an *academic from abroad* really had the audacity to say the following:

"Up to now the speakers mentioned only two great powers, the Imperial Diet and the Emperor, to whom they intended to appeal in order to bring about the dismissal of the Ministers; but the greatest power, the people, has been forgotten! *We must appeal to the people and must try to influence it employing every possible means. We must raise a storm against the Government, and must work towards this end in every possible way, even using Mephistophelian means. We must use the press, posters and discussions to achieve this.*" [354]

Printed according to the newspapers

Published in English for the first time

NEWSPAPER REPORTS OF MARX'S SPEECH IN THE FIRST WORKERS' ASSOCIATION OF VIENNA ON AUGUST 30, 1848

[*Die Constitution* No. 133, September 1, 1848]

Dr. Marx spoke about the workers, especially the German workers abroad.—The national workshops and the latest workers' revolution in Paris. He asserted that the German workers could be proud that a considerable number of those deported were their compatriots.—The Chartists in England and the recent Chartist movements. England and the complete emancipation of the workers of Europe. Belgium.

[*Der Volksfreund* No. 109, September 3, 1848]

Dr. *Marx*, editor of the [*Neue*] *Rheinische Zeitung*, greeted the Association and said that he felt it an honour to speak also to a workers' association in Vienna, as he had already done in Paris, London and Brussels.

Printed according to the newspapers

Published in English for the first time

REPORT OF MARX'S LECTURE ON WAGE LABOUR AND CAPITAL AT THE MEETING OF THE FIRST WORKERS' ASSOCIATION OF VIENNA ON SEPTEMBER 2, 1848[355]

...Dr. Marx delivered a fairly long lecture on wage labour and capital. He said in his introduction that all revolutions are social revolutions. Capital consists not of money, but of raw materials, instruments of production and articles of consumption; wage labour produces capital as distinct from the products. The assertion that the interests of the capitalist and of the wage labourer are identical is false. Along with division of labour, competition among the workers grows and wages fall; but this occurs still more owing to the use of machines. Production costs determine wages. Civilisation does not increase the well-being of the workers, but does the opposite. Taxes and the price of the necessities of life increase.

The lecturer spoke also about the remedies that had been tried and their inadequacy, such as, for example, Malthus' theory of over-population. The workhouses in England. Industrial training. Abolition of protective tariffs and of taxes. Finally, he stated that conditions must improve because not all the workers are used as workers, but part of them are maintained....

First published in *Die Constitution* No. 136, September 5, 1848

Printed according to the newspaper

Published in English for the first time

REPORT OF PLATOON LEADER MENTÉS
OF THE COLOGNE CIVIC MILITIA

Third Standard   Company No. XVI

Report

of the 5th Platoon of the Standard Guard of September 1, 1848

Absent from the standard guard without excuse:

Corporal Herr C. Mohr	Sculptor
ditto " Ferd. Rhien	Pharmacist
Militiaman J. A. Fischer	Cap-maker
ditto G. Weerth	Editor of the *Neue Rheinische Zeitung*
ditto E. Dronke	ditto
ditto F. Engels	ditto
ditto F. Schnabel	Cap-maker[a]
ditto C. Kayser	Merchant
ditto R. Kayser	ditto
ditto M. Olzem	ditto
ditto Jac. Schmidt	Shoemaker
ditto Fried. Greven	Butcher
ditto Wm. Engels	Garment-maker
ditto Joh. Struben	ditto
ditto Ign. Wieners	—
ditto J. P. Mohr	Roofer
ditto M. Woocker	Grocer
ditto C. Deckker	—

Cologne, September 2, 1848

Platoon leader
M. Mentés

Printed according to the manuscript
Published for the first time

---

[a] In the original the whole line is crossed out and the following note inserted: "he turned up".— *Ed.*

REPLY

No. 201 of the *Breslauer Zeitung* publishes a report from Berlin that knight Schnapphahnski[356] has bought many shares in the *Neue Rheinische Zeitung* and for this reason the series of feature articles about him has come to an end, because it is not possible for a newspaper to wage a polemic against its own shareholders. The allegedly democratic *Düsseldorfer Zeitung* considers itself bound to reproduce this insinuation in its columns. Whatever concoctions it may be desired to invent in Berlin, a *Silesian* newspaper ought to have known that this assertion was a lie and why it was a lie. Unfortunately for it, however, the treacherous assertion comes too late. No. 92 of the *Neue Rheinische Zeitung*, which was published long before the arrival of No. 201 of the *Breslauer Zeitung*, contains the continuation of the feature articles in question. Moreover, the *Neue Rheinische Zeitung* is the newspaper of a party and has already given sufficient proof that it is not to be bought.

**The Responsible Publishers
of the *Neue Rheinische Zeitung***

First published in the supplement to the *Neue Rheinische Zeitung* No. 93, September 3, 1848

Printed according to the newspaper

Published in English for the first time

LEGAL PROCEEDINGS
AGAINST THE *NEUE RHEINISCHE ZEITUNG*

Cologne, September 5. Yesterday one of our editors, *Friedrich Engels*, was again summoned to appear before the examining magistrate in the investigation against Marx and consorts,[a] but this time not as a witness but as co-accused. The preliminary investigation has ended, and if the Public Prosecutor's office does not make any further proposals, the Council Chamber will shortly have to decide whether Marx, Engels and Korff will have to appear before the Assize Court on the charge of insulting or libelling Chief Public Prosecutor Zweiffel and the six policemen.

First published in the *Neue Rheinische Zeitung* No. 95, September 6, 1848

Printed according to the newspaper

Published in English for the first time

---

[a] See this volume, p. 566.—*Ed.*

ADDRESS
TO THE GERMAN NATIONAL ASSEMBLY IN FRANKFURT ADOPTED BY A PUBLIC MEETING HELD IN COLOGNE ON SEPTEMBER 7, 1848[357]

An armistice with Denmark, which has been ratified by Prussia, has been presented by the Prussian Government to the Imperial Government, and by the Imperial Government to you.

The undersigned German citizens resident in Cologne protest against this armistice, and, considering:

1. that Prussia has concluded this armistice on the basis of an authorisation issued by the Imperial Regent[a] but not countersigned by any responsible Imperial Minister, and hence legally invalid;

2. that Prussia has exceeded this authorisation in every point thus pursuing only the interests of absolutism and its own, un-German plans;

3. that no political agreement may be concluded without *previous* authorisation of the National Assembly;

4. that this armistice forces the victorious German troops to an ignominious retreat, instals a Danish Government in Schleswig-Holstein and Lauenburg, betrays to Denmark the Provisional Government, which arose from the revolution and was recognised by Germany, and all its decisions; withdraws the Schleswig troops from the German High Command and delivers Schleswig-Holstein to civil war;

5. that whereas Germany has constantly fought the revolution in Italy, Posen and Prague, the Danish war is the only one in which Germany defends the revolution against legitimism and absolutism;

---

[a] Archduke John of Austria.— *Ed.*

request you: to *reject* the armistice concluded by Prussia in violation
of the authorisation and in defiance of the Central Authority and the
National Assembly, and to defend the revolution in Schleswig-
Holstein even at the risk of a European war, and never again to
entrust the present Prussian Government with diplomatic negotiations on behalf of Germany; and, finally, to declare that Germany
will on no account force the Danish-speaking North Schleswig to
become a part of Germany against its will.

Cologne, September 7, 1848

First published in the *Neue Rheinische
Zeitung* No. 98, September 9, 1848

Printed according to the newspaper

Published in English for the first
time

MINMINUTES OF THE COMMITTEE MEETING
OF THE COLOGNE WORKERS' ASSOCIATION
HELD ON SEPTEMBER 11, 1848

After reading the minutes of the previous meeting, the secretary, Citizen Kalker, declared that because of his departure from here, which would take place tomorrow, it would no longer be possible for him to give his services as secretary of the Association and that he herewith handed over his functions to the Association.

Thereupon Citizen Blum jun. was proposed as secretary and accepted.

The latter then took the floor and related the detailed circumstances of the arrest of himself and Citizen Salget last Sunday evening in Wesseling by the Burgomaster of that place.[a] For, on their way back to Cologne, after visiting a Workers' Association founded earlier in Cassel, they visited the Workers' Association in Wesseling; they had spoken there about social reform for barely a quarter of an hour, when Geier, the local Burgomaster, suddenly appeared accompanied by a policeman, arrested them, and placed them in custody in the latter's house, but next morning, with the most friendly civility, he let them go home peacefully.

President Moll thereupon asked Citizen Blum whether he had perhaps promised the Burgomaster of Wesseling not to take any steps against him, and when the question was answered in the negative, he moved that, to safeguard their rights and prevent similar illegal and arbitrary arrests, the meeting should decide to take the necessary steps, namely through the courts, which was agreed unanimously.

Citizen Röser requested the managing committee of the Society to invite the Workers' Association in Frechen to the public meeting to

[a] See this volume, p. 426.—*Ed.*

be held on the 15th in Worringen. The secretary was instructed to comply.

Citizen Dronke: We have now reached a point which could be more important and fraught with more consequences than many might perhaps think. The Government of Action has fallen, along with its world-enchanting financial plans. But let us not assume that we are now at the goal of our desires, or that anything will be done for us; let us not even count on getting a Government of the Left. On the contrary, we now have the prospect of a Government which does not even belong to the Chamber and will consist of people from the past, von Vincke etc. Behind such a Government stands absolutism in all its grandeur, all its insolence and arrogance. It will probably wish to disperse the Chamber with the aid of Pomeranian bayonets, and then the struggle between monarchy and nation will be inevitable. Perhaps while we are sitting here they are already fighting on the barricades in Berlin.

Thereupon the meeting turned to the social question, and President Moll remarked that we had come to a halt on the question whether an organisation of work was possible or not.[358] People often threw at us the failure of the national workshops in France[359] in order to prove that an organisation of work was impossible.

Citizen Engels made a lengthy speech on this subject. His speech was received with great applause.

After a written reply from the local Town Council had been read, concerning the request that the expenses of our delegates to the workers' congress in Frankfurt[360] be defrayed, in which the Town Council asks for further details, the meeting was closed.

Voluntary contributions amounted to 11 silver groschen and 7 pfennigs.

First published in the *Zeitung des Arbeiter-Vereines zu Köln* No. 33, September 21, 1848

Printed according to the newspaper

Published in English for the first time

LETTER WRITTEN BY VON KÜHLWETTER, MINISTER OF THE INTERIOR, TO KARL MARX [361]

To *Dr. Marx*, Esquire, in *Cologne*

In reply to your submission of the 23rd of last month,[a] I have to inform you that I cannot consider it illegal that for the time being the Royal Government in Cologne has rejected your request to be accorded the status of Prussian, since you do not possess a *right* to naturalisation; for your status of Prussian became extinct under Paragraph 20 of the law of December 31, 1842, Statute Book 1843, p. 17, by your acceptance of the Deed of Release which you requested for the purpose of emigrating to North America in the year 1845,[362] of which you also availed yourself when you settled abroad. A claim to readmission, however, is neither conferred on the emigrant by that law nor can it be derived from the decision of the Prussian Assembly of March 30 of this year nor from general legal principles.

Berlin, September 12, 1848

Minister of the Interior
von Kühlwetter

First published in the *Frankfurter Zeitung und Handelsblatt* No. 176, June 27, 1913

Printed according to the manuscript

Published in English for the first time

---

[a] See this volume, pp. 407-10.— *Ed.*

MASS MEETING
AND THE COMMITTEE OF PUBLIC SAFETY

Cologne, September 14. We return to the subject of yesterday's mass meeting and its results, since these have caused a fairly considerable sensation in our city.

The mass meeting on the Frankenplatz was opened shortly after 12 o'clock by Herr W. Wolff, who briefly explained its purpose and proposed that Herr H. Bürgers should preside over it. Herr Bürgers, who was elected by acclamation, came on to the platform and gave the floor again to Herr Wolff, who then proposed that a Committee of Public Safety be formed to represent the parts of the population of Cologne not represented in the existing legal authorities. Herr F. Engels seconded the motion, which was supported also by Herr H. Becker and Herr E. Dronke. The proposal was adopted amid stormy applause by the audience of at least 5,000-6,000 persons, with only five votes against, after no opposer had come forward despite repeated invitations. It was then decided to fix the number of members of the Committee at 30, and these 30 were elected.[363] Since these included also two, Gottschalk and Anneke, who were under arrest, two substitutes for them were also elected.

Herr F. Engels then proposed the following address to the Berlin Assembly:

To the Assembly which is to agree on the Prussian Constitution in Berlin.

The undersigned citizens of Cologne,
considering:

that the Assembly which is to agree on the Prussian Constitution has made it the bounden duty of the Government to issue without further delay the decree decided on August 9 concerning reactionary efforts of officers so as to calm the country and also avoid a breach with the Assembly [a];

that in consequence of this decision the Auerswald-Hansemann Government has been dismissed and the King has charged Imperial Minister Beckerath, who has just been overthrown, to form a new Government;

that Herr Beckerath by no means affords the requisite guarantees for implementing the decision of the Assembly; and that, on the contrary, in view of his known counter-revolutionary sentiments, an attempt to dissolve the Assembly is to be expected;

that an Assembly elected by the people for reaching agreement on the Constitution between King and people cannot be unilaterally dissolved, because otherwise the Crown would not be on a level with, but *above* the Assembly;

that a dissolution of the Assembly would therefore be a coup d'état;

call upon the [members of the] Assembly,

in the event of an attempt to dissolve the Assembly, to do their duty and defend their seats even against the force of bayonets.

This address was unanimously adopted, following which the meeting came to an end.

Although numerous delegates from the Citizens' Association were present in the upper parts of the square, and although it is said that a number of well-known "wailers"[364] did their utmost to recruit rowdies by persuasion and the offer of money, and furthermore although policemen in plain clothes were present in fairly large numbers, nevertheless the meeting was skilful enough to prevent all attempts at disturbing the peace.

Meanwhile the commanders of the civic militia were sitting in the Town Hall and debating what to do, for some of them considered that disturbances were bound to occur. In the middle of their deliberations the door opened and the leaders of the Citizens' Association burst into the room, declaring that the Committee of Public Safety was the first step towards revolution, that Cologne was in danger and the red republic on the verge of being proclaimed,

---

[a] See this volume, pp. 417-18.—*Ed.*

584   Appendices

and that if the civic militia by itself was insufficient to maintain order, the *Citizens' Association with all its resources* would put itself *at the disposal of Herr von Wittgenstein*! Herr von Wittgenstein was adroit enough to refuse this offer and to refrain also from calling any of the civic militia to arms. The consequences proved how right the civic militia was on this occasion.

Not satisfied with this, while the mass meeting was still in progress, the gentlemen of the Citizens' Association posted up copies of a "Protest", which we reproduce below. Within five minutes the Protest, which was *unsigned*, disappeared without trace from every part of the city. Towards evening it reappeared as a leaflet in bold type, printed at the press of the *Kölnische Zeitung* and distributed to subscribers to this newspaper. This time it had the following amusing introduction:

Cologne, September 13, 1848

The so-called democrats want to exploit the alarm caused by the latest decisions of the Assemblies in Frankfurt and Berlin in order to regain the ground they have increasingly lost and to provoke a conflict at all costs. With this aim, too, the significance and danger of the friction between the army and the citizens which occurred in Cologne on the 11th of this month has been recklessly depicted with deliberate exaggeration and exploited for criminal purposes.[365] By means of a wall-poster, even this morning a mass meeting was convened to be held in the open air at midday, and this meeting actually elected by acclamation a list of persons who had been proposed and agreed upon in advance, to a Committee of Public Safety.

It is unquestionably true that no one should recognise such an authority, which has arisen from a casually assembled mass of people, bypassing the existing official bodies, and that the members of this committee, should they presume to act as such, at once make themselves liable to legal proceedings. It is however better to prevent crimes than to punish them after they have been committed and perhaps claimed many victims.

Hence it is our duty to warn all citizens and to call their attention to the present danger.

To this end, the following protest is issued, together with an appeal:

Protest

The formation of a Committee of Public Safety is the first step towards

Revolution.

Whoever wants true freedom and order is invited to support the existing authorities with all his might, to oppose the criminal efforts of a minority and to protest against the formation of a Committee of Public Safety.

In particular, all members of the civic militia are urged to do their duty and energetically protect law and order. The pretended danger from the army is non-existent, but the real danger arises from the formation of a Committee of Public Safety.

Several members of the managing committee of the Cologne Citizens' Association.

The Committee of Public Safety held its first meeting yesterday evening and in the first place decided to file this amusing protest, and the gentlemen of the Citizens' Association will evidently have to be satisfied with that. The Committee elected a president,[a] a secretary[b] and three members of an Executive Committee.[c] Furthermore, it adopted a communication addressed to the *Regierungspräsident*, the Commandant's office, the Town Council, and the command of the civic militia, in which it notified these authorities of its formation and informed them that it would use all legal means to pursue the aim of maintaining calm, in agreement with the authorities wherever possible, but at the same time watching over the preservation of the people's rights. It resolved moreover to announce this by means of a wall-poster to the inhabitants of Cologne. We shall publish both documents tomorrow.

This morning, people's minds have already been to some extent set at rest. People laugh at yesterday's alarm which caused them to see in the Committee a Provisional Government, a *comité de salut public*, a conspiracy for a red republic, in short, everything but what it actually is: a *committee* elected directly and publicly by the people, a committee which undertakes the task of representing the interests of the part of the population not represented in the legally instituted authorities, a committee which operates only in a legal way and has no intention of wanting to arrogate any other authority than the moral influence which the right of free association, the laws, and the confidence of the electors allow it to exert.

First published in the *Neue Rheinische Zeitung* No. 103, September 15, 1848

Printed according to the newspaper

Published in English for the first time

---

[a] Hermann Becker.— *Ed.*
[b] Funk.— *Ed.*
[c] Weyll, Bernigau and Moll.— *Ed.*

MASS MEETING IN WORRINGEN

Cologne, September 18. Yesterday a large public meeting took place at Worringen. From Cologne five or six large Rhine barges, each with a few hundred persons, and with the red flag at the prow, made the trip down the Rhine. More or less numerous delegations were present from Neuss, Düsseldorf, Krefeld, Hitdorf, Frechen and Rheindorf. The meeting, which was held in a meadow at the side of the Rhine, comprised at least 6,000-8,000 persons.

Karl *Schapper* from Cologne was appointed chairman, and Friedrich *Engels* from Cologne secretary. On a proposal put by the chairman, the meeting declared unanimously, except for one vote, in favour of a republic, and in fact for a democratic social republic, a *red republic*.

On the proposal of Ernst *Dronke* from Cologne, the same address to the Berlin Assembly that had been adopted the previous Wednesday at the meeting on the Frankenplatz in Cologne (in which the Assembly was called upon, in the event of its being dissolved, not to give way even before the force of bayonets [a]) was also unanimously adopted by the Worringen meeting.

On the proposal of Joseph *Moll* from Cologne, it was decided to *recognise* the Committee of Public Safety elected at the public meeting in Cologne and on the motion of a member of the meeting three hearty cheers were given for this Committee.

---

[a] See this volume, pp. 582-84.—*Ed.*

On the proposal of Friedrich *Engels* from Cologne, the following address was unanimously adopted:

To the German National Assembly in Frankfurt.

The German citizens here assembled hereby declare that if as a result of the resistance of the Prussian Government to the decisions of the National Assembly and the Central Authority a conflict should arise between Prussia and Germany, they will be ready to sacrifice their lives and property on the side of Germany.

Worringen, September 17, 1848

On the proposal of Schultes from Hitdorf it was resolved that the *Kölnische Zeitung* did not represent the interests of the Rhine Province.

In addition, there were speeches by W. *Wolff* from Cologne, F. *Lassalle* from Düsseldorf, *Esser* from Neuss, *Weyll, Wachter, Becker* and *Reichhelm* from Cologne, *Wallraf* from Frechen, *Müller,* a member of the Worringen Workers' Association, *Leven* from Rheindorf, and *Imandt* from Krefeld. The proceedings concluded with a short speech by Henry *Brisbane* of New York, the well-known editor of the democratic-socialist *New-York Tribune.*

During the meeting, news came from a trustworthy source that it was intended "on Tuesday to send the 27th Regiment again to Cologne, to draw in also the remaining battalions of the regiment, to provoke conflicts between the soldiers and the citizens, and to take advantage of this occasion to proclaim the city in a state of siege, to disarm the civic militia, and in short to deal with us in the same way as with Mainz".[a]

In case this report should actually prove to be well founded and a clash take place, the inhabitants of the areas around Cologne present at the meeting promised their help. In fact, the people from Worringen are only waiting to be called upon for them to appear on the scene.

Let the ex-commander of the civic militia, Herr Wittgenstein, take note of this.

First published in the *Neue Rheinische Zeitung* No. 106, September 19, 1848

Printed according to the newspaper

Published in English for the first time

[a] See this volume, pp. 20 and 23.—*Ed.*

DECISION OF THE MASS MEETING[366]

The favour of reprinting is requested.

PROCLAMATION

The citizens assembled in a mass meeting in Cologne on September 20,[a]
considering:

that the decision of the Frankfurt National Assembly of the 16th, approving the dishonourable armistice with Denmark, is a betrayal of the German people and of the honour of German arms,

declare:

Article 1. The members of the Frankfurt so-called National Assembly, with the exception of those who have announced to the people their readiness to resign, are traitors to the people;

Article 2. The fighters at the barricades in Frankfurt have rendered a meritorious service to the fatherland.

This proclamation is to be distributed as widely as possible by wall-posters and through the press.

---

[a] A separate leaflet with the text of the Proclamation was also issued. In this leaflet the introductory phrase was printed in the following form: "The citizens assembled in a mass meeting, which was summoned by the Committee of Public Safety, the Democratic Association and the Workers' Association, in Cologne on September 20...."— *Ed.*

The office of the *Neue Rheinische Zeitung* is prepared to accept contributions for the support of the insurgents and their families.[a]

First published in the *Neue Rheinische Zeitung* No. 110, September 23, 1848

Printed according to the newspaper

Published in English for the first time

---

[a] In the leaflet this sentence is replaced by the following text: "The office of the *Neue Rheinische Zeitung* has consented to accept contributions in aid of those who fought on the barricades in Frankfurt and their families, and it will forward them to Deputy Schlöffel from Silesia for appropriate use.

"The other democratic newspapers will undoubtedly act in a similar way."— *Ed.*

ANNOUNCEMENT
OF THE RESPONSIBLE PUBLISHERS
OF THE *NEUE RHEINISCHE ZEITUNG*

TO OUR SUBSCRIBERS

During the state of siege imposed on Cologne, when the pen has to submit to the sabre, the
NEUE RHEINISCHE ZEITUNG
has been forbidden to appear and for the time being is unable to fulfil its obligations to its esteemed subscribers.

We hope, however, that the exceptional situation will continue only for a few days more, and then during the month of October we shall be able to ensure the dispatch of our newspaper to our subscribers in an *enlarged format*, with *new powerful means* for its support, the more punctually because before long the printing will be done by a new rapid printing-press.

Cologne, September 28, 1848

THE RESPONSIBLE PUBLISHERS

Published as a leaflet

Printed according to the leaflet

Published in English for the first time

ANNOUNCEMENT
OF THE RESPONSIBLE PUBLISHERS
OF THE *NEUE RHEINISCHE ZEITUNG*

TO OUR SUBSCRIBERS

According to the assurance of the office of the Fortress Commandant received in reply to our inquiry, the state of siege will end in Cologne on October 4 and accordingly the

NEUE RHEINISCHE ZEITUNG

WILL APPEAR AGAIN ON OCTOBER 5.[367]

We take this opportunity, therefore, to invite the friends of our paper, with references to the circular of September 28, to subscribe for the 4th quarter, and accordingly to notify the nearest post-office as soon as possible.

New equipment will enable us in future to avoid any irregularity in dispatch.

The subscription rate for three months in Cologne is 1 taler 15 silver groschen, and in all other places in Prussia 1 taler 24 silver groschen 6 pfennigs. Advertisements are 1 silver groschen 6 pfennigs per 8-point line of column width (4 columns per page) or the equivalent space.

Cologne, September 30, 1848

THE RESPONSIBLE PUBLISHERS

Published as a leaflet

Printed according to the leaflet

Published in English for the first time

INVITATION TO SUBSCRIBE
TO THE *NEUE RHEINISCHE ZEITUNG*

The *Neue Rheinische Zeitung* was quite unjustifiably suppressed for some days by the armed reaction during the state of siege imposed on the city of Cologne. After today's lifting of the state of siege, the *Neue Rheinische Zeitung* will *once more defend the democratic interests of the whole people with energy and circumspection. This is just now the more essential since we have all seen with what brazen ruthlessness the armed reaction has come out in the most recent period in opposition to the freedom justly won by the people.* Making this announcement to supporters of democracy, we ask them at the same time for really numerous subscriptions for the fourth quarter now commencing, since the democratic newspapers, which moreover encounter hostility from many sides, *especially need the active co-operation of their supporters.*

For Cologne, the subscription per quarter costs 1 taler 15 silver groschen. In Prussia outside Cologne it is 1 taler 24 silver groschen 6 pfennigs. Outside Prussia the printed matter mail charges in the foreign country concerned have to be added.

Advertisements: per 8-point line of column width (4 columns per page) or the equivalent space, cost 1 silver groschen 6 pfennigs.

Cologne, October 3, 1848.

H. Korff

Responsible Publisher
of the *Neue Rheinische Zeitung*

Published as a leaflet

Printed according to the leaflet

Published in English for the first time

WARRANT FOR THE ARREST
OF HEINRICH BÜRGERS AND FRIEDRICH ENGELS

Warrant for arrest. The persons described below have taken refuge in flight from the investigation instituted against them on account of crimes envisaged in Articles 87, 91 and 102 of the Penal Code. On the basis of the order for their appearance in court issued by the examining magistrate here, I therefore request all authorities and officials whom it may concern to be on the look-out for them and, if discovered, to arrest them and have them brought before me.

Cologne, October 3, 1848

For the Chief Public Prosecutor,
Public Prosecutor **Hecker**

Description. I. Name: *Joh. Heinr. Gerhard Bürgers*; occupation: writer; place of birth and residence: Cologne; religion: Catholic; age: 28 years; height: 5 feet 7 inches; hair, eyebrows and eyes: brown; forehead: round; nose: thin; mouth: medium; beard: brown; teeth: good; chin and face: oval; complexion: healthy; figure: slender; language: German.

II. Name: *Friedrich Engels*; occupation: merchant; place of birth and residence: Barmen; religion: Evangelical; age: 27 years; height: 5 feet 8 inches; hair and eyebrows: dark blond; forehead: ordinary; eyes: grey; nose and mouth: well-proportioned; teeth: good; beard: brown; chin and face: oval; complexion: healthy; figure: slender.

First published in the *Kölnische Zeitung* No. 271, October 4, 1848

Printed according to the newspaper

Published in English for the first time

BLACK LIST

Cologne, October 13. A very well-informed friend in *Brussels* writes to us:

"*Engels* and *Dronke* were arrested and transported across the frontier in a prison van only because they were imprudent enough to give their names.[a] A worker from Cologne, *Schmitz*, who is supposed to have played an active part in the freeing of Wachter, shared the same fate. The fact is that the Brussels police had a long list of persons who have fled from Cologne. Thus the Belgian police were accurately informed also about the alleged participation of Schmitz in the freeing of Wachter."

Is perhaps acting Police Superintendent *Geiger* informed about the authors and senders of this black list?

First published in the *Neue Rheinische Zeitung* No. 116, October 14, 1848

Printed according to the newspaper

Published in English for the first time

---

[a] See this volume, pp. 459-61.—*Ed.*

FROM THE MINUTES
OF THE COMMITTEE MEETING
OF THE COLOGNE WORKERS' ASSOCIATION
ON OCTOBER 16, 1848.
ENTRY OF MARX'S SPEECH
IN CONNECTION WITH HIS ASSUMPTION
OF THE PRESIDENCY

The acting President, Citizen Röser, stated that Dr. Marx had acceded to the request of the deputation sent to him from the Association that he should put himself at the head of our Association, and he therefore asked him to take his seat.

Dr. Marx: His position in Cologne was precarious. The reply he had received from ex-Minister Kühlwetter to his request for renaturalisation[a] was tantamount to a concealed order for his expulsion. He would, of course, lodge a protest against it in the National Assembly. On the other hand, he was to be tried at the Assize Court for an alleged press offence. Moreover, owing to the temporary dispersion of the editorial board of the *Neue Rheinische Zeitung* he was overburdened with work. Nevertheless, he was ready, provisionally until Dr. Gottschalk was set free, to accede to the desire of the workers. The Government and the bourgeoisie ought to realise that, despite their acts of persecution, there were always persons to be found who would be ready to put themselves at the disposal of the workers.

Dr. Marx then spoke in some detail about the revolutionary activities of the German workers abroad, and in conclusion stressed their outstanding role in the recent Vienna revolution. He therefore proposed an address to the Vienna Workers' Association. (Adopted with acclamation.)...

The President's proposal (concerning the rules of procedure) was that the first hour should be devoted to the interests of the Association (i.e. to its internal and external affairs), that during the

---

[a] See this volume, p. 581.—*Ed.*

second hour social and political questions should be discussed, and
that the meeting should begin at 8.30. (Adopted.)...

First published in the *Zeitung des Arbeiter-*   Printed according to the newspaper
Vereines zu Köln No. 40, October 22, 1848
                                                      Published in English for the first
                                                      time

FROM THE MINUTES
OF THE GENERAL MEETING
OF THE COLOGNE WORKERS' ASSOCIATION
ON OCTOBER 22, 1848

The President, Dr. *Marx*, opened the meeting with some remarks about the system of indirect election.

Citizen Röser: We have received a request to send a delegate to the Democratic Congress to be held in Berlin on the 26th of this month.[a] In this connection, however, the question arises whether the Workers' Association should send someone separately or together with the Democratic Association. At the last committee meeting of your Association decision was taken in favour of the former alternative, namely to act independently, but it remains for the general meeting to give its approval and in connection with such acceptance it is essential that the question of cost should be taken into account. Therefore I move:

That we elect a delegate to represent us alone, and that we levy a voluntary contribution to cover the expenses.

The motion was adopted and the contributions fixed at a minimum of one silver groschen....

' Citizen Beust was proposed and elected delegate to the Congress in Berlin.

The President, Dr. Marx, and the Vice-President, Citizen Röser, were confirmed in their official positions by the meeting....

First published in the newspaper *Freiheit, Brüderlichkeit, Arbeit* No. 2, October 29, 1848

Printed according to the newspaper

Published in English for the first time

---

[a] See this volume, pp. 490-92.— *Ed.*

FROM THE MINUTES
OF THE COMMITTEE MEETING
OF THE COLOGNE WORKERS' ASSOCIATION
ON NOVEMBER 6, 1848.
ENTRY RELATING TO MARX'S REPORT
ON THE EVENTS IN VIENNA

... The President, Dr. Marx, gave a short report on the events in Vienna and stressed especially that it was only as a result of the manifold betrayal on the part of the bourgeoisie there that it became possible for Windischgrätz to capture the city....

First published in the newspaper *Freiheit, Brüderlichkeit, Arbeit* No. 6, November 12, 1848

Printed according to the newspaper

Published in English for the first time

NOTES
AND
INDEXES

NOTES

[1] "Demands of the Communist Party in Germany" were written by Karl Marx and Frederick Engels in Paris between March 21 (when Engels arrived in Paris from Brussels) and March 24, 1848. This document was discussed by members of the Central Authority, who approved and signed it as the political programme of the Communist League in the revolution that broke out in Germany. In March it was printed as a leaflet, for distribution among revolutionary German emigrant workers who were about to return home. Austrian and German diplomats in Paris informed their respective governments about this as early as March 27, 28 and 29. (The Austrian Ambassador enclosed in his letter a copy of the leaflet which he dated "March 25".) The leaflet soon reached members of the Communist League in other countries, in particular, German emigrant workers in London.

Early in April, the "Demands of the Communist Party in Germany" were published in such German democratic papers as *Berliner Zeitungs-Halle* (special supplement to No. 82, April 5, 1848), *Düsseldorfer Zeitung* (No. 96, April 5, 1848), *Mannheimer Abendzeitung* (No. 96, April 6, 1848), *Trier'sche Zeitung* (No. 97, April 6, 1848, supplement), *Deutsche Allgemeine Zeitung* (No. 100, April 9, 1848, supplement), and *Zeitung für das deutsche Volk* (No. 21, April 9, 1848).

Marx and Engels, who left for Germany round about April 6 and some time later settled in Cologne, did their best along with their followers to popularise this programme document during the revolution. In 1848 and 1849 it was repeatedly published in the periodical press and in leaflet form. Not later than September 10, 1848, the "Demands" were printed in Cologne as a leaflet for circulation by the Cologne Workers' Association both in the town itself and in a number of districts of Rhenish Prussia. In addition to minor stylistic changes, point 10 in the text of the leaflet was worded differently from that published in March-April 1848. At the Second Democratic Congress held in Berlin in October 1848, Friedrich Beust, delegate from the Cologne Workers' Association, spoke, on behalf of the social question commission, in favour of adopting a programme of action closely following the "Demands". In November and December 1848, various points of the "Demands" were discussed at meetings of the Cologne Workers' Association.

Many editions of the "Demands" published during the revolution and after its defeat have survived to this day in their original form, some of them as copies kept in the police archives.

At the end of 1848 or the beginning of 1849 an abridged version of the "Demands" was published in pamphlet form by Weller Publishers in Leipzig. The slogan at the beginning of the document, the second paragraph of point 9 and the last sentence of point 10 were omitted, and the words "The Committee" were not included among the signatories.

In 1853, an abridged version of the "Demands" was printed, together with other documents of the Communist League, in the first part of the book *Die Communisten-Verschworungen des neunzehnten Jahrhunderts*, published in Berlin for purposes of information by Wermuth and Stieber, two police officials, who staged a trial against the Communists in Cologne in 1852.

Later Engels reproduced the main points of the "Demands" in his essay *On the History of the Communist League*, published in November 1885 in the newspaper *Sozialdemokrat*, and as an introduction to the pamphlet: K. Marx, *Enthüllungen über den Kommunisten Prozess zu Köln*, Hottingen-Zürich, 1885.

English translations of the "Demands of the Communist Party in Germany" appeared in the collections: *The Communist Manifesto of Karl Marx and Friedrich Engels* with an introduction and explanatory notes by D. Ryazanoff, Martin Lawrence, London (1930); K. Marx, *Selected Works*, Vol. II, ed. V. Adoratsky, Moscow-Leningrad, Co-operative Publishing Society of Foreign Workers in the USSR (1936); ibid., New York (1936); *Birth of the Communist Manifesto*, edited and annotated, with an Introduction by D. J. Struik, International Publishers, New York, 1971, and in other publications. p. 3

² The letter to the editor of the *Populaire* and the Declaration are in Engels' handwriting. Both documents were drawn up at the end of March 1848 after Engels' arrival in Paris and reflect the struggle which the leaders of the Communist League were waging against those German petty-bourgeois emigrant leaders in Paris, Herwegh and Bornstedt among others, who intended to speed up revolution in Germany by moving in a volunteer legion organised by using private donations and subsidies from the Provisional Government of the French Republic. Appeals to enlist were accompanied by demagogic appeals to the patriotic and revolutionary sentiments of German emigrants. Marx, Engels and other members of the Central Authority of the Communist League spoke out against the adventurist nature of such plans to "export revolution" and advised German workers instead to return to their home country individually in order to take part in the revolutionary events that were brewing there. "We opposed this playing with revolution in the most decisive fashion," Engels later wrote in his work *On the History of the Communist League*. "To carry out an invasion, which was to import the revolution forcibly from outside, into the midst of the ferment then going on in Germany, meant to undermine the revolution in Germany itself, to strengthen the governments and to deliver the legionaries ... defenceless into the hands of the German troops."

The letter and the Declaration were first published in English in the journal *Science and Society*, 1940, Vol. IV, No. 2. The first publication in the language of the original appeared in the collection *Der Bund der Kommunisten. Dokumente und Materialien*, Bd. I, 1836-1849, Berlin, 1970. p. 8

³ The *German Democratic Society* (below it is called the Society of German Democrats) was formed in Paris after the February revolution of 1848. The society was headed by petty-bourgeois democrats, Herwegh, Bornstedt (the latter expelled from the Communist League) and others, who campaigned to raise a volunteer legion of German emigrants with the intention of marching into

Germany. In this way they hoped to carry out a revolution in Germany and establish a republic there. Late in April 1848 the volunteer legion moved to Baden where it was dispersed by government troops.   p. 8

4 The *German Workers' Club* was founded in Paris on March 8 and 9, 1848, on the initiative of Communist League leaders. The club's aim was to unite German emigrant workers in Paris, to explain to them the tactics of the proletariat in a bourgeois-democratic revolution, and also to counter the attempts of the bourgeois and petty-bourgeois democrats to stir up the German workers by nationalist propaganda and enlist them into the adventurist invasion of Germany by volunteer legions. The club successfully arranged the return of German workers one by one to their home country to take part in the revolutionary struggle there.   p. 9

5 On March 29, 1848, the supplement to No. 89 of the *Trier'sche Zeitung* carried a report from Paris, dated March 24, in which the activity of the German Democratic Society (see Note 3) was criticised. This article was apparently written by one of Marx's followers in the Communist League, probably with Marx's help. The author vehemently denounced the idea of an armed invasion of Germany by the volunteer legion and stated that the German Workers' Club associated with the Communist League had nothing to do with this venture.

Deeply hurt by this article, the leaders of the German Democratic Society sent Marx a note signed by Bornstedt, Löwenfels, Börnstein, Volk and Mayer in which they demanded the author's name. The reply is published here from a copy made by Engels. After Marx had rejected their demand, one of the society's leaders, Herwegh, wrote a memorandum for the German periodicals (on April 3, 1848), in which he justified the idea of a volunteer legion and venomously attacked communists.   p. 10

6 Marx's letter was published in *L'Alba* on June 29, 1848, with the following introductory note by the editors: "We publish the following letter received from Cologne to show what feelings the noble-minded Germans entertain towards Italy; they ardently wish to establish fraternal relations between the Italian and German peoples, whom European despots have tried to set against each other."

The reply by the editors of *L'Alba*, signed by L. Alinari, is quoted in Engels' article "Germany's Foreign Policy" (see this volume, p. 167).

An English translation of this letter was published in the magazine *Labour Monthly* No. 5, 1948, and in the collection: Karl Marx and Frederick Engels, *Selected Correspondence* (Moscow, 1955, London, 1956).   p. 11

7 This statement of the editorial board was printed in the first number of the *Neue Rheinische Zeitung*, which appeared in the evening of May 31, but was dated June 1, 1848. (In English the statement was published in the magazine *Labour Monthly* No. 5, 1948, and in the collection: Karl Marx and Frederick Engels, *Articles from the "Neue Rheinische Zeitung". 1848-49*, Progress Publishers, Moscow, 1972.)

Marx and Engels began to plan the publication of a German revolutionary paper as far back as March 1848 when they were still living in Paris. On March 26 and 28, 1848, Engels wrote about this plan to his brother-in-law Emil Blank.

The publication of a proletarian newspaper was regarded by Marx and Engels as an important step towards a mass party of the German proletariat, which, they believed, should be founded on the basis of the Communist League. On their arrival in Germany, they realised that the conditions for creating such a party were not yet ripe: the German workers were disunited; their immaturity and lack of organisation made them easy prey to narrow craft and petty-bourgeois influences and particularist moods, while the Communist League, for which there was no sense in continuing secret activities during the revolution, was too weak and small in number to be instrumental in consolidating the workers. Marx and Engels realised this after studying the reports submitted by the Central Authority emissaries on the situation in the League's local communities. In this context, the role of a newspaper in influencing the masses, in their ideological and political education and consolidation, seemed peculiarly important. The paper could be used for political guidance of the activities of Communist League members, who were instructed by Marx and Engels to avail themselves of every legal opportunity and join the emerging workers' associations and democratic societies.

Marx and Engels decided to publish the paper in Cologne, the capital of the Rhine Province, one of the most economically and politically advanced regions in Germany. The new paper was given the name of the *Neue Rheinische Zeitung* to emphasise that it was to continue the revolutionary-democratic traditions of the *Rheinische Zeitung*, which Marx had edited in 1842 and 1843. Taking account of the specific circumstances, with the absence of an independent mass workers' party in Germany, Marx, Engels and their followers entered the political scene as a Left, actually proletarian, wing of the democratic movement. This determined the stand of the *Neue Rheinische Zeitung*, which began to appear under the subtitle "The Organ of Democracy".

When they started the paper, Marx and Engels had to cope with serious financial difficulties as well as with the opposition from sectarian elements in the Communist League (Hess, Anneke and others), who intended to publish a purely local sheet under a similar title. In April and May 1848, Marx and Engels worked hard selling shares in the paper, finding contributors and establishing regular contacts with democratic periodicals in other countries. The editorial committee was known for its unanimity of views, well-co-ordinated work and strict division of functions.

As a rule, Marx and Engels wrote the editorials formulating the paper's stand on the most important questions of the revolution. These were usually marked "*Köln" and "**Köln". Sometimes editorial articles marked with one asterisk were printed in other sections under the heading of news from Italy, France, England, Hungary and other countries. In the early months of the paper's existence Marx was fully occupied with administrative and organisational matters and most of the leading articles were written by Engels. In addition to this, Engels also contributed critical reviews of debates in the Berlin and Frankfurt National Assemblies, articles on the national liberation movements in Bohemia, Posen and Italy, and on the war in Schleswig-Holstein, revolutionary developments in Hungary and political life in Switzerland. Wilhelm Wolff contributed articles on the agrarian question, on the condition of the peasants and their movement, particularly in Silesia. He was also responsible for the current events section. Georg Weerth wrote feuilletons in verse and prose. Ernst Dronke was for some time the *Neue Rheinische Zeitung* correspondent in Frankfurt am Main and wrote several articles on Poland. Ferdinand Wolff was for a long time one of the paper's correspondents in Paris. The only article which Heinrich Bürgers wrote for the *Neue Rheinische Zeitung* was almost entirely rewritten by Marx. Ferdinand Freiligrath, who became one of the paper's editors in October 1848, published his own verses.

The *Neue Rheinische Zeitung* was a daily paper (from September 1848 it appeared every day except Monday). Its editors often published a second edition on one day in order to supply their readers with prompt information on all the most significant revolutionary developments in Germany and Europe; supplements were printed when there was too much material to be squeezed into the four pages of the number, while special supplements and special editions printed in the form of leaflets carried the latest and most important news.

The consistent revolutionary tendency of the *Neue Rheinische Zeitung,* its militant internationalism and political accusations against the Government displeased its bourgeois shareholders in the very first months of the paper's existence; its editors were persecuted by the Government and attacked in the feudal-monarchist and liberal-bourgeois press. Following the appearance of the paper's first number, which carried Engels' article "The Assembly at Frankfurt" (see this volume, pp. 16-19), a large number of the shareholders withdrew their financial support, and articles in defence of the June uprising of the Paris proletariat frightened away most of the rest. The editors now had to rely on German and Polish revolutionary circles for funds.

To make Marx's stay in the Rhine Province more difficult, the Cologne authorities, on instructions from Berlin, refused to reinstate him with the rights of Prussian citizenship (which Marx had renounced in 1845); on several occasions he and other editors of the *Neue Rheinische Zeitung* were summoned to court. On September 26, 1848, when a state of siege was introduced in Cologne, several democratic newspapers, the *Neue Rheinische Zeitung* among them, were suspended. To avoid arrest, Engels, Dronke and Ferdinand Wolff had to leave Germany for a time. Wilhelm Wolff stayed in Cologne but for several months lived illegally. When the state of siege was lifted, the paper resumed publication on October 12, thanks to the great efforts of Marx who sank all his ready money into the paper. Until January 1849, the whole burden of the work, including editorial articles, lay on Marx's shoulders since Engels had to stay out of Germany (in France and Switzerland).

Persecution of the *Neue Rheinische Zeitung* editors by the legal authorities and the police was intensified, particularly after the counter-revolutionary coup in Prussia in November-December 1848.

In May 1849, when the counter-revolution went into the offensive all over Germany, the Prussian Government issued an order for Marx's expulsion from Prussia on the grounds that he had not been granted Prussian citizenship. Marx's expulsion and repressions against other editors of the *Neue Rheinische Zeitung* caused publication of the paper to be ceased. Its last issue (No. 301), printed in red ink, came out on May 19, 1849. In their farewell address to the workers, the editors of the *Neue Rheinische Zeitung* said that "their last word will everywhere and always be: *emancipation of the working class!*" p. 15

[8] The *September Laws,* promulgated by the French Government in September 1835, restricted the rights of jury courts and introduced severe measures against the press. They provided for increased money deposits (caution money) for periodical publications and introduced imprisonment and large fines for publication of attacks on private property and the existing political system. p. 15

[9] The opening session of the all-German National Assembly, the purpose of which was to unite the country and draft a Constitution, took place on May 18, 1848, in Frankfurt am Main at St. Paul's Church. Among the deputies elected in various German states late in April and early in May, there were 122 government officials, 95 judges, 81 lawyers, 103 teachers, 17 manufacturers and wholesale dealers, 15 physicians and 40 landowners. The liberal deputies, who were in the majority,

turned the Assembly into a mere debating club, incapable of taking any resolute decisions.

In writing this and the following articles concerning the debates in the Frankfurt National Assembly, Marx and Engels made use of the stenographic reports which later appeared as a separate publication, *Stenographischer Bericht über die Verhandlungen der deutschen constituirenden Nationalversammlung zu Frankfurt am Main*, Frankfurt am Main and Leipzig, 1848-1849.

Engels' article was first published in English in the collection: Karl Marx and Frederick Engels, *Articles from the "Neue Rheinische Zeitung". 1848-49*, Progress Publishers, Moscow, 1972.   p. 16

10 At the sitting of the Frankfurt National Assembly on May 19, 1848, the liberal Deputy Raveaux proposed that Prussian deputies elected to both the Berlin and Frankfurt Assemblies should have the right to be members of both. The Berlin Assembly, i. e. the Prussian National Assembly, was convened on May 22, 1848, to draft a Constitution "by agreement with the Crown". The Assembly was elected under the electoral law of April 8, 1848, by universal suffrage and an indirect (two-stage) voting system. Most of the deputies belonged to the bourgeoisie or liberal bureaucracy.   p. 17

11 *The limited understanding of a loyal subject*—an expression used by the Prussian Minister of the Interior von Rochow. In his letter of January 15, 1838, addressed to the citizens of Elbin who expressed their dissatisfaction at the expulsion of seven oppositional professors from the Hanover Diet, Rochow wrote: "Loyal subjects are expected to exhibit due obedience to their king and sovereign, but their limited understanding should keep them from interfering in affairs of heads of state."   p. 18

12 The *Preparliament*, which met in Frankfurt am Main from March 31 to April 4, 1848, consisted of representatives from the German states, most of its delegates being constitutional monarchists. The Preparliament passed a resolution to convoke an all-German National Assembly and produced a draft of the "Fundamental Rights and Demands of the German People". Although this document proclaimed certain rights and liberties, including the right of all-German citizenship for the residents of any German state, it did not touch the basis of the semi-feudal absolutist system prevalent in Germany at the time.
                                                                 p. 18

13 The *seventeen "trusted men"* who represented the German governments were summoned after the March revolution in Germany by the Federal Diet, the central body of the German Confederation (which was founded in 1815 by the Congress of Vienna). The "trusted men", among them Dahlmann, von Schmerling, Uhland and Bassermann, met in Frankfurt am Main from March 30 to May 8, 1848, and drafted an all-German Imperial Constitution based on constitutional-monarchical principles.

The *Federal Diet* consisted of representatives of the German states. Though it had no real power, it was nevertheless a vehicle of feudal and monarchical reaction. After the March revolution of 1848, reactionary circles in the German states tried to revive the Federal Diet and use it to undermine the principle of popular sovereignty and prevent the democratic unification of Germany. p. 18

14 Auerswald's decree, dated May 22, 1848, and published on May 23, 1848, in the *Preussische Staats-Anzeiger* No. 21, p. 215, included Raveaux's proposal (see Note 10).   p. 19

[15] The article was first published in English in the collection: Karl Marx, *On Revolution*, ed. by S. K. Padover, New York, 1971 ("The Karl Marx Library" series), Vol. 1.   p. 20

[16] On May 22, 1815, Frederick William III who, during the war with Napoleonic France, had to respond to the demand for a Constitution, issued a decree in which he promised "popular representation", that is, to set up Provincial Assemblies of the Estates in Prussia and to convoke an all-Prussia representative body. All that ever resulted from these promises, however, was the law of June 5, 1823, which created Provincial Assemblies of the Estates with limited, advisory functions.
The *German Confederation*—see Note 13.   p. 20

[17] *Lazzaroni*—a contemptuous nickname for declassed proletarians, primarily in the Kingdom of Naples. They were repeatedly used by the absolutist Government in the struggle against liberal and democratic movements.   p. 25

[18] The reference is to the "cordial agreement" (*entente cordiale*) between France and England in the early period of the July monarchy (1830-35). The "agreement", however, proved unstable and was soon followed by intensified contradictions.
                    p. 25

[19] *Sanfedists* (from *santa fede*—holy faith)—supporters of the papacy who joined terrorist gangs to fight against the Italian national liberation movement.   p. 25

[20] On *August 10, 1792*, the monarchy in France was overthrown by a popular uprising in Paris. The sculpture of a dying lion by Thorwaldsen was installed in Lucerne some time later, to commemorate the Swiss guards who were killed defending the royal palace.
On *July 29, 1830*, the Bourbons were overthrown in France.
In *July 1820*, the Carbonari, aristocratic and bourgeois revolutionaries, rose in revolt against the absolutist regime in the Kingdom of Naples and succeeded in having a moderate liberal Constitution introduced. Intervention by the powers of the Holy Alliance, however, led to the restoration of the absolutist regime in Naples.
On all these occasions Swiss mercenaries were used by the counter-revolutionary forces.   p. 26

[21] The reference is to treaties concluded between the middle of the fifteenth and the middle of the nineteenth centuries between Swiss cantons and European states for the supply of Swiss mercenaries.   p. 26

[22] An article dealing with this subject was originally written by Heinrich Bürgers, but Marx editorially deleted half of it and rewrote the rest (see Marx's letter to Ferdinand Lassalle of September 15, 1860).
An English translation of this article was first published in the collections: Karl Marx and Frederick Engels, *Articles from the "Neue Rheinische Zeitung". 1848-49*, Progress Publishers, Moscow, 1972, and Karl Marx, *The Revolutions of 1848. Political Writings*, Vol. 1, London, Penguin Books, 1973.   p. 27

[23] In 1848-49 the advocates of a bourgeois constitutional system in Germany called the republican democrats "agitators" (*Wühler*) and these in turn called their opponents "wailers" (*Heuler*).   p. 28

[24] On March 29, 1848, the Camphausen Government in which Hansemann held the post of the Minister of Finance replaced the Government of Count Arhim-Boitzenburg, which had been formed on March 19, 1848, when revolution broke out in Prussia.

In writing this and other articles concerning the Prussian National Assembly, the authors made use of the stenographic reports, which later came out as a separate edition entitled *Verhandlungen der constituirenden Versammlung für Preussen 1848*, Berlin, 1848.

The article was first published in English in the collection: Karl Marx, *The Revolutions of 1848. Political Writings*, Vol. 1, London, Penguin Books, 1973.

p. 30

[25] The *United Diet*—an assembly of representatives from the eight Provincial Diets of Prussia, similarly based on the estate principle. The United Diet sanctioned new taxes and loans, discussed new Bills and had the right to petition the King.

The First United Diet, which opened on April 11, 1847, was dissolved in June, following its refusal to grant a new loan. The Second United Diet met on April 2, 1848, when the Camphausen Ministry was in office. It passed a law on the elections to a Prussian National Assembly and sanctioned the loan. The United Diet session was closed on April 10, 1848.

p. 32

[26] See Note 10.

p. 33

[27] According to tradition, around 390 B. C. the Gauls captured Rome with the exception of the Capitol, whose defenders were warned of the approaching enemy by the cackling of the geese from the Temple of Juno.

p. 33

[28] In this article Engels describes one of the episodes in the war between Germany and Denmark over Schleswig and Holstein.

By the decision of the Congress of Vienna (1815) the duchies of Schleswig and Holstein were incorporated into the Kingdom of Denmark in spite of the fact that Germans constituted the majority of the population in Holstein and in Southern Schleswig. Under the impact of the March revolution, the national liberation movement of the German population grew in strength and assumed a radical and democratic nature, becoming part of the struggle for the unification of Germany. Volunteers from all over the country rushed to the aid of the local population when it rose up against Danish rule arms in hand. Prussia, Hanover and other states of the German Confederation sent to the duchies federal troops, under the command of the Prussian General Wrangel, who entered Jutland on May 2. The Prussian Government, however, declined to take a firm stand on the Schleswig-Holstein issue, for it feared a popular outbreak and an intensification of the revolution. The liberal majority of the Frankfurt National Assembly also cherished secret hopes of an agreement with the Danish ruling circles, at the expense of national unity. Things were complicated by the intervention of Britain, Sweden and Russia in favour of Denmark, and their demand that federal troops be withdrawn from the duchies. (In this connection, Engels alludes to the Note of May 8, 1848, which Chancellor Nesselrode handed in to the Berlin Cabinet and in which this demand was accompanied by the threat of a break between Russia and Prussia.)

All these circumstances had a negative effect on the military operations against Denmark undertaken by the German federal troops and volunteer detachments.

The report on the defeat of the German federal troops appeared on May 30, 1848, in No. 11179 of the *Börsen-Halle,* and was then reprinted in most of the German papers. In English it appeared on June 3 in *The Times* No. 19880.

p. 34

29 The reference is to the presidents of the Provincial Diets of the Estates, which were formed in 1823 and consisted of heads of princely families, representatives of the nobility (the latter enjoying the greatest influence), and representatives of towns and rural communities. The competence of the Diets was limited to local economic and administrative problems. They could also express opinions on government Bills submitted for discussion. p. 36

30 See Note 25. p. 36

31 The article was first published in English in the collection: Karl Marx, *The Revolutions of 1848. Political Writings,* Vol. 1, London, Penguin Books, 1973.

p. 39

32 An allusion to the speech which the French lawyer André Dupin addressed to the Duke of Orléans (representative of the younger branch of the Bourbons), made King of the French by the July revolution of 1830. In his speech, Dupin emphasised that the Duke of Orléans was elected "not *because* he was a Bourbon but *although* he was a Bourbon". This was an answer to the question whether the King should adopt the name of Philippe VII or Louis Philippe. p. 40

33 Concerning the German-Danish war over Schleswig-Holstein see Note 28.

p. 42

34 The army of the anti-French coalition, in which Prussian forces participated, defeated Napoleon's army in the vicinity of Berlin at the battles of *Grossbeeren* (August 23, 1813) and *Dennewitz* (September 6, 1813). p. 42

35 Excerpts from an announcement published in the supplement to the *Berliner Zeitungs-Halle* No. 128, June 4, 1848, under the title "Berliner Tagesgeschichte" [Sicherheits-Ausschutz], are quoted in this article with some digressions. p. 46

36 In February 1846, the Prussian police in Posen tracked down the leaders of preparations for a national liberation uprising in Poland and carried out wholesale arrests. As a result, a general uprising aimed at restoring Poland's independence was staved off and only sporadic outbursts occurred (among them an unsuccessful attempt by a group of Polish revolutionaries to capture the Posen fortress on March 3). Only in the Republic of Cracow, which since the Congress of Vienna had been under the joint control of Austria, Russia and Prussia, did the insurgents gain power on February 22 and create a National Government of the Polish Republic, which issued a manifesto abrogating all feudal obligations. The Cracow uprising was suppressed in early March 1846 and, in November, Austria, Prussia and Russia signed a treaty incorporating the free city of Cracow into the Austrian Empire. p. 47

37 In late April and early May 1848, Berlin was the scene of a compositors' strike for higher wages and shorter working hours. The workers disregarded the threat of deportation, and succeeded in forcing their employers to abandon an attempt to make them sign, as a condition of agreement, a statement in which the workers would acknowledge their "errors" and repent. p. 47

[38] The article was first published in English in the collections: Karl Marx and Frederick Engels, *Articles from the "Neue Rheinische Zeitung". 1848-49*, Progress Publishers, Moscow, 1972, and Karl Marx, *The Revolutions of 1848. Political Writings*, Vol. 1, London, Penguin Books, 1973. Excerpts from it appeared earlier in the collection: Karl Marx, *On Revolution*, ed. by S. K. Padover, New York, 1971, under the title "A United German State", which was supplied by the editors.
p. 48

[39] The Left wing of the Frankfurt National Assembly consisted of two factions: the Left (Robert Blum, Karl Vogt and others), and the extreme Left known as the radical-democratic party (Arnold Ruge, Friedrich Wilhelm Schlöffel, Franz Zitz and others). Though the sympathies of the *Neue Rheinische Zeitung* were with the extreme Left wing rather than with more moderate groups of democrats, it criticised the former for their vacillations and halfway stand on the basic problems of the German revolution—abolition of feudal survivals and unification of the country.
p. 48

[40] See Note 13.
p. 49

[41] The *Holy Roman Empire of the German Nation* was founded in 962 and lasted till 1806. At different times, it included the German, Italian, Austrian, Hungarian and Bohemian lands, Switzerland and the Netherlands, forming a motley conglomeration of feudal kingdoms and principalities, church lands and free cities with different political structures, legal standards and customs.
p. 50

[42] The *agreement debates* (*Vereinbarungsdebatten*) was the name given by Marx and Engels to the debates in the Prussian National Assembly, which met in Berlin in May 1848 to draft a Constitution "by agreement with the Crown" according to the formula proposed by the Hansemann-Camphausen Government. Marx and Engels labelled the Berlin Assembly, which adopted this formula and thereby rejected the principle of popular sovereignty, the "Agreement Assembly" and its deputies "the agreers".
p. 53

[43] The reference is to the treaty signed by Russia and Prussia on March 29, 1830, on the extradition of deserters, prisoners of war and criminals. A secret declaration adopted simultaneously with the agreement made persons guilty of political offences also subject to extradition. The governments of both countries used this convention in their struggle against the Polish national liberation movement.
p. 53

[44] Abbreviation for *Preussische Seehandlungsgesellschaft* (Prussian Sea Trade Society). This trade credit society, founded in 1772, enjoyed a number of important state privileges. It offered large credits to the Government and actually played the part of banker and broker. In 1904 it was made the Prussian State Bank.
p. 54

[45] According to the *Verordnung wegen der künftigen Behandlung des gesammten Staatsschulden-Wesens* (Decree on the Future Handling of All Government Debts), issued in Prussia on January 17, 1820, new loans and government debts had to be guaranteed by the forthcoming Prussian Assembly of the Estates, as well as by the Government.
p. 55

[46] After the March revolution of 1848, an insurrection of the Poles broke out in the Duchy of Posen for liberation from the Prussian yoke. The Polish peasants and artisans took an active part in this together with members of the lesser nobility.

The Prussian Government was forced to promise that a committee would be set up to carry through the reorganisation of Posen (creation of a Polish army, appointment of Poles to administrative and other posts, recognition of Polish as an official language etc.). Similar promises were given in the Convention of April 11, 1848, signed by the Posen Committee and the Prussian Commissioner. On April 14, 1848, however, the King of Prussia ordered that the Duchy of Posen be divided into an eastern Polish part and a western "German" part, which was not to be "reorganised". During the months following the suppression of the Poles by Prussian troops that broke the Convention, the demarcation line was pushed further and further east and the promised "reorganisation" was never carried out.

p. 57

[47] In the table of contents of this issue of the *Neue Rheinische Zeitung*, the article is listed under the title "A New Partition of Poland", but the text itself begins with the heading "The Seventh Partition of Poland". This refers to the decree issued on June 4, 1848, by General Pfuel, the commander of Prussian troops in Posen, which further extended the territory of the western "German" part of the duchy at the expense of its eastern "Polish" part, which was to be "reorganised" as promised by the Government, but never was (see Note 46). This was the fourth time that the line of demarcation was pushed further east to the detriment of the Polish population (the three previous occasions were April 14, April 22 and May 2, 1848). Ironically calling this the "seventh partition of Poland", Engels shows it to be a continuation of the policy of appropriation of Polish lands by the European powers. This found reflection in the three partitions of Poland (by Prussia, Austria and Russia) at the end of the eighteenth century (1772, 1793, 1794-95); in the transfer to Russia (by Napoleon, under the Peace Treaty of Tilsit concluded in 1807) of a part of Polish territory in exchange for recognition of the Duchy of Warsaw, created by Napoleon as a vassal state; in the decision of the Congress of Vienna (1815), which abolished the Duchy of Warsaw and once again sanctioned the annexation of the Polish lands by Prussia, Russia and Austria, and also in Austria's annexation of the free city of Cracow in 1846.

p. 64

[48] The reference is to the return of the Prince of Prussia to Berlin (on June 4, 1848) from England, where he had fled during the March revolution.

p. 67

[49] Following the unsuccessful revolutionary action of the Paris workers on May 15, 1848, the Constituent Assembly adopted a decree on the reorganisation of national workshops, and steps were taken to abolish them altogether; a law was passed banning gatherings in the streets, a number of democratic clubs were closed and other police measures taken.

p. 68

[50] *Repealers*—supporters of the repeal of the Anglo-Irish Union of 1801, which abrogated the autonomy of the Irish Parliament. Ever since the 1820s, the demand for the repeal of the Union became a mass issue in Ireland. In 1840, a Repeal Association was founded whose leader, Daniel O'Connell, proposed a compromise with the English ruling circles. In January 1847 its radical elements broke away from the Association and formed an Irish Confederation; representatives of its Left revolutionary wing stood at the head of the national liberation movement and in 1848 were subjected to severe repression.

p. 68

[51] The *Committee of Fifty* was elected by the Preparliament (see Note 12) in April 1848, mainly from among the representatives of its constitutional monarchist majority, with moderate republicans receiving only 12 seats. The Committee rejected the

proposal of the Federal Diet (see Note 13) to create a directory of three men to constitute a provisional Central Authority of the German Confederation.

At the beginning of June 1848, a similar proposal was submitted to the Frankfurt National Assembly. As a result of the debate, the Assembly decided on June 28 to form a provisional Central Authority composed of an Imperial Regent and an Imperial Ministry.   p. 68

52 The *"property of the entire nation"* — the words inscribed by armed workers in Berlin on the walls of the palace of the Prince of Prussia, who had fled to England during the March revolution of 1848.   p. 68

53 The reference is to the republican insurrection in Baden, led by the petty-bourgeois democrats Friedrich Hecker and Gustav Struve, which was crushed in April 1848. The main regions of the insurrection were the Lake district (Seekreis) and the Black Forest (Schwarzwald).   p. 68

54 See Note 23.   p. 70

55 On June 9, 1848, the Frankfurt National Assembly rejected a Bill bringing the approval of any future peace treaty with Denmark within the Assembly's jurisdiction. The Assembly thus avoided taking any responsibility for the final settlement of the Schleswig-Holstein question and allowed the Federal Diet complete freedom of action on this issue.   p. 72

56 Part of this article was first published in English in the collection: Karl Marx and Frederick Engels, *Articles from the "Neue Rheinische Zeitung". 1848-49*, Progress Publishers, Moscow, 1972.   p. 73

57 The decree on the press, by Frederick William IV, published on March 18, 1848, cancelled the censorship of periodicals and introduced caution money (from 500 to 2,000 talers) instead as a guarantee against the publication of anti-government articles; this system existed in Prussia until the adoption of the 1874 press law.
                                                                                p. 73

58 This was how the conflict between the King and the United Diet (see Note 25) in 1847 was described in government circles.   p. 73

59 On March 24, 1848, soldiers and non-commissioned officers killed on the night of March 18 during the popular insurrection were buried at the Invaliden Cemetery in Berlin. In their public announcements the authorities deliberately underestimated the number of casualties in order to disguise the extent of the fighting and to cover up the fact that the troops had been beaten by the people.   p. 74

60 Among the Left deputies of the Prussian National Assembly were Johann Jacoby, Georg Jung, Karl d'Ester and Benedikt Waldeck.   p. 75

61 On June 3, 1848, the Berlin National Assembly debated a motion that members of the Assembly should join the march, organised by students, to the grave of the revolutionary fighters who had fallen in March; the motion was rejected by a majority vote.   p. 76

62 On May 15 and 26, 1848, there was a popular armed uprising in Vienna to defend the gains achieved during the March revolution. This forced the Austrian

Emperor Ferdinand I to proclaim the manifestos of May 16 and June 3, in which he made a number of new concessions; among other things, he gave the status of Constituent Assembly to the Imperial Diet, which was about to be convened.

p. 79

[63] *Wends*—the German name for the Labe Slavs who, in the early Middle Ages, occupied the territory between the Elbe (Labe) and the Oder (Odra). In the middle of the eleventh century, while fighting against German and Danish expansion, they formed an early feudal confederation, which existed till the first third of the twelfth century; it also comprised a group of West-Slavonian tribes living on the Baltic coast (future Pomerania), who were ethnically close to the Wends.

p. 82

[64] In this article the outcome of the Cologne by-election of June 14, 1848, is compared with that of the general election that had taken place on May 10, 1848. Both were elections of deputies to the Frankfurt National Assembly.

The article was first published in English in the collection: Karl Marx, *The Revolutions of 1848. Political Writings*, Vol. 1, London, Penguin Books, 1973.

p. 87

[65] *Citizens' associations* (*Bürgervereine*), consisting of moderate liberal elements, arose in Prussia after the March revolution. Their aim was to preserve "law and order" within the framework of a constitutional monarchy, and to combat "anarchy", i. e. the revolutionary-democratic movement.

p. 87

[66] The *Democratic Society* in Cologne, which met in Franz Stollwerk's Café, was founded in April 1848. Among its members were small proprietors, workers and artisans. Marx and Engels took an active part in the management of the Society. At the meetings, Marx, Engels and other members of the editorial staff of the *Neue Rheinische Zeitung* managed to get certain resolutions adopted which unmasked the anti-revolutionary policy of the Prussian Government and condemned the irresolute conduct of the Berlin and Frankfurt Assemblies. A year later, when Marx and his followers took practical steps to create an independent mass party of the proletariat, they decided to sever all organisational links with petty-bourgeois democrats, and withdrew from the Democratic Society. Nevertheless they continued to give support to the revolutionary actions of democratic forces in Germany.

p. 87

[67] Enraged by the disavowal of the March revolution by the Prussian National Assembly (see this volume, pp. 73-86), workers and artisans from Berlin stormed the arsenal on June 14, 1848, in order to arm the people in readiness to defend the gains of the revolution. This was, however, a spontaneous and unorganised action and military reinforcements as well as civic militia detachments quickly dispersed and disarmed the people.

p. 89

[68] Influenced by the revolutionary action of the working people of Berlin, the Prussian National Assembly adopted a resolution of June 15, 1848, which declared that the Assembly "does not need the protection of the armed forces but instead places itself under the protection of the people of Berlin".

p. 89

[69] *During the night of August 4, 1789*, the French Constituent Assembly, under the impact of the growing peasant unrest, announced the abrogation of a number of feudal obligations which had already been abolished by the insurgent peasants.

p. 89

[70] *On March 21, 1848*, Frederick William IV, frightened by the barricade fighting in Berlin, issued an appeal "To My People, and the German Nation" in which he promised to set up a representative institution based on the estate principle, and to introduce a Constitution, ministerial responsibility, public trials, juries etc.
p. 89

[71] This article was first published in English in the magazine *Labour Monthly*, 1948, Vol. XXX, No. 4, and also in the collections: Karl Marx and Frederick Engels, *Articles from the "Neue Rheinische Zeitung". 1848-49*, Progress Publishers, Moscow, 1972, and Karl Marx, *The Revolutions of 1848. Political Writings*, Vol. 1, London, Penguin Books, 1973.
p. 91

[72] See Note 46.
p. 91

[73] The *Slav Congress* met in Prague on June 2, 1848. It was attended by representatives of the Slav countries forming part of the Austrian Empire. The Right, moderately liberal wing, to which Palacký and Šafařik, the leaders of the Congress, belonged, sought to solve the national problem through autonomy of the Slav countries within the framework of the Habsburg monarchy. The Left, radical wing (Sabina, Frič, Libelt and others) wanted to act in alliance with the revolutionary-democratic movement in Germany and Hungary. Radical delegates took an active part in the popular uprising in Prague (June 12-17, 1848), which was directed against the arbitrary rule of the Austrian authorities, and were subjected to cruel reprisals. On June 16, the moderate liberal delegates declared the Congress adjourned for an indefinite period.
p. 91

[74] After the suppression of the Prague uprising, the Czech liberals took the lead of the national movement, which they turned into an instrument against the revolutionary-democratic forces of Germany and Hungary, and into a prop for the Habsburg monarchy and, indirectly, for Russian Tsarism. This was the reason why the *Neue Rheinische Zeitung* denounced this movement in the months that followed.
p. 93

[75] See Note 59.
p. 98

[76] The reference is to the wars waged by the peoples of Europe against Napoleonic France in 1813-14 and 1815, following the defeat of Napoleon's army in Russia in 1812. These were, indeed, of a contradictory nature and their character was affected by the counter-revolutionary aims and expansionist policy of the ruling circles in the feudal monarchical states fighting on the side of the anti-French coalition. But especially in 1813, when the struggle was aimed at liberating German territory from French occupation, they turned into a genuinely popular national liberation war against foreign oppression. In this passage, Engels ridicules the over-patriotic zeal with which the representatives of Germany's ruling classes speak of the 1813-14 and 1815 wars. Later, when once again considering that period of the history of Germany, Engels in a series of articles entitled "Notes on the War" (1870) stressed the progressive nature of the people's resistance to Napoleon's rule and in his work *The Role of Force in History* (1888) wrote: "The peoples' war against Napoleon was the reaction of the national feeling of all the peoples, which Napoleon had trampled on."

The battle of the nations at *Leipzig* (October 16-19, 1813) ended with victory for the Russian, Prussian, Austrian and Swedish troops over Napoleon's forces.

At the battle of *Waterloo* (June 18, 1815) Napoleon's forces were defeated by British and Prussian troops commanded by Wellington and Blücher.
p. 98

[77] Most Prussian fortresses capitulated to the French without a fight after the defeat of the Prussian troops at Jena and Auerstedt (October 14, 1806). The fortress of Cüstrin, for instance, surrendered to a small French detachment on November 10, 1806, and Magdeburg, with its many-thousand-strong garrison and artillery, was surrendered by General Kleist on November 8, 1806, after the first salvo fired by the French from light field mortars.   p. 99

[78] *Code civil*— French code of civil law of 1804 known as the *Code Napoléon*. This Code was introduced by Napoleon into the conquered regions of Western and South-Western Germany and remained the official law of the Rhineland even after that region's union with Prussia.   p. 103

[79] The Prussian General Pfuel ordered the heads of captured insurrectionists in Posen in 1848 to be shaved and their arms and ears branded with lunar caustic (in German *Höllenstein*, i. e. stone of hell). This was how he got the nickname "von Höllenstein".   p. 104

[80] The assault upon the arsenal on June 14, 1848 (see Note 67) led to a ministerial crisis in Prussia and the downfall of the Camphausen Government. The conservative and aristocratic members of the Government, Kanitz, Schwerin and Arnim, resigned on June 17. An attempt to reorganise the Government failed and on June 20 the entire Ministry resigned.

The article was first published in English in the collections: Karl Marx, *On Revolution*, ed. by S. K. Padover, New York, 1971 ("The Karl Marx Library" series), and Karl Marx, *The Revolutions of 1848. Political Writings*, Vol. 1, London, Penguin Books, 1973.   p. 107

[81] The Camphausen Government began its activities on *March 30, 1848*. At about the same time, a national liberation uprising broke out in Posen and was cruelly suppressed by this Government (see Note 46).   p. 107

[82] The reference is to the national liberation war against Austrian domination. On March 18, 1848, a popular armed uprising broke out in Milan, the capital of Lombardy; and after five days of bitter fighting the Austrian troops were driven out. The Austrians were also driven out of the Venice region, where a republic was proclaimed. On March 25, Charles Albert, King of Sardinia (Piedmont), declared war on Austria in the hope of exploiting the patriotic movement in his own dynastic interests. In April, the Italian army won a number of minor victories in the vicinity of Verona, but the hesitant policy of Charles Albert resulted in a serious defeat for the Italians at Custozza on July 25, 1848, and the Austrian army under the command of Field Marshal Radetzky reoccupied Milan on August 6. On August 9, Charles Albert concluded an armistice, which aroused vehement popular protests. Once again Lombardy found itself under the yoke of the Austrian Empire.

Fighting was resumed in March 1849, but the Sardinian forces were routed on March 21-23 at the battles of Mortara and Novara.   p. 109

[83] The Provisional Government of Lombardy was formed on March 22, 1848, after the Austrian troops had been driven out of Milan; its members were mainly moderate liberals.   p. 109

[84] *Pandours*— soldiers of the Austrian army, whose irregular infantry units were recruited mainly in the South-Slav provinces of the Austrian Empire.   p. 109

85 The article was written a few days before a new Government which replaced the
Camphausen Ministry was finally formed. The formal head of the new
Government—the so-called Government of Action (June 26-September 21,
1848)—was Rudolf von Auerswald, a dignitary close to the Court; Hansemann,
one of the candidates for the post of Prime Minister, remained the Minister of
Finance just as he had been under Camphausen, but was the actual leader of the
Government. Representatives of the Right groups, such as Milde and Gierke,
entered the Ministry together with some of the former Ministers. Karl Rodbertus,
one of the leaders of the Left Centre, was also a member of the Government, but
he soon resigned from his post.   p. 111

86 An allusion to the speech from the throne made by Frederick William IV at the
opening of the United Diet on April 11, 1847. The King said he would never agree
to grant a Constitution which he described as a "written scrap of paper".
   The words "bourgeois grain and wool merchants" refer to Camphausen who, in
his youth, engaged in oil and corn trading, and to Hansemann who started his
commercial career as a wool merchant.   p. 115

87 An English translation of this article was first published in the collection: Karl
Marx, *On Revolution*, ed. by S. K. Padover, New York, 1971 ("The Karl Marx
Library" series), under the title "Prussia's Feudal Reforms".   p. 117

88 *Liege money*—dues which the feudal lord was entitled to receive on the
selling of a vassal estate.   p. 117

89 See Note 69.   p. 118

90 *Patrimonial jurisdiction*—the right of landlords to pass judgment upon their
peasants and to fine them; limited in Germany in 1848 and abolished in 1877.
                                                                       p. 118

91 The Bill on the establishment of *mortgage banks* envisaged the founding of
annuity-offices for the realisation of the redemption of peasant obligations under
terms extremely favourable to the landlords. The bank was to advance
compensation to the landlords amounting to eighteen times the value of the
annual obligations of the peasants, the latter having to pay back this sum within 41
years.   p. 118

92 Between 1807 and 1811, the Ministers Stein and Hardenberg carried out certain
agrarian reforms in Prussia. In October 1807, serfdom was abolished but all the
feudal obligations of the peasants remained. In September 1811, the peasants
received the right to redeem their obligations on the condition that they
surrendered up to half of their land to the landlord or paid a corresponding sum
of money. In 1845, the amount of the redemption payment was established at
twenty-five times the value of annual feudal dues.   p. 118

93 The article was first published in English in the collection: Karl Marx and
Frederick Engels, *Articles from the "Neue Rheinische Zeitung". 1848-49*, Progress
Publishers, Moscow, 1972.   p. 119

94 Following the revolutionary action of the Viennese masses on May 15, 1848,
Emperor Ferdinand and his Court fled to Innsbruck, a small town in Tyrol, which
became the mainstay of feudal aristocratic counter-revolution.

Engels is referring to the spontaneous rising of textile workers in Prague towards the end of June 1844. The revolt, in the course of which mills were destroyed and machines smashed, was brutally crushed by Austrian troops.

p. 119

95 The full title of this Committee, which was set up in Vienna during the revolutionary events of May 1848, was the Committee of Citizens, the National Guard and Students for Maintaining Safety and Order and Defending the Rights of the People.

p. 120

96 By referring to Windischgrätz as the Tilly of Prague Engels is comparing him with Johann Tilly, the army commander of the Catholic League during the Thirty Years' War, famous for the savage way he dealt with the Protestant population of conquered towns as well as for his military pillage.

p. 120

97 The national guard—an armed civic militia that was formed in Paris at the beginning of the French revolution of 1789-93 and existed, with intervals, till August 1871. During the February revolution of 1848, a considerable section of the national guard took the side of the insurgents, but in the course of the Paris uprising in June 1848 the Provisional Government employed the national guards of bourgeois districts in the fight against the workers.

p. 121

98 In the Neue Rheinische Zeitung this item was followed by a report on the events in Paris printed in smaller type and based, apparently, on the French newspapers which had just arrived. Part of it read: "The immediate cause of the new uprising was measures directed at abolishing the national workshops—censuses of the workers, expulsion of workers who were not born in Paris to their native parts or to Sologne to build canals, introduction of piecework in the remaining workshops etc.—as well as the law on reintroduction of caution money for journals, open attacks (see today's issue of our paper, 'Paris', June 22) on the popular press, debates in the National Assembly so closely resembling those in the Chamber of Peers under Louis Philippe that even the noble knight Montalembert, in his speech at the session on the 22nd, said the same things, in a somewhat different form, which he had said shortly before the February revolution in defence of money-bags, the law against street gatherings etc."

The report quoted at length the French newspaper Journal des Débats politiques et littéraires's account of the events of June 22 in Paris. It was hostile towards the insurgents and misrepresented their conflict with the Minister of Public Works, Marie, a moderate republican and spokesman of the Government. For this reason the Neue Rheinische Zeitung's report ended with a warning: "It should not be forgotten that the Journal des Débats, which printed this report, is an old Court sheet and Marie is an advocate of the law against street gatherings and the man of the National."

p. 121

99 This refers to the address sent by the electors of Berncastel to August Reichensperger, their deputy in the Prussian National Assembly, expressing their indignation at his conduct, and that of other deputies from the Rhine Province, during the debate on the revolution: their vote to pass on to the agenda was considered repudiation of the revolution.

p. 122

100 The reference is to the Labour Commission that met at the Luxembourg Palace under the chairmanship of Louis Blanc. This was set up on February 28, 1848, by the Provisional Government under pressure from the workers, who demanded a

Ministry of Labour. The Commission, in which both workers and employers were represented, acted as mediator in labour conflicts, often taking the side of the employers. The revolutionary action of Paris workers on May 15, 1848, led to the end of the Luxembourg Commission, since the Government disbanded it next day.

National workshops were instituted by a government decree immediately after the February revolution of 1848. The Government thus sought to discredit Louis Blanc's ideas on the organisation of labour in the eyes of the workers and, at the same time, to utilise the workers of the national workshops organised on military lines in the struggle against the revolutionary proletariat. Revolutionary ideas, however, continued to gain ground among workers employed in the national workshops, and the Government took steps accordingly to limit the number of workers employed in them, to send some off to public works in the provinces etc. This caused great indignation among the Paris proletariat and was one of the reasons for the June uprising. After its suppression, the Cavaignac Government issued a decree disbanding the national workshops (July 3, 1848).

On June 7, 1848, the Constituent Assembly passed a *law against gatherings.* Any violation of this law was punishable by imprisonment of up to ten years.

p. 124

101 The *mobile guard* was set up by a decree of the Provisional Government on February 25, 1848, to fight against the revolutionary masses. These armed units consisted mainly of lumpenproletarians and were used to crush the June uprising in Paris.

p. 125

102 The *Palais Royal* was the residence of Louis XIV from 1643; in 1692 it became property of the Orléans branch of the Bourbons. Following the February revolution of 1848 it was proclaimed state property and its name was changed to Palais National.

p. 125

103 The reference is to the *Café Tortoni* on the boulevard des Italiens; when the Stock Exchange was closed, business transactions were carried on in this café and its vicinity. As distinct from the official Stock Exchange, the Café Tortoni and the adjacent district became known as the "small Stock Exchange".

p. 125

104 The *municipal guard of the republic* (also known as the republican guard) — a detachment of 2,600 men subordinated to the Prefect of Police — was formed on May 16, 1848, by decree of the French Government, frightened by the revolutionary action of the Paris workers on May 15. The republican guard fulfilled police functions in Paris.

p. 126

105 This article was first published in English in the collection: Karl Marx and Frederick Engels, *Articles from the "Neue Rheinische Zeitung". 1848-49*, Progress Publishers, Moscow, 1972.

p. 128

106 An article published in *The Northern Star* No. 557, June 24, 1848, under the title "The New Rhenish Gazette" stated: "*Neue Rheinische Zeitung* is the title of a new daily journal lately started at Cologne. This journal, which announces itself 'the organ of the democracy', is conducted with singular ability and extraordinary boldness; and we hail it as a worthy, able, and valiant comrade in the grand crusade against tyranny and injustice in every shape and form. The principal editor is Dr. *Marx*, one of the ablest of the defenders of Labour's rights in Europe. The assistant editors include W. Wolff, of Breslaw, a sterling democrat; Dr.

Dronke, of Coblentz, ex-state prisoner; F. Wolff, of Cologne (was ten years in Paris); H. Bürgers (of Cologne, a favourite popular orator, and member of the first popular assembly at Frankfort): Frederick Engels, whose able writings have often graced the columns of the *Star;* and George Weerth, a name honourably known to our readers as the unmasker of the Freetrade delusionists at the celebrated Brussels Conference. We wish our contemporary a long career of usefulness and victory."

p. 129

[107] Words from the French patriotic song based on the Song of the Girondists from *Chevalier de Maison-Rouge,* a play by Alexandre Dumas (father) and Auguste Maquet which was staged in 1847. The words and music of the refrain are taken from Rouget de Lisle. The song won wide popularity not long before the 1848 revolution and was known as "the second *Marseillaise*".

p. 130

[108] See Note 76.

p. 131

[109] The *Society of the Rights of Man and the Citizen* was a democratic organisation that arose during the July monarchy. Led by Armand Barbès, Aloysius Huber and others, the Society united a number of clubs in the capital and the provinces and fought for the implementation of the Jacobin Declaration of the Rights of Man and the Citizen adopted in 1793. Some of the members of this Society were leaders of the June uprising. For instance, the retired officer Kersausie, Chairman of the Society's Committee of Action, drew up a plan for an armed uprising which was partially carried out during the June events in Paris.

p. 133

[110] The reference is to the heroic defence of Saragossa during the Spanish people's war of liberation against Napoleon's rule. The city was twice besieged by the French (from June to August 1808 and from December 1808 to February 1809) and it was only after the second siege, during which over 40,000 of its defenders perished, that Saragossa surrendered to the superior forces of the French.

p. 135

[111] The *municipal guard of Paris,* formed after the July revolution of 1830, was subordinate to the Prefect of Police and used to suppress popular uprisings. Following the February revolution of 1848, the municipal guard was disbanded.

p. 138

[112] The *Île Louvier,* separated from the right bank by a narrow branch of the Seine, was connected with the mainland in 1844, forming a stretch between the boulevard Morland and the Henry IV embankment.

p. 142

[113] An allusion to the fact that, in suppressing the proletarian uprising, the republican guard undertook police functions similar to those of the monarchist municipal guard.

p. 142

[114] A passage from this article by Marx was later included in the first article of the series "From 1848 to 1849" (subsequently published by Engels under the title *The Class Struggles in France),* printed in the journal *Neue Rheinische Zeitung. Politisch-Ökonomische Revue* in 1850.

An English translation of this article was first published in 1851 under the title "June 29, 1848" in No. 16 of the Chartist weekly *Notes to the People* which was edited by Ernest Jones. Later translations appeared in England and the United

States between the 1920s and the 1940s. In 1972 the article was published in the collection: Karl Marx and Frederick Engels, *Articles from the "Neue Rheinische Zeitung". 1848-49*, Progress Publishers, Moscow, and in 1973 in the collection Karl Marx, *The Revolutions of 1848. Political Writings*, Vol. 1, London, Penguin Books.

p. 144

115 The party which formed around the daily paper *Le National* in the 1840s was composed of moderate republicans headed by Armand Marrast; it was supported by the industrial bourgeoisie and a section of the liberal intellectuals.

The party that supported the French daily *La Réforme* consisted of democrats and republicans headed by Ledru-Rollin; petty-bourgeois socialists led by Louis Blanc were also associated with it.

p. 144

116 The *Executive Committee* (the Commission of the Executive Government)—the Government of the French Republic set up by the Constituent Assembly on May 10, 1848, to replace the Provisional Government which had resigned. It survived until June 24, 1848, when Cavaignac's dictatorship was established.

p. 144

117 The *dynastic opposition*—an oppositional group in the French Chamber of Deputies during the July monarchy (1830-48). The group headed by Odilon Barrot represented the views of the liberal industrial and commercial bourgeoisie, and favoured a moderate electoral reform, which they regarded as a means of preventing revolution and preserving the Orléans dynasty.

p. 147

118 The *legitimists* were supporters of the Bourbon dynasty, which was overthrown in 1830. They upheld the interests of the big hereditary landowners.

p. 147

119 See Note 49.

p. 148

120 The reference is to an official poster which appeared in the streets of Paris on June 26 announcing that "the insurgents have been defeated, the struggle has ceased, and order has triumphed over anarchy".

p. 152

121 This article was first published in English in the collection: Karl Marx and Frederick Engels, *Articles from the "Neue Rheinische Zeitung". 1848-49*, Progress Publishers, Moscow, 1972.

p. 157

122 The reference is to the Paris uprising of June 5-6, 1832, prepared by the Left wing of the republicans as well as by members of secret societies including the Society of the Friends of the People. The uprising flared up during the funeral of General Lamarque, an opponent of Louis Philippe's Government. The insurgent workers threw up barricades which they defended with great courage and persistence.

p. 158

123 The royalist uprising in Paris on 12 and 13 Vendémiaire (October 4 and 5), 1795, was suppressed by the republican troops under the command of General Bonaparte.

p. 161

124 An abridged English translation of this article was first published in the magazine *Labour Monthly*, London, 1923, Vol. 5, No. 1, pp. 32-33. The article was published in full in the collection: Karl Marx and Frederick Engels, *Articles from the "Neue Rheinische Zeitung"*, 1848-49, Progress Publishers, Moscow, 1972.

p. 165

[125] On July 25, 1792, the Duke of Brunswick, commander-in-chief of the Austro-Prussian army fighting against revolutionary France, issued a manifesto, in which he threatened to raze the whole of Paris to the ground.   p. 165

[126] In 1785 an uprising against the rule of the aristocracy and the Catholic clergy who supported William of Orange broke out in the Netherlands. The uprising, which was led by the republican bourgeoisie, deposed William of Orange. Two years later, however, with the help of Prussian troops, he again became the Stadholder of the Netherlands.   p. 165

[127] Under an agreement between Britain, France and Russia concluded at the London Conference of 1830, Greece, whose people rose in revolt against Turkish rule in 1821 and won national independence, was to become a monarchy. The Bavarian Prince Otto was made King of Greece in 1832 while still a minor. He arrived in Greece accompanied by Bavarian troops and high officials and ruled as Otto I. This rule was strongly opposed by the Greek people.   p. 165

[128] At the Congress of the Holy Alliance (a covenant of European monarchs founded on September 26, 1815, on the initiative of the Russian Emperor Alexander I and the Austrian Chancellor Metternich), which began in Troppau in October 1820 and ended in Laibach in May 1821, the principle of intervention in the internal affairs of other states was officially proclaimed. Accordingly, the Laibach Congress decided to send Austrian troops into Italy to crush the revolutionary and national liberation movements there. French intervention in Spain with similar aims was decided at the Congress of Verona in 1822.

Ypsilanti was a Greek patriot who made an unsuccessful attempt to raise a revolt against Turkish rule in March 1821. He fled to Austria, was arrested and imprisoned until 1827.   p. 165

[129] In the 1820s and 1830s Austria and Prussia supported the clerical and feudal party headed by Dom Miguel, which opposed any measures designed to restrict absolutism in Portugal.   p. 165

[130] Austria and Prussia supported Don Carlos, who in 1833 started a civil war in Spain in order to win the throne with the help of the clerical and feudal party.   p. 165

[131] See Note 36.   p. 166

[132] See Note 83.   p. 167

[133] The party of the *National*—see Note 115.

The *party of Thiers* united bourgeois politicians with royalist tendencies supporting the Orléans dynasty and voicing their opinions in the newspaper *La Constitutionnel*. Before February 1848, they upheld a monarchy with republican institutions and thereafter a republic with monarchical institutions.

The *dynastic opposition*—see Note 117.   p. 168

[134] The *Executive Committee*—see Note 116.

The *September Laws*—see Note 8.   p. 168

[135] The reference is to the clashes between Prussian troops stationed at Trier and its citizens on May 2, 3 and 4, 1848, provoked by the authorities. On the order of

Schreckenstein, commander of the 2nd Army Corps, the civic militia of Trier was disbanded.   p. 171

[136] See Note 8.   p. 171

[137] The *Holy Hermandad*—a league of Spanish cities founded at the end of the fifteenth century with the co-operation of the royal authorities who wanted to make use of wealthy townspeople in their fight against the feudal magnates in an attempt to establish royal absolutism. From the middle of the sixteenth century the armed forces of the Holy Hermandad carried out police functions. Thus the police in general has often been ironically labelled the "Holy Hermandad".   p. 177

[138] Anneke spoke at the meeting of the Cologne Workers' Association (see Note 245) which took place at the Gürzenich Hall on June 25, 1848, to debate the setting up of a united commission which was to consist of representatives from the three democratic organisations of Cologne: the Democratic Society, the Workers' Association and the Association for Workers and Employers.   p. 178

[139] The *Code pénal*—the penal code adopted in France in 1810 and introduced into the regions of Western and South-Western Germany conquered by the French. The *Code pénal* and the *Code civil* remained in effect in the Rhine Province even after the region was annexed by Prussia in 1815. The Prussian Government attempted to reduce the sphere of its application and reintroduce the Prussian Penal Code: a whole series of laws and decrees were promulgated designed to guarantee feudal privileges. These measures, which met great opposition in the Rhineland, were annulled after the March revolution by the decrees issued on April 15, 1848.   p. 178

[140] On March 3, 1848, Anneke was arrested together with Gottschalk and Willich because they had helped to organise a mass meeting in Cologne. All three were accused of "incitement to revolt and founding an illegal association". They were released from prison on March 21, 1848, on the royal amnesty.   p. 178

[141] The *Köslin address*—on May 23, 1848, junkers and officials of the town of Köslin (Pomerania) issued an appeal to the Prussian population to march on Berlin to crush the revolution.   p. 181

[142] These countries were the chief markets for Prussia's spinning and weaving industry. They were lost even before the revolution of 1848 and 1849.   p. 182

[143] The Prussian General Pfuel ordered the heads of captured Polish insurgents in Posen to be shaved in order to humiliate them.   p. 182

[144] During the summer of 1848, a special detachment of armed men dressed in civilian clothes was set up in Berlin. These persons were to be used in addition to the regular police to break up street gatherings and mass demonstrations. Another of their functions was to gather intelligence. These special policemen were called "constables" by analogy with the special constabulary employed in England to disperse the Chartist demonstration on April 10, 1848.   p. 185

[145] At the close of the session of July 4, 1848, the Prussian National Assembly decided to grant the committee investigating the events at Posen unlimited authority. Contrary to all parliamentary rules, representatives of the Right attempted to

organise a vote on a motion to limit the powers of the committee. The deputies of the Left walked out of the Assembly in protest. The Right made use of this to pass the motion prohibiting the committee from travelling to Posen and interrogating witnesses and experts on the spot. Thus the Assembly's original decision was illegally annulled. For debates on the Posen committee see this volume, pp. 57-61, 195-98 and 200-07.   p. 188

[146] On April 8, 1848, during a secret mission on behalf of the King of Prussia Major Wildenbruch handed a Note to the Danish Government. It stated that Prussia was not fighting in Schleswig-Holstein in order to rob Denmark of the duchy but merely in order to combat "radical and republican elements in Germany". The Prussian Government tried every possible means to avoid official recognition of this compromising document.   p. 191

[147] The article was published in a special supplement to the Neue Rheinische Zeitung No. 39, and also in No. 40 of this newspaper where it was dated "Cologne, July 9".   p. 199

[148] See Note 145.   p. 201

[149] The Thirty Years' War, 1618-48 — a European war, in which the Pope, the Spanish and Austrian Habsburgs and the German Catholic princes rallied under the banner of Catholicism and fought against the Protestant countries: Bohemia, Denmark, Sweden, the Republic of the Netherlands and a number of German states. The rulers of Catholic France — rivals of the Habsburgs — supported the Protestant camp. Germany was the main arena for this struggle, the object of plunder and territorial claims. The Treaty of Westphalia (1648) sealed the political dismemberment of Germany.   p. 202

[150] The Long Parliament (1640-53) — the English Parliament which was convened by Charles I and became the constituent body of the English revolution.
                                                                         p. 206

[151] On October 20, 1842, the Rheinische Zeitung published a Bill on divorce which was being secretly prepared in government quarters. This started a broad public discussion of the Bill in the newspapers. The publication of the Bill in the Rheinische Zeitung and the blunt refusal of its editors to name the person who had sent in the text of the Bill was one of the reasons for the suppression of the Rheinische Zeitung. For details see present edition, Vol. 1, pp. 274-76 and 307-10.   p. 208

[152] Kamptz — member of the Central Investigation Commission in Mainz (see Note 308), which was instituted in 1819 by decision of the conference of German states. He was one of the instigators of the campaign against the representatives of the opposition among students, intelligentsia and other liberal elements; known as the "demagogues", they upheld Germany's unity and constitutional reforms.
Black, red and gold — the colours of the national liberation movement in Germany.   p. 208

[153] See Note 139.   p. 209

[154] On the motion of the Democratic Society (see Note 66), the popular meeting that gathered in Cologne at the Gürzenich Hall on July 9, 1848, adopted an address to

the Prussian National Assembly in which the activities of the Auerswald-Hansemann Government were denounced and the Prussian Assembly was asked to declare the Ministry "divested of the confidence of the country".   p. 210

[155] See Note 149.   p. 212

[156] *Svornost*—the Czech national militia formed after the revolutionary events of March 1848 in the Austrian Empire. It was recruited mainly from among students. Its main detachment guarded the Czech Museum in Prague where the Slav Congress was in session (see Note 73). During the June uprising in Prague, this detachment was disarmed and arrested by government troops. The Austrian authorities disbanded the national militia even though it was commanded by moderate representatives of the Czech movement (Baron Karel Villány) who disapproved of the insurgents.   p. 213

[157] *Fictitious purchases*—business transactions concluded for a definite period during which no transfer of goods or securities takes place. The speculative element arises from the difference between rates of exchange on the market and commodity prices.   p. 224

[158] See Note 44.   p. 229

[159] The first article, dated "Cologne, July 17", from the cycle "The Debate on Jacoby's Motion", was first published in English in the collection: Karl Marx and Frederick Engels, *Articles from the "Neue Rheinische Zeitung". 1848-49*, Progress Publishers, Moscow, 1972. All the other articles in this cycle are published in English for the first time.   p. 232

[160] On June 28, 1848, the Frankfurt National Assembly decided to set up a provisional Central Authority consisting of the Imperial Regent (Archduke John of Austria) and an Imperial Ministry. Since the Central Authority had neither a budget nor an army of its own, it possessed no real power.
    In the Prussian National Assembly the formation of a provisional Central Authority was debated at the session of July 11, 1848, when Johann Jacoby tabled this motion on behalf of the Left deputies.   p. 232

[161] See Note 13.   p. 232

[162] See Note 12.   p. 234

[163] The *Customs Union* (*Zollverein*) of the German states, which established a common customs frontier, was founded in 1834 and headed by Prussia. Brought into being by the necessity for an all-German market, the Union embraced all the larger German states with the exception of Austria.   p. 236

[164] *Vendée*—a department in Western France; during the French Revolution the centre of a largely peasant-based royalist uprising. The word "Vendée" came to denote counter-revolutionary actions.   p. 237

[165] See Note 149.   p. 238

[166] The *Anti-Corn Law League* was founded in 1838 by the Manchester factory owners Cobden and Bright. By demanding unrestricted free trade, the League fought for the abolition of the Corn Laws, which established high tariffs on imported

agricultural produce in order to maintain high prices on the home market. In this way, the League sought to weaken the economic and the political position of the landed aristocracy, as well as to cut workers' wages. The struggle between the industrial bourgeoisie and the landowning aristocracy over the Corn Laws culminated in their repeal in 1846.   p. 238

[167] On April 2, 1848, the republican minority headed by Friedrich Hecker and Gustav Struve walked out of the Preparliament (see Note 12), to show its opposition to the policy of compromises pursued by the liberal majority. They counted on support among broad circles of the revolutionary-minded population in Southern and Western Germany, particularly in Baden. Frightened by the growth of the republican movement, the Baden Government decided to increase its army, asked for military assistance from neighbouring German states and issued an order for the arrest of the republican Joseph Fickler, who was denounced by the liberal Karl Mathy. These measures led to the republican uprising on April 12, 1848, under the leadership of Hecker and Struve. Ill-prepared and lacking organisation, the uprising was crushed by the end of April.   p. 239

[168] In most German states elections to the Frankfurt National Assembly were indirect. Under the law of April 8, 1848, the Prussian National Assembly too was elected by two-stage voting.   p. 248

[169] See Note 13.   p. 249

[170] An English translation of this article was first published in the collection: Karl Marx, *The Revolutions of 1848. Political Writings*, Vol. 1, London, Penguin Books, 1973.   p. 250

[171] In June 1848, Danish and Prussian plenipotentiaries met at Malmö (Sweden) to negotiate an armistice in the war over Schleswig-Holstein (see Note 28). An agreement was reached on July 8 and approved by the King and the Prussian Government, but the commander-in-chief, General Wrangel, refused to sign it because it was obviously disadvantageous to the German side. The armistice was signed in a modified form on August 26, 1848 (see Note 271).   p. 253

[172] See Note 41.   p. 253

[173] An ironical allusion to the Magna Carta Libertatum — a deed which the insurgent barons of England forced King John to sign on June 15, 1215. Magna Carta introduced certain limitations on the royal prerogative, primarily to the advantage of the big feudal lords. Some concessions were also granted to the knights and the townspeople.   p. 257

[174] See Note 17.   p. 259

[175] On the armistice negotiations with Denmark see Note 171.
    The article was first published in English in the collection: Karl Marx and Frederick Engels, *Articles from the "Neue Rheinische Zeitung". 1848-49*, Progress Publishers, Moscow, 1972.   p. 266

[176] See Note 13.   p. 266

[177] The *Sound tax* was a toll which, from 1425 to 1857, Denmark collected from all
foreign vessels passing through the Sound.   p. 268

[178] The *Workers' Congress* met in Berlin between August 23 and September 3, 1848, on
the initiative of several workers' organisations. At this Congress, many workers'
associations united into the Workers' Fraternity. The programme of the Congress
was drawn up under the influence of Stephan Born and set the workers the task of
implementing narrow craft-union demands, thereby diverting them from the
revolutionary struggle. A number of its points bore the stamp of Louis Blanc's and
Proudhon's utopian ideas. The editors of the *Neue Rheinische Zeitung* did not
approve of the general stand taken by Born, but they refrained from criticising his
views in the press, bearing in mind the progressive nature of the endeavour to
unite workers' associations. The programme of the Workers' Congress was
published in the *Neue Rheinische Zeitung* (No. 31, July 1, 1848) as a report from
Berlin without editorial comment.   p. 271

[179] On April 6, 1848, the Posen Assembly of the Estates rejected the proposal of the
Prussian Government to incorporate the Grand Duchy of Posen into the German
Confederation (see Note 13).   p. 273

[180] The government Bill on the compulsory loan was submitted to the Prussian
National Assembly on July 12, 1848.   p. 278

[181] *Sliding scale*—a way of regulating tariffs on imported grain products practised in
England during the operation of the Corn Laws, a system of raising or lowering
tariffs in proportion to the fall or rise of grain prices on the home market. One set
of sliding-scale regulations was introduced by the Peel Ministry in 1842.
                                                                              p. 281

[182] On *special constables* see Note 144.
On *Fickler's arrest* see Note 167.   p. 288

[183] The *First Democratic Congress* in Frankfurt am Main was held between June 14 and
17, 1848; it was attended by delegates from 89 democratic and workers'
associations from different towns in Germany. The Congress decided to unite all
democratic associations and to set up district committees headed by the Central
Committee of German democrats, with headquarters in Berlin. Fröbel, Rau and
Kriege were elected members of the Central Committee and Bayrhoffer, Schütte
and Anneke—their deputies. Even after this decision, the democratic movement
in Germany still lacked unity and organisation because of the weakness and
vacillations of its petty-bourgeois leaders.

The Congress discussed the political programme and organisational structure
of the democratic party. A programme point that ran as follows was adopted:
"There is only one acceptable constitution for the German people: a democratic
republic, i.e. a system under which the whole society is responsible for the
freedom and welfare of its every member." However, nothing definite was said
about the ways to attain this aim.   p. 289

[184] Moderate liberal elements in Germany, adherents of the constitutional monarchy,
began to unite into constitutional associations and clubs, headed by the
Constitutional Club in Berlin, and into citizens' associations (see Note 65).
Associations of Right-wing forces sprang up alongside them, particularly in
Prussia, such as the Prussian associations (*Preussenvereine*) and the counter-
revolutionary Association for the Protection of Property and the Well-Being of All

Classes. Catholic organisations in the Rhine Province—associations of Pius IX (*Piusvereine*)—which campaigned for a moderate constitutional programme resorting to demagogical phraseology, joined either the liberal or the reactionary camp.   p. 289

[185] This article was first published in English in the collections: Karl Marx and Frederick Engels, *Articles from the "Neue Rheinische Zeitung"*. *1848-49*, Progress Publishers, Moscow, 1972, and Karl Marx, *The Revolutions of 1848*. *Political Writings*, Vol. 1, London, Penguin Books, 1973.   p. 290

[186] Feudalism was abolished, and juries and the *Code Napoléon* were introduced in the Rhine Province during the French Revolution and Napoleon's Empire. Feudal relations were not restored in the Rhineland even after its incorporation into Prussia (1815) where remnants of feudalism survived in spite of the reforms of 1807-11, allowing redemption of feudal obligations.

The Bill abolishing feudal obligations was submitted to the Prussian National Assembly by the Minister of Agriculture Gierke on July 11, 1848, and discussed on July 18.   p. 290

[187] See Note 88.   p. 293

[188] See Note 69.   p. 295

[189] This article was first published in English in the magazine *Labour Monthly*, 1948, Vol. XXX, No. 8, and later in the collection: Karl Marx and Frederick Engels, *Articles from the "Neue Rheinische Zeitung"*. *1848-49*, Progress Publishers, Moscow, 1972.   p. 296

[190] Under the Poor Law of 1834 the only relief available to the poor who were fit for work was admission to a workhouse. These were dubbed "Poor Law Bastilles".   p. 296

[191] In 1824, under mass pressure the English Parliament repealed the ban on trade unions. However, in 1825 it passed a Bill on workers' associations confirming the repeal of the ban on the trade unions but vigorously limiting their activities. Merely to urge workers to join a union and take part in a strike was considered, for example, as "coercion" and "violence" and was liable to criminal prosecution.   p. 297

[192] This refers to bloody clashes between workers and police in Birmingham, Glasgow, Newcastle and Sunderland in 1839. The most significant event was the Newport rising in November 1839, due to the deplorable conditions of the South-Wales miners and growing discontent after Parliament had turned down the Chartist petition and a number of popular Chartist agitators (Henry Vincent and others) were arrested. The leaders of the insurrection intended it to lead to a general armed struggle for the People's Charter. Three poorly armed insurgent detachments (numbering 3,000 men) entered Newport at dawn on November 4 but were dispersed by troops and police who had been brought in advance. On January 13, 1840, the leaders of the insurgents were sentenced to capital punishment which was commuted to transportation as a result of a protest campaign.

When Parliament rejected the second Chartist petition in August 1842 in conditions of economic crisis and growing poverty, disturbances broke out in some of the industrial districts in England. In Lancashire and in a considerable part of Cheshire and Yorkshire strikes assumed a general nature and in some places (Stockport, Preston and others) they turned into spontaneous revolts. The Government responded with mass arrests and severe sentences for Chartist leaders.   p. 297

[193] See Note 166.   p. 299

[194] The fight for legislative restriction of the working day to ten hours began in England as early as the end of the eighteenth century, and from the 1830s on large sections of the workers became involved in it. In an attempt to use this popular slogan against the industrial bourgeoisie, representatives of the landed aristocracy supported the Ten Hours' Bill in Parliament. The Bill limiting working hours for women and young children was passed by Parliament on June 8, 1847.   p. 299

[195] This refers to the battle of Custozza, near Verona, between the Austrian army, under the command of Radetzky, and Piedmont troops under the command of King Charles Albert. The fighting went on for three days, from July 23 to 25, without bringing decisive victory to either side. Eventually the Austrian command mustered superior forces and dealt a heavy blow at the Piedmont troops, who were scattered largely due to poor generalship which doomed them to inaction at the decisive moment.   p. 305

[196] In the battle of *Curtatone* (five kilometres from Mantua) on May 29, 1848, the Austrian troops forced the Tuscany corps, which fought on the side of the Piedmont army, to retreat. The resistance offered by this corps, however, enabled the Piedmont troops to regroup their forces and on May 30, in the battle of Goito, to hurl back the Austrians to their former positions. Nevertheless, the Piedmont command failed to make use of this success.   p. 305

[197] This article was first published in English in the collection: Karl Marx, *The Revolutions of 1848. Political Writings,* Vol. 1, London, Penguin Books, 1973.
   In this article the phrase "secret treaties with Napoleon" refers to the *Treaty of Tilsit* signed in July 1807 by France, Russia and Prussia. In an attempt to split the defeated powers, Napoleon made no territorial claims on Russia and even managed the transfer of part of the Prussian monarchy's eastern land to Russia. He consolidated an alliance with Alexander I when the two emperors met in Erfurt in the autumn of 1808. At the same time, this treaty imposed harsh terms on Prussia, which lost nearly half its territory to the German states dependent on France, had to pay indemnities, had its army limited etc. However, Russia, as well as Prussia, had to sever alliance with England and, to her disadvantage, join Napoleon's Continental System. Napoleon formed the vassal Duchy of Warsaw on Polish territory seized by Prussia during the partitions of Poland at the end of the eighteenth century, and planned to use the duchy as a springboard in the event of war with Russia. Sharp contradictions between France and Russia led to Napoleon's campaign against Russia in 1812.   p. 307

[198] This refers to the "Appeal to the Germans" issued on March 25, 1813, in Kalisch after the defeat of Napoleon's Grand Army in Russia in 1812. The Russian Tsar and the King of Prussia called upon the Germans to fight Napoleon and demagogically promised them freedom and independence. It later transpired that the monarchs' intention was to use the national liberation movements to strengthen the feudal monarchies and privileges of the nobility.   p. 308

[199] For the *congresses of the Holy Alliance* held in *Laibach* and *Verona*, see Note 128.

The delegates of the states forming the German Confederation held a conference in Carlsbad in August 1819. On the initiative of the Austrian Chancellor Metternich and with the approval of the Russian Tsar, measures of struggle against the opposition movement were worked out. The decisions of the conference were approved by the Federal Diet (see Note 13) on September 20, 1819. The Carlsbad decisions envisaged the introduction of preliminary censorship in all German states, strict supervision of universities, prohibition of students' societies, establishment of an investigation commission to suppress so-called demagogues.   p. 308

[200] See Note 164.   p. 309

[201] See Note 12.   p. 310

[202] The first partition of Poland took place in 1772 between Prussia, Austria and Russia.   p. 310

[203] See Note 146.   p. 310

[204] This refers to the *Polish national liberation uprising of November 1830-October 1831.* The majority of its participants were revolutionary nobles (the *szlachcics*) and its leaders came from the ranks of the aristocracy. It was suppressed by Russian troops, with the support of Prussia and Austria. In spite of its defeat, the uprising was of major international significance because it diverted the forces of counter-revolution and thwarted their plans regarding the bourgeois revolution of 1830 in France and the 1830-31 revolution in Belgium.   p. 311

[205] This refers to the rescripts by Frederick William IV of February 3, 1847, convening the United Diet, in which the King referred to the laws on estates representation promulgated in Prussia between the 1820s and the 1840s. The convocation of the United Diet (see Note 25) was presented by the King as implementation of his earlier promises to introduce a Constitution.   p. 311

[206] An allusion to the suppression of the Cracow national liberation uprising in 1846 by Austrian troops and the abolition of the status of the free city of Cracow ("the Cracow Republic") by decision of the three powers — Austria, Prussia and Russia (see Notes 36 and 47).   p. 311

[207] In the summer of 1848, the anti-feudal movement and the struggle for complete liberation from the yoke of the Turkish Sultan grew in intensity in the Danube principalities (Moldavia and Wallachia), which formally remained autonomous possessions of Turkey. The movement in Wallachia grew into a bourgeois revolution. In June 1848, a Constitution was promulgated, a liberal Provisional Government was formed and George Bibesco, the ruler of Wallachia, abdicated and fled from the country.

On June 28, 1848, twelve-thousand Russian troops entered Moldavia and in July of the same year, Turkish troops also invaded the country. Intervention helped to restore the feudal system and the subsequent entry of Turkish troops into Wallachia, with the consent of the Tsarist Government, brought about the defeat of the bourgeois revolution.   p. 311

[208] Grave economic difficulties (almost universal crop failure) and natural calamities (cholera epidemics and devastating fires) exacerbated the class contradictions in

Russia in the spring and summer of 1848. This year witnessed the rise of the
peasant movement, cholera "riots" in St. Petersburg and Riga and popular revolts
in some gubernias, for example, in Vladimir Gubernia. An important seat of
revolutionary ferment was the Kingdom of Poland.   p. 312

209 The item was printed in the column "French Republic". It deals with the Press Bill
submitted to the French Constituent Assembly at the end of July 1848 and widely
discussed in the German press. The Bill provided for severe punishment for
insult, in the press, of the authorities, attacks on property, religion and family
principles. It was passed by the Assembly on August 9-11, 1848.   p. 314

210 The *Neue Rheinische Zeitung* of July 6, 1848, carried a report received from
Ewerbeck, its Paris correspondent, under the heading "Bakunin". The author
reported the current rumour that Mikhail Bakunin was in the secret service of
Nicholas I and that George Sand was in possession of evidence to this effect. Such
rumours circulated among Polish emigrants even before the 1848 revolution. On
July 16, the *Neue Rheinische Zeitung* reprinted Bakunin's statement to the editors
of the *Allgemeine Oder Zeitung* in which he refuted these accusations. It also carried
Bakunin's letter to George Sand asking her to make a public statement testifying
to the falsity of the rumour, which discredited him as a revolutionary. On August
3, Marx received George Sand's letter to the *Neue Rheinische Zeitung* through the
Polish democrat Kościelski and immediately published it with an introductory
note from the editors.

In 1853 certain English newspapers accused Marx of having used the *Neue
Rheinische Zeitung* to spread insinuations against Bakunin. Early in September
1853 Marx refuted these charges — the authors of which were emigrants hostile to
proletarian revolutionaries — in statements to the editors of the *Morning Advertiser*
and the *People's Paper* (see present edition, Vol. 12). In the statement to the
Morning Advertiser he recalled that the *Neue Rheinische Zeitung* had published
Bakunin's letters of self-acquittal and the relevant letter of George Sand; he also
quoted the editors' introductory note to this letter.

Subsequently, in his letter to Lassalle written on March 3, 1860, Marx gave the
following description of this episode: "I printed in the *Neue Rheinische Zeitung* a
denunciation of Bakunin received from two different sources in Paris, the one
being a Pole I knew and the other — the *Paris lithographic bulletin*, which would
anyway have circulated this denunciation to *all* papers even if *I* had not printed it.
The fact that the accusation was made *publicly* was in the interest of the cause as
well as of Bakunin himself. I reprinted *immediately* Bakunin's refutation which
appeared in the *Neue Oder Zeitung*. Kościelski, whom Bakunin sent to Cologne in
order to challenge me to a duel, examined the *letters from Paris* and became
convinced that as an editor I was *in duty bound* to have the denunciation printed (it
appeared as a report with no comments). *Thereupon* he wrote to Bakunin
informing him that he could no longer represent his interests. Kościelski became
one of the best and most treasured friends of the *Neue Rheinische Zeitung*. I gave
public satisfaction to Bakunin in the *Neue Rheinische Zeitung* and made it up with
him when we met in Berlin in August 1848. Subsequently (in 1851) I broke a lance
defending him in the *Tribune*." (This refers to "Revolution and Counter-
Revolution in Germany", an article which Engels wrote for Marx and in which
he highly praised Bakunin as a participant in the Dresden uprising of May
1849.)   p. 315

211 An allusion to the closest entourage of Frederick William IV (the Gerlach brothers, Radowitz and other prominent figures with counter-revolutionary aspirations).   p. 320

212 Proudhon's speech is set forth and quoted in this article according to newspaper reports. The full text of Proudhon's speech at the session of the French National Assembly on July 31, 1848, was published in *Compte rendu des séances de l'Assemblée nationale*, Vol. II, Paris, 1849, pp. 770-82.   p. 321

213 The *Inquisition proceedings*—a form of criminal proceedings under absolutism, which allowed extremely wide powers to judges, who combined the functions of prosecutor and examining magistrate, trial in camera, and the use of torture to obtain evidence. The Inquisition proceedings became particularly notorious in Catholic Church courts and especially those of the Holy Inquisition which examined crimes of heresy.   p. 325

214 *Lettres de cachet*, i.e. warrants for arrest signed by the King of France at the time of the absolute monarchy. Any person could be imprisoned without investigation or court proceedings.   p. 326

215 See Note 92.   p. 328

216 The *threshing gardeners (Dreschgärtner)*—the name applied in some places in Germany, particularly in Silesia, to dependent peasants who rented a plot of land with a house from the landowner and, in return, had to work for him (mainly harvesting) for a small payment in cash or in kind.   p. 330

217 *Banalities* (the original has *Zwangs- und Bannrechte*)—feudal lords' right to impose taxes on peasants for the obligatory use of flour mills, wine presses etc. owned by feudal lords.   p. 331

218 Traditional holidays with carnivals in Belgium to celebrate its separation from Holland and its independence proclaimed at the time of the 1830 revolution.   p. 336

219 The debates on the Grand Duchy of Posen were held in the Frankfurt National Assembly on July 24-27, 1848.   p. 337

220 See Note 47.   p. 337

221 Engels refers to the repeated promises of Frederick William III to introduce a Constitution in Prussia based on the estate principle.   p. 338

222 This refers to the cowardly and servile conduct of the Prussian bureaucracy after the defeat of Prussia by Napoleonic France in the battles of Jena and Auerstedt in October 1806 (see also Note 77).   p. 342

223 The treaties signed by Russia, Prussia and Austria in Vienna on May 3, 1815, and the Final Act of the Congress of Vienna signed on June 9, 1815, which legalised the abolition of the Duchy of Warsaw established in 1807 by Napoleon and a new partition of the Polish lands between Austria, Prussia and Russia, pledged that representative bodies and national political institutions would be set up in all

Polish lands. In Posen this resulted in the convocation of an assembly of the estates endowed with advisory functions.   p. 343

[224] See Note 36.   p. 344

[225] The *Convention of Jaroslawiec* was concluded between the Posen Committee of Polish insurgents and the Prussian Commissioner General Willisen on April 11, 1848. It stipulated that the Polish insurgents were to lay down their arms and disband. In return, the Poles were promised the "national reorganisation" of Posen, i.e. the formation of a Polish army, the appointment of Poles to administrative and other posts and recognition of Polish as an official language. However, the Convention was treacherously violated by the Prussian administration, and the national liberation movement in Posen was brutally suppressed by Prussian troops. The border between the western ("German") part of the Duchy of Posen, which was not liable to reorganisation, and the eastern (Polish) one, was shifted further to the east. The promised "reorganisation" was never carried out.   p. 346

[226] See Note 149.   p. 346

[227] The *chambers of reunion* (*chambres de réunion*) were set up by Louis XIV in 1679-80 to justify and provide legal and historical grounds for France's claims to certain lands in neighbouring states, primarily in the territory of Germany; these lands were subsequently occupied by French troops.   p. 347

[228] The *Polish Constitution of 1791* expressed the aspirations of the progressive sections of the nobility and urban bourgeoisie. It abolished the *liberum veto* (the principle that resolutions of the Diet could only be passed unanimously) and the elective monarchy, provided for a Government responsible to the Diet and granted the urban bourgeoisie various political and economic rights. The Constitution was directed against feudal anarchy and aimed at strengthening the Central Authority; it also alleviated to some extent the position of peasant serfs by recognising the legal force of commutation agreements between landowners and peasants. As a result of the revolt of the nobility and the interference on the part of Catherine II of Russia and Frederick William II of Prussia, the Constitution was repealed in 1792-93 and a second partition of Poland between Russia and Prussia took place.   p. 351

[229] The majority of deputies to the Frankfurt National Assembly were members of the liberal *Centre* which, in its turn, was split into two factions—the *Right Centre* (Dahlmann, Gagern, Bassermann, Mathy, Mevissen and others) and the *Left Centre* (including Mittermaier, Werner and Raveaux). The deputies of both centres were supporters of the constitutional monarchy.   p. 354

[230] On August 6, 1848, troops of all German states were, by an order issued by the Imperial Minister of War Peucker on July 16, 1848, to take the oath of allegiance to the Imperial Regent Archduke John at the celebration parade. Frederick William IV, who himself claimed to be the Supreme Commander of the Armed Forces of the German Confederation, cancelled the parade in Prussia appointed for August 6.   p. 359

[231] Janiszewski apparently quoted the following words by Jean Jacques Rousseau addressed to the Poles: "If you cannot prevent the enemy from swallowing you

up, try at least to prevent him from digesting you." See also his work *Considérations sur le gouvernement de Pologne, et sur sa réformation projette.*   p. 366

[232] At a session of the Frankfurt National Assembly on August 7, 1848, Deputy Brentano spoke in favour of amnesty for the participants in the Baden republican uprising and for their leader Hecker. The Right-wing deputies kept interrupting Brentano and finally forced him to leave the rostrum.   p. 368

[233] Paragraph 6 of the *Fundamental Rights of the German People* worked out by the Frankfurt National Assembly as part of the future Constitution (it was adopted on August 2, 1848) abolished all estates privileges and all titles not connected with office.   p. 368

[234] Don Carlos who, in 1833, appeared as a pretender to the Spanish throne against Isabella, daughter of King Ferdinand VII, referred to the 1713 law prohibiting succession to the throne along the female line. In 1838-40, Lichnowski took part in the civil war unleashed by Don Carlos and was promoted to the rank of brigadier-general.   p. 370

[235] *Wasserpolacken*— original name of ferrymen on the Oder who were mainly natives of Upper Silesia; subsequently it became widespread in Germany as a nickname of Silesian Poles.   p. 370

[236] The *Albigensian wars* (1209-29) were waged by the feudal magnates of Northern France, together with the Pope, against the movement of townspeople and the lesser nobility, supported by peasants, in Languedoc, in the south, who were seeking independence from the north. This movement took the form of a "heresy", being directed against the power and doctrine of the Catholic Church as well as against the secular power of the feudal state. And its adherents were called "Albigenses" from the city of Albi, one of their main centres. The Albigensian heresy was wiped out after twenty years of war, and a considerable part of Languedoc annexed to the lands of the French kings. The whole of Languedoc was annexed to France in 1271, retaining, however, a measure of self-government which was finally abolished at the time of the absolute monarchy.   p. 372

[237] See Note 73.   p. 374

[238] During the Cracow national liberation uprising in 1846 (see Note 36) the Austrian authorities provoked clashes in Galicia between Ukrainian peasants and detachments of Polish insurgents. When the uprising was suppressed, the participants in the peasant movement in Galicia were severely persecuted.   p. 375

[239] The *Wahl-Manifest der radicalen Reformpartei für Deutschland* written by Ruge and published in *Die Reform* No. 16, April 16, 1848, proclaimed "the editing of the *rationale* of events" as the main task of the National Assembly.   p. 377

[240] The reference is to one of the legends woven round the foundation of the Swiss Confederation, the origin of which dates back to the agreement of the three mountain cantons of Schwyz, Uri and Unterwalden in 1291. According to this legend, representatives of the three cantons met in 1307 in the Grütli (Rütli) meadow and took an oath of loyalty in the joint struggle against Austrian rule.   p. 377

241 This refers to a system of general treaties set up by the Vienna Congress (September 1814-June 1815) which embraced the whole of Europe, with the exception of that part then incorporated in Turkey. The decisions of the Congress helped to restore feudal order, perpetuated the political fragmentation of Germany and Italy, sanctioned the incorporation of Belgium into Holland and the partitions of Poland and outlined measures to combat the revolutionary movement.   p. 378

242 *Lamartine's manifesto* (of March 4, 1848) — a circular of the Minister of Foreign Affairs on the foreign policy principles and goals of the Provisional Government of the French Republic.   p. 378

243 On July 27, 1848, the Frankfurt National Assembly approved the decision passed earlier by the Federal Diet (see Note 13) to include a number of regions of the Grand Duchy of Posen into the German Confederation, sanctioned the powers vested in the twelve deputies elected from these regions (though the Polish population had refused to take part in elections to the Frankfurt Parliament), confirmed the demarcation line established by General Pfuel in Posen after the repeated transference of this line further east and obliged the Prussian Government "to guarantee the security of Germans residing in Posen".

   This decision aroused strong indignation in democratic circles in Germany. For example, on August 11, a general meeting of the Cologne Democratic Society, presided over by Marx, adopted a resolution of protest against the Frankfurt Assembly decisions on the Polish question and sent it to the Assembly (see this volume, pp. 564-65).   p. 381

244 See Note 230.   p. 383

245 For the Cologne Democratic Society, see Note 66.

   The *Cologne Workers' Association* — a workers' organisation founded by Andreas Gottschalk on April 13, 1848. Its 300 members had increased to 5,000, the majority of whom were workers and artisans, by the beginning of May. The Association was led by the President and the committee, which consisted of representatives of various trades. The newspaper *Zeitung des Arbeiter-Vereines zu Köln* was the organ of the Association, but from October 26 it was replaced by the *Freiheit, Brüderlichkeit, Arbeit.* There were a number of branches of the Association. After Gottschalk's arrest, Moll was elected President on July 6 and he held this post till the state of siege was proclaimed in Cologne in September 1848, when he had to emigrate under threat of arrest. On October 16, Marx agreed to assume this post temporarily at the request of Association members. In November Röser became acting President and on February 28, 1849, Schapper was elected President and remained in this post until the end of May 1849.

   The majority of the leading members (Gottschalk, Anneke, Schapper, Moll, Lessner, Jansen, Röser, Nothjung, Bedorf) were members of the Communist League.

   During the initial period of its existence, the Workers' Association was influenced by Gottschalk who, sharing many of the views of the "true socialists", ignored the historical tasks of the proletariat in the democratic revolution, carried on sectarian tactics of boycotting indirect elections to the Federal and Prussian National Assemblies and came out against support of democratic candidates in elections. He combined ultra-Left phrases with very legalistic methods of struggle (workers' petitions to the Government and the City Council etc.) and supported the demands of the workers affected by craft prejudices etc. From the very beginning, Gottschalk's tactics were resisted by the supporters of Marx and Engels. At the end of June a change-over took place under their influence in the activities of the Workers' Association, which became a centre of revolutionary agitation among the workers, and from the autumn of 1848 onwards, also among the peasants. Members of the Association organised democratic and workers' associations in the vicinity of Cologne, disseminated revolutionary literature, including the "Demands of the Communist Party in Germany", and carried on among themselves education in scientific communism through the study of Marx's writings. The Association maintained close contact with other workers' and democratic organisations.

When, in the spring of 1849, Marx and Engels took steps to organise the advanced workers on a national scale and actually started preparing for the creation of a proletarian party, they relied to a considerable extent on the Cologne Workers' Association.

The mounting counter-revolution and intensified police reprisals prevented further activities of the Cologne Workers' Association to unite and organise the working masses. After the *Neue Rheinische Zeitung* ceased publication and Marx, Schapper and other leaders of the Association left Cologne, it gradually turned into an ordinary workers' educational society.   p. 384

[246] Paragraph 1 of Article 1 of the *Fundamental Rights of the German People* worked out by the Frankfurt National Assembly was adopted at its session of July 21, 1848, with the following wording: "Every German possesses the general German right of citizenship from which it accrues that a citizen of every separate state enjoys all rights of a naturalised citizen of another state."   p. 384

[247] After the battle of Custozza (see Note 195) the Piedmont troops retreated. On August 4, 1848, they were defeated near Milan, into which the Austrian army of Radetzky entered on August 6. On August 9, 1848, an armistice was concluded under which Piedmont undertook to withdraw its armed forces from the cities and fortresses of Lombardy and Venice, thus surrendering them to the Austrians.

This article was first published in English in the collection: Karl Marx and Frederick Engels, *Articles from the "Neue Rheinische Zeitung". 1848-49*, Progress Publishers, Moscow, 1972.   p. 385

[248] *Carbonari*—members of bourgeois and aristocratic revolutionary secret societies which appeared in Italy in the early nineteenth century. They fought for national independence and unification of Italy and at the same time demanded liberal-constitutional reforms. The Carbonari played an important role in the revolutionary developments in the kingdoms of Naples and Sardinia early in the 1820s and also during the revolutionary struggle in Italy against Austrian rule and local feudal monarchies in the 1830s.

During the revolution of 1821 in Piedmont, Prince Charles Albert of Carignano made overtures to the Carbonari and they appointed him regent. However, afraid to lose his right to the Sardinian Crown if events took an unfavourable turn, he fled from Turin, abdicated his regency and helped to suppress the movement.   p. 386

[249] The battle of *Goito* (May 30, 1848) was part of the hostilities between the allied Italian forces and Austrian vassals, which started with the battle of Curtatone (see Note 196).

The battle of *Mozambano* (July 24, 1848) was an episode in the battle of Custozza (see Note 195) between the Piedmont and Austrian armies.

In both cases, the Piedmont Command proved incapable of energetic action against the enemy and of taking advantage of successes achieved at separate sectors along the front.   p. 388

250 See Note 248.   p. 389

251 Quotations are taken from the rescript of Frederick William IV dated March 18, 1848, on the speeding up of the convocation of the United Diet (see Note 25).   p. 390

252 See Note 246.   p. 391

253 This is a list of the battles between the Austrians and the French during the French Revolution, the Directory, the Consulate and the Empire, in which the Austrian army was defeated at Jemappes (November 6, 1792), at Fleurus (June 26, 1794), at Millesimo (April 13-14, 1796), at Rivoli (January 14-15, 1797), at Neuwied (April 18, 1797), at Marengo (June 14, 1800), at Hohenlinden (December 3, 1800), at Ulm (October 17, 1805), at Austerlitz (December 2, 1805), at Wagram (July 5-6, 1809).   p. 396

254 *Sonderbund*—a separatist union formed by the seven economically backward Catholic cantons of Switzerland in 1843 to resist progressive bourgeois reforms and defend the privileges of the church and the Jesuits. The decree of the Swiss Diet of July 1847 on the dissolution of the Sonderbund served as a pretext for the latter to start hostilities against other cantons early in November. On November 23, 1847, the Sonderbund army was defeated by federal forces.   p. 396

255 On the defeat of the Piedmont army at Custozza on July 25, 1848, see Note 195. On July 26-27 the Austrians routed the Piedmont troops at Volta and on August 6, 1848, occupied Milan.   p. 396

256 See Note 238.   p. 396

257 The revolution of 1848 in Italy, followed by revolutionary events in other European countries, was started by the people's uprising of January 12 in Palermo and the successful armed struggle in Sicily against the absolute monarchy of the Neapolitan Bourbons.   p. 397

258 This article was first published in English in the collection: Karl Marx and Frederick Engels, *Articles from the "Neue Rheinische Zeitung". 1848-49*, Progress Publishers, Moscow, 1972.   p. 399

259 For the storming of the arsenal, see Note 67.
    On August 21, 1848, meetings and demonstrations were held in Berlin against the assault, engineered by reactionary forces, on members of the Democratic Club in Charlottenburg (then a suburb of Berlin). The demonstrators demanded the resignation of the Auerswald-Hansemann Ministry and the punishment of those involved in the incidents in Charlottenburg; they also threw stones at the building in which Auerswald and other Ministers met. The Government retaliated with further repression.   p. 400

260 This refers to Prussia's participation in the wars of the anti-French coalition against Napoleon in 1813-14 and 1815 (see Note 76).   p. 400

[261] See Note 235.   p. 400

[262] This article was first published in English in the collection: Karl Marx and Frederick Engels, *Articles from the "Neue Rheinische Zeitung"*. *1848-49*, Progress Publishers, Moscow, 1972.   p. 402

[263] The armistice between Sardinia and Austria concluded on August 9, 1848 (see Note 247), was originally to last six weeks but was prolonged. It was annulled on March 12, 1849, but soon after hostilities were resumed the Sardinian army was defeated, Charles Albert abdicated and Victor Emmanuel II, the new King, again concluded an armistice with the Austrians on March 26.   p. 402

[264] On August 21, 1848, workers' disturbances started in Vienna, caused by the growth of unemployment and the Government's decree on the reduction of wages. On August 23 the national guards of bourgeois and aristocratic districts opened fire on unarmed workers who were protesting against this measure. The counter-revolutionaries who supported Emperor Ferdinand (who returned to Vienna from Innsbruck on August 12) and his court camarilla, and were preparing to attack the achievements of the revolution, took advantage of the situation, which had undermined the unity of the democratic forces.   p. 402

[265] This article was first published in English in the collection: Karl Marx and Frederick Engels, *Articles from the "Neue Rheinische Zeitung"*. *1848-49*, Progress Publishers, Moscow, 1972.   p. 404

[266] The so-called *Risquons-Tout trial*, held in Antwerp from August 9 to 30, 1848, was a fabrication of the Government of Leopold, the King of the Belgians, against the democrats. The pretext was a clash, which took place on March 29, 1848, between the Belgian Republican Legion bound for its home country from France and a detachment of soldiers near the village of Risquons-Tout not far from the French border. Mellinet, Ballin, Tedesco and other principal accused were sentenced to death, but this was later commuted to 30 years imprisonment, and still later they were pardoned.   p. 404

[267] The *German Workers' Association* was founded by Marx and Engels in Brussels at the end of August 1847, with the aim of politically educating German workers residing in Belgium and spreading the ideas of scientific communism among them. Its best cadres were members of the Communist League and it maintained contacts with Belgian workers' and democratic associations. Its activities ceased soon after the February revolution of 1848 in France when its members were arrested and deported by the Belgian police.   p. 406

[268] On his arrival in Cologne on April 11, 1848, Marx successfully applied to the Cologne City Council for citizenship. However, the decision was subject to approval by the local royal authorities who were slow in answering. At the beginning of August 1848, after four months' delay, Marx was informed that his application had been turned down. The conduct of the Cologne authorities aroused indignation in the city's democratic circles. The Cologne Democratic Society sent a deputation demanding that police measures against Marx should cease (see this volume, pp. 562-63). In reply to Marx's complaint, the Prussian Minister of the Interior Kühlwetter approved the decision of the local authorities on September 12, 1848 (see this volume, p. 581). Although the protest campaign

prevented reactionary circles from carrying out their schemes with regard to Marx immediately, he was in danger of being deported from Prussia as a "foreigner". Subsequently, the Prussian Government deported Marx for alleged "violation of the right of hospitality". This act and repressive measures against other editors of the *Neue Rheinische Zeitung* caused the newspaper to cease publication in May 1849.   p. 407

269 Under the impact of the March revolution in the German states, the Federal Diet (see Note 13) established by its special decision of March 30, 1848, the representation quota to the German National Assembly. On April 7, an amendment to this decision was approved which extended the right to vote and to be elected to political refugees who returned to Germany and were reinstated in German citizenship.   p. 408

270 See Note 12.   p. 408

271 On August 26, 1848, an armistice for the term of seven months was signed between Denmark and Prussia in the Swedish city of Malmö. The armistice provided for a ceasefire between Prussia and Denmark, replacement of the provisional authorities in Schleswig by a new Government to be formed by the two contracting parties (the representatives of the Danish monarchy predominant), separation of the troops of Schleswig and Holstein, and other onerous terms for the national liberation movement in the duchies. The revolutionary-democratic reforms which had been introduced were now virtually eliminated. Though the Prussian ruling circles had waged the war against Denmark in the name of the German Confederation, they sacrificed all-German interests to dynastic and counter-revolutionary considerations when they concluded the armistice. They were also prompted by the desire to avoid complications with Russia and Britain, which supported Denmark. Nonetheless, as Engels foresaw, on September 16, the Frankfurt National Assembly approved by a majority vote the armistice concluded in Malmö.   p. 411

272 This editorial note was published in parentheses at the end of the article "The Financial Project of the Left" in the *Neue Rheinische Zeitung*. It gave the following information:
   "*Berlin*, Sept, 6. The deputies Waldeck, Zenker, Anwandter, Krackrügge, Reuter, d'Ester, Stein, Elsner, Otto, Behrends, Jacoby, Schultz and others on the Left have placed the following financial plan before the National Assembly:
   "The Ministry is empowered to issue paper money to the sum of — million talers at 3 $^1/_3$ per cent interest and to be redeemed in twenty consecutive years against an annual sum of — million talers.
   "This paper money will bear the name 'Prussian interest-bearing notes'."
   The author then lists the terms of issue and circulation of the above-mentioned "interest-bearing notes" and quotes the opinion of the Left-wing deputies on the advantages of their financial project. The following consideration is given particular mention:
   "The above plan will provide the Government with the means it needs to meet the requirements of the state and save it from resorting either to the hated measure of a compulsory loan or the expensive one of a loan from individual bankers....
   "By issuing smaller denominations the interest-bearing notes plan will satisfy the pressing need for a freer circulation of capital, which does not occur in the

case of a loan ... make it possible to exchange government bonds, which are sluggish in circulation and exposed to big fluctuations in exchange, for interest-bearing notes; it will also give the private individual and every worker the chance to invest his savings at interest without losing his disposal of them and free him from the cumbersome savings-banks and from the intermediary of bankers with their usual deductions for commission.

"The interest-bearing notes plan will entice out of its hiding-place and bring into circulation the ready cash at present lying unproductively in the hands of timid capitalists and as a necessary consequence promote the flow of ready cash back to the state banks, while at the same time impeding the export abroad of coined metal. This can only be to the benefit of the country....

"The same security that in any case would have to be put up by the Government for any loan will form the security for the Prussian interest-bearing notes, but this plan spares the Government the humiliation of having to haggle with foreign bankers over the amount to be gained by the latter at the expense of Prussia; the plan also gives the Government a favourable opportunity to show the world that Prussia possesses sufficient means within itself to pay for its requirements, thereby reinforcing the confidence of the Prussian people in their own strength and emancipating them from the arbitrary power of foreign usurers."   p. 416

[273] On August 9, 1848, in view of the frequent sorties of Prussian officers, the Prussian National Assembly voted for the proposal of Stein, a deputy of the Left, requesting the Minister of War to issue an army order to the effect that officers opposed to a constitutional system were bound to quit the army. Despite the National Assembly's decision, Schreckenstein, the Minister of War, did not issue the order; so Stein tabled his motion for the second time at the session of the National Assembly on September 7. As a result of the voting, the Auerswald-Hansemann Ministry had to resign. Under the Pfuel Ministry that followed, the order though in modified form was issued on September 26, 1848, but this also remained on paper.   p. 417

[274] This refers to the visit of Frederick William IV to Cologne on August 13-15, 1848, in connection with the festivities to mark the sixth centenary of the laying of the cornerstone of St. Peter's Church.   p. 420

[275] This article was first published in English in the collection: Karl Marx and Frederick Engels, *Articles from the "Neue Rheinische Zeitung". 1848-49*, Progress Publishers, Moscow, 1972.   p. 421

[276] See Note 146.   p. 424

[277] Re *August 10, 1792*, see Note 20.

During *May 31-June 2, 1793*, the Girondist Government representing the republican circles of the industrial and commercial bourgeoisie, which strove to prevent the further development of the revolution, was overthrown by the masses in Paris. Twenty-nine Girondist leaders were expelled from the National Convention (later on, many of them took part in counter-revolutionary conspiracies and riots), and the revolutionary-democratic dictatorship of the Jacobins was established in France.   p. 425

[278] The second, third and fourth articles of this series (dated September 12, 13 and 15) were published in the *Neue Rheinische Zeitung* under the title "Crisis".

Excerpts of the third article were first published in English in the magazine *Labour Monthly*, 1948, Vol. XXX, No. 9, and in the collection: Karl Marx, *On Revolution*, ed. by S. K. Padover, New York, 1971; all these articles were published in English in full in the collections: Karl Marx and Frederick Engels, *Articles from the "Neue Rheinische Zeitung"*. *1848-49*, Progress Publishers, Moscow, 1972, and Karl Marx, *The Revolutions of 1848*. *Political Writings*, Vol. 1, London, Penguin Books, 1973.   p. 427

279 Decrees (*ordonnances*) issued by the King of France on *July 26, 1830*, abolished freedom of the press, dissolved Parliament and changed the electoral law, reducing the electorate by seventy-five per cent. These emergency measures taken by Charles X's Government led to the July 1830 bourgeois revolution in France as a result of which the Bourbon monarchy was replaced by the Louis Philippe liberal monarchy.

On *February 24, 1848*, the Louis Philippe monarchy was overthrown and the Second Republic proclaimed in France.   p. 430

280 In his message of September 10, 1848, Frederick William IV agreed with the view of his Ministers that the resolution passed by the Prussian National Assembly on September 7, 1848 (see Note 273), was an infringement of the "principle of constitutional monarchy", and approved their decision to resign as a protest against the Assembly's action.   p. 430

281 This refers to Stein's proposal accepted by the Prussian National Assembly on August 9 on the resignation of reactionary officers (see Note 273). The Assembly passed a resolution couched in rather mild terms after it had discussed the situation in the army following the shooting down on July 31 by the garrison of the Schweidnitz fortress in Silesia of the civil guard and townspeople, as a result of which 14 people were killed and 32 seriously wounded. The Minister of War was asked to warn officers to abstain from "reactionary tricks", and it was recommended that they resign from the army if they disagreed with the resolution. The Auerswald-Hansemann Ministry raised no objection because it was sure the deputies would not demand the faithful implementation of the resolution. But the Minister of War's non-observance of the Assembly's recommendations led to a conflict between the Government and the Assembly and to a ministerial crisis.
                                                                            p. 432

282 *Vendée*—see Note 164.
The Constituent Assembly in France (*Constituante*) held its sessions from July 9, 1789, to September 30, 1791.   p. 432

283 On September 13, 1848, a clash took place between the soldiers and officers of the 1st and 2nd Regiments of the Guards stationed in Potsdam. This was provoked by the Command detaining a letter written by the soldiers to Deputy Stein and the National Assembly thanking them for adopting the September 7 resolution on the resignation of reactionary officers. During these disturbances the lower ranks at one point resorted to building barricades. Cuirassiers of the Guards stationed in Nauen refused to obey their officers and attack the civil population.   p. 433

284 In 1648 Frederick William, the Elector of Brandenburg, supported the candidature of John Casimir to the Polish throne; in 1656, after taking advantage of the King of Poland's difficult situation he concluded a military pact with Charles Gustav, King of Sweden, and supported his claims to the Polish crown. In

the war of 1655-60 between Sweden and Poland, he manoeuvred between the warring parties and thus secured the final incorporation of Eastern Prussia in Brandenburg.

On April 5, 1795, in Basle, Prussia concluded a separate peace treaty with France, the first anti-French coalition having already begun to disintegrate.

In November 1805, Russia and Prussia concluded a convention in Potsdam on joint action against Napoleonic France. The Prussian Government undertook to join the third anti-French coalition (Britain, Austria, Russia and Naples), but after the defeat sustained by the Austrian and Russian armies at Austerlitz, it renounced its obligations.   p. 435

285 This refers to the debate in the Frankfurt National Assembly in the summer and autumn of 1848 on the status of Limburg, a province of the Kingdom of the Netherlands, then part of the German Confederation. Numerous explanations on this subject were offered to the Assembly by representatives of the so-called Central Authority (the Imperial Ministry).   p. 435

286 This article was first published in English in the collections: Karl Marx, *On Revolution*, ed. by S. K. Padover, New York, 1971, and Karl Marx and Frederick Engels, *Articles from the "Neue Rheinische Zeitung". 1848-49*, Progress Publishers, Moscow, 1972.   p. 436

287 After the Ministers sent in their resignation, Frederick William IV, in his message of September 10, 1848, while expressing his agreement with their motives for resigning, asked them to carry out their duties pending the appointment of successors.   p. 436

288 This article was first published in English in the collection: Karl Marx and Frederick Engels, *Articles from the "Neue Rheinische Zeitung". 1848-49*, Progress Publishers, Moscow, 1972.   p. 439

289 On September 16, 1848, the Frankfurt National Assembly ratified the Malmö armistice by a majority vote. This evoked profound indignation among democratic circles and the broad masses. On September 17 the citizens of Frankfurt and the surrounding neighbourhood held a mass protest meeting at which they demanded that the Assembly be dissolved and a new representative body set up. The Imperial Government countered by summoning Prussian and Austrian troops to Frankfurt. An insurrection broke out the next day, but the poorly armed people sustained a defeat despite their stubborn barricade fighting. Unrest in many parts of Germany, particularly in the Rhineland, and another attempt at a republican uprising in Baden on September 21, were an echo of the Frankfurt events.

The first article on the Frankfurt uprising had no title because it was published in the supplement to the *Neue Rheinische Zeitung* which had no table of contents.

The article was first published in English in the collection: Karl Marx and Frederick Engels, *Articles from the "Neue Rheinische Zeitung". 1848-49*, Progress Publishers, Moscow, 1972.   p. 442

290 On September 21, 1848, a Ministry headed by Pfuel was formed in Prussia by royal order. It consisted of top officials and high-ranking officers. Outwardly its attitude towards the National Assembly was one of loyalty, but actually the Pfuel Ministry sought to organise and unite the counter-revolutionary forces. Pfuel and

his colleagues paved the way for the overtly counter-revolutionary Government of Count Brandenburg (November 8, 1848), which accomplished a coup d'état in Prussia.   p. 448

291 See Note 23.   p. 448

292 The Committee of Public Safety consisting of 30 people was formed by the democratic and workers' organisations of Cologne at their mass meeting on September 13, in view of the ministerial crisis in Prussia, the menace of a counter-revolutionary coup and the increasing popular unrest in the Rhine Province aroused by the armistice with Denmark concluded at Malmö. The editors of the *Neue Rheinische Zeitung*, including Marx, Engels, Wolff, Dronke and Bürgers, as well as the leaders of the Cologne Workers' Association Schapper and Moll, were elected among its members. The Committee of Public Safety became a guiding centre of the Cologne solidarity movement with the Frankfurt insurgents and of the mass struggle against encroachments on the revolutionary gains and democratic freedoms by the Prussian authorities, who started openly to persecute members of democratic and proletarian organisations.   p. 450

293 The public meeting at Worringen (near Cologne), at which, besides the townspeople, peasants from the neighbouring villages were present, was called by the workers' and democratic organisations on September 17, 1848. It played an important part in rallying the masses to fight against the counter-revolution. The meeting recognised the Committee of Public Safety in Cologne, adopted an address supporting the protest made by democratic circles against the armistice between Prussia and Denmark and declared for a democratic social republic in Germany. For details on the meeting see this volume, pp. 586-87.   p. 451

294 See Note 23.   p. 452

295 See Note 137.   p. 452

296 The Cologne authorities, frightened by the upsurge of the revolutionary-democratic movement, resorted to police persecution and on September 26, 1848, placed the city in a state of siege "to safeguard the individual and property". The military commandant's office issued an order prohibiting all associations that pursued "political and social aims", cancelled all meetings, disbanded and disarmed the civic militia, instituted courts martial and suspended publication of the *Neue Rheinische Zeitung* and a number of other democratic newspapers. On October 2 the protest campaign made the Cologne military authorities lift the state of siege, and on October 3 subscription to the *Neue Rheinische Zeitung* was resumed. However, Marx was not able to resume publication of the newspaper until October 12 because of lack of funds and because Engels and Dronke had had to leave Cologne, under threat of arrest.   p. 455

297 In English, this article was first published in an abridged form in the magazine *Labour Monthly*, 1948, Vol. XXX, No. 10, and in full in the collections: Karl Marx, *On Revolution*, ed. by S. K. Padover, New York, 1971, Karl Marx and Frederick Engels, *Articles from the "Neue Rheinische Zeitung"*. *1848-49*, Progress Publishers, Moscow, 1972, and Karl Marx, *The Revolutions of 1848. Political Writings*, Vol. 1, London, Penguin Books, 1973.   p. 457

298 A popular uprising that took place in Vienna on October 6-7, 1848, was sparked off by the orders of the Austrian Government to dissolve the Hungarian Diet and

send Austrian troops to the Croatian Ban Jellachich who, supported by the Imperial Court, had started a counter-revolutionary campaign against Hungary but sustained defeat at the hands of the Hungarian revolutionary troops on September 29. The masses, headed by the petty-bourgeois democrats, prevented the Vienna garrison from marching on Hungary and, after fierce fighting, captured the city. The Austrian Emperor and his court fled to Olmütz (Olomouc) on October 7, 1848, and were later followed by the Ministry. The majority of Czech deputies to the Austrian National Assembly (*Reichstag*) who belonged to the national-liberal party departed for Prague in haste.   p. 457

[299] The reference is to the holidays held in September 1848 to mark the eighteenth anniversary of the Belgian revolution of 1830.   p. 459

[300] This article was first published in English in the collections: Karl Marx, *On Revolution*, ed. by S. K. Padover, New York, 1971, and Karl Marx, *The Revolutions of 1848. Political Writings*, Vol. 1, London, Penguin Books, 1973.   p. 462

[301] At the session of the Prussian National Assembly on September 29, 1848, Deputy d'Ester demanded that the Government lift the siege of Cologne and call the Cologne Garrison Headquarters to account for unlawful actions.   p. 462

[302] On October 2, 1848, a group of counter-revolutionary bourgeois in Cologne (Stupp, Ammon and others) handed an address to the Prussian National Assembly in which they stated that the demand that the siege of Cologne be lifted put forward by d'Ester and supported by the Rhine Province deputies Borchardt and Kyll allegedly "does not reflect the mood and opinions of the burgh- ers".   p. 462

[303] See Note 245.   p. 463

[304] For *Stein's Army Order* see Note 273.
On September 17, 1848, the commander of the Brandenburg military area, General Wrangel, issued an army order which demanded that "public law and order" be secured, threatened "elements who were against law" and called upon the soldiers to rally around their officers and the King.   p. 463

[305] When the popular unrest in Cologne provoked by the arrests of democratic and workers' leaders on orders of the Cologne authorities was at its highest, Marx and his associates called upon the workers to refrain from premature armed actions and from succumbing to provocation in a situation unfavourable for the revolutionary forces. Marx uttered this warning at the meeting of the Cologne Workers' Association in the Kranz Hotel on September 25, 1848, and later at a popular meeting in the Eiser Hall attended by members of the Cologne Democratic Society.   p. 464

[306] Thiers' work published in the newspaper *La Constitutionnel* in September and October 1848, was later printed in pamphlet form under the title *De la propriété*, Paris, 1848.   p. 467

[307] Thiers' speech was a reply to the proposal made by Deputy Turck to found a state mortgage bank with a fixed rate of exchange.   p. 467

[308] The *Direct Commission of Mainz* was founded in 1819 by decision of the Carlsbad conference of German states (see Notes 152 and 199) to investigate "tricks of the

demagogues", i.e. for the struggle against the opposition movement in the
German states. The Commission, whose members were appointed by the
individual governments of the German states, was authorised to hold direct
inquiries and make arrests in all the states of the German Confedera-
tion.   p. 472

309 The reference is to the "law on the protection of the Constituent National
Assembly and the officials of the Central Authority" according to which offences
against National Assembly deputies and the officials of the Central Authority were
punishable by imprisonment. This law was a repressive measure adopted by the
Frankfurt National Assembly majority and the Imperial Government on October
9, 1848, i.e. after the September uprising in Frankfurt.
    Black-red-golden—a symbolic combination of colours signifying the unity of
Germany.   p. 473

310 In September 1848 Turkish troops supported by the Tsarist Government
occupied Wallachia to suppress the national liberation movement. In Bucharest,
they were guilty of bloody outrages against the civil population. The proclamation
published by the Turkish government commissioner Fuad Effendi declared the
necessity of establishing "constitutional order" and "eliminating all vestiges of the
revolution".   p. 473

311 See Note 86.   p. 474

312 See Note 273.   p. 476

313 On events of August 23 in Vienna see Note 264.
    On October 5, 1848, it became known in Vienna that Austrian troops were to be
sent to suppress the Hungarian national liberation movement and that a battalion
of grenadiers had received marching orders. This news caused general
indignation and a popular uprising on October 6 and 7.   p. 477

314 See Note 133.   p. 478

315 On May 15, 1848, a popular uprising in Naples, caused by King Ferdinand II's
infringement of constitutional rights, was savagely crushed (see this volume,
pp. 24-26), declassed elements (lazzaroni) being active in its suppression.
    Early in September 1848 Neapolitan troops sent by Ferdinand II to suppress
the revolutionary movement in Sicily bombarded the town of Messina for four
days and, having captured it, committed violent outrages. Ferdinand earned for
himself the derisive nickname "Bomba".
    The capture of Milan by Austrian troops on August 6, 1848, was accompanied
by outrages against the population.   p. 481

316 See Note 18.   p. 481

317 In the summer of 1848 the Cologne Public Prosecutor's office was already trying
to start legal proceedings against the editors and the publisher of the Neue
Rheinische Zeitung, accusing them of insulting the Public Prosecutor and police in
connection with the newspaper's defence of the arrested leaders of the Cologne
Workers' Association Gottschalk and Anneke (see this volume, pp. 176-79). In the
autumn, the Cologne Public Prosecutor Hecker issued orders to bring to trial
Marx, the editor-in-chief, and Korff, the newspaper's responsible publisher, for

printing a number of articles, including the proclamation "To the German People" written by the republican Friedrich Hecker. Despite the negative findings of the examining magistrate, who in October 1848 stated that there were insufficient grounds for prosecution, the Public Prosecutor's office insisted on pressing its accusations and, in addition, put forward new ones (see Marx's article "Three State Trials against the *Neue Rheinische Zeitung*", present edition, Vol. 8). Another charge was brought against Marx for his participation in the revolutionary movement as a leader of the Cologne democratic organisation. p. 485

318 See Note 310. p. 485

319 See Note 139. p. 486

320 The reference is to the opposition of Marx and his followers in March 1848 to the plan of the German legion of volunteers to enter Germany with the aim of starting a revolution; this plan was supported by Herwegh, Bornstedt and others (see Note 2). p. 488

321 The *Deutsche Volkszeitung* for April 17, 1848, published a report from Paris which censured the German communists' negative attitude towards Herwegh's plan. p. 488

322 This article was first published in English in the collections: Karl Marx, *On Revolution*, ed. by S. K. Padover, New York, 1971, and Karl Marx, *The Revolutions of 1848. Political Writings*, Vol. 1, London, Penguin Books, 1973. p. 490

323 The reference is to the *Second Democratic Congress* which was held in Berlin from October 26 to 30, 1848. Here, a new Central Committee of German democrats (d'Ester, Reichenbach, Hexamer) was elected, the question of constitutional principles was discussed and the "Declaration of the Rights of Man" adopted. However, the motley composition of the Congress led to discord and differences on the main issues. In response to the proposal of the Left-wing representatives to appeal to the people to support the Viennese insurgents, the majority of the delegates, who were against it, walked out. But the appeal was adopted by the rest of the delegates. Though worded in a bombastic style, it actually contained merely an appeal for aid from German governments which were manifestly hostile to revolutionary Vienna. On the whole, instead of adopting resolute measures to mobilise the masses for struggle against counter-revolution, the Congress limited itself to passing sterile and contradictory resolutions.

It took a more consistent and radical position during the discussion of the social question on October 30. Several points of the "Demands of the Communist Party in Germany" were made the basis of the practical proposals of the reporter on this question (the reporter being a delegate from the Cologne Workers' Association Beust) which were submitted for discussion by the Congress to all democratic societies. p. 490

324 See Note 23. p. 491

325 This article was first published in English in the collections: Karl Marx, *On Revolution*, ed. by S. K. Padover, New York, 1971, and Karl Marx and Frederick

Engels, *Articles from the "Neue Rheinische Zeitung". 1848-49*, Progress Publishers, Moscow, 1972.   p. 493

326 An ironical allusion to the previous political activities of Brüggemann who for his participation in the student opposition movement and his support for freedom of the press at the Hambach festivities (1832), was sentenced to death for "high treason". This sentence was later commuted to life imprisonment. During the amnesty in 1840 Brüggemann was pardoned.   p. 497

327 The *Neue Rheinische Zeitung* gives reports on events in Vienna from the above-mentioned *Preussische Staats-Anzeiger*, and the *Allgemeine Oder-Zeitung*.   p. 497

328 This article was first published in English in the collections: Karl Marx, *On Revolution*, ed. by S. K. Padover, New York, 1971, and Karl Marx and Frederick Engels, *Articles from the "Neue Rheinische Zeitung". 1848-49*, Progress Publishers, Moscow, 1972.   p. 498

329 *Slovanská Lípa*—a Czech national society founded at the end of April 1848. The leadership of the society in Prague was in the hands of moderate liberals (Šafařík, Gauč), who joined the counter-revolutionary camp after the Prague uprising in June 1848, whereas the provincial branches were mostly led by radicals. p. 498

330 During the French Revolution, Koblenz was the centre for the counter-revolutionary émigrés.   p. 499

331 See Note 238.   p. 499

332 This article was first published in English in the collection: Karl Marx, *On Revolution*, ed. by S. K. Padover, New York, 1971.   p. 503

333 The *Academic Legion*—a student military organisation set up in Vienna in March 1848. Each faculty of the University formed a detachment divided into companies. The majority of the Legion were radical democrats. Lecturers and professors of the University as well as writers, poets, journalists and doctors, made up part of the Legion. The Legion played an important part in the revolutionary movement in Austria in 1848.   p. 503

334 See Note 101.   p. 505

335 Frederick Engels' travel notes "From Paris to Berne" have survived in the form of an unfinished fair copy. Prior to his trip the following events took place: On September 26, 1848, a state of siege was declared in Cologne and an order to arrest some of the editors of the *Neue Rheinische Zeitung*, Engels among them (see this volume, p. 593), was issued. Engels emigrated to Belgium and, together with Dronke who joined him en route, arrived in Brussels; but the Brussels police arrested both of them and, on October 4, deported them from Belgium (see this volume, pp. 459-60). On October 5, Engels and Dronke arrived in Paris. After a few days, Engels, who had almost no ready money, started on foot for Switzerland. About November 9 he reached Berne via Geneva and Lausanne, where he stayed for a while. Engels began writing his travel notes in Geneva, as evidenced by the original title to the manuscript, "From Paris to Geneva". The manuscript is appended with two sheets of sketches drawn by Engels en route (see illustrations between pages 508 and 509 of this volume) between Auxerre (France) and Le Locle (Switzerland).

On the first sheet there are the following designations (in angular brackets are names crossed out by Engels; in square brackets—inexact names of localities in the manuscript):

1) Route from *Auxerre to Chalon* with marks:
"Auxerre—Saint-Bris—Vermenton—Pont aux Alouette—Lucy le Bois—Avallon—⟨Rouvray⟩—Saulieu—⟨in the direction of Dijon⟩—Chanteaux—Rouvray—in the direction of Dijon—Arnay-le-Duc—Château—(a long village)—here I went to the post-office—coal mines—an inn—a beautiful valley, wine—the same—Chagny—Chalon."

2) Route from *Beaufort to Geneva* with marks:
"Beaufort—Orgelet—Ain—Moirans—Pont du Lizon [in the manuscript Pt. d'Ison]—Saint-Claude—La Meure—Mijoux—Gex—Ferney—Succony—Geneva."

On the same sheet there are several drawings, including one of a rider in the Hungarian uniform. There are also discernible names:

Czechs	Croats	Serbians	Poles
Magyars	Illyrians	Bosnians	Ruthenians
Slovaks	Slovenes	Bulgarians	

On the second sheet there are the following designations:

1) Route from *Auxerre to Geneva* with marks:
"Auxerre—Saint-Bris—Vermenton—Pont aux Alouette—Lucy le Bois—Avallon—⟨Rouvray⟩—Saulieu—Arnay-le-Duc—a long village—Ivry—La Cange—Chagny—Chalon—Saint-Marcel—Louhans—Beaufort—Orgelet—Ain—Moirans—two mountains—Pont du Lizon [in the manuscript Pt. d'Ison]—Saint-Claude—La Meure—Mijoux—Gex—Geneva."

2) Route from *Moirans to Saint-Claude* with marks:
"Moirans—wind mills—Pont du Lizon [in the manuscript Pt. d'Ison]—Saint-Claude."

3) Route from *Geneva to Le Locle* with marks:
"Geneva—Bellerive—Coppet—Nyon—Rolle—Aubonne—Morges—Cossonay—La Sarraz—Orbe—Yverdon—Saint-Croix—Fleurier—Travers—Les Ponts—Le Locle."

An ethnographic note and drawings appended to the manuscript suggest that Engels stopped writing his travel notes when, at Marx's request, he started on an article "The Struggle in Hungary" (see present edition, Vol. 8). p. 507

336 *Chant du départ* (A Marching Song)—one of the most popular songs of the French Revolution. It also remained popular later.
Mourir pour la patrie—see Note 107. p. 513

337 See Note 100. p. 517

338 The *maximum laws* and the *law against buying up food supplies* (June 26, 1793; in the manuscript Engels uses the German transliteration *Akkapareurs* for the French word *accapareur*—meaning "usurer", "profiteer") were adopted by the Convention under pressure from the masses, who were demanding fixed prices and effective measures against profiteers in food at a time of deepening food crisis and rising prices. The first maximum adopted on May 4, 1793, introduced fixed prices for grain; the decree of September 11, 1793, fixed a single price for grain and flour; on September 29, 1793, fixed prices on other staple goods (second maximum) were introduced. p. 520

[339] All the three receipts are in Engels' handwriting. p. 533

[340] The address "To All Workers of Germany" on behalf of the Mainz Workers' Educational Association was drafted by the emissary of the Communist League who arrived from Paris, member of the Central Authority Karl Wallau, and Communist League member Adolf Cluss. The address was published in several democratic newspapers. On April 8, 1848, on their way to Cologne, Marx and Engels stopped at Mainz where, together with the local communists, they discussed the further plan of action aimed at preparing ground for a mass party of the German proletariat with the Communist League forming its nucleus.

p. 535

[341] On December 1, 1845, Marx, then residing in Brussels, asked officially to be relieved of his Prussian citizenship with the intention of depriving the Prussian authorities, who were making attempts to get him expelled from Belgium, of any opportunity to interfere in his affairs. After the March revolution of 1848 in Germany Marx returned to his homeland and applied for Prussian citizenship.

He wrote his application to the police office on the second day after his arrival in Cologne. The rough copy of the application has also survived. The fair and the rough copy of the application are written in an unknown hand; the signature, place and date are in Marx's handwriting. The fair copy differs considerably in some places from the rough one, which mentions Marx's intention to publish the *Neue Rheinische Zeitung*. Apparently Marx thought better about informing the police of this.

On April 18 Marx was summoned to Police Inspector Hünermund who wrote an account of Marx's statement. From the text of the account (see next document) it is evident that Marx declined once again to reveal to the police his plans to publish a newspaper.

Subsequent events showed that Marx had good reason not to trust the police. The Cologne regional police office deliberately delayed answering his application and, after the publication of the *Neue Rheinische Zeitung*, it firmly rejected it. In a report to the Minister of the Interior, the regional police office described the editors of the newspaper as very dangerous revolutionaries who were striving to overthrow the existing system. *Oberpräsident* of the Cologne Province Eichmann called Marx the "soul" of the *Neue Rheinische Zeitung*, stressing that he was "the most prominent figure among the republicans of Cologne". The Prussian Government did their best to induce the Cologne police to take measures against the activities of the editor-in-chief of the revolutionary newspaper. This was why Marx was refused Prussian citizenship (see this volume, pp. 407-10). p. 537

[342] This document is not included among those kept in the police archives, connected with granting Marx Prussian citizenship. Apparently it was given back to Marx. p. 538

[343] This document reflects events prior to the publication of the *Neue Rheinische Zeitung* and gives new information on the situation in which Marx and his followers were campaigning for the foundation of a truly revolutionary proletarian organ. Before his arrival in Cologne, Marx, who was already planning this publication, got to know from Georg Weerth's letter that Hess and Anneke, members of the Cologne communities of the Communist League, intended to found a democratic newspaper of the same title. An announcement of the publication of a new paper printed in the *Kölnische Zeitung* on April 7, 1848, above their signatures showed that it was going to be an ordinary local petty-bourgeois

paper, having nothing to do with the class struggle of the proletariat and lacking any understanding of the true tasks of the German revolution. The announcement evoked different responses: various rich bourgeois offered financial advice, petty-bourgeois intellectuals offered to collaborate, Communist League members expressed astonishment at the paper's programme. Marx and Engels hastened their return to Germany.

On April 11, 1848, they arrived in Cologne and at once started to discuss the idea of a newspaper with Communist League members. Marx and his followers succeeded in strengthening their position. Hess, who was barred from taking part, left Cologne for Paris.

Much effort was made to settle issues with the democrats who, as one of the conditions for supporting the newspaper, demanded a repudiation of republican propaganda; financial problems were also acute, since the cautious attitude of the Rhenish bourgeois towards Marx and Engels' convictions greatly reduced the financial sources for the newspaper. In mid-April, Engels went to Barmen, Elberfeld and other towns to seek out shareholders.

The decision to include Heinrich Bürgers, who was prone to the petty-bourgeois influence, on the editorial board of the newspaper was a compromise. Bürgers wrote the prospectus, published here, in the spirit of petty-bourgeois socialism, in a moderate and ellusive tone (even the bourgeois *Elberfelder Zeitung* mentioned on April 30, 1848, the "indefinite expressions" of this "socialist republican document"). The prospectus, however, expressed the intention of publishing an all-German political newspaper rather than a local sheet and the necessity of paying attention to the social question and the condition of the "workers' estate". It also proved the importance of choosing Cologne—the centre of the Rhine Province, the most progressive in Germany—as the place of its publication. The names of the editors were not mentioned. Although by that time it had already been decided that Marx would be editor-in-chief, the composition of the editorial board was not yet settled.

. Displaying great resourcefulness and persistence in overcoming political and financial difficulties, Marx succeeded in enlisting on the editorial board true proletarian revolutionaries, thus ensuring a clear revolutionary line for the *Neue Rheinische Zeitung*. In a brief space of time he completed the formidable organisational preparations for a daily political newspaper. At the end of May, the newspapers of the Rhine Province and other parts of Germany announced that the *Neue Rheinische Zeitung* would begin publication on June 1, 1848.   p. 539

[344] Before the March revolution of 1848, there existed in Cologne a Communist League community which included d'Ester, Daniels, Bürgers, Anneke, Gottschalk and others, the majority being under the influence of the "true socialists". At the beginning of April 1848, the community was joined by Communist League members who had returned from emigration. As seen from the minutes published in this volume, soon after the arrival of Marx and Engels in Cologne sharp differences arose between them and Gottschalk. This document is signed by Bürgers and Moll, the leaders of the community; Marx was present at the sitting as the President of the Central Authority of the Communist League.   p. 542

[345] The meeting of the shareholders who financed the *Neue Rheinische Zeitung* was held at the end of May 1848, and a provisional committee was elected consisting of Hermann Korff, Karl Wachter and Georg Weerth who apparently undertook the final editing of the Articles. The document was discussed at meetings of shareholders on June 18 and 21; in July, the Articles, printed as a separate pamphlet by Wilhelm Clouth, were sent to the shareholders.

From the very beginning, differences arose between shareholders and editorial board. Many of the shareholders, displeased at the revolutionary trend of the newspaper, refused their contributions. They were particularly disturbed by the articles in defence of the proletarian uprising in Paris in June 1848. This led to the editor-in-chief, Marx, seeking other financial sources (the aid of the German and Polish democrats etc.) including his own personal means.   p. 543

[346] Hermann Becker, one of the leaders of the Cologne Democratic Society, despite Marx's objections, invited Wilhelm Weitling who had returned from emigration to address a general meeting.

In his speech delivered on July 21, 1848, Weitling, who called himself "a democrat, socialist and communist", proclaimed as a vital task of the revolution the establishment of a dictatorial Provisional Government consisting of a narrow circle of persons—"very keen people", having in mind himself as the sole dictator. Like Gottschalk, Weitling ignored the bourgeois-democratic character of the revolution and called for immediate and revolutionary fulfilment of his utopian plans for social transformation, considering that political questions merely distracted from the main aim. At the next meeting of the Democratic Society on August 4, Marx gave his reply. We can only judge the contents of his speech from this newspaper report. The author of this highly imperfect report, apparently, did not clearly understand the meaning of Marx's speech and some propositions are therefore presented in very confusing and inexact manner.

In his speech, Marx dealt especially with the peculiarities of the German revolution and its vital task: to eliminate the remnants of feudalism. In his controversy with Weitling, Marx stressed the close connection between political and social struggle, the inseparability and interdependence of political and social demands. The principal difference between Marx's position and that of Weitling was also manifest in the issue of the form of government which should be established after the victory of the revolution. Emphatically rejecting the idea of a one-man dictatorship, Marx saw the necessity to establish a revolutionary-democratic dictatorship founded on the union of those classes which had accomplished the revolution—proletariat, peasantry and petty bourgeoisie.   p. 556

[347] The First Rhenish District Congress of Democratic Associations was held in Cologne on August 13 and 14, 1848. Marx and Engels took part in the work of the Congress.

It was proposed that regional committees should be organised of representatives of democratic associations, with their headquarters in a number of cities. The Regional Committee of the Rhine Province and Westphalia was to have its seat in Cologne. The Central Committee of the three democratic associations in Cologne (see Note 348), which was organised prior to the Congress, was confirmed as the Rhenish Regional Democratic Committee, which included, besides its President Schneider II, Marx, Schapper and Moll. Under the influence of the Communist League members—deputies to the Congress—a resolution was passed on the necessity of conducting work among the factory proletariat and also among the peasants. The Congress recommended that every possible support be rendered to the democratic press (this primarily concerned the *Neue Rheinische Zeitung*).   p. 558

[348] The Central Committee of the three democratic associations of Cologne—the Democratic Society, the Workers' Association and the Association for Workers and Employers—was organised at the end of June on a decision of the First

Democratic Congress in Frankfurt am Main. This Committee functioned as the Regional Committee until the convocation of the Rhenish Congress of Democrats. Marx was its member.   p. 558

[349] The document is written in an unknown hand, but signed by Marx.   p. 561

[350] This protest was made on August 11, 1848, at a general meeting of the Cologne Democratic Society. The meeting was presided over by Marx (see this volume, p. 562).   p. 564

[351] In its address "To the German People" on April 6, 1848, the Committee of Fifty, which was elected by the Preparliament in April 1848 (see Note 51) and consisted mostly of liberals, called for support for activities aimed "at returning Poles their homeland". This call was, however, very vaguely worded.   p. 564

[352] Marx went to Vienna to strengthen ties with the democratic workers' organisations and to collect funds for the publication of the Neue Rheinische Zeitung in view of the refusal of many shareholders to subsidise the newspaper after it came out in defence of the Paris insurgents. Marx left Cologne on August 23, and stayed for a few days in Berlin, where he met Left-wing deputies of the Berlin National Assembly, the Russian revolutionary Mikhail Bakunin and other democrats.

Marx arrived in Vienna on August 27. The next day, at a meeting of the Democratic Association, he spoke against the representative of the Berlin Central Committee of Democrats, Julius Fröbel, who supported the proposal to petition the Emperor to dismiss Minister of Labour Schwarzer—the main culprit in the bloody clashes between the bourgeois national guard and the workers in Vienna on August 23, 1848. Marx was opposed on principle to conciliating monarchs. On August 30 Marx delivered a lecture to the first Vienna Workers' Association on the June insurrection in Paris, noting that German emigrant workers had taken part in it, and on September 2 lectured on wage labour and capital. During his talk with the leader of the German-Bohemian faction in the Austrian National Assembly (Reichstag) Borroš, he was convinced that the national antagonism between Czechs and Germans did not extend to relations between the workers of the two nationalities since these were united by common class interests.

On his way back, Marx visited Dresden and again Berlin. Here he attended sessions of the Prussian National Assembly and met the Polish revolutionary Kościelski who in the name of the Polish democrats later sent him two thousand talers for the publication of the Neue Rheinische Zeitung. About mid-September Marx returned to Cologne.   p. 568

[353] Reference to Paris is apparently made because of the passport Marx had on him, issued by the Paris police office on March 30, 1848 (see illustrations between pages 408 and 409 of this volume).   p. 569

[354] This excerpt was in the retrospective review signed PBS and published in the supplement to the Wiener Zeitung. The author of the review wrote with overt hostility about the "encroaches" of the Left organisations, criticising "a certain association"—this refers to the Vienna Democratic Association—because it let foreign politicians "drastically criticise" the measures of the Austrian Government and breed "distrust". Having cited Marx, the author exclaims: "For me these words are unforgettable as they reflect all the chasm, all plans of this party."   p. 571

355 On September 8, 1848, the *Neue Rheinische Zeitung* published the following note by its Vienna correspondent Müller-Tellering concerning this report: "At today's sitting of the first Vienna Workers' Association Marx delivered a speech on the social-economic question." p. 573

356 In a series of satirical articles, Georg Weerth ridiculed the Prussian reactionary Prince Lichnowski under the name of the knight Schnapphahnski. The articles "Life and Deeds of the Famous Knight Schnapphahnski" were published unsigned in the *Neue Rheinische Zeitung* in August-September and December 1848. p. 575

357 The public meeting in Cologne at which this address was adopted in connection with the debates on the ratification of the armistice at Malmö (see Note 289) in the Frankfurt National Assembly, was convened on the initiative of the *Neue Rheinische Zeitung*, as may be judged from the extant handwritten notes which Marx wrote later (at that time he was away). Engels apparently took part in the drafting of the address. The editorial board of the *Neue Rheinische Zeitung* published the text of the address in the editorial marked "Cologne, September 8" and supplied it with the following note: "Last night a public meeting was held in Rauch's Riding School to protest against the Prussian-Danish armistice and against the Prussian civic militia law which has been partially passed. Although the posters announcing the meeting were put up only late in the morning, the large hall, which holds no fewer than two and a half thousand people, was filled to overflowing, and at least twice that number were turned away because there was no room...." p. 577

358 During the summer of 1848, the Cologne Workers' Association discussed the social question. Marx's followers (Schapper, Moll and others) were trying to explain to the workers the groundlessness of utopian plans to transform society on the basis of existing capitalist relations, like Louis Blanc's scheme to create a workers' association with the aid of the state ("organisation of labour"), and other similar petty-bourgeois socialist projects. Engels made a detailed report, but its content was not noted in the minutes. The Cologne discussion on the social question was of great importance for the dissemination of the ideas of scientific communism among the workers. p. 580

359 See Note 100. p. 580

360 On July 15, 1848, an Artisans' Congress opened in Frankfurt to work out the Trade Rules. As apprentices were not admitted to the Congress by the worker-masters, the former convened their own congress on July 20 and invited representatives from the workers' associations. The work of the Apprentices' Congress lasted, with intervals, till September 20. At the Congress along with the protest against the narrow position of the Artisans' Congress and the criticism of the Trade Rules the following ideas were widespread: the ideas of the German economist Winkelblech (who took part in the work of both congresses) on the re-establishment of guilds, his theory of "federal socialism", and the desire to evade political questions. The Apprentices' Congress supported the idea of establishing the all-German Workers' Union with the aim of improving the workers' conditions and proposed to the National Assembly that a "social Parliament" be convoked and a "social Ministry" be formed. p. 580

[361] A copy of this letter sent to the Cologne regional administration is extant. The postscript runs as follows: "The copy of the above-mentioned instruction is sent to the royal regional administration for information, being at the same time a reply to the notice of the 20th of last month on remission of the application."   p. 581

[362] In his letters to Görtz, the Chief Burgomaster of Trier, of October 17 and November 10, 1845 (see present edition, Vol. 4), Marx supported his request to be released from Prussian citizenship by stating his intention to emigrate to the United States of America (no other documents testifying to this intention are available). In accordance with this, the letter of *Regierungspräsident* of Trier von Auerswald to *Oberpräsident* of the Rhine Province and the Minister of the Interior of November 6, 1845, concerning Marx's release from citizenship mentions the same motive. Officially Marx was released from Prussian citizenship on December 1, 1845.   p. 581

[363] On the election of Marx, Engels and other editors of the *Neue Rheinische Zeitung* to the Cologne Committee of Public Safety see Note 292.   p. 582

[364] The *Citizens' Association*— see Note 65.
      Wailers— see Note 23.   p. 583

[365] On September 11, 1848, soldiers of the 27th Regiment billeted in Cologne clashed with citizens supported by the democratic part of the civic militia.   p. 584

[366] This proclamation was published in the *Neue Rheinische Zeitung* without title and also as a separate leaflet the title of which is given here. The text of the leaflet differs somewhat from the version printed in the newspaper. Different wording is given in the footnotes.   p. 588

[367] Because of its lack of funds and other difficulties the publication of the *Neue Rheinische Zeitung* was resumed not on October 5 but 12, 1848.   p. 591

NAME INDEX

A

ist; deputy to the Prussian National Assembly (Left Centre) in 1848.— 207

Aschoff von— Prussian general, commandant of Berlin; during April and May 1848 commanded the Berlin civic militia.— 46,47

d'Aspre, Constantin, Baron (1789-1850) — Austrian general, took part in suppressing the 1848-49 revolution in Italy.— 386

Attila (d. 453) — King of the Huns (433-53).— 387

Auersperg, Karl, Count von (1783-1859) — Austrian field marshal, commander of the troops in Lower Austria during the revolution of 1848-49; took part in suppressing the Vienna uprising in October 1848.— 491, 503

Auerswald, Alfred von (1797-1870) — Prussian Minister of the Interior (March-June 1848).—19

Auerswald, Rudolf von (1795-1866) —Prussian statesman, liberal aristocrat, Prime Minister and Minister of Foreign Affairs (June to September 1848).— 38, 96, 106, 170, 172, 174, 183-85, 191, 194, 210, 217, 229, 240, 267, 269, 303, 417, 430, 435, 583

Augusta, Marie Luise Katharina (1811-1890) — wife of William, Prince of Prussia.— 106

B

Bakunin, Mikhail (1814-1876) — Russian revolutionary and writer, an ideologist of the Narodnik trend and of anarchism.— 315

Ballin, Felix (born c. 1802) — Belgian democrat, member of the Democratic Association in Brussels, one of the defendants at the Risquons-Tout trial.— 405, 406

Baltzer, Wilhelm Eduard (1814-1887) — German preacher; deputy to the Prussian National Assembly (Left wing) in 1848.— 243

Barbarossa—see *Frederick I* ("*Barbarossa*" or "*Redbeard*")

Barbès, Armand (1809-1870)—French revolutionary, a leader of secret societies during the July monarchy; deputy to the Constituent Assembly in 1848; sentenced to life imprisonment for his participation in the popular insurrection of May 15, 1848, and pardoned in 1854; emigrated to Belgium.—155

Barrot, Camille Hyacinthe Odilon (1791-1873) — French politician, leader of the liberal dynastic opposition until February 1848; from December 1848 to October 1849 headed the Ministry, which relied on a monarchist coalition.— 440

Bassermann, Friedrich Daniel (1811-1855) — German politician, represented the Baden Government in the Federal Diet during the 1848-49 revolution; deputy to the Frankfurt National Assembly (Right Centre).— 17, 237, 313, 464, 489

Bastide, Jules (1800-1879) — French politician and journalist, an editor of the newspaper *Le National* (1836-46); moderate republican, Minister of Foreign Affairs from May until December 1848.— 135, 377, 480, 481

Baudin, Charles (1784-1854) — French admiral.— 25

Bauer (died c. 1850) — Prussian official in Krotoschin (Posen); deputy to the Prussian National Assembly (Left Centre) in 1848.— 196, 197

Bauer, Heinrich (b. 1813) — prominent figure in the German and international working-class movement, a leader of the League of the Just, member of the Central Authority of the Communist League; shoemaker.— 7, 9, 533

Bauerband, Johann Joseph (1800-1878) — German lawyer; deputy to the Prussian National Assembly (Right wing) in 1848.— 207, 302

Baumstark, Eduard (1807-1889) —German professor; deputy to the

Democratic Association in Brussels; one of the accused at the Risquons-Tout trial.— 335, 405-06, 461

Mentés, M.— platoon leader in the Cologne civic militia.— 574

Metternich-Winneburg, Clemens Wenzel Lothar, Prince (1773-1859) — Austrian statesman and diplomat; Foreign Minister (1809-21) and Chancellor (1821-48); a founder of the Holy Alliance.— 92, 387, 396

Meusebach, von— Prussian official; deputy to the Prussian National Assembly (Right wing) in 1848.— 58

Mevissen, Gustav von (1815-1899) —German banker; deputy to the Frankfurt National Assembly (Right Centre) in 1848-49.— 194

Meyendorf, Pyotr Kazimirovich, Baron (1796-1863)—Russian diplomat; envoy to Berlin (1839-50).— 313

Mieroslawski, Ludwik (1814-1878)— prominent figure in the Polish national liberation movement; took part in the insurrection of 1830-31, in the preparations for the uprising of 1846 and in the 1848-49 revolution; later, a leader of the moderate wing of Polish democratic emigrants; sympathetic to Bonapartism.— 354, 375

Miguel, Maria Evarist (Miguel Maria Evaristo de Braganza) (1802-1866) — King of Portugal (1828-34).— 165, 311

Milde, Karl August (1805-1861) — Silesian manufacturer, moderate liberal; in 1848 Minister of Trade in the Auerswald-Hansemann Ministry (from June to September), President of the Prussian National Assembly (Right wing).— 33, 57, 59, 85, 106, 199, 219, 238, 262, 304, 313, 400, 418

Minutoli, Julius, Baron von (1805-1860) — Prussian official and diplomat; Chief of Police in Berlin in 1847 and 1848.— 46, 47

Mirabeau, Honoré Gabriel Riqueti, Comte de (1749-1791) — leading figure in the French Revolution, advocate of constitutional monarchy.— 102, 237

Mittermaier, Karl (1787-1867) — German lawyer, moderate liberal; a leader of the Left Centre in the Frankfurt National Assembly in 1848.— 239

Mohl, Robert von (1799-1875) — German lawyer, moderate liberal; deputy to the Frankfurt National Assembly (Left Centre) in 1848; Imperial Minister of Justice (1848-49).— 473

Mohr, C.— sculptor, corporal in the Cologne civic militia.— 574

Mohr, J. P.— roofer, member of the Cologne civic militia.— 574

Moll, Joseph (1813-1849) — prominent figure in the German and international working-class movement, a watchmaker by trade; a leader of the League of the Just, member of the Central Authority of the Communist League; President of the Cologne Workers' Association (from July to September 1848), member of the Rhenish District Committee of Democrats; killed in battle during the Baden-Palatinate uprising in 1849.— 7, 9, 452, 454, 463, 533, 542, 558, 579, 580, 585, 586

Moltke, Karl, Count von (1798-1866) — Schleswig-Holstein statesman, leader of the Danish counter-revolutionary party; from September 1848 head of the Provisional Government of Schleswig-Holstein formed after the armistice between Prussia and Denmark.— 412, 413, 447

Monecke, Edmund— German student, democrat.— 176

Montesquieu, Charles Louis de Secondat, Baron de la Brède et de (1689-1755) — French philosopher and sociologist, Enlightener.— 204, 206, 236, 246, 336, 430

Moritz, Daniel Samuel— Prussian judicial official; deputy to the Prussian Nation

INDEX OF LITERARY AND MYTHOLOGICAL NAMES

INDEX OF QUOTED
AND MENTIONED LITERATURE

WORKS BY KARL MARX AND FREDERICK ENGELS

Marx, Karl
The June Revolution (this volume)
— Die Junirevolution. In: *Neue Rheinische Zeitung* No. 29, June 29, 1848.—478

Legal Proceedings against the "Neue Rheinische Zeitung" (this volume)
— Gerichtliche Untersuchung gegen die "Neue Rheinische Zeitung". In: *Neue Rheinische Zeitung* No. 37, July 7, 1848.—207, 208

Legal Proceedings against the "Neue Rheinische Zeitung" (this volume)
— Gerichtliche Untersuchung gegen die "Neue Rheinische Zeitung". In: *Neue Rheinische Zeitung* No. 41, July 11, 1848.—314

The "Model State" of Belgium (this volume)
— Der "Musterstaat" Belgien. In: *Neue Rheinische Zeitung* No. 68, August 7, 1848.—482

The Poverty of Philosophy. Answer to the "Philosophy of Poverty" by M. Proudhon (present edition, Vol. 6, pp. 105-212)
— Misère de la philosophie. Réponse à la Philosophie de la misère de M. Proudhon. Paris-Bruxelles, 1847.—324

Revolution in Vienna (this volume)
— Revolution in Wien. In: *Neue Rheinische Zeitung* No. 114, October 12, 1848.—496

Engels, Frederick

The Agreement Debates on the District Estates (this volume)
— Vereinbarungsdebatten über die Kreisstände. In: *Neue Rheinische Zeitung* No. 56, July 26, 1848.—317

The Berlin Debate on the Revolution (this volume)
— Die Berliner Debatte über die Revolution. In: *Neue Rheinische Zeitung* Nos. 14-17, June 14-17, 1848.—89

The Danish Prussian Armistice (this volume)
— Der dänisch-preussische Waffenstillstand. In: *Neue Rheinische Zeitung* No. 99, September 10, 1848.—439

Details about the 23rd of June (this volume)
— Details über den 23. Juni. In: *Neue Rheinische Zeitung* No. 26 (special supplement), June 26, 1848.—159

The Frankfurt Assembly Debates the Polish Question (this volume)
— Die Polendebatte in Frankfurt. In: *Neue Rheinische Zeitung* Nos. 70, 73, 81, 86, August 9, 12, 20, 26, 1848.—368, 373, 375, 395

The German Citizenship and the Prussian Police (this volume)
— Das deutsche Reichsbürgerrecht und die preussische Polizei. In: *Neue Rheinische Zeitung* No. 73, August 12, 1848.—393, 407

Germany's Foreign Policy (this volume)
— Auswärtige deutsche Politik. In: *Neue Rheinische Zeitung* No. 33, July 3, 1848.—271

The "Kölnische Zeitung" about the June Revolution (this volume)
— Die "Kölnische Zeitung" über die Junirevolution. In: *Neue Rheinische Zeitung* No. 31, July 1, 1848.—479

The Prague Uprising (this volume)
— Der Prager Aufstand. In: *Neue Rheinische Zeitung* No. 18, June 18, 1848.—119

Marx, K. or Engels, F.
Arrests (this volume)
— Verhaftungen. In: *Neue Rheinische Zeitung* No. 35, July 5, 1848.—186, 208

The Downfall of the Camphausen Government (this volume)
— Sturz des Ministeriums Camphausen. In: *Neue Rheinische Zeitung* No. 23, June 23, 1848.—466

The Hansemann Government (this volume)
— Das Kabinett Hansemann. In: *Neue Rheinische Zeitung* No. 24, June 24, 1848.—170

WORKS BY DIFFERENT AUTHORS

Ariosto, L. *L'Orlando furioso.*—364

Aristoteles. *Politica.*—264

Arndt, Ernst Moritz. *Des Deutschen Vaterland.*—371
— *Der Freudenklang.*—400

Bakunin, M. *Erklärung.* In: *Ostdeutsches Athenäum,* supplement to the *Neue Oder-Zeitung für Kunst, Wissenschaft und Literatur* No. 151. 1848; *Neue Rheinische Zeitung* No. 46 (supplement), July 16, 1848.—315

Beaumarchais, P. A. C. de. *La folle journée, ou le mariage de Figaro.*—264

Becker, N. *Der deutsche Rhein.*—154

[Benkert, F. G.] *Joseph Bonavita Blank's ... Kurze Lebens-Beschreibung.* Würzburg. 1819.—337

DOCUMENTS

Verhandlungen der deutschen constituirenden Nationalversammlung zu Frankfurt am Main, Frankfurt a. M. und Leipzig, 1848-1849, Bd. 2.—357

Allgemeine Gewerbeordnung. Vom 17. Januar 1845. In: *Gesetz-Sammlung für die Königlichen Preussischen Staaten* No. 5, Berlin, 1845.—332

Allgemeines Landrecht für die Preussischen Staaten.— 178, 226, 250, 317, 342, 432

Aufruf an die Deutschen, Kalisch, March 13(25), 1813.—309

[*Aufruf des demokratischen Kongresses in Berlin an das deutsche Volk,*] October 29, 1848. In: *Volksblätter* No. 44, October 31, 1848: *An das deutsche Volk.*—490-91

Bekanntmachung, Berlin, June 1, 1848. In: *Königlich privilegirte Berlinische Zeitung von Staats- und gelehrten Sachen* No. 127, June 3, 1848.—46-47

Bekanntmachung in Betreff der Demarkationslinie. Posen, 4. Juni. In: Preussischer Staats-Anzeiger No. 35, June 6, 1848.—64

Belgian Constitution of February 7, 1831.—205, 333

Code civil— see *Code Napoléon*

Code Napoléon. Edition originale et seule officielle. Paris, 1808.—103, 187, 250, 290, 318, 520, 521

Compte rendu des séances de l'Assemblée nationale, T. 1-10, Paris, 1849-1850, T. 1, 2, 4 (Marx and Engels did not use this source directly, but through newspaper articles).—135, 137, 140, 148, 149, 155, 160, 168, 169, 321-24, 440, 467-71, 525-26

Declaration wegen Einziehung und künftiger Verwaltung der geistlichen Güter, ingleichen der Starosteien und anderer königl. Güter in Südpreussen und der von der ehemaligen Republik Polen neuerlich acquirirten Provinzen, Berlin, July 28, 1796.—348

Le décret relatif aux attroupements armés ou non armés, June 7, 1848. In: *Compte rendu des séances de l'Assemblée nationale,* T. 1, Paris, 1849.— 124, 168-69

Le décret relatif aux crimes et délits commis par la voie de la presse, August 11, 1848. In: *Compte rendu des séances de l'Assemblée nationale,* T. 2, 3, Paris, 1849-1850.— 314

Edikt den erleichterten Besitz und den freien Gebrauch des Grund-Eigenthums, so wie die persönlichen Verhältnisse der Land-Bewohner betreffend, October 9, 1807. In: *Sammlung der für die Königlichen Preussischen Staaten erschienenen Gesetze und Verordnungen von 1806 bis zum 27sten Oktober 1810,* Berlin, 1822.—118, 328

Edikt die Regulirung der gutsherrlichen und bäuerlichen Verhältnisse betreffend, September 14, 1811. In: *Gesetz-Sammlung für die Königlichen Preussischen Staaten,* Berlin, 1811, No. 21.—328

Edikt über die Einführung einer allgemeinen Gewerbe-Steuer, October 28, 1810. In: *Gesetz-Sammlung für die Königlichen Preussischen Staaten,* Berlin, 1810, No. 4.—331

Edikt wegen der Mühlen-Gerechtigkeit, und Aufhebung des Mühlen-Zwangs, des Bier- und Branntwein-Zwangs in der ganzen Monarchie, October 28, 1810. In: *Gesetz-Sammlung für die Königlichen Preussischen Staaten*, Berlin, 1810, No. 4.—331

Entschädigungsgesetz zur allgemeinen Gewerbeordnung, January 17, 1845. In: *Gesetz-Sammlung für die Königlichen Preussischen Staaten*, Berlin, 1845, No. 5.—332

Entwurf des Strafgesetzbuchs für die Preussischen Staaten, nebst dem Entwurf des Gesetzes über die Einführung des Strafgesetzbuches und dem Entwurf des Gesetzes über die Kompetenz und das Verfahren in dem Bezirke des Appellationsgerichtshofes zu Köln, Berlin, 1847.—317-18

Entwurf einer Verordnung über Ehescheidung, vorgelegt von dem Ministerium für Revision der Gesetze, im Juli 1842. In: *Rheinische Zeitung für Politik, Handel und Gewerbe* No. 293 (supplement), October 20, 1842.—208

Entwurf eines Gesetzes betreffend die Ausschreibung einer Zwangs-Anleihe, July 10, 1848. In: *Stenographische Berichte über die Verhandlungen der zur Vereinbarung der preussischen Staats-Verfassung berufenen Versammlung*, supplement to the *Preussische Staats-Anzeiger*, Bd. 1, Berlin, 1848.—278-86

Entwurf eines Gesetzes über die Errichtung der Bürgerwehr, July 6, 1848. In: *Stenographische Berichte über die Verhandlungen der zur Vereinbarung der preussischen Staats-Verfassung berufenen Versammlung*, Bd. 1, Berlin, 1848.—227, 256-64

Entwurf eines Gesetzes wegen unentgeltlicher Aufhebung verschiedener Lasten und Abgaben, July 10, 1848. In: *Stenographische Berichte über die Verhandlungen der zur Vereinbarung der preussischen Staats-Verfassung berufenen Versammlung*, Bd. 1, Berlin, 1848.—290-95

Entwurf eines interimistischen Pressgesetzes. In: *Kölnische Zeitung* No. 201 (first supplement), July 19, 1848.—250-52

Entwurf eines Verfassungs-Gesetzes für den preussischen Staat, May 20, 1848. In: *Stenographische Berichte über die Verhandlungen der zur Vereinbarung der preussischen Staats-Verfassung berufenen Versammlung*, Bd. 1, Berlin, 1848.—72, 89, 96, 252

Der Erste Vereinigte Landtag in Berlin 1847, Th. 1, Berlin, 1847.—115, 474

Flottwell [, E. H. von]. *Denkschrift des Oberpräsidenten Herrn Flottwell ueber die Verwaltung des Gross-Herzogthums Posen, vom Dezember 1830 bis zum Beginn des Jahres 1841*, Strasburg [1841].—357, 368

Friedrich Wilhelm III. *Verordnung über die Organisation der Landwehr*, March 17, 1813. In: *Gesetz-Sammlung für die Königlichen Preussischen Staaten*, Berlin, 1813, No. 7.—343, 355, 411, 449, 559

Friedrich Wilhelm IV. [*Ansprache an die Deputation der Frankfurter Nationalversammlung beim Kölner Dombaufest*,] August 14, 1848. In: *Kölnische Zeitung* No. 229, August 16, 1848.—474

— [*Antwort an die Deputation der Berliner Nationalversammlung*,] October 15, 1848. In: *Berliner Zeitungs-Halle* No. 241, October 18, 1848.—474

— [*Antwort an die Deputation der Bürgerwehr*,] October 15, 1848. In: *Berliner Zeitungs-Halle* No. 241, October 18, 1848.—476
— [*Antwort auf das Entlassungsgesuch der Minister*,] Sanssouci, September 10, 1848. In: *Neue Rheinische Zeitung* No. 102, September 14, 1848.—430, 436

Fuad Mehemmed. *Manifest an die Bojaren und an Euch Einwohner der Walachei aller Klassen*, Bucharest, September 13-25, 1848. In: *Neue Rheinische Zeitung* No. 118 (supplement), October 17, 1848: *Bukarest, 28. September.*—473, 485

Gesetz, betreffend den Schutz der constituirenden Reichsversammlung und der Beamten der Centralgewalt, October 9, 1848. In: *Stenographischer Bericht über die Verhandlungen der deutschen constituirenden Nationalversammlung zu Frankfurt am Main*, Frankfurt a. M. und Leipzig, 1848-1849, Bd. 4.—473

Gesetz über die Erwerbung und den Verlust der Eigenschaft als Preussischer Unterthan, so wie über den Eintritt in fremde Staatsdienste. Vom 31. Dezember 1842. In: *Gesetz-Sammlung für die Königlichen Preussischen Staaten*, Berlin, 1843, No. 2.—408, 409

Gesetzbuch über Strafen, Köln, 1812.—178, 209-11, 250, 251, 405, 486, 487, 593

Il Governo provvisorio alla Nazione Germanica, Milano, April 6, 1848. In: *Raccolta dei decreti, avvisi, proclami, bulletini ec. ec. emanti dal Governo provvisorio, dai diversi comitati e da altri dal giorno 18 Marzo in avanti*, Milano, 1848.—167

Griesheim [, K. G. von]. *Bekanntmachung*, Berlin, June 15, 1848. In: *Neue Rheinische Zeitung* No. 19, June 19, 1848.—97

Grundrechte des deutschen Volkes. In: *Stenographischer Bericht über die Verhandlungen der deutschen constituirenden Nationalversammlung zu Frankfurt am Main*, Bd. I-II, Frankfurt a. M. und Leipzig, 1848.—249, 252, 288, 368, 384, 391, 443

Jansen [, J. J.]. [*Aufruf an die Mitglieder des Arbeiter-Vereins und Bürger von Köln.*] Köln, July 3, 1848. In: *Neue Rheinische Zeitung* No. 35, July 5, 1848.— 178

Kabinettsorder vom 28sten Oktober 1807, betreffend die Aufhebung der Erb-Unterthänigkeit auf sämmtlichen Preussischen Domainen. In: *Sammlung der für die Königlichen Preussischen Staaten erschienenen Gesetze und Verordnungen von 1806 bis zum 27sten Oktober 1810*, Berlin, 1822.— 328

Kartel-Konvention, unterzeichnet von den Bevollmächtigten Sr. Majestät des Königs von Preussen und Sr. Majestät des Kaisers von Russland, Königs von Polen,... ratifizirt und ausgewechselt am 3. Juli 1844. In: *Gesetz-Sammlung für die Königlichen Preussischen Staaten*, Berlin, 1844, No. 22.—53-54

Königliche Ordre an das Staats-Ministerium, betreffend die nationale Reorganisation des Grossherzogthums Posen, April 26, 1848. In: *Reden, Proklamationen, Botschaften, Erlasse und Ordres Sr. Majestät des Königs Friedrich Wilhelm IV.*, Berlin, 1851.— 346

Konstytucja 3-go Maja 1791 r. Ustawa Rzadowa.—351, 354, 372

[*Kösliner Adresse,*] May 23, 1848. In: *Neue Rheinische Zeitung* No. 14, June 14, 1848.— 181

Lamartine, A. *Manifeste à l'Europe. Circulaire du ministre des affaires étrangères aux agents diplomatiques de la République française*, [March 4, 1848,] Paris, 1848.— 378

Loi sur les crimes, délits et contraventions de la presse, et des autres moyens de publications, September 9, 1835. In: *Lois Déitrots, Ordonnances, Réglements et avis du conseil-d'état,* T. 35, Paris, 1836.— 15, 171, 250

[*Manifest der Linken in der Frankfurter Nationalversammlung.*] In: *Neue Rheinische Zeitung* No. 7, June 7, 1848.—48-52

Motivirtes Manifest der radikal-demokratischen Partei in der konstituirenden Nationalversammlung zu Frankfurt am Main. In: *Neue Rheinische Zeitung* No. 6, June 6, 1848.—48-52

Nesselrode. [*Circular to All Russian Embassies.*] In: *Frankfurter Oberpostamts-Zeitung* No. 210 (second supplement), July 28, 1848: *St. Petersburg, 6. Juli. Die russische Note.*— 307-13

Patent die ständischen Einrichtungen betreffend. Vom 3. Februar 1847. In: *Gesetz-Sammlung für die Königlichen Preussischen Staaten,* Berlin, 1847, No. 4.— 311

Patent wegen beschleunigter Einberufung des Vereinigten Landtages, March 18, 1848. In: *Reden, Proklamationen, Botschaften, Erlasse und Ordres Sr. Majestät des Königs Friedrich Wilhelm IV.,* Berlin, 1851.— 390-91

Proclamations of the Vienna Town Council. In: *Neue Rheinische Zeitung* No. 133 (second supplement), November 3, 1848: *Berlin, 1. Nov. (Über die Kapitulation Wiens).—* 498

[*Programm des Arbeiterkongresses in Berlin.*] In: *Neue Rheinische Zeitung* No. 31, July 1, 1848: *Berlin, 29. Juni. Arbeiterparlament.*—271

Protest mehrerer Vorstands-Mitglieder des Kölner Bürger-Vereins, September 13, 1848.—584

Protokolle der Deutschen Bundesversammlung vom Jahre 1848, Frankfurt am Main, 1848.—408-09

Przyluski, L. [*Die Korrespondenz des Erzbischofs von Posen, Przyluski, mit dem Berliner Kabinett.*] In: *Neue Rheinische Zeitung* Nos. 5, 7, 10, 14, 38, 39, June 5, 7, 10, 14, and July 8 and 9, 1848, and also in the book, [Brodowski, Kraszewski und Potworowski.] *Zur Beurtheilung der polnischen Frage im Grossherzogthum Posen im Jahre 1848,* Berlin [1848].—201, 338

Sebaldt. *Warnung.* In: *Trier'sche Zeitung* No. 169, June 17, 1848.— 95

Stenographischer Bericht über die Verhandlungen der deutschen konstituirenden Nationalversammlung zu Frankfurt am Main, Frankfurt a. M. und Leipzig, Bd. 1-9, 1848-1849, Bd. 1-4 (Marx and Engels did not use this source directly, but through newspaper articles).—16-19, 72, 109, 110, 232, 235, 249, 288, 337, 338, 340-43, 344, 345-48, 353-58, 360-62, 364-72, 373, 374, 376, 377, 378, 379, 414, 421, 439, 440

Stenographische Berichte über die Verhandlungen der zur Vereinbarung der preussischen Staats-Verfassung berufenen Vesammlung, supplement to the *Preussische Staats-Anzeiger,* Bd. 1-3, Berlin, 1848 (Marx and Engels did not use this source directly, but through newspaper articles).—30-32, 37, 38, 45, 53-61, 66, 67, 72-86, 89, 94, 96-100, 117, 118, 170-75, 180-85, 189-93, 195-98, 201-07, 216-23, 226-37, 238-41.

— No. 273, September 29, 1848: *Nouvelles de Paris d'aujourd'hui.*—467
— No. 286, October 12, 1848: *Bruxelles, le 11 octobre, Revue Politique.*—467

Le Journal d'Anvers No. 243, August 31, 1848: *Affaire de Risquons-Tout. Verdict du Jury.*—406

Journal des Débats, July 30, 1848: *Paris, 29 juillet.*—168

Kölnische Zeitung Nos. 281, 285, 290, 293, 294, 300, 301, 303, October 8, 12, 17, 20, 21, 27, 28, 30, 1847. Series of articles on Proudhon's work *Système des contradictions économiques ou Philosophie de la misère.*—324
— No. 161, June 9, 1848: *Berlin, 6. Juni. Versammlung zur Vereinbarung der preussischen Verfassung.*—66-67
— No. 175, June 23, 1848: *Berlin, 20. Juni.*—116
— No. 176 (special supplement), June 24, 1848: *Köln, Samstag 24. Juni, abends 10 Uhr.*— 152, 154
— No. 179 (supplement), June 27, 1848: *Paris, 24. Juni, 11 Uhr.*— 155
— No. 179 (special supplement), June 27, 1848: *Paris, 25. Juni, 10 Uhr morgens.*— 134-35
— No. 179 (special supplement), June 27, 1848: *Paris, 25. Juni, 11 Uhr.*— 152
— No. 180 (special supplement), June 28, 1848: *Paris, 26. Juni.*— 152
— No. 181, June 29, 1848: *Köln, 28. Juni. Die Pariser Ereignisse.*— 152-56, 479
— No. 182, June 30, 1848: *Berlin, 27. Juni.*—171
— No. 203, July 21, 1848: *Köln, 20. Juli. Die Debatte über den Jacobyschen Antrag.*—242, 244, 246
— No. 211, July 29, 1848: *Köln, 28. Juli. Die europäische Revolution und die Handelsfreiheit.*—296
— No. 215, August 2, 1848: *Köln, 31. Juli.*—319-20
— No. 256, September 16, 1848: *Berlin, 12. Sept.*—436
— No. 265, September 27, 1848: *Köln, 26. Sept.*—462
— No. 268, September 30, 1848: *Köln, 29. September. Die Barrikaden in Köln.*—462, 464
— No. 297 (special supplement), November 3, 1848: *Köln, 2. November, 10 Uhr abends.*—497
— No. 299, November 5, 1848: *Berlin, 3. Nov.*—501
— No. 299, November 5, 1848: *Breslau, 2. Nov.*—501

Le Libéral Liégeois No. 218, September 1, 1848: *Liège, le 1ᵉʳ septembre 1848* (leading article).—406

The London Telegraph No. 122, June 26, 1848 (leading article).—150, 151

Le Moniteur belge. Journal officiel No. 212, July 30, 1848: *Emigration aux Etats-Unis de l'Amérique du Nord.*— 333
— No. 213, July 31, 1848: *Exportations.—Marchandises belges.*—335

Morgenbladet No. 322 (supplement), November 18, 1846: *Skandinavisme og Danmark.*—423

La Nation, October 7, 1848.—459-60
— October 10, 1848.—461

Neue Berliner Zeitung No. I (supplement), June 20, 1848: *London, 15. Juni.*— 113, 114

Neue Rheinische Zeitung. Organ der Demokratie No. 1, June 1, 1848: *Wien, 25. Mai, Morgens 7 Uhr.*—457
— No. 1, June 1, 1848: *Brüssel, 30. Mai.*—460
— No. 25 (special supplement), June 25, 1848: *Berncastel, 18. Juni.*—122
— No. 29, June 29, 1848: *Paris, Schluss der Sitzung der Nationalversammlung vom 25. Juni.*—140
— No. 30, June 30, 1848: *Paris, 27. Juni.*—156
— No. 31 (supplement), July 1, 1848: *Paris, 28. Juni.*—169
— No. 33, July 3, 1848: *Französische Republik.*—167, 169
— No. 40, July 10, 1848: *Berlin, 7. Juli.*—199
— No. 47, July 17, 1848: *Berlin, 14. Juli (Pressgesetz).*—250
— No. 49, July 19, 1848: *Stuttgart, 15. Juli.*—249
— No. 50, July 20, 1848: *Heidelberg, 17. Juli.*—249
— No. 62, August 1, 1848: *Mailand, 25. Juli.*—305, 327
— No. 62, August 1, 1848: *Mailand, 26. Juli. Mittags.*—305, 327
— No. 64, August 3, 1848: *Paris, 31. Juli...*—*National-Versammlung.*—321
— No. 72, August 11, 1848: *Kopenhagen, 5. August.*—382
— No. 92, September 2, 1848: *Köln, 1. Sept. (Die Debatte über Aufhebung der Standesprivilegien. Schluss).*—575
— No. 103, September 15, 1848: *Köln, 14. Sept.*—450
— No. 127, October 27, 1848: *Wien, 21. Oktober.*—503

The Northern Star No. 558, July 1, 1848: *Liberty, Equality, Fraternity.*—478
— No. 559, July 8, 1848: *The Counter-Revolution.*—478

L'Observateur Belge No. 272, September 30, 1848.—467

La Presse No. 4499, October 19, 1848: *Question italienne. Dernière phase de la médiation anglo-française (Communication).*—480

Preussischer Staats-Anzeiger No. 90, August 2, 1848: *Berlin, 1. August.*—317

La Réforme, July 2, 1848: *Paris 1ᵉʳ juillet. La conspiration de la calomnie.*—478
— No. 289, October 18, 1848: *Paris, 17 octobre. La Conciliation et l'amnistie.*—478-79

The Times No. 19383, October 2, 1848: *London, Monday, October 2, 1848. The perfect tranquillity...*—460

695

INDEX OF PERIODICALS

L'Alba. Giornale politico-letterario—an Italian democratic newspaper published in Florence in 1847-49.—11, 12, 167, 271

Allgemeine Oderzeitung—a German newspaper published in Breslau (Wrocław) in 1846-49; in 1848 voiced democratic views.—501

Allgemeine Zeitung—a German conservative daily founded in 1798; from 1810 to 1882 it was published in Augsburg.—154, 305, 464

Arbeiter-Zeitung—see *Zeitung des Arbeiter-Vereines zu Köln*

Die begriffene Welt. Blätter für wissenschaftliche Unterhaltung—a monthly published by Wilhelm Jordan in Leipzig in 1845-46.—360

Berliner Zeitungs-Halle—a German daily published by Gustav Julius in Berlin from 1846; in 1848-49 it was a leading democratic newspaper.—7, 119, 399, 401, 436, 437, 448

Berlinische Nachrichten von Staats- und gelehrten Sachen—a German newspaper published in Berlin from 1740 to 1874. In 1848-49 it took a constitutional-monarchist stand.—436

Börsen-Halle. Hamburgische Abendzeitung für Handel, Schiffahrt und Politik—a German daily published from 1805.—270

Breslauer Zeitung—a German daily founded in Breslau in 1820; in the 1840s voiced liberal views.—497, 501, 575

La Concordia—an Italian liberal daily published in Turin in 1848-49.—271, 272

Die Constitution. Tagblatt für constitutionelles Volksleben und Belehrung—a democratic newspaper which appeared in Vienna from March to October 1848; its editor was L. Häfner.—572, 573

Le Constitutionnel—a French daily published in Paris from 1815 to 1817 and from 1819 to 1870; in the 1840s it voiced the views of the moderate wing of the Orleanists

696 Index of Periodicals

and during the 1848 revolution became the mouthpiece for the monarchist bourgeoisie (the Thiers party).—154, 156, 187, 467, 479

Daily News—an English liberal newspaper, which appeared under this title in London from 1846 to 1930 as an organ of the industrial bourgeoisie.—461

Débats—see *Journal des Débats politiques et littéraires*

Deutsche Allgemeine Zeitung—a German newspaper published under this title in Leipzig from 1843 to 1879; until the summer of 1848 it voiced conservative views and later liberal ones.—213

Deutsche Jahrbücher für Wissenschaft und Kunst—a Young Hegelian literary and philosophical journal published under this title in Leipzig from July 1841 under the editorship of Arnold Ruge. In January 1843 it was closed down and prohibited throughout Germany.—380

Deutsche Volkszeitung—a German democratic daily published in Mannheim in April 1848 under the editorship of Julius Fröbel and Eduard Pelz.—488, 536

Deutsche Zeitung—a German daily published in Heidelberg under the editorship of Georg Gervinus from 1847 to September 1848; then, up to 1850, it appeared in Frankfurt am Main; it supported constitutional monarchy and unification of Germany under Prussian hegemony.—69, 115, 116, 325, 464

Düsseldorfer Zeitung—a German daily published under this title in Düsseldorf from 1826 to 1926.—575

L'Emancipation—a Belgian daily founded in Brussels in 1830.—188

Faedrelandet—a Danish newspaper published in Copenhagen from 1834 to 1839 weekly, and then daily; in 1848 it was the semi-official organ of the Danish Government.—253, 254, 267, 268, 269, 434, 435, 446-47

Frankfurter Journal—a German daily published in Frankfurt am Main from the seventeenth century up to 1903.—213

Frankfurter Oberpostamts-Zeitung—a German newspaper published in Frankfurt am Main from 1619 up to 1866; it was owned by Thurn und Taxis princes; during the 1848-49 revolution it was the organ of the Imperial Regent and Imperial Ministry.—307, 472, 473

La Fraternité de 1845. Organe du communisme—a workers' monthly of the Babouvist trend, published in Paris from January 1845 to February 1848.—298

Freiheit, Brüderlichkeit, Arbeit—a German newspaper, organ of the Cologne Workers' Association, published in Cologne from October 26, 1848, twice a week. On January 14, 1849, Gottschalk's followers made an attempt to substitute it by the *Freiheit, Arbeit*, a newspaper disavowed by the leaders of the Association; the paper resumed publication on February 8, 1849, and appeared up to the middle of 1849.—597, 598

Gazzetta di Milano—an Italian newspaper published from 1816 to 1875; until the late 1850s it was the official organ of the Austrian authorities in Northern Italy.—487

Gervinus Zeitung—see *Deutsche Zeitung*

SUBJECT INDEX

A

Absolutism— see *Monarchy, absolute*
Academic Legion— 503
Agitation— 239, 298, 423
Agricultural chemistry— 470
Agriculture— 3, 342, 363, 468-71
  See also *Agricultural chemistry*
Alsace— 423
Analogy, historical— 51, 351
Anti-Corn Law League— 238, 299
Aristocracy, landed— 55, 118, 119, 298, 299, 351, 354, 363, 373, 433, 520
Arming, arms— 3, 73, 96, 180, 260, 437
Army
  — its organisation after victorious democratic revolution— 3
  — as component part of state apparatus— 77, 437
  — mercenaries— 25, 26, 165
  — Austrian— 11, 109, 257, 387, 395, 396
  — Danish— 42, 436
  — Prussian— 34, 43, 69, 85, 107-09, 227-28, 257, 258, 262-63, 264-65, 283, 355, 383, 400, 431, 433, 438
  — of German states— 42, 165
  — of the Two Sicilies— 25, 388
  See also *Arming, arms*; *Artillery*; *Military, the*; *Military art*
Articles of consumption— 4
Artillery— 161
Associations of workers— 297
Athens— 512
Austria— 92-93, 109
  — political system— 350

  — history— 396
  — national question— 11
  — and Germany— 11, 396, 400
  — and Hungary— 165
  — and Italy— 11, 92, 165, 167, 386, 387, 396, 397, 400, 403, 421, 487
  — and Portugal— 165
  — and Russia— 350
  — and Polish lands— 11, 92, 350-51, 373
  — and Slavs— 91-93
  See also *Austro-Italian War of 1848-49*; *Bourgeoisie, Austrian*; *Hungary*; *Revolution of 1848-49 in Austrian Empire*; *Working class of Austria*
Austro-Italian war of 1848-49— 109-10, 212, 305-06, 376, 385-89, 395-97, 400, 402, 421, 473
Autocracy— 116, 363

B

Baden republican uprising (April 1848) — 68, 239, 245, 368
Banks— 4, 118, 470, 484, 485
Barbarism— 116, 351, 423
  See also *Feudalism*
Belgium— 165, 333-36, 404, 405, 423, 483-85
  — social and political system— 333, 484-85
  — economic conditions— 333-35, 483-84
  — foreign trade— 334